Global social

Crossing borders, blurring boundaries

Edited by Carolyn Noble, Helle Strauss and

Brian Littlechild

SYDNEY UNIVERSITY PRESS

First published by Sydney University Press
© Individual contributors 2014
© Sydney University Press 2014

Reproduction and Communication for other purposes
Except as permitted under the Act, no part of this edition may be reproduced, stored in a retrieval system, or communicated in any form or by any means without prior written permission. All requests for reproduction or communication should be made to Sydney University Press at the address below:

Sydney University Press
Fisher Library F03
University of Sydney NSW 2006
AUSTRALIA
Email: sup.info@sydney.edu.au

National Library of Australia Cataloguing-in-Publication Data

Other Authors/	Noble, Carolyn, editor
Contributors:	Strauss, Helle, editor
	Littlechild, Brian, 1953–, editor
Title:	Global social work: crossing borders, blurring boundaries, edited by Carolyn Noble, Helle Strauss and Brian Littlechild
ISBN:	9781743324042 (paperback)
	9781743324059 (ebook: epub)
	9781743324066 (ebook: mobipocket)
Notes:	Includes bibliographical references
Subjects:	Social service--International cooperation
	Social work education
	Human services--International cooperation
Dewey Number:	361.3

Cover design by Miguel Yamin
Cover image © iStock.com/MichelIsola

Contents

Contents

Preface

The editors of this book share a long-term interest in working internationally for social work education as well as locally and nationally in their respective countries and communities of practice. Each has played a key role in the International Association of Schools of Social Work (IASSW), serving in various capacities over several years. Their current roles are as co-chairs (Carolyn and Brian) and committee member (Helle) of the IASSW publication committee and in these roles they are responsible for developing publications of value to the international community that the IASSW serves.

It was in this committee that the idea of a global book on social work education began to germinate. The idea was to gather curricula on social work programs from as many regions as possible to showcase what was being taught in various cultural, sociopolitical and regional contexts. While many texts were being published focusing on international social work and the complexity of working and talking about social work across borders and cultures, there were no such books on what was actually informing the curricula in countries where social work was taught.

But we didn't want to stop there. We acknowledge that social work education theory and practice is current, relevant and transformative if it is informed by contemporary debates, critical reflections and research. That is, scholarship must reflect upon and challenge current thinking and thus generate new ideas. Here we set out to compile a collection of work by eminent scholars, which has an international focus. Our idea to do this was based on the premise that no such gathering of programs and ideas from as wide a field as we had in mind had yet been undertaken. It was an exciting project, an exciting idea.

Taking the proposal from the publications committee to the full board of IASSW was the first step in furthering this project. Given full support from the board for this initiative, we then set about forming the book's content and structure, contacting possible contributors and looking for a publisher. The IASSW global conference to be held in Melbourne in 2014 was a key point to work back from.

A clarion call across the membership and beyond yielded the current content focusing on the many elements that make up social work education. In response we have educators from Mexico, Argentina, Chile, Spain, south and east Africa, the Caribbean, Indonesia, Eastern Europe, Canada, the United Kingdom, Aotearoa/New Zealand, Australia, South Korea, Nepal, the United States of America, India and Hong Kong talking about their programs. An eclectic mix of ideas and unique identities that inform many of the social work programs in these countries emerged from their efforts. We are grateful for all their contributions, for sharing their ideas and salient features of their courses and the philosophical and pedagogical practices that underpin their programs.

To complement this information on curricula the editors approached eminent authors from across the globe whose work we were familiar with and asked them to submit what we called seminal ideas emanating from their long careers in social work education as teachers, researchers and scholars. Their response resulted in a wide range of scholarship.

We have organised authors' contributions into eight parts. These are: 'Theory of social work', 'Social work as a profession', 'The development of social work education courses', 'The social work curriculum', 'Social work and the welfare state', 'Social work and social change', 'Social work and political activism', and 'The past and the future of social work'. Threaded throughout these sections are discussions on the philosophical bases of social work, social work education as transcending disciplinary and professional boundaries, and salient lessons from long-term activists. In exploring these themes, *Global social work: crossing borders, blurring boundaries* addresses issues regarding commitments to human rights, social action, and the desire to challenge traditional orthodoxies and take social work discourse in new, albeit challenging directions.

We are thankful to each other for this book, which is a truly international collaboration based on friendship and cooperation. Born out of our shared belief of the importance of global interdependence, this edited collection builds on the strength of local and national practices, a respect for cultural influences, and the acknowledgment that sociopolitical contexts should underpin all our actions and theoretical understandings.

We hope you will agree with us that the depth of scholarship these authors have given us will continue to influence the current and future developments of social work programs across the globe as ideas cross borders and blur boundaries.

Carolyn Noble
Helle Strauss
Brian Littlechild

Part 1
Theory of social work

1

Towards identifying a philosophical basis of social work

Carolyn Noble and Mark Henrickson

Social work has absorbed and adapted major theories from related disciplines since its inception as an applied discipline over 100 years ago. These positions have been used to construct its ethical underpinnings and its epistemological standpoint. In this chapter we revisit this activity and address two questions: can we act as practitioners before we are fully cognisant of the ontological and philosophical position informing our practice? Is it possible to have a unitary, core 'truth to act' in light of the current globalisation of cultural norms, intercultural influences and challenges to intellectual traditions as being patriarchal, colonial and monocultural? Social workers must critically engage with philosophical and theoretical writings in order to understand the bases and implications of their practice decisions. Equally, however, a philosophy of social work must be dynamic, intersubjective and dialogic, and propose that we co-create theory, knowledge and praxis with our clients.

Why a philosophy of social work?

Social work has emerged as an international discipline and is now practised in many countries around the world: the International Federation of Social Workers claims membership from at least 90 different countries (International Federation of Social Workers, n.d.). A key question for the discipline now is what are the shared understandings about the world, communities and individuals that allow social workers from Beijing, Buenos Aires, New York, Durban, Suva, Mumbai, Helsinki or the remote Australian Outback to talk cogently with one another? That is, what is social work and its praxis, and what, if any, shared understandings or unifying philosophy can be identified?

It is important to acknowledge at the outset that social work research and pedagogy have been established on the foundations of European knowledge and worldviews (Sung-Chang & Yuen-Tsang 2008). These worldviews have been enshrined in the dominant language of social work knowledge discourse, English. In the postmodern era our discussions about social work must occur in the context of globalisation (Desai 2000). As we write this chapter the definition of social work itself is being reviewed and revised, and this review acknowledges multiple knowledges and the existing hegemony of Western knowledge discourses. The definition review acknowledges this multiplicity by encouraging regional and even national amplifications of the international definition of social work.

Across the globe we can discern a common feature of social work in its drawing on a number of interdisciplinary theories for its praxis (e.g. cognitive behavioural theories, psychodynamic, ecological, general systems, etc.), which is often cited as a strength: we take the best theories of other disciplines that are consistent with social work values and ethics, and through praxis give them a social work 'flavour'. However, the diversity of theoretical approaches to praxis can also be seen as a weakness, encouraging many theories to exist side by side (Soifer 1999) without a framework for deciding what theory to use when, and treating all theories as more or less equally valid. Fook (cited in Bell 2011) notes that a philosophy of social work is necessary to establish a framework theory of theories, in order to avoid an unsystematic eclecticism that might proffer contradictory approaches to practice from equally contradictory ontological positions. Other attempts to explore a uniquely philosophical position find social work scholars renouncing exclusivist logical positivism and its research and practice methodologies, while at the same time recognising the inevitable limitations and difficulties of an exclusivist postmodernism with its multiple truths (Hugman 2003). Others have challenged the notion of having to choose between positivism and postmodernism (Thomas 2004). However, in the marketised, neoliberal funding and practice context that prevails throughout much of the world, social workers are increasingly pressured by funders and governments into positivist research and 'outcomes-driven' service delivery paradigms (Peile & McCouat 1997).

In an age of economic austerity, how can social work explain and justify itself, its research and service delivery paradigms to funders and governments, let alone to each other and service users? Unlike the creative arts, we cannot be satisfied with a position that says that 'we know it when we see it'. And in multidisciplinary practice environments such as health and mental health care, how does social work explain what it does (and does not do) to other disciplines and professions?

This discussion is an opportunity for social work not only redefine itself but to redefine what we mean by 'profession' in light of what we 'know' to be true. While we do not propose to take up the professionalism debate in detail in this chapter, we note that a fundamental characteristic of a profession is that it has a coherent (or systematic) science (knowledge) and learning. However, as noted above, it has been repeatedly proposed that social work lacks such a coherent philosophy, or theory of theories (Göppner 2012; Göppner & Hämäläinen 2007) necessary to engage in a critical discussion about itself as a profession, and it is quite possible that a social worker, when asked to name a social work philosophy, might find him or herself mumbling something about eclecticism, assuming the doing (praxis) explains the thinking (theory) about what it does and why.

In order to explore a philosophy of social work, we need to set out a framework of what social work is (ontology), what social workers know (epistemology), and how to assess who we are and what we know. The development of a philosophy of social work would go some way to providing cogent responses to questions about what social work is, what it does, and why it does what it does, and the activities and issues with which it concerns itself. This chapter is presented as a dialogue between the two authors as a way of teasing out some of the difficulties and approaches to this topic, and by way of engaging in the heuristic that we will propose.

What do we mean by philosophy?

C: I have always been intrigued by philosophy as much as I have been influenced by theory, and the ideas it posited. This conversation is an opportunity to explore that interest and its relevance to my current thinking about theory. Philosophers are interested in the abstract, born from curiosity, a desire to understand something and articulate the logical process of arriving at that understanding. Looking for principles that govern the flow of ideas, philosophers are primarily concerned with rules of inference (i.e. each step of the argument flows the laws of logic) and the conclusions drawn are then posited as true and valid. This has been its practice since Socrates and Plato when rational science was heralded as the paragon of rational activity, as the way of knowing in the examination of the natural world and this process of inquiry would also inform the exploration of the social world. Essentially philosophy involves a premise such as 'Pleasure is the ultimate good' or 'How do we explain evil if there is an all powerful loving god?' (Epicurus) or with questions such as 'Can reason discover truth independent of experience?' or 'Are there limits to our effort to know?' To these questions propositions are posited which are then tested by logical argument supported by evidence, and conclusions are then drawn. While knockdowns in conclusions are rare, the challenge is more likely in the beginning premise. So another premise or question is devised and following the same logical formula another conclusion is put forward. This framework is regarded as a benchmark against which all cognitive endeavours must be measured (Fay 1996). How it links with its aesthetic sensibility or affect, and how that creed is coloured, expressed and portrayed to others, hint at a more complex philosophy than its first beginnings. This is important when we look beyond the Western philosophising to explore the more contemporary philosophy arising as a result of the contributions from Indigenous and Eastern philosophers, feminist philosophers and critiques from critical realists, social constructivists and multiculturalism.

It seems to me that people engage with philosophy and philosophical ideas to get something out of it, so its significant contribution to social work is how it can be used or applied. There is no inherent pre-determined path leading from philosophical ideas about the big questions to ideas about how to achieve a particular end or outcome, e.g. how to enact equality, justice, democracy, personal agency and ethical behaviours. It is left to theorists to take these premises and construct political, social, economic and cultural beliefs (theories) around them that can motivate action or inform social practices or, in social work's case, a praxis from which to act. For example, how philosophy elucidates questions like 'What is virtue?', 'What is existence and its authenticity?', 'What is cause and effect?', 'What does it means to be human?', 'What is truth?', 'What is knowledge?', 'What is equality?' and what is meant when we talk about wellbeing, peace and happiness is used to inform political, religious, educational and social theories (to mention just a few uses). Theories emerge to fill the gap between the philosophical and the contextual – the psychological, social, economic, cultural and political practices that are deemed to follow if the premise is to be acted upon. When applied to social work this philosophical inquiry and the actions that follow that inquiry have a particular resonance. My interest has led to my exploring a philosophy of social work with the knowledge of 30 years of social work scholarship behind me. This is especially pertinent in the current changing environment facing social work and the many ideas informing its practice as well as its desire to shore up its professional standing.

It is my premise that a philosophy of social work is important not only to identify what social work is, but also what it is not, and what it does not do. Beginning with Plant's (1970) attempt to map the logical geography of the social and moral theory informing social casework (the dominant method at the time) and Ragg's (1977) philosophical analysis of social casework which began the move away from the technical application of its early beginnings to exploring its normative underpinnings, there have been spasmodic attempts to articulate a philosophical position. Plant, Lesser and Taylor-Gooby's work (1980) explored the philosophical foundations of concepts such as welfare obligations, rights of welfare and concepts of community, and McDermott's (1975) collection of essays on self-determination and related concepts on liberty, human equality, rights and right conduct, freedom and persuasion by philosophers and social theorists is still an important reference. Clark and Asquith's (1985) work on social work and philosophy discusses the meaning and application of important insights from social philosophy including ideology, theory and professional ethics. Each of these early works introduced philosophical debates into the emerging profession's discourse, resulting in the breadth of philosophical musings explored here that have found their way into social work ontology. Social work needs to think as well as do.

M: I accept wholeheartedly the notion that social work's values and ethics are essential elements in establishing what a philosophy of social work is; Popper acknowledged this as an essential difference between the social and natural sciences (Stokes 1997). However, I challenge the notion that 'philosophy' is some kind of ontological entity with which social work must develop some kind of relationship. Social work is simultaneously theoretically and praxis-based. Indeed, Payne's somewhat confusingly named 'modern social work theory' (Payne 2005) (which I think should be called 'post-modern theory') reminds us that social work theory has moved beyond a catalytic, top-down heuristic, where social work is done to clients, to a heuristic where clients are active co-creators of social work theory and practice, together with social workers, and practice settings. Social workers above all understand themselves as practitioners, whatever their area of work, and any social work philosophy, however ontological, must be informed by its values and praxis.

C: Philosophical inquiry is not a static process and on reading philosophical works one can spot all sorts of shifts in concerns that mirrored and reflected social changes of the time. For example, philosophical ideas on what a good life is, what justice is, what equality is, and even what society is, can be understood in terms of changes in society's rational expectations, as well as the changes resulting from the impact of sociopolitical and cultural events (e.g. the emergence of Confucianism, Buddhism, Hinduism, Christianity and Islam, the influence of the European Renaissance and the Enlightenment, the challenge to positivism, the critiques offered by post-structuralism and the rise in social constructivism, critical realism and multiculturalism) (Garvey & Stangroom 2012, 370). The feminist challenge to the hegemony of men dominating the world of ideas also gave Western philosophy a shakeup. We need to take these developments on board. I argue for a re-thinking of philosophy and its continuing usefulness to social work theory, practice and professional standing because of the old Hellenic tradition of 'there is something good about argument itself, for the community and the individual' is worth revisiting (Benton & Craib 2011, 182). I think any discussion about the source of these ideas is essential before undertaking any form of practice: which ideas and in what context are also important to explore.

M: I agree with you completely that philosophy and social values are dynamic, and informed by the social, political, economic and intellectual environments from which they emerge. That is one of the challenges we face in social work. While until the last century much of the development of social ideas happened relatively independently in different parts of the world, with the advent of globalisation—technology that allows almost instantaneous communications of even the most trivial thoughts, the relative ease of travel, and as you yourself put it, 'the metaphorical shrinking of time and place' (Noble 2013, 346) — ideas spread quickly. Cultures are increasingly homogenised, and the domestic concerns of a region quickly become available to the entire world. Yet the spread of ideas is not the same as their adoption: the widely variant treatments of women, ethnic and cultural minorities, sexual and gender minorities, and refugees and migrants, are examples of ways the world holds on to its local tribalism. This means that any global social work ontology must also take into account—or even privilege— indigenous and local epistemologies and cultures, while at the same time engaging with them from the standpoint of social work's own values. You seem, however, to be suggesting that any philosophy of social work must therefore be relativist, and that pursuing any one, unitary ontology is not going to be a useful or productive undertaking. I can almost hear our readers and colleagues saying that we've given up before we've begun. But a dynamic, dialogic, interactive ontology can be a philosophy just as much as a static, unitary philosophy. In dialogue social work recognises the dynamism that inheres within our epistemology and generalises it to ontology.

C: I am not sure I am arguing for or against one ontology as such but I am arguing for social work to revisit the discipline of philosophy and its ontological underpinnings as well as its premises when exploring theories for practice which determine how we act with and for clients. Let me continue my case.

Social work is a human activity with specific ideas about social and human interaction with its own aims, assumptions, values, morals and actions. Questions like 'What is a good life?', 'What does being human mean?', and 'What is society' are the kind of questions social workers ask when being reflective about our discipline base and these questions are philosophical in nature.

M: These questions are also highly contextual to time, place, and even person, and the questions social workers ask are things like 'What is a good life here and now, and what does that mean to this person?'

C: Nevertheless, if being reflective about one's practice and motivations, assumptions as well as one's beliefs, morals, ethics and values, and making them available to public and private scrutiny and internal and external accountability is important for a profession's integrity, then the discipline of philosophy is helpful. Further if we want to dig deep into the core of social work's knowledge base, its fundamental meanings, its core values, beliefs, attitudes, knowledge, its priorities, and more broadly what professional bodies suggest practitioners and educators spend time attending to and why, then philosophical inquiry is an important disciple to help navigate this maze and its continual quest for answers can help the profession be more systematic in this reflective investigation.

Understanding human nature and acting in the social, economic, cultural and political arena has enormous consequences on the lived lives and aspirations of those who receive the results of these interventions (individuals, families, communities, nation states and the environment). For example, when social workers engage with people in their most intimate lives, making judgments, proposing alternatives, they are also making statements about who they are and what their professional discourse is saying about the nature of the world, about the nature of human beings and society, as well as about the nature of help-ing and the assumptions about the helping process. More broadly their interventions also say something about important concepts, i.e. 'What is the purpose of living and being in this world?' and 'What is important about their work and their position in it?' which then provides justifications about the what, why and how of social work's involvement in the lives of clients, in the framing of the policies and practices that impact on their wellbeing. These interventions need to be more than whims; these actions need, in my opinion, to be consciously informed by logic or analytical philosophy when applied in practice and ac-cessible on reflection. The justification of each intervention or interpretation, judgments made, policies formed, or what action or non-action has occurred must then by necessity be made in moral, ethical, social, cultural and political terms within an ontological frame-work which can be articulated when required, either in professional terms or individual practice terms. Social work theories can provide a structured set of concepts that help un-derstand the subject matter concerned, while philosophical reasoning can light the path of cognitive inquiry. An engaged practice can be enhanced by philosophical reasoning.

Many social work theories rest upon the surface or insubstantial understanding of the texts from which they are borrowed, so an ontological examination and discussion of the intervention and sociopolitical, cultural and psychological consequences of these theories is needed. A transparency of actions requires not only an understanding of the rules of engagement associated with a particular practice theory but deeper more onto-logical explanation of what is assumed underneath in the deeper meaning embedded in these actions. Also, undertaking this examination provides opportunities for practitioners and clients to challenge their assumed participation and understanding of this engagement with the individual worker, the agency and the profession more broadly.

M: I agree that an ontological examination and discussion of the consequences of any particularly theory is required. I hold, however, that this discussion cannot be held exclu-sively amongst social workers as 'experts'. These discussions must be inclusive of clients and other stakeholders. Some of the resistance to the professionalisation of social work—and even formal social work qualifications— is that in developing a philosophy, or theory or knowledge base we have distanced ourselves from our grass, flax or bamboo roots from which we have always derived our authority. Remember that even in the early Settlement House movement the community was the expert, and the worker was the student of the community teacher. This critique becomes moot, however, if we include those roots in our discussions, and stakeholders become co-creators of theory in a particular context. That is not to suggest that social work should ever abandon its values and ethics in that context, but that through engagement all voices are heard and valued. I also acknowledge, however, that this notion will challenge the notion of social workers as government functionaries administering or enforcing government policies. That, in my view, is not social work, but rather a catalytic, top-down administration of pre-determined policies and programs to achieve pre-established outcomes.

C: Ideas are not identical or symmetrical to actions; indeed what actions and responses are chosen can unleash a chain of unforeseen responses which then posit a whole range of different reflections about that interaction and each person's reaction to it and so on. It seems to me that practitioners need to have considered the possible consequences of their actions or at best have a firm idea of their intentions already framed by a philo-sophical investigation. This questioning or philosophical investigation will consequentially result in deeper questions than the insightful accounts of the rules being followed. Knowing the technicality of what practitioners are doing should not obviate the need for a why question. The why question involves deep reflections, rather than unreflective taken-for-granted routinised or rehearsed responses. Many practitioners and scholars recognise this process as involving reflection (Schön 1983). But in the philosophical sense it involves an archaeological exploration, rather than a faithful descriptive account of actions or preferences which are often automatic and unreflective (Steel & Guala 2011).

M: What you are calling 'archaeological exploration' I am calling a dialogic, iterative hermeneutic. Unlike archaeology, the social worker cannot undertake this excavation in isolation: it must be interactive.

C: The practice of asking deep questions might, as Benton and Craib (2011) argue, irreversibly alter the idea, position or practice in such a way that new investigations are needed, hinting that engaging in reflection is not a smooth and uncomplicated process.

M: Indeed! It rarely is.

C: The much repeated adage that 'Life is complex' has resonance here. However, in complex situations, social workers have to meet an immense variety of challenges and demands, much of which requires 'practice wisdom'. Practice wisdom entails acquiring and testing a stock of routinised, casual knowledge, often not fully articulated, to be deployed, but nevertheless deployed with great skill and competence. However, and here's the concern, at key moments when ethical, political, cultural and social dilemmas emerge, roadblocks are encountered, ambiguities and contradictions are exposed; if there are gaps between the doing and the thinking and being able to give an explicit account of what was done and the embedded meanings, then a lot is at stake. Professional integrity, transparency, accountability and efficacy are all up for questioning and challenge. This is where an exploration of the genealogy of ideas can be influential in giving a public account of practice and making it transparent for all to see.

M: Accountability is essential, and assessing the genealogy of an action or decision (because it will be the action or decision and its consequences that will be scrutinised, not only the idea) is important. I am simply suggesting that if a social worker reserves to herself the concept of expert knowledge then she will have disempowered the client (however we construct that term). And if the client shares in the decision, then the client shares a certain amount of responsibility.

Traditionally understood, philosophy is a way of living, or, in this context, working. Perhaps we can now recognise that there is not just one way, but ways of living and working. Wittgenstein wrote that rule-following only makes sense in the context of a community able to monitor applications of the rule; a successful rule is therefore exactly what the community says it is (Gunnell 2009). In an increasingly globalised world, identifying a consensus about what a single rule, or philosophy, or praxis, should be, exactly, would be a daunting enterprise at best. Social work is above all relational: one cannot 'do' social work on one's own; it requires an other, or client, be that other an individual, family, group, community, organisation or policymaking body. Perhaps the best we can hope for is that our global social work community commits to ongoing dialogue about what a successful ontology and praxis are in each context. This means that social work can and must define itself, and not be reliant on outsiders to define us. This would seem to put an end to the issues that Flexner (1915) (who was not a social worker) raised a hundred years ago about social work not being a profession because it did not meet his traditional criteria of a profession. In addition, we have relied too heavily on validation from government policies to recognise who we are and what we do: regulation, for instance, must come from within the profession, not from external bodies. The management of risk, which is the primary purpose of external regulatory bodies, only makes sense in a neoliberal, managerialist environment. It is in this context that Dominelli (in Bell 2011) calls for a collectivist, inclusive ontological foundation for social work, particularly in the marketised context of contemporary practice. Where there is a robust social work environment, the social work community, like any professional community, is very capable of regulating itself. Managerialism, and its attempt to manage risk, assaults the autonomy and discretion of social work and increases bureaucracy and control (Rogowski 2010). Multiplicity, diversity and dialogue are social work's challenge to subordination to managerialism, which is a despairing ideology; why settle for merely managing risk if we believe we can find solutions to social problems?

An objective, unitary ontology is not only not likely in the applied social sciences, but it is not useful: the interpreter, the interpretation, as well as the thing that is interpreted are all in constant and dynamic relationship with each other. Wittgenstein stressed that interpretation is an action that 'hangs in the air along with what it interprets' (cited in Gunnell 2009, 603). An iterative, dialogic, hermeneutic model of truth-seeking will be of most value to the dynamic kind of social work which we recognise in the 21st century, where the social worker, the client, and the relationship between the client and the work are all in constant, dialogic relationship. This kind of dynamism will be frustrating, and possibly make no sense to the positivist or 'natural' scientist. However, Popper proposed that social sciences are different from natural sciences (Stokes 1997), and indeed rejected the notion that reason can reveal the true nature of anything (Parvin 2011) because no-one can foresee all the potential consequences of their proposals. The philosopher of science Alfred North Whitehead proposed that mutuality and interdependence are essential aspects of an applied philosophy (Schmidt 1967): each occasion (or in our context, each interaction) merges into the next natural occasion to create something new. Thus, all occasions and relationships are perpetually made new through their encounters with other occasions and relationships. It requires what Buber called a 'Thou' relationship with a client (Buber 1958 [1923]). This conceptualisation is an excellent fit for social work, since social work practitioners do not claim authoritative, expert knowledge, but allow ourselves to be changed and transformed through our interactions with our clients. Our reflective practice (Schön 1983) shapes and informs our practice philosophy, which in turn reflexively forms a hermeneutic philosophy of social work. One of the models that comes close to this idea is the integrated practice model (Keen & O'Donoghue 2005), which suggests that the practitioner is in a relationship with self, and environment of the self, the other/client and the environment of the other/client.

Why do we need a philosophy of social work?

C: So we agree that we need to engage with a philosophy of social work; it is how we define what that might be and how we reach that end that we need to explore. Before we do that I would like to make one last plea for a less fluid philosophy for these reasons. We need a philosophy of social work because, while social workers have not been shy about adopting ideas from the social sciences and philosophers in the development of the professional discourse, they have been adopted and adapted with, I would argue, only a surface level analysis.

For example, Chenoweth and McAuliffe (2012, 60–62) provide a summary of the main philosophical utilities used in social work as the basis for its moral and ethical base, underpinning many of the current and past ideas that have formed the numerous social, political and cultural theories and their epistemologies that have been adopted/adapted into its scholarship and practice. This is important knowledge for us to know and adopt/adapt to the situation but it is also important knowledge to be familiar with at a much deeper level than contemporary social work scholars acknowledge. Parton and O'Byrne (2000) and Aymer and Okitikpi (cited in Bell 2011) also advocate for a move from surface-level theory to deeper exploration of these ideas; a distillation proffered by philosophy in terms of exploring its underlying ontology, epistemology, as well as its logical, ethical, moral and political implications. Without this deep engagement with the philosophical ideas in their context and totality, social work theories and critical assumptions underpinning them are buried so deeply that awareness is lost or never explored, risking (knowingly or unknowingly) using theory and its application inappropriately uncritically and inconsistently. We need a philosophical practice to unpack a whole lot of ideas obscured when simply put together in the form of a general matrix to guide practice (Beddoe & Maidment 2009; Bell 2011). Meaney (2001) argues that without a sustained focus on re-imaging the ontological foundations of social work we risk building (more) elaborate epistemological facades (cited in Bell 2011, 414). Indeed many regard the survival of social work as a profession is dependent on getting its act together and beginning to seriously engage with its philosophical assumptions and making them explicit (Bell 2011). Indeed I would argue that social work, in its uncritical grab of *grandes idées* and their uncritical absorption into social work academic and practitioner discourse has also undermined social work efficacy nationally and internationally. The project of getting a universally agreed definition of social work could be seen as way of revitalising social works' ontological position.

M: I agree that we social workers have largely adopted philosophical ideas somewhat uncritically; that is a challenge to educators, however. Our task as social work educators is to resist a model of social workers as technicians (which has been occasioned by the current managerialist environment and the reality that in many countries government is the largest employer of social workers) and ensure that social work students are thoroughly grounded in philosophy and theory, and can engage critically with philosophy. We need to place at least as much weight on philosophy and critical thinking as we do on field placements. That, I think, would move us a long way towards greater parity with allied disciplines, and towards establishing ourselves as a profession. The tension is for us to do this in a way that retains our praxis skill-set. Nevertheless, I suggest that this is not a philosophy of social work, but an engagement of social workers with a knowledge base of philosophical traditions.

C: The task then, if we want to shore-up social work's professional identity and purpose in the current sociopolitical, economic and cultural context is to begin an re-engagement with philosophy as a matter of urgent concern. So the question as to how to distil or sort through the many philosophical explanations and their theoretical trajectories becomes crucial. In addressing this question we can see some progress; social work scholars have come to align their thinking with notions of critical thinking and reflection, deep questioning and thick description, transformative learning and interpretative analysis, cultural evolution, social constructionism and relativism and multiculturalism, each with its own corpus, though rarely acknowledged (White, Fook & Gardner 2012). How, then, can social work save itself as a profession with integrity and applicability? The challenge is for social workers to reconcile possibly radically different ontological positions and articulate its knowledge base situated within a panoply of social science and philosophical musings. More importantly, is there a philosophy of social work that can lead its rescue?

M: I accept wholeheartedly the notion that social work's values and ethics are essential elements in establishing what a philosophy of social work is; as we've seen, Popper acknowledged this as an essential difference between the social and natural sciences (Stokes 1997). However, I challenge the notion that 'philosophy' is some kind of ontological entity with which social work must develop some kind of relationship. As I suggested earlier, I think that a social work philosophy differs from a social worker's engagements with different philosophies. Social work is simultaneously theoretically and praxis-based. You seem to be arguing that thinking comes first, then the doing and that the thinking must have a logical and sustainable flow to it. I am suggesting that social work combines the thinking with the doing and vice versa as an interrelated and relational exercise. This exercise is underpinned by a process philosophy that is dynamic, interactional, relational and dialogic, and in which ideas are only realised in its praxis, which also is interactive.

What does this mean for social work teaching and practice?

M: I think the way forward for us is to agree that there are simultaneously two discussions which intersect with each other. Firstly, we have identified a discussion about social workers' critical engagement with an array of philosophical traditions and writings; the second discussion is about a how to create a philosophy of social work. Both, I think, are necessary. Social workers must critically engage with a broad array of philosophical and theoretical writings in order to understand the bases and implications of their practice decisions. Critical engagement with something called 'philosophy' can place us on a more equal footing with our professional colleagues in other human service disciplines, and move us beyond merely being technicians, or implementers of manualised policies and practices. Here is where social work will become a danger to neoliberal and managerialist policies; this is something our Latin-American colleagues have known and understood for decades. Encouraging this engagement is, in the first instance, a task for social work educators. Equally, however, a philosophy of social work must be intersubjective and dialogic; a philosophy of social work says that we co-create theory, knowledge and praxis with our clients. A philosophy of social work is informed by our internationally agreed values and ethics, just as our praxis must be grounded in a coherent philosophical framework. It is those agreed values and ethics, together with our integration of those values into our practice, that allow social workers from all over the world to have cogent conversations with each other. A philosophy of social work is not a unitary ontology, nor does it need to be: a philosophy of social work is dynamic, critical, and engaged with clients and the intersection of their multiple environments, and the array of philosophies, values and ethics which inform us as social workers.

C: Yes, let's agree on this position.

References

Beddoe, L. & Maidment, J. (2009). *Mapping knowledge for social work: critical intersection*. Melbourne, VIC: Cengage Learning.

Bell, K. (2011). Towards a post-conventional philosophical base for social work. *British Journal of Social Work*, 42(3): 408–23. DOI: 10.1093/bjsw/bcr073.

Benton, T. & Craib, I. (2011). *Philosophy of social science: the philosophical foundations of social thought*. London: Palgrave Macmillan.

Buber, M. (1958 [1923]). *I and thou*. (2nd edn.) Trans. by R. G. Smith. NY: Charles Scribner's Sons.

Chenoweth, L. & McAuliffe, D. (2012). *The road to social work and human service practice* (3rd edn). Melbourne, VIC: Cengage Learning.

Clark, C. & Asquith, S. (1985). *Social work and philosophy: a guide to practice London*. London: Routledge & Kegan Paul.

Desai, M. (2000). Curriculum planning for the history of social work. *Indian Journal of Social Work*, 61(2): 231–36.

Fay, B. (1996). *Contemporary philosophy of social science: a multicultural approach*. Oxford: Blackwell Pub.

Flexner, A. (1915). Is social work a profession? Retrieved on 24 December 2013 from www.socialwelfarehistory.com/social-work/is-social-work-a-profession-1915/.

Garvey, J. & Stangroom, J. (2012). *The story of philosophy: a history of Western thought*. London: Quercus.

Göppner, H. J. & Hämäläinen, J. (2007). Developing a science of social work. *Journal of Social Work*, 7(3): 267–85. DOI: 10.1177/1468017307084071.

Göppner, H. J. (2012). Epistemological issues of social work science as a translational action science. *Research on social work practice*, 22(5): 542–47. DOI: 10.1177/1049731512442250.

Gunnell, J. G. (2009). Can social science be just? *Philosophy of the Social Sciences*, 39(4): 595–621. DOI: 10.1177/0048393109335330.

Hugman, R. (2003). Professional values and ethics in social work: reconsidering postmodernism. *British Journal of Social Work*, 33(8): 1025–41. DOI: 10.1093/bjsw/33.8.1025.

International Federation of Social Workers (n.d.). What we do. Retrieved on 27 December 2013 from ifsw.org/what-we-do.

Keen, M. & O'Donoghue, K. (2005). Integrated practice in mental health social work. In M. Nash, R. Munford & K. O'Donoghue (eds), *Social work theories in action* (pp. 80–92). London: Jessica Kingsley.

McDermott, F. E. (1975). *Self-determination in social work: a collection of essays on self-determination and related concepts by philosophers and social work theorists*. London: Routledge & Kegan Paul.

Meaney, M. (2001). Nature, nurture, and the disunity of knowledge. *Annals of the New York Academy of Sciences*, 935(1): 50–61.

Noble, C. (2013). Social work and the Asia Pacific: from rhetoric to practice. In C. Noble & M. Henrickson (eds), *Social work education: voices from the Asia Pacific* (pp. 343–66). Sydney: Sydney University Press.

Parton, N. & O'Byrne, P. (2000). *Constructive social work: towards a new practice*. NY: St Martin's Press.

Parvin, P. (2011). The rationalist tradition and the problem of induction: Karl Popper's rejection of epistemological optimism. *History of European Ideas*, 31(3): 257–66. DOI: 10.1016/j.histeuroideas.2010.10.005.

Payne, M. (2005). *Modern social work theory* (3rd edn). Basingstoke, UK: Palgrave Macmillan.

Peile, C. & McCouat, M. (1997). The rise of relativism: the future of theory and knowledge development in social work. *British Journal of Social Work*, 27(3): 343–60.

Plant, R. (1970). *Social and moral casework*. NY: Routledge.

Plant, R., Lesser, H. & Taylor-Gooby, P. (1980). *Political philosophy and social welfare: essays on the normative basis of welfare provision*. NY: Routledge.

Ragg, N. (1977). *People not cases: a philosophical approach to social work*. London: Routledge & Kegan Paul.

Rogowski, S. (2010). *Social work: the rise and fall of a profession?* Bristol: Policy Press.

Schmidt, P. F. (1967). *Perception and cosmology in Whitehead's philosophy*. New Brunswick, NJ: Rutgers University Press.

Schön, D. (1983). *The reflective practitioner*. NY: Basic Books.

Soifer, S. (1999). Social work: a profession in search of a paradigm. *Indian Journal of Social Work*, 60(1): 50–56.

Steel, D. & Guala, F. (eds) (2011). *The philosophy of social science reader*. London: Routledge.

Stokes, G. (1997). Karl Popper's political philosophy of social science. *Philosophy of the Social Sciences*, 27(1): 56–79. DOI: 10.1177/004839319702700104.

Sung-Chang, P. & Yuen-Tsang, A. (2008). Bridging the theory–practice gap in social work education: a reflection on an action research in China. *Social Work Education*, 27(1): 51–69. DOI: 10.1080/02615470601141383.

Thomas, P. E. (2004). Towards the development of an integral approach to social work: implications for human behavior theory and research. *Journal of Human Behavior in the Social Environment*, 9(3): 1–13. DOI: 10.1300/J137v09n03_01.

White, S., Fook, J. & Gardner, F. (2012). *Critical reflection in context: applications in health and social care*. Milton Keynes, UK: Open University Press.

2

Transnational social work: a new paradigm with perspectives

Isidor Wallimann

In the course of its professionalisation, social work seems to have got trapped in national social policy frames while our world is increasingly marked by transnational processes. Due to its structural location within nation states, therefore, social work generally has its hands tied to adequately respond to 'globalisation', particularly in the almost total absence of transnational or world social policy frames. Given this situation, what can the profession do? This chapter explores how social work could experience a professional renaissance by explicitly reflecting its role and activities from a transnational perspective. First is explored what a transnational social work perspective is, and what it is not. Second, the possible locations are identified as to where transnational social work could already be practiced. Third, key knowledge dimension are identified for the entire social work field to move forward in adopting a transnational perspective in training, research, service delivery systems and practice.

Social work (understood here to include social work and social pedagogy) is a young profession and owes its legitimacy, status and economic standing primarily to developments after World War 2. While previous pioneers of social work laboured hard to get the profession established, national social policy gave them little support at the time, be it in Europe, the US, or elsewhere. Social services did not enjoy a high priority then, since social policy's prime concern was to broadly establish social insurance systems and to better safeguard the population against the risks of capitalism. To the extent that these systems needed personnel for their administration, recruitment took place outside of social work. Social workers, if at all, were given official functions primarily in conjunction with health and welfare services. Even in the years immediately after World War 2, it must be recognised that social services did not rank high on the social policy priority list. Therefore, when we observe that social work became a legitimate profession after World War 2, this has primarily been so within the last 40 years of the 20th century. By then, the social insurance systems had been broadened so as to cover (in most cases) the entire population of Northern Europe and North America. At the same time also the coverage had become qualitatively better than ever before.

Granted, this path of social work development as a recognised profession is associated with the history of social policy development in 'developed countries' (DCs). It would be a leap of faith, however, to assume that social work in 'less developed countries' (LDCs) today is on a very different track. Though social work training has spread throughout the world, the volume and density of social work services in LDCs still remains rather low. More important, since LDCs typically have little developed social insurance and social services delivery systems, social work there still suffers from lack of official professional recognition and formal embedding. Social work still tends to take place 'outside any welfare state' structure. It mostly tends to operate within a 'private' NGO space. In addition, social work graduates often do not find jobs in the field for which they were trained. Social work has not (yet) become an integral part of a larger system of social problem management and remains a 'marginal' profession outside DCs.

Professionalised social services arrived, historically speaking, late in the development of the welfare state, both in volume and differentiation. In the 1970s volume and differentiation began to grow, however, at a very rapid pace so that some might even speak of a social services explosion. A look at employment and budget indicators would strongly reflect this observation, and the growth in social work education (measured by the number of schools and social work degrees awarded for a range of competences and responsibilities) points to this great expansion at the time. In part, social work functioned to directly complement various components of the social insurance system. But, depending on the country, important growth for social work services took place without being directly linked to the social insurance system in the 'developed world'.

The above analysis suggests that social work obtained its acceptance within national – though different – social policy frames and that the early pioneers and advocates of social work as a (new) profession could not rely on national social policy frames to enhance what they were struggling for. Or, expressed in another way, as social work became an established (new) profession it was simultaneously straight jacketed by the respective national social policy frames. It had little reason to develop a horizon to transcend national perimeters in social analysis and professional action. This is not to say that there would not have been sufficient reason to develop social work perspectives transcending national boundaries. There definitely was, as can be illustrated by migration flows affecting both Europe and North America, and by such things as the North–South dialogues and the preoccupation with 'Third World' social and economic development. The absence of national social policy frames confining social work in perspective and action, then, would explain why the pioneer advocates for professionalised social work in North America and Europe so strongly emphasised the importance of an international perspective. It was the international perspective that helped them at the time to understand certain social processes, problems and challenges facing the populations of their concern. Migration, imperialism and exploitation, and colonial and imperialist wars were major components to their international perspective. Their international perspective was framed by these components and debates around them, though it then differed from our 'global perspective' marked by decades of continued globalisation since.

Now that social work has become an established profession with steadily more individuals trained for it (in and outside universities), what should make us believe that social work would ever be in a position to transcend the national social policy frames confining it? What current and future developments might be so compelling as to necessitate social work to be reflected and daily practiced with an international perspective?

One answer to this question might be found in the rapid trend to integrate economic and social spaces beyond national perimeters although no new (transnational) social policy frames are created to substitute the old (national) ones. The European Union – and to a lesser extent the North American Free Trade Agreement (NAFTA) – would testify to this. Both are transnational processes to integrate social and economic spaces with one exception: social policy tends to remain subject to national authority. In so doing, they follow the subsidiarity principle.

Another part of the answer might be sought in a trend that has been named 'globalisation'. Both the EU/NAFTA and the globalisation process would increasingly call for a perspective that transcends the hitherto common national focus in social work. Even though social work remains confined to national social policy frames, transnational processes will tend to impose an international perspective on them in general, and for social work in particular. Therefore, we may expect social work with an international perspective to become much more important in theory, research and practice.

Transnational, international and global social work

This chapter focuses on the ways in which social work could (or must) be conceived and practiced from more than a national perspective. 'Transnational' could be the term used for social work that transcends the now dominant national focus. 'International' could be used to designate social work with an orientation toward social process between two or more nations. International social work might be termed 'global social work' when the focus is on what has been called 'world system', implying that very many, if not all, nations are seen to be in an interactive process.

It is suggested here to use the term 'transnational social work'. It seems to optimally capture what we mean by social work having a need to extend its perspective beyond national boundaries. Furthermore, 'international' or 'global' social work can be subsumed under it.

Based on these reflections, transnational social work is not:

1. a national juxtaposition of social work development and practice
2. a national comparison of social policy frames and the role social work plays in them
3. a comparison of social work curricula and training practices between nations or schools of social work from different countries
4. an international exchange of students, teachers and practitioners
5. an international cooperation in social work training or research
6. an international social work conference
7. social work in international NGOs unless certain requirements are met (see discussion below)
8. social work in national NGOs or government organisations active abroad unless certain requirements are met
9. multicultural social work unless certain requirements are met.

While it is true that the above may lead the national perspective to be extended, they do not in themselves constitute transnational social work. However, they may be vehicles to facilitate a transnational perspective. Only specific ways to conceive practice and reflect social work can lead to it being transformed from one with a national to one with a transnational dimension and quality.

In this chapter, we understand the transnational perspective in social work as one that cuts across all areas of social work. This view significantly differs from what is generally discussed under 'global', 'international' or 'transnational' social work in the literature. Here, it is proposed that transnational social work be regarded like gender that, if systematically included as a variable, may drastically alter social work both in theory and practice. Likewise, given a problem relevant to social work, additional insights for social work theory and action may result when queried for transnational dimensions. Clearly, the national dimension would be transcended even when the response to a problem remains – or must remain – nationally (or even locally) anchored. 'The national' becomes transnational, as in gender studies 'the private' becomes political. As a result, social work would in theory and practice assume a radically different quality. It would undergo a change from the inside out, so to say.

For example, the response to unemployment or poverty may be anchored on the local or national level. With the transnational focus added, however, this response may qualitatively be very different and, thus, change social work practice and with it possibly also the social policy of which it is a part. Of course, it can always be argued that the better and more effective way would be to anchor the response to unemployment and poverty in a transnational or even global policy frame, since such a frame would by its very nature have to transcend any national focus. There is no reason to dispute such a claim, if the problem addressed can thus be dealt with in a more optimal way. Nonetheless, it remains true that a transnational perspective in social work enables social work practice to better cope with transnational processes, even in the absence of transnational or global policy frames. Thus, unemployment at home may be differently understood if seen as an element of transnational processes through which it may be caused. For instance, knowledge of what economists call 'structural adjustments in the global division of labour' may subsequently lead to different modes of intervention and social work practice.

New social work theory and practice due to a paradigmatic shift

If conceived as suggested here, how much would a transnational perspective change contemporary social work theory and practice? It is hard to say. However, given the ongoing transnational processes of today, and the cumulative outcomes generated by them in the recent past and the foreseeable future, it would be reasonable to assume that many segments of social work theory and practice would experience significant change.

Surprisingly, even in social work fields that are commonly thought of as being a response to a purely 'local' or even a micro social problem, like the family, might undergo change. What is deemed a purely local or national problem may indeed prove to be a 'false' perception – a limited and limiting focus on the micro level, or when social work intervention suffers from an ethnocentric 'national bias' structured into the national policy frame from within which social work delivers services. The unquestioned focus on the national dimension could even be labelled as 'chauvinist social work' given the trend towards transnational processes like migration and the need to recognise and accept in this context a multitude of family patterns 'uncommon' to a particular nation and its family policy frame.

How much would social work focusing on the needs of families change if transnational labour markets, migration and ethnicity were systematically included in analysis and intervention? How, then, would social work be differently practiced pertaining to issues in child rearing, divorce, recombined families, families separated by transnational distance, transnational extended family systems, etc? Again, it is likely that the transnational perspective would change – probably significantly – the ways in which social work in this field would be reflected and practiced.

Responses to alcohol abuse could be a case in point. How much of social work theory and practice in this area of intervention might change after having considered migration, ethnicity and cultural differences in drinking and alcohol abuse patterns? How much would change when internationalised lifestyle patterns are brought into the picture, and with them the international trade and advertising for alcoholic beverages by giant multinational conglomerates? By taking into account such transnational dimensions, it is reasonable to expect that theory and practice relating to alcohol abuse – its prevention, therapy and stabilisation – would undergo significant differentiation and change.

Social work renaissance through the transnational perspective

The above are just a few of many examples that serve to illustrate the powerful influence a transnational perspective – understood as a focus on transnational processes (the salient dimensions of interaction among nations) – would have on social work. Think how a transnational perspective might influence industrial social work, youth work, social work in the health and criminal justice system, community development, etc. There is little doubt that, if systematically applied, a transnational perspective would be of considerable significance to social work theory and practice – be it of the proactive or the reactive type. It could even lead to a professional renaissance associated with a new professional development cycle.

Given the magnitude of contemporary transnational processes, it might be objected that social work in most areas has long ago begun to reflect and practice from a transnational perspective. Not doing so – so is the claim – would have yielded unsatisfactory results for too long. Social work practice has by necessity been doing for some time what is here espoused as a renaissance project for social work. Youth work, community development, family work and other fields have, it may be asserted, for many years been confronted with transnational processes and globalisation. Therefore, the field had no other choice but to practice social work from a transnational perspective.

It would certainly be false and unwarranted to maintain that social work has nowhere been practised with a transnational perspective. Without any doubt, many stellar projects and intervention methods could be found to document the improvement a transnational perspective has brought and could bring to the field. However, how persistently and systematically has the transnational perspective been employed, including in the fields mentioned above that obviously are good 'candidates' for doing so? How systematically has research in social work proceeded to include a transnational perspective? And how many social work training sites are making the international perspectives an explicit part of the curriculum? Closer scrutiny seems to suggest that transnational perspectives have been employed rather sparsely, irregularly and, above all, not explicitly.

What can be observed for 'gender', recognised for many years as a salient variable to be systematically included in all areas of social work, should also hold for the 'transnational perspective'. While 'gender' may have become an explicit variable in some social work education, research and practice, the 'transnational perspective' lags far behind in comparison. Neither, however, has adequately become a dimension firmly embedded in social work theory and practice. Worse, in many cases where 'gender' has 'officially' become a part of reflecting on and practising social work, it may have remained lip service or ritualistic behaviour. That the 'transnational perspective' might to some extent also suffer the same fate is to be expected. However, both 'gender' and the 'transnational perspective' are too important as dimensions to be employed only ambivalently.

Transnational organisations, international social policy frames and transnational social work

Social work operating within a national social policy frame has been the focus so far. It was suggested that the nature of social work theory and practice would in all likelihood change considerably by including a transnational perspective. However, it may be asked, is there social work that already operates within some international social policy frame? If so, where would we be able to locate such international social policy frames in the absence of a world government? Three settings come to mind where social work might be practiced with a transnational perspective or be embedded in a transnational policy frame:

1. the United Nations and its NGOs
2. NGOs that are not part of the UN, but working in an international context
3. national government organisations working in international contexts.

To be sure, a vast number of social workers are employed within national social policy frames, not within international ones. Therefore, it seems to be more pressing to insist on the importance of a transnational perspective for social work still operating – and, given present world structures, probably for many years to come – within a national policy frame. This, however, does not preclude that social work services delivered through organisations such as are listed above do not exist or will not grow in volume in the near future.

At the same time, it must be asked to what extent internationally active NGOs are themselves subject to and subordinated to national social policy frames when active in a particular country or, for that matter, in 'a world of countries'. Since all NGOs (and organisations of foreign governments) are but guests to the country in which they work, they are by nature of this status, and at the risk of expulsion, subject to that country's rules. Therefore, it is not true that social work services offered through internationally operating NGOs is by necessity also 'transnational social work'. On the contrary, it is reasonable to believe that most internationally operating NGOs are 'in business' because they excel in offering solutions tailored to existing national social policy frames. Therefore, we are led back to the claim already made above that social work as a profession would undergo significant change if it managed to introduce a transnational perspective even when it is practised from within an internationally active NGO.

Are international NGOs, however, not in the advantageous position to practise social work with an international perspective? They are, indeed. The potential for international NGOs to practise international social work as understood here lies in the fact that, as a corporate body, they may have accumulated significant knowledge of transnational processes. International NGOs also have significant knowledge about social policy frames that could be designed for dealing with problems related to transnational processes. Given this knowledge base, they possess a ready-made potential to be applied towards arriving at a transnational perspective in social work. This is only so, however, if the host country does not confine such NGOs to operate exclusively from a national perspective.

An example for the above could be found with NGOs that are active in community development and community organising. An NGO, for instance, may have acquired knowledge of migration patterns from a less developed country (LDC) to a developed one. It may know much about social problems related to migration in the country of origin, and it may equally know much about social problems which tend to be generated by migration upon arrival in the country of destination. Assuming that the same NGO is active in both the country of origin and that of destination, it may decide to coordinate its activities by employing a transnational perspective. This may, for instance, lead the NGO to simultaneously coordinate community development projects in the LDC with those for the same migrant group in the country of destination. In so doing, it may mitigate both problems related to emigration and problems related to immigration. Furthermore, it might decide to channel migrants' resources, such as remittances and knowledge, in such ways as to enhance the migrants' 'home' region development.

While various other examples of transnational social work practice within NGOs could certainly be found, we have little knowledge of the volume and nature of such practice. When and where do NGOs practice transnational social work? In which fields of social work do they tend to do so? How much of the total volume of NGO social work is guided by a transnational perspective as it is understood here? Do they do so on principle, or only when given the opportunity by the host country? Similar questions could equally be posed to UN agencies or to national government agencies working abroad.

We might too hastily conclude that UN organisations (such as UNESCO, UNICEF, FAO and others) deliver social work services anchored in a transnational perspective. First, as mentioned above, UN organisations, too, are guests to the countries in which they operate and, therefore, subject to national social policy frames. Second, even though UN organisations may strive to establish global standards in education, health, nutrition, income, fertility, human rights, etc., the social services may nevertheless be provided from a purely national perspective. Expecting a country to meet a given global standard – and to assist them in achieving it – does not imply that social work services (to the extent that they may be a part of this effort) will be designed from a transnational perspective.

The above reflections would lead to the conclusion that UN organisations may very well operate under an international policy frame, such as global standards for member countries. Following the UN, other international NGOs may also subscribe – where meaningful – to the same global standards, adopt their own version thereof or develop new international policy standards in addition. Such additional standards could pertain to gender, salaries and benefits, environment, transparency and accountability, etc.

In general, internationally active NGOs could be categorised as follows:

1. NGOs without global standards and without a transnational perspective underlying their social work services
2. NGOs with global standards in terms of internal functioning and project goals, but without a transnational perspective underlying their social work services

3. NGOs whose work is wholly or in part anchored in a transnational perspective regard-less of whether or not there is adherence to international goals or standards.

It is only the last mentioned NGOs that are of interest here, since we refrain from categori-cally labelling social work services delivered through international NGOs as 'transnational social work'.

Educating for transnational social work – key knowledge dimensions

If transnational social work is based on a perspective that takes into account the effects of transnational processes between two or more nations, what could be understood under 'transnational processes'? Here, a very general concept shall be advanced. A 'transnational process' shall include three features:

1. An interaction and/or exchange pattern between two or more countries – possibly all countries. The nature of this exchange may be economic or not.
2. An interaction and/or exchange pattern persistent enough to produce recognisable and articulated, undesired 'external effects' for one or more of the exchange partners.
3. A spillover onto other countries. Positive and negative external effects of exchange may spill over and, thereby, affect third parties.

If transnational social work is an activity that deals with transnational processes, reflects upon them, and considers their effects when designing social services, what could be some of the knowledge dimensions salient to social work with an international perspective? Let us consider some:

1. Mobility. Exchange processes can consist of the mobility of capital, goods and services, labour power and information culture. All can have negative effects in terms of social problems, calling for social work services. Therefore, it may be important to know what causes migration, by what patterns does the working population migrate, what problems may be generated due to migration and which ones may be generated by labour immigration. The same questions could be asked pertaining to the flows of cap-ital, goods, services and information. What problems arise in the country from which they flow and in the country to which they flow? Additionally, which social prob-lems are generated by the environmental impact mobility in general has on nature and populations. Here, both the energy consumed by the mobility of goods, services and labour, and as a result of moving materials from one ecological system to another, must be taken into account.
2. Unequal exchange. The very quality of an exchange process can equally give rise to problems to which social work may be called upon to respond. Thus, exchange can be more or less equal. Accordingly, a transnational social work perspective would entail knowledge about unequal exchange processes alluded to by terms such as 'un-equal exchange', 'fair and unfair trade', 'unequal development', 'underdevelopment', 'development of underdevelopment', 'transfer of value', 'exploitation', 'environmental destruction', etc.
3. Transnational conflicts. Transnational exchange patterns may lead to conflict-ridden interaction patterns. These in turn may lead to additional problems beyond those caused by 'exchange' in the more narrow sense. Thus, attempts to correct for exchange

relations deemed unacceptable by any party may spiral into a conflict pattern assuming, to some extent, a life of its own. The outcome of such conflicts might even be war. Therefore, a transnational social work perspective would incorporate knowledge about behaviour in conflict situations including knowledge about how conflicts can be escalated or de-escalated.

4. Internal national conflicts and national aggression. Internal national conflicts may spill over to affect other nations, in which case a problem becomes transnational. Refugee migration and other problems come to mind. Equally, in the case of aggression, problems may be imposed on other countries. Thus, the transnational social work perspective would be cognisant of such processes and incorporate knowledge pertaining to them.

5. Transnational cooperation in social policy. Given globalisation and the increased volume of transnational exchange and labour flows, national social policy frames are here and there beginning to be harmonised or even be opened up a bit or complemented by policy elements based on transnational social policy cooperation. Comparative knowledge about various national social policy frames and the transnational cooperation around them is increasingly important for social work with a transnational perspective.

The key knowledge dimensions suggested here are points of orientation for degree programs, continuing education, social work research, and for structuring service delivery systems. Making them an integral part of the field illustrates in more detail how transnational social work as a transversal perspective can be conceived. At the same time, it will begin to move the profession into a transformative process and renaissance to better respond and cope with the ongoing transnational processes and globalisation.

Conclusions

A glance at the history of social work suggests that the founding pioneers of social work were very concerned with transnational processes at the time. They looked beyond their immediate spheres of social work intervention. While social work then had a smaller spectrum of activity than today – it was very often situated in the context of international migration, poverty, education, social and cultural integration – it was accompanied by a 'transnational perspective'. At the same time, this transnational perspective was politically articulated in various forms on national and international levels. With increased professionalisation and the emergence and development of the welfare state, however, the transnational perspective seemed to have lost ground. The more social workers were trained to be certified professional, the more the social work perspective became 'nationalised'. National social policy frames, and social work to be done in them, took centre stage.

Social work as a profession became 'hostage' to the 'welfare state' as the main employer. As a result, social work today is almost exclusively practised with a national perspective, to the exclusion of a transnational one. At the same time, though, social work has been confronted with a phenomenal 'globalisation wave' and an immense qualitative and quantitative change in transnational exchange processes. Clearly, there is a significant dissonance between the social policy frame within which social work is mostly embedded and the challenges posed on many fronts by the sheer magnitude in recent transnational exchange processes. What can be done to mitigate this dissonance?

It is suggested here to infuse the predominant national focus with a transnational perspective in all of social work training, research and practice. This, so it is suggested, will strongly influence the way social work is being reflected, taught, researched and practised within national policy frames, and will lead to an opening toward transnational or global policy frames. Successfully introduced, the transnational perspective could bring social work and the entire field into a renaissance. To some extent, transnational NGOs might serve a useful role in this effort. At the same time, however, it is here concluded that transnational NGOs are guests in the countries in which they work and, therefore, confined to national policy more than is often surmised. In situations of serious social policy conflicts, NGOs could be curtailed or even expelled. Nevertheless, be it from within a transnational NGO or from within a national policy frame, the nature of practicing social work would significantly change once it has learned to adopt a transnational perspective.

Reference note

The above is meant to be a synthetic text written against the background of the literature cited in the bibliography. The cited literature is comprehensive for the English and German language areas. The bibliography, however, does not tend to include publications too removed from 'transnational social work' as understood here, and as delineated above.

References

Borrmann, S., Klassen, M. & Spatscheck, C. (2007) (eds). *International social work: social problems, cultural issues and social work education*. Opladen, Germany: Budrich.

Cox, D. & Pawar, M. (2006). *International social work: issues, strategies, and programs*. London: SAGE Publications.

Deacon, B. (2009). *Global social policy and governance*. London: SAGE Publications.

Elsen, S. (2007). *Die Ökonomie des Gemeinwesens: Sozialpolitik und Soziale Arbeit im Kontext von gesellschaftlicher Wertschöpfung und –verteilung*. Weinheim, Germany: Juventa.

Erler, M. (2007). *Soziale arbeit. Ein lehr – und arbeitsbuch zu geschichte, aufgaben und theorie*. Weinheim, Germany: Juventa.

Ferguson, L.M., Lavelette, M. & Whitmore, E. (eds) (2005). *Globalisation, global justice, and social work*. London: Routledge.

Frank, A. (1994). *The world system: five hundred years or five thousand?* London: Routledge.

Frank, A. (1979). *Dependent accumulation and underdevelopment*. NY: Monthly Review Press.

Frank, A. (1978). *World accumulation: 1492–1789*. NY: Monthly Review Press.

Friedlander, W. (1949). Some international aspects of social work education. *Social Service Review*, 23(2): 204–10.

Grossmann, A. (1983). Mass working class sex reform organisations in the Weimar Republic. In I. Wallimann & M. Dobkowski (eds), *Towards the Holocaust: the social and economic collapse of the Weimar Republic* (pp. 265–93). Westport: Greenwood Press.

Hamburger, F. (ed.) (2009). *Innovation durch Grenzüberschreitung*. Bremen: Europäischer Hochschulverlag.

Healy, L. & Asamoah, Y. (eds) (1997). Global perspectives in social work education. A collection of course outlines on international aspects of social work. Alexandria, VA: Council of Social Work Education.

Healy, L. (1988). Curriculum building in international social work: toward preparing professionals for the global age. *Journal of Social Work Education*, 24(3): 221–28.

Healy, L., Asamoah, Y. & Hokenstad, M. (eds) (2003). Models of international collaboration in social work education. Alexandria, VA: Council of Social Work Education.

Hering, S. & Waaldijk, B. (eds) (2002). *Die Geschichte der sozialen Arbeit in Europa (1900–1960): Wichtige Pionierinnen und ihr Einfluss auf die Entwicklung internationaler Organisationen.* Leverkusen, Germany: Budrich.

Herrmann, P. (2009). *Social quality: looking for a global social policy – attempting an approximation to the analysis of distances of social systems.* Bremen, Germany: Europäischer Hochschulverlag.

Homfeldt, H. & Reutlinger, C. (eds) (2009). *Soziale Arbeit und Soziale Entwicklung.* Baltmannsweiler, Germany: Schneider-Verlag Hohengehren.

Homfeldt, H., Schröer, W. & Schweppe, C. (2008) (eds). *Soziale Arbeit und Transnationalität. Herausforderungen eines spannungsreichen Bezugs.* Weinheim, Germany: Juventa.

Internationale Konferenz für Sozialarbeit (1975). *Industrialisation and Social Work.* Köln, Germany: Carl Heymann.

Kersting, H. & Riege, M. (eds) (2001). Internationale Sozialarbeit. Schriften des Fachbereiches Sozialwesen der Fachhochschule Niederrhein. Band 29. Mönchengladbach, Germany: Fachhochschule Niederrhein.

Kniephoff-Knebel, A. (2006). *Internationalisierung in der Sozialen Arbeit.* Schwalbach: Wochenschau Verlag.

Lesnik, B. (ed.) (1997). *Change in social work: international perspectives in social work.* Farnham, UK: Ashgate.

Lindio-McGovern, L. & Wallimann, I. (eds) (2009). *Globalisation and third world women: exploitation, coping and resistance.* Burlington, VT: Ashgate.

Lorenz, W. (2006). *Perspectives on European social work.* Opladen, Germany: Budrich.

Lorenz, W. (1994). *Social work in a changing Europe.* London: Routledge.

Lyons, K., Manion, K. & Carlsen, M. (2006). *International perspectives on social work: global conditions and local practice.* NY: Palgrave Macmillan.

Mende, U. (1972). *Internationale Sozialarbeit.* Neuwied, Germany: Luchterhand.

Payne, M. & Askeland, G. (2008). *Globalisation and international social work: postmodern change and challenge.* Aldershot, UK: Ashgate.

Rappo, A. & Wallimann, I. (2004). Auswüchse der Privatisierung in der Sozialen Arbeit. New Public Management, KonsumentInnen ohne Wahl und privatisierte Herrschaft. In *Reader des wissenschaftlichen Beirats von Attac, Die Privatisierung der Welt* (pp. 200–05). Hintergründe, Folgen, Gegenstrategien. Hamburg, Germany: VSA.

Razavi, S. & Hassim, S. (eds) (2006). *Gender and social policy in a global context: uncovering the gendered structure of 'the social'.* Basingstoke, UK: Palgrave Macmillan.

Sanders, D. (1977). Developing a graduate social work curriculum with an international cross-cultural perspective. *Journal of Education for Social Work*, 13(3): 76–83.

Schilling, J. & Zeller, S. (2007). *Soziale Arbeit. Geschichte, Theorie, Profession.* München: Reinhardt.

Staub-Bernasconi, S. (1995). *Systemtheorie, soziale Probleme und Soziale Arbeit: lokal, national, international.* Bern, Switzerland: Haupt.

Tan, N.-T. & Envall, E. (eds) (2000–2004). *Social work around the world*, vols 1–3. Bern, Switzerland: IFSW Press.

Whebi, S. (2008). Teaching international social work: a guiding framework. *Canadian Social Work Review*, 25(2): 117–32.

3

Transcending disciplinary, professional and national borders in social work education

Silvia Staub-Bernasconi

The following contribution addresses the questions: Is social work education prepared to promote the goals of the 'Global Agenda for Social Work and Social Development – Commitment to Action' presented to the United Nations in Geneva in 2012 by the three international associations (International Association of Schools of Social Work [IASSW], International Federation of Social Workers [IFSW] and International Council on Social Welfare [ICSW])? What changes in education and practice are needed, when social work and social policy are focused on a transnational frame? The starting hypothesis is that the influences of globalisation and world society on social problems cannot be ignored anymore. What does this mean for the organisation of the disciplinary knowledge, the professional mandate and its ethical base in human rights, social justice and democracy? Are they 'globalisable'? And, as a consequence, how could we overcome the deep dividing line between micro and macro practice? How this could be done is illustrated with two examples: first, the development of social care-chains for the problem of deportation of migrants or asylum-seekers; and second, world-poverty, which requires influencing social cause chains.

Globalisation and world-society – two independent, but since 1945 interdependent, constellations

In many texts and discussions globalisation is a phenomenon which developed at the middle or end of the 20th century and means mainly economic globalisation. However, to make 'globalisation' a synonym for Westernisation, Americanisation or capitalism is an incorrect Eurocentric view of world society. Arabic, Indian or Chinese influences are much older and lasted much longer – over 1000 years or even more. Of course, globalisation has also to do with capitalism, but the expansion and colonisation of Spain and Portugal were examples of feudal colonisation. Genova and Venice were motivated by capitalism, but always in a fragile partnership with Byzantines, the Mongols, the Mamelukes and finally the Ottomans. Only since the rise of the Netherlands and England can one identify clear capitalististic colonisation and exploitation, defined as the dominant search for profit in trade relations. Thus, capitalism is only one source of globalisation. Other sources are the missionary impetus of monotheistic religions and the political goals of power-regimes to establish a hegemonic order over parts of the world or even dominance over the whole world (Menzel 2007, 55–57).

Following from this short historical overview, globalization can be described as a process within world-society, but not identical to it. Therefore I shall use the concept of world-society as the broader concept. Heintz (1982) describes world-society as a system of social units and different system-levels, which show a characteristic structure and processes of reproduction and change. A second idea, more often the strong conviction of many citizens and politicians, that the national history, its level of socioeconomic development and technical as well as cultural accomplishments are completely home- and self-made, leading to a fundamental ethnocentric prejudice leading to harmful superiority feelings over the rest of the world. And these can be harmful to migrants who try to get a small share or dividend for their and their descendants' benefit. Third, in relation to social work, there are other factors which narrow the perspective on world-society:

- the successful universal cultural colonisation by the neoliberal agenda decided in Washington in 1989 (see later) which means a forced focus on work with individual clients as units of help with privatised, self-caused social problems which have to be solved by self-responsibility, self-management, self-empowerment
- the cultural persuasion or even dogma that social justice and democracy can be guaranteed only within a national state context and that they can be practised only when they are codified as nationally institutionalised law and legislation; and finally the sociostructural characteristic of the roles set as members of different social systems.

If one has to practise dominantly internal roles within the family, the social agency (e.g. direct casework with clients, not having to address transformation of privatised troubles into public issues), it is difficult to develop a perspective of a world citizen. The gender-related division of labour between internal and external social roles of social systems is a broad topic of feminist theory which is also relevant for the size of the social space envisioned by individuals (Heintz & Obrecht 1980). Education cannot in the face of these serious obstacles produce miracles, but it can try to develop the relevant disciplinary, professional and practice guidelines for transcending local and national borders, some of which I shall discuss in the next sections.

World-society as subjective perceived reality and transdisciplinary framework for social work

The historical start for the reorganisation of the international order and the slow consolidation of word-society as a social structure of subsystems and interdependent social levels is 1945, the end of World War 2. The process of de-colonisation (still today not completed) and the founding of many new nation-states created the conditions for a new worldwide field of interaction. The old and new states started to describe themselves as sovereign entities, but having an institutionalised supra-national interaction platform at the United Nations and other emerging supra-national organisations. States and many individuals shared the idea of human rights and the development of common political, economic and educational institutions which transcend on national barriers and thus the North–South as well as the East–West divide. Supported by the worldwide student revolt of the 1960s and 70s people began to define social differences in economic and educational terms; they saw income development within and between nations as social injustice and claimed wellbeing and freedom for all individuals. There was a scientific and political search for the common development of transnational social policies to reach this goal.

With the fall of the Soviet regime in 1989 followed by the declaration of the Washington Consensus in the same year, this development was stopped. Prime ministers, politicians, diplomats and a legion of lobbyists with vested interests celebrated – with many inhabitants of the Western societies – the 'death of socialism' and founded the World Trade Organization (WTO). Its new world policy-document – called the Washington Consensus (1989) – begins with the following first article: 'The most important goal of economy is growth; economic growth produces jobs, wealth, development, equality and democracy'. This credo is followed by nine articles – the effects of them we know by now very well as:

- economic globalisation; opening all borders for the free trade of goods, social services, capital, investment (yet not in human beings)
- privatisation, deregulation, constraining the role of the state
- global free trade, not local production is the source of wealth
- reduction of taxes for entrepreneurs and corporations
- restriction of the role of the state concerning health, education and social welfare (i.e. opening them up for the free market of insurance companies)
- unrestricted competition of all against all to promote (output-oriented, efficient) performance (Meyer 2009).

The WTO regime with its ten neoliberal articles of faith began to colonise almost the whole world – not only the economic development and consumption, but also politics, education, culture, health, social welfare, many systems of legislation and last, but not least, social work and social policy (Meyer 2009).

World-society defined by people and by theoretical disciplines

World-society can't be seen and observed. Yet it is a fact of life, more precisely a fact which affects the life of people worldwide. They have to live with this fact, even if they don't want to know about it and its influence upon them, their life perspectives and decisions – e.g. to open a bank account or not, to stay where they are born or to migrate or seek refuge in another area or country. But when they feel in some way affected by it, they construct an image of it mainly determined by their social membership, cultural affiliation and personal codes, as well as aspirations, interests and goals.

How do social work practitioners, faculty members, field instructors define world-society? Looking at the literature, the bulk of contributions focuses on individuals, families, small groups, ethnic groups, then in rapidly declining numbers on local communities – ending at the national borders. Conferences and journals about international social work are mainly a collection of very interesting accounts about social work endeavours, problems, goals and successes without identifying influences from or for a broader social context. If we want to go a step further, we have to have a disciplinary notion of world-society. Society is today a worldwide complex interaction field of individuals with multiple or no memberships in social micro-, meso- and macro-systems. Thus the object base of human development, sociology, politics, economy, cultural studies etc. has to be within the frame of world-society. One can hardly find a social problem –poverty, unemployment, forced migration, displacement, discrimination, racism, sexism, classism, religious and other intolerance, traffic in children and women, political persecution and torture and last but not least wars – which doesn't have distinct causes in the structure and dynamics or processes of world-society (Heintz 1982; Wobbe 2000).

The approach outlined by Heintz (1982) and Wobbe (2000) identifies the following transnational sub-systems interacting in different ways to understand the dynamics of world-society, namely:

- the transnational stratification system of the world-population, which encompasses the position of the individuals along the dimensions of education, occupation, income and urbanisation and their evaluation of these social structures in relation to need satisfaction, freedom versus oppression, (ill)egality, (in)justice etc. – all are topics of ecology, psycho-biology, psychology, social psychology, sociology and cultural studies;
- the transnational economic system of transnational corporations – and the more recent development, the increasing power of the financial industry – a main topic of economic theory;
- the international state-system of the hegemonic political-military-power-system – a main topic of political science;
- the transnational intercultural system – symbol-systems as philosophy, religion, science, ethics, ethnic subcultures, public discourses – transported by internet communication and social media.

This theoretical approach must be accompanied by a conceptualisation of world-society as a multi-level structure of social actors and social systems: the individual, family, group, local community and organisational levels which are already very familiar in social work texts. But in a globalised world we have to add the national, regional/continental, inter- and supra national level. So, the question is: what could teaching and practice include, if social work, or at least a part of it, should be one of the many players in a globalised world-society?

The global agenda for social work and social development 2012

A program for strengthening social work's role in setting an agenda for global action was recently developed, enlarged and reinforced in 2012 by an international document of the IASSW, IFSW and ICSW called 'Global agenda for social work and social development – commitment to action', presented at the United Nations. It states:

> We believe that now is our time to work together, at all levels, for change, for social justice, and for the universal implementation of human rights, building on the wealth of social initiatives and social movements. We ... recognise that the past and present political, economic, cultural and social orders ... have unequal consequences for global, national and local communities and have negative impacts on people. (IASSW, ICSW, IFSW 2012)

These inequalities are listed as:

- only a minority of the world's population has access to the respect, protection and fulfilment of human rights through national states
- poverty, followed by damaged wellbeing and poor health due to unjust and poorly regulated economic systems, non-compliance to the international standards of labour conditions and lack of corporate social responsibility
- missing respect of cultural diversity and the right to self-expression, especially for indigenous and first nation peoples
- disruption of supportive, caring social relationships in families and communities
- victims of direct and indirect violence, such as war, ethnic/religious conflicts, natural disasters, pollution and climate change (IASSW, ICSW, IFSW 2012).

The list of social problems closes with an international, regional and national commitment to advocate for a new world order which makes a reality of respect for human rights and dignity. It addresses a different structure of human relationships, promoting social and economic justice and community participation in governance, environmentally sensitive development, and finally ensuring appropriate education, practice and research for the implementation of these goals. One can read the document as one possible alternative answer to the policy program of the Washington Consensus of 1989 which has not only neglected, but suppressed any reference to the needs of people and their wellbeing, to social problems, social justice and social rights. Its assumption is that economic growth is the panacea for everything. This urges social work to clarify the following central issues: the (re)definition of the relevant societal context within which it operates and accordingly the scope of its professional mandate; old and new actors for social change, and the way of linking social micro-, meso-, and macro-practice which I shall call the development of transnational 'social work chains' (Staub-Bernasconi 2012).

The professional triple-mandate of social work – a mandate for social work without borders

A common assumption is that social work has a double mandate, one of the client and one of the social agency, sometimes characterised as 'help and control'. Yet, the profession has in fact a triple-mandate: from the client, the social agency and the profession itself. The third mandate of social work has two dimensions, namely science-based interventions (in common with other professions) and the explicit orientation towards human rights and social justice as professional ethics. In a world-society with very different political regimes, legislation and cultural differentiations, social work must also be possible in nations which aren't welfare states, and the same should also hold for those that are considered as corrupt or even failed states (Gore 1969; Midgley 1997, 2000). In these cases social workers might not be able to refer themselves to a national consensual, official professional code. Yet, they still can rely on the common documents of the international associations IASSW/IFSW/ICSW – which are also relevant for social workers not organised in a national association.

The third mandate gives to social work the possibility to formulate a self-defined mandate based on the identification of pressing, unfulfilled needs, social injustice, violence, and human rights violations in general without having to wait for a mandate from society or a state which may never come. Ideally, it should get it from the people in distress – if possible in combination with and with support from social movements, NGOs or philanthropic efforts – in short, from civil society. The idea is not so new, but has to be revitalised: professional social work started in many countries with initiatives by self-mandated women – be it through direct help in the local community or social policy and legislation on the national level and even for world politics, e.g. in relation to suffrage and World War 1 (Addams and the Women of Hull House; Alice Salomon from Germany, Clara Ragaz from Switzerland, Radlinska from Poland). Today we know of 'doctors without borders', followed by 'reporters without borders' and an initiative in Switzerland called 'law without borders'. Inspired by John Ruggie, UN Special Representative of the Secretary-General for business and human rights, this NGO alliance calls on parliaments to make regulations law in order to oblige companies and their worldwide subsidiaries to implement human rights and environmental protection. At the same time it opens the way for individuals, groups and populations who are damaged or come to grief to access the judicial system. The central idea is that corporations should be responsible for the whole production chain from the beginning regardless of the country of residence of their headquarters.

While the universality of scientific, transdisciplinary epistemology and research procedures is – sometimes more, sometimes less – accepted, social work has to face the fact that the universality of human rights is partially contested; for example, as Western colonisation in the guise of charity. It was a big issue at the Vienna World Conference of 1993 where most of the national delegates reinforced the idea of the universality and indivisibility of human rights. This was possible, despite dictators from Asian and African states ignoring the claims for the liberty and democracy of their populations and the many NGOs present there. Yet the claim for the universality of human rights is still an important and critical issue of the mandate of social work. To support this claim, I restrict myself to four arguments (see Staub-Bernasconi 2011, 2014).

First, analysing the rich literature about philosophical, religious and secular-humanist approaches to human dignity and human rights, I suggest that there is only one approach left for the justification of the universality of human rights as a minimal ethic, which doesn't colonise and/or exclude individuals, minorities of every kind or even national indigenous populations (first nation peoples), namely: the one which refers to the biological, psychological, social and cultural needs common to all human beings and the manifold consequences if their fulfilment is violated. As almost all international social work theories refer in some way to human needs, it might be plausible that their fulfilment must be (legally) universally protected. Yet needs should not be confused with wishes and aspirations mainly influenced by socialisation and the cultural context (Antweiler 2007). The violation of needs have a long history of individual and public articulation and transformation into values of freedom, participation/democracy and social justice (see the history of slavery; the Freedom Charter of the ANC during the apartheid regime; the liberation movements in Latin-America; the Hong-Kong Asian Charter formulated by hundreds of NGOs; the first claims during the Arabic Revolutions since 2011). Second, contextual, subcultural philosophical, ethnic or religious adaptations of human rights are acceptable, unless they legitimise the violation of human rights. Third, there can be no subordination of the individual person under the declared absolute superiority of social systems of any size – from family to organisations, nations etc. This refers to the problem of oppression, dictatorship in the name of a superior social whole. The same holds for the subordination of social systems under the absolute superiority of the individual in the name of an unlimited freedom; for example, for property and economic trade which doesn't care about the breakdown or destruction of social relations and social rules which guarantee needs-fulfil-ment for all individuals – meaning here the whole world population. If one doesn't divide the UN Declaration into its two parts – the liberal and the social rights – then we have a model of human beings as, 'individuals in social contexts'. Finally, the supra-national law of human rights is a yardstick for the analysis of the legitimacy of a national law systems and their implementation. Not only in nation-states, but also the preamble of continen-tal, African, Asian and Islamic human rights declarations agree with the universality of human rights, but don't accept international interventions threatening their sovereignty. This paradox must be understood as an understandable safeguard in the face of European colonisation history. To tackle this paradox seems to be perhaps the most difficult and is shown by the long learning process nations have to go through, such as the actual prob-lems of the International Judicial Court in The Hague.

The task for teaching 'social work without borders' in the face of its triple mandate will then be, first, to place its long and large tradition of needs-based social work and social policy into the broader framework of human rights and human dignity (Ife 2001; Reichert 2003; Wronka 2008); second clarification – if religious, ethnic, political or other particular worldviews which ignore or negate human rights or replace them by inhuman world-views or theories. But the main task of social work and social policy will be to try to introduce – as far as possible – human rights as a regulative idea into the main topics of education and practice on the national and international levels (Staub-Bernasconi & Wronka 2012; Staub-Bernasconi 2014).

More specifically, social work and social policy will have to join in the discussions about the possibility to transnationalise their meta-values of social justice and democracy (see Addams 1902), which means the overcoming of the dogma that they can only be guar-anteed in and through a nation-state, and that they can exist only when they are codified as nationally institutionalised law. What then do I mean by the 'globalisation' of social and democratic citizenship?

The universalisation of social justice

Distributive social justice as a topic of social policy has been until today a national-eth-nocentric enterprise. 'Theories of global justice will either point to facts about our nature as human beings . . . and are motivated by what we share simply by virtue of being hu-man [non-relational approaches] . . . or to the fact that we share certain institutions or are bound together in some other significant way [relational approaches cf Rawls]' (San-giovanni 2007 cited in Armstrong 2012, 25). Global or transnational social justice is, according to Armstrong (2012), 'any theory which suggests that there are some entitle-ments of justice which have global scope and . . . that there are some duties of justice which have global scope'. This means that there are certain things we are obliged to do, or not to do (17).

John Rawls (1973 in Armstrong 2012, 76–86), the most cited philosopher of social jus-tice confines it mainly to the liberal rich societies and their individuals sharing the idea of free and equal citizens, an idea which is – in his eyes – not widely accepted. To impose this scheme of justice on non-liberal societies would be illegitimate and hurt the principle of tolerance. Even Rawls (1999 cited in Armstrong 2012, 76–86) is indifferent to the fact that there are rich and poor societies and that the rich societies might profit from the re-sources, cheap labour, former slavery and colonisation structures of the poor ones. Yet he accepts the duty of rich societies to assistance having a defined, 'target and cut-off-point'. For him global distributional justice neglects the responsibilities of peoples for their own wealth and poverty which are homemade – actually a generalisation of the neoliberal view of self-made social problems by the individual and thus the self-responsibility of solving them. Thomas Pogge calls this position 'explanatory nationalism' (2002, 139–145). According to Mario Bunge a society has to be internally and externally just, fulfilling the needs – not wishes – of its population and not hindering the economic, social and cultural development and thus need-fulfilment of the other societies (1989, 372).

The universalisation of democracy

Concerning the universalisation of democracy, we know many highly problematic examples of legitimising democracy through wars. There are prominent theoreticians who regard the idea of a global democracy as 'unachievable' or 'that its advocates are barking to the moon' (Archibugi, Koenig-Archibugi & Marchetti 2012). Yet a new generation of scholars (such as David Held, Richard Falk, Jürgen Habermas) point out that democracy has become widely, albeit not universally accepted as the only (best?) way to legitimate political power (Archibugi et al., 2) and have thus developed different models of global democracy such as: confederalism, federalism and polycentrism (6–14) or intergovernmentalism, global governance and global polity (22–46). Many forms are combinations of two or three types. What is common to all conceptions, is the vision of a system of global governance that is responsive and accountable to the preferences of the world's citizens and works to reduce political inequalities among them (Archibugi et al. 2012). Governance may, but need not, be provided by a 'government'. It could also mean the reform of international organisations such as the UN, especially the Security Council and the WTO.

The discussion of the pros and cons of all these models isn't possible within this chapter. But what one should remember is a book of one of our own theoreticians about democracy, Jane Addams 'Democracy and Social Ethics' (1902). She introduced the notion of 'integral democracy' which requires the sharing and division of power starting with social work, continuing within the family, the industry or economic and educational system and finally in politics. In addition she requires that political democracy based on the equality of citizens and procedural fairness should be enlarged by the social dimension of social justice (for the concept of integral democracy see also Bunge 2009, 351–401).

Castles and Davidson (2000) discussing the many problems of migrants (difficult social integration, pressure for cultural assimilation, rejection, and discrimination) and immigration societies (emergence and segregation of ethnic minorities as consequence of discrimination, the racialisation of the nation-state), try to show that a theory of citizenship for a global society must be based on separation between nation and state. This means a new type of state that is not constituted exclusively or mainly around the nexus of territoriality and belonging. Yet in a world of migrants and ethnic groups, citizenship cannot be blind to cultural belonging. The political mechanisms that make people into citizens must take account of both of their rights as individuals and their needs, interests and values as members of social and cultural collectives. Reconciling the individual and the collective is the key problem of citizenship for a globalised society and is discussed extensively in their book.

What follows, then from all this for the conception of and teaching a social work practice to answer the social problems caused by the social structure and development of world-society as well as to the policy-program of the 'global agenda of social work'? Many texts dealing with this question suggest vaguely what 'one should do' or they describe what social workers have already done working in international organisations. Teaching transnational social work requires something more precise: the theory-/science-based design of action guidelines which show how one can surmount the deep dividing line between micro- and macro-practice transcending national borders.

Social work chains as general action principle for the development of concerted actions of micro- meso- and macro-practice

Although one could feel completely powerless and thus reject world-society as an empirical, theoretical and normative framework of social work, it would be a mistake to define it as an unchangeable global stratification– and power– or oppression–system influencing social subsystems and their individuals in a strict one-way top-down-model with no chance to react to and actively reshape it. World society is also the product of the perceptions, interpretations, interests and resulting activities of individuals and collective actors with very different power sources and embedded in different power structures who identify and use accessible social action spaces and opportunities to realise their goals. So how can we teach this perspective? Here are examples which follow the assumption that world-society can be at least partially influenced by social work by gaining definitional (scientific) power over social problems caused by the structure and dynamics of world-society, by organising and linking micro- meso- and macro-practice together, and by building networks, coalitions and join social movements and/or NGOs which share approximately the same goals and are themselves organised or at least oriented along the mentioned different action-levels. These are the ingredients of what I call the conception and development of social work chains through trying to build professional social work chains or to influence social work chains.

Establishing transnational social care chains: human rights concerns and the deportation of unwanted migrants and asylum seekers

To diagnose the influence of the transnational social subsystems of world-society upon individuals I try to show it with the following example.

A young woman with a physical disability (as member of the transnational social stratification system of the world population) came to Switzerland because she heard that there are camps where asylum seekers could work for at least four years (perception, relevance and use of the transnational stratification system to migrate from a country with low to a country with high socioeconomic development). She (as member of the political-military power system) was sent back to the Kosovo. There she lives with her 80-year-old father. He was a partisan during World War 2 (as member of the hegemonic political-military power system) and (as member of the national stratification system) has a very small pension. It's just enough to pay the rent for the one-room apartment and each day some yoghurt, eggs, burek and onions for him and his daughter. In the kitchen, which serves also as living room, next to the television (member of the transnational intercultural system), there is a model of the Eiffel tower of Paris. The father was married twice. Both women went back into their family because he forbade them to go out and even to look out of the window (patriarchal oppression in the family system). The young woman isn't able to – as most of the women of her age – find a job (exclusion from the local and national socioeconomic system). Individuals with disabilities don't get state subsidies as long as they can move on their own (exclusion from the social security system of the nation-state). She can't find a man who will marry her yet she has seven abortions behind her.

The main scholarly texts about migration demand from social work the best possible societal integration of migrants and refugees using intercultural sensitivity and trauma work as well as anti-discriminatory, anti-racist practices. What is almost completely neglected are the problems following deportations which grow in number since the nation states in the European Union restricted their immigration laws and made it more and more difficult to cross their borders. According to these laws everything is correct. But is legality also ethically legitimate, e.g. considering the human right of being recognised everywhere as a person before the law or the right to freedom of movement and residence within the borders of each state (Articles 6, 7, 13, 14 of the UN Declaration)? Does the mandate of social work end at the national or European border? The woman above returns not only in deplorable, violent conditions, which have destroyed her dignity, social relations and physical integrity; in addition she is sent into a social vacuum with no person or organisation to which she could go for help. What about youngsters sent back after turning 18 years old without having a chance to get education or vocational training and jobs in their home country? Are their 'career' possibilities illegal labour, criminality, prostitution or joining a politically radical organisation? Many succeed in returning illegally to an immigration country so that one could speak of a permanent rotation of migration – problems between nations (Verschiebebahnhof), where all try to solve them by their national laws almost without success – not to speak of the thousands of deaths of the 'boat-refugees'.

One action-theoretical answer to these deportation problems should be the systematic development of social care chains for deported individuals and families through institutionalised cooperation between social welfare organisations of the country from which they were deported and organisations of the home country if they are willing to cooperate. Such arrangements exist already for victims of human trafficking. A second necessity on the national-state level is the development and promotion of the idea of global democratic and social citizenship and the adaptation of national legislation so that immigrants in the country to which they have immigrated get access to social rights such as education, work, social medicine and welfare. But their status as political citizens of the nation-state remains very fragile or is quite often denied, if right-wing-populism or racism is strong or growing. (Soysal 1994, Castles & Davidson 2000; Yeates 2001) In this case they should be able to rely on the status of a world-citizen and bearer of human rights. Furthermore, the plea for an engagement with socioeconomic development in poor regions or countries to stop the main causes of migration must be on the public agenda. In sum, the complex theoretical and practical task is to plan a coalition with actors representing each social level which is relevant for problem solving, so that there can be a continuous information flow and coordinated social actions.

Influencing social cause chains of harm: world poverty and human rights

Poverty on a local or national level and its consequences has been present at the historical beginning of social work. Today, most people in northern countries know, at least through the media that there is – far away – poverty and extreme poverty. The Treaty of Lisbon had a goal to cut down worldwide poverty by 50% by 2015. By now it is clear that this goal won't be reached (Pogge 2002, 195).

But for the media poverty statistics and millions of deaths because of poverty, malnutrition, avoidable diseases is not an issue for 'breaking news'. Why information is not morally salient to the people in rich nations has cultural and structural causes. The cultural causes are common assumptions and perceptions in rich countries, which systematically ignore worldwide poverty and negate the responsibility of transnational justice Pogge (2002, 6–11). They highly favour the popular ideas that:

- poverty is a national and thus internal matter produced by the corrupt local and national elites
- world poverty is so great a problem that it simply cannot be eradicated in a few years, at least not at a cost that would be bearable for the rich societies. It would greatly damage our lives and communities and thus is clearly politically unfeasible
- the history of failed attempts at development show that one is throwing money out of the window, and sharing money and bread with everybody would be hungry and poor
- preventing poverty deaths is counter-productive because it will lead to overpopulation and hence to more poverty deaths in the future (this is a neo-Darwinian thesis)
- world poverty is disappearing anyway. The popularity of this assumption in the developed world has less to do with actual trends than with people being eager to believe the rhetoric of politicians, economists, and organisations such as the World Bank taking good care to define and measure poverty so as to show improvement. (Pogge 2002, 139–45)

Pogge (2002) calls these ideas 'explanatory nationalism' which means that everything which exists and happens in world-society is explained with internal national structures and processes. The rich countries believe only in the success in producing economic wealth, forgetting their history of worldwide colonisation and actuality of exploitation of cheap labour and precious resources and – in the last 20 years – overlooking the enormous enrichment mainly of the (neofeudal) upper class according to their undemocratic, self-made law systems. And they use the same national frame to blame the poor and developing countries for their 'bad domestic policies and institutions that stifle, or fail to stimulate, national economic growth and engender national economic injustice' (Pogge 2002, 140). This view entirely ignores the influences of the actual geopolitical context with its domination of the transnational economic and autonomous financial industry system over the national economies and governments of the poor, but also the rich countries. Emancipated middle- and upper-class women forget that they could study, get a job and support their own family due to support from very low-paid, unregulated housework of women migrating from far away, who leave their own children behind in their home country.

Sociostructural causes: the transnational economic system as parallel society with laws and social rules without democratic legitimation

The main sociostructural causes for world-poverty are according to Pogge (2002), Fischer-Lescano & Möller (2012) the social rules of the World Trade Organization, World Bank, the International Monetary Fund and their sub-organisations, which have established a transnational economic system supported by a law system which is not democratically legitimate, and which systematically discriminates against the developing countries. It is a Lex Mercatoria of a parallel society, conceived by our prime ministers, politicians, diplomats, delegates, lawyers and lobbyists. They installed judicial courts with social laws of free trade, the right to property for huge corporations and private global investors freed of taxation, yet rising high taxes for import goods and state subsidies for national goods which expropriate huge populations from their resources, their economic development and export-chances. In other words, the transnational economic system since 1989 creates its own laws which it needs to establish its world hegemony and force national politics to suggest that there isn't enough money for education, health and social security/welfare. These mechanisms – legalised by the Lex Mercatoria – explain why there can be no concomitant social development and progress in spite of high rates of economic growth in the (financial) business and industry – in general, but also in the rich societies of the north (Wilkinson & Pickett 2009) and even in the dependent poor countries under the WTO regime. Since the financial crisis of 2008 even the existing national social legislations, the European Social Charter and the UN covenant on social rights are irrelevant – not only, but especially for Greece, Spain and Portugal. A new treaty called the Transatlantic Trade and Investment Partnership is in the pipeline which, if implemented, will be the death of any financial state autonomy (Wallach 2013).

Influencing social cause chains of harm: implementing the negative principle of doing no harm

The harm caused by the described cultural and sociostructural determinants can be defined as follows. One harms the poorest of the world when one:

- hinders the fulfilment of their needs which is a violation of human, especially social rights
- is not able to develop an alternative oranisational design – or social cause chain – which follows the rule of 'do no harm' which means to protect the poor from human rights violations by social actors and their organisations (Pogge 2009, 32).

Pogge's suggestions don't aim primarily at the social distribution of wealth (for this goal see Shue 1996). He thinks that it is too difficult and slow to change the morals of people in rich countries. His goal is to change the social rules of the supra-national organisations ruling world-society with no democratic legitimate.

What then could be the role of transnational social work chains in influencing the chains of social harm according to a concerted multi-level strategy? I suggest the following steps:

- the meta-reanalysis of poverty-narratives and studies all over the world in different sociocultural contexts – using multiple research methods – to show empirically the harm to the individual, familial or local community level (see McGillivray & Clarke 2006; Banerjee & Duflo 2012; Duflo 2010; Cox & Pawar 2006)

- the organisation of social platforms on the local or national level to report, anonymously or publicly, cases of bonded labour, discrimination, exploitation, oppression, corruption etc., followed by marches claiming land, clean water, food, medical services etc., which in fact identify the actors causing poverty
- the strengthening of human and social rights on the nation-state level using the instruments of state and NGO reports to the UN, followed by a monitoring of the state activities concerning the recommendations of the UN Committee on Economic, Social and Cultural Rights
- external campaigning and internal lobbying for the democratisation of the supranational organisations such as WTO, World Bank, International Monetary Fund, European Union, and their sub-organisations, together with alliances of actors, politicians, open-minded economic leaders and experts who support the democratisation claims (for a precise blueprint see Stiglitz 2006)
- diffusion of counter knowledge negating the different myths surrounding the causation of and thus responsibility for world poverty.

Concerted action within such a transnational network would have to coordinate the information-flow from the bottom to the top and back again, as well as the plans and evaluated effects of social actions on each level. It seems that young generations worldwide use the rapidly growing 'transcultural subsystem' of general and social media much more intensively, systematically and in creative ways for social protest, virtual communities and concrete social action than social workers and their teachers. To construct the suggested 'social work chains' and with them forms of critical knowledge to disrupt the inhuman chains these media are indispensable. But their use must be based on disciplinary knowledge and research about world-society and social problems, a clear professional mandate and a social practice linking micro-, meso- and macro-levels of social action.

References

Addams, J. (1902). *Democracy and social ethics*. NY: Macmillan.

Antweiler, C. (2007). *Was ist den Menschen gemeinsam? Über Kultur und Kulturen*. Darmstadt, Germany: Wissenschaftliche Buchgesellschaft.

Archibugi, D., Koenig-Archibugi, M. & Marchetti, R. (2012). *Global democracy*. Cambridge: Cambridge University Press.

Armstrong, C. (2012). *Global distributive justice*. Cambridge: Cambridge University Press.

Banerjee, A. & Duflo, E. (2012). *Poor economics: a radical thinking of the way to fight global poverty*. Philadelphia, PA: Public Affairs.

Bunge, M. (1989). *Treatise on basic philosophy*, vol. 8, *Ethics: the good and the right*. Dordrecht, Netherlands: Reidel Publishing.

Castells, M. (1996). *The rise of the network society*. Oxford: Blackwell.

Castles, S. & Davidson, A. (2000). *Citizenship and migration: globalisation and the politics of belonging*. London: Macmillan.

Cox, D. & Pawar, M. (2006). *Internationale social work: issues, strategies, and programs*. London: SAGE Publications.

Duflo, E. (2010). *Le développement humain. Lutter contre la pauvreté*. Seuil, Paris.

Fischer-Lescano, A. & Möller, K. (2012). *Der Kampf um globale soziale Rechte*. Berlin: Wagenbach.

Gore, M.S. (1969). Social work and its human rights aspects. In International Council on Social Welfare (ed.), *Social welfare and human rights: proceedings of the XIVth International Conference on Social Welfare* (pp. 56–68), August 1968, Helsinki, Finland.

Healy, L.M. (2002). Internationalizing social work curriculum in the 21st century. In N. Tan & I. Dodds (eds), *Social work around the world*, vol. 2, *Agenda for global social work in the 21st century* (pp. 179–94). Berne, Switzerland: IFSW Press.

Heintz, B. & Obrecht, W. (1980). Die sanfte Gewalt der Familie. In G. Hischier, R. Levy & W. Obrecht. *Weltgesellschaft and Sozialstruktur*. Diessenhofen, Switzerland: Rüegger.

Heintz, P. (1982). *Die Witgesellschaft im Spiegel von Ereignissen*. Diessenhofen, Switzerland: Rüegger.

Huntington, S.P. (1996). *The clash of civilizations: remaining of the world order*. NY: Simon & Schuster.

McGillivray, M. & Clarke, M. (eds) (2006). *Understanding human wellbeing*. NY: United Nations University Press.

Menzel, U. (2007). Was ist Globalisierung oder die Globalisierung vor der Globalisierung. In M.A. Ferdowsi (ed.), *Weltprobleme* (6th edn) (pp. 23–57). Bonn, Germany: Bundeszentrale für politische Bildung.

Meyer, J.W. (2009). *World society*. Oxford: Oxford University Press.

Midgley, J. (2000). Globalisation, capitalism and social welfare: a social development perspective. *Canadian Social Work*, special Issue, *Social Work and Globalisation*, 2: 13–28.

Midgley, J. (1997). *Social welfare in global context*. Thousand Oaks, CA: SAGE publications.

Pogge, T.W. (2002). *World poverty and human rights: cosmopolitan responsibilities and reforms*. Cambridge: Polity Press.

Reichert, E. (2003). *Social work and human rights*. NY: Columbia Press.

Shue, H. (1996). *Basic rights: subsistence, affluence, and US foreign policy* (2nd edn). Princeton, US: Princeton University Press.

Staub-Bernasconi, S. (2014). Soziale Arbeit und Menschenrechte. Opladen, Germany: Barbara Budrich.

Staub-Bernasconi, S. (2012). Human rights and their relevance for theory and practice. In L. Healy, M. Link & J. Rosemary (eds), *Handbook of international social work. Human rights, development, and the global profession* (pp. 30–37). Oxford/NY: Oxford University Press.

Staub-Bernasconi, S. (2012). Global agenda for social work. Partnering with the United Nations – human rights and social work. Retrieved on 22 April 2014 from www.avenirsocial.ch/fr/cm_data/ GLOBAL_AGENDA_-_Staub_-_UN_GENF_26.3.2012.pdf.

Staub-Bernasconi, S. (2011). Human rights and social work – philosophical and ethical reflections on a possible dialogue between East Asia and the West. *Journal of Ethics & Social Welfare*, 5(4): 331–47

Staub-Bernasconi, S. (2010). Human rights – facing dilemmas between universalism and pluralism/ contextualism. In D. Zavirsek, B. Rommelspacher & S. Staub-Bernasconi (eds), *Ethical dilemmas in social work – international perspectives* (pp. 9–24). Ljubljana, Slovenia: Faculty of Social Work University of Ljubljana.

Staub-Bernasconi, S. & Wronka, J. (2012). Human rights. In K. Lyons, T. Hokenstad, M. Pawar, N. Huegler & N. Hall (eds), *The SAGE handbook of international social work* (pp. 70–84). London: SAGE Publications.

Stiglitz, J.E. (2006). *Making globalisation work*. NY: Norton.

Wallach, L. (2013). TAFTA – die grosse Unterwerfung. *Le Monde Diplomatique*, (1): 16–17

Wilkinson, R. & Pickett, K. (2009). *The spirit level – why more equal societies almost always do better*. London: Penguin Books.

Wobbe, T. (2000). *Weltgesellschaft*. Bielefeld, Germany: Transcript Verlag.

Wronka, J. (2008). *Human rights and social justice: social action and service for the helping and health professions*. Thousand Oaks, CA: SAGE Publications.

Yeates, N. (2001). *Globalisation and social policy*. London: SAGE Publications.

4

Educating social workers without boundaries through the Intercultural Social Intervention Model (ISIM)

María-José Aguilar-Idáñez and Daniel Buraschi

Some innovative and replicable aspects about the main contents of one educational program for social workers in Spanish are presented. The program is based on the critical analysis of implicit models and the development of intercultural competences. Our Intercultural Social Intervention Model (ISIM) is the central axis (theoretical and practical) of the educational program, which is used and inspired by other practice theoretical models and perspectives from the south and the north: concientización or consciousness raising model, anti-oppressive model, empowerment and advocacy model, and the transformative mediation model; though adapted to multicultural realities with more complexity and diversity than those in which the mentioned models developed. It is an international postgraduate program which is open to final-year bachelor students of social work. The program combines remote instruction (off-line and online activities) and on-campus activities (face-to-face online classes and workshops, practices in the field, collaborative groups, etc.).

> No problem can be solved by the same consciousness which created it.
>
> Albert Einstein

In our program we teach professionals to advocate for vulnerable groups, making them aware of processes for implementing empowerment at an individual and collective level, in different countries and multicultural social contexts. Our innovative program in social work education is ten years old and is based on the critical analysis of implicit models (unconscious and frequently ethnocentric) and the development of intercultural competences (mindset and skillset). We have developed a model called Intercultural Social Intervention Model (ISIM) which is the central axis (theoretical and practical) of our educational program. ISIM is used and inspired by other practice theoretical models, theories and perspectives from the south (mainly) and the north: concientización or consciousness raising model (Freire 1967 to 1996; Boal 1978; Kaplún 1983, 1985), anti-oppressive model (Solomon 1976), empowerment and advocacy models (Rose & Black 1985), and the transformative mediation model (Bush & Folger 1994), etc. We have adapted all the models to multicultural realities with complexity and diversity to a greater extent than those in which they were developed, and added clearer practice and application components.

From the academic point of view, our program is also innovative because it is directed at international students (up until now people from 21 different countries have taken part in it). It includes degree and post-degree training, and the teachers have very diverse training profiles, with practical experience in several countries of the north and of the south (Europe and Latin America). The practices are carried out in different countries, always in multi-ethnic and culturally diverse contexts. It is also the only social work education program in Spanish with these characteristics, and our graduates and postgraduates have a very high percentage of employment. The following sections describe some of the relevant aspects of our training, which can be applicable to other contexts.

Educational program foundation

The reasons for the educational program 'Migration and cultural diversity' are new realities which offer new opportunities to education of social workers.

Cultural diversity constitutes a central issue of increasing importance in current societies. Cultural pluralism is, therefore, a fact that represents new challenges and opportunities for social work: practical challenges of an intellectual, emotional, political and ethical nature, and specific technical challenges. But migration is also a reality that offers social workers new opportunities, since cultural diversity opens new possibilities of professional action and makes us critically rethink and reformulate traditional interventions. This circumstance, in addition, makes us reflect in depth about our professional praxis, our action and thinking frameworks. It confronts us with the commitment of our professional mission, values and principles of social work.

As a consequence of globalisation, social workers are immersed in constant change processes. The fact of migration, and the intercultural challenge it implies, imposes on social workers the necessity of continuous training and updating, especially in aspects that are not traditionally considered in the curriculum. The focus on the most disadvantaged and excluded people is an inherent element in this profession, and the intercultural challenge can help us reclaim it in these times of strong pressure against the welfare state, of uncertainty and disorientation over our professional role, and of loss of initiative in many social, political, university, etc. interventions. In these difficult moments for the Welfare State, social work has to 'swim upstream' against a competitive, individualist and exhausted society where populist and demagogic currents that encourage racism and xenophobia are dominant. In this context, traditional procedures, tools, theoretical frames, training, resources, and the way of conceiving professional attention within social services, no longer help and are no longer effective.

Authors and experts in different countries have warned of the necessity of a new professional training and our program aims to provide an effective response to this challenge (Ronnau 1994; Legault 1997; Verbunt 1994, 1999, 2004; Lévesque 2004, 2006; Fook 2004, 2012; Aguilar 2004, 2006, 2008, 2010, 2011a, 2011b, 2013; Aguilar & Buraschi 2012; Payne & Askeland 2008; Novak & van Ewijk 2010; among others). We consider that it is necessary to develop new knowledge and skills, as well as personal sensitivity and new attitudes in the way of being and acting professionally. It is an educational process where it is essential to put together an intellectual attitude of openness towards the 'other' along with a deep self-analysis and self-discovery, integrating cognitive and affective elements in our reflections.

Aims and approach: professionals in critical-transformative intercultural perspective

Our goal is to teach professionals advocacy for vulnerable groups, to make them capable of implementing processes of empowerment at an individual and collective level. To achieve it, the educational program offers an axiological, theoretical, methodological and practical training in terms of professional intervention with migrants (particularly in the field of intercultural mediation, although not exclusively), as well as knowledge, skills and abilities in research applied to the international migration field and intercultural studies, and all of that from an interdisciplinary perspective of social intervention and a critical-transforming intercultural focus.

The dominant social intervention models reflect the diverse response methods that are usually given to the management of our societies' diversity. These models have proved to be ineffective in the field of civic cohabitation for an inclusive citizenship. The more frequent responses are the following three:

- Subaltern assimilation: a model based on the absorption of ethnic-cultural minorities, with these minorities ending up occupying a subaltern position within the social structure.
- Culturalist racism: a perspective that 'racialises' cultural differences, reducing people's complexity to a few simplistic categories.
- Intercultural aesthetic: consisting of a superficial celebration of cultural diversity, more similar to colonial exoticism than to the intercultural perspective.

The limitations and weaknesses of these three responses make impossible the construction of an inclusive citizenship, impeding the transformation and overcoming of inequalities and power asymmetries in the different social groups' intercultural coexistence. It is necessary, therefore, to develop an intercultural critical and transforming response, that is, a valid alternative to overcome those barriers, inequalities and asymmetries that are inherent in the three mentioned responses. Interculturalism is a type of normative response to the fact of cultural plurality, which is based on an effective coexistence, learning, and mutual enrichment. This focus differs from and is opposed to other normative responses such as 'assimilation' of minority cultures by the majority culture and is an alternative to the mere 'mutual tolerance' of a certain multiculturalism ('equal but separated'). The intercultural focus we propose is critical because it implies the deconstruction of the subaltern assimilation and the culturalist racism as well as the overcoming of certain reductionist forms of understanding interculturalism. Our model is also transforming because it proposes rethinking our way of conceiving identity, culture, participation and citizenship.

Our critical-transforming focus of interculturalism is not limited to the recognition of the difference and the promotion of positive interaction between people or groups with different referential cultural horizons; it also supports the fight against social, economic and political inequalities as well as ethnic, racial and cultural discriminations.

Theoretical and practical central axis

Implicit models, ethnocentrism and prejudice of social workers

The implementation of social politics destined for the integration of migrant people depends in large part on professional practice. Social workers have been professionally socialised in monocultural and north-occidental clinic-therapeutic types of intervention models, which have not proved to be the most appropriate to address intervention within the new cultural diversity realities. In short, not all the theoretical and methodological professional intervention models in the social field are appropriate, opportune or pertinent if we analyse them from an intercultural perspective, especially from the point of view of the construction of an inclusive citizenship.

We should clearly distinguish the difference between an implicit and explicit intervention model. The social intervention explicit model is a reflexive and coherent set of thoughts and concepts referring to principles, theories, strategies and actions, built on the basis of population categories that then draw a social intervention guide related to a specific problem. Implicit models are, for their part, a referential frame and a simplified and schematic construction of reality that provide an explanation of it and form a general referential outline that guides practice in an unreflective way.

Although it may be embarrassing and hard to accept, we need to become aware of the fact that frequently our way of working with and for migrant people is based on assumptions and stereotypes that can reproduce new ways of racism and that prevents us from recognising the real necessities of people.

In our designs of intervention programs, our way of understanding social problems and our quotidian work practices with migrant people, implicit models may be found. These implicit models of intervention are the frame through which we interpret, understand and act. These implicit intervention models systematically reproduce a specific action with immigrants and their problems, and a specific vision of migrating people, their context, their resources and problems. Very often, these models are based on universalising schemes from particular concepts that exacerbate cultural differences. We should not forget that the way of framing a problem determines the way of solving it; in fact, the larger difficulty for an effective social intervention is based on a wrong framing of the problem (false, distorted, reductionist or biased view) that prevents us from finding its solution.

An intervention model is a coherent set of thoughts and concepts referring back to theories, feelings, attitudes and actions built upon the base of population categories that draw a social intervention guide in relation to specific problems. Models are, therefore, a simplified and schematic construction of reality that provide an explanation of it and create a general referential scheme that guides subsequent practice. Implicit models depend upon and are configured as a result of the interrelationship of various elements: how the situation of the problem that is expected to be solved is defined; what interests are at stake; which are the dominant values; what are the strategies that are considered more acceptable to deal with the problem; how the people involved are defined – in particular, which roles and status have they been assigned and what relationship they should have between them. These elements reflect the values, beliefs and prejudices of the professional worker; from these elements and their interrelations derive the specific nature that is established between the social agent and the immigrant 'user', as well as the specific and operational forms of that professional intervention (methodological orientation, procedures, etc.). Professionals' awareness of the presence of these implicit models is not common, and, as a result, only explicit models are addressed in training and professional exercise. Incoherence and contradiction between the explicit and the implicit models is very frequent, since the implicit models are usually at an unconscious level.

Ethnocentric culturalism as a basic process of implicit models

The logic behind the dominant models within social intervention is a process we term 'ethnocentric culturalism'. It is a process of social construction of reality based on rigid, ethnocentric, essentialist categories imposed on migrant people. Ethnocentric culturalism comprises three elements, intimately related: imposed categorisation, ethnocentrism and culturalism.

Imposed categorisation: this is the construction of a classification system that has the power of reproducing and creating what, apparently, limits itself to description only. The way of thinking and categorising migrant people determines the intervention style. We should not forget the institutional and social worker's constructions and discourses are dominant and usually prevail over the definitions of the migrant people themselves; in this sense it has the power of normalising and naturalising arbitrary categories. There are three major common groups of metaphors to categorise migrant people: metaphors that define the migrant person as victim, metaphors that define them as a menace, and metaphors that categorise the migrant person as deprived.

1. The victim category is the one that defines those people as vulnerable, passive, defenceless, and unable to face problems and be owners of the migratory project itself.
2. The menace category emphasises the danger certain migrant people can represent for our values, our beliefs or for the welfare state. Migrant people are principally conceived of as a problem.
3. The vision of the migrant person as deprived is based on an ethnocentric vision of what we consider 'normal', being centred on the supposed cultural, social, economic, linguistic, etc., deficits of immigrants.

Categorisation implies a process of reduction of the complexity of the migrant person to one or few of their supposed characteristics. From this point of view implicit models are a device of reduction and invisibilisation of part of social reality. We often do not take into account the previous history, focusing our attention on the problems and not on the ability of people to face their difficulties; we invisibilise certain social and conjunctural factors, the multiple identities and cultural complexity of the migration process. This way the migrant person loses the possibility of self-defining themselves – the definition of their identity does not belong to them. Indifference and exclusion are subtle forms of racism, because they deny the complexity of the subject, and even deny them the consideration of it, to turn them into a mere object.

The other characteristic of the 'ethnocentric culturalism' process is that we usually apply our analytic categories to other social realities, forgetting that important differences do exist: we adapt the reality to the categories instead of adapting the categories to the reality. That is, we think the categories we use in our job are universal and can be applied in all the contexts; but this is false.

Finally, the last element of the 'ethnocentric culturalism' process is the exaggeration of the cultural factor and the essentialisation of the culture. We interpret people's behaviours only by their belonging (real or supposed) to a certain culture, confusing social differences with cultural differences. This way the inability of the state (and lack of will) to satisfactorily solve the problems is hidden, and cultural differences are used as a front to cover the debates the society does not want to face.

This tendency is especially noticeable in the integration problem's diagnosis and analysis phase: delinquency, school failure, and poverty are explained through the cultural variables as 'religion features', 'mentality', 'orientation towards present', 'fatalism', etc. This intervention model tends to make poverty exotic, underestimates the economic and social factors and overestimates cultural factors. The diagnosis is still being framed as an exterior assessment of the interested subjects who are not consulted or included to actively take part in it. Frequently, intervention projects are formulated without taking into consideration the participation of all participants, reducing the potential effectiveness of the interventions. The immigrant is usually classified as 'good' or 'bad' depending on their more or less concordance with social rules, with the marginalisation situation perceived as maladjustment, lack of will, or deviance that has to be corrected to 'normalise' their behaviours.

Our Intercultural Social Intervention Model (ISIM)

Apart from the critical analysis of the implicit models in the professional practice, our training program applies a critical-transforming intercultural focus to social intervention, developing guidelines for the construction of an Intercultural Social Intervention Model (from this point forward 'ISIM') based on the deep comprehension of the Other, on the development of intercultural empathy, and on the acquisition of intercultural competences. Intercultural social intervention is not about including new intervention tools, but about transforming our way of thinking and living cultural diversity, including cognitive and affective factors.

We have to take into account that the majority of the professionals have been socialised within ethnocentric and monocultural backgrounds and they often do not have the tools to manage the uncertainty and the stress generated by the relationship with people whose behaviours we cannot understand or foresee. In this context, the incomprehension is double: we do not know how to interpret foreign behaviours (explicative uncertainty) and we do not get to foresee the possible reactions (predictive uncertainty). That means that, in order to work effectively in a multicultural space, good will and positive attitudes towards diversity are not enough; it is necessary to have the competences to understand diversity and manage conflicts effectively. Our values and beliefs may not be enough when we face complex and ambiguous situations. Values and beliefs must be accompanied by knowledge, skills, attitudes and dexterities that let us manage effectively conflictive and ambiguous situations. Without these competences the intercultural encounter can turn into a cultural clash that ends up creating racism and xenophobia.

The ISIM explicit model is formulated from theoretical analysis of the dominant forms of discourse and racism of the elite groups (Van Dijk 2000), including institutional racism put into practice through policies and social interventions. It has other theoretical references: in the proposals of anti-oppressive social work (initially elaborated by Bárbara B. Solomon 1976); in the concepts of empowerment and advocacy (Rose & Black 1985), and in the transformative mediation model (Bush & Folger 1994). From the model operability point of view, the more relevant theoretical-practical inspiration is the awareness or consciousness raising and liberation focus that started in Latin America with Paulo Freire's work, particularly his proposal of 'problematising education' and 'dialogicity' in liberating education (1967), pedagogy of the oppressed (1970), hope pedagogy (1992) and autonomy pedagogy (1996). These proposals are also applied in the Oppressed's Theatre of Boal (1978) – in its Latin-American and European versions – as well as in different 'popular education' Latin-American programs, particularly promoted by the Latin American Council for Adult Education (CEAAL).

In our model the social worker uses strategies of empowerment to reduce, delete, fight or invert the negative valuations that, from society as a whole in general, and from power and its groups in particular, immigrants are subjected to. Utilisation and strengthening of mutual support networks; the usage of training, skills and technologies transference; training to take decisions and organise; interpreting, etc. are some examples of these strategies, where the conflict is not denied but identified and people work with it and from it when it is necessary. This model demands a compromise to keep socio-educative services and social intervention programs effectively egalitarian as well as to face negative valuations, even within technical-professional and institutional culture.

The emphasis is then on implementing dialogue, comprehension and development processes, using concepts, techniques and strategies from emancipatory and radical social work to promote the improvement and the self-determination of the participants. That is, for the development of skills that let people, organisations and communities improve by themselves by way of actions, and boost the necessary social change so that situations are more fair and equitable.

In this perspective, the social worker has a very different and diverse role: contrary to the classic role of expert manager and organiser, in our model they need to be a facilitator, a contributor, a defender, a mediator, and a trainer, depending on the dynamics generated by the intervention process. Our action is thus turned into a strengthening emancipatory pedagogic and political instrument of organisations, people and groups. The self-determination concept is a basic foundation of this model, that defines itself as a group of interrelated skills, such as: skills to identify and express necessities; establish objectives or expectations and draw up an action plan to achieve them; identify resources; make rational selections between alternative courses of action; develop appropriate attitudes to achieve the objectives; evaluate results, etc.

Social intervention is aimed at the self-determination of immigrants in multicultural contexts. It is necessary, in order to do this, to offer an intercultural training process to the professionals, to avoid social intervention turning, although involuntarily, into a reproduction of social inequalities.

Intercultural competences in ISIM

In the ISIM intervention model we propose the acquisition of a group of intercultural competences in social work, based on the contributions of Chen and Starosta (1996), Byram (1997), Aneas (2003) and Sclavi (2003). We define intercultural competences as a body of knowledge, attitudes and skills that allow the professionals to work effectively in multicultural contexts, contributing to intercultural cohabitation. It is not only about behaving in a pertinent way and adapting to different contexts, but about transforming relationships to contribute to transform the entire society.

Following Milton Bennett's proposal (1986), we can differentiate between different intercultural competences dimensions: mindset and skillset. The first one makes reference to a way of looking at the world and includes cognitive, emotional and attitudinal aspects that are transferable to all the specific competences and that we can term the intercultural mind: tolerance towards ambiguity, focus on and curiosity towards diversity, mental flexibility, creativity, among others. The second term makes reference to the behavioural aspects, specific capacities and necessary strategies to work effectively with people and groups with different cultural models. According to our model, specific competences of the professionals that work in multicultural models are: intercultural awareness; comprehension of other reference cultural frames; intercultural sensitivity; intercultural assertiveness; and creative management of conflicts.

Intercultural awareness

Paulo Freire formulated the awareness concept to describe the personal and social transformation process the oppressed people start when they become aware of the oppression logic that sustains the power relationships in which they are involved. The interesting aspect of the awareness concept is that it not only makes reference to the domination concept, but also to the oppression models that structure the oppressed's minds. We can apply this concept to relationships between people in multicultural contexts and talk about intercultural awareness as the raising of awareness of our implicit pre-assumptions, beliefs and implicit values that, often automatically, have an influence in our interpretations of the world and our behaviour(s). As we have seen in the first part of this chapter, these implicit models are often invisible barriers that prevent us from understanding other frames of reference, communicating effectively and managing conflicts and reproducing stereotypes, prejudice and unequal relations.

The awareness of the own cultural horizon in general, and of the implicit models that guide our social intervention in particular, is the first step to develop intercultural competences since this 'is our way of looking at the one that very often keeps the others in their more limited belonging, and is also our way of looking at the one that can free them' (Maalouf 1998, 7).

The comprehension of other reference frames includes the attitudes, knowledge and skills that let us understand people that do not share our same reference frame and/or situation in pluricultural contexts. It is based on the ability of researching diversity through 'dynamic maps', a group of hermeneutical keys that represent a flexible guide towards comprehension and let us change our way of identifying a problem. In this sense this is a fundamental competence in the diagnosis role of the social worker. The starting point does not only have to be the analysis of the problems, but the competences of migrating people, their networks, social and cultural capital as well as their resilience. The fundamental questions of our diagnosis should not be 'Which are the factors that determine the vulnerability of migrant people?' but 'Which are the factors that have often been determining for the success histories of these people?'. It is about revalidating resilience, the ability of facing adversity and to keep moving forward, it is about taking into consideration the previous history of migrant people, their practices, support networks, characteristics of the recipient society, environment, social climate in a certain moment, protective factors, internal resources and abilities, their opportunities and vital dynamism (Aguilar 2013).

Regarding the transnational and socio-communitarian dimension of the migrating experience, it must be emphasised that, in the majority of the cases, professional intervention of social services usually is developed from diagnosis models (characteristic of occidental clinic perspectives), that usually tend to define reality based on the characteristics of the offer, without seriously considering the communitarian exploration of potentialities and internal resources.

Intercultural sensitivity is a competence that includes emotional self-awareness, positive attitude towards diversity and intercultural empathy. For this last one we understand an empathy form that is effective in pluricultural contexts. With empathy we are seeking to understand the experience of the other person to understand within our own frame. It is a way of leaving a narcissistic vision but not an ethnocentric one. When we try to put ourselves 'in other's shoes' we are actually putting ourselves 'in our shoes'. Sclavi (2003) proposes the exotopy concept, to define the effort of recognising the autonomous perspective of the other, a perspective with its own sense, not reducible to ours. In empathy we isolate and decontextualise some features of the other's experience to understand it from our cultural frame; this way, in reality, we are not going out of ourselves, but we project our way of feeling and living an experience. Exotopy generates another way of empathy, intercultural empathy, a process in which the other person does not play a passive role, but an active one, and collaborates with us in the construction of a shared sense of affective experience. In this sense we can define 'intercultural empathy' as the skill to make experience out of aspects from reality in a different way than how it would have been done from our reference frame through the collaborative construction of the sense of affective experience.

Intercultural assertiveness is the 'skill to negotiate the cultural meanings and act communicatively in an effective way according to the multiple identities of participants' (Chen & Starosta 1996, 358). Being assertive in multicultural contexts means knowing how to identify our own communicative styles; recognise the communicative style of other people and groups; know how to create communication channels; and have the ability to conceptualise, explain oneself, present oneself in an appropriate way, reach an acceptable grade of reciprocal comprehension and manage interaction appropriately and effectively.

Finally, creative management of conflicts is the ability to use exploratory resolution strategies based on a complex analysis of conflicts, the restructuring of relationships (Bush & Folger 1994) and the generation of alternatives based on the construction of a new common reference frame (Sclavi 2003).

Pedagogical design

> Educating is not transmitting knowledge, but creating the necessary conditions for its construction.
>
> Paulo Freire

The pedagogical design of the program allows the achievement of these intercultural critical-transforming analysis and intervention abilities, through a series of innovative elements. As an example, we mention the following:

Professor and lecturer selection: more than 40 European and Latin-American professors take part in the program. All of them are internationally prestigious specialists in their respective fields and share analytical critical frames, as well as a personal commitment to social entities and movements in the fight against the different means of discrimination in each of their countries. The profile is very interdisciplinary (social workers, sociologists, anthropologists, pedagogues, jurists, psychologists, doctors, demographers, lawyers, sociolinguists, etc.). Many of them have had training in more than one of these disciplines.

Candidate students selection: the postgraduate program is also open to degree (bachelor) students. Candidates from any country and from different professional fields with social influence can take part. This profile for selection ensures a great cultural diversity in the learning group, with interdisciplinary profiles and different perspectives and vital experiences, which are very important to ensure the success of the training program.

Selection and design of training contents: the training contents have been designed so that the students progressively acquire critical analysis ability of the reality inherent in our analytical framework, apart from increasing their self-awareness. In all the training modules cognitive and affective contents are incorporated, to achieve the acquisition of intercultural empathy from the beginning of the program. This means the contents do not superimpose or overlap themselves, but they are supported by each other, in a constructive and sequenced way. Contents are updated throughout all the courses. In the online discussion forums graduated students of the program and all the teachers take part.

Contents sequencing: in our program there are no subjects, but sequenced and successive training modules, that allow a learning building process in such a way that the students go on maturing personally as they advance in training, and go on becoming aware of their own reference frames (especially implicit). Abilities and attitudes from ISIM are also gradually acquired, especially from the third month after entry.

Theory-practice integration: all the methodological and theoretical knowledge is applied to practice. Knowledge is oriented to action. The result of the integration-application of knowledge and critical reflection for them to practice and work in the field is evaluated. All the materials and workshops incorporate cognitive and emotional elements, as a way of progressively developing intercultural empathy ability, tolerance towards ambiguity and open-mindedness towards the Other.

Study and observational analysis in empathic perspective: in the majority of the modules, critical and self-critical reality observation exercises are included. The fact that all the international students live in their own countries boosts enrichment and exchange of experiences. One of the strengths of the program is precisely this: each student has the experience of their own context, and also the direct experience of the other contexts where their colleagues live, so they can share dialogue and collaborative work in their studies and solution of practical cases.

Study and solution of cases in a cooperative way: diverse perspectives are used, such as critical incidents analysis, learning based on problems, participative auto-diagnosis, participative planning, etc. Collaborative solutions are encouraged before the realisation of the individual work and exercises.

Fieldwork: from the fourth month of training and afterwards, all the modules include practical work that the student has to do in their own context and field, with the tutorial orientation of professors. The three last months of the program are exclusively supervised practices, that are carried out in the country and region that the student decides upon, always in multicultural and complex contexts.

Conclusions

Implicit ethnocentric and culturalistic models have important consequences in social interventions with immigrants: they reproduce an unequal and asymmetric social relationship system, reinforce the image of migrant people as a 'group of social exclusion' and obstruct the autonomy and integration process. The demands of migrant people and the insufficient responses of the traditional intervention models may generate stress, uncertainty and anxiety, but are, also, an important occasion to revise our intervention methods, an opportunity to be conscious of the limitations of our analysis scheme and rethink our intervention models.

Given the unconscious character of implicit models, the development of processes to raise awareness about the existence of these models is an indispensable requirement. Professional training for social work must add these proposals. All the process is about being conscious that the categories we usually consider neutral are, often, closely related with a cultural context, and in some cases based on reductionist ethnocentric pre-assumptions. In addition, new alternative intervention models, adapted and coherent with the values, principles and compromises of social work, should be learned during training. Our ISIM intercultural social intervention model is a theoretical-practical, systematic and effective proposal for social work in contexts of cultural diversity when the goal is to achieve an actually inclusive and equalitarian citizenship. The ISIM model is critical-transforming, emancipatory, and empowering, it supports and stimulates individuals and groups to develop their skills to solve their problems and take decisions, and this model at the same time advocates for a structural change towards a fairer society. At an individual level, results include control of the situation, sociability and behaviours aimed at action. In organisations, results include the development of organisational networks, fundraising and policy re-definition. In the community, results are the creation of social inclusion projects, pluralist cohabitation and construction of collective projects of environment and life quality improvement.

References

Aguilar, M.J. (2013). *Trabajo social: concepto y metodología*. Madrid, Spain: Editorial Paraninfo-Consejo General de Trabajo Social.

Aguilar, M.J. (2011a). Ciudadanía intercultural y animación: una experiencia innovadora para el empoderamiento de colectivos inmigrantes. *Journal Sociocultural Community Development and Practices*, 1: 22–47. Retrieved on 17 April 2014 from www.atps.uqam.ca/numero/n1/pdf/ATPS_AguilarIdanez_2010.pdf.

Aguilar, M.J. (2011b). El racismo institucional en las políticas e intervenciones sociales dirigidas a inmigrantes y algunas propuestas prácticas para evitarlo. *Documentación Social*, 162: 139–166.

Aguilar, M.J. (2010). Modelos de intervención social con inmigrantes e interculturalidad: un análisis crítico. Inguruak. *Revista Vasca de Sociología y Ciencia Política*, special issue, *Monográfico especial 'Sociedad e Innovación en el siglo XXI'*, Febrero: 77–94.

Aguilar, M.J. (2008). Ciudadanía intercultural: Materiales y propuestas desde la Sociología Visual [DVD]. Albacete, Spain: GIEMIC-UCLM.

Aguilar, M.J. (2006). Inmigración, integración e interculturalidad. In A. Alted et al., (eds), *De la España que emigra a la España que acoge* (pp. 556–69). Madrid, Spain: Fundación Francisco Largo Caballero y Caja Duero.

Aguilar, M.J. (2004). Trabajo social intercultural: una aproximación al perfil del trabajador social como educador y mediador en contextos multiculturales y multiétnicos. *Portularia: Revista de Trabajo Social*, 4: 153–160. Retrieved on 17 April 2014 from dialnet.unirioja.es/servlet/articulo?codigo=860428.

Aguilar, M.J. & Buraschi, D. (2012). El desafío de la convivencia intercultural. *REMHU: Revista Interdisciplinar da Mobilidade Humana*, 38: 27–43. Retrieved on 17 April 2014 from www.csem.org.br/remhu/index.php/remhu/article/viewFile/298/273.

Aneas, A. (2003). Competencias interculturales transversales en la empresa: un modelo para la detección de necesidades de formación. Tesis doctoral del Departamento de Mètodes d'Investigació i Diagnòstic en Educació. Barcelona: Universitat de Barcelona. Retrieved on 17 April 2014 from hdl.handle.net/2445/42451.

Baldwin, M. (2011). Resisting the EasyCare model: building a more radical, community-based, anti-authoritarian social work for the future. In M. Lavalette (ed.), *Radical social work today: social work at the crossroads* (pp. 187–204). Bristol: Policy Press.

Bhatti-Sinclair, K. (2011). *Anti-racist practice in social work*. Basingstoke, UK: Palgrave Macmillan.

Bennett, M.J. (1986). A developmental approach to training intercultural sensitivity. *International Journal of Intercultural Relations*, 10(2): 179–86.

Boal, A. (1978). *Jeux pour acteurs et non-acteurs. Pratique du theatre de l'opprimé*. Paris: Maspero.

Bush, R. & Folger, J. (1994). *The promise of mediation*. San Francisco, CA: Jossey-Bass.

Byram, M. (1997). *Teaching and assessing intercultural communicative competence*. Clevedon, UK: Multilingual Matters.

Chen, G.M. & Starosta, W.J. (1996). Intercultural communication competence: a synthesis. In R.B. Brant (ed.), *Communication yearbook 19*. Thousand Oaks, CA: SAGE Publications.

Fook, J. (2012). *Social work. A critical approach to practice* (2nd edn). London: SAGE Publications.

Fook, J. (2004). Some considerations on the potential contributions of intercultural work. *Social Work & Society*, 2(1): 83–86.

Freire, P. (1996). *Pedagogía da autonomía- Saberes Necessários à prática Educativa*. São Paulo, Brazil: Paz e Terra.

Freire, P. (1992). *Pedagogia da esperança: um reencontro com a Pedagogia do oprimido*. Rio de Janeiro, Brazil: Paz e Terra.

Freire, P. (1970). *Pedagogía del oprimido*. Montevideo, Uruguay: Tierra Nueva.

Freire, P. (1967). *Educação como prática da liberdade*. Rio de Janeiro, Brazil: Paz e Terra.

Kaplún, M. (1985). *El comunicador popular*. Quito, Ecuador: CIESPAL.

Kaplún, M. (1983). *Hacia nuevas estrategias de comunicación en la educación de adultos*. Santiago, Chile: UNESCO.

Langan, M. (2011). Rediscovering radicalism and humanity in social work. In M. Lavalette (ed.), *Radical social work today: social work at the crossroads* (pp. 153–63). Bristol: Policy Press.

Lavalette, M. & Ioakimidis, V. (2011). International social work or social work internationalism? Radical social work in global perspective. In M. Lavalette (ed.), *Radical social work today: social work at the crossroads* (pp. 135–51). Bristol: Policy Press.

Legault, G. (1997). Social work practice in situations of intercultural misunderstandings. *Journal of Multicultural Social Work*, 4(4): 49–66. DOI: 10.1300/J285v04n04_04.

Lévesque, J.A. (2006). Training social workers in intercultural realities: a teaching model to counter unreasoned affectivity and contribute to the development of reflective judgment. In F. Pons et al. (eds), *Towards emotional competences* (pp. 229–48). Aalborg, Denmark: Aalborg University Press.

Lévesque, J.A. (2004). L'anthropopédagogie: une méthodologie au service d'un modèle de développement du jugement réflexif. Recherche-action, recherche systémique? Questions vives. *État de la recherche en éducation*, 2(3): 123–32.

Maalouf, A. (1998). *Identidades asesinas*. Madrid, Spain: Alianza Editorial.

Novak, J. & Van Ewijk, H. (2010). From assimilation to intercultural competences: a challenge for social work. In H. Van Ewijk (ed.), *European social policy and social work: citizenship-based social work* (pp. 130–39). NY: Routledge.

Núñez, C. (1989). *Educar para transformar, transformar para educar*. San José, Costa Rica: Grupo Alforja.

Okitikpi, T. & Aymer, C. (2010). *Key concepts in anti-discriminatory social work*. London: SAGE Publications.

Payne, M. & Askeland, G.A. (2008). *Globalisation and international social work: postmodern change and challenge*. Aldershot, UK: Ashgate.

Ronnau, J. P. (1994). Teaching cultural competence: practical ideas for social work educators. *Journal of Multicultural Social Work*, 3(1): 29–42. DOI: 10.1300/J285v03n01_04.

Rose, S.M. & Black, B.I. (1985). *Advocacy and empowerment: mental health care in the community*. Boston, MA: Routledge & Kegan Paul.

Sclavi, M. (2003). *Arte di escoltare e mondi possibili*. Milan, Italy: Bruno Mondadori.

Solomon, B. (1976). *Black empowerment: social work in oppressed communities*. NY: Columbia University Press.

Van Dijk, T. (2000). New(s) racism. In S. Cottle (ed.), *Ethnic minorities and the media* (pp. 33–49). Buckingham, UK: Open University Press.

Verbunt, G. (2004). *La question interculturelle dans le travail social. Repères et perspectives*. Paris: La Découverte.

Verbunt, G. (1999). Le problème des migrants et la formation des travailleurs sociaux. In J. Demorgon & E.M. Lipiansky (eds), *Guide de l'interculturel en formation* (pp. 35–41). Paris: Retz.

Verbunt, G. (1994). *Les obstacles culturels aux apprentissages*. Paris: Centre National de Documentation Pédagogique.

5

Indigenism and Australian social work

Christine Fejo-King

Indigenism is a concept that has emerged over the last 20 years as a result of the engagement of Indigenous academics with research. It is a way of claiming a space within research for Aboriginal knowledge systems and ways of knowing, being and doing. However, in Australia, Indigenism and Indigenist theory and practice have not been confined to research alone, it has been embedded within Aboriginal and Torres Strait Islander social work for a number of decades. This chapter will introduce Indigenism and Indigenist theory and practice in social work, as it was developed in the Australian setting in the 1970s, identify how it has evolved and illustrate how it has impacted on both Australian social work and national policies and practices. The chapter will then move on to explore how Indigenism and Indigenist theory can inform social work theory and practice into the future.

Researchers position themselves in their research projects to reveal aspects of their own tacit world, to challenge their own assumptions, to locate themselves through the eye of the 'other', and to observe themselves observing. This lens shifts the observer's gaze inward toward the self as a site for interpreting cultural experience. The approach is person-centred, unapologetically subjective, and gives voice to those who have often been silenced. (Settee 2007, 117)

The citation above by Settee helps to set the framework for what will follow in this chapter. While Settee is speaking about research, her words also have meaning within the education and practice setting. Indigenism is an unapologetically subjective perspective and practice by indigenous researchers and academics, that opens the indigenous worldview and knowledge systems to non-indigenous practitioners and researchers. This chapter is a small step in introducing how indigenism has been developed and is being progressed in Australian social work today and how it might progress in the future.

The theories and concepts known as indigenist ideology, indigenism and indigenist theory have been developed by indigenous academics and researchers around the world in the margins of the disciplines of social work, education, science, law and many others for a number of years. These theories and concepts acted as a means of incorporating Aboriginal ways of knowing, being, and doing (Arbon 2008; Churchill 1996; DiNova 2005; Martin

2008; Rigney 1997, 2001; Ramsden 2002; Sinclair et al. 2009; Smith 1999, 2012; West 2000) within these disciplines to claim a space, and place for practice and research methodologies that privileged indigenous knowledges.

This chapter introduces, defines and examines what is meant by an indigenist ideology, indigenism, and indigenist theory and then explores how they have already been included into social work education, theory, practice and research in Australia and how these practices might be extended and strengthened into the future. To set the scene, a number of stepping-stones are positioned to allow us to move to the point where the concepts identified above can be introduced and discussed.

The stepping-stones begin with a brief re-visit to the historical beginnings of social work in Britain and America and the ideology that supported it. A second stepping-stone is the identification of two American women who had a lasting impact on social work throughout the world. The third stepping-stone is a brief introduction to how social work began in Australia. This section will include an identification of the different imperatives that informed the beginnings of indigenous social work practice as it contrasted to the practice of non-indigenous social workers.

The chapter then seeks to answer a number of questions. Firstly, why did indigenous academics and researchers believe it was necessary to develop indigenist theory and praxis? Secondly, what has been achieved through this movement? Thirdly, how might this information be incorporated into the schools of social work, guide the development of theories of the south, and inform social work practice and research into the future, while still maintaining its unique indigenist ontology, epistemology, axiology, methods and methodology?

Furthermore, in introducing indigenism and indigenist theory into social work education, a major consideration must be the need to identify ways to prevent the mining and colonisation of indigenous ontologies and epistemologies. This form of practice has been and continues to be condemned, both nationally and internationally (Bin-Sallik 2003; Bishop 2005; Fejo-King 2013; Foley 2002, 2003; King 2011; Martin 2008; Smith 1999, 2012; Rigney 1999). These concerns continue today as raised at the recent 2nd International Indigenous Social Work Conference (July 2013) in Winnipeg, Canada.

Placing some stepping stones

Before moving forward it would be helpful to define what is meant by the terms ontology, epistemology, theory, and working in the margins as they relate to this chapter. An ontology can be described as 'the theory of the nature of existence, or the nature of reality' (Wilson 2008, 33). The central question embedded within ontology is 'What is real?' This is an interesting question, as reality can be different for each person or groups of people, as we all experience and interpret the world differently. Some different ontologies that have been identified in the literature include the Western, Eastern, and indigenous; however, there are many others.

An epistemology is 'the study of the nature of thinking or knowing. It involves the theory of how we come to have knowledge' (Wilson 2008, 33). Often an epistemology is developed without conscious thought; it can be influenced by our standpoint (gender, economic position, ethnicity, culture, lived experience, religious background and/or political perspective) and is intrinsically connected to our ontology. It is often unmarked and unnamed, it is just there in the background, used every day as a litmus test against which we measure everything we come into contact with as it causes us to ask, 'How do I know what is real' (Wilson 2008, 33).

A theory is a short way of naming a group or set of knowledge systems about a specific topic. Anzaldúa made the following insightful comments about theory:

> What is considered theory in the dominant academic community is not necessarily what counts as theory for women of colour. Theory produces effects that change people and the way they perceive the world. Thus we need theories that will enable us to interpret what happens in the world, that will explain how and why we relate to certain people in specific ways, that will reflect what goes on between inner, outer and peripheral 'I's within a person and between the personal I's and the collective 'we' of our ethnic communities. (Anzaldúa cited in Pattanayak 2013, 87)

Working in the margins can be understood to be work happening on the outside of the main text or dominant discourse and/or social work context. It is similar to when you read a book and make notes in the margins. These comments can be cross-references, comments of agreement or disagreement, or they can be different ways of achieving the same goal using particular ontologies and epistemologies that may not have been considered by the author. They may also be comments of support for what has been written, or expand upon them.

The beginnings of social work

In their book *Unfaithful angels: how social work has abandoned its mission*, Specht and Courtney (1994) examined the roots of social work and explained that for the Western world, the forerunners of social work were patronage, piety, the Poor Laws, and philanthropy. Each of these concepts formed the basis of a different strategy to address poverty, initially in Britain and later in America. These concepts became so embedded within social work education, theory and practice that elements of each can still be found today in social work around the world.

In the 1980s, two very influential American women, with diametrically opposite ideologies, also had a lasting impact on social work. These women were Jane Addams and Mary Richmond. Jane Addams is often viewed as 'the mother of structural social work'. She focused on changing society through the use of existing structures and strengths of the community. To achieve this goal she examined the systems that resulted in poverty and utilised social change mechanisms, such as women's suffrage and child labour laws, to bring about positive change (Margolin 1997).

Mary Richmond on the other hand is often viewed as 'the mother of casework', which included surveillance and the keeping of detailed case-notes. This is also viewed as the beginning of individual social work (Margolin 1997). Margolin highlights the influence of these women when he states, 'social workers may claim Jane Addams as their source of inspiration, but they do Mary Richmond' (4).

Apart from the issues of structural versus individual social work, another tension within social work has to do with care versus control. Specht and Courtney (1994) also highlighted that there is a dilemma for social workers, who are often called upon to enact state and government policies of social control, with regard to the protection of children and particular groups of adults.

This issue can sometimes be viewed as a dilemma because this role can conflict with the social justice aspirations of social work and can create an increased risk of burnout for social workers (Margolin 1997). The other risk for social workers is that the people they are working with can come to view them as 'Jekyll and Hyde' type characters (Fejo-King 2013). This means that social workers might say to people that they are trying to help them, whilst at the same time enforcing policies that the people see as biased, cruel or evil (Blackstock 2009). This affects the way clients view social workers and, therefore, the ability of the social worker to build relationships of trust with the client or client group (Calma & Priday 2011).

Social work was imported to Australia as a mature profession from Britain and America and first taught at the University of Sydney in 1940. Qualifying graduates were employed either as social service workers in a hospital setting, or as child welfare officers (Camilleri 2005; University of Sydney 2012). This identifies the roots of Australian social work as being firmly embedded in the West and within the Richmond framework.

The beginnings of Aboriginal and Torres Strait Islander social work

Due to past government policies and restrictions, very few Aboriginal and Torres Strait Islander peoples were able to access tertiary education until the 1970's, when Australian Government policies changed and Aboriginal and Torres Strait Islander peoples had access to tertiary education for the first time. The South Australian Institute of Technology (SAIT) became the first educational institution to take Aboriginal and Torres Strait Islander students in large numbers, from around the country. These students moved to Adelaide and began their learning journey. Initially, two courses were offered – Community Development and/or Social Work – with exit points being at the certificate or associate diploma level. A social work degree was not offered.

The lack of degree-level studies did not act as a barrier to the students gaining employment. However, it meant that none of the social work graduates of SAIT were eligible for membership with the Australian Association of Social Work (AASW). It also meant that these students were not the decision makers and team leaders in the areas they were working in. Leadership of these positions were held by non-indigenous social workers, psychologists and other professionals with a degree as a base line entry.

These practices bought about critical reflection on the part of Aboriginal and Torres Strait Islander social workers, resulting in the development and progressing of Aboriginal Terms of Reference (ATR) (Kickett 1992). I use this terminology because in the 1970's the terms indigenist, indigenism, and indigenist theory and practice, had not yet been named. Further information about Aboriginal and Torres Strait Islander social work in Australia and the way in which it was embedded within indigenist ideology, indigenism, indigenist theory and practice will be discussed later in the chapter. The next section will focus on defining these concepts.

An indigenist ideology, indigenism, and indigenist theory and practice

Indigenism has been the way in which indigenous researchers and academics have claimed a space for Aboriginal knowledge systems within research over the last twenty years. This section unpacks what is meant by an indigenous theory and identifies two major theorists, the first from the United States of America, and the second from Australia.

By exploring what is meant by an indigenist ideology, we are able to identify who could be considered an indigenist, and then address what is meant by indigenism, indigenist theory and practice. Figure 5.1 is a beginning point to understanding these concepts, offering some insights around how each of these concepts flow, connect and interact.

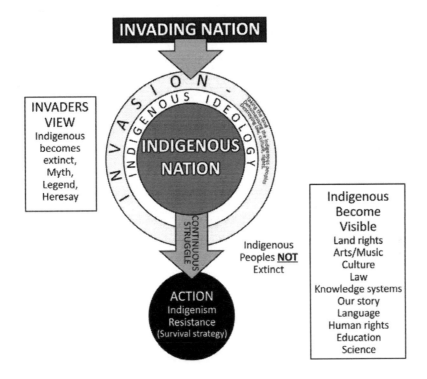

Figure 5.1 Origins of indigenism: contributing factors.

From this diagram, it becomes clear that an indigenist ideology is developed as a result of the invasion of an indigenous nation or land mass by another nation; in the case of Australia, the invading nation was Britain. The major reason for invading and colonising another group's homeland has throughout history been connected to one country needing or wanting more land or access to the natural resources of another group (LaRocque 2010).

In the process of the invasion and colonisation of Australia there were numerous instances of genocide, ethnic cleansing, murder and the removal of Aboriginal and Torres Strait Islander children (Haebich 2000; King 2013; Moses 2004). These practices were not confined to Australia alone – the indigenous peoples of the United States of America and Canada also shared similar experiences (Churchill 1997; King 2011; Sinclair 2007). It is in response to these and other atrocities that an indigenist ideology is developed.

Ward Churchill (1996), a controversial native American academic and enrolled member of the United Keetoowah Band of Cherokee, First Nations Peoples of the United States of America, refers to an indigenous ideology when he says, 'very often in many of my writings and lectures, I have identified myself as being "indigenist" in outlook'(509). In the context of indigenism, what Churchill refers to as an 'outlook' I refer to as an indigenous ideology. It is a way of thinking that is based on a particular worldview, and the lived experiences and values of colonised indigenous peoples. It calls for action that seeks the recognition of their sovereignty and human rights in order to achieve social justice and self-determination. The indigenous person or activist who employs these tactics is then identified by Churchill as being an indigenist.

Using Churchill's description of himself, pulling it apart and examining each statement in detail offers great insights that support the notion that an indigenist is an Indigenous person whose:

> highest priority . . . is the rights of their people and to achieve this goal they draw on the traditions, knowledge and values of indigenous peoples from around the world. (Churchill 1996, 509)

According to Churchill, the indigenist uses the knowledge gained through these traditions, values and ways of knowing, being and doing in order to 'advance critiques of, . . . conceptualise alternatives to, the present social, political, economic, and philosophical status quo' (Churchill 1996, 509).

Lester-Irabinna Rigney, an Aboriginal educator from South Australia adds depth to Churchill's work by asserting that Indigenism is, 'multi-disciplinary with the essential criteria being the identity and colonising experience' of the Indigenous writer (Rigney 2001, 1). Using the insights offered by both Churchill and Rigney, it becomes clear that indigenous theory and practice is developed and informed by the struggle for the rights of indigenous peoples. This struggle then becomes the highest priority in the political life of an indigenist, often emerging as activism. Further, it is this body of knowledge – the ontologies and epistemologies of indigenous peoples of the world, rather than the ontology and epistemology of the dominant non-indigenous world – that guides the thoughts and actions of the indigenist.

What is Indigenist theory and practice?

Indigenist theory is one of emancipation and empowerment, developed by indigenous academics and researchers both nationally and internationally, which works toward a paradigm shift that privileges indigenous knowledges. To illustrate how indigenist theory works in practice, two examples are shared here around validating indigenism and indigenist theory.

Example 1: Developing a moral compass

This example deals with the research process of my PhD journey and is found in the paper, 'Decolonising research from an Australian Indigenous research perspective' (King 2005). At that time I was not aware of the developing indigenist theory. However, on analysing what was written in that article with regard to the inward moral search that I undertook, through the questions I asked myself and what emerged through this process, it can be clearly identified as being grounded in an indigenist ideology that resulted in indigenist theory in practice. What assisted me in getting to this point was the theoretical frame within which the questions I asked of myself were placed.

These questions were, firstly, was it appropriate for me as an Aboriginal woman to undertake research that would be fully focused upon my people? Secondly, what was the motivation behind my wanting to undertake this research? Thirdly, what if any benefits would flow on to my family, communities and nations in particular, and what if any benefits might also flow on to other Australian Indigenous peoples? Fourthly, what foundations might my research be built upon? In other words, what ideology would frame my research? (2).

These questions were used to develop the moral compass shown in Figure 5.2, which I drew up and kept in a prominent position in my study so that I would see it each time I sat down to work. It then guided my research process (Fejo-King 2013). Over time, the moral compass was refined to its current depiction as shown below.

Figure 5.2 My moral compass.

Example 2: Validating Indigenism and Indigenist theory

In order to find the connections between my use of stories, learning circles, the connection of all things, and to find a way to describe how this connection works and what it meant for me, I undertook a search, not knowing in advance where I would be led. The search was undertaken over a period of four weeks and began with the word 'metaphor'. However, I found this this was too narrow and constricting to describe the phenomena that I was focused on. I then moved on to analogy, allegory, epic, grand theory, cosmos, unity and finally to cosmology which is described as being the 'science or theory of the universe' (Collins Australian Concise Dictionary 2001).

On locating this word I felt that it warranted further investigation, so I did a Google search, but added the word 'indigenous' before cosmology. It was encouraging to find that many other First Nations scholars had also found their way to this definition and contributed to it.

Sinclair included in indigenous cosmology concepts such as ceremonies, and 'All my relations', which she viewed as one of the most significant symbols of indigenous cosmology. Translated to English from different indigenous languages, the term means the same thing and is used in the same context. For Sinclair, the concept of 'All my relations' captured the essence of Indigenous spirituality. She offered the following quote to illustrate what this concept meant for her and in doing so adds depth to this chapter. King (1990) as cited by Sinclair (2007) states that:

> 'All my relations' is first a reminder of who we are and our relationship with both our family and our relatives. It also reminds us of the extended relationship we share with all human beings. But the relationships that Native people see goes further, the web of kinship extending to the animals, to the birds, to the fish, to the plants, to all the animate and inanimate forms that can be seen or imagined. More than that, 'all my relations' is an encouragement for us to accept the responsibilities we have within this universal family by living our lives in a harmonious and moral manner. (King 1990, 1 cited in Sinclair 2007, 89)

Bringing the indigenist view as shared by King and Sinclair into Australian social work would mean that there needs to be a clear understanding by the schools of social work and social work educators, that an indigenist ideology and indigenism are embedded within the hearts, minds and hands (Kelly & Sewell 2001) of indigenous social work students, academics and educators. These then equate to practice and guide and shape what we do, just as it did for Churchill, Rigney, King and Sinclair.

This practice of the heart, learned through lived experiences and gained over many lifetimes of our ancestors, is then reflected in the knowledge and understandings indigenous students bring with them to the education system and which is often not validated (Baikie 2009; Fejo-King 2013). It is also reflected in the way that indigenous academics teach, the theorists introduced and studied, and the strategies and tactics indigenous practitioners advocate, the types of struggles they support and the nature of the alliances they enter into (Churchill 1996, 509).

This then raises two major questions: the first being how can an indigenous ideology, indigenism, and indigenist theory be successfully integrated into Australian social work education? The second is what are the challenges to including, developing and delivering these ways of knowing, being and doing (Arbon 2008; Martin 2008), within a social work setting when the majority of the educators are not indigenous?

Are Indigenism and Indigenist education, theory and practice new to Australian social work?

In addressing the first question, I do not believe or support the assertion that these concepts are new to Australian social work. Rather, they can be seen as an example of an instance of theory catching up to practice, as shown by within an Australian context, the inception of Aboriginal organisations such as Aboriginal Health Services (AHS) and the National Aboriginal Community Controlled Health Organisation (NACCHO), the Secretariat for National Aboriginal and Islander Child Care (SNAICC), the Link Up services and Aboriginal legal services and land councils. Even the inquiry into the removal of Aboriginal children from their families, more commonly known as the 'Stolen Generations', is grounded in indigenism and indigenist theory in practice; when comparing them to the definitions provided by Rigney and Churchill, the connections are clear. However, the social work that contributed to the development of the services identified above pre-date the naming of the terms and practices described as indigenism, indigenist theory and practice.

Indigenism, indigenist theory, practice and research are 'new' buzz-words within Australian social work and are being treated as though they are new concepts within Australian social work. As clearly illustrated throughout this chapter, I argue that this is not the case. I assert that Aboriginal and Torres Strait Islander social workers developed education, theory and practice from within this framework in the 1970s and perhaps even earlier, as the impetus for their practice, which was very different to the dominant form of social work being practised in this country. For Aboriginal and Torres Strait Islander social workers the focus, aim and objectives of their practice was indigenist because it was founded on and informed by these ideological perspectives, but undertaken by 'unqualified' indigenous social workers and so was pushed to the margins of Australian social work.

To treat this form of practice as though it is the new wonder kid on the block that should be embraced by all is, I believe, illustrative of the arrogance of whiteness within Australian social work and the continued marginalisation of Aboriginal and Torres Strait Islander social workers, who have been engaged in this form of practice for decades as already noted throughout this chapter. To help put things into perspective, it is well worth remembering the following view:

> By not looking at where [we've] come from, [we] cannot know where [we] are going, or where it is [we] should go. It follows that [we] cannot understand what it is [we] are to do or why. In [our] confusion, [we] identify with the wrong people, the wrong things, the wrong tradition. [We] therefore inevitably pursue the wrong goals and objectives, putting last things first and often forgetting the first things altogether, perpetuating the very structures of oppression and degradation [we] think to oppose. (Churchill 1996, 510)

I suggest that it is within social work research that indigenous ideologies, theories and practices are new. This is as a direct result of the engagement of indigenous social work academics in this very Western activity and that these concepts have been introduced to social work theory, education and practice, as a means of ensuring cultural safety for the indigenous researchers and indigenous groups involved in the research.

Further, it is asserted that, in the 1970s, indigenist theory and practice in the form of Aboriginal Terms of Reference (ATR) were developed in Australian social work as a critical response by Aboriginal and Torres Strait Islander social workers to the cultural abuse experienced by our peoples.

These theories and practices emerged from the desperate needs of Aboriginal and Torres Strait Islander peoples to access services that were not being delivered, to challenge dominant systems of oppression, to achieve social justice and self-determination. This focus on systematic change also places the social work developed and practised by Aboriginal and Torres Strait Islander social workers at that time firmly within the Addams tradition.

Muriel Bamblett of the Secretariat of National Aboriginal and Islander Child Care Agency (SNAICC) defined cultural abuse as being:

> when the culture of a people is ignored, denigrated, or worse, intentionally attacked. It is abuse because it strikes at the very identity and soul of the people it is aimed at; it attacks their sense of self-esteem, it attacks their connectedness to their family and community. (Bamblett 2007)

The question that must be asked here is, 'Does Bamblett's definition of cultural abuse fit what has and is being done to Aboriginal and Torres Strait Islander social workers through the discounting of their work, their self-esteem and their achievements in the rush by the broader social work community to embrace the terms indigenism, indigenist theory and practice today?' If the word culture is replaced in the quote above with the word 'practice', it raises a whole different perspective, therefore different considerations of social workers credibility and achievements and could well be viewed as lateral violence in an Australian social work setting.

The challenges of including Aboriginal and Torres Strait Islander ontology and epistemology into the Australian social work curriculum

Indigenism, indigenist theory and practice are about indigenous peoples, acting for indigenous peoples, using indigenous ways of knowing, being and doing (Arbon 2008; Martin 2008) to achieve the best possible outcome for their peoples. It is about insider knowledge being applied politically, socially, economically, ethically and morally. It is also about indigenous leadership. This being the case, it is essential that any social work research, discussion, books or programs about indigenist ideology, indigenism, indigenist education, theory and practice in social work in Australia, be developed and led by indigenous researchers, academics and practitioners. The practices advocated here fit within an indigenist ideology, Aboriginal terms of reference, and culturally congruent practices that ensure cultural safety as shown in Figure 5.3 below.

Therefore, this ensures that this initiative does not become an exercise in mining and stripping of Indigenous knowledge systems, and the discounting of the work of Aboriginal and Torres Strait Islander social workers for an extended period. Ensuring that indigenism and indigenist theory and practice are not taught by non-indigenous researchers and academics, or practised by non-indigenous social workers, will certainly be a major concern for indigenous Elders, communities, academics, researchers and social workers.

This is a huge challenge given that there is such a small number of Indigenous academics currently employed within the schools of social work. This then bring us to another vital question: 'Where does that leave non-indigenous social workers?' I propose that it is as allies, which will be introduced and discussed next.

The role of non-indigenous social work allies

The term ally was used during the 2nd International Indigenous Social Work Conference held in Winnipeg, Canada (July 2013), to describe non-indigenous social workers and others who support the goals, aspirations, ways of knowing, being and doing (Arbon 2008; Martin 2008), and cultural protocols of indigenous peoples of the world. The support offered by allies included mentoring, support, talking for, working shoulder to shoulder with, and ensuring that indigenous knowledges were not colonised, misused or misinterpreted. Allies acknowledged at each point the leadership, expertise and value of the lived experience of their indigenous peers and were guided by them around how best to work within indigenous contexts, to achieve the empowerment and social justice goals of these groups.

From the example just shared, it is proposed that the role of allies can be progressed in similar ways in the Australian setting. However, some more specific ally support could be offered through the following five points. These points are: first, recognising the work undertaken by Aboriginal and Torres Strait Islander social workers from the 1970s onward, as the practice of these social workers was firmly placed within the Addams approach to social work and has achieved outcomes that have changed the Australian political and social environment, to meet the social justice needs of Aboriginal and Torres Strait Islander Australians.

Second, social workers examine and learn from what has been happening in the margins of social work in Australia and document this practice and include it into the history

Figure 5.3 The cycle and aim of indigenist theory.

of social work in Australia. This will enrich social work in this country, and reveal hidden knowledge and strengths within social work practice that have existed in the margins for over 40 years.

Third, that in the search for 'getting it right', we do not 'get it wrong', by not making the connections between Aboriginal Terms of Reference and what has been happening in the margins of dominant social work in Australia for the past 40 years. Our allies should be working to empower the indigenous social work that began in the 1970s and that continues today. This will bring about and enhance reconciliation rather than causing further marginalisation.

Fourth, that the Reconciliation Action Plan that was initiated by the AASW be updated, concluded, launched and rolled out across all states and territories, with the role of allies being added.

Fifth, understanding the role of allies and working from that position, rather than as colonisers mining indigenous knowledges. Working as allies will enable non-indigenous social workers to participate in indigenism and indigenist theories and practices in a positive way.

Conclusions

This chapter not only introduces the concepts of indigenism and indigenist theory and practice, it calls for the recognition of the work undertaken by Aboriginal and Torres Strait Islander social workers in the margins of Australian social work for the past 40 years. It also calls for the recognition of Aboriginal Terms of Reference (ATR) as the forerunner of the terms indigenism and indigenist theory in Australian social work.

A number of questions were raised and answered throughout the chapter around what is an indigenist ideology, who is an indigenist and how can indigenism and indigenist theory be taught within the schools of social work and in practice settings. Examples of indigenism and validating indigenist theory and practice were shared within the chapter, as a means of illustrating different uses of these theories.

The chapter also provided insights into how non-indigenous social work academics and researchers can participate in indigenist education, theory and practice as allies. Examples of how allies worked and were spoken about at the recent 2nd International Indigenous Social Work Conference in Winnipeg, Canada, were shared to provide insights and paths to the future. Additionally five points have been identified that would allow Australian social workers to immediately take up the role of allies in the Australian context.

Importantly, a number of challenges and cautions have been raised about not forgetting where we have come from, in an effort to prevent terms that could discount the practice of many indigenous social workers of the past 40 years, who have worked in the margins of dominant social work in Australia. It should be remembered that it was these social workers who, through their efforts and the efforts of their allies of the time, changed the landscape of Australian politics and policies through activism and structural change very successfully in the past.

References

Arbon, V. (2008). *Arlathirnda Ngurkarnda Ityirnda: being – knowing – doing: de-colonising Indigenous tertiary education*. Teneriffe, QLD: Post Pressed.

Baikie, G. (2009). Theorising a social work way-of-being. In R. Sinclair, M.A. Hart & G. Bruyere (eds), *Wícihitowin: Aboriginal social work in Canada*. Black Point, NS: Fernwood Publishing.

Bamblett, M. (2007). Presentation at the ATSIS Out of Home Care, Conference. Canberra.

Bin-Sallik, M. (2003). Cultural safety: let's name it! *The Australian Journal of Indigenous Education*, 32: 21–28.

Bishop, R. (2005). Freeing ourselves from neocolonial domination in research: a Kaupapa Māori approach to creating knowledge. In N.K. Denzin & Y.S. Lincoln (eds), *The SAGE handbook of qualitative research*. Thousand Oaks, CA: SAGE Publications.

Blackstock, C. (2009). The occasional evil of angels: learning from the experiences of Aboriginal peoples and social work. *First Peoples Child & Family Review*, 4(1): 28–37.

Calma, T. & Priday, E. (2011). Putting Indigenous human rights into social work practice. *Australian Social Work*, special issue, *Australian Indigenous Social Work and Social Policy*, 64(2): 147–55.

Camilleri, P. (2005). Social work education in Australia: at the 'crossroads'. Retrieved on 22 April 2014 from hdl.handle.net/10272/245.

Churchill, W. (1997). *A little matter of genocide: holocaust and denial in the Americas 1492 to the present*. San Francisco: City Lights Books.

Churchill, W. (1996). *From a native son: selected essays on Indigenism 1985–1995*. Boston, MA: South End Press.

Collins Australian Concise Dictionary (2001). 5th edn. Bath: William Collins Sons & Co. Ltd., Bath Press.

DiNova, J.R. (2005). *Spiraling webs of relation: movements towards an Indigenist criticism*. NY: Routledge.

Fejo-King, C. (2013). *Let's talk kinship: innovating Australian social work education, theory, research and practice through Aboriginal knowledge*. Canberra, ACT: Christine Fejo-King Consulting.

Foley, D. (2003). Indigenous epistemology and Indigenous standpoint theory. *Social Alternatives*, 22(1): 44–52.

Foley, D. (2002). Indigenous standpoint theory. *Journal of Australian Indigenous Issues*, 5(3): 3–13.

Haebich, A. (2000). *Broken circles: fragmenting Indigenous families 1800–2000*. Fremantle, WA: Fremantle Arts Centre.

Kelly, A. & Sewell, S. (2001). *With head heart and hand: dimensions of community building* (4th edn). Brisbane, QLD: Boolarong Press.

Kickett, D. (1992). *Aboriginal terms of reference: a paradigm for the future*. Perth, WA: Curtin University.

King, C. (2011). How understanding the Aboriginal kinship system can inform better policy and practice: social work research with the Larrakia and Warumungu Peoples of the Northern Territory. PhD thesis, Australian Catholic University, Canberra.

King, C. (2005). Decolonising research from an Australian Indigenous research perspective. Presentation for the 7th Indigenous Researchers Forum, Cairns, QLD.

King, T. (ed.) (1990). *All my relations: an anthology of contemporary Canadian native fiction*. Toronto, Canada: McClelland & Stewart Ltd.

LaRocque, E. (2010). *When the other is me: native resistance discourse 1850–1990*. Winnipeg, Canada: University of Manitoba.

Margolin, L. (1997). *Under the cover of kindness: the invention of social work*. Charlottesville, VA: University of Virginia Press.

Martin, K.L. (2008). *Please knock before you enter: Aboriginal regulation of outsiders and the implications for researchers*. Teneriffe, QLD: Post Pressed.

Moses, A.D. (ed.) (2004). *Genocide and settler society: frontier violence and stolen Indigenous children in Australian history*. NY: Berghahn.

Pattanayak, S. (2013). Social work practice in India: the challenge of working with diversity. In H.K. Ling, J. Martin & R. Ow (eds), *Cross-cultural social work: local and global* (pp. 87–100). Yarra, VIC: Palgrave Macmillan.

Ramsden, I.M. (2002). Cultural security and nursing education in Aotearoa and Te Waipounamu, PhD thesis, Victoria University, Wellington. Retrieved on 6 March 2006 from culturalsafety.massey.ac.nz.

Rigney, L.I. (2001). A first perspective of Indigenous Australian participation in science: framing Indigenous research towards Indigenous Australian intellectual sovereignty. *Kaurna Higher Education Journal,* 7: 1–13.

Rigney, L.I. (1999). *The first perspective: culturally safe research practices on or with Indigenous peoples.* Paper presented at the Chacmool Conference, University of Calgary, Calgary, Canada.

Rigney, L.I. (1997). Internationalisation of an Indigenous anti-colonial cultural critique of research methodologies: a guide to Indigenist research methodology and its principles. In *Research and development in higher education: advancing international perspectives*, vol. 20), pp. 626–29. Milperra, NSW: Higher Education Research and Development Society of Australasia (HERDSA).

Settee, P. (2007). Pimatisiwin: Indigenous knowledge systems, our time has come, PhD Thesis, University of Saskatchewan, Saskatoon, Canada. Retrieved on 22 April 2014 from library2.usask.ca/theses/available/etd-04302007–084445/unrestricted/settee_p.pdf.

Sinclair, R. (2007). All my relations – native transracial adoption: a critical case study of cultural identity, PhD thesis, University of Calgary, Calgary, Canada.

Sinclair, R., Hart, M.A. & Bruyere, G. (eds) (2009). *Wichihitowin: Aboriginal social work in Canada.* Black Point, NS: Fernwood Publishing.

Smith, L.T. (2012). *Decolonising methodologies: research and Indigenous peoples* (2nd edn). NY: Zed.

Smith, L.T. (1999). *Decolonising methodologies: research and Indigenous peoples* (1st edn). NY: Zed.

Specht, H. & Courtney, M.E. (1994). *Unfaithful angels: how social work has abandoned its mission.* NY: Free Press.

University of Sydney (2012). Social work at the University of Sydney: seven decades of distinction. Retrieved on 22 April 2014 from sydney.edu.au/education_social_work/about/history/social_work.shtml.

West, E. (2000). An alternative to existing Australian research and teaching models. The Japanangka teaching and research paradigm: an Australian Aboriginal model, PhD thesis, University of South Australia, Adelaide, SA.

Wilson, S. (2008). *Research is ceremony: Indigenous research methods.* Black Point, NS: Fernwood Publishing.

Part 2
Social work as a profession

6

Envisioning a professional identity: charting pathways through social work education in India

Vimla V. Nadkarni and Sandra Joseph

This paper presents an overview of social work as a profession in India, tracing its historical beginnings, philosophical base, dominant practice perspectives, its relevance in the country's current socioeconomic and politico-cultural context and its impact on emerging trends in global practice. It also aims to stimulate discussion on the possible ways through which Social Work education can make significant contributions in the wake of the changing trends in state responsibility towards the poor and marginalised and in doing so carve its professional identity in order to gain its rightful status in Indian society.

Historical beginnings

The profession of Social Work in India marked its platinum jubilee in the year 2012. Seventy-five years and more have been critical in the establishment of the profession as an independent helping profession, interdisciplinary in nature and based on a foundation of traditional Social Work methods and skills, values and ethics built around humanitarian principles with a combination of several religio-cultural philosophies rich to the nation. The Western legacy of professionalisation of Social Work continues in several developing countries that have adopted an American–Eurocentric model. The initiation of Social Work education in India was based on Western thought and pedagogy.

Professionalisation of Social Work began with practice in Mumbai (erstwhile Bombay) in 1936 under the leadership of Sir Clifford Manshardt, an American missionary, at the Nagpada Neighbourhood House (settlement house for family welfare). He became the founder-director of the Sir Dorabji Tata Graduate School of Social Work which began with a Diploma in Social Service Administration. In 1964, the School became the Tata Institute of Social Sciences (a Deemed University) which offered a Master of Arts Degree in Social Work.

In the 1950s and 1960s several schools of Social Work started in other parts of the country with faculty who completed doctoral studies in the US. This was a major factor, particularly for the growth of postgraduate degrees in Social Work with specialisations in clinical and non-clinical Social Work. Social Work educators have written extensively on the urgent need to indigenise the curriculum. Writings of Gore (1965), Dasgupta (1968), Banerjee (1972), Desai (1985), Siddique (1987), Desai (2004), Saldanha (2008) and recently by Bodhi (2011) have strongly criticised the Western models and made emphatic deliberations on the need for a newer and relevant curriculum design for Social Work practice in India.

It was in the 1970s also that the concept of integrated methods and integrated social work practice entered the curricula of several Social Work programs across the country. This led to a greater emphasis on the interface between macro and micro practice using the systems framework for social change (Pincus and Minahan 1973). Studies reveal the persistence of American influence over the curriculum and issues relating to adapting Western Social Work values to the Indian culture (Nagpaul 1993; Mandal 1989; Srivastava 1999). When professional Social Work was 'imported' to India from the West, it was squeezed into the social fabric and forced to deal with several local factors. Thus, the experience of professional Social Workers is complex and requires a constant dance between different systems and cultural ideologies (Kuruvilla 2005).

Philosophical base of social work

Given India's diverse socioeconomic and politico-cultural milieu, it is no easy task in identifying a single philosophical base for the profession's existence. As discussed earlier, the context in which Social Work education emerged in India drew heavily on the American curricula given its historical beginnings of partnership between the Tata Trust and the US Education Technical Mission with the Council of Social Work of America (Gore & Gore 1977). In retrospect, the dependence on Western ideologies to a large extent deferred the indigenisation processes of the profession, perpetuating rigid curriculum structures which did not evince sufficient credibility, support and recognition from entities that govern the country's development or education. However, the arduous journey towards greater integration of indigenous knowledge and practice frameworks continues.

Social service in India stems from deep-rooted religious beliefs. It existed in the form of almsgiving and charity to the poor and needy, creation of shelters and kitchens, and institutions for orphans and elderly, the destitute, and beggars. Philosophies of welfare and humanitarianism that arose from deep-rooted religious beliefs and practices of Hinduism, Buddhism, Jainism, Islam, Christianity and indigenous beliefs were at some point the driving forces behind education and practice of Social Work in India. Kulkarni asserted that the Indian model is indigenous and the aberrations, if any, are minor (Kulkarni 1993). A few schools integrated India's distinguished lineage in the freedom movement and adopted the thinking of world renowned philosophers such as Gandhi, Swami Vivekananda and Tagore in their curriculum (Kumar 1998). Yet some other schools emphasised the value of human rights, empowerment and social justice as their core values in their curriculum.

Increasingly, the trend is that missions of schools are influenced by their affiliations and political interests of governing members and trustees or on faith and missionary enthusiasm. Today there are several central, state, private and deemed universities with: departments/faculty/schools of social work. Departments of social work are located in state or national health and mental health academic institutions, and social work courses are taught in social science departments in a state or central university. These programs claim to be secular in their curriculum development and teaching approaches. There are also Social Work degree programs offered by faith-based 'minority-labelled' institutions (Report of the Consultation on National Network of Schools of Social Work for Quality Enhancement of Social Work Education in India 2012).

Dominant perspectives on education and practice

Perspectives for practice have changed with the changing economic and political developments in the country. From charity and reform it gradually moved to welfare and subsequently to development and more recently to human rights and social justice. However, this has not been observed as a linear progress; rather, all forms of practice perspectives are known to exist simultaneously.

A historic meeting in 1964 of professional Social Workers with Gandhian workers led to the realisation that while Gandhian workers accepted the need for education and training, professionals recognised that Social Work needed to move beyond ameliorative work to social action so as to remedy the roots of social malaise and to change the social order (Dasgupta 1967 cited in Desai and Narayan 1998, 537, 538). As observed by Gore and Gore (1977, 265–66), curative Social Work through casework dominated in the Social Work programs (cited in Mandal 1995). It de-emphasised the needs of social and economic development, promotion of preventive services and social action – the prime need of the country in the post-independence era.

Social Action, Social Policy and Social Administration as important courses were emphasised in the Review Committee Report of the Second University Grants Commission (Mandal 1995, 539). These areas were identified in the National Curricular Review in 1988–1990 undertaken by the University Grants Commission. According to Pathak and Siddigui (from Mandal 1995, 539) several educators have observed that Social Work education has not pursued in practice what it has professed (Pathak 1980; Siddiqui 1984 cited in Mandal 1995, 539). However, field-based practice as a response to emerging issues in health education, women's rights, reproductive and sexual health, HIV/AIDS, child rights, etc. has moved ahead with the times. This movement is seen in the shift from a clinical-based remedial approach to a rights-based approach, more concerted use of empowerment methodologies, social action and involvement in policy efforts.

At the turn of the 20th century, labour welfare persisted as a social work specialisation in the form of human resource management, although it lost its 'Welfare and Social Work' practice features. The focus continues to be on industry and the organised sector in quite a few schools that offer the specialisation. More recently the issue has been brought to the fore for debate but the dichotomy of whether it falls in the purview of social work education and practice in India still looms large, being contested in several conferences and seminars.

Global influences in India

Similar to other nations, particularly in the global South, globalisation has posed tremendous challenges for the profession with its accompaniment of privatisation and neoliberalisation, bringing both benefits and negative effects to people. Those who are on the fringes of Indian society – the rural and urban poor, the homeless, malnourished children and women, dalits (lower castes), tribals and sexual minorities – are bearing the brunt of some of the negative fall-out of the rapidly increasing emphasis on economic growth and focus on foreign direct investment. Studies show lower rates in development indicators among the marginalised sections, the most economically and socially backward populations in India. Discrimination on the basis of caste, class, gender, age, religion, disability and sexual orientation are issues which need attention both from the global to the local context.

Economic growth and development continues to be the priority of the Indian polity. Natural resources are exploited and people are being ousted from their roots. There are social movements against expansion of industries like mining for steel or coal, hydropower or nuclear power projects that are neither environment friendly nor people friendly. 'Contemporary Social Work issues in India cannot be addressed without a shift to a more politically aware definition of the profession, guiding both national and international goals for Social Work. Standards that support equity and human rights as well as focusing on adjustment are necessary to address these issues in the global context' (Alphonse et al. 2008).

In the globalised world, protecting the ecosystem is not just the responsibility of a single country but is an international political issue. Ecological social work or social work on environmental issues and environmental justice including climate change are emerging as critical areas for curriculum and practice in India. New epidemics are appearing while old ones are re-emerging. According to the National Family Health Survey (NFHS), 43% of India's children remain underweight and an estimated 88% between six and 24 months are anaemic. More recently mobility has become a major issue for development and health workers.

Use of digital communication and social media has shrunk the world and has opened up many avenues for sharing of resources, campaigning on common fronts, and attracting support from people around the globe on several issues. With the opening up of the Indian Government towards foreign universities setting up campuses in India, without an Indian partner, the impact on higher education in India will necessarily go through a sea change in its intake of students, its curricular design and its quality of output. This phenomenon will also impact upon social work education in the country, a cause for reflection and action.

Fortunately, despite the pressures to give in to globalisation demands, Social Work has maintained a fair balance, and continues to support the development of health and education as human rights (as seen in the National Rural Health Mission and the Right to Education Bill). Working with the State means also having to deal with the issues of poor governance of welfare programs where the allocated resources are not reaching the poorest of the poor in both the urban and rural areas. The big challenge is how education of Social Work should be positioning itself in India given the strong global influences.

Shift from problem perspective to development perspective

A very significant paradigm shift in social work curriculum was the move from a 'social problem perspective' to a 'developmental perspective' in the analysis of social issues. This was greatly influenced by the World Summit on Social Development in 1995 in Copenhagen that led to the United Nations focusing on key social development themes. Social work educators were thus influenced to integrate development concerns and issues in the curriculum. This perspective was also integrated in the National Social Work Curriculum (University Grants Commission 2001). Since the turn of the century, social work teachers have been joining hands with human rights groups to protect the rights of children, women, prisoners, activists, etc. Social work colleges in India too are gradually incorporating the human rights perspective in their curriculum, pioneering programs and policy change to protect the rights of the child, the girl child, women, and the right to education, health and livelihood. This is in keeping with the United Nations Human Development Reports (United Nations Development Programme 2007 and 2009) adopted by the International Association of Schools of Social Work (IASSW) and the International Federation of Social Workers (IFSW).

The education of social work in several institutions by and large complies with the requirements of their respective university standards. The absence of a body that would govern social work education and practice in the country seems to be a big setback in the development of the profession in the country. However, a few institutions incorporate the suggestions made in the Global Standards.

Though international social work is not a dominant practice perspective, there is a growing trend towards teaching international social work. The Indian Government is encouraging universities to open their doors to international students, and compete in the global market. More departments and schools are thus linking with international social work programs through teacher and faculty exchanges and online courses. 'International Social Work' is gradually becoming a popular course among Indian students, especially those who vie for higher studies abroad. Programs abroad are also seeking new sites for field placements for their students in developing countries and India is providing ample opportunities for this movement of foreign students coming for short-term or semester internships earning credits in their home university. The government of India permits international students through a Home Ministry providing the opportunity for students to study in India. This also provides an opportunity of creating an international movement of social work alumni around the world to work together on the common cause of reducing inequalities, support for the cause of human rights and social justice for the poor. This freedom to innovate is feasible in universities or colleges with an autonomous status and where legal procedures are less cumbersome.

Nevertheless, efforts to indigenise the curriculum tailored to meet the local needs of the Indian population as well as equip students with the required knowledge on international influences and international practice are on the rise in several schools. There is an attempt at discourse on anti-oppressive practice in the development of dalit and tribal social work. Social work educators in the country are also leading special centres on social exclusion and human rights that conduct research and practice with special reference to minority and oppressed populations.

Local influences on social work pedagogy

The knowledge base for social work education in India is interdisciplinary in nature. For an in-depth understanding of society, human behaviour and societal development, foundation courses span a wide range of disciplines like psychology, sociology, medicine, psychiatry, economics, law, management and administration. Methods courses – Case Work, Group Work, Community Organisation, Social Work Research, Welfare Administration, and Social Policy Analysis and Development – provide the core skills base. History and Philosophy of Social Work, Ideologies and Perspectives, Social Development and Social Problems are covered as essential and core courses.

State influence on social work curriculum

In 1990, the University Grants Commission set up a Curriculum Development Cell for Social Work Education at the Tata Institute of Social Sciences. The 1990 report suggests that while core subjects remain common across social work programs, there are attempts made to tailor the curriculum to regional needs. A unified and holistic approach in the curriculum may not be the answer to solving diverse social challenges. The mission and goals of social work education, that are adopted from the International definitions of the International Association of Schools of Social Work (www.iassw-aiets.org), the International Federation of Social Workers (www.ifsw.org), and the National Accreditation and Assessment Council (www.naac.gov.in), vary in terms of institutional goals, regional challenges, cultural practices, religious emphases, human rights and justice values and a range of other contexts in which schools are established.

All courses are subject to approval of Boards of Studies and Academic Councils appointed by universities and/or the University Grants Commission. In very few instances, departments or schools have experimented with more generic areas of study like micro and macro practice, social welfare and social development. Students are required to select either of the domains. The School of Social Work at Tata Institute of Social Sciences, Mumbai, offers nine master's level degree programs in social work in nine specified thematic areas prioritising needs emerging from the changing social, economic, political, and cultural scenarios in the country and available expertise (www.tiss.edu).

Fieldwork education comprises several components which are organised across the semesters. The basic framework across most programs is made up of field orientation and observation visits, rural camps, study tours, block placements and concurrent fieldwork under the supervision of a field and faculty supervisor. Government and non-government organisations are identified where students gain a wide exposure to the social realities of the poor and marginalised. They get hands-on experience of working with people at different levels including systems-based interventions, policy and advocacy work.

The major gap is that universities in India fail to recognise the uniqueness of the social work curriculum with its field practice laboratory and view it on similar lines to other departments. This has led to a lack of academic support for fieldwork training which is an exclusive requirement of the profession. Fieldwork gets further diluted in social work courses offered through distance and online programs. Social workers graduate from these courses most often without adequate field supervision.

Due to the increasing emphasis on research and publications, both national and global, social work educators have been encouraged by higher education bodies, such as the University Grants Commission and those Universities supported by central and state governments, to research and publish and demonstrate high quality in areas of research. There is a dearth of provision in creating proactive scholarship among social work academics in India. The burden of performance on the educators increases with the balancing of several tasks simultaneously: teaching, fieldwork supervision, research and writing. Though these are core responsibilities of the social work educator, processes that can enhance and enable better performance need attention.

Continuing faculty development and field engagement

Education and training in the discipline of social work is far more complex in view of its unique nature. To create a cadre of competent professional social workers requires competent teachers and practitioners who together form a pool of educators created from a praxis of reflections on theory and practice. Most social work educators are trained social work professionals who qualify through passing the UGC governed National Eligibility Test or the state governed State Level Eligibility Test (www.ugcnetonline.in) to teach at the college level. Giving priority to past or simultaneous practice experience is always an advantage. They further qualify with an MPhil or PhD in social work. Schools of social work are required to mandatorily employ such qualified personnel in the teaching profession. Faculties are also required to complete certain refresher courses for career advancement.

A major challenge is the lack of faculty development programs or refresher courses tailored specifically for enhancing capacities of educators. Retaining competent faculty is a major challenge owing to the larger sociopolitical, financial and infrastructural constraints that draw them to more fulfilling and greener pastures, even outside the country. The need for a strong body or network of schools that weaves together the diversities in teaching and learning methodologies, and ensures high quality in the education and training patterns in the country, is apparent.

The profession is not governed by an exclusive council or a body that oversees the areas of social work practice. Therefore no rigid or clearly marked boundaries exist in the country. Social work practitioners do not require a licence as would doctors, lawyers, nurses, etc. This has led to several other disciplines entering the domain of social work practice. Educational programs such as Human Rights, Development Studies, Health Management, Human Resource Management, Rural Management, Urban Studies etc. are becoming independent disciplines or professions, which were once an integral part of the domain of social work. One tends to agree with Darvill et al. that:

> in future Social Workers are likely to be employed less in social services and Social Work departments and more in multi-disciplinary and multi-agency settings. In these settings integration of different skills and professional groups is the norm, and this varies according to the requirements of user centered services, greater social inclusion and new ways of working. (Darvill et al. 2001, 4)

The profession is going through the process of re-establishing a national association of social work educators in the country. Educators are spearheading this effort to create a credible body that will monitor and enhance the quality of social work education and practice in India. This effort has taken on a distinct and clear-cut structure in the recent past in the formation of a National Network of Schools of Social Work (Nadkarni & Desai 2012). In a recent consultation, a group of senior educators from the network met at Tata Institute of Social Sciences to launch the Indian Association of Social Work Education (IASWE). This association is expected to chart new pathways for enhancing the competency and visibility of the profession through its educational programs.

Indigenous social work theory and practice

One of the most obvious pathways towards creating an identity for social work in India would be to evoke indigenous theoretical and practice frameworks. With English as the medium of instruction in most schools, the indigenisation of social work is grossly stunted. Students from the vernacular (regional language) medium face difficulties in coping with English as a medium of instruction and expression. Some slim efforts have been made to develop literature in regional languages. The absence of indigenous literature in practice has led to the poor quality of referencing and preparing home-based and classroom assignments. Nevertheless, India has a wealth of literature and creative writings in regional languages relevant to social work education and practice; such literature can be made available in local languages. This will go a long way in augmenting social work knowledge in the country. 'As far as the Indian context is concerned, there is a growing realisation among contemporary Social Work educators and practitioners alike that there cannot be one overarching indigenous Social Work knowledge base' (Bodhi 2011, 290).

Field action through colleges/schools/departments has been supported as a pedagogical tool to test and evolve indigenous social work practice. These projects that start with micro-level practice become model programs supported by relevant ministries in the government; they influence national programs and policy, serve as learning centres for social work students, paraprofessionals and faculty. Several major initiatives in the country range from work with the most marginalised populations to remedying existing clinical and social systems or creating new ones.

Several indigenous projects are emerging as models to replicate. For example, CHILD-LINE India Foundation (www.childlineindia.org.in), which started as a helpline for street children, has demonstrated the need to reach out to children through the rights-based approach and policy development on child protection. It is today a national scheme fully sponsored by the Ministry of Child and Women Development. Inclusive education for all children through the NGO, 'Pratham' (www.pratham.org), started as a pilot project to attract poor children of preschool age to school, as a collaboration of the College of Social Work in Mumbai and a social entrepreneur. This has become an institutionalised (registered) movement with branches all over the country and abroad. Integrating the concepts of social entrepreneurship with social work, a sustainable partnership in the era of globalisation has been forged.

Social work colleges in some parts of the country have been very sensitive to their local needs and emerging challenges. Indigenous practice models have also been developed in the fields of disaster prevention and response, relief and rehabilitation of displaced persons, HIV/AIDS and new emerging diseases, dalit and tribal social work.

Concerns and challenges

The complex Indian reality

The Indian social reality is a complex and multi-dimensional one. Its social, economic, cultural and political factors capped by its invasive caste, class and gender system call for more careful and deeper analytical understanding of India's reality and a social work response that will necessarily have to be multidimensional. 'The high degree of ethnic heterogeneity and dynamic interface of gender-caste-tribe-religion-class reality coupled with the dialectical relationship between the "traditional-modern" and "conservative-progressive" subsumed within an overarching frame of institutionalised exclusion and oppression in the form of caste, is indeed a colossal task to comprehend' (Bodhi 2011, 292).

The current scenario calls for a curriculum that will depart from its traditional trajectory and move towards one that will equip students with liberatory and emancipatory ideologies, theories and practice of social transformation with radical underpinnings that will respond to the complex Indian social realities. It is in these contexts that social work education will have to take responsibility and work towards gaining its rightful recognition in the complex Indian reality.

Need to reposition human resource management

With increasing focus on the services and manufacturing sector in India, there is today great demand for management skills in business and industry. In this era of an unregulated labour market, there is increasing need for human resource management and skills in project planning and development as well as monitoring and evaluation. The response of social work has been to cater to these capacity-building needs by initiating postgraduate degrees in these areas which have been the territory of management schools. In turn, management schools are also preparing managers and social entrepreneurs for the social sectors.

In the current context where management is the buzzword for any professional whether in business, health, education or social welfare, there is a danger of social work losing its people-centred focus. In the process of over-professionalisation, the compassion and empathy of working with people at the grassroots is replaced by quantitative performance-oriented targets such as the University Grants Commission's Annual Self-Assessment for Performance Based System Indicators and Scores for promotion of teachers (www.ugc.ac.in) measuring efficiency and effectiveness of social work practice.

Need for more bachelor level programs

The second major issue has been that social work education in India began with postgraduate programs rather than undergraduate programs. The first undergraduate degree in social work began in 1974 at the College of Social Work, Nirmala Niketan, Mumbai University. The current scenario is that most of the colleges/departments prefer to run postgraduate programs again due to the jobs available in the government and non-government sectors. Only very few five-year integrated social work programs are offered which start after junior college (12 years of formal education in India).

In the context of graduate education in India, a bachelor's professional degree is viewed as the foundation for any profession and the student is expected to complete a professional master's degree for professional practice in that specialisation. The social work undergraduate program provides the basics in the social sciences or in social work; the social work graduates are more motivated to work as field practitioners.

Advocacy for creating positions for social work at the bachelor's level is imperative. This is part of the process of making social work education more relevant to Indian socio-cultural settings. There is a need to attract social workers at younger ages so as to mould them into socially aware citizens and effective social workers. Youth social workers have to become socially aware and active citizens whose rights are embedded not merely in personal entitlements, and grounded in location but grounded in personhood. It is essential to incorporate diversity into our understanding of social rights (Drover 2000).

People-centredness vs elitism

Professionalisation has been said to create elitism in social work where the field is dominated by the urban middle class. According to Siddiqui (1984), the priority for offering of courses is the easily available job placements and this influences the selection of students who fit into these jobs (cited in Desai and Narayan 1998). The Second Review Committee Report strongly advocates that the profession of social work should be non-elitist both in the content and pedagogy as well as in the social class from which the students hail:

> These developments and the rise of the middle classes have been increasingly making the job of structural Social Work challenging, so much so that Social Work is experiencing an identity crisis in India. (Rao 2011, 38)

For students with rising costs of living, the dilemma remains – an elitist job with high salary or a development organisation with comparatively low salary and no perks. There is also now greater opportunity for international jobs and projects. There is a danger of focusing more on projects and consultancy instituted by foreign funding agencies with little relevance to the country's needs. Institutions of social work education in India, who face serious resource crunches, find it increasingly difficult to address these issues.

Need for social work professionals at different levels

According to Fook, the autonomy of all professionals is challenged in the current context. Managers and bureaucrats are taking control of professional practice due to the increased emphasis on managerialism and changed funding arrangements. Thus, the assumptions are being questioned. Professional identities are being undermined and professional boundaries are weakened. Jobs are represented in fragmented skill or program-based terms, rather than holistic professional terms. Competition between different professional groups increases as each one struggles for territory and ascendancy (Fook 2002). Midgley and others view globalisation as involving complex processes with both positive and negative impacts. Social work education has to build student and faculty capacity to critically assess these processes and anticipate the challenges (Midgley 2000).

In a workshop on 'Perspectives for Social Work Training: 2000 AD', the alumni of TISS were divided in their opinions about the future thrust of training. While the majority advocated for focus on conscientisation of the marginalised, the minority preferred the established remedial orientation of social work and clinical social work which was urban- and middle-class oriented (Desai 1991).

Institutions could encourage academic activism through critical research, policy-level interventions and by expressing solidarity and support with people-centred movements (Desai & Narayan 1998, 547). As social workers, we need constantly to translate and communicate what the values and goals of social justice mean to different people and groups (Desai & Narayan 1998, 547).

Considering its size, diversity, poverty levels and increasing disparities, India needs a range of trained social workers – the paraprofessionals, the graduates and the postgraduates, along with the doctoral-level research practitioners who will work with a holistic perspective at a variety of levels and catering to a variety of needs. 'We need the ability to transfer our knowledge and skills in any setting' (Fook 2002, 28).

There is also the realisation that there are many more players involved in these processes besides the trained social workers. Joining hands with them to work towards social transformation on a robust foundation of theory and values should be the goal of social work education. The greatest challenge is to 'be the change you want to see in the world'. A majority of schools need to work towards establishing high quality social work education programs.

Based on the need for a transformative paradigm for social work education, the National Network of Schools of Social Work members developed objectives to make social work education emancipatory and transformative to create an inclusive and just society; set minimum required standards of curriculum, re-emphasising its ethical foundations; created a universally accessible repository of high quality knowledge, resources, expertise and processes of sharing with schools across the country; achieve visibility for the profession through structures that engage state, civil society, and industry; established linkages and databases that connect and inform all responsible stakeholders; strived to improve standards through accreditation systems and periodic reviews; and created representative scientific associations to explore various facets of social work, taking responsibility for collective advocacy and action (Nadkarni 2012).

Need for a core curriculum framework

The need for a national curriculum when there is extreme diversity in the country is a question often debated in some fora of social workers. Conceptualising a core framework for social work theory and practice through praxis, that would serve as the foundation for the social work curriculum, is the need of the day. This framework could then be developed further regionally to integrate the local social and developmental issues.

A national consultation to achieve this was organised by the National Network of Schools of Social Work spearheaded by the Tata Institute of Social Sciences. However, it was observed that there was a need for greater conceptualisation and re-imagining of social work education. Efforts to collate the emerging fields of practice and in-depth analysis on various components of social work education is being carried out. A Social Work Education Observatory as the mechanism to develop and digitise indigenous knowledge resources and disseminate them to all corners of the country has been envisaged. This would serve as the knowledge hub that would create country-wide classrooms for imparting basic courses and specialised courses and thus enable students to access knowledge resources and lectures through web-based systems.

This implies that all institutions would need to develop the technological base, trained staff, ongoing training and sufficient resources to access the knowledge hub. The National Network will moot the idea for continuous enhancement of knowledge, promote active research to inform social sector policy evaluation, and change and develop IT and digital library networks to share knowledge and learning resources so that students located in any part of the country are able to access quality teaching offered from schools of social work.

Conclusions

While social work in India has not created a visible identity for itself nor has a marked territory for practice, the fraternity is aware of the insightful prediction that the social work professional 'will increasingly be required to work in more than one task-specific team simultaneously, and change teams thereafter. They will have key roles in setting up, maintaining and changing teams' (Darvill et al. 2001, 4).

An important aspect that is critical to envisioning a professional identity for the profession in India is to chart out a clear curriculum that emphasises critical and analytical thinking to enable students to commit themselves in working towards development needs of the poor and marginalised people: the dalits, the indigenous people, children, women, girls, the socially stigmatised and all groups that are increasingly deprived of social safety nets with the reducing investment of the government in social sectors. Indian social work educators need to continuously tailor programs and update themselves on current knowledge frameworks in order to carry forward a professional approach in the plans for work, especially in the most poor and backward areas of the country. In doing so, the profession of social work will gain its rightful recognition and acceptance in Indian society. The task may be uphill but it will move towards the achievement of what social work definitions portend in all the major bodies of social work education in the world.

References

Alphonse, M., George, P. & Moffatt, K. (2008). Redefining social work standards in the context of globalisation: lessons from India. *International Social Work*, 51(2): 145–15. Retrieved on 22 April 2014 from isw.sagepub.com/cgi/content/abstract/51/2/145.

Banerjee, G. (1972). Papers in social work: an Indian perspective. Bombay: Tata Institute of Social Sciences.

Bodhi, S.R. (2011). Professional social work education in India, a critical view from the periphery, discussion note 3. *The Indian Journal of Social Work*, 72(2): 230.

Darvill, G., Green, L., Hartley, P. & Statham, D. (2001). The future of social work; stimulus paper for consultation – national occupation – standards for social work. NY: NISW & LMG Associates.

Dasgupta, S. (1968). *Social work and social change: a case study in Indian village development*. Boston: Extending Horizon Books.

Dasgupta, S. (1967). *Towards a philosophy of social work in India*. New Delhi: Popular Book Services.

Desai, A. (1985). Foundations of social work education in India and some issues. *Indian Journal of Social Work*, 46(1): 41–57.

Desai, M. & Narayan, L. (1998). Challenges for social work profession; towards people-centred development. In M. Desai, A. Monteiro, L. Narayan (eds), *Indian Journal of Social Work*, special issue, *Towards People-Centered Development (Part 2)*, 59(1): 531–58.

Desai, M. (2004). *Methodology of progressive social work education*. New Delhi: Rawat Publications.

Desai, M. (1991). Issues concerning the setting up of social work specialisations in India. *International Social Work*, 34(1): 83–95.

Drover, G. (2000). Redefining social citizenship in a global era. *Canadian Social Work*, special issue, *Social Work and Globalization*, 2(1): 13–28.

Fook, J. (2002). *Social work: critical theory and practice*. London: SAGE Publications.

Gore, M. (1965). *Social work and social work education*. Bombay: Asia Publishing House.

Gore, P. & Gore, M. (1977). *Social work education in India*. Bombay: Tata Institute of Social Sciences.

Kulkarni, P.D. (1993).The Indigenous base of social work profession in India. *The Indian Journal of Social Work*, 54(4): 555–65.

Kumar, A. (1998). Gandhi, Tagore and professional social work. *The Indian Journal of Social Work*, 59(2): 696–701.

Kuruvilla, S. (2005). Social work and social development in India. In L. Ferguson (ed.), *Globalisation, global justice and social work*. London: Routledge.

Mandal, K.S. (1995). India. In T. D., Watts., Elliott & N.S. Mayadas (eds), *International handbook on social work education* (pp. 356–65). Westport: Greenwood Press.

Mandal, K.S. (1989). American influence on social work education in India and its impact. *International Social Work*, 32(4): 303–09.

Midgley, J. (2000). Globalisation, capitalism and social welfare: a social development perspective. *Canadian Social Work*, special issue, *Social Work and Globalisation*, 2(1): 13–28.

Nadkarni, V. (2012). National network on schools of social work – a proposal. National network meeting with the planning commission. Mumbai: Tata Institute of Social Sciences.

Nadkarni, V. & Desai, K. (2012). *National consultation on national network of schools of social work for quality enhancement of social work education in India*. Mumbai: School of Social Work, Tata Institute of Social Sciences.

Nagpaul, H. (1993). Analysis of social work teaching material in India: the need for indigenous foundations. *International Social Work*, 36(3): 207–20.

Pincus, A. & Minahan, A. (1973). *Social work practice: model and method*. Itasca, IL: Peacock.

Rao, V. (2011). Social policy, justice and democratic rights: a critical view of social work in India today. *ERIS Web Journal*, 2. Retrieved on 17 April 2014 from periodika.osu.cz/eris/dok/2011-02/justice_and_democratic_rights_vidya.pdf

Saldanha, D. (2008). Towards a conceptualisation of social action within social work: teaching social action as a dialogue between theoretical perspectives and between theory and practice. *Indian Journal of Social Work*, 69(2): 111–37.

Siddiqui, H.Y (1987). Towards a competency based education for social work. *Indian Journal of Social Work*, 48(1): 23–32.

Siddiqui, H.Y. (ed.) (1984). *Social work and social action*. New Delhi: Harnam Publications.

Srivastava, S.P. (1999). Addressing the future of professional social work in India. *The Indian Journal of Social Work*, 60(1): 119–39.

United Nations Development Programme (2009). Human development report. Overcoming barriers: human mobility and development. Retrieved on 17 April 2014 from hdr.undp.org/en/media/HDR_2009_EN_Complete.pdf.

United Nations Development Programme (2007). Human development report. International human development indicators. Retrieved on 17 April 2014 from hdrstats.undp.org/en/countries/country_fact_sheets/cty_fs_IND.html.

University Grants Commission (2001). UGC model curriculum: social work education. New Delhi: UGC. Retrieved on 17 April 2014 from www.ugc.ac.in/oldpdf/modelcurriculum/social_work_education.pdf.

7

Social work education in Indonesia: challenges and reforms

Fentiny Nugroho and Kanya Eka Santi

The social work profession in Indonesia has not yet become a desirable occupation that parents would like their children to take up, as opposed to a doctor or an engineer. This is partly because the profession is not widely known yet in Indonesia. Why is this the case? It is a relatively new development in Indonesia, which began around the late 1950s when the Ministry of Social Affairs commenced to recruit social workers as its employees. Furthermore, the term 'social worker' is not considered attractive as an occupation. In Indonesia, social work philosophy is 'helping people to help themselves'. The concept of a 'helping profession' is not regarded as based on science and knowledge, because in the daily life of Indonesian society 'helping others' is common, because the general nature of Indonesian society is still in a close relationship, so they tend not to feel the need for a 'helping profession'. Research conducted by the Asian Pacific Association for Social Work Education (APASWE) revealed that in the country many people do not know about the profession of social work. For those people, volunteers are social workers (Sasaki 2013).

This condition is a major challenge that must be faced by social work / social welfare education in Indonesia. How can we make efforts to make social work widely known, and social work become a desired profession? This chapter will discuss the debates around social work, which incorporate challenges encountered and the efforts made for social work development.

Debates and contextual analysis

Who is a social worker?

In Indonesia there are still debates around social work. Firstly, according to the general public and volunteers, anyone who works in the field of social welfare is called a 'social worker'. Especially in the field, they feel that it is non-professional social workers who mainly assist them in dealing with their problems. In contrast, social workers take the view that not everybody who works in the field of social welfare is a social worker; some of them are professional social workers, while others are volunteers. For this latter group, social workers are those who have graduated from a bachelor or 'Diploma 4' program in social welfare.

Misperception about the profession of social workers in Indonesian society is one of the main factors that make the profession less attractive, because to them helping can be done by everyone, without specific education. Thus, a 'helping profession' is not considered as a profession; especially in this society, helping/social support can be obtained from the extended family and neighbours. In order to affirm that the social worker is a professional, the association of social workers in Indonesia is called the Indonesian Association of Professional Social Workers (IPSPI). The society's views on the profession of social work cause the professional social workers to encourage and facilitate the issuance of Law No. 11/2009 on Social Welfare. According to this law, someone who has not graduated from a school of social welfare cannot be called a professional social worker; they are called welfare workers (tenaga kesejahteraan sosial) and volunteers. The stipulation of Law No. 13/2011 on the poorest of the poor, and Law No. 11/2012 concerning the child judicial system, demonstrate the growing recognition of social work as a profession in Indonesia. In line with the establishment of the Asean Social Work Consortium in Manila (the Philippines), the Indonesian Social Work Consortium was founded in 2011.

Social work reform in Indonesia began especially with the issuance of the Law on Social Welfare No 11/2009, which recognised the 'professional social worker' as a graduate of a social work school. This law clearly distinguishes the role from the 'volunteer' and 'welfare worker' who may come from other disciplines. This Act was reinforced by the Regulation of Minister of Social Affairs No.108/2009 on the Certification of Professional Social Workers and Welfare Workers, as well as the Regulation of Minister of Social Affairs No.107/2009 on Accreditation of Social Welfare Institutions.

To improve the quality of education in Indonesia, the Ministry of Education and Culture requires the accreditation of the delivering university, as well as undergraduate, masters and doctoral programs once every five years. This is conducted by the National Accreditation Board of Higher Education. Especially for departments of social welfare, accreditation is the process of monitoring the program and assuring the quality of graduates.

In line with these social work reforms, the Indonesian Association of Social Work / Social Welfare Education (IPPSI), which is an organisation consisting of 37 Indonesian schools to develop social work/social welfare education in Indonesia, formulated a standardised national curriculum. It consists of 19 core courses (57 credits) that must be taken by students of the bachelor level. Overall they must pass 144 credits to earn a bachelor's degree. Within the remaining 87 credits, there is an ample space for school members to design courses in accordance with the features of curriculum at the respective universities, incorporating the strengths of the school, as well as the local culture and the existing human resources.

The Ministry of Education requires that to be a lecturer in a Bachelor program, one must minimally hold a master's degree. In addition, to teach in the master's program, one must have obtained a PhD degree. Currently in Indonesia there are two schools – University of Indonesia and University of Padjadjaran – that have programs from a bachelor to doctorate. Besides an academic degree, a faculty member requires a number of credits for his/her promotion namely, in teaching, research/scholarly work, community services, and supporting aspects such as involvement in committees and organisations both on campus and off campus. For lecturers of a department of social welfare, the community service activities enrich their practice experiences and skills, which are very important for teaching. As social work is an applied science, the schools invite practitioner guest lecturers to teach. In formulating the national core courses to standardise social work education in the country, IPPSI refers to the needs of local and national levels, as well as the global curriculum standard. The curriculum also incorporates the rules on the competence-based curriculum established by the Higher Education section of the Ministry of Education and Culture. The competences consists of: the foundation of personality; mastery of knowledge and skills; ability to work; attitudes and behaviours in the work according to the level of expertise as well as the understanding of the 'rules' of the society.

Most of the elements in the 'Global Standards for Social Work Education and Training', which are formulated by the International Association of Schools of Social Work (IASSW) and the International Federation of Social Workers (IFSW) (see www.iassw-aiets.org), have been adopted in the core curriculum of social welfare education, such as courses on Sociology for Social Workers and Psychology for Social Workers, which in the Indonesian core curriculum are put together to be one course called 'Social Work/Welfare Theories'. The other courses taken from the Global Standards are: Human Behavior and Social Environment, Ethics and Human Rights in Social Work, Human Service Management, Social Planning and Policy Analysis, Social Work Research, Supervision and two Practicum. For the course on social work methods, IPPSI made changes. If previously there was only one course on Social Work Methods, in the formulation of new core curriculum, which adopts the Global Standards, the method course has added the courses/subjects as follows: Social Work Practice with Individuals and Family, Social Work Practice with Groups, and Social Work with Organisations and Community. So altogether there are four courses on intervention methods (Sewpaul & Jones 2004). This is a more appropriate design, as the essence of social work is helping clients to deal with their problems; therefore, the intervention methods must be a major feature. Similarly, a course on Social Work Practice in Multicultural Society, which had not previously been included in the national curriculum, at present has become a core course in accordance with global standards. As the core courses, they are compulsory for social work students all over Indonesia.

In the core curriculum, students must minimally undertake two placements. The first is 'a concurrent placement' (two days a week), the second is 'a block placement' (four days a week). In preparation for placement, there is a briefing for students to review skills that so far have been taught in class. Placement is a very important component in social work education because through placements the students can practice to develop themselves in the application of theories, values and skills for helping clients.

Based on the above description, it is obvious that social work practice – the same as other professions – is based on theories, values/ethics and skills, which cannot be undertaken by those without social work or social welfare education.

Social work or social welfare?

The second debate concerns whether to use the term 'social work' or 'social welfare'. In Indonesia, the school name is 'Department of Social Welfare Science', although in daily English translation people call it 'Department of Social Welfare'. In general, all over the world the school's name is 'Social Work School' or 'Social Work Department', although there are some schools, such as the University of California, Berkeley, and in South Korea that use the name 'School of Social Welfare'.

Figure 7.1 This photo was taken by Dina Hidayat, a student who is doing her placement with an agency dealing with child trafficking. In a trafficking prevention program, together with the agency's staff, the student makes a banner, which is installed in one of the villages, where many trafficking cases occur. This banner states 'Come on, together we protect our village from human trafficking, free-sex and child sexual exploitation'. This banner is part of the prevention program.

Those who tend to use the term 'social welfare' argue that this is more appropriate because it is regarded to be a broader term than 'social work' and more suitable for developing countries. 'Social welfare' also includes 'intervention' against governments, both at local and national levels; for example, through advocacy on government policies. This intervention is required to achieve people's wellbeing. This is highlighted, for example, in the curriculum of the Department of Social Welfare at the University of Indonesia and also reflected in its vision, mission and objectives (Faculty of Social and Political Sciences, University of Indonesia 2009). Furthermore, social workers should be concerned with the impact of global policies on human lives and the disadvantaged and carry out concrete actions for dealing with those. This means that the government is also a 'client' who needs to be helped/changed for the society's best interests. Those who are likely to use the term 'social work' state that social work is also broad, as it includes micro, mezzo and macro levels. These three levels are described in Kirst-Ashman (1993).

However, referring to the thoughts of Midgley (1995) on social development, it appears that social welfare is wider than social work because it includes social work, social policy/administration and social development. Based on observations, it seems that to some extent the development of social work / social welfare in Indonesia is related to development theories, such as modernisation and dependency theories. During the 1960s or early 1970s when the modernisation theory began to be widely applied in many developing countries, including Indonesia, social workers in the country tended to develop clinical social work, similar to that in the West (developed countries). Based on this theory, developing countries should imitate the West in order to be developed countries (Foster-Carter 1986: Roxborough 1979). Everything that comes from the West was seen to be good. Therefore, it is not surprising that at the time casework and group work, which are both widely used in Western countries, were also frequently employed in developing countries, including Indonesia.

Nevertheless, when the dependency theory was introduced in the 1970s, there was a view that relations with the West can create dependency and underdevelopment as occurred in Latin America. As a result, there was emerging awareness in developing countries that they did not need to imitate the West (Foster-Carter 1986). In regard to social work, there was a slight change in trends: in developing countries, community development started becoming popular. Khinduka, for example, states that for developing countries, where massive poverty is a major problem, community development is more appropriate (Khinduka 1971). Although casework and group work are still relevant, apparently these methods are not quite suitable. Moreover, social planning and policy also became very important. Their role at a state level (not only at the program level) is critical to the welfare of citizens.

In connection with the debate over social work or social welfare, Indonesian social work practitioners and educators have decided to accommodate both; for example, for education associations, it is expressed as the Indonesian Association of Social Work / Social Welfare Education. In general, the direction of education is moving toward both social work and social welfare. For example, some universities such as the School of Social Welfare (under the Ministry of Social Affairs) and the University of Padjadjaran focus on learning and strengthening the practice of social work. Widuri School of Social and Political Sciences emphasises more clinical social work, while the University of Indonesia, for example, gives more focus on social welfare as learning objectives. With this broader scope, this university offers competence in the field of social development for its students.

Is social welfare a science/discipline?

The third debate concerns if it is right to use the name 'Department of Social Welfare Science'? Is social welfare a science/discipline? Some say that it is not a science; social welfare is a field, and social work is a profession. However, there are also those who regard social welfare a science, specifically social science, with reference to Zastrow (2004). He states that social welfare is 'both an institution and an academic discipline'. As a discipline, social welfare is based on knowledge and theories, and there are also linkages with other disciplines such as health.

Social work / social welfare education in Indonesia emphasises three aspects: knowledge, values/attitudes and skills. Related to the knowledge aspect, social work is eclectic, so students must learn about many theories from various disciplines like politics, economics, anthropology, sociology, psychology, health and so on. Certainly, beside these, the students learn about social work / welfare theories, such as critical theory, empowerment theory, organisational theory, behavioural theory, etc. At some schools, the students also learn the development theories, such as modernisation theory, dependency theory, world system theory and globalisation.

Figure 7.2 This photo shows the living conditions of the poor in a slum area. In rural areas there are even more people living in severely disadvantaged conditions. Social workers must help these people to help themselves. Photo by Novi Kartika.

IPPSI claims that, through undergraduate education, the graduates have developed general competence, namely as empowerment agents, problem solvers, social welfare analysts and agents of change. Theories, values/ethics and skills are three important aspects underlying the competencies to be achieved. Thus, social work / social welfare is 'science' and 'art'. Theory and knowledge represent 'science', whereas the application of the theory requiring values and skills represents 'art'.

In Indonesia, nearly all social welfare science departments are administered within universities, specifically under the umbrella of faculties of social and political sciences, except for schools such as the School of Social Welfare in Bandung. Being under the Ministry of Social Affairs is beneficial because the ministry can facilitate its human resource development; on the other hand, the school is bound by an obligation to educate primarily for future Ministry of Social Affairs employees – although the students are not absolutely bound to be its employees – so to some extent the school is expected to make attempts to fulfil the ministry's needs for example, in terms of certain practice areas. Thus, students are prepared to apply their knowledge directly and are ready to work. However, most social welfare schools are under the university; consequently, as a department, social welfare is a science. At the beginning of the establishment of the Social Welfare Department, the Minister of Education asserted that if we wanted to be under the university/faculty, it should be as a science, the same as nursing science, international relations science, etc.; if not, it should be placed outside the university. This is one of the most important decisions made by the founders, which is still in operation today.

As a science, there are linkages with other professions such as health professions. For example, there are similarities in the university-compulsory courses to be undertaken by social welfare students and students of other faculties. Additionally, the university-level service is a multidisciplinary activity, which involves students from all faculties, including the Faculty of Social and Political Sciences (Department of Social Welfare being part of this), Faculty of Public Health or Faculty of Medicine. With such cooperation, social welfare and medical students carry out a program together, applying their respective science and approaches. Furthermore, many students of the Social Welfare Department carry out placements in health settings. It is expected that in medical case management, psycho-social aspects of the patients are also considered in diagnosis.

Based on data from IPPSI, schools of social welfare can be distinguished based on their administering ministry. There are at least three ministries, namely, the Ministry of Education and Culture, Ministry of Social Affairs, and the Ministry of Religion. The schools under the Ministry of Education and Culture can be classified into state and private universities. The difference of ministry affects the curriculum applied in each school, especially for courses beyond the core curriculum. For example, at the universities under the Ministry of Religion, there is an emphasis on an Islamic-based curriculum that corresponds to the core business of the Ministry of Religion which is Islamic religious education, in addition to the compulsory courses for Indonesian universities in all disciplines. Consequently, there are many courses that must be taken by the students which affect the space for enhancing social work core skills.

Challenges and efforts for development

In Indonesia, most books used for teaching originally come from the West and are in English. Therefore, the Bridging Professional Social Work foundation helps to publish some books in the Indonesian language and also does translation. This foundation, which is led by Professor Martha Haffey, gives great support for the development of Indonesian social work, both educational and professional. This foundation took some initiatives, such as establishing a Social Work Practice Resource Centre. The other international organisations, Save the Children and UNICEF, also support the enhancement of the social work profession, especially the establishment of social work systems in relation to child welfare. These organisations, in cooperation with the Ministry of Social Affairs, conducted research on Quality of Child Care in Children's Social Institutions (Martin, Florence and Sudrajat 2007) which triggered the emergence of awareness about the importance of building a system of social work. The research findings confirm that child protection services cannot be implemented properly in the absence of professional social workers. In this case, all components of social work from policy, education, quality of graduates, to the mandates for social work practice, are incorporated in the system. Moreover, because it is realised that the development of the social work profession relies heavily on education, Save the Children provides IPPSI with great support.

Nowadays nearly all educational institutions think about internationalisation, including schools of social welfare. The Education Act also encourages collaboration with international institutions. To implement this, the universities in Indonesia established a dual degree program with universities abroad that includes collaboration over student/staff exchange and research. However, despite the emphasis on internationalisation, social welfare education programs encourage and provide great opportunities to the local cultural dimensions. For example, in a course on poverty, the students learn about national (government policy) and global aspects which to some extent worsen poverty; they learn the theories of poverty that derive from the West, but local factors are also discussed, in terms of both local cultural values and local government policy; for example, discussing the lives of an ethnic group in Borneo Island. One of their agricultural products is bananas. The people have a value/belief that they cannot cut the clump of banana trees; if they do, it will lead to a big problem for their family members, such as illness or death. Yet according to modern agricultural science, in a grove of trees there should not be too many banana trunks. If there are too many, then the fruit will be small and poorly produced. Therefore, some of them have to be cut down to only about 3–4 trees. Because they have such beliefs, their banana products are undervalued because they are below market quality standard. This affects their economic conditions.

Through the discussion of cultural factors, it is expected that when the students graduate and become social workers, they may be more sensitive and understanding of local culture, both positive and negative. The social worker is a change agent. Thus, if there are cultural factors that need to be changed, social workers can do it with sensitivity and empathy. The culturally relevant education is also explored by Gray and Coates (2008).

Social work education institutions bear a moral responsibility to make the profession become well-recognised and respected and to prevent their graduates being unemployed. Therefore, they conduct continuous promotion initiatives, create an attractive curriculum design and ensure that the Schools produce high quality graduates. To achieve the expected quality, the Schools make efforts to meet the standards of higher education in accordance with the requirements established by the National Accreditation Board of Higher Education. Moreover, IPPSI as an umbrella of Indonesian schools of social work / social welfare, facilitates the implementation of a core curriculum as a national standard for social work/social welfare education. This curriculum also includes the Global Standard established by IASSW and IFSW. However, the national standard does not stand alone; this needs to be in line with the standards of practice set by the Indonesian Association of Professional Social Workers and the National Board for Profession Certification (BNSP). This agency is in charge of certifying all professions in Indonesia. Furthermore, the implementation of a practicum for most schools remains a problem. This relates to the low hours available for practicum, the limited number of supervisors and the lack of practice carried out by the lecturers of social work / social welfare schools. As a result, integration of theory and practice that should be transferred between the school supervisor (lecturer) and field supervisor can not take place optimally. Looking ahead, this condition is certainly a challenge considering the more complex global issues that increasingly demand competent graduates. Global challenges will be bigger within the ASEAN community by 2015. The job market for Indonesian social workers will be more competitive than from other ASEAN countries. Social work leaders in Indonesia have to make more significant efforts to improve the quality of practice and the work of the lecturer/supervisor. IPPSI has already held training on practicum and supervision. There are clearly more training events/workshops required on practicum and supervision, as well as the micro, mezzo and macro skills, because when we talk about competition in the job market, the mastery of skills plays an important role. This condition needs to be anticipated even though there is data that in 2013 there were 139,000 social workers needed, while at present approximately 15,000 people are available.

From the period 2010–2013 several initiatives have been undertaken by the Indonesian Association of Social Work/Social Welfare Education to develop social work and overcome the challenges faced by social work education in Indonesia. The activities include:

- National Workshop on Core Competence of Social Work and Definition of Social Work
- National Workshop on Core Curriculum; Seminar with APASWE on Development of Social Work Education: Indonesia and Asia Pacific Perspectives
- National Workshop on the Guidelines of Core Curriculum Contents
- Training on practicum; Seminar with IASSW on Social Work Education in Indonesia: Indigenous and International Perspectives
- The International Conference on Social Welfare in the ASEAN Region, in collaboration with the Ministry of Social Affairs and the other social work leaders
- The Indonesian Social Work Consortium (IPPSI is one of the leaders of this consortium) in collaboration with the International Consortium for Social Development-Asia Pacific, held an International conference: 'Envisioning New Social Development Strategies Beyond Millennium Development Goals'
- National Workshop on the Competencies of Postgraduate Students of Social Work / Social Welfare Science and Learning Outline for Practicum
- National Workshop on finalisation of Learning Outline / Lesson Plan for Practicum 1 and Practicum 2
- Social work supervision training for lecturers of social work / social welfare schools
- Workshop on Piloting of Core Curriculum of Social Work / Social Welfare Education.

To implement the Regulation of Minister of Social Affairs No. 108/2009 on the Certification of Professional Social Workers and Welfare Workers, as well as the Regulation of Minister of Social Affairs No. 107/2009 on Accreditation of Social Welfare Institutions, the process of social worker certification and social welfare institutions accreditation has been achieved. The accreditation of the institutions not only helps to improve their quality, but also enables the process of making social workers a profession that is widely recognised, because employing social workers at the institutions is a key feature in their achieving an A-grade in accreditation.

The other progress identified is the accommodation of human rights perspectives in social work / social welfare education. In economic globalisation, where individualism, greed and wealth are important aspects in human life, the idea of human rights provides an alternative moral reference. Human rights are very important for those who work in the human services in general and for social workers in particular. Social work is the profession of human rights; human rights pose many issues and dilemmas faced by social workers, which can be seen in a new perspective.

Human rights provide a moral basis for social work practice, both at the micro-level with clients, as well as community development and policy advocacy. Human rights have developed over three generations (Ife 2001, 24–42):

1. First generation of human rights: civil and political rights. This includes the right to vote, the right to freedom of speech, freedom of assembly, the right to equal treatment before the law, citizenship rights, privacy rights, right to disagree, the right to freedom of religion, the right to participate in society, the right to be treated with dignity, the right to security, freedom from discrimination, intimidation, torture and coercion.

2. Second generation of human rights includes social, economic and cultural rights. It is the right of individuals or groups to receive various social services in order to realise their full potential as human beings. The rights include the right to work, the right to adequate wages, the right to housing, the right to adequate food and clothing, the right to education, the right to adequate health care, and the right to social security. Based on the second generation of human rights, apparently poverty is a violation of human rights.

3. Third generation of human rights includes new rights which are meaningful when linked to the collective level. It is the rights of communities, populations, or nations, not individuals, although individuals can also obtain benefit from the realisation of these rights.

The rights include the right to economic development, the right to benefit from world trade and economic growth, the right to live in a cohesive and harmonious society, environmental rights (for example, breathing with no air pollution, rights to water, etc.). So, if the global free-trade policy causes misery to people, it would be considered a human rights violation.

The National Association of Social Workers (US) (see www.socialworkers.org/) states that human rights are basic knowledge and a foundation of social work theory.

Social work intervention which is based on human rights incorporates:

- the rejection of oppression for example, of policies that cause misery for the poor, gender inequality, etc.
- empowerment to overcome unjust structures. It is important to understand the experiences of marginalised groups
- the practice of cultural competency and sensitivity: cultural understanding, non-discrimination
- feminist practice: concern with unjust structures. All humans have the right to be free from oppression and discrimination.

Based on the above description, it seems that the implications for education should be as follows:

1. educational process: inclusive, non-discriminatory, open to various opinions (Millam 2011).
2. The curriculum should include, among others:

- critical theory
- advocacy
- gender, feminist perspective
- developing network skills (government and non-government organisations)
- poverty issues
- methods to increase social awareness
- cultural understanding and tolerance and cross-cultural sensitivity (Devore 1986; Bhatti-Sinclair 2011).

All the efforts above have begun to show positive results, which gives the impression of a growing appreciation toward the profession. However, although this successful scenario occurs at the University of Indonesia and although people suggest that one school cannot represent all school members of IPPSI, we still face challenges such as those related to society's recognition of the social work profession. Based on a survey conducted by the Department of Social Welfare, University of Indonesia, in 2010/2011 and another survey implemented by the university in 2010, the research findings demonstrate that on average the waiting length for graduates to get jobs is between 2.4 and 3 months. The Indonesian social work leaders and activists continuously work hand in hand and their struggle will continue.

Conclusions

Indonesian social work is currently still facing challenges which must be dealt with in more effective ways, otherwise it will become a serious threat for social work development in the country. The challenges stretch from basic to the complex ones. So far there have been many efforts to address the issues and make a positive impact.

References

Bhatti-Sinclair, K. (2011). *Anti-racist practice in social work.* Hampshire: Palgrave Macmillan.
Devore, W. & Schlesinger, E.G. (1986). *Ethnic-sensitive: social work practice.* Columbus: Charles E. Merril Publishing Company.
Faculty of Social and Political Sciences, University of Indonesia (2009). Guidance for the Curriculum and the Compilation of Academic Regulations. Depok: Faculty of Social and Political Sciences, University of Indonesia.
Foster-Carter, A. (1986). *The sociology of development.* Ormskirk: Causeway Press Ltd
Gray, M., Coates, J. & Yellow Bird, M. (eds) (2008). *Indigenous social work around the world: toward culturally relevant education & practice.* Aldershot, UK: Ashgate.
Ife, J. (2001). *Human rights and social work.* Cambridge: Cambridge University Press.
Khinduka, S.K. (1971). Social work and the Third World. *Social Service Review,* 45(1): 62–73.
Kirst-Ashman, K.K. & Hull, G.H. (Jr) (1993). *Understanding generalist practice.* Chicago: Nelson-Hall Publishers.
Martin, F. & Tata, S. (2007). *Someone that matters: the quality of care in childcare institutions in Indonesia.* Jakarta: Save the Children UK, The Ministry of Social Affairs (DEPSOS) &UNICEF. Retrieved on 24 April 2014 from www.savethechildren.org.uk/sites/default/files/docs/someone-that-matters_1.pdf.
Midgley, J. (1995). *Social development: the developmental perspective in social welfare.* London: SAGE Publications.
Millam, R. (2011). *Anti-discriminatory practice.* London: Continuum.
Roxborough, I. (1979). *Theories of underdevelopment.* Atlantic Highlands, NJ: Humanities Press.
Sasaki A. (ed.) (2013). *(Professional) social work and its functional alternatives.* Tokyo: Social Work Research Institute Asian Center for Welfare in Society (ACWelS), Japan College of Social Work & Asian and Pacific Association for Social Work Education (APASWE).
Sewpaul, V. & Jones, D. (2004). Global standards for the education and training of the social work profession. Adopted at the General Assemblies of IASSW and IFSW, Australia. Retrieved on 22 April 2014 from cdn.ifsw.org/assets/ifsw_65044–3.pdf.
Zastrow, C. (2004). *Introduction to social work and social welfare.* Pacific Grove, CA: Brooks Cole Publishing Company.

8

Social work education in South Asia: diverse, dynamic and disjointed?

Bala Raju Nikku

Social work, claiming to be a global profession, is struggling for its legitimate identity in South Asia. South Asia is home to over one-fifth of the world's population, making the region one of the most populous and culturally, economically, socially and politically diverse geographical regions. Like the variations across the region, there exist key differences in the growth, establishment, nature and practice of social work education which is dynamic, diverse but also disjointed. Imparting social work education in countries of South Asia is a challenging task due to political instabilities, multicultural issues and low professional recognition. Using a comparative approach, this chapter analyses the initiation, growth and knowledge base of social work programs and addresses key epistemological challenges. By doing so, it suggests revisiting social work curricula and teaching practices in the region. Divided in to five sections, this chapter provides a regional view of the status of social work education and argues for crafting indigenous social work knowledge and practices, teaching and practice innovations, and human resource development of social work educators and students in this vast and diverse region.

South Asia as a distinct region

South Asia is home to over one-fifth of the world's population, making the region both the most populous and most densely populated geographical region in the world. South Asia is a distinct geographical entity comprising eight countries: Afghanistan, Bangladesh, Bhutan, India, Nepal, Pakistan, Sri Lanka and the Maldives (situated in the Indian Ocean). The countries of South Asia are very diverse and are part of global flows of people, goods, services and ideas. Different forms of governance, language, religion, culture and markets make this region a vibrant one in global political, economic, social and cultural affairs.

About 40% of the world's absolute poor live in this region. It also contains nearly 400 million or half of the world's non-literate population. The modernisation of education in South Asia started after the end of World War 2 in 1945 and has continued over successive decades, but the process is far from complete.

Out of eight countries of South Asia, three are land locked (Nepal, Afghanistan and Bhutan) and six are included as the least developed countries (LDCs) currently in the world. The LDCs represent the poorest and weakest segment of the international community. The political, economic, social and cultural milieu of the South Asia region offers vast potential for social work. The cultures and philosophies of this region are rich and diverse. Social work, like the diversity of people, is not a homogeneous entity in the region. Different models of social welfare and social work have developed over the past decades.

Despite the existence of the South Asian Association for Regional Cooperation (SAARC), there is a lack of a regional human rights mechanism to protect and promote human rights in the region as a whole. South Asia region has the world's largest conflict-affected population – around 71 million. Given the vast population of the South Asia region subjected to exploitation, natural disasters, and marginalisation induced by the various structural inequalities and less resource entitlements, social work plays a crucial role in providing a range of services leading to crafting of robust families and communities in the region. Professional social workers can play a vital role in helping children and youth to access education, health care, entitlements to food and shelter, and empowerment and protection of elders, people with disabilities, the poor and vulnerable, to name a few.

South Asian social work and global influences

The changing nature of social problems and new threats to the wellbeing of individuals, families and communities are not only common to South Asian countries. Social work education has enjoyed respect and recognition in the West, especially for the first half of the 20th century. Unfortunately, in a vigorously changing South Asian region, it may take a few more years or decades for social work to be recognised as a full profession by the respective states, though it has much to offer to the wellbeing of citizens. As practice and extension of remit are basic essential elements of professional social work, educating young people in social work is not a difficult task as ample opportunities are available for practice and extension of remit in the region.

Abraham Flexner in 1915 raised a critical question: is social work a profession? Since then, many social work academics, institutions and practitioners have contributed their working lives to the development of the social work knowledge base, skills development and practice standards that ultimately transformed social work from the status of a vocation to a profession that is globally relevant. However, Social Work continued to receive internal and external criticisms and self-reflection making the profession more resilient. The South Asian region is no exception to this phenomenon.

In the Asian region, departments/schools of social work began under missionary leadership, mainly originating from influence and patronage of Western countries. As a result, indigenous methods of social service were largely ignored and emphasis was laid upon using Western concepts, theories and techniques. South Asia was no exception to this trend. One of the early such 'transplants' was the Tata Institute of Social Sciences established originally as the Sir Dorabji Tata Graduate School of Social Work in Mumbai, western India, in 1936. The initial dependence on foreign materials and concepts continued to dominate and led to the application of Western notions in local practices. This historical neglect also resulted in non-inclusion of indigenous materials, case studies, and social action techniques in the social work curricula and training.

In the period after World War 2, the profession was globalised, as schools of social work proliferated across the South, invariably with cultural assumptions originating in the North (Healy 2001; Midgley 1981). The second wave of influence came right after World War 2 in the form of United Nations assisted social work education and training with an objective of strengthening social work education in South Asia. As a result, American models of social work and values travelled and were transplanted into schools of social work initiated in Pakistan and Bangladesh. This led to the further US influence on the ethnocentrism of social work training in the South Asian region. Scholars like Nagpaul (1972) termed this as cultural imperialism and Professor James Midgley of the US called it 'professional imperialism', the term used to characterise the way in which social work on the Western model has been introduced to Third World countries (Midgley 1981). The profession's growth has been characterised as 'academic colonialisation' (Atal 1981), mirroring political and scientific colonisation (Clews 1999).

A third factor that influenced South Asian social work education is the dissatisfaction with social workers trained in India and other countries because their skills and knowledge are not US-specific. These schools lacked insights into Asian problems and lacked suitable staff for training students of social work from developing Asian countries. After completion of their studies a number of them did not return home; among those few who returned, they became ambivalent about their role and relevance. As a result, many returned to America and have contributed to social work education there.

Social work education in the region: diversity

India

Social work in India has a long history, originating from a pre-modern charitable response of individuals or groups of people to address the problems of society, and evolving to the more modern professionalisation of social work underlined by formal training in theory and practice (Palattiyil & Sidhva 2012). Social work was introduced into India in the 1930s by North Americans eager to share the new treatment methods that were proving successful in helping many Americans to handle personal problems. India, receptive to new approaches, then began under American leadership the development of schools of social work based on the American model and adopting all its basic principles (Howard 1971). These social workers came to colonial India with a sense of adventure and excitement in introducing their ideas into a new culture. As a result, in 1936, the first school of social work, now known as Tata Institute of Social Sciences, was established. The first undergraduate degree in generic social work was started in 1974 in the Nirmala Niketan College of Social Work in Mumbai.

Prompted by domestic as well as global demand, social work education in India is said to be on an expansionary route. In the last 25 years the number of departments offering social work under private colleges has increased due to demand for social workers in India in the non-governmental organisations (NGOs) and private sector. The increasing marketisation, outsourcing, and Western-style human resource policies are impacting the world view of Indian social workers.

Major schools of social work are teaching structural social work within the radical paradigm, but practice occurs within the community arena, thus lacking the depth and vigour that social activism strategy entails (Palattiyil & Sidhva 2012). Despite its 75 years of the social work education history, India has not been able to come up with national standards for social work education, coherence in curricula, or implement a licensure procedure; nor could it form a national association of social workers to implement and regulate the professional standards. The enactment of a National Bill on social work is necessary not only in the contemporary scenario of the unregulated and haphazard growth of social work profession (without any uniform norms of education and practice) but also to get social work to a respectable, deserving place in the mainstream of professions in India. Despite the efforts by eminent social work educators, formation of a national association of schools of social work with regulatory powers and resources remains a challenge given the lack of statutory recognition of social work as a profession. A national network of schools for quality enhancement of social work education in India was launched at the Tata Institute of Social Sciences (TISS) during May 2012, with an aim to address some of these quality issues (IFSW 2010, 2012).

India is currently witnessing a sea change in the attitudes and aspirations of its one billion plus population. In all this, social work education could not be left unaffected. Contemporary social work issues in India cannot be addressed without a shift to a more politically aware definition of the profession, guiding both national and international goals for social work (Alphonse, George & Moffatt 2008).

Pakistan

In Pakistan, the first in-service training course, sponsored by the government of Pakistan and the United Nations Technical Assistance Administration (UNCTAA), trained its first 65 Pakistani social workers in 1953 (Rehmatullah 2002, 1). After the in-service training courses, a degree course in social work started in Punjab University in November 1954 and a postgraduate degree in 1956. From 1954 to 1962, Punjab University continued the professional training requirements for the then West and East Pakistan. In East Pakistan (now Bangladesh), however, the University of Dhaka started an MA course in social work in 1958 and admitted candidates from Karachi and other parts of Pakistan. Subsequently from 1958 onwards, the Universities of Dhaka, Karachi, Peshawar, Hyderabad and Balochistan started master degree programs (see Graham et al. 2007).

Rehmatullah, a pioneer of medical social work, was one of the members of the first in-service training course that began on 2 October 1952 and lasted till 2 April 1953. Thereafter she studied at Columbia University New York and obtained her master's degree in social work with a major in social administration. She described in her seminal book *Social welfare in Pakistan*, the country's 50-year history with social work as one of lost promise. The profession 'started [in the 1950s] with high idealism and a desire to practice new unconventional methods'. But it 'became victim of political and bureaucratic designs of the powers that be at a given period in time'. In the process, some of its programs and services survived, others fell by the wayside. The profession continues to have 'Western oriented methods of problem solving', and 'it still falls short of the original ideal of developing indigenous social work literature of our own and developing Pakistani methodology' (Rehmatullah 2002, 180). It must, in short:

> rise again into a scientific program, to review the achievements as well as its failures, and inject new blood into it [and it must] reshape the practice of social work in the context of

our strong family system as advised by the first UN advisors who came to Pakistan fifty years ago . . . It is time to recover the sense of reality. Crutches like those offered by the 'development experts' have served their time. Now we should walk on our own feet, on our own paths, dream our own dreams, not the borrowed ones from the West. (Rehmatullah 2002, xiv, 457)

Currently, social work is taught as a two-year bachelor program (BA) in several colleges affiliated to universities and a four-year BS program in selected universities. The master and PhD programs are available in few Universities: presently, the University of Punjab Lahore, University of Sargodha, Islamia University of Bahawalpur, Bahauddin Zakariya University in Multan, and Government College Faisalabad located in Punjab province. The University of Peshawar (KPK province), University of Quetta (Balochistan), University of Karachi and University of Jamshoro (located in Sindh province) are offering the MA in social work. There are private colleges that are also offering Master's in Social Work, for example, Greenwich University (Sindh province), Punjab College, Joharabad Khushab (Punjab province), in addition to many government universities. Commenting on the past, current and future trends of social work in Pakistan, Mohamad Jafar, a lecturer at the Islamia University of Bahawalpur, Punjab, noted that

sixty years of social work history in Pakistan could not achieve the status of full profession. The NGOs are focusing on community development and the government sector focusing on institutional practices such as child and women welfare, prison reforms etc. Despite the rich history, social work education is still struggling for achieving quality standards. There is a need for creating further opportunities for higher training i.e. Master's and PhD in the country. For a population of 180 million a handful of colleges and universities that are offering social work are not able to train enough and quality human resources to bring desired changes and make an impact in the society. (Personal communication, 20 November 2013)

Bangladesh

Social work education also travelled to Bangladesh when it was given independence from Pakistan. The advent of academic social work in Bangladesh has arisen from the recommendations made by UN experts on welfare for the establishment of a program of professional welfare practice. The recommendation highlighted the need for scientific knowledge in the solution of acute and large-scale social problems (Watts, Elliott & Mayadas 1995). In response to the proposal for the establishment of a school of social work, the government established the College of Social Welfare and Research Center in 1958, and it commenced its educational program in the academic year 1958–59 with 15 students registered for an MA degree in social welfare at the University of Dhaka (Ahmadullah 1986; Taher and Rahman 1993). The College of Social Welfare and Research Center, the first social work school of Bangladesh, was merged with the University of Dhaka (DU) as the Institute of Social Welfare and Research (ISWR) in 1973. Currently, the Institute of Social Welfare and Research at Dhaka University runs a two-year MA degree in social welfare and a three-year BA Honours degree in social work. The College of Social Work under Rajshahi University also runs a three-year Honours degree in social work.

Currently, several more universities have started social work programs. To produce local knowledge, the institute at Dhaka University has now set up the Bangladesh Social Work Teachers Association for developing indigenous materials. Efforts are also being made to translate the standard foreign textbooks to make learners familiar with basic social work concepts in the Bengali language.

Sri Lanka

The Department of Social Services was set up in 1948, under the recommendation of a Royal Commission headed by Sir Ivor Jennings, and the department was entrusted with implementation of social welfare schemes for disabled people in Sri Lanka.

The Institute of Social Work was thus created in 1952 in Colombo, the first formal attempt to establish professional social work in the country. Dr Dorothy Moses, first principal of the YWCA School of Social Work (later the Delhi School of Social Work under Delhi University), provided the initiative to create the Ceylon Institute of Social Work in 1952. The School of Social Work has become part of the National Institute of Social Development (under the Ministry of Social Services and Social Welfare).

In 2005 the National Institute of Social Development became a degree granting authority (BSW) (Chandraratna 2008). The master programs in social work (MSW) were established in 2008 (Zaviršek and Herath 2010). The National Institute of Social Development (NISD) is an institution of higher learning in social work education in Sri Lanka established by the National Institute of Social Development Act No. 41 of 1992. It is recognised by the University Grants Commission of Sri Lanka as a degree awarding institution in Sri Lanka. After the tsunami disaster of 2004, the need for social workers became greater, and the University of Colombo started to develop a stream of social work within the Department of Sociology together with the University of Ljubljana (Lešnik and Urek 2010). Recently the University of Ruhuna has started a Community Development Diploma Programme and the University of Kelaniya and University of Perdeniya are planning to introduce courses in social work (Zaviršek and Herath 2010). According to expert estimates there were some 800 practicing social workers, while the country would need 'about 30,000 trained social workers' (Lešnik and Urek 2010, 273).

Nepal

Nepal is relatively young when it comes to introduction of social work education compared to India, Pakistan, Bangladesh and Sri Lanka. Only in 1996 was the first department of social work with Kathmandu university affiliation started with the support of Nirmala Niketan, an Indian social work school. The initiation of social work education in Nepal was largely under the purview of affiliated colleges of the universities (Nikku 2012a). Almost all of these colleges providing social work are located in Kathmandu, the capital city of Nepal, resulting in restricted access to social work education for students from poor and disadvantaged rural areas of Nepal.

One of the main issues for social work education in Nepal is the lack of coherence and focus on promotion of social work values. The social work training of the three different universities that currently exist in Nepal promote different values and methods of social work. For example, Purbanchal University promotes rights-based values, Kathmandu University focuses more on clinical social work and Tribhuvan University bases its approach more on generic social work (Nikku 2009).

Another important issue is crafting indigenous social work in Nepal and bringing coherence into the social work curricula that is suitable for the current needs of Nepalese society. The evidence suggests that the social work curricula developed over a period of time (1996–2005) under three different Universities in Nepal had signs of indigenous efforts in developing social work curricula suitable to train social workers relevant for Nepal and its growing needs.

The Nirmala Niketan School of Social Work in India helped St Xavier's college in Nepal to prepare a three year bachelor of social work program that was subsequently approved by Kathmandu University in 1996. Similarly the Tribhuvan University curriculum development centre renamed one of the courses titled 'Social Service' to 'Social Work' and added supervised fieldwork hours as a requirement (Nikku 2011).

In 2005, Purbanchal University constituted a subject committee to prepare the social work curricula for both bachelor and master programs. The subject committee (the author of this paper is a member of this committee) is aware of the discourses on indigenous and Western models of social work and utilised the opportunity to reflect on the models of social work. Over many discussions and debates a curriculum that is suitable to the country's current needs has been prepared and approved by the university. An analysis of the three social work curricula shows that Purbanchal University, as mentioned previously, adopted a social development model grounded in rights-based social work, Kathmandu University focuses on clinical social work and Tribhuvan University is focused more on social service (Nikku 2010).

The social work curriculum of Purbanchal University shifted from a clinical social work focus to a rights-based model. This social work curriculum would serve as the first comprehensive resource available in the country for other colleges, training centres, and government and non-government organisations for planning and programming of rights-based training in Nepal and beyond. The course structure includes relevant principles, guidelines and references that could be easily adapted to the specific situations on the ground and target groups to be trained (Nikku 2010, 2011).

The title 'social worker' is rather loosely used and abused in the context of Nepal. Anyone in social service work, including politicians, claims that they are doing social work. There is no clear formal definition stated and adopted either by the University Grants Commission of Nepal or by any government agencies such as the Ministry of Social Welfare. However, the Department of Social Work at Kadambari College, initiated in 2005 (an affiliate of Purbanchal University and a founding member of Nepal School of Social Work), together with other like-minded agencies, came up with the following definition:

'Social Worker' in the context of Nepal refers to new graduates and current practitioners (both Nepalese and other nationals) with recognised social work qualifications, i.e. Degree in Social Work (BSW or MSW) or a Graduate Diploma in Social Work or a recognised Social Work qualification. These qualifications should be recognised or acceptable to associations like the Singapore Association of Social Workers and or International Association of Schools of Social Work (IASSW), until a formal definition of social worker is adopted by the Nepal Association of Social Workers which is not yet formed.

The Nepal School of Social Work came up with another definition for social service practitioners who are already involved in providing direct services to clients and working in NGOs and international non-governmental organisations (INGOs). This is to make the public aware of the different roles and to protect the rights of the trained social workers in Nepal. Currently, the Nepal School of Social Work with other likeminded people and institutions is also lobbying for accreditation and registration systems to be introduced in Nepal. It states:

> 'Social Service Practitioners' are those who are working in the capacity of social workers performing social work functions for the major part of their work but are without relevant social work qualifications like BSW and MSW. Executive directors, program executives, youth workers, field social workers, case workers, who are not formally trained in social work per se but are performing social work functions for the major part of their work can qualify to be accredited as Social Service Practitioners if they meet the entry requirements for Social Service Practitioners. They can become accredited Social Workers if they go on to acquire a recognised Social Work qualification and also fulfill the other entry requirements for accreditation.

To sum up briefly, among many professions in Nepal, social work professionals can play crucial roles in response to Nepal's post-conflict problems. Unfortunately the state of the Nepalese State is so weak that the social work profession has not been recognised formally by the government. The case of Nepal shows evidence of a country where social work education is at the nascent stage, with a need for a critically reflective framework based on student-centred practices that is crucial to professional development (Nikku 2012a).

Bhutan

The review suggests that there are no opportunities available for professional social work education in Bhutan to date.

Maldives

The Ministry of Gender and Family of Maldives and the University of Newcastle, Australia, supported by UNICEF, helped the Maldives College of Higher Education to offer a one-year Advanced Certificate in Social Service Work in 2007 (Plath 2011).

Afghanistan

The country has a history of turmoil and conflict, especially in the past 30 years. These conflicts have had a dramatically deleterious impact on the education system within Afghanistan. University campuses became relative war zones, which resulted in a shattered infrastructure and forced many faculty members into exile and/or intellectual isolation. Some faculty members were even killed for their commitment to education (Tierney 2006). The relevant ministries are trying to introduce social work education. In May 2006, the Ministry of Labour, Social Affairs, Martyrs and Disabled (MoLSAMD) launched the National Strategy for Children At-Risk (NSFCAR), supported by UNICEF. The government recognises that professional social workers are critical to the effective delivery of family support and child protection services in Afghanistan. One of the key tenets of the NSFCAR is the development of staff trained as child protection social workers. Social work does not yet exist as a 'profession' in Afghanistan. There is no school of social work or other accredited training program. There are no standardised tools, quality benchmarks for service delivery, or established minimum standards of care. Relevant legislation and policy is outdated at best, and is absent otherwise (UNICEF Afghanistan 2009).

Social work education in South Asia: dynamic and disjointed

Throughout its rather young history, social work has been marked by extensive disputes and self-criticism about its role and identity in the global North and South (Hugman 2008). From Flexner (1915) and Greenwood (1957/1976) to Fisher (1973) and beyond, social workers have heard criticisms of social work and social work education. In addition, a series of invited papers and rejoinders from Stoesz and Karger, Brij Mohan, Sowers and Dulmus in *International Social Work* journal in 2009 is a valuable source of historical material for social work educators such as the current author from South Asia to understand the development and dynamics of social work education in other parts of the world. In this section, I further show how social work education in South Asia also reflects these contradictions and conflicts evident elsewhere.

Kendall in 1950 argued that in each country, social welfare, social service, social work, social development, whatever you name it, is a dynamic activity. The report stated, 'no definition of social work can be formulated that would be accepted in all countries and might be put forward as an "international definition"' (Kendall 1950, 88). These observations apply equally well to this region. Taking into account social work development across the globe, there are abundant opportunities for social work to grow in the South Asia region. The fact is that there are countless challenges due to the variations and differences of educational systems and standards within the region.

Hammoud (1988) also documented the possible value conflicts across social work in different countries due to cultural and political differences. The South Asia region is no exception to these views. The social work educators in the countries of the region have argued that global social work definition and global social work standards might be of help but difficult to implement due to the local needs and diversity. Nadkarni (2010) in her editorial for the *Journal of Social Work Education* highlighted the nature of social work in Asia that applies to South Asia too:

Social work education in Asian countries today faces several challenges and opportunities. Social work education in Asian countries also needs to address problems arising from untrammelled growth accompanied by ecological destruction and climate change. Development itself has thus become a generator of conflict because of competing land use issues involving the haves and the have-nots in these countries . . . The recognition of professional social work and the need for quality social work education in Asia has been moving at a slow pace. (Nadkarni 2010, 15)

Levels of social work education

The general objectives of social work education, which provides students with the value system and ethical standards of the profession, providing basic knowledge and developing skills and competencies to perform the social worker role, have remained across all the countries within the region with some modifications in order to suit to a particular country's religion and other requirements.

Social Work education is found at different levels in the countries of the region. India has all levels of education at bachelor's, master's, postgraduate and PhD levels and even distance education, compared to Bhutan (for example) with less than one million people that does not even have one bachelor's program in social work in the entire country. In Nepal (30 million people) there are two bachelor's programs (BA in social work and bachelor's of social work) and one master's program is available.

In Sri Lanka (20 million people) there is certificate, bachelor's and master's level available at one institution. Both Bangladesh and Pakistan offer both bachelor's and master's level of training but are facing competition from other courses and lack of educators and resources for the department to offer social work. Currently, the four social work schools, namely the Institute of Social Welfare and Research of Dhaka University, and departments of social work in Rajshahi University, Shahjalal University of Science and Technology, Jagannath University and National University, have been offering courses at four levels: four year graduation with honours, one year master's, MPhil and PhD.

The Maldives (0.4 million people) is currently offering a certificate level whereas Afghanistan (30 million people) is trying to develop a curriculum for special training of social work officers. This suggests that at present there is a wide variety of levels, and quantity of provision, that exists in the different countries.

Educational opportunities at the PhD level in social work are lacking in all the countries except in India and Bangladesh, and this has affected the training of social work educators and researchers. The doctorate education in social work provided in Indian schools also needs scrutiny as the quality varies. The doctorate education in social work is to prepare students for leadership roles in administration and policy, more advanced and specialised practice, research and teaching. So there is a need for developing such programs using international experiences in the region for renewal of social work education.

Licensure and professional social work organisations

In none of the countries in the region, irrespective of the history of social work education and its development, has a licensure procedure been adopted, nor are strong professional bodies such as national associations of social workers functioning. The exceptions are Sri Lanka and Bangladesh which claim some form of associations, but they are not strong and therefore able to influence the social work trajectory in their own countries. The Sri Lankan Association of Social Workers was founded in 1962 and the Association of Social Workers in Bangladesh seems to not be functioning anymore. In India some States have formed state level associations, but again to date a national association could not be formed due to regional differences, lack of national legislation and social work leadership.

International social work

Is there any need for international social work teaching and practice in the South Asia region? This question seems pertinent especially when social work is disjointed in this region. Communications with colleagues from the region, especially from India and Nepal at the 2010 joint world social work and social development conference at Stockholm, and email exchanges suggest that there is a significant need for, and interest in, teaching and practicing international social work in South Asia. Given the diversity and cultural and political issues present within the region, it is a fertile ground for international social work teaching and practice.

The current president of the International Association of Schools of Social Work (IASSW) is a professor from the Tata Institute of Social Sciences, India. The author of this chapter is currently serving as a member of the executive board of IASSW, is from India and worked in Nepal. Faculty members from the Sri Lankan School of Social Work and Institute of Social Welfare and Research, Dhaka University, are serving on the executive board of APASWE, providing evidence that social work educators from this region are actively associated with the regional and global social work organisations. There is also evidence that many schools from India, Pakistan, Bangladesh, Sri Lanka, and also countries like Nepal where social work education is just beginning, have made linkages with schools of social work around the globe to further strengthen the social work education and profession in the region (Nikku 2012b).

International organisations like the IASSW, International Federation of Social Workers (IFSW) and International Council of Social Welfare (ICSW) and regional organisations such as APASWE can play an important role in strengthening social work education in the South Asian region. A brief analysis shows that their presence in the region is weak, suggesting that there is a need for social workers from this region to actively participate, develop partnerships and share their concerns at these international and regional forums and make use of these bodies to strengthen social work in their own countries.

Social welfare programs and policies

From the above brief presentation on the status of social work in each of the countries in the region, we can conclude that social work has taken a back seat in most, if not, all the South Asian nations which do not provide social services and care as a matter of right for citizens, but do so on the basis of political needs and agendas. The wellbeing of the professional workforce who work for the wellbeing of others is also at a crossroad. Social work as a helping profession is in need of help. The level and scope of social welfare services and the role of civil society in each of these countries are also very varied.

South Asia is home for many non-governmental organisations in which trained social workers seek employment. The nonprofit sector, with its roots in volunteerism, increasingly plays a central role in South Asia's cultural, economic and social development. Throughout the region nonprofit organisations provide vital services especially to the poor and marginalised, address significant needs of communities, and are increasingly important alternative delivery mechanisms for needed services of citizens.

In the last 25 years or so, due to growing disenchantment with the functioning of the government and the fear that the 'market' may not reach everywhere, NGOs have increasingly been recognised as a 'third' institutional pillar for the development of an economy. Most of the activities carried out by the NGOs are on behalf of the government, making them mere implementation agencies. The constraints and challenges South Asian NGOs face are excessive governmental control, a project-based culture and, more importantly, they lack a proper management system and model of their own. To cope with management problems, NGOs are heavily dependent on corporate sector management, which, most of the time, negates the values of this sector (Rahman 2007, 223). Many NGOs are not in a position or do not have the mandate to employ professional social workers as their employees. This leads to a problem of continuity in committed leadership as many NGOs do not have policies in place to prepare successive leaders. Social Work, though a young profession in the region, might provide answers to these issues.

Working with Muslim clients and communities

Around 62% of the world's Muslims live in South and Southeast Asia, with over 1 billion adherents (Pew Forum 2012). Pakistan, Bangladesh and India from the South Asia region are included in the world list of top 10 countries with the largest Muslim populations. India has the world's second-largest Muslim population (next to Indonesia) in raw numbers (roughly 176 million) though Muslims make up just 14.4% of India's 1.2 billion total population. The three countries of Pakistan, Bangladesh and India together account for about one-third of the global total Muslim population. This will have implications on how social work education is structured, course content and what values and philosophy are taught and practiced. Social work knowledge and skills in a particular country are socially constructed. A brief analysis of social work curricula in the countries clearly shows the evidence that they are influenced by Western models and hence not entirely culturally relevant to this region and particularly the Muslim dominant countries. In contrast, increasingly, models of social work emphasise the importance of understanding clients' worldviews for effective social work, and integration of spirituality in social work is increasingly being called for (Barise 2005). Further efforts are needed for localisation of social work within Muslim contexts (Sarker & Ahmadullah 1995) in the region.

Voices of social work educators

Social Work is contextual, yet increasingly crossing boundaries and national borders in South Asia. As discussed above, several key factors have challenged and influenced social work education and practice in this region. In addition, social work educators played a crucial role. Many challenges were reported by social work educator colleagues irrespective of their location in the region. Some educators (especially from Nepal and Sri Lanka) shared that it is very difficult for them to separate practice from teaching as their countries are going through transitions and conflicts and social work is yet to be recognised. Many social work educators from this region saw themselves as academic activists and are working closely with a range of practitioners, bureaucrats and policymakers who are often not trained in formal social work. Many of them also reported that there are not enough academic opportunities to progress compared to their counterparts in other (especially Western) parts of the world. Chan and Ng argued that 'it is important for social work teachers to adopt a holistic practitioner-researcher-educator role in their everyday practice in order to create the necessary impact to effect change' (2004, 312). To further illustrate the point, I present some voices which show the plight of social work educators:

In Nepal it is a young and emerging profession. It is only since about 16 years that social work education has been initiated in Nepal. There is less recognition in our profession by the state and other development organisations which is the biggest challenge. Another challenge is we do not have a social work association and hence it is difficult to intervene in serious social problem cases in the society. (Samjhana Oli, social work educator with seven years of experience at Nepal School of Social Work)

None of the Sri Lankan public universities offer SWE [social work education]. Only one institution provides diploma, degree and master degree in Social Work. The institution is under the purview of the Ministry of Social Services. The social work profession is not legalised yet. (Sri Lankan social work educator with 15 years of teaching experience)

Conclusions

I must acknowledge and admit that the analysis of the material for this chapter has deliberately used broad generalisations to make a point and to emphasise the differences between social work education and practice in respective countries to put the regional differences in focus.

In this chapter, I presented the status and scope of social work education in the South Asian region, which is in various stages of maturity as an academic discipline and a profession. Despite the diversity, common threads we see in the life and work experiences of social work educators and practitioners are: commitment to social justice, social work values and ethics, skills and competencies. One of the major challenges in the region is to indigenise social work literature (theories and practice) in order to reflect local culture and values. Another goal is to encourage indigenous social work practices to train social work graduates with appropriate skills and attitudes.

It is evident in this chapter that the presence and influence of social work education in the region is growing over the years and more departments/schools of social work have been established in the past decade. The caution here is in relation to the mushrooming growth of social work departments in affiliated colleges of Universities in India, leading to lower quality standards. The lack of clear state support for social work education in Pakistan and Bangladesh also needs to be analysed and addressed. Afghanistan needs immediate help in initiating social work training to be able to help the country's ongoing reconstruction process. At the same time the lack of presence of schools of social work or educational opportunities for professional social work in Bhutan and Maldives may be a point for further reflection. The presence of only a few schools in Nepal and Sri Lanka needs further assistance nationally and internationally and can make crucial contributions to the growth of social work in South Asia.

Social work education in the South Asia region is facing an uncertain future within the academy as it has to compete with other market-oriented disciplines. The social work educational programs are yet to gain public and state support and perceived relevance. There exist tensions among the Universities and institutions offering social work at different levels due to their differences in mission, purpose and values. In a healthy environment these differences should be serving as a springboard of ideas rather than hurdles. Despite these tensions, social work education has contributed to training of staff who in turn directly or indirectly contributed in addressing social issues in the region. In addition, social work education and practice in this region has been shaped by different forces such as religion, political situation, availability of trained staff and donor influences in a particular country in the region. Social work knowledge and skills are socially constructed. The rich diversity of this region should trigger innovations in social work practice in working with different cultural and religious client groups.

To conclude, this chapter provides a valuable but brief comparison of, and discussion on, the social issues and status of social work education in the respective countries of the region. It also presents the formal and informal social welfare systems and the role social work education could play. This chapter also shows how social work in the South Asia region is diverse and also divided, and argues for an indigenous base of social work knowledge. It calls for a unified approach and recognises the need for governments, university administrators, and international and regional organisations to come forward to help social work educators and leaders to strengthen social work training and practice in their respective countries. I further argue for a common base of social work knowledge and praxis for South Asia as a distinct political and cultural region. I have also tried to raise further discussion on how social work institutions, academics, development practitioners and the state can further promote the process of academic and professional renewal in the region.

This chapter is dedicated to Shireen Rehmatullah of Pakistan and Armaity Desai of India, the founding President of the Asian and Pacific Association for Social Work Education (APASWE), for their lifetime passion to build social work scholarship.

References

Ahmadullah, A.K. (1986). Presidential address, report of the Seminar of Bangladesh Social Work Teachers Association, Dhaka.

Alphonse, M., George, P. & Moffatt, K. (2008). Redefining social work standards in the context of globalisation: lessons from India. *International Social Work*, 51(2): 145–58.

Atal, Y. (1981). *Building a nation: essays on India*. Delhi: Abhinav.

Barise, A. (2005). Social work with Muslims: insights from the teachings of Islam. *Critical Social Work*, 6(2): 73–89. Retrieved on 22 April 2014 from www1.uwindsor.ca/criticalsocialwork/social-work-with-muslims-insights-from-the-teachings-of-islam.

Chan, C.L.W. & Ng, S.M. (2004). The social work practitioner-researcher-educator: encouraging innovations and empowerment in the 21st century. *International Social Work*, 47(3): 312–20.

Chandraratna, D. (2008). *Social work: education & practice: a Sri Lankan perspective*. Colombo, Sri Lanka: Vijitha Yapa Publication.

Clews, R. (1999). Cross-cultural research in aboriginal rural communities: a Canadian case study of ethical challenges and dilemmas. *Rural Social Work*, 4: 26–32.

Fisher, J. (1973). Is casework effective? A review. *Social Work*, 18(1): 5–20.

Flexner, A. (1915). Is social work a profession? In *Proceedings of the National Conference of Charities and Corrections, 1915* (pp. 576–90). Chicago: Hildmann Printing.

Graham, J.R., Al-Krenawi, A. & Zaidi, S. (2007). Social work in Pakistan: preliminary insights. *International Social Work*, 50(5): 627–40.

Greenwood, E (1957). Attributes of a profession. *Social Work*, 2(3): 45–55.

Hammoud, H.R. (1988). Social work education in developing countries: issues and problems in undergraduate curricula. *International Social Work*, 31(3): 195–210.

Healy, L. (2001). *International social work: professional action in an interdependent world*. NY: Oxford University Press.

Howard, J. (1971). Indian society, Indian social work: identifying Indian principles and methods for social work practice. *International Social Work*, 14(4): 16–31.

Hugman, R. (2008). Social work values: equity or equality? A response to Solas. *Australian Social Work*, 61(2): 141–45.

International Federation of Social Workers (IFSW) (2012). Indian social work education: quality enhancement network launched. Retrieved on 22 April 2014 from ifsw.org/news/quality-enhancement-of-social-work-education-in-india/.

International Federation of Social Workers IFSW (2000). General meeting. Montreal, Canada. Retrieved on 22 April 2014 from www.ifsw.org/en/p38000265.html.

Kendall, K. (1950). *Training for social work: an international survey*. Lake Success, NY: Department of Social Affairs, United Nations.

Lešnik, B. & Urek, M. (2010). Traps of humanitarian aid: observations from a village community in Sri Lanka. *European Journal of Social Work*, special issue, *Race and Ethnic Relations*, 13(2): 271–82.

Midgley, J. (1981). *Professional imperialism: social work in the Third World*. London: Heinemann Educational Books.

Nadkarni, V. (2010). Editorial, social work education. *The International Journal*, 29 (8), 815–17.

Nagpaul, H. (1972). The diffusion of American social work education to India: problems and Issues. *International Social Work*, 15(1): 3–17.

Nikku, B.R. (2012a). Building social work education and the profession in a transition country: case of Nepal. *Asian Social Work and Policy Review*, 6 (3), 252–64

Nikku, B.R. (2012b). Global agenda on social work and social development: voices from South Asian social work. In N. Hall (ed.), *Social work around the world*, vol. 5, *Building the global agenda for social work and social development*. Berne: IFSW Press.

Nikku, B.R. (2011). Evolution of social work in Nepal: opportunities and challenges in a transition society. In S. Stanley (ed.), *Social work in countries of the East* (pp. 327–45). Washington, DC: Nova Science.

Nikku, B.R. (2010). Social work education in Nepal: major opportunities and abundant challenges. *Social Work Education: The International Journal*, special issue, *Challenges for Social Work Education in the Asian Context*, 29(8): 818–30.

Nikku, B.R. (2009). Social work education in South Asia: a Nepalese perspective. In Noble et al. (eds), *Social work education: voices from the Asia Pacific* (pp. 341–62). Melbourne: The Vulgar Press.

Palattiyil, G. & Sidhva, D. (2012). Guest editorial. Social work in India. *Practice: Social Work in Action*, 24(2): 75–78.

Pew Forum (Pew Research Center's Forum on Religion and Public Life) (2012). Washington, DC: Pew Research Centre.

Plath, D. (2011). Social work capacity building in the Maldives. In S. Stanley (ed.), *Social work in countries of the East* (pp. 347–67). Washington, DC: Nova Science.

Rahman, Mustaghis-ur- (2007). NGO management and operation: a South Asian perspective. *Journal of Health Management*, 9 (2): 223–36.

Rehmatullah, S. (2002). *Social welfare in Pakistan*. London: Oxford University Press.

Sarker, A.H. & Ahmadullah, A.K. (1995). Bangladesh. In T.D. Watts, D. Elliott & N.S. Mayadas (eds), *International handbook on social work education* (pp. 367–88). Westport, CT: Greenwood Press.

Taher, M. & Rahman, A. (1993). Social work in Bangladesh: problems and prospects. *Indian Journal of Social Work*, 4. Mumbai: Tata Institute of Social Sciences.

Tierney, W. (2006). Transformation, reform, and renewal in Afghanistan. *International Educator*, 15(5): 14–18.

UNICEF Afghanistan (2009). Advocacy paper 5, Social work curriculum development. Retrieved on 22 April 2014 from www.crin.org/docs/Social%20Work%20Curriculum%20Development%20Advocacy%20Paper%205%20February%202009.pdf

Watts, T.D., Elliott, D. & Mayadas N.S. (eds) (1995). *International handbook on social work education*. Westport, CT: Greenwood Press.

Zaviršek, D & Herath, S.M.K. (2010). 'I want to have my future, I have a dialogue': social work in Sri Lanka between neo-capitalism and human rights. *Social Work Education: The International Journal*, 29 (8): 831–42.

9

Social work education and family in Latin America: a case study

Carolina Muñoz-Guzmán, Sandra Mancinas and Nelly Nucci

The chapter develops a comparative analysis of three social work programs applied in three Latin-American countries, to answer the question whether these programs do or do not include teaching about families in a way that students are prepared for, enabling clients to challenge and transcend oppressions that disempower them (Dominelli 2002). To attain that goal, we identified three key dimensions that help students in achieving a comprehensive sociopolitical and integrated analysis about familial contexts, and constitute basic content in social work programs that should provide 1) acknowledgement of social and demographic changes, 2) a critical approach to social policies our states are adopting, and 3) a dialogue with vulnerable and marginalised families about their needs and the challenges they experience. Through analysis of each case and cross-case analysis, we answer the question guiding the study and propose some future challenges.

The purpose of this chapter is to develop a comparative analysis across three Latin-American countries on how social work education about families reflects expression of two main features for practice: families in their own private domains (referring to conformation of domestic spaces of social reproduction) and family policy carried out in each country (Argentina, Chile and Mexico). The approach social work education may have towards these two factors becomes crucial in order to understand the achievement of social work's professional mission of transcending oppressions and accomplishing empowerment of people (Dominelli 2002), and is particularly relevant for the Latin-American region, given the centrality of the family in Latin-American people's everyday life; social work and families are intrinsically merged in most of the public and private actions oriented towards social welfare.

In Latin America, social work schools began including families as a particular subject of study in their programs during the period of post-reconceptualisation and after the breakdown produced by the social movement of reconceptualisation through the 1960s and 70s, as a result of academic and professional debates on epistemological theory perspectives and methodological options for social work. From these discussions the institution of family became relevant for the academic field because it is one of the main subjects that social work interacts with. Family was acknowledged then as an organisation where the key social reproduction of its members occurs.

In regard to the post-reconceptualisation, the process is a reaction to the prior Latin-American movement of reconceptualisation of social work. Social work in the 1960s questioned its professional practice as one profoundly influenced by society's economic and political forces, and marked by apathy in response to inequities caused by structural sources of oppression over excluded groups in society. Assuming a critical perspective of capitalist societies (Faleiros 2011; Netto 1976), this movement was based on a Marxist analysis of capitalism, searching for transformations of social structures, critically analysing social work's daily practices, and questioning its servile disposition towards dominant social structures.

The process following this movement, post-reconceptualisation, brought a new search for the foundations of the profession, based on a critical appraisal of the reconceptualisation outcomes. Basically, the previous process was accused of being too ideological, and there was a new focus on working with families, which replaced the traditional work with the individual case, and made broader the intervention towards groups and communities, based on renovated conceptual and epistemological frameworks as well as intervention methodologies.

For those who support the idea of social work as a profession that interacts with social actors (families, groups, communities and institutions) searching for solutions to daily life complexities, the study of life conditions and family organisation in each socio-historical context becomes significant, as well as the distribution of social reproductive responsibilities of the state, the market and families. The members of families request different resources to satisfy their needs; those resources are their labour activities (paid or domestic labour), as well as formal and informal cross-over points indicating exchange relations and mutual help relations (Jelin 2000). The relationship between families and social work professionals occurs in institutional contexts related to social policy, conforming fields of power relations affected by time and space.

Therefore, how students of social work are taught about family conformations will tell us about how social work thinks about the relationship between the family relationship and the state and wider society; how social work envisages and carries out research with families; how it answers questions in relation to what aids or obstructs the development of the capacity to care; and how social work deliberates about the fields of power where social work intervenes. The approach to these key topics will elucidate how social work education in the Latin-American region tackles a vital subject for students and practitioners alike: the role of social workers in enabling their clients to challenge and transcend oppressions that disempower them (Dominelli 2002).

This chapter is devoted, then, to compare social work education about families in the Latin-American region, taking three case studies as theoretical samples. Three schools of social work were studied in their teaching of social work and families; specifically, the modules dedicated to family are reviewed. The structure of the chapter justifies first the relevance of teaching about families for social work. Secondly, it discusses how social contexts have changed in Latin-American societies, producing a tension between development, globalisation and public action, presenting a number of issues between the political/economical approaches in each country in serving the poor/excluded. These discussions identify the emergence of key dimensions that need to be acknowledged in the curricula of social work education in order to ensure its fidelity to social work principles of social justice.

Latin America: a changing society

Nowadays it is undeniably the case that the whole world is immersed in transformations: post-modernity and globalisation have wrought effects on many structures, including one of the most core institutions: the family. It is understood as 'a social institution, the most representative of the human systems, based on socio-ecological relations with the environment and the cultural context to which it belongs and represents' (Quintero 2001, 7). The importance of family lies in its centrality for society to function. Therefore, if sociocultural contexts change family will change too, and vice versa.

'Concepts, definitions, measurements and perceptions of family life, family policies and policies that impact on families are not constant over time or space' (Hantrais 2004, p.1), because they need to respond to an increasingly complex family structure; social work education is challenged too to respond to the new plurality of family life. This is expressed in decreasing fertility rates, increases in rates of divorce and separation of families, and changes in gender roles. All of the three countries under study in this chapter are affected by these tendencies.

To face these challenges, social work education needs to acknowledge and give legitimacy to new family conformations as well as study family policies from a critical stance, because these become the instruments to support families in coping with complex needs. The critical perspective in social work education becomes a core approach, to prepare students to support families in challenging structures that disrupt egalitarian relations among individuals, families and communities (Dominelli 2002). An approach of this nature should lead to family policies ensuring gender equality, reconciliation of work and family life without making undue demands on women, intergenerational solidarity, lifelong learning, and the expansion of day-care systems for children, among others.

New family configurations are emerging rapidly in the Latin-American region but are still considered as atypical families; previously the family could only possibly be conceived as a two-parent structure, as an unbreakable morally, legally and religiously sanctioned structure, whilst today it becomes more evident that a hegemonic model of the family does not seem to belong to the era of globalisation (Quintero 2001, 9). According to Arriagada (2007), the traditional family is no longer the main household structure in Latin America, due to modifications of the basic conditions of life affected by globalisation and modernisation. These conditions are related to urbanisation, and then linked to industrialisation (demographic shifts and modifications in the production process), an expansion of female employment and new consumption patterns, as well as new ways of employment and consumption and greater access to, but more segmented, social services (education, health, among others).

Key demographic shifts are expressed in the decrease of birth rates: in Chile the current birth rate is 0.99%, one of the lowest in Latin America. The decrease has been drastic; in the last 40 years this rate has decreased 54% (INE 2012). In México fertility rates have also decreased from 5.7 children per woman in 1976 to 2.2 in 2006 (INEGI 2009). As for Argentina, the birth rate has decreased from 1970 (23 per thousand) to 2012 (17 per thousand), as well as the average number of children per woman of 1.4 or more per year: in 1979, 3.73; 1990, 2.99; 2000, 2.48; and in 2010, 2.21.

Naturally, this has affected family size. In Chile, between 1992 and 2002, the average number in a family was reduced from 4 to 3.6 people; by 2012 this average was 3.28 family members per group. In Mexico, family size was reduced from 6 children per woman in 1975 to 5 in 1979, 4 in 1985, 3 in 1994 and 2.2 in 2000. Even though these trends are observed in different continents, the speed of change in such a short period may provoke particular difficulties in the society to adjust to such a radically different scenario, especially if family has been a core institution, as we will see later.

The basic idea of a 'nuclear family' as the model for the design of family policies is currently challenged by demographic trends in the region. The three countries show new types of family conformations as well as transformations in the family life cycle, based on the postponement of the arrival of the first child, and the decrease of the average size of households. Although the most common familial organisation is still the nuclear two-parent household with children, increasingly it is observable in the three countries that this configuration is changing towards new ones, such as single-parent households with children, unmarried cohabitation and an incremental increase in the number of divorced couples. New patterns in marriages, divorces, re-marriages etc. contribute to a different family landscape.

The former transformations in the three countries have affected gender roles. Increasingly there are more households headed by women, with a weakening of the male breadwinner and female career model. Sources of transformation are anchored also in improvements of social indicators like longer life expectancy, a rise in general schooling and education, especially for women, and increase of female access to the workforce. However, it is observable that there is an unequal access to these improvements through the different socioeconomic groups, negatively affecting lower socioeconomic groups. Certain changes in family conformations and practices are affecting mainly higher income groups, such as schooling and female access to the labour market. Other changes negatively affect poor families; in the three countries there has been a rise in the number of female-headed households in the poorest families. These groups are characterised by women holding mostly non-qualified jobs and family responsibilities, which means that they have young children, school age children and teenagers to care for as well as work responsibilities. This information concords with empirical evidence establishing that young households with small children or of school age have more probabilities of being in disadvantage and poverty than those households with parents at a more advanced stage in life (Kaztman & Filgueira 2001).

These families are also characterised by their low school attainment. In Argentina, Mexico and Chile, the relationship between education and income is relatively stable until 12 years of education, after which additional years of education increases income. According to Raczynski (2000), most of the adults from families living under the basic subsistence line and in poverty have not completed twelve years of education, limiting their access to better paid jobs. Their low attainment influences also their children's school achievement. According to the United Nations Economic Commission for Latin America and the Caribbean (2007), in Latin America the educational level of parents plays a more important part than income in explaining children's educational performance, negatively affecting results, school dropout, and predicting low educational attainment. Low educational level of poor families impacts also their precarious economic status, expressed in a range of activities with common employment patterns: non-standard employment, being underpaid and under-protected by labour laws, and often insecure employment, affecting particularly women, who not only have precarious access to the labour market, but see themselves as restricted by cultural patterns.

Modernity in the family would be expressed as the exercise of democratic rights, autonomy of their members and more equity, but it becomes fractured when families have to struggle against market competitiveness and the unequal distribution of wealth, a feature of Latin-American societies. Inequality is the reality for many Latin-American families; Jelin (1998) claims that Latin-American families carry out the functions of social support and protection when it comes to responding to social and economic crises (unemployment, death, low incomes); the family then appears as a strategic resource of great value, which is an outcome related to governments' social, political and economic options.

Therefore, demographic shifts, new types of family structure, changes in the family life cycle and transformation in gender practices are general trends in Chile, Argentina and Mexico, but certainly with different features. Chile and Argentina are located in the southern part of South America, while Mexico is in North America. Chile has been considered an archetype of privatisation and the neoliberal economy with social policies as strategies for economic growth. However, this is a country where a neoliberal model of development has increased the already present forms of socioeconomic stratification, affecting Chileans' perception of economic and social insecurities, inequity and lack of trust in others and institutions (UNDP 2009; Marcus 2004). In Chile political power is concentrated in the executive branch, which initiates most legislation, and is highly centralised, with presidential appointment of the regional executives and the provincial governors. Argentina and Mexico are different; both have federal states leading to a decentralisation of power, favouring regional variation according to local needs.

Even though in these countries there is decentralisation, it does not necessarily bring more equity. In Mexico economic policy had produced an important negative effect in income distribution. According to Székely (1995), some measures such as privatisation and financial liberalisation have led to a concentration of resources' ownership in few people. This, in a country historically unequal, unavoidably means that differences tend to expand. A similar situation is found in Argentina, where the federal system isn't always favourable to equality; there are large inequalities between provinces. As a neoliberalist model was installed, inequalities and poverty growing with it transformed the role of the market which has become a regulator of social risks, and the state only attends to extreme situations. Consequently, people's needs were conceptualised as residual rights of specific groups, and assistance policies assumed the character of compensatory policies. Resources to families in poverty were given only from targeted programs.

Political and economic approaches frame the type of welfare regime implemented in each country, and the kind of family involvement in it. The next section reviews theories of welfare regimes and how they can be apply to the countries under study.

Welfare regimes and social policy in Latin America

The acknowledgement and critical review of types of welfare regimes affecting families gives to the family a clearer perspective. To compare social policy from a social work viewpoint, there are several frameworks to guide the discussion; one of these is the typology introduced by Esping-Andersen in *The three worlds of welfare capitalism* (1990). Later debate about this typology has led to criticisms of it and this critique in Europe has led to the development of more sophisticated models of comparison (Hantrais 2004). Currently, the review of the social investment approach becomes a crucial means of appraisal for social work to analyse the relation between social policies and families (Jenson 2009; Morris & Featherstone 2010).

Esping-Andersen (2000, 53) claimed that in welfare regimes the family must not be considered as only a shelter of privacy and a place of consumption, but also as one of the most important actors, whose decisions and behaviour influence directly the welfare state and labour market. This view is shared in Latin America; Jelin (2005) proposes considering the family as an organic part of broader social processes that include productive and reproductive dimensions; cultural patterns, political systems, labour markets and social network organisations, in a way that demographic processes such as fecundity, divorce, ageing, among others, are as much part of family processes as social, economic and cultural processes, with all interrelated to public policy.

Hantrais (2004) suggested a categorisation with four 'regimes' of family: de familialised, partly defamilialised, familialised, and refamilialised types of welfare states.

> These regimes reflect different ways to mix social service providers with family responsibilities, leading to highly variable consequences in terms of the role of the family, but also in terms of resource distribution between richer and poorer, men and women, generations, immigrants and natives, etc. (Nygren, in press)

Under these classifications, in the three countries under study, a liberal and conservative welfare mix is recognisable, combining familialised and defamilialised policies. In the case of Mexico – and following here the classification of Esping-Andersen (2000) – Mexico's social welfare regime is closer to the Mediterranean model. Social policy appears strongly familialised, influenced by patronage and the Catholic Church. In Mexico, families have been made responsible for solving family problems in cases where protection systems are weak; in practice, the family, particularly the poor ones, is the only institution that ameliorates the effects of economic crisis, unemployment and disease (González de la Rocha 2006, 3). Family has been regarded as a central body to improve the level of success of social policy (Székely 2003). These features are also seen in the Chilean case.

These approaches are not free from economic options taken by these countries. We have identified in different stages for México, Chile and Argentina an economic liberalisation approach (Sheahan 1997, 7). The model has brought negative effects for these countries' poorer socioeconomic groups, even though direct social aid has been promoted to lessen the impact on the poor through the implementation of methods that do not interfere with markets. These policies led to a divided society, because they caused marginalisation and the risk of social exclusion.

Following Hantrais (2004), we will understand partially defamilialised policies as those that in their discourse appear supportive of families, but stay far from intervening in private life, reducing coordination between policy actors (Hantrais 2004, 202). These policies are seen frequently under liberal approaches, based more in risks than rights. Familialised policies often appear to be influenced by Catholic social doctrine and the principle of social support, i.e. social policies are aimed at addressing situations where primary social networks (especially the family) fail. Thus, a familialised system does not mean 'pro-family' but rather proposes policies in which family members are primarily responsible for the welfare of the rest of the family.

A deeper critical scrutiny of Latin American welfare mix and family policies is found in Jenson (2009). The author has claimed that, currently in Latin America, neoliberalism is being replaced by the social investment perspective.

> In the social investment perspective the state may have a legitimate role if it acts to increase the probability of future profits and positive outcomes. This objective-setting in future terms is exemplified by the overriding concentration, now shared by policy communities in Europe and Latin America, on breaking the intergenerational cycle of poverty and disadvantage rather than on ending poverty (ECLAC 2007, Chapter V, for example) (Jenson 2009, 450)

The focus of this approach is represented by the value of present investment for future returns and the value of policy based on its outcomes. Spending strategies as well as policy instruments are shaped by the social investment perspective's underpinning ideas, preferring life-course perspectives instead of cross-sectional measures of the here-and-now, or the increase of the value of asset building. All of these shifts in ideas about time and about appropriate policy instruments buttress new ideas and practices about social citizenship (Jenson 2009). The new perspective privileges structural adjustments that 'make markets the distributors of wellbeing, families responsible for their own opportunities, and the community sector the final safety net' (Jenson 2009, 454).

The effect of this perspective on family policies is the reconfiguration of a 'rights dimension' by giving a 'child focus' to social rights (Jenson 2001; Jenson & Saint-Martin 2003 in Jenson 2009, 458). Examples of this are found in programs like 'Oportunidades' in Mexico, 'Plan Nacional de Familias por la inclusión social' in Argentina, and 'Chile crece contigo' in Chile. It also has been expressed in the extensive use of conditional cash support programs as preferred policy instruments, which demand from citizens some pre-specified actions (Jenson 2009).

Underlying this approach is a dilemma for social workers when working in child welfare. In a context where there is a rise of formal early intervention to invest in children, legislation supports family involvement:

> yet the prevailing political and social environment seeks to position vulnerable families outside of mainstream discourses and services, and resists their ongoing involvement in the welfare of their children. (Morris & Featherstone 2010, 563)

According to Morris and Featherstone (2010, 563):

> a number of problematic binaries have operated, such as children versus parents, and hardworking families who can access modernised support services versus the small number of failing 'high-risk high-cost' families . . . Furthermore, as we have suggested above, families within this group, alongside others, have also been called upon by government policies to provide care often with inadequate resources or rights available to them.

The new perspective then, with its child-centred and human capital emphases of the social investment strategy, ends up strengthening the idea of children who should be invested in, to achieve future success and social cohesion, with the help of parents controlled by the state, while the social work focus is on families who were defined as failures (Jenson 2009).

Therefore, the challenges for social work education and family issues are complex, and require a comprehensive sociopolitical and more integrated analysis. It is not only about acknowledging social and demographic changes our societies are going through, nor only about studying critically the social policies our states are adopting; it is also about what Morris and Featherstone (2010) claim as an urgent need 'dialogue with vulnerable and marginalised families about their needs and the challenges they experience . . . what risks they consider they pose'. Social work education on family issues must ensure social workers are able of understanding 'how we know what we know and how that knowledge is grounded in connectivity within everything that we do' (Bellefeuille & Ricks 2010, 1241).

In the current context, with a strong preeminence of liberal and social investment approaches, social projects are predefined, and only poor and inadequate primary research with such families has been carried out (Nixon & Parr 2008) to inform those projects. For instance, in Chile the focus has been on professionals' implementation capacities, but weak attention has been given to how difficulties are experienced by families. Are all these challenges acknowledged and addressed in social work education on families? This is the analysis we carry out to finish this chapter.

Neoliberalism and critical perspectives as factors affecting anti-oppressive social work

The analysis of our case studies is led by the question of whether the social work programs in the three selected Latin-American social work schools include teaching about families in a way that is conducive to discarding top-down and hierarchical relations with people, and promoting more dialogical and collaborative relationships (Dominelli 2002). To attain that goal, we have identified three key dimensions that help students in achieving a comprehensive sociopolitical and integrated analysis about familial contexts, constituting how basic content in social work programs should provide 1) acknowledgement of social and demographic changes, 2) a critical approach to social policies our states are adopting, and 3) a dialogue with vulnerable and marginalised families about their needs and the challenges they experience.

To study the social work programs from three different Latin-American countries, the analysis was carried out within each case and across countries. Therefore each case is now analysed as a unit, in order to develop later a comparative analysis across the three countries.

In the case of Mexico, the social work program from Universidad de Nuevo León currently is in transition from a program that analysed family issues from Urie Bronfrenbrenner's systems theory perspective and gave special attention to sociodemographic change and its repercussions on how families reconfigure their composition. However, the fact that the specific module teaching familial transformations is optional does not ensure that all social work students get these fundamental contents. The second characteristic of this first program is its descriptive approach to the neoliberal model applied in Mexican society, which is seen clearer in the module Social Theories II; in it there is not a critical discussion about the impact of the model on social production and reproduction of families.

Lastly, in the module Social Policies and Social Work, even though it is focused on discussing sectorial social policies implemented in the country, families' interpretations and appraisal of these policies are absent in the contents of the program. In addition, there is no special validation of families' contribution and responsibility in the success of the policies' outcomes.

The second highlighted program in the Mexican case shows the general tendency of national educational policies aiming for the development of competences, with an emphasis on a practical approach. In this program there is an emphasis on two main theoretical constructs – general system theories and human development – which are based on motivational schools of thought coming from existentialism and the psychology of Carl Rogers; this program replaced the module Social Work with Families, which included the understanding of sociodemographic variables affecting policies and family intervention. Although other programs such as Approaches to Social Work, Socio-communitarian Human Development, and Law, include the family unit as one of the objects of study, the focus of the teaching is placed on the attainment of specific skill-based educational outcomes. Therefore, there is not a clear fidelity in these two programs to the three core dimensions identified earlier for our analysis.

In the Argentinean case, based on the Universidad Nacional de Cordoba, contents related to demographic transformations and new familial conformations are covered by the module Scenarios, Processes and Subjects; this includes topics that contribute to the understanding of social actors: socioanthropological, cultural, psychosocial and human development contents. These contents are studied again in the module Theories, Spaces and Strategies of Intervention, which deepens the interpretative efforts to understand the meaning families give to their daily lives. The dimension related to political-economic contexts and their impact on family life is covered in this case in several sub-modules (Social Policy, Health and Public Policy, Education and Public Policy) which are articulated within a larger area of intervention strategies that studies concepts of and state interventions on families. Both modules also incorporate families' daily practices as strategies to live and cope that should be part of considerations about professional intervention.

In the Chilean case, based on the Pontificia Universidad Católica de Chile, there are only two modules whose contents give special attention to the family as a whole connected with the rest of the spheres of social life; these are Social Work and Families and Social Policy and Family. Because of the short time invested in these subjects, the challenge of teaching about sociodemographic change and family reconfigurations is achieved to an extent, but the capacity to review policy approaches is restricted to the descriptive level, rather than a critical appraisal of them and their impact on family life. Achieved to a lesser degree has been the response to the challenge of listening to the voice of the families to integrate this in reflexive practices to improve interventions.

Additionally, the particular approaches used to understand family issues, such as Urie Bronffrenbrenner's systems theory, ecological perspectives, and strengths perspective bring the risk of giving responsibility only to clients in solving their crises, instead of developing more holistic understandings about the disempowerment these families experience.

The general review of the three programs shows limitations in Mexico and Chile to fully embrace the unique role social work has advocated: 'educate students to be change agents and to enable clients to alter their social environments' (Reisch 2013). However, it seems to be that Argentina has kept its loyalty to social work's mission, and we have tried to find some answers to why this might be the case.

One reason for the strong differences between different countries is the degree of autonomy universities have from higher education policies. In Argentina, state universities have sustained an important defence of civic education and responsibility towards society in their curriculum. Even though this autonomy was interrupted during many periods by both democratic and military governments, some measure of university reform was established in the years following the end of the dictatorship in 1983. During these critical periods there was a strong reflexive action among the body of social work professionals and faculties allowing some filters against the neoliberal logic that was preeminent at that time in the country. In 1995 there emerged a point of inflection from the faculty body convening a Specificity of Social Work and Professional Training.

> This meeting allowed the rethinking of the academic training in terms of the ethical-political dimension, theoretical-epistemological dimension and methodological-instrumental dimension, as it recognises the need to rethink Social Work and reinforce our explanatory theories, and produce new knowledge to confront the profound contextual transformations. (Acevedo et al. 2007, 5)

Consequently and consistently over time there have been academic meetings arranged dedicated to discuss the training and curriculum reform processes in social work careers. There is clearly an important heterogeneity and diversity in social work training in Argentina. However, there is also an agreement about how social work programs should seek to strengthen critical perspectives and transfer them into teaching and practice.

Mexico and Chile have been affected by a strong regulation of the higher educational system, leaving few spaces for autonomy that protects the particular emphases and commitments social work has. Specific aspects jeopardising social work's mission have been recognised by Reisch (2013, 715) in regard to US social work education:

> the growing stratification of social work faculty; the increased reliance on untested online methods of education; and the emphasis on quantitative 'outcomes' as indicators of educational success. At the same time, social work education in the US has been unable to respond effectively to the implications of demographic and cultural diversity.

The constant effort in Mexico and Chile to attain American's standards have put social work schools under pressure to achieve outcomes that are not always compatible with professional values, and the lack of a strong corporative defence has reduced the capacity to subvert this, especially when funds are dependent upon achieving state goals.

This last point raises a second difference between Argentina's case and the other two cases. Unlike Argentina, although in Mexico and Chile there are professional organisations and councils, these are still weak in their contribution to building professional cohesion and a strong corporative defence (Ribeiro et al. 2007). Currently, in Mexico there is the Mexican Association of Educational Institutions of Social Work, which states that one of its objectives is to improve the academic level of social work, but has not issued any statement about the intrusion of the neoliberal logic in the training of social workers. In Chile, practitioners' associations and the discipline of social work appear fragmented, limiting its already limited influence.

A third difference is in the critical approach of the programs to the neoliberal effects on social policies, strategies and instruments. It seems that the Argentinean programs better acknowledge the negative effects of social investment perspectives, and this is achieved by emphasising an approach to reality from hermeneutical perspectives that gives central-ity to relational ties with clients. In contrast, the use of perspectives coming from ecological theory and systems theory in Mexico and Chile relates more to a vision centred on the satisfaction of individual needs (Jani & Reisch 2011). The impact can be seen then in 'an emphasis on individual change, rather than social action' (Reisch 2013, 723).

Lastly, if we look at the general distributions of modules in each program, there are policy modules dedicated to teach macroeconomics, legal regulations, and social analy-sis among other relevant subjects. However, if the implications of the labour market, legal frameworks and changing social action are not problematised, then few steps can be achieved to help students in raising resistance and change from their practices. On the contrary, the risk of adapting to the 'disciplinary regime' of neoliberalism becomes higher (Reisch 2013, 71).

Conclusions

From within and a cross case analysis it clearly appears that the three programs achieve the first dimension identified as key to promote social work's mission: the programs under study acknowledged demographic and sociocultural changes in family life. However, this first accomplishment is minimised in two cases, Mexico and Chile, because these are not so strong in applying a critical approach in the modules reviewing policy approaches, and do not provide the means for students to listen to the voice of the families, to integrate it in reflexive practices to improve interventions. The risk these deficiencies bring to social work education is the lack of a comprehensive analytical capacity in social work profes-sionals, which becomes a barrier to re-think policies and programs implemented in each country. The outcome, then, is professionals with few skills to offer in cooperative interac-tion with families, helping them to recover intimacy and trust.

Our analysis led us to articulate the trends of higher education in Mexico and Chile that had a rigid conceptualisation of quality, produced by weak critical appraisal of social policies. The consequence is a threat for the role of the family in regard to resource distribution between different groups and genders and a tendency to an unquestioning ac-ceptance of market-oriented solutions.

In Argentina these trends have been resisted by a strong corporative defence of social workers, demonstrated in collaborative actions that are sufficiently empowered to prevail upon social work ethics, developing the capacity to fight successfully for professional au-tonomy. This last aspect has been aided by the higher education autonomy from market forces. We would now question if neoliberalism has been working against social work ed-ucation, and is it not time to do something?

References

Acevedo, P., Garma, M.E. & Peralta, M.I. (2007). Document no. 2: discussion. Produced by Commission Directive FAUATS (Argentinean Federation of Social Work Academic Programs). Retrieved on 5 June 2014 from fauats.blogspot.com.au/p/documentos.html.

Arriagada, I. (2007). *Familias latinoamericanas. Diagnóstico y políticas públicas en los inicios del nuevo siglo.* Santiago, Chile: CEPAL.

Bellefeuille, G. & Ricks, F. (2010). Relational inquiry: a child and youth care approach to research. *Children and Youth Services Review,* 32(10): 1235–41. DOI: 10.1016/j.childyouth.2010.04.013.

Dominelli, L. (2002). *Anti-oppressive social work theory and practice.* Houndmills, UK: Palgrave Macmillan.

ECLAC (Economic Commission for Latin America and the Caribbean) (2007). *Social cohesion: inclusion and a sense of belonging in Latin America and the Caribbean.* NY: United Nations.

Esping-Andersen, G. (1990). *The three worlds of welfare capitalism.* Cambridge: Polity Press; Princeton: Princeton University Press.

Esping-Andersen, G. (2000). *Fundamentos sociales de las economías postindustriales.* Barcelona, España: Ariel.

Faleiros, V. (2011). Desafíos del trabajo social frente a las desigualdades. *Emancipação, Ponta Grossa,* 11(1): 117–28. DOI: 10.5212/Emancipacao.v.11i1.0009.

González de la Rocha, M. (2006). Familias y política social en México. El caso de oportunidades. Paper presented at the conference Welfare Regime and Social Actors in Inter-Regional Perspective: The Americas, Asia and Africa. Austin, University of Texas. Retrieved on 16 April 2014 from lanic.utexas.edu/project/etext/llilas/cpa/spring06/welfare/delarocha.pdf.

Hantrais, L. (2004). *Family policy matters: responding to family change in Europe.* Bristol: Policy Press.

INE (Institute Nacional de Estadística) (2012). *Estadísticas demográficas.* Santiago, Chile: INE.

INEGI (Instituto Nacional de Estadística, Geografía e Informática) (2009). *Estadísticas históricas de México 2009.* Retrieved on 1 October 2014 from www.inegi.org.mx/prod_serv/contenidos/espanol/bvinegi/productos/integracion/pais/historicas10/EHM2009.pdf.

Jani, J. & Reisch, M. (2011). Common human needs, uncommon solutions: applying a critical framework to perspectives on human behaviour. *Families in Society,* 92(1): 13–20. DOI: 10.1606/1044-3894.4065.

Jelin, E. (2005). Las familias latinoamericanas en el marco de las transformaciones globales: hacia una nueva agenda de políticas públicas. In I. Arriagada (ed.), *Políticas hacia las familias, protección e inclusión sociales* (pp. 69–88). Santiago: CEPAL.

Jelin, E. (2000). *Pan y afectos. La transformación de las familias.* San Pablo: Fondo de Cultura Económica.

Jelin, E. (1998). *Pan y afectos: la transformación de las familias.* Buenos Aires: Fondo de Cultura Económica.

Jenson, J. & Saint-Martin, D. (2003). New routes to social cohesion? Citizenship and the social investment state. *Canadian Journal of Sociology,* 28(1): 77–99.

Jenson, J. (2009) Lost in translation: the social investment perspective and gender equality. *Social Politics,* 16(4): 446–83.

Jenson, J. (2001). Re-thinking equality and equity: Canadian children and the social union. In J. Broadbent (ed.), *Democratic equality: what went wrong?* (pp. 111–29). Toronto: University of Toronto Press.

Kaztman, R. & Y Filgueira, F. (2001). *Panorama de la infancia y la familia en Uruguay.* Montevideo: Universidad Católica del Uruguay.

Marcus, B. (2004). Growth without equity: inequality, social citizenship, and the neoliberal model of development in Chile. Paper presented to the Faculty of the Graduate School of the University of Texas, Austin.

Morris, K. & Featherstone, B. (2010) Investing in children, regulating parents, thinking family: a decade of tensions and contradictions. *Journal of Social Policy and Society,* 9(4): 557–86.

Netto, J.P. (1976). La crisis del proceso de reconceptualización del servicio social. In N. Alayón (ed.), *Desafío al servicio social. ¿Crisis de la reconceptualización?,* vol. 20 (pp. 85–105). Argentina: Colección Desarrollo Social Humanitas Argentina.

Nixon, J. & Parr, S. (2008). Family intervention projects – sites of resilience, resistance and domination. In M. Barnes & D. Prior (eds), *Subversive citizens: power, agency and resistance in public policy* (p. 20). Bristol: Policy Press.

Nygren, L. (in press). Family complexity and social work: a comparative study of family-based welfare work in different welfare regimes. NORFACE Welfare State Future Application Template Outline Proposal.

Quintero, Á. (2001). Escenarios contemporáneos de la familia: familia, ciudadanía y transformación social desde la dimensión humana. Paper presented at XVII Seminario Latinoamericano de Escuelas de Trabajo Social, Lima, Perú.

Raczynski, D. (2000). Chile: progress, problems, and prospects. In Morales-Gomez, D., Tschirgi, N. & Moher, J. (eds), *Reforming social policy: changing perspectives on sustainable human development* (pp. 45–82). Ottawa, Canada: International Development Research Center United Nations Economic Commission for Latin America and the Caribbean.

Reisch, M. (2013). Social work education and the neo-liberal challenge: the US response to increasing global inequality. *Social Work Education: The International Journal*, 32(6): 715–33. Retrieved on 22 April 2014 from dx.doi.org/10.1080/02615479.2013.809200.

Ribeiro, M., López, R. & Mancinas, S. (2007). Trabajo social y política social en México. *Revista Internacional de Ciencias Sociales y Humanidades*, Julio–Diciembre. Tamaulipas: SOCIOTAM. Retrieved on 16 April 2014 from www.redalyc.org/pdf/654/65417208.pdf.

Sheahan, J. & Williams, C. (1997). Effects of liberalisation programs on poverty and inequality: Chile, Mexico, and Peru. *Latin American Research Review*, 32(3): 7–38. Retrieved on 22 April 2014 from www.jstor.org/stable/2503996.

Székely, M. (2003). Lo que dicen los pobres. *Cuadernos de Desarrollo Humano*, vol. 13. México, DF: Secretaria de Desarrollo Social.

Székely, M. (1995). Aspectos de la desigualdad en México. *El Trimestre Económico*, 62(2): 201–43. 62.

UNDP (2009). Desarrollo humano en Chile. La manera de hacer las cosas 2009. Programa de Naciones Unidas para el Desarrollo, Santiago.

Part 3

The development of social work education courses

10

Social work education in the Caribbean: charting pathways to growth and globalisation

Letnie Rock and Cerita Buchanan

> Professional social work education began in the English-speaking Caribbean
> in 1961. Over time there has been a gradual development of undergraduate
> and graduate social work programs in the region. These programs which
> vary in some respects are delivered in multidisciplinary departments in col-
> leges and universities in the region. In every institution a small number of
> social work faculty members deliver social work training which focuses on
> preparing social workers to practice in the Caribbean or elsewhere. In addi-
> tion to the core courses and electives taught in these programs there is the
> requirement of a supervised internship that takes place within social service
> agencies. This internship may vary in duration and intensity according to the
> level of the training offered. Most programs have a regional orientation but
> faculty are being encouraged by the Association of Caribbean Social Work
> Educators (ACSWE) to use the IASSW/IFSW Global Standards to bench-
> mark for excellence.

The Caribbean region is subdivided into English-, Dutch-, Spanish- and French-speaking
territories as a result of their history of colonisation. Due to this divide, there is little consensus and holistic identity about the Caribbean in terms of history, problems, resources,
policies, and programs and this has influenced social work education as it developed in the
countries of the region (Dolly-Besson et al. 1983). The social work programs as they evolve
are not homogenous and the English-, Dutch-, French- and Spanish-speaking countries all
have different approaches to the delivery of social work education. Some programs adopt
a North American approach to training but ensure that Caribbean content is infused in
the curriculum while others have a predominantly European orientation. The European
orientation is particularly noticeable in the programs that are delivered in countries that
have remained territories of European countries. For example, social work education as
offered in the Dutch-speaking Caribbean countries of Aruba and Curacao is still influenced by the philosophy surrounding social work education in the Netherlands. Thus, it
is not very compatible with local needs. However, the local faculty have recognised a need
to move away from a Eurocentric approach to practice to a greater Caribbean slant and
as a result the universities in these Dutch territories are trying to make their social work

programs more culturally relevant by adding Caribbean content into the social work curriculum (Baker & Maxwell 2012).

This chapter provides an overview of the past and current delivery of social work education in the English-speaking Caribbean. It will discuss the programs and the methods presently used in preparing students for practice. The status of social work education vis-a-vis educational programs in the allied professions, the internationalisation of the curriculum and the use of the Global Standards in program and curriculum development will be included in the discussion. The programs offered by The University of the West Indies will be used as the specific point of reference.

Before 1838 (emancipation of the slaves), social welfare services were virtually non-existent in the British Caribbean colonies because of the nature of the slave plantation economy. Little provision was made for the wellbeing of the ex-slaves following emancipation and over time the sociopolitical conditions of the masses in the British colonies became so dire that it led them to revolt in 1937 (Augier et al. 1970). The British Government investigated the cause of the unrest in its colonies through the Moyne Commission in 1938. Following the investigation, a report was written known as the Moyne Report (Maxwell 2002). Based on the recommendations of the report, the British Government passed a Colonial Development and Welfare Act in 1940 which established a Colonial Development and Welfare Fund. Funding for social programs in the colonies was provided from this fund through the Colonial Development and Welfare Office in Britain (Augier et al. 1970). This assistance by the British Government in the early 1940s led to the development of social welfare systems and the introduction of social work in the region. Thus, it can be said that social welfare services in the British West Indies developed as a mandate of the British Colonial and Welfare Office (Maxwell 2002; Dolly-Besson et al. 1983), out of a need for social and economic justice and to meet the welfare needs of the poor and disadvantaged. Social welfare agencies were set up in some colonies including Barbados, Guyana, Jamaica and Trinidad. Persons were appointed as social welfare officers and sent to universities such as Swansea, the London School of Economic and the University of Edinburgh in the United Kingdom for professional social work training (Maxwell et al. 2003; Dolly-Besson et al. 1983). A decade later it was documented in a Colonial Development and Welfare Report that 'the climate of public opinion in the West Indies has changed, and there is more acceptance of the need for skilled professional direction of social work' (Colonial Development and Welfare Report 1953 as cited in Maxwell 2002). These early services were delivered using the welfare model and the casework approach to practice in countries such as Barbados and Trinidad (Dolly-Besson et al. 1983). In Jamaica, 'the emphasis was on community development' (Dolly-Besson et al. 1983, 3). The casework approach was passed down through the years but social work education in the Caribbean has been trying to move practitioners away from this old method of social work intervention which tends to encourage client dependency, to a more dynamic, pragmatic, developmental and empowering approach to helping through a focus on ecological and empowerment theories and the strengths perspective.

Maxwell (2002) gives an excellent account of the development of social work in the English-speaking Caribbean. He maps the transition from the pre-20th century colonial era through the post-1938 (World War 2) period to the end of the 20th century. He highlights the provision of state sponsored poor relief that catered to the basic needs of people through a welfare model and makes reference to the employment of the first social welfare officers in the region. He mentions the early initiatives that were undertaken to professionalise social services in the region. These included professional training for the newly appointed social welfare officers in the 1940s and 1950s 'to perform as multifunctional social work practitioners' (19), and the streamlining of the social services to serve the needs of a varied clientele. He also briefly notes the measures that were taken over the years 'to provide training and professional education for the social workers staffing the various service agencies' (29). These included the development of the two year professional certificate program offered by the University of the West Indies (UWI) Mona in 1961 and the expansion of social work education across the region to the University of Guyana in 1970 and to two other campuses of UWI, the Cave Hill and St Augustine Campuses in 1988 and 1990 respectively. Maxwell (2002) also acknowledges the role of various non-governmental organisations in the development of social work and social welfare services in the English-speaking Caribbean in the first part of the 20th century and describes the growth of the government social services sector in countries of the region during the latter part of the century.

The history of social work and social work education in the English-speaking Caribbean is still being written but much has been documented by Caribbean scholars (Rock 2013; Baker & Maxwell 2012; Watkins & Holder-Dolly 2012; Rock 2011; Nettleford 2005; Maxwell et al. 2003; Maxwell 2002; Dolly-Besson et al. 1983). 'These scholars agree that formal social work education was started in the English-speaking Caribbean in 1961 when a two-year professional certificate course was introduced at the Mona Campus' (Rock 2013, 735). This program later developed into a full-fledged three year baccalaureate program in 1970 (Maxwell et al. 2003; Dolly-Besson et al. 1983). Today the Mona Campus also offers the MSW which was started in 1993. The second oldest program in the English-speaking Caribbean was started in 1963 by the UWI Social Welfare Training Centre in Jamaica. This developed into a four-month certificate course in social work for paraprofessionals. This program still exists today and brings together students from all over the Caribbean to train in Jamaica. Over the last three decades several other tertiary-level institutions in the Caribbean also began to offer social work programs either at the certificate, diploma or degree level. However, none of these programs are offered through schools or departments of social work. They are located in college or university departments which also offer programs in other disciplines such as political science, psychology and sociology. This presents challenges for the social work programs as they have to compete for the scarce resources available in the departments (Maxwell et al. 2003).

Context and philosophical underpinnings of social work education in the Caribbean

Social work services in the Caribbean have been growing in response to the varied social needs of the people and social work education is increasingly being seen as critical to enable the preparation of social workers for professional practice with vulnerable populations. In 2013 there are over 18 tertiary-level institutions in over 19 countries in the Caribbean region which have taken on the mandate of offering social work training. Five of these programs are located in Jamaica, four in Trinidad and Tobago and two in Barbados. With the introduction of online social work programs by UWI Open Campus in 2009, persons in 17 Eastern Caribbean countries can also have access to social work education. The programs offer various qualifications. These include the certificate in social work, the associate degree in social work, the baccalaureate and master degree and the PhD degree which is offered by two of the programs. The baccalaureate degree (BSc and not BSW) is the most common qualification offered (Baker & Maxwell 2012, 385). The certificate programs are often year long and are geared towards meeting the educational needs of paraprofessionals engaged in social work related duties. The diploma and associate degree programs are generally two years in duration and the baccalaureate programs are three years in duration if undertaken on a full-time basis. There are a few programs which offer introductory (4–6 months) certificate courses and 12 month diploma programs.

The institutions that offer social work programs in the Dutch and English-speaking Caribbean include the four campuses of the University of the West Indies (Cave Hill Campus, Barbados; Mona Campus, Jamaica; St Augustine Campus, Trinidad and Tobago; and the Open Campus), Northern Caribbean University (Jamaica), the University of the Southern Caribbean (Trinidad and Tobago), the University College of Trinidad and Tobago; the University College of the Bahamas, Barbados Community College, The Sir Arthur Lewis Community College, St Lucia, the University of Aruba, University of the Netherland Antilles (Curacao), the University of Guyana, The International University of the Caribbean (St Kitts and Nevis), Jamaica Theological Seminary, Montego Bay Community College (Jamaica), TA Marryshaw Community College (Grenada), the University of Belize, the Caribbean Nazarene College (Jamaica) and the College of Science, Technology and Applied Arts of Trinidad and Tobago (COSTAATT). The philosophical approach to the delivery of social work education as well as the curricula content of these programs differ and there are efforts by the Association of Caribbean Social Work Educators (ACSWE) to get the programs to use the Global Standards as a way of ensuring that they use basic international guidelines in the planning and delivery of social work education. The programs delivered by the four campuses of UWI are harmonised to some degree to facilitate the transfer of students from one program to another if they so desire.

At the inception of the certificate program in social work at the Mona Campus in 1961, the countries of the English-speaking Caribbean were colonies of Britain and this early course was patterned to a large extent after existing programs in social administration at universities in the UK (Watkins & Holder Dolly 2012; Maxwell et al. 2003; Dolly-Besson et al. 1983). When the Mona baccalaureate program was instituted in 1970 it also had a British orientation but 'there was a significant modification of the program in the mid-1970s bringing it more in line with the professional requirements in North America and Britain' (Maxwell et al. 2003, 13). As other programs emerged in the English-speaking Caribbean, they gravitated towards the North American approach to the preparation of students, not only because they tended to adopt the Mona model but because some of the faculty members had received their professional training in North America (Maxwell et al. 2003). Additionally, because of the dearth of Caribbean social work literature for teaching, the books and much of the materials used in the programs were authored by North American and European scholars. A decade ago Maxwell et al. (2003) cited this as a matter for concern and challenged faculty members to increase their research output as a way of producing indigenous theories and textbooks. However, the situation still exists and the lack of local empirical literature presents some epistemological challenges for the programs since students receive little grounding in the theory and concepts of the Caribbean reality that would enable them to have a greater understanding of the problems that exists in their own locales. However, it must be emphasised that Caribbean thought and experiences are being increasingly infused into the curriculum with the understanding that there are cultural considerations and challenges to fully adopting non-Caribbean paradigms and models of practice.

It should be noted, however, that a number of Caribbean social work scholars, including faculty of the University of the West Indies, have produced some excellent publications against the odds. Some have written chapters in edited social work text books and articles in journals which are disseminated internationally and there are manuals and other materials with a Caribbean focus that are produced by local social work faculty. The Association of Caribbean Social Work Educators (ACSWE) has provided two vehicles for Caribbean social work colleagues to share their research and scholarship. These are the Biennial Social Work Educators' Conference and the *Caribbean Journal of Social Work*, a peer-reviewed journal that was initially funded by a grant from the International Association of Schools of Social Work (IASSW) and the University of Connecticut, School of Social Work, US. The journal has been published since 2002 and has become a useful medium for the dissemination of indigenous social work research and other scholarly writing with a Caribbean focus (Rock 2013). However, the rallying call for Caribbean social work faculty to pursue a program of culturally relevant social work research to guide policy and build models of intervention that can fully inform practice with Caribbean populations (Maxwell et al. 2003; Rock & Valtonen 2002) still remains. A major obstacle is that the programs in the region have a small number of social work faculty members who are burdened with many teaching and related responsibilities which afford them little opportunity to engage in scholarly research and writing.

Delivery of social work education

Within UWI, social work education is delivered mainly by faculty who hold qualifications in social work. There are some PhD trained faculty but most people hold the MSW as their most advanced qualification. There is a general understanding and appreciation of the skills and knowledge base required to be a social work educator and this is considered when hiring new social work faculty members who usually have a wealth of on-the-ground experience of different kinds, which underpins their teaching. However, non-UWI programs do not follow this requirement and will employ faculty who hold a BSc and/or master's degree in psychology, in counselling or a related discipline. Thus, without a social work qualification or social work experience, people are hired as faculty to teach social work. This compromises the standards of the profession. It is a very troubling issue, and so there needs to be consensus among programs in the region about the skill set and knowledge base required for teaching in the discipline. Today many of the social work lecturers who are employed in the regional institutions have been trained in North America or the Caribbean and to a lesser extent in Europe.

An important task for ACSWE is to establish that social work education which involves students in an internship in a social service setting is the professional training for social workers. Although the length of classroom instruction and the duration of the internship may differ according to the course of study being undertaken, the internship is a most critical component of social work training. ACSWE also needs to encourage institutions that offer social work programs to use the Global Standards for the Education and Training of the Social Work Profession (www.iassw-aiets.org/global-standards-for-social-work-education-and-training 'the Global Standards') as a guide for program development, employment of staff, recruitment of students, and the organisation, administration and governance of the program. Advocacy regarding licensing and registration of social workers in the Caribbean must become the mission of trained social workers in the region.

The general aims of the social work programs offered by UWI are: (1) to create a cadre of social work trained professionals suitably qualified to intervene in the lives of persons who are vulnerable and at-risk, to motivate, empower and help these individuals lead fulfilled lives; and (2) to produce graduates who are mature, work ready, attuned to clients, who have the ability to advocate on behalf of persons for social and economic justice and who understand the nature of national, regional and global social problems. The missions of the social work programs tend to be aligned with the mission of their institutions. Although the syllabi are designed to a large extent to reflect the Caribbean reality, they also incorporate a global perspective. The curricula of the programs do vary based on the level of the qualification being offered but a generalist approach is usually adopted at the undergraduate level. The generalist approach to practice focuses on the empowerment of clients and knowledge is grounded in the strengths perspective, systems theory and ecological theory. Psychological theories are also incorporated where applicable. This generic approach to preparing students to work with individuals, families, groups and communities is useful as it exposes students to all levels of practice – micro, meso, and macro – and helps to position young graduates for the social work job market. It also equips them in a singular way to work within the local social service system, as they acquire broad skills for networking and collaborating across different areas of the human services.

The curricula of the undergraduate programs include courses in social work, psychology and sociology and core courses in social work ethics, counselling, developmental and abnormal psychology, social research and statistics, work with individuals and families, group work theory and practice, community organisation, social work administration, social policy, and human behaviour or at least some variation of these. Apart from the core social work theory and practice courses, students usually have access to a wide range of electives. These will vary from program to program but may include courses in 'crisis intervention and areas relevant to special population groups, such as abused and neglected children, the elderly, disabled, substance abusers and persons affected by and infected with HIV/AIDS. Students may also take advantage of electives offered in other disciplines' (Rock 2013, 738). This approach to training is necessary because in recent times the bachelor level graduate in the region is being sought to fill roles in many sectors such as HIV/AIDS, trauma and grief counselling, domestic violence intervention, child abuse prevention, and substance abuse management. As graduate education expands in the region, some of the jobs in these niche areas are being filled by MSW graduates.

'At both the undergraduate and graduate levels the social work course content is infused with modules on the history of the profession, human rights, social and economic justice, social work principles, values and ethics' (Rock 2013, 737). The coordinators of the programs are also encouraged to periodically renew their curricula to keep them current.

The supervised internship (practicum) in a social service agency is an important part of the social work curriculum in all programs and at all levels of certification. The structure of this practicum may vary across programs. For example, 'the curriculum of the current B.Sc. Social Work program at The University of the West Indies Cave Hill Campus in Barbados combines two years of classroom coursework and one year of field instruction' (Rock & Ring 2010) while the Mona and St Augustine campuses deliver a concurrent placement. The length of the placement (hours of work in the agency) usually varies according to the level of training – certificate versus degree. What is common is the intensive exposure of the student on internship to work with vulnerable populations and in areas such as probation and correctional services, child services, welfare and social service programs, substance abuse management, victim support, community development, HIV/AIDS, clinical services (hospital and mental health), social service administration and management, and school social work, among others. The Global Standards state that 'field education should be sufficient in duration and complexity of tasks and learning opportunities to ensure that students are prepared for practice' (Sewpaul & Jones 2004) and also that 'issues regarding cultural and ethnic diversity, and gender analysis are to be represented in the fieldwork component of the program' (10).

The internship is generally supervised by a trained faculty member and/or field placement coordinator and in each agency by an agency supervisor who is suitably qualified to support the student and provide practice guidance in the agency. However, due to the limited number of openings for internships in traditional social work agencies, students may be placed in non-traditional settings where there may not be suitably qualified practicing social workers to supervise the student. In such cases the practicum coordinator provides direct supervision to the student. The internship affords students the opportunity to engage clients in the agency setting and to 'integrate the theory learned in the classroom with practice' (Rock & Ring 2010, 177). A strong component of this internship at UWI is a weekly Field Integrative Seminar which allows students to process and assess their level of engagement in the agency, their success in applying the theory learned in the classroom to their work with clients, their own suitability for the social work profession, and benefit from peer support. As social work and psychology programs have increased in the region and as the number of students in these disciplines has grown, there is an increasing demand for supervised internships for students in social service agencies. In small countries such as Barbados this has led to great difficulty in procuring agency placements and created a need for social work students and faculty to look beyond the borders of their own country and be prepared to engage in internships in other countries of the region or internationally.

Graduate social work education is delivered mainly by the three UWI Campuses, Mona, Cave Hill and St Augustine. Graduate students are given the opportunity to pursue the MSW in clinical social work, administration and management, community and policy practice or HIV/AIDS (Baker & Maxwell 2012). A master's degree in mediation studies is also delivered under the auspices of the Social Work program at the St Augustine Campus. New MSW programs are beginning to emerge as other universities in the region are getting involved in graduate social work education.

The internationalisation of social work education

Social work programs in the English-speaking Caribbean are placing great importance on cultural relevance and working with diversity. The UWI endeavours to ensure cultural relevance and reliability by including information about the local peoples' beliefs, customs and general way of life in the social work curriculum. The Caribbean has a mix of peoples, and although most persons are of African descent, there are various ethnic groupings and indigenous populations (Baker & Maxwell 2012) and therefore social workers must be appropriately trained to work with the local populations and with cultural sensitivity.

Knowledge of the local scene and cultural underpinnings in client case management, community engagement, clinical practice in hospitals, schools and other settings is essential for the social worker. This is supported by Dominelli (2012) who states that 'emphasis on the local is important because this is the space where everyday life practices occur' (45). However, Healy (2002) notes that while working in their own countries, social workers also need to know how global issues impact their various clients, their agencies and others around them and how to deal with others who come to their countries. She also states that the practitioner comes into contact periodically with situations that require knowledge beyond the borders of his/her own country and that 'social work programs should prepare students to understand and address the local manifestations of global problems' (4). Furthermore, the local social work programs 'exist within institutions and communities that are trying to survive in the turbulent, global environment and this in itself creates a tremendous impact on the profession' (Rock 2013, 738) as it develops in the region.

Internationalisation and globalisation are terms used frequently in reference to social work education and practice. In social work education internationalisation may be introduced via the curriculum. Dominelli (2012) defines internationalisation as 'those processes whereby people interact across national borders, cultures, traditions, and everyday life routines through organisations that link the local with the global and vice-versa to promote human wellbeing through egalitarian practices' (45). There are a variety of models and possibilities when internationalising the social work curriculum (Hokenstad 2012; Healy 2012), and social work programs in the English-speaking Caribbean have approached the internationalisation of their curricula in different ways. For example, the practice models and perspectives used in the programs in the English-speaking Caribbean are of North American and/or Eurocentric origins and therefore strongly influence the delivery of social work education in the region. Additionally, international content is purposefully infused into the curriculum and students and staff are afforded opportunities for exchange and engagement to share best practices and knowledge of what is happening in the profession globally so as to maintain a global reach in the programs. Students and faculty also participate in international exchanges. Living in a global world is a factor that is increasingly emphasised through courses that include content on global development and global social issues, global models of practice and international case studies. A focus on human rights also engages students in the Caribbean in discussion on the UN international conventions and treaties.

Caribbean programs have a history of training students to work not only in their own countries and throughout the region but internationally on graduation. Apart from classroom instruction the campuses of UWI make gallant efforts to prepare students for the global marketplace including through international linkages. Many Caribbean families also have ties with relatives who have migrated and so the Caribbean social work graduate is also increasingly migrating in search of work or further study. These graduates are often recruited by agencies abroad and they need to be able to make the transition (Rock 2013). Some agencies in countries such as the US, UK, and Canada may require Caribbean graduates to pursue short courses in order to become registered and gain license to practice in their country but this is not considered a barrier. The Caribbean and International Social Work Conferences which are held in the Caribbean biennially, and the agreements and memoranda of understanding (MOUs) that are signed with other international universities and which facilitate international student and faculty exchanges also promote the internationalisation of Caribbean programs (Rock 2011). Students from the Mona, Cave

Hill and St Augustine campuses participate in international exchange programs annually. Social work educators must be aware that, in whichever part of the globe they work, their students need exposure to the world view.

Some Caribbean social work programs and by extension their faculty are members of IASSW and the North American and Caribbean Association of Schools of Social Work (NACASSW). The Cave Hill program was involved in a global group work project with international partners and the International Association of Social Work with Groups. Membership in these bodies and the presentations made by faculty from the Caribbean in International conferences, meetings and seminars foster international visibility, allow persons from the region to make a contribution to social work education at the international level and contribute to the transfer of information.

The Global Standards for Education and Training of the Social Work Profession

'The purpose of social work is to promote human wellbeing, human rights and social justice, with special attention to those who are marginalised by society, experiencing oppression, poverty or disability' (Huxtable et al. 2012, 232). The Global Standards which were adopted by IASSW and IFSW in 2004 and made available via their websites to social workers around the world promote the purpose of social work. These standards constitute guidelines for program development and are basically the ideals to which social workers and social work programs may aspire as they work towards enhancing their approach to the profession.

The social work programs in the Caribbean have been made aware of the Global Standards through various media including the IFSW (www.ifsw.org) and IASSW (www.iassw-aiets.org) websites and ACSWE. However, there is no empirical evidence that the programs, apart from those offered on the UWI campuses, have used these standards as a framework in the development of their programs or in the renewal of their curricula. The UWI programs are subject to a quality assurance review every five years and in 2006 one of the recommendations of the Social Work Self-Assessment Team for the Cave Hill Campus was that the Global Standards be shared with and reviewed by the campus administration as a way of gaining support for needed resources for program development. In the review of the social work program of the St Augustine Campus in 2011, 'the transferability between countries of quality standards for both teaching and research' (Taylor & Rock 2011, 365) was discussed. The UWI programs have therefore sought to use the standards as guidelines to help ensure that their programs are of a sufficient standard and quality that students are adequately prepared for professional practice. Careful thought is given by faculty to the core curriculum of their program and the Global Standards which address the 'domain of social work', the 'domain of the social worker', 'methods of social work practice', and the 'paradigm of the profession' provide useful information. Objectives with regards to cultural and ethnic diversity, and gender analysis, social work values and ethics and human rights are also incorporated into the curricula as suggested in the Global Standards. The Global Standards have proven to be most useful as a point of reference and to bring added credibility to small social work programs which are being delivered in small island developing states.

Conclusions

Today, almost 73 years after the recommendations of the Moyne Report, and 52 years since the first social work education program was offered at the Mona Campus, there are numerous 'state-sponsored social services created along the lines of the welfare systems found in the former or current colonial states' (Baker & Maxwell 2012, 384) throughout the Caribbean. There are also several social work education programs that are being offered by tertiary institutions. However, despite this growth in services and programs, the social work profession is still fighting for recognition in the Caribbean as many persons including politicians equate charity and voluntarism with professional social work. In fact the mindset of many persons is that the church welfare worker and other 'do-gooders' who provide assistance to the poor are social workers. This has caused some problems for the profession since social service agencies continue to hire non-social work trained personnel to perform social work duties and bachelor level trained psychology and sociology graduates are employed as social workers. While it may be useful to employ persons in allied fields to perform social work related duties in countries of the region where there are not enough professionally trained social workers, this practice is unacceptable in those places where programs are graduating social workers on an annual basis. The local professional associations often make a response to this practice as they seek to establish that social work is a profession in its own right. In Barbados the professional association has worked with government to establish various categories for the employment of persons who perform social work or social work related duties in government social service agencies. The same is true for the Jamaica Association of Social Workers (JASW www.gojasw.org) which launched the new code of ethics (gojasw.org/wp-content/uploads/213/12/COE1.pdf) for Jamaican professional social workers and allied professionals last year (June 2012). This group is now assiduously pursuing licensing and registration of its members. Although social workers are recognised for their work with vulnerable populations and their role in the creation of social policies to address social issues, they need to be licensed and registered to uphold their unique professional status.

In social work education the responsibility is to continue to train persons to the highest level in the profession and maintain accreditation of programs. This includes the delivery of quality postgraduate education (MSW and PhD) and continuing education for social work practitioners and supervisors. Thus far, there are only a few universities in the region including three of the UWI campuses which offer MSW and PhD social work programs in social work. It can be said that UWI is leading in postgraduate social work education (Baker & Maxwell 2012). Many of the other programs, although not yet ready to offer graduate level training in social work, also need to aspire to offer graduate education so that more students can study to the highest level in the profession without having to go abroad. It is also necessary for coordinators of the social work programs in the region to meet periodically to review their curricula so that programs benefit from new trends and insights and seek ways to address the regional and global demands impacting the profession as well as the emerging social issues in the region. The programs also need to work towards professional accreditation and the professional associations toward the licensing and registration of social workers in the Caribbean. Much of this is a work in progress but it will determine how and when social work will achieve professional recognition throughout the Caribbean region.

Social work in the English-speaking Caribbean emerged out of a need for equality and social justice for the people of the region. Today the programs are being encouraged to adopt a rights-based approach to practice as they intervene with individuals, families, groups and communities. The quest for social justice is critical and must affect legislation, policy and program organisation. The global agenda on social work and social development (www.iassw-aiets.org/global-agenda) challenges social workers globally to commit to a number of agenda action items including the 'promotion of social and economic equalities'.

Social work education in the Caribbean is advancing amid the challenges which include limited financial resources to deliver programs and fund research activity, a paucity of local empirical research to drive the development of indigenous theories, a limited number of professionally trained agency supervisors to supervise students on internships, few faculty members holding the PhD qualification, scarcity of social work jobs for graduates and the employment of non-social work personnel to perform social work duties in social agencies, the perceived low status of the profession, the lack of licensing and registration of social workers and the lack of an accreditation system for programs (Rock 2013; Watkins & Holder Dolly 2012).

References

Augier, F.R., Gordon, S.C., Hall, D.G. & Reckford, M. (1970). *The making of the West Indies*. Jamaica: Longman Caribbean Ltd.

Baker, P.A. & Maxwell, J. (2012). Social work in the Caribbean. In L. M. Healey & R. Link (eds), *Handbook of international social work: human rights, development and the global profession* (pp. 383–87). NY: Oxford University Press.

Dolly-Besson, J., Wint, E. & Brown, C. (1983). Social work and social development: a departmental statement. Paper presented at the UWI Faculty of Social Sciences 21st Anniversary Conference, Mona, Jamaica, 21–25 March.

Dominelli, L. (2012) Globalisation and indigenisation: reconciling the irreconcilable in social work? In K. Lyons, T. Hokenstad, M. Pawar, N. Huegler & N. Hall (eds), *The SAGE handbook of international social work* (pp. 39–55). London: SAGE Publications.

Healy, L.M. (2012). Defining international social work. In L.M. Healey & R. Link (eds), *Handbook of international social work: human rights, development and the global profession* (pp. 9–15). NY: Oxford University Press.

Healy, L.M. (2002). Internationalising the social work curriculum in the twenty-first century. *Journal of Social Work*, 1(1): 1–15.

Hokenstad, T. (2012). Social work education: the international dimension. In K. Lyons, T. Hokenstad, M. Pawar, N. Huegler & N. Hall (eds), *The SAGE handbook of international social work* (pp. 163–78). London: SAGE Publications.

Huxtable, M., Sottie, C.A. & Ulziitungalag, K. (2012). Social work and education. In K. Lyons, T. Hokenstad, M. Pawar, N. Huegler & N. Hall (eds), *The SAGE handbook of international social work* (pp. 232–48). London: SAGE Publications.

IASSW & IFSW (2004). Ethics in social work: statement of principles. Retrieved on 26 October 2013 from www.iassw-aiets.org.

Maxwell, J. (2002). The evolution of social welfare services and social work in the English-speaking Caribbean (with major reference to Jamaica). *Caribbean Journal of Social Work*, 1: 11–31.

Maxwell, J., Williams, L., Ring K. & Cambridge, E. (2003). Caribbean social work education: the University of the West Indies. *Caribbean Journal of Social Work*, 2: 11–35.

Nettleford, R. (2005). Social work for Caribbean people: perspectives from home and abroad. *Caribbean Journal of Social Work,* 4: 8–12.

Rock, L.F. (2013).The role of social work in advancing social development in the English-speaking Caribbean. *Social Work Education: The International Journal,* 32(6): 734–47. Retrieved on 21 October 2013 from dx.doi.org/10.1080/02615479.2013.809201.

Rock, L.F. (2011). Social work education in the English-speaking Caribbean: the University of the West Indies. *Social Dialogue,* 1: 48–52.

Rock, L.F. & Ring, K.A. (2010). Evaluating the one-year block placement in field instruction. *Social Work Review,* 9(4): 175–84.

Rock, L.F. & Valtonen, K. (2002). Identifying a program of social work research in the Eastern Caribbean. *Journal of Eastern Caribbean Studies.* 27(3): 49–68.

Sewpaul, V. & Jones, D. (2004). Global standards for the education and training of the social work profession. Adopted at the General Assemblies of IASSW and IFSW, Australia. Retrieved on 22 April 2014 from cdn.ifsw.org/assets/ifsw_65044-3.pdf.

Taylor, I. & Rock, L. F. (2011) Editorial. *Social Work Education: The International Journal,* 30(4): 365–66. Retrieved on 26 October 2013 from dx.doi.org/10.1080/02615479.2011.573921.

Watkins, J. & Holder Dolly, J. (2012). Social work in North America and the Caribbean. In K. Lyons, T. Hokenstad, M. Pawar, N. Huegler & N. Hall (eds), *The SAGE handbook of international social work* (pp. 166–79). London: SAGE Publications.

11

Social work education and training in southern and east Africa: yesterday, today and tomorrow

Rodreck Mupedziswa and Refilwe P. Sinkamba

In Africa, social work is considered a young profession, as it was imported from the West at the beginning of the last century. Critics have expressed concern that African social work education, because of its Western roots, lacked appropriateness and relevance. Many institutions in southern and east Africa have heeded the call to strive for relevance. Studies, however, reveal that enormous challenges have been encountered in attempts to realise relevance, while at the same time ensuring adherence to IASSW Global Standards. The impediments have included problems in generating indigenous teaching materials, lack of resources, lack of appropriate field placements, etc. Using empirical data, this paper commences by chronicling the historical development of social work education and training in Southern and East Africa, before surveying its current state, and concluding with comments on prospects for the future.

Social work education in Africa: yesterday

Social work education in Africa has a colonial heritage having been imported from the Western world, especially Europe, in the last century (Mwansa 2011; Mupedziswa 2001). There has been disgruntlement around issues of relevance and appropriateness of social work in Africa. In the 1970s, African scholars (Midgley 1981; Ragab 1982; Safari 1986; Kaseke 1991; Hall 1990; Mupedziswa 1992; Osei-Hwedie 1993b) began to express discontent regarding the type of social work that was being 'foisted' on the people of the continent. The then umbrella body for social work education and training in Africa (Association of Social Work Education in Africa (ASWEA) 1982, 11) added its voice to these concerns by observing that:

> African social work must proceed from remedial social work – foreign by nature and approach – to a more dynamic and more widespread preventive and rehabilitative action which identifies itself with African culture in particular and with the socioeconomic policies of Africa in general.

Commentators contended that to become relevant, the social work profession in Africa had to assume a developmental orientation, and this had to start at the level of education and training.

Social work education and training in Africa began in the 1930s in such countries as Egypt and South Africa. In the case of South Africa, the Jan Hofmeyer College was one of the early institutions established in 1924, while in Egypt the Higher Institute for Social Work in Cairo was among the first in 1946. In Ghana the School of Social Welfare Accra had its humble beginnings around 1946. Ten years later in 1956, the teaching of social work commenced at the University of Ghana. The 1960s saw more schools of social work being established in Africa, including the School of Social Work in Zimbabwe in 1964 and the Oppenheimer College of Social Science in Zambia which was absorbed into the University of Zambia in 1965.

The School of Social Work at the University of Khartoum in the Sudan was established in 1969. In Ethiopia, a fully fledged university department of social work was launched in 1966. The Department of Social Work, University of Botswana, was established in 1985. According to Midgley (1981, 61), by 1973 the International Association of Schools of Social Work (IASSW) had 25 schools of social work from Africa in its register. The numbers of social work education institutions have continued to increase; for example, Uganda currently boasts 21 institutions offering social work.

Programs offered

The various social work education and training institutions in Africa have offered a diversity of programs. Certainly not all of them have offered high quality qualifications in social work. Criteria used to determine quality of training have included admission requirements, length of training and affiliation to universities. On the basis of such criteria, the United Nations (1971) reported that in the 1970s there was a relatively small number of independent or university-based schools of social work in African countries, and that most of the personnel in the field were without advanced education or professional qualifications.

Some institutions could not be regarded as professional schools of social work because of the nature of their offerings. A number of African countries had community development training centres which did not train social workers per se. Thus, in Africa discrepancies were evident in terms of training standards of different institutions. There were also variations in the extent to which these different institutions conformed to international standards, guidelines and expectations. Even so, they all purported to train personnel who were expected to promote the general social welfare of the people. In Africa, the length of training and qualifications awarded by different schools of social work have clearly not been standardised (Mupedziswa 2001; Osei-Hwedie 1993b).

Overview of traditional curricula in use

In many countries in Africa, social work education and training programs were first established either by outsiders, mostly from the West who doubled as consultants, or at least with the assistance of local practitioners who had been trained in the West, hence who had a Western orientation. Consequently, the curricula that were adopted reflected the Western influence. Some of the Western countries had so much influence that they even offered generous scholarships to train students from the developing countries (Midgley 1981). Some of the scholars that were offered these scholarships, upon returning from abroad, perpetuated the Western influence.

According to Midgley (1981, 72), studies of the curricula of schools of social work in developing countries (those in Africa included) carried out in the 1960s revealed that the content of social work training in these countries conformed with Western, particularly American, approaches. The curricula of these institutions thus had many features which were in tandem with those of the Western world (Mupedziswa 2005). For example, the teaching of social work methods emphasised Western techniques and themes of case work, group work and community organisation. This observation was corroborated by Ragab (1982) and Muzaale (1987), who expressed concern over the inappropriateness of the approaches. Such an orientation of social work education would not assist students to relate theory and practice in the classroom as they acquire principles, values and ethics (Mupedziswa 2001; Mupedziswa 2005; Mwansa 2010).

Research done in this regard also made some disturbing discoveries with respect to literature used in social work education and training in Africa. Most African schools of social work were found to be dependent on Western social work literature and, sadly, few efforts had gone into developing indigenous teaching materials. Referring to the situation in Asia, Nagpaul (1972) lamented that it was unfortunate the schools of social work in that part of the world were dependent on Western literature. He admonished that the Western textbooks used had been written with a Western audience in mind. The same could be said about the African situation. As long ago as 1964 a report of a Consultant Team for the Study of Schools of Social Work in Africa (Economic Commission for Africa 1973) had similarly noted with regret that social work educators in the continent were having to consult foreign textbooks which they and the students found difficult to use as a foundation for professional training and practice and whose content was not applicable to their situation. This problem appears to have continued unabated in some institutions. Indeed, the majority of the textbooks currently in use in Africa have neither taken cognizance of indigenous social, economic and political conditions nor the contribution of African social scientists (Mwansa 2010).

Apart from classroom instruction curricula, there is also the fieldwork element. In most schools of social work in Africa, students have been placed (for fieldwork attachment) with various agencies such as government departments, hospitals, psychiatric and rehabilitation units, parastatal organisations, private industry, mines, local authorities and non-governmental organisations (NGOs). Preoccupation has been with urban placements at the expense of rural placements. Njau (1986, 93), for example, commenting on the situation at the University of Nairobi, Kenya, had this to say:

> Out of 40 weeks of fieldwork in 3 years of (degree) training, the students have an option to work in the rural areas for only 8 weeks of their second year block (fieldwork) placement, if they chose to do so. The rest of the time is spent in fieldwork in and around Nairobi.

Institutions elsewhere in the continent have had similar experiences; and while some, like Makerere University in Uganda, have taken steps to do something about this anomaly (Ankrah 1987), many others have not.

Safari (1986) has identified a number of challenges associated with choice of placements in social work education and training institutions in Africa:

1. shortage of suitable staff in agencies (i.e. to supervise students)
2. competition for a limited number of places for fieldwork
3. limited opportunities to explore suitability of agencies which take students
4. lack of suitable accommodation for students and supervisors
5. To the four problems noted above could also be added lack of financial resources which limits the placement choices (Mupedziswa 2001).

These challenges have been confirmed by researchers who recently conducted a study of 25 social work institutions in southern and east Africa (Hochfeld et al. 2009). While these challenges might be experienced in both urban and rural areas, they are mostly prevalent and acute in rural rather than urban areas.

The problem of the shortage of suitable staff to supervise students in agencies, for example, is mostly a rural phenomenon. In many African countries the vast majority of trained personnel prefer to work in urban areas, partly because of the 'urban biased' nature of the education system they went through, but also because most employment opportunities are concentrated in urban areas, and so is infrastructure.

Lack of proper accommodation for students and supervisors may be both an urban and a rural problem, but it is more acute in the rural situations. Generally students going on urban placements can easily arrange to stay with relatives and/or friends. But such an arrangement is for obvious reasons only possible in very rare occasions in rural settings. The concern about competition for a limited number of field places is more of an urban than a rural problem because, due to urban bias, fieldwork in many African countries is concentrated in urban areas.

As education and training institutions in Africa have grown and expanded, it has become more and more difficult to find placements for students. The limited budgets for fieldwork training have also made it virtually impossible to send students to places that are too far away and scattered all over the countryside. Safari (1986) echoed this concern, and explained that it is the prohibitive costs involved that make it difficult for institutions in Africa to consider rural placements. Njau (1986, 93) also expressed reservations about using rural placements, especially due to the distances involved. She noted that,

> The distance between some rural agencies and the social work training institutions (which are mainly urban based) makes it difficult for trainers to identify suitable rural fieldwork agencies and fieldwork supervisors, and they therefore prefer to place students in nearby agencies where communication and effective supervision can be carried out.

Yet as the number of social work education institutions increases, there will be a need to focus on rural placements as urban placements cannot absorb everyone. Also, as institutions move in the direction of a developmental social work approach, rural placements become an imperative.

Social work education in Africa today: debate over relevance and appropriateness

Issues around flaws of the traditional curricula spelt out above triggered the debate over relevance and appropriateness in the 1970s. Appropriateness refers to the most suitable method (of intervention in a given situation) based on an understanding of the context of the needs in the particular situation and an understanding of what would be the most effective method or combination of methods to achieve the goals of social work intervention in that situation (Willmore 1985, 24). In order to realise relevance, there is a need to employ appropriate strategies and methodologies. Without use of such appropriate strategies and methods, the goals of relevance and appropriateness would almost certainly remain a pipe dream. The two concepts (relevance and appropriateness) therefore go hand in glove.

Many commentators (e.g. Hampson 1987; Mupedziswa 1992) have argued that the concept of relevance is in itself a positive, progressive and pragmatic idea, and that it is not only a useful concept but central to the debate; hence it needs to be analysed at two related levels, namely at the level of theory and of practice. They do, however, concede that realising relevance remains a Herculean task, especially where it relates to social work in Africa in particular. The greatest concern relates to what constitutes relevant aspects and also how to realise that relevance.

As noted, the concept of relevance, as it relates to social work, can be analysed at two levels – i.e. at the theory and practice levels. The social work profession in Africa has for several decades now been embroiled in debate over how best to realise relevance. In 1971 the Fifth United Nations International Survey of Social Work Training (UN 1971) addressed the issue of relevance, acknowledging in the process the inappropriateness of American social work theories to programs of other societies. Some authors (e.g. Khinduka 1971; Lasan 1975) also addressed the issue of relevance in the context of social work theory and practice, reaching similar conclusions in as far as its central role in social work is concerned.

At the level of social work theory (i.e. education), the argument has been that efforts must be made (particularly in Africa) to come up with relevant theories that would hopefully better inform practice. Thus, relevance, when addressed in relation to theory, focuses more on the need for social work education to be appropriate to the needs of social work practice in a given situation.

When considering the concept of relevance in the context of social work practice, three basic schools of thought seem to predominate: these could be referred to as the conservative, the pragmatic, and the radical schools of thought. The conservative school would argue that there is no need to tamper with existing forms of practice which, by accident of history perhaps, happen to be Western in origin. What needs changing is the environment to enable it to suit these existing Western approaches, as basically the approaches are tested and tried, with universal appeal and application. The pragmatic approach, on the other hand, would argue, among other things, that social work scholars in the developing world should not expend energy and waste effort striving to reinvent the wheel as such but should simply work towards attempting to modify existing theories, irrespective of the fact that they originate from the West. Where a theory hails from is immaterial; what matters is its potential efficaciousness. Finally, the radical approach would dismiss the arguments presented above and urge practitioners to change strategies and models completely and come up with new approaches that are more relevant to local situations. It calls for the development of new theories better suited to situations in the developing world.

The critics of the conservative view (Ragab 1982; Midgley 1981; Ankrah 1987, etc.) argue persuasively that the most critical constraint seems to be the Western theories and methods that the social work profession in Africa has lavishly employed, and which are neither appropriate nor effective. Because the theories and methods are inappropriate then, they cannot be expected to address meaningfully the question of relevance (Chitereka 2009). The critics further note that the Western models are narrow, remedial and curative in nature; that these models tend to ignore the issue of traditional forms of welfare and hence they come short as they are not rooted in local culture, that they focus on individual pathologies (e.g. crime, prostitution, delinquency etc.) at the expense of structural issues imbued in the rubric of poverty, i.e. issues like homelessness, unemployment, etc. (Chitereka 2009; Mupedziswa 2005; Midgley 1981).

The two approaches (conservative and pragmatic) differ slightly in the way they approach the pertinent question of realising relevance. While the pragmatic approach admonishes against throwing away Western theories, as all that is needed is modification of these theories to suit local conditions (Midgley 1981), the radical approach is more revolutionary, arguing as it does that there is indeed a need to discard Western theories and methods in favour of locally developed new theories rooted in local tradition and culture (Mwansa 1992; Osei-Hwedie 1993b; Ragab 1982).

Context is also an important factor when considering the concept of relevance. It should be noted that social work practice does not occur in a vacuum; it happens in sociocultural, economic and political contexts. In fact, in countries like Egypt for instance (Walton & El Nasr 1988), the religious element is considered just as important as other related factors. The concept of relevance therefore has to be tackled in relation to a host of related factors, including sociocultural and socioeconomic contexts. Very often there has been a tendency to ignore the political dimension, important though it may be. And yet relevance can only be realisable if the political context is taken into cognisance (Ankrah 1987). It is the sum total of these various dimensions or contexts that will provide a conducive atmosphere for realisation of relevance.

Social work education in Africa today: towards a social development approach

The debate on relevance and appropriateness, meant to steer social work in Africa in the direction that will enable it to realise relevance, has culminated in calls to adopt a developmental approach. The social development package comes with a number of new concepts. The next few paragraphs consider the concept of social development, before an attempt is made to unpack some of the key related concepts.

Social development concept

Efforts to realise relevance in social work education and practice in Africa have, as noted above, culminated in calls for the adoption of a social development orientation. Social development is a relatively new and in some ways revolutionary perspective on addressing social problems. Social work educators and practitioners alike have not yet achieved consensus as to its content and practice requirements (Muzaale 1987), although scholars like Patel (2007), Midgley (1997, 1996) and Gray (1996) have made serious attempts to unpack this concept. Sanders (1982) defined social development as a process of planned institutional change to bring about a better fit between human needs and social policies and programs. The concept describes a radical change of mission, knowledge base and practice skills in social work. Muzaale (1987) added that social development can be viewed as the proposed package of social work's contribution to the redefinition of the content, objectives, methods and social structures of development. Its core skills include policy analysis, planning, community organisation, program evaluation and social advocacy. Hollister (1982) observed that the knowledge base of social development includes a mastery of the ingredients of social structures, economic structures and political structures.

The concept of developmental social work emerged in the wake of calls by African scholars for social work in Africa to move away from the remedial, residual, social control thrust to focus more attention on an approach which emphasises social change. Commentators (e.g. Muzaale 1987; Osei-Hwedie 1993b) explained that in traditional social work the emphasis had been on relief type of welfare assistance. Muzaale (1987) observed that the recent failures of development programs to reduce poverty in developing countries in general and Africa in particular had led social workers to question their own practice paradigm and redefine the purpose of development.

Social development is seen as a holistic approach to development which encourages the maximum participation of people, particularly the marginalised, in collaboration with the various agencies. Hall (1990, 149) explained that, 'A social development orientation in social work means that social work as a profession can begin to address issues of structural inequality and social disadvantage'. This view is corroborated by Elliott (2012, 103) who states that 'Social development offers a progressive model of social work practice with goals of social justice, and empowerment of the oppressed, the marginalised, or excluded population'. The approach is preventive and proactive rather than remedial and reactive, aiming at long-term change for the benefit of the majority of a country's population. Social development advocates for self-reliance and participation, and stresses the need for enhancement of people's capacity to work for their own welfare and that of the society. Thus, empowerment and capacity building are considered important elements in this approach (Mupedziswa 1988, 2001).

Paira (1982) postulated that the broad mission of social development is to contribute to the emergence and maintenance of a society in which organisations and institutions are more sensitive and responsive to human needs. This contention is corroborated by de Graaf (1986) who emphasised the element of people's control over their resources. He argued that social development should involve the capacity of the people to control, utilise and increase their resources, adding that a community which does not control its infrastructural arrangements can be a victim of external factors.

Selected concepts in social development perspective

There are a number of concepts which are in tandem with a social development orientation to which social work education in Africa has been urged to pay particular focus; namely indigenisation, authentisation, radicalisation, reconceptualisation and recontextualisation. Commentators have argued that all these concepts ought to be viewed not as multifarious strategies but merely as tools for achieving the same goal – that of realising relevance through promotion of the social development approach.

Indigenisation: this is a concept characterised by appropriateness, which means professional social work must be appropriate to the needs of different countries (Midgley 1983, 170). Shawkey (1972, 3) has referred to indigenisation as a process of adapting imported ideas to fit local needs. Indigenisation therefore emphasises modification of imported ideas to fit local needs. African scholars who subscribe to this view do not call for a reinvention of the wheel (Mupedziswa 1992), but rather, adaptation of existing methods and theories with a view to making them more relevant to the needs of Africa. Critics (e.g. Hall 1990) have argued that indigenisation simply entails modification of existing models of social work, to suit different cultural contexts, and this may not be sufficient. The critics would prefer to see much more than the apparently 'cosmetic' changes implied in indigenisation.

Authentisation: Ragab (1982, 21) defines authentisation as, 'The identification of genuine and authentic roots in the local system, which would be used for guiding its (i.e. the community's) future development in a mature, relevant and original fashion'. It refers to the creation or building of a 'domestic model of social work' (Walton & El Nasr 1988, 136) in light of the social, political and economic characteristics of a particular country. The approach contends that each country should develop its own theory and practice, based on its own experience, for its own use. This new thinking admonishes social work training institutions and practitioners alike to be wary of applying social work principles from the West indiscriminately, without due regard for appropriateness. Critics, however, regret that the approach is too theoretical and hence unworkable. They argue that the building of a domestic social work implies reinvention of the wheel, which is a total waste of resources (Mupedziswa 1992). Proponents of this view have been accused by some scholars of being 'fundamentalist' in their approach to issues, as evidenced by some of the jargon they employ.

Reconceptualisation: this concept relates to the reformulating of concepts so that they fall in line with efforts to empower the marginalised groups in society. The term has its roots in Latin America where it was influenced by the work of Paulo Freire's conscientisation approach and also liberation theology. It denotes building new 'constructs' on the basis of these observations. Osei-Hwedie (1993a) observed that reconceptualisation 'makes room for adaptation and modification of old ideas, knowledge and process of practice as well as the emergence of new ones, all in the effort towards appropriateness of social work professional education and practice'. Reconceptualisation aims to raise the consciousness of individuals and society. Activities incorporated in the reconceptualisation concept include consciousness raising, training, organising and social mobilisation, with the basic aim of liberation of the human being. In the context of this approach, schools of social work would be expected to organise programs in such a way that they work critically with organisations and institutions that serve the masses (Molina 1992), achieving a dialectic interaction of theory and practice and developing a new image of social work in the social consciousness by society; a school which responds totally to the realities of the present.

Radicalisation: this refers to a disposition to make a marked departure from the usual or the tradition to effecting extreme changes in existing views, behaviours, conditions or institutions (Ankrah 1987). Radicalisation has to do with getting to the root of issues in social development. It thus refers to developing a practice paradigm with African roots. Ankrah (1987, 9) argues, 'To radicalise roles is to prescribe behaviours that directly address the conditions of Africa, not those pervading elsewhere'. The calls for radicalisation have come in the wake of a realisation that the models currently operational in Africa are at best ineffective, and at worst weak and inappropriate. Mwansa (1992, 2) observed that for social work to be meaningful to the process of social development in Africa today, it must depart from its current liberal manner of practice to adopt a more pragmatic, radical approach. Ankrah (1987) opined that there is an imperative that African social work finds a way from the slavish replication of inherited forms. Critics have, however, dismissed it as a Marxist approach which by definition is violent and whose ultimate aim is the overthrow of the existing sociopolitical institutions. Others view it as being a method of confrontation and a violent way to bring about change.

Recontextualisation: this focuses attention on attempts to put social work in Africa into its proper perspective (Mupedziswa 2005). It attempts to achieve this by urging the social work profession to revisit the conditions and circumstances under which social work is taught and practiced in the continent, with a view to recasting its orientation (Mupedziswa 2001). The concept urges social workers to consider alternative forms of operation, based on an analysis of various factors in the local social system, including power and the constellation of forces at work in a given situation. It further urges the profession in Africa (as elsewhere) to select those alternatives that are likely to deal most effectively with a particular situation and circumstances (Molina 1992). Recontextualisation calls for vigilance on the part of the social work profession in Africa, to ensure the profession is not caught unprepared for this. The term also implies that practice is determined by theoretical considerations based on having put each problem in its proper context in terms of social, economic, cultural and political considerations. Critics, however, observe that there is very little if anything to distinguish this concept from the others discussed before it.

Challenges in promoting the developmental social work approach in Africa

Over the last few decades, many social work education and training institutions in Africa have heeded the call to move in the direction of developmental social work. A study by Hochfeld et al. (2009) entitled 'Developmental social work education in Southern and East Africa' found that all 25 institutions of social work education that responded to the study (including those from Ethiopia, Tanzania, Uganda, South Africa (Rwanda) had aligned their programs in the direction of a developmental social work approach. However, they all reported facing challenges of different types, and these are considered below.

One challenge related to the fact that there is a general lack of indigenous materials for use in schools of social work in Africa. Social work literature used in African institutions is Westernised material from Europe, America, Australia and other countries. Consequently, students and educators remain frustrated because the literature used is unable to appreciate African culture and its diversity (Mwansa 2011). Hence, the call to synthesise the Western theories and models based on African values and culture in an effort to have an appropriate social work education that is specific to the African population (Mwansa & Kreitzer 2012). Due to the nature of the curriculum that is heavily Westernised, there is a lack of fitness-for-purpose between social work education and the service needs of the communities (Hutton & Mwansa 1996; Mupedziswa 2005, 2001).

Curricula which lack relevance have been noted to be a major problem in most social work institutions in Africa. This problem is critical, particularly given that it is the curriculum that will ultimately determine the type of graduate who will be churned out. Graduates who are trained using inappropriate curricula are likely to turn out to be a liability to the social work profession in the continent as they might perpetuate inappropriate forms of social work. Such graduates are also likely to show little commitment to change. It has been observed that Africa lacks curriculum experts who would normally assist in curriculum development efforts. Agouba (1976, 54) corroborated this by noting that there was limited expertise for curriculum design and also often different understandings of the concept of social work among African social work educators.

In most African countries the number of social workers that graduate each year is negligible. In addition, there has been the perennial problem of the 'brain drain' (Mupedziswa & Ushamba 2006). A few countries (e.g. in the Great Lakes Region) still do not have social work (professional) training programs of their own. Thus, limited output of trainees is a problem which often has a ripple effect in the African continent. The build-up of training resources in the field of social work in Africa thus ensures just a minimum supply of workers required in the existing social work field.

The problem of inadequate resources is not unique to the field of social work in Africa. However, in the social work education field, this problem has often severely impeded programs. In many African countries the classrooms are cramped and equipped with inadequate or inappropriate materials for meaningful learning. Agouba (1976, 54), writing a few decades ago, pointed out that lack of adequate funds to improve, promote and expand training, or to increase staff numbers, were common problems in many schools of social work in Africa. The situation has hardly changed over the years. The shortage of staff has sometimes resulted in part-time educators being recruited, but some of them may not have the correct orientation or commitment to the goals of appropriateness and relevance. Many schools of social work in Africa, because of shortage of resources, depend largely on donated books from the West, some of which are old editions, besides being inappropriate for the local situation (Mupedziswa 2001). A further problem is that although local materials are increasingly becoming available, many of these remain unpublished due to limited resources.

Similarly, there is limited research carried out locally that can be used as literature for the classroom (Mwansa 2010). Coupled with this are challenges regarding the class assignments given to the students. The Western literature provides case studies that are totally different from the actual scenarios in Africa, and this often poses a great challenge when students are faced with cases during practice, as some of the theories learned are not applicable there. There is a need for transformation of social work education with a view to reorienting the curricular and teaching methods to synthesise with indigenous information so that social work can be effective and relevant (Osei-Hwedie & Rankopo 2008).

Schools of social work in Africa have also often had to grope in the dark as a result of unclear national policies with regard to the position and role of the social work profession. Some governments, because they are not well acquainted with this relatively young human service profession, have tended to at worst ignore the profession completely, and at best do little to acknowledge this profession's pertinent role in national development. In instances where governments support tertiary education through loans and grants, sometimes social work students have been discriminated against through either lack of support or inadequate support (Mupedziswa 2005).

The lack of well defined, stable social policies in various African countries has also caused problems in terms of designing training programs that will address national needs.

Ideally, it is on the basis of clear social policies that schools of social work can attempt to base or relate education and training of their professionals. Because of such constraints, however, social work education sometimes lags behind and inadequately responds to the pressing problems faced in the continent.

There are often two types of Western trained personnel teaching in social work institutions in Africa today. One category comprises the expatriates, born, bred and trained in the West, who make their way to Africa for a variety of motives. While some are motivated by a genuine desire for cross-fertilisation of ideas and experiences and a desire to help in the development and promotion of social work education in Africa, others may come for adventure and even personal aggrandisement. It is the latter category that has set the clock backwards where advancement of relevant social work education in the continent is concerned. However, even with those who are committed, who mean well, sometimes their Western bias and background has not helped matters where issues of appropriateness of models of education and training are concerned.

The second category relates to social work educators who are locally bred but who opt to go and train as social workers in the West. Many of these are wittingly or unwittingly influenced by their Western training, and have at times wrought havoc where attempts to promote appropriate local education programs are concerned. Again while some such persons genuinely believe their Western training is superior, and hence Western oriented social work programs should prevail in Africa, others will be committed to change but, unwittingly, their Western background will distort their good intentions. It must be stressed that not all African social work educators trained in the West suffer from this effect; there are some who have used their Western training to advantage by employing that knowledge to critically look at local conditions and proceeding to do something about these. However, this breed of Western trained local educators who have kept their heads above water is very rare in Africa.

Social work in Africa tomorrow: the way forward

Social work education and training in Africa has come a long way. The profession, however, suffers from lack of relevance and appropriateness in terms of practice knowledge, value base, philosophy and ideology. There have been concerted calls for these institutions to adopt a developmental social work approach in order to realise relevance. Many of the institutions have heeded this call and have proceeded to embrace the developmental approach. Naturally they have encountered challenges along the way. What is encouraging though is that many of the institutions have tried to do something in terms of addressing the challenges. Clearly, social work educators in Africa have to be proactive in the struggle for their profession to realise relevance. Only in that way can the tomorrow of social work in Africa be expected to be bright.

References

Agouba, M. (1976). 'Africa' in social realities and the social work response. NY: IASSW.

Ankrah, M. (1987). Radicalising roles for Africa's development: some evolving practice issues. Journal of Social Development in Africa, 2(2): 17–29.

Association of Social Work Education in Africa (ASWEA) (1982). *Survey of curricula of social development training institutions in Africa*. Addis Ababa, Ethiopia: ASWEA.

Chitereka, C. (2009). Social work practice in the developing continent: the case of Africa. *Advances in Social Work*, 10(2): 144–56.

de Graaf, M. (1986). Catching fish or liberating man: social development in Zimbabwe. *Journal of Social Development in Africa*, 1(1): 7–26.

Economic Commission for Africa (1973). Preliminary survey for the establishment of a regional training research centre for social development in Africa. Addis Ababa, Ethiopia: Economic Commission for Africa.

Elliott, D. (2012). Social development and social work. In L. Healy & R. Link (eds), *International social work: human rights, development, and the global profession* (pp. 102–08). NY: Oxford University Press.

Gray, M. (1996). Towards an understanding of developmental social work. *Social Work Practice*, 1(96): 9–12.

Hall, N. (1990). *Social work training in Africa: a fieldwork manual*. Harare: Journal of Social Development in Africa.

Hampson, J. (1987). Realising relevance. *Journal of Social Development in Africa*, 2(2): 2–4.

Hochfeld, T., Mupedziswa, R., Chitereka, C. & Selipsky, L. (2009). Developmental social work education in Southern and East Africa. Centre for Social Development in Africa, University of Johannesburg.

Hollister, D. (1982). The knowledge and skills bases of social development. In D. Sanders (ed.), *The developmental perspective in social work* (pp. 16–23). Honolulu: University of Hawaii School of Social Work.

Hutton, M. & Mwansa, L.K. (1996). *Social work practice in Africa: social development in a community context*. Gaborone: Print Consult.

Kaseke, E. (1991). Social work practice in Zimbabwe. *Journal of Social Development in Africa*, 6(1): 33–45.

Khinduka, S.K. (1971). Social work in the Third World. *Social Science Review*, 45(1): 14–23.

Lasan, D.B. (1975). Indigenisation with a purpose. *International Social Work*, 18(1): 76–94.

Midgley, J. (1997). *Social development*. London: SAGE Publications.

Midgley, J. (1996). The developmental perspective in social welfare: transcending residual and institutional models. *Social Work Practice*, 1(96): 2–8.

Midgley, J. (1981). *Professional imperialism: social work in the Third World*. London: Heinemann.

Molina, L. (1992). Poverty and transformation: advances and new themes in social work education and practice in Latin America. In International Associational of Schools of Social Work (ed.), *New reality of poverty and struggle for social transformation. Plenary papers and abstracts of 25th International Congress of Schools of Social Work, Lima, Peru* (pp. 66–71). Vienna: International Associational of Schools of Social Work.

Mupedziswa, R. (2005). Challenges and prospects of social work services in Africa. In J.C. Akeibunor & E.E. Anugwom (eds), *The social sciences and socio-economic transformation in Africa* (pp. 271–317). Nsukka: Great AP Express Publishing.

Mupedziswa, R. (2001). The quest for relevance towards a conceptual model of development social work education and training in Africa. *International social work*, 44(3): 285–300.

Mupedziswa, R. (1992). Africa at the crossroads: major challenges for social work education and practice towards the year 2000. *Journal of Social Development in Africa*, 7(2): 19–38.

Mupedziswa, R. (1988). Popular participation as a strategy for empowerment and capacity building among underprivileged groups: the case of Zimbabwe. In C. Guzzetta & F. Mittwoch (eds), *Social development and social rights* (pp. 12–19). Vienna: International Association of Schools of Social Work.

Mupedziswa, R. & Ushamba, A. (2006). Challenges and prospects: social work practice in Zimbabwe in an environment of economic meltdown. In N. Hall (ed.), *Social work: making a world of difference* (pp. 163–172). Oslo: International Federation of Social Workers & Fafo.

Muzaale, P. (1987). Rural poverty, social development and their implications for fieldwork practice. *Journal of Social Development in Africa*, 2(1): 75–87.

Mwansa, L.K. (2011). Social work education in Africa: whence and whither? *Social Work Education*, 30(1): 4–16.

Mwansa, L.K. (2010). Challenges facing social work in Africa. *International Social Work*, 53(1): 129–36.

Mwansa, L.K. (1992). Radical social work practice: the case of Africa. Paper presented at the Department of Social Work, National Field Supervisors Seminar, the University of Botswana, Gaborone.

Mwansa, L. & Kreitzer, L. (2012). Social work in Africa. In K. Lyons, T. Hokenstad, M. Pawar, N. Huegler & N. Hall (eds), *The SAGE handbook of international social work* (pp. 393–407). London: SAGE Publications.

Nagpaul, H. (1972). The diffusion of America social work education to India: problems and issues. *International Social Work*, 15(3): 13–17.

Njau, W.P. (1986). Social development training with special reference to rural fieldwork. In J. Hampson & B. Willmore (eds), *Social development and rural fieldwork* (pp. 13–20). Harare: School of Social Work.

Osei-Hwedie, K. & Rankopo, M. (2008). Developing culturally relevant social work education in Africa: the case of Botswana. In M. Gray, J. Coates & M. Yellow Bird (eds), *Indigenous social work around the world: toward culturally relevant education & practice* (pp. 203–19). Aldershot, UK: Ashgate.

Osei-Hwedie, K. (1993a). Putting the 'social' back into 'work': the case for the indigenisation of social work practice and education in Africa. Special report. Cape Town: Institute of Indigenous Theory and Practice.

Osei-Hwedie, K. (1993b). The challenge of social work in Africa: starting the indigenisation process. *Journal of Social Development in Africa*, 8(1): 19–30.

Patel, L. (2007). Social development and curriculum renewal in an African context. *The Social Worker Practitioner–Researcher*, 17(3): 363–77.

Paira, J. (1982). Dynamics of social development and social work. In D. Sanders (eds), *The developmental perspective in social work*. Hawaii: University of Hawaii School of Social Work.

Ragab, I.A. (1982). *Authentization of social work in developing countries*. Tanta: Integrated Social Services Project.

Safari, J. (1986). The role of fieldwork in the training of social workers. In J. Hampson & B. Willmore (eds), *Social development and rural fieldwork* (pp. 27–33). Harare: School of Social Work.

Sanders, D. (ed.) (1982). *The developmental perspective in social work*. Hawaii: University of Hawaii School of Social Work.

Shawkey, A.M. (1972). Social work education in Africa. *International Social Work*, 15(3): 38–46.

United Nations. (1971). *Training for social welfare. Fifth international survey: new approaches in meeting manpower needs*. NY: United Nations, Department of Economic and Social Affairs.

Walton, R. & El Nasr, M. (1988). Indigenisation and authentisation in terms of social work in Egypt. *International Social Work*, 31(2): 28–47.

Willmore, B. (1985). Training for flexibility in choice of method in social work practice. Case study. Master's in Social Work research report. University of Zimbabwe, Harare.

12

The current status and future challenges of social work education in South Korea

In-young Han and Jung-won Lim

> The growth in the number of social workers in the past six decades has been accompanied by a dramatic shift in social work education in South Korea. However, the quality of social work education was not fully considered. Thus, this chapter sets out the history and current status of social work education in South Korea, and discusses the contemporary challenges and the future of social work education in South Korea. First, current status and issues regarding academic programs, curricula, field education, and the social work licensure system are addressed. The challenges for social work education in South Korea are then discussed. The areas of accreditation reviews to verify each program, course development beyond the licensure examination, the improvement in the quality of field education, and efforts to improve social work competencies are all then examined.

A social work education program was first established at Ewha Womans University in the middle of the 20th century with a limited number of classes in casework (Hong, Kim, Lee & Ha 2011). Since then, social work and welfare in South Korea has grown rapidly. According to the *Korean social work statistical yearbook* (Korea Association of Social Workers 2012), there were 556 graduate and 482 undergraduate programs in social work and social welfare, and 505 vocational schools offered a specialised program in social work in 2010. Recently, web-based social work education as well as continuing education programs have been expanding. Approximately 57 web-based 'cyber colleges' and 66 continuing education centres offer social work education. Nationally, there is a significant number of general social service agencies, as well as social welfare agencies for specific populations (i.e. people with disabilities, the elderly); these agencies have a significant role in a variety of settings within the social work educational field. These programs produced 492 social work educators (faculty members), and a total of 110,082 licensed social workers who hold a level 1 social work certification in 2013. Of these licensed social workers, 751 mental health social workers, 666 medical social workers, and some school social workers are working toward obtaining additional certificates in specific settings.

In accordance with the current numbers of academic programs, field education settings, educators, and licensed social workers, there are numerous issues and challenges for social work education in South Korea. These challenges may be a consequence of social work scholars' concerns about the rising number of social work education programs and the concurrent changes in social welfare policy and social problems in South Korea. Koreans in the social work profession have made short- and long-term commitments to manage the diverse social problems in Korea; thus, the social work profession can be said to be in a development phase. At the same time, social work education is expected to expand continuously to address diverse learning needs and to provide high-quality educational opportunities. The recognition of recent changes and challenges in social work education as well as the attempts to improve social work education in South Korea may help to establish the legitimacy of the field in terms of official educational standards. The purpose of this chapter is to describe the history and current status of social work education in South Korea and to discuss the contemporary challenges and the future of its social work education. Issues related to academic programs, curricula, field education, and the social work licensure system will be addressed.

The history of Korean social work education

The first social work education program began at the Ewha Womans University in 1947. Since then, several universities in South Korea (e.g. Kangnam University, Seoul National University) have established departments of social work. Social work education in South Korea has been modified to respond to education reforms, but the underlying values and functions of social work undergo gradual changes. Generally, Korean social work education can be categorised into three stages: (1) the Department of Social Work era (1950–1960); (2) the Department of Social Welfare era (1970–1980); and (3) the Department of Family, Society, and Welfare era (1990–current).

The Department of Social Work era

An important trait of Korean social work education is that the department of social work was created before social welfare policies and standards of clinical practice were established. This characteristic differentiates South Korea from other nations, such as the United States or Japan, where the principles of social work practice and social work education were established before social work education was implemented. Lee and Nam (2005) argue that Koreans simply imported the social work education system of the United States, as if they were transplanting an organ, without considering how the clinical experiences, experiments and research, philosophies and social movements would apply in a South Korean context. However, the system was also imported for a practical reason: during the first stage of social work education, many Korean educators obtained doctoral degrees in the United States and were then hired at universities in South Korea. Their employment at universities stimulated the development of a new social work education system that was based on the missions of schools of social work in the United States. Thus, courses on the traditional social work practices, ethics and values in the United States have been included in the social work curriculum. For example, casework, group work, community-based organisation, human rights and social justice were required topics in social work education during this stage. However, there were limitations on the ability to practice social work skills and values in the South Korean cultural context: social services in the public and private sectors were not linked to social work education, and people in social work service agencies did not fully understand the social work service delivery systems or social work education.

The Department of Social Welfare era

In the 1970s, South Korea made significant efforts to achieve economic growth, and the South Korean Government prioritised the economic development of poor communities. In response, social work students focused on volunteer activities to promote development in poor communities, which is one aspect of social work practice. While social work education programs in the United States focused on integrative social work methods in the 1970s, the core content in social work education programs in South Korea continued to include traditional social work practices, such as individual, group, and community-based organisational practices. This trend continued until the middle of the 1990s, and many Korean educators learned through trial and error (Lee & Jung 2012). When politics and values in South Korea gradually shifted toward supporting the welfare society, several social work educators began discussing their educational identities. During this stage, the number of social work programs in South Korea increased rapidly, and social work education in the United States emphasised the interaction between micro and macro social work practices. In colleges and universities in South Korea, departments of social work became departments of social 'welfare'.

The Department of Family, Society, and Welfare: the globalisation era

As the open education movement grows in South Korea, new education systems have emerged, including the school system (called 'hack-boo-jae' in Korean), the double-major system, and minimum-grade-for-credit system. During this stage, the number of private universities has increased significantly as higher education has been popularised in South Korea. While social work education in the United States has been implemented at the master's level, social work education in South Korea has primarily focused on undergraduate programs that are based on the school system and the minimum-grade-for-credit system. Consequently, one challenge has been to effectively provide social work knowledge, skills, and abilities that balance micro and macro practical approaches, theory and practice, and science and skills with an education that includes social work values, philosophies and ethics. This situation has caused confusion regarding the identities and professionalism of social work and welfare academics and education programs; thus, diverse changes have been made in social work policies and the new licensure system which embrace status-related and organisational tactics. That is, according to the Social Welfare Service Act, the social work licensing examination has been administered by the government since 2003. With the diverse changes in social work education, the number of programs has increased to more than 550 graduate and 480 undergraduate programs in social work and social welfare. These programs have produced more than 70,000 social workers who work in diverse areas of social work practice, including the micro, mezzo, and macro sectors.

The current status of social work education in South Korea

Academic programs

There are several types of social work education programs in South Korea. At the bachelor's level, four-year and two-year colleges provide social work education. At the master's level, professional graduate programs, general graduate programs, and special graduate programs offer social work and welfare courses for professional or academic social workers. As another vehicle of social work education, web-based educational institutes, which are known as 'cyber colleges', deliver academic programs completely online. Continuing education programs offer a broad spectrum of post-secondary learning activities, and programs provide social work education to non-traditional students who require non-degree career training, workforce training, or formal personal enrichment courses. Because each program has a different mission and different goals and values, the quality of the academic courses, field practices, educators and students varies. For example, social work programs that are provided by two-year colleges, cyber colleges and continuing education institutions are designed to produce personnel who can work in general social service agencies. These programs tend to provide social work education so that students can meet the minimum academic requirements to obtain a level 2 social work certification. Although the duties performed by social workers holding a level 2 social work certification are similar to those of social workers holding a level 1 social work certification (e.g. counselling, referral, program development, policy proposals, etc.), social workers holding a level 2 social work certification do not have opportunities such as higher-level promotions, higher salaries, management/supervision, and establishment of social work agencies. Thus, because the missions and values of social work education programs differ, the quality of social work education depends on the educational setting.

Table 12.1 shows the numbers of academic programs that provided social work education in 2007 and 2010. According to the *Korean social work statistical yearbook* (2012), the number of departments of social welfare increased to 31 in 2010, and the number of departments that are similar to social welfare increased to 242. The number of social welfare educational agencies increased by 130% from 2007 to 2010. While the quality of social work education differs according to the type of academic setting or program, the significant increases in the number of social work education programs indicate that social work has been integrated into Korean culture, and social work education is continuing to expand in South Korea.

Social work curriculum

The Korean Council on Social Welfare Education (KCSWE) currently attempts to standardise the social work curriculum, as the official educational standards did not appropriately guide the social work curricula in colleges and universities. For example, in many social work programs, the link between theory and practice is weak, and there is often no attempt to combine academic education with field education. In fact, one responsibility of the KCSWE is to evaluate and accredit undergraduate and graduate social work and welfare programs; however, the KCSWE is not currently conducting accreditation reviews to verify that each program is appropriate.

Table 12.1 Social work education programs in South Korea in 2007 and 2010 (Korean social work statistical yearbook 2012).

		Departments of social welfare (social work)		Departments of social welfare–related majors		Total	
		2007	2010	2007	2010	2007	2010
Professional colleges		51	71	60	434	111	505
Two-year and four-year colleges		115	147	93	335	209	482
Graduate schools	General	51	65	10	165	61	227
	Special	90	118	81	189	171	307
	Professional	8	10	16	12	24	22
Cyber colleges	Two-year college	2	1	6	7	8	8
	Four-year college	13	11	12	38	25	49
Total		331	423	278	1177	609	1600

Nevertheless, the KCSWE recommended 35 courses for achieving the required competencies for the social work profession. The recommendations serve as a resource for social work educators in curriculum development. In addition, the 35 courses help students who are enrolled in a minor in social work or who are interested in obtaining a social work degree through a continuing education program to obtain the eligibility requirements for a level 2 social work certification. Generally, the courses are categorised into four domains: (1) required courses that prepare students for the social work licensure examination, (2) required courses with material that is not included on the social work licensure examination, (3) elective courses, and (4) optional courses. The first domain refers to the required courses that are included in the social work licensure examination as eligibility requirements for a level 1 social work certification (e.g. Human Behavior and Social Environment, Social Work Practice, etc.). The second domain refers to courses that are required for credits but are not included in the social work licensure examination, but students who would like to obtain a level 2 social work certification are encouraged to take these courses (e.g. Introduction to Social Welfare and Social Work Field Instruction). The third domain includes elective courses that should be taken for credits to obtain a level 2 social work certification, and students are required to take at least four courses (e.g. Family Welfare, Social Work Practice for the Elderly, etc.). Finally, there are several optional courses that are neither required nor elective. Certain social work programs offer these courses based on students' needs and national and international trends (e.g. Family Therapy, Poverty, etc.). Courses categorised into each domain are detailed in Table 12.2.

Table 12.2 Required and elective courses in social work and welfare program courses (Korea Association of Social Workers 2012).

	Courses
Required courses (examination courses)	Human Behaviour and Social Environment
	Research Methods for Social Welfare
	Social Work Practice
	Skills & Techniques for Social Work Practice
	Community-based Social Services and Practice
	Social Welfare Policy, Social Welfare Administration
	Introduction to Social Welfare Law
Required courses (non-examination courses)	Introduction to Social Welfare
	Social Work Field Instruction
Elective courses	Family Welfare, Correctional Social Welfare
	Social Work Practice for the Elderly
	The Study of Social Problems, Social Security
	History of Social Welfare, Social Welfare Ethics
	Statistics for Social Welfare, Child Welfare
	Volunteer Management, Social Welfare for the Handicapped
	Mental Health, Social Work in Mental Health
	Social Welfare for the Youth
	Program Development and Evaluation, School Social Work
Optional courses	Family Therapy, Poverty, Theories of Welfare States
	Case Management

Field education

Field education is an integral part of the social work and welfare programs in South Korea. According to section 2.1 of the Enforcement Ordinance of Social Welfare Service Act, corporations, institutes, agencies and groups that are related to social work and welfare are used as field instruction sites. To qualify as a field supervisor, social workers should (1) hold a level 1 social work certification and have at least three years of social work experience or (2) hold a level 2 social work certification and have at least five years of social work experience. A minimum of 120 hours of field experience is required, and a maximum of three credits can be earned for one field placement. Generally, students can decide whether to complete the field placement during the summer/winter vacation or during an academic period (spring/fall). If the students are engaged in the field placement during an academic period, they are required to work eight hours per week and can complete their placement after a minimum of 120 hours. If students are in the field during a vacation, they are required to work eight hours per day and five days per week to complete the minimum 120 hours (Korea Association of Social Workers 2010).

The field education standards for social work and welfare programs are that field settings should provide social work education from qualified field supervisors. The basic field supervisor qualification is a level 1 social work certification. Field supervisors with a master's degree are required to have taken the field practice course at least one time during their academic program. Additionally, field supervisors should have at least 5 years of post-master's social work experience and should have supervisory experience. Field supervisors with a doctoral degree are required to have taken the field practice course at least one time during their academic program and should have at least one year of post-master's social work experience that included supervisory experience.

Generally, the field practice experience begins with the basic tasks of field experience and clinical practice, including orientation and administrative tasks. The orientation includes an introduction to agencies and regions, client-related practices, the attitudes and roles of students, the overall schedule, and assignments. In addition, the preparation and submission of case and daily reports are reviewed. The administrative tasks are associated with the management and preparation of agency operations and budgets as well as decision-making processes. Next, the students are engaged in diverse activities, including case management, individual and group therapy and programs, community-based social work practice and organisation, and social development. The content of social work field practices is dependent on students' preferences and on the needs of social service agencies. Students may be actively involved in individual counselling, family counselling and therapy, social surveys, or community-based approaches. During the field experience, students are required to submit progress notes for case interventions and daily activity notes. Table 12.3 indicates the number of students who were engaged in field experiences in 2012.

Social work licensure system

The major focus of social work education in South Korea has been to prepare students for the social work licensure examination (Hong et al. 2011). According to section 11.3 of the Enforcement Ordinance of Social Welfare Service Act, the Korean Government requires that people take a national examination to obtain a level 1 social work certification. For a level 2 social work certification, undergraduate students take at least 10 required courses and four elective courses related to social work and welfare, which is the equivalent of a bachelor's degree. Graduate students must major in social welfare or social work (other majors are not allowed) and take six required courses and two elective courses, and they must complete one social work field experience; this coursework is equivalent to a master's or doctoral degree. The required courses for the social work licensure examination are grouped into three categories: (1) basic social welfare (i.e. Human Behavior and Social

Table 12.3 Average number of students engaged in social work field practice in 2012 (*Korean social work statistical yearbook* 2012).

		The number of schools	%
Average number of students engaged in social work field practice per semester (N=479)	Mean (SD)	67.11 (95.88)	
Average number of students in charge of social work field practice per faculty	≤10	100	20.9
	11~30	209	43.7
	31~50	106	22.2
	51~100	53	11.1
	>100	10	2.1
	Total	478	100.0

Environment/ Research Methods for Social Welfare); (2) social work practices (i.e. Social Work Practice, Skills & Techniques for Social Work Practice, Community-based Social Services and Practices); and (3) social welfare policy (i.e. Social Welfare Policy, Social Welfare Administration, Introduction to Social Welfare Law). The Social Welfare Service Act in South Korea requires that social workers receive at least eight social work continuing education credits per year to maintain the social work certification. The continuing education system caters to professionals at different levels and in different careers. Figure 12.1 indicates the number of licensed social workers in South Korea.

With the general social work licensure examination, several specialties, such as mental health social workers, medical social workers, and school social workers, have established their own certification and training programs. For example, to obtain the level 2 mental health social work certification, the Korean Association of Mental Health Social Workers (KAMHSW) requires that students receive at least one year of training in mental health education agencies after passing the social work licensure examination. In the training agencies that are assigned by the Ministry of Health and Welfare, the trainees should receive a total of 1000 hours of training, including 150 hours for theoretical education, 830 hours for practical education, and 20 hours for academic activities. The level 1 mental health social workers should hold at least a master's degree in social work/welfare and must be trained by mental health professional agencies for at least 3 years. After obtaining a level 2 certification, trainees should receive at least five years of training in mental health agencies, a mental health centre, social rehabilitation facilities, long-term mental health facilities, an alcohol counselling centre, or other counselling centres. Trainees should also obtain more than 20 points related to mental health academic activities and pass the qualification test of the Korean Association of Mental Health.

In 2008, the Korean Association of Medical Social Workers (KAMSW) established a certification system for the purposes of enhancing the professionalism of social workers in health care settings, providing differentiated health care services, and managing the quality of health care services. In addition, the KAMSW organises the training system for trainees who want to work in medical care settings.

School social workers have received school social work education and training in addition to field experiences in school social work settings, but the Korean Government does not provide any qualification regulations for school social workers. As a private section, the qualification committee in school social work permits people who have trained at least 20 hours per year to commit to being a school social worker.

Associations for social work education

Three associations represent social work education: (1) the Korean Council on Social Welfare Education (KCSWE), (2) the Korea National Council on Social Welfare (KNCSW), and (3) the Korea Association of Social Workers (KASW). Each association has a different mission and plays a different role in improving the quality of social work education in South Korea. We will briefly introduce the major activities and primary roles of each association.

The Korean Council on Social Welfare Education (KCSWE)

The KCSWE was established in 1966 for the purposes of improving networks with international agencies and developing social work education. The major activities include conducting research on social work education curriculum, releasing publications related to social work education, and coordinating curricula among national and global social work agencies. The KCSWE is composed of the following seven committees: general af-

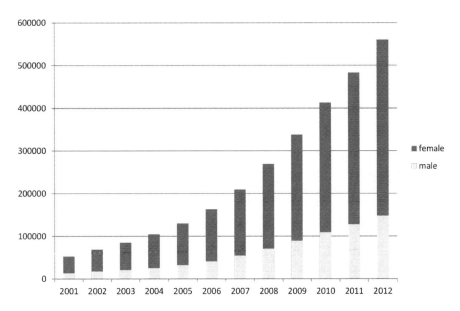

Figure 12.1 Change in the total number of licensed social workers in South Korea (*Korean social work statistical yearbook* 2012).

fairs, education, international, external cooperation, evaluation and accreditation, editing, and credentials and membership. Beyond the responsibilities and duties of each committee, the KCSWE disseminates guidelines for social work courses, holds annual meetings with the committee chairs, and evaluates social work education programs.

Korea National Council on Social Welfare (KNCSW)

As a public organisation that was established by the Social Service Act, the KNCSW's diverse activities contribute to the development of social welfare in South Korea, such as coordinating and consulting on efforts to promote the private sector of social welfare, developing policy, conducting surveys and research, providing education and training, performing volunteer activities, conducting informational business, and implementing activities for economically disadvantaged and underserved populations. The KNCSW's major functions and responsibilities include the following: (1) developing social work research and surveys, (2) preparing policy-related proposals, (3) educating and training social workers, (4) promoting social welfare, (5) engaging in fundraising for social services and research, (6) creating publications, (7) supporting and collaborating with city and provincial social welfare agencies, (8) coordinating with internal social work agencies, (9) promoting volunteer activities, (10) developing social work services and resources, (11) developing informational projects, and (12) conducting other social work services that are assigned by the Ministry of Health and Welfare. Since the revision of the Social Service Act in 1998, all social welfare agencies are required to be evaluated and accredited at least once every three years; thus, the KNCSW is responsible for reviewing and evaluating the qualifications of all social work agencies. In addition, the KNCSW operates the Volunteer Management System, operates the food bank, and manages under-served populations.

Korea Association of Social Workers (KASW)

According to the Social Service Act section 46, the KASW is the support organisation for social workers. The KASW develops and disseminates professional knowledge and skills, provides social work education and training for quality improvement, and increases the welfare of social workers. The major activities include developing and disseminating professional knowledge and skills for social work and welfare, providing education and training for social workers' professional practices, conducting surveys and research related to social welfare, creating publications, and providing educational opportunities and collaborations with national and international social work professionals. The KASW comprises 16 associations for social workers in cities or provinces. In addition, the KAMSW, KAMHSW, and Korean Society of School Social Work are members of the KASW. The KASW manages a continuing education centre that administers the level 1 certification test and provides over 8 hours of continuing education per year for social workers. To maintain their qualifications, social workers are required to enrol in courses on social welfare ethics and values, social work practices, social welfare policy and laws, social welfare administration, and research methods in social welfare.

Contemporary challenges and the future of social work education in South Korea

The growth in the number of social workers in the past 6 decades has been accompanied by a dramatic shift in social work education in South Korea. Given that many people were interested in becoming social work professionals and were motivated to attend social work programs for different reasons, professional social workers must be successfully and continuously trained to meet their professional goals. Although social work education in South Korea has been growing at a fast rate, the quality of social work education (i.e. academic programs, curriculum, field education, and the social work licensure examination), which should align with an increase in the quantity of programs, was not fully considered. In fact, social work education in South Korea should consider two issues related to educational and social welfare policy goals. First, social work and welfare programs at colleges and universities are generally designed to prepare professional social workers for different types of clients. Second, social workers can be employed by several types of social service agencies that all depend on social welfare policies to satisfy the needs of their consumers and providers (Lee & Nam 2005). Given that social welfare policy in South Korea currently requires social workers to play diverse roles and to serve diverse functions in social service agencies, a vision is necessary to improve the quality of services and to develop systems of social work education in South Korea.

First, there are many different types of social work education programs in South Korea, and each type has a unique educational mission and set of objectives. The KCSWE recently announced that only 77 schools were registered in the KCSWE, which indicates that only 16% of the schools are registered KCSWE members. Given that the KCSWE disseminates guidelines for social work and welfare courses and evaluates social work education programs, all schools should register with the KCSWE so that they can provide appropriate and systematic social work education. The KCSW should also initiate and conduct accreditation reviews to verify each program.

Second, most of the social work and welfare curriculum is based on the social work licensure examination; courses that are not included in the licensure examination are rarely considered. Furthermore, courses are still based on the content and culture of the United States, and the course content does not always consider the South Korean context (Hong & Han 2013). To improve students' competencies, the social work and welfare curriculum should reflect current social problems and international changes. For example, issues related to multiculturalism and diversity have been raised as a result of the rising rate of immigration in South Korea; thus, courses related to international social work and cultural diversity should be included in the social work and welfare curriculum.

Koreans also face other diverse issues that have not been considered. For example, foreign workers, women immigrants by marriage, mixed race children, and people who have relocated from North Korea (known as 'sae-ter-min' in Korean) are becoming clients. Professional social workers need to provide diverse social services that can help these clients adjust in new social environments. Meanwhile, the international standard for social work education requires that social work education address diversity (Han & Kim 2006). A number of social work programs at colleges and universities in South Korea include courses related to international and multicultural social work in their curricula. For example, the graduate school of social welfare at Ewha Womans University offers classes such as International Social Work and Cultural Diversity and Social Work Practice (Hong et al. 2011). The underlying purpose of the current curricula on multiculturalism is to educate the future generation of social workers about the importance of social development and joint collaborations with other countries, particularly underdeveloped countries. To achieve this purpose, courses should be developed to enhance cultural competency through joint collaboration and partnership between social workers and social service agencies for ethnic minorities and immigrants in South Korea. Beyond the social work licensure examination, the following courses on social changes and trends may be valuable: Human Sexuality and Social Work Practice, Unification and Social Welfare, Understanding Social Enterprise in Theory and Practice, Military Social Work, Cultural Diversity and Social Work Practice, International Social Work, International Cooperation for Regional Development, and Regional Study and International Volunteerism.

Third, the qualification standards for field experience supervisors in South Korea are insufficient for providing the appropriate practical skills and competencies to students. Specifically, to be an academic supervisor, the qualification standards require at least one year of practical social work experience under the supervision of an individual with a doctoral degree; these academic supervisors do not have enough practical social work experience to provide student supervision. Furthermore, the field supervisors in the field tend to provide practice-focused supervision only, which does not appropriately link the experience with academic knowledge and skills. For two-year colleges and cyber colleges, the field education is not long enough to be regulated by a systematic and organised manual.

Currently, the minimum required time for field education is 120 hours. In fact, that amount of time is relatively and absolutely limited to applying academic knowledge and skills to field settings, acquiring experiences related to social work values, and practicing concrete skills with clients. Most social work programs in the United States require approximately 1000 hours for two-year master's programs. Consequently, additional hours should be required to provide experience in social work skills and values.

In addition to increasing the qualifications of supervisors and the amount of time in the field, the core content of field education should be enhanced to improve the quality of field education. During the orientation, academic supervisors at schools and universities should address the goals, attitudes, ethics, expectations and emotional feelings of students in relation to their field placements. The KASW recently standardised the process of obtaining field supervisor and academic supervisor certifications. To obtain the certifications, courses on the theory of supervision, field administration, writing proposals for field supervision, attitudes and roles for field supervisors, case management, program development and evaluation, resource development in non-profit organisations, organisation management and administration, and regulation for financial accounting are offered. Supervision-related continuing education programs should enhance the capabilities of field supervisors (Jang 2011). In addition, each agency should support supervisors who require additional attitude, skill and knowledge development.

Fourth, the KCSWE recently redefined courses to standardise social work education in South Korea, and courses to pass the social work licensure examination were established. This development implies that the minimum requirements for social work education were standardised to follow the regulations of the Social Work Act in South Korea. For example, to be a certified medical social worker or mental health social worker, students are required to receive training in field settings for a certain time period before entering the actual field. General social workers who are employed in general social service agencies must also receive annual continuing education. While regulations regarding social work and welfare have been established, efforts to address the working conditions of social workers, such as salary, conflicts and the environment, are relatively undeveloped. Indeed, compared to other professionals, the salaries of social workers are lower and their rate of leaving the profession is higher. Furthermore, everyone who passes the social work licensure examination automatically receives the level 1 certification, which allows individuals to work in a social work setting without receiving additional training in social work practices. To improve both social work competencies and job satisfaction in the social work field, people should be sufficiently educated to apply their knowledge and skills to clients. Consequently, additional professional training after obtaining the certification may be necessary to improve workers' individual competencies and to translate their skills into real-life practice. Furthermore, a positive relationship between the schools and social service agencies will be helpful to enhance the quality of social work education, increase skills and knowledge that can be applied to practice, better understand social changes, and maximise the engagement of students in field settings.

Conclusions

This chapter addresses many of the efforts to enhance social work education in South Korea and the challenges in this process. These efforts reflect the growth in social work education in South Korea. However, these efforts do not always reflect the true gaps and challenges in the goals of social work education in South Korea. Nonetheless, the challenges do suggest further areas for increased attention, including variation in the quality of academic programs; the need for curriculum development within bachelor's, master's, and doctoral education programs; content on working with new clients; differentiating skills and practice preparation; barriers to interactions between students and faculty; faculty development; collaborative efforts between schools and field sites; the quality of the social work licensure examination; continuing education for licensed social workers; and engagement in global issues. We hope that this chapter promotes the improvement of social work education in South Korea and challenges us to think about the similarities and differences in social work education between South Korea and other countries.

References

Han, I.Y. & Kim, Y.J. (2006). Case of diversity education in Korea. *Korean Journal of Social Welfare Education*, 2(1): 105–20.

Hong, J.S. & Han, I.Y. (2013). Call for incorporating cultural competency in South Korean social work education. In C. Noble, M. Henrickson & I. Y. Han (eds), *Social work education: voices from the Asia Pacific* (pp. 3–28). Sydney: Sydney University Press.

Hong, J.S., Kim, Y.S., Lee, N.Y. & Ha, J.W. (2011). Understanding social welfare in South Korea. In S.B.C.L. Furuto (ed.), *Social welfare in East Asia and the Pacific* (pp. 41–66). NY: Columbia University Press.

Jang, S.M. (2011). Collaboration between field education faculty and field supervisor in Korea. In C. Noble & M. Henrickson (eds), *Social work field education and supervision across Asia Pacific* (pp. 45–63). Sydney: Sydney University Press.

Korea Association of Social Workers (2012). *Korean social work statistical yearbook*. Seoul: Ministry of Health and Welfare.

Korea Association of Social Workers (2010). Social work field practice: survey and guideline. Seoul: Ministry of Health and Welfare.

Lee, H. S. & Jung, F. R. (2012). *Social work practice*. Seoul: Chungminsa Publishing.

Lee, H.K. & Nam, C.S. (2005). Fifty years' history of social welfare education in Korea – in the context of institutionalisation of social welfare and universalisation of higher education. *Korean Journal of Social Welfare Education*, 1(1): 69–95.

Part 4
The social work curriculum

13

Social work education in Aotearoa/New Zealand and Australia

Barbara Staniforth and Carolyn Noble

> Aotearoa/New Zealand and Australia have unique histories which have strongly shaped the development of social work education within their settings. This chapter explores the commonalities and differences of each country in relation to the development of the profession and the provision of social work education. Particular emphasis is placed upon the role of Aotearoa/New Zealand's bicultural status and Australia's incorporation of indigeneity in the shaping of the delivery and curricula within social work education. This chapter also explores how social work education in the South Pacific is offering a valuable contribution to the development of an indigenous-centred social work education.

Social work education posits itself both as a universal (global) and local endeavour. However, the International Association for Schools of Social Work's (IASSW) Global Standards (Sewpaul & Jones 2004), while encouraging sufficient interpretation and application at local levels, provides quite concrete criteria on such things as: social work's core purpose; program objectives and outcomes; standards regarding core curricula (including field education); staffing; school structure, administration and governance; and a code of conduct for the social work profession as a way of setting the benchmark for professional standards for both education and practice. This prescription, we argue, introduces tensions as to how the global and the local (indigenous models of social work education) are to be balanced. While Aotearoa/New Zealand and Australia's professional associations also set concrete criteria governing national education standards for social work practice, there has been a more conscious attempt to privilege and include the indigenous voices to enrich and enhance the educational project. This is despite the history of oppression and displacement of indigenous peoples, the traditional landowners before white settlement. How this inclusion has been undertaken will be presented in this chapter.

While we, the authors, are both white female academics and as such we recognise the role in colonisation that our ancestors have played, we have been fortunate to teach in programs where strong indigenous voices have shaped the way that social work is taught and practiced. Therefore we have chosen to focus this chapter on the influence of our countries' histories and indigenous contributions as one way of addressing the tension between the global and the local in curricula design and delivery.

Historical settlement: Australia

The impact of European settlement in Australia continues to have a profound impact on the indigenous peoples of the land – socially, culturally, politically and educationally. Australian Aboriginal culture is believed to be among the oldest continuous cultures in the world (Bennett 2013). The word Aboriginal is a unitary construct that deflects attention away from the rich diversity in Aboriginal communities. At the time of white settlement there were believed to be about 700 tribal groups and languages in common use, each placing a different emphasis on kinship, relationships with families, each other, and the ecosystem of the land and country. While contact with its nearest neighbour, Indonesia, dated well before the 15th century, was based on trade and cultural exchanges, the European contact was motivated by colonisation and control over the country's wealth, resources, land and peoples. So in 1770 when Captain Cook arrived in Australia he declared Botany Bay and Sydney Cove as the first of many British settlements across this vast land. Ignoring the indigenous peoples, the British settlers declared the land and area as terra nullius (empty land) and ready for colonisation, sending convicts to populate the land on their release from custody (Bennett 2013). The British imported their system of governance and culture, including their welfare system based on the Poor Laws introduced in Britain in 1601, relying on the church and its parishes for the provision of welfare for the 'destitute and homeless', mainly women and children. Post-colonisation, the newly federated states assumed the role of providing welfare assistance as Australia moved towards a universal welfare system when the social and economic impact from the Great Depression of the 1930s and both World Wars resulted in previously viewed deserving citizens uprooted into poverty and unemployment as a result of structural factors outside their control (Chenoweth and McAuliffe 2012). A welfare state continues in some form today with the state and federal governments providing assistance for their citizens in health, education, social planning and the development and delivery of social and welfare services to mitigate against social impacts such as poverty, crime and unemployment which resulted from rapid industrialisation and uneven urban growth.

Australian Aboriginals and Torres Strait Islander peoples have their own histories of human problems and ways of addressing them; mostly passed down by oral traditions. However, when the state assumed responsibility for the welfare of Australian Aboriginals starting in the latter part of the 18th century to the present day, the policies have moved from protectionism, to assimilation, to cultural genocide, to recognition of past harms, to cultural protection and self-determination (Bennett 2013). In addition to the Indigenous population, Australian welfare politics were also influenced by selected immigration from peoples from Europe, the Pacific and more latterly Asia as well as a small number of refugees from war-torn countries from across the globe resulting in a growth of a vibrant multicultural society. In brief, Australia's welfare policies have been forged in the tensions between its colonial settlers, its indigenous inhabitants and more latterly its immigration policies and practices, creating both a bicultural and multicultural society, also with its own inherent tensions.

Historical settlement: Aotearoa/New Zealand

The indigenous people of Aotearoa/New Zealand are the Māori (also referred to as Tangata Whenua, or people of the land) who are the descendants of the great Polynesian ocean explorers who are said to have settled in Aotearoa/New Zealand in the 13th century (King 2003). By the 16th century most of the country had been settled and the beginnings of tribal Māori society were in evidence. In 1769 Captain James Cook of the British Royal Navy arrived (King 2003). While the French arrived soon after, like Australia, the country was to be colonised by the British. Unlike Australia, however, the Crown recognised that Tangata Whenua had rights, and in 1840 the Crown and different Māori Chiefs throughout the country signed the Treaty of Waitangi (Te Tiriti o Waitangi), which would become the founding document of Aotearoa/New Zealand. As in Australia, the English imported a welfare system similar to the English Poor Laws, which became the basis upon which Aotearoa/New Zealand's welfare system for Pakeha (European settlers) would be based. Different systems were initially put in place for the Māori, and Pakeha settlers (Tennant 1989). Colonisation, death by imported European disease, land confiscation and other factors would all play a devastating role for Māori and relations between Māori and non-Māori would form a significant backdrop of the country's development.

The evolution of social work as a profession

For both Australia and Aotearoa/New Zealand, formal social work was initially a global endeavour, being imported from the UK and the US. The developing trajectories, however, were to be influenced by their local contexts. Their indigenous peoples, social and economic movements as well as the space that they occupied geographically would all play a part in creating a social work identity unique to each country.

Nash (2001) and Walsh-Tapiata (2004) acknowledge that Māori were engaged in many of the roles and tasks associated with social work in terms of care for their own communities many years prior to colonisation. Formal social work, in its professional Western construct, was, however, quite slow to emerge in Aotearoa/New Zealand.

Post-colonisation, many people would become engaged in roles that would soon become known as social work; however, they did not identify them as such. For example, child welfare workers, school teachers and nurses carried on social care functions without identifying them as being unified within the umbrella of social work.

It was not until 1964 that the New Zealand Association of Social Work was formed (which would later become the Aotearoa/New Zealand Association of Social work in 1998). It became a member of the International Federation of Social Work (IFSW) in the same year (Nash 2001) and is a current member of IASSW as well.

Two issues were significant in the development of social work in Aotearoa/New Zealand. The early development of social work concurred with a widening recognition that the rights of indigenous people had been violated. In 1980, the South African Springboks rugby team was due to tour Aotearoa/New Zealand. A movement developed within the country to halt this tour on the grounds of South Africa's apartheid regime and the fact that black players were prohibited from playing. This movement concurred with protests that demanded return of Māori lands that had been stolen over the previous generations. Social work was at times seen to be linked with an oppressive state and to represent the interest of maintaining the status quo. Divisions occurred within the profession. These divisions became linked to the second significant issue in terms of the profession's development: that of the drive towards a more professional identity for social work (Staniforth 2010). Those pushing for increased educational requirements for social work and registration of social work were seen to be separate from those with a more grassroots (often identified as flax roots in Aotearoa/New Zealand) who were seen to be more concerned with professional status than the wants and needs of the people, and more particularly oppressed people. 'The emphasis on the professionalism of social workers and their academic training was seen as discriminating against people who were often qualified by life and culture to do the work more effectively' (Ministerial Advisory Committee on a Perspective for the Department of Social Welfare 1986, 23). While voluntary registration for social workers came into effect in 2003, the debate continues of whether to allow non-qualified social workers into the professional association, and there is a continued push to make registration of social workers mandatory.

Social work's professional and educational identity and development are currently held and maintained by four key stakeholders. These include the Council for Social Work Education of Aotearoa New Zealand (CSWEANZ), the Aotearoa New Zealand Association of Social Workers (ANZASW, which includes the Takawaenga o Aotearoa (Māori) social work caucus), the Social Workers Registration Board (SWRB) and the newest member, the Tangata Whenua Social Worker's Association (TWSWA) which was formed and launched in 2009 (personal correspondence, M. Scott, 28/08/2013).

In Australia social work was also initially influenced by the UK and US experiences and scholarship; however, a localised practice model was quick to develop post-World War 1. From the 1880s there were philanthropic endeavours as well as faith-based organisations delivering services and programs to help marginalised people, especially women and children who were destitute, and activists worked tirelessly to create a better and more equitable society. In particular, in New South Wales, it was social activists in the national women's association that influenced the establishment of social work as a beginning profession from as early as the 1800s (Chenoweth and McAuliffe 2012).

In Australia, the period after World War 2 saw the rise of a welfare state and social workers' role in the assessment and provision of welfare services and social, emotional and financial support, designed to help mitigate the effects of changing social conditions. Up until the late 1970s in Australia, the welfare systems were committed to providing universally for their citizens, and services were developed with the prime aim of enhancing the wellbeing of the whole community. However, all from the late 1980s, with increasing concern about the growth in welfare spending and an ideological shift away from supporting the community to encouraging individuals and families to take more responsibility for their care, the influence of neoliberal ideology heralded a decline in publicly funded services, reduction in universal entitlements, and a move towards more scrutiny and accountability of individual welfare provisions and programs (Lavalette 2011). Managerialism, competition and privatisation dominated the welfare discourse. Government funded services diminished, human services programs and provisions were contracted outside of the state and the private-for-profit services were strengthened as a result. This changing landscape has created new tensions for social workers. With the rise in the more conservative neoliberal philosophy determining public policy, social workers, as government employees, are increasingly finding themselves in the middle between enacting polices that support the more conservative elements of the current status quo and ones that advocate for a shift in power to the least powerful – a key philosophical underpinning of social work's commitment to social justice, human rights and an empowered citizenry.

As social work progressed over the decades a number of unsuccessful attempts have been made to achieve registration in Australia and these continue. Registration is seen by the Australian Association for Social Workers (AASW) as an important process to ensure the ongoing legitimacy of social work as a profession in the human services industry and to shore up practitioners' rights to practice independently, claim government financial support and protect consumers from harm as well as holding social work more accountable for this work (Chenoweth and McAuliffe 2012). The debate continues.

In 1972 the then Australian federal labour government adopted the policy of self-determination for indigenous communities to decide on the pace and nature of their future development. Aboriginal specific services were established such as the Department of Aboriginal Affairs, Aboriginal Legal Aid medical services and housing and welfare schemes (Green and Baldry 2012). In 1997, land rights legislation was passed and the Royal Commission into Aboriginal Deaths in Custody was established in 1987. In 1990, Aboriginal and Torres Strait Islander Commission (ATSIC) was legislatively established while Eddie Mabo successfully challenged the terra nullius notion in 1992, thus recognising that indigenous peoples were the first inhabitants of the country. The Native Title Act (1993) followed and many other initiatives to improve cultural relations and undo the long-term cultural harm suffered by the indigenous peoples were established. In 1997 and then in 2007 the issues of the stolen children and child sexual abuse were addressed, and in 2007 the Australian Government gave the indigenous peoples a national apology, which gave all Australians some hope for a different future. These developments have had an important influence on the development of an indigenous approach to social work education and recognition by the profession to acknowledge this history and social work's past and ongoing obligation to Aboriginals and Torres Strait Islander Australians (Green and Baldry 2012).

Evolution of social work education in Australia and New Zealand

Australia

In Australia the first social work training was offered by institutes that were separate from the universities as early as the 1920s. These institutes offered specific training in particular areas of practice and the formalisation of university-based qualifications came in the 1940s when universities in Sydney, Melbourne and Adelaide began offering specific social work training. By 1976 there were 11 schools of social work across Australia offering bachelor degrees and today there are 29 Universities offering programs in both undergraduate and postgraduate professional qualifications as well as postgraduate research, MSWs, DSWs and PhD programs. This growth is linked to the expansion of the tertiary sector and the growth in demand for social and human services workers. When social work moved from the institutes to the universities, a more generic curriculum was developed, with employers and academics exerting their influence on what should be included in the programs, with the professional association having the final say (Chenoweth and McAuliffe 2012).

The Australian Association for Social Workers (AASW), established in 1946, regulates the training of practitioners through its role in the national accreditation of programs and hence the graduates that enter the profession. It also disciplines members who have been found to have acted unethically and will withdraw accreditation of courses if standards, resources, governance and curricula fall below its nationally set criteria. Current curricula guidelines encourage a more radically informed approach to practice by including a structural analysis in the theory and practice strands and more latterly the new Australian Social Work Educational Accreditation Standards (ASWEAS 2012) encourage full incorporation of alternative cultural knowledge into the educational curricula with important flow-ons into practice, policy and research. Further, Australian social work academics have led the epistemological challenge to the more conservative and individual (case work and case management) approach to include broader critical social analysis both nationally and internationally. For example, the consideration of a multi-cultural practice which promotes the acceptance of diversity and difference in both theory and practice, in order to reflect the concerns of the multifaceted nature of the community in which it is located, is a required aspect of curricula. So too is the need to internationalise the curricula by including more international literature, exploration of other countries' culture and context of practice, and encouraging the link with international issues and local practices. A strong commitment to social justice, human rights, gender and minority groups' democracy is reflected in its ontological foundations. A key core curricula consideration is the inclusion of Aboriginal and Torres Straits knowledge and practice across the programs as well as in stand-alone units of study (where possible).

The baseline qualification is a four year undergraduate program but a two-year postgraduate Master of Social Work (Qualifying) (MSW[Q]) has more recently emerged for people with under-graduate qualification in cognate areas in the human services. The usual social science knowledge (social systems, psychology, political economy, law, sociology, philosophy) and social work theory and methods, and practice competencies and extensive field education make up the curricula. Programs can be offered on or off campus or online as long as students are on campus for five days each academic year. The issue of field placements continues to pose difficulties in both countries as the length of time (1000 hours) and availability of agencies willing to take students are a constant concern.

Aotearoa/New Zealand

The history of social work education in Aotearoa/New Zealand has been written in detail by Nash in her 1998 doctoral thesis. In this she indicates that professional social work education emerged relatively late in Aotearoa/New Zealand. While, like in Australia, there was a system of social security in place that was meant to serve its population from cradle to grave (*The Social Security Act 1938*), the government at the time saw the expressed need for social work as an indictment on its much lauded welfare state. As a result, the first social work education program (first intake 1950), located at Victoria University in Wellington (the nation's capital), was not permitted to call itself such, with the qualification being named the Diploma in Social Sciences. This was a two-year postgraduate diploma that produced a very limited number of graduates, not nearly enough to meet the need for qualified social workers at that time. It would be approximately another 25 years before undergraduate social work programs would be established with Massey University on the North Island and University of Canterbury on the South Island. The two-year Diploma of Social Work followed in 1980, situated in the Auckland Teacher's College (now the University of Auckland). From the mid-1980s onward, numerous social work diplomas, certificate and degree programs were developed. These were situated mainly in universities, polytechnic institutes and in wānangas (tertiary education providers that provide programs from a Māori cultural perspective).

The Aotearoa New Zealand Association of Social Workers (ANZASW) initially provided accreditation for social work education programs. With the advent of the *Social Workers Registration Act 2003*, this task was assumed by the Social Workers Registration Board, which currently provides accreditation to programs, which enables graduates from those programs to achieve provisional registration upon graduation (SWRB 2013b). There are currently 17 institutions in the country that provide either a qualifying bachelor's degree (three or four years) or master's degree in 'social work' (SWRB 2013a). The SWRB has signalled to institutes that the minimum requirement will shift from a three-year undergraduate qualification to a four-year qualification, which will take effect from 2017 (SWRB 2013b). This is a development that has been praised by some as it brings Aotearoa/New Zealand into line with many other countries, and decried by others as it has the potential to make the qualification less accessible to groups such as Māori due to increased costs and longer time away from the family or the workforce that will be required.

Contribution indigeneity has made to social work education

We have discussed that both countries began their education programs through importing ideas from overseas, and we note the reflexive nature of globalisation as both countries have borrowed from, and contributed to, international discourses surrounding social work education and practice. Part of this contribution has been made through the knowledge, skills and values of our countries' indigenous peoples, and other people native to the Pacific whose knowledge, educational processes and ideas form part of the 'local' of each country, and have much to offer the global. We have chosen to explore two aspects of how indigenous process and knowledge have contributed to social work education. From Australia we discuss some of the ways that indigeneity is embedded in the curricula, while from Aotearoa/New Zealand we focus more specifically on theory.

Australia

The Australian Social Work Education and Accreditation Standards (2012) specifically deem that all Australian social work courses cover ATSI attitudes, values, knowledge and skills as core curricula. Further, the preamble for both the AASW Code of Ethics (2010) and the AASW newly formed Practice Standards (2013) note great advances in developing a collaborative and integrated social work response to issues ATSI peoples face. Each of these documents begins by stating:

1. Social work acknowledges the Aboriginal and Torres Strait Islander peoples, the First Australians, whose lands, winds and waters we all now share, and pay respect to the unique values, and their continuing and enduring cultures which deepen and enrich the life of our nation and communities.
2. Social workers commit to acknowledge and understand the historical and contemporary disadvantage experienced by Aboriginal and Torres Strait Islander peoples and the implication of this for practice.

3. Social workers are responsible for ensuring that their practice is culturally competent, safe and sensitive. (Briskman 2007; Zubrzycki and Crawford 2013; Green and Baldry 2012)

Further, each of these commitments requires curricula that support its implementation. In summary, this is done in several ways. The first is incorporating an indigenous world view – 'ways of knowing' – as well as 'ways of being' and finally 'ways of doing' (see Australian Social Word Education and Accreditation Standards 2012, section 3.3.4; 20–24). The second is to show respect for ATSI peoples and for non-white peoples to challenge racism and oppression in practice and educational processes, and work to address their consequences. The third is to review how the history of social work has been influenced by colonisation and how as a consequence 'white politics' and 'whiteness' dominate its epistemology and pedagogy and to work at decolonising its impact. Fourth is to link social justice and human rights in developing an anti-racist practice that informs the development as well as research and policy changes. The fifth is to acknowledge the resilience of ATSI peoples, and their strengths and survivorship in the face of extensive racism, oppression and the trauma of dispossession from their land and the legacy of the Stolen Generations. Sixth is to acknowledge the importance of working communally rather than individually. Seventh is to work in true and real collaboration in both the classroom and the workplace in the development of an Indigenous social work. In essence to open up dialogue by inviting yarning, learning and listening to indigenous peoples as they talk and act from their lived experiences and provide them in the curricula. Finally (although not exclusively) to incorporate a critically reflective aspect to education and supervision in order to begin the work outlined above.

We, along with others (Zubrzycki and Crawford 2013; Green and Baldry 2012) would argue that an important contribution that this scholarship offers social work education more generally is of 'turning the lens' on whiteness within educational content and processes and actively redressing the fact that indigenous peoples are at the bottom of the communities' race-aligned hierarchies. The constant question and challenge for social work education is how to continue to address this situation in the curricula, the classroom, practice and the profession more broadly. The contribution of ATSI scholars in defining ways of including indigeniety in the social work curricula as outlined above is an important way forward. Aotearoa/New Zealand has also made some strides forward in these regards.

Aotearoa/New Zealand

Aotearoa/New Zealand is a relatively small country sitting in the middle of the South Pacific region. It has evolved a unique identity based on its Māori heritage and pioneer spirit. A reflexive relationship has also existed with the many Pacific Islands that surround it. All these influences have played a part in how social work education has evolved and is currently delivered.

One of the distinguishing features of Aotearoa/New Zealand's colonisation was the signing of the Treaty of Waitangi (Te Tiriti o Waitangi) between the British Crown and some of the chiefs of Aotearoa/New Zealand. The key points of the treaty were that Māori chiefs gave the Queen governance over the land, that Māori chiefs were given exercise of chieftainship over their lands, villages, and property or treasures, and that Māori would have the same protection and rights accorded to British subjects (State Services Commission 2005, 15). Controversy surrounded the treaty, however, as more than one version was signed (three in English and one in Māori). Key terms were confused in the translation, which would cause significant misunderstandings and conflict in the years to come (Ruwhiu 2013). Regardless of these controversies, the Treaty established the foundation of biculturalism within the country and entrenched the rights of Māori people as Tangata Whenua. As described earlier, formal social work education was just establishing a 'critical mass' at a time when the social fabric of the country was shifting from being a relatively conservative agriculturally-based country to a country that would become known for speaking out against human rights abuses, including the ones occurring on its own soil. Social work's identity was closely aligned with these developments.

In 1986 the government commissioned a report into practices within the Department of Social Welfare that found extensive evidence of institutional racism in the provision of service and the department itself. The report, known as Puao te Ata tu, would become a seminal document in social work education and practice (Hollis-English 2012). The family group conference, which entrenches the rights of whanau (extended family) and is used in child welfare decision-making and young offender restorative justice programs, emerged from this report. These approaches have been deemed to be more in line with Māori cultural world views and practices.

In 1993 the social work association, ANZASW, developed a code of ethics and bicultural code of practice. A bilingual (Māori and English) version was adopted in 2007. This code of ethics, as well as the code of conduct developed by the SWRB, form the basis on which schools of social work base their teaching and curricula around ethics and practice.

During the course of the evolution of social work education, there has been a parallel development of programs developed and delivered by Māori academics for Māori students, often delivered through wanangas (which have also had a number of non-Māori students) as well as recognition that students in 'mainstream' programs needed to become more aware of the Māori world (te ao Māori) and to gain competence in being able to work with Māori clients. The ANZASW lists one of its practice principles as 'The social worker demonstrates a commitment to practicing social work in accordance with the Code of Ethics (2007) and an understanding of Te Tiriti o Waitangi Articles 1, 2, 3 and 4' (ANZASW 2007) while the SWRB requires that social workers demonstrate the competence to practise social work with Māori (SWRB 2010a).

Some training programs have specific papers or courses devoted to working with Tangata Whenua, while others embed the whole of their programs within this context. While much of the content taught in social work programs in Aotearoa/New Zealand still resonates with Western theories and models, Māori models of wellbeing have also been embedded within social work curriculum. Durie's (1985) Māori model of wellbeing, Te Whare Tapa Wha, uses a metaphor of the walls of the meeting house, which need to be in balance to hold up the house. These walls are hinengaro (thoughts and emotions), wairua (spirituality), whanau (family) and tinana (physical). They are also held up by a strong foundation of relationship to the whenua or the land. Māori ceremonies and processes, such as that of the powhiri, have also been adopted within social work practice. These include the use of karakia (prayer), waiata (song) and the joining together over kai (food) (Munford and Sanders 2010; Webber-Dreadon 1999).

While concepts such as 'evidence-based practice' or 'practice-based evidence' have influenced what is taught, in New Zealand this has often been filtered through a critical lens in terms of what constitutes evidence, and a growing recognition about the importance of the inclusion of Tangata Whenua and other groups' voices in determining what works in practice. Ruwhiu notes that all social work in New Zealand should be familiar with the history of Tangata Whenua/Tauiwi (people who have come from elsewhere) relations and the importance of the narrative in the formation of identity and concepts of wellbeing (2013).

While discussion around the how social work is conceptualised and taught within the various Pacific Islands is beyond the scope of this paper, we acknowledge the influence and contribution that Pacific Island peoples have made upon social work education and practice. Pasifika models of wellbeing have also been included in 'mainstream' social work education.

The most well-known of the Pacific Island models is the Samoan Fonofale Model (Polutu-Endemann 2001). Developed by Polutu-Endemann, this model has similarity to the previously discussed Whare Tapa Wha Model. In this model, the fale (meeting house) is held up by different posts (pou-tu). These posts are representative of the spiritual (fa'aleagaga), mental (mafaufau), physical (fa'aletino) and 'other' realms of wellbeing, such as gender, age, sexuality and socioeconomic status, which sit on a foundation of the extended family (aiga). These are held in place by culture, or the roof of the fale, and sit within context, time and environment (Mafile'o 2013).

As Ruwhiu (2013) espouses three important considerations in becoming competent to work with Māori, Faleolo provides guidelines (2009) for achieving cultural validity in social work education. These include establishing a social work curriculum where cultural content is 'strong, authoritative and equitable' (153); incorporating assessments that utilise cultural knowledge and practices, and acknowledging parables as culturally valid knowledge (153).

While social work in Aotearoa/New Zealand is deemed to occur within a bicultural context, the country itself has become increasingly multicultural in terms of its makeup. The ANZASW has particular interest groups for African, Chinese, Filipino, Indian, and

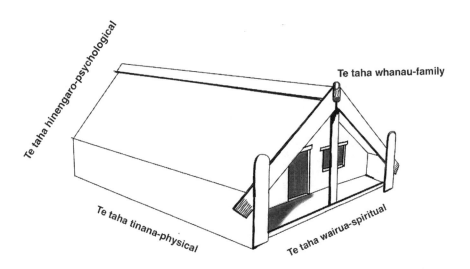

Figure 13.1 Te whare tapa wha (Durie 1985).

Pasifika social workers (ANZASW 2013). These groups serve to provide a mutual connection for social workers from various minority ethnic groups and can also act as consultants in relation to policy, research and practice. The core competencies of the SWRB indicate that social workers must demonstrate 'competence to practice social work with different ethnic and cultural groups in Aotearoa/New Zealand' (SWRB 2010b).

Conclusions

Like many places in the world, the tensions between the global and the local are felt within the Australian, New Zealand and South Pacific contexts. The contribution of Aotearoa/New Zealand's bicultural status on the development of social work and Australia's attempt to include indigeniety into the social work curricula are making some progress in breaking down the institutional barriers that decades of white privilege has created. This also has implications for the promotion of effective cross-cultural practice and enables social workers to work not only with indigenous communities but other ethnicities characteristic of Australia and Aotearoa/New Zealand's multicultural populations. While links with international and global contexts are important, it is in the local that significant changes can occur.

Just as the proposed new definition of social work, which is emerging from extensive cross-cultural and cross-national collaboration and consultation, needs to hold the balance of global and local, so does social work's educational curriculum. Schools of social work will need to be proactive in ensuring that their students are adequately prepared for both

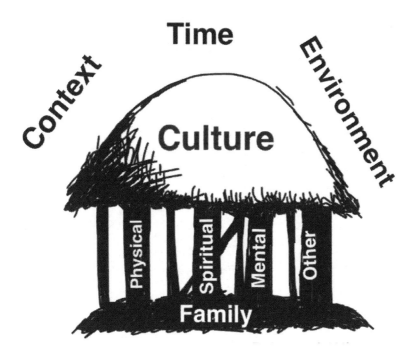

Figure 13.2 Fonofale model (Polutu-Endemann 2001).

the local and the global contexts. We hope that some of the examples put forward in this chapter are helpful in providing ideas on ways forward within these dialectical tensions as both our countries move towards celebrating the incorporation of indigenous histories, voices and learning in their social work programs.

The authors would like to acknowledge the images created by Dr Simon Nash.

References

Aotearoa New Zealand Association of Social Workers (ANZASW) (2013). Governance, 2013. Retrieved on 22 April 2014 from anzasw.org.nz/about/topics/show/60-governance-2013.

Aotearoa New Zealand Association of Social Workers (ANZASW) (2007). Bilingual code of ethics. Christchurch, New Zealand: Author.

Australian Association for Social Workers (AASW) (2013). Practice standards. Retrieved on 22 April 2014 from www.aasw.asn.au/document/item/4551.

Australian Association for Social Workers (AASW) (2012). Australian social work education and accreditation standards, 2012. Retrieved on 22 April 2014 from www.aasw.asn.au/document/item/3552.

Australian Association for Social Workers (AASW) (2010). Code of ethics. Retrieved on 22 April 2014 from www.aasw.asn.au/document/item/1201.

Bennett, B. (2013). The importance of Aboriginal and Torres Strait Islander history for social work students and graduates. In B. Bennett, S. Green, S. Gilbert & D. Bessarab (eds), *Our voices: Aboriginal and Torres Strait Islander social work*. Melbourne: Palgrave Macmillan.

Briskman, L. (2007). *Social work with Indigenous communities*. Melbourne: The Federation Press.

Chenoweth, L. & McAuliffe, D. (2012). *The road to social work and human service work*, 3rd ed. South Melbourne: Cengage Learning Australia.

Durie, M. (1985). A Māori perspective of health. *Journal of Social Sciences and Medicine*, 20(5): 483–86.

Faleolo, M. (2009). Culturally valid social work education: a Samoan perspective. In. C. Noble, M. Henrickson & I.Y. Han (eds), *Education for social work: voices from the Asia-Pacific* (pp. 149–72). Melbourne: Vulgar Press.

Green, S. & Baldry, E. (2012). Indigenous social work in Australia. In B. Bennett, S. Green, S. Gilbert & D. Bessarab (eds), *Our choices: Aboriginal and Torres Strait Islander social work*. Melbourne: Palgrave Macmillan.

Hollis-English, A. (2012). Pūao-te-ata-tū: informing Māori social work since 1986. *Aotearoa New Zealand Social Work, Te Komako edition*, 24(3, 4): 49–64.

King, M. (2003). *The Penguin history of New Zealand*. Auckland, New Zealand: Penguin Books.

Lavalette, M. (ed.) (2011). *Radical social work today: social work at the cross roads*. Bristol: Policy Press.

Mafile'o, T. (2013). Pasifika social work. In M. Connolly & L. Harms (eds), *Social work: contexts and practice* (3rd edn, pp. 138–50). South Melbourne: Oxford University Press.

Ministerial Advisory Committee on a Māori Perspective for the Development of Social Welfare (1986). Puao-te-ata-tu. The report of the Ministerial Advisory Committee on a Māori perspective for the Department of Social Welfare. Wellington, New Zealand: Department of Social Welfare.

Munford, R. & Sanders, J. (2010). Embracing the diversity of practice: indigenous knowledge and mainstream social work practice. *Journal of Social Practice: Psychotherapeutic Approaches in Health, Welfare and the Community*, 25(1): 63–77.

Nash, M. (2001). Social work in Aotearoa/New Zealand: its origins and traditions. In M. Connolly (ed.), *Social work in New Zealand: contexts and practice* (pp. 32–43). Auckland, New Zealand: Oxford University Press.

Nash, M. (1998). People, policies and practice. Social work education in Aotearoa/New Zealand/New Zealand from 1949–1995. PhD thesis, Massey University, Palmerston North, New Zealand.

Polutu-Endemann, F.K. (2001). Fonofale model of health. Paper presented at the workshop on Pacific models for health promotion, 7 September 2009, Wellington, Massey University. Retrieved on 22 April 2014 from www.hauora.co.nz/resources/Fonofalemodelexplanation.pdf.

Ruwhiu, L. (2013). Making sense of indigenous issues in Aotearoa/New Zealand. In M. Connolly & L. Harms (eds), *Social work: contexts and practice* (3rd edn, pp. 138–50). Melbourne: Oxford University Press.

Sewpaul, V. & Jones, D. (2004). Global standards for the education and training of the social work profession. Adopted at the General Assemblies of IASSW and IFSW, Australia. Retrieved on 22 April 2014 from cdn.ifsw.org/assets/ifsw_65044–3.pdf.

Social Workers Registration Board (2013a). Schedule 1: current recognised New Zealand social work qualifications. Retrieved on 22 April 2014 from www.swrb.govt.nz/new-applicants/recognised-qualifications.

Social Workers Registration Board (2013b). The process for recognition/re-recognition of social work qualifications in New Zealand. Policy statement. Retrieved on 29 April from www.swrb.govt.nz/doc-man/policies-1/41-the-process-for-recognition-re-recognition-of-social-work-qualifications-in-new-zealand-1.

Social Workers Registration Board (2010a). Competence to practise social work with Māori. Policy statement. Retrieved on 29 April from www.swrb.govt.nz/doc-man/policies-1/29-competence-to-practise-social-work-with-maori-1.

Social Workers Registration Board (2010b). Competence to practise social work with different ethnic and cultural groups. Policy statement. Retrieved on 29 April from www.swrb.govt.nz/doc-man/policies-1/30-competence-to-practise-social-work-with-different-ethnic-and-cultural-groups-1.

Staniforth, B. (2010). Counselling in social work in Aotearoa/New Zealand: the historical, political and socio-cultural evolution. *Aotearoa NZ Social Work Review*, 22(3): 3–14.

State Services Commission (2005). The story of the treaty. Part 1. Wellington, New Zealand: The Treaty of Waitangi Information Programme.

Tennant, M. (1989). *Paupers and providers: charitable aid in New Zealand*. Wellington, New Zealand: Allen & Unwin/Historical Branch.

Walsh-Tapiata, W. (2004). The past the present and the future: the New Zealand indigenous experience of social work. *Social Work Review*, 16(4): 30–37.

Webber-Dreadon, E. (1999). He Taonga Mo o Matou Tipuna (a gift handed down by our ancestors): an indigenous approach to social work supervision. *Social Work Review*, 11 (4): 7–11.

Zubrzycki, J. & Crawford, F. (2013). Collaboration and relationship building in Arboriginal and Torres Strait Islander social work. In B. Bennett, S. Green, S. Gilbert & D. Bessarab. *Our voices: Aboriginal and Torres Strait Islander social work*. Melbourne: Palgrave Macmillan.

14

Social work education in the United States: beyond boundaries

Clara Shockley and Frank R. Baskind

Today in the United States of America, social work education at the baccalaureate, master's, and doctoral levels enjoys high demand, while continuously evolving in response to its environment and the changing context of professional practice. This chapter explores the salient features that propel American social work education towards excellence. These include the Council on Social Work Education's Educational Philosophy and Educational Standards (EPAS); the credentials and scholarship of the faculty who craft the programs and curricula; accreditation standards that address global awareness; the values and ethics of the profession; and economic and social justice through a lens of cultural competency. Contemporary issues in American higher education also are identified to illustrate social work education's responses to evolving trends in university teaching.

With an explosive demand for social workers for service in health care, mental health, social services, and other areas, the education of social workers currently enjoys a dynamic confluence of development and historical contribution. According to the US Bureau of Labor Statistics, the growth forecast for social work jobs in the US for the period 2010 to 2020 is 25%, where the anticipated growth of the national average for all professions is 14% (Bureau of Labor Statistics 2014). Likewise, US social work education currently possesses among the strongest vitality, demand and discovery in its history, with over 100,000 individuals enrolled in the US for social work study in both full- and part-time study. Through development of evolving best practices techniques and the shared knowledge across disciplines, social work education is positioned for growth and impact in the future. Informed by an emphasis on ethical practices and keenly aware of concern for cultural competence, social work education in the US works towards inclusion of ideas, individuals and best practices.

In the US, social work education involves completion of degrees at the baccalaureate, master's and doctoral levels, with a strong emphasis on continuing education for practitioners, scholars and leaders of social work. Institutions of higher learning in the US typically require four years of study for the baccalaureate degree and two years of full-time or its equivalent study to fulfil the master's degree.

The baccalaureate degree is pursued by those who seek a career as a beginning professional social work practitioner. The BSW degree involves four years of full-time study or equivalent, with a multidisciplinary general education curriculum that leads to the last two years learning ethics and values, practice theories, and social welfare policy, research knowledge, and field practicum internships essential for social work practice. It is the first professional degree preparing students for generalist social work practice. The MSW requires two years of full-time study or equivalent, and equips the social worker with knowledge and skills for advanced practice in a variety of different fields of practice.

Regarding the number of US social work students for the 2012 academic year, baccalaureate enrolment is 52,789 full-time students with 7279 part-time students. For MSW graduate programs, student enrolment is 34,484 full-time and 19,351 part-time (CSWE Annual Statistics 2012). For the most recent period for which numbers are available (2012), 15,946 baccalaureate and 22,441 master's degrees were awarded (CSWE 2014).

Number of social work degree programs

In conjunction with growth of social work demand, the number of social work programs has grown over the past several decades in the US Today there are 490 accredited baccalaureate programs, which offer studies to meet the Bachelor of Social Work degree, and also, as of June 2013, there are 228 accredited social work programs that offer the Master of Social Work degree. As of October 2013, there are 19 BSW programs in candidacy status working towards initial accreditation and ten new MSW programs in candidacy status working towards initial accreditation (CSWE 2013).

For MSW studies, advanced concentrations generally are in Direct Clinical Practice, or Macro Practice. Within these concentrations there may be areas of focus that may include Gerontology, International Policy and Practice Issues, Physical, Mental and Behavioral Health, Organisational Management and Leadership, and Community Organising, Planning and Development. Professional development and the related continuing education are expectations of practicing and licensed social workers, and key elements of the network of social workers across academia and regional and local settings and communities where US social workers live and work. This open-minded exchange of ideas continues to ensure quality social work education in the US

The Council on Social Work Education

The development, implementation, and oversight of social work educational standards in the US are coordinated by a non-profit organization with the mission to validate the quality and content of social work education nationally. The Council on Social Work Education (CSWE) in the US is an 'association of social work education programs and individuals that ensures and enhances the quality of social work education for a professional practice that promotes individual, family, and community wellbeing, and social and economic justice' as described on their website at www.cswe.org. Oversight of US social work education includes graduate and undergraduate programs at both the baccalaureate and master's levels. Originating in 1952, CSWE connects social welfare agencies, individual social workers, plus educational institutions and members across the profession, for the advocacy and advancement of sound social work education for best practices, cultural learning and advocacy and furtherance of social work education (CSWE 2014).

Accreditation

Commission on Accreditation (COA)

As the governing body, CSWE has oversight of the delivery of social work education to ensure quality and practice competency in the US. Within the Council on Social Work Education, there is a unit that holds the responsibility for the accreditation standards that define this competency and ensure that the educational intentions for social work meet them. The Commission on Accreditation (COA) within CSWE develops standards for accreditation, moving the conceptual aspects required within social work educational programs into standards. The Council on Social Work Education serves as the sole accreditation source for social work education in the US, and holds recognition from the Council for Higher Education Accreditation (CHEA). Other programs recognised by CHEA include the Council on Occupational Education, the Middle States Commission on Higher Education, and the Western Association of Schools and Colleges.

CHEA is a liaison group designed to provide accountability and transparency for the public regarding fulfilment of the guidelines for accreditation. Thus, CHEA, which is sanctioned by the US federal government as the group that recognises CSWE as source for social work education accreditation standards, confirms completion of the standards and makes them public. A not-for-profit, self-regulating agency, CHEA maintains accreditation requirements for social work education and these then sanction CSWE's accreditation of educational programs for social work education.

These guidelines of accreditation establish standards that educational institutions fulfil for professional social work education. Periodic re-assessment of accreditation and accreditation standards generate the guidelines by which CSWE reviews how and where quality social work education is delivered. Such competence involves careful and detailed standards, which are systematically reviewed, studied and updated by the COA, which is comprised of 25 members chosen as being committed to fair and impartial standards. Most noteworthy of the standards is the focus on continuous assessment and improvement of the program and its curriculum.

Educational Policy and Accreditation Standards (EPAS)

As one critical component of its oversight of accreditation for social work education, CSWE maintains standards for accreditation, articulated in its Educational Policy and Accreditation Standards (EPAS). CSWE's *EPAS Handbook* articulates the components of the following standards for accreditation: program mission and goals, explicit curriculum, implicit curriculum, and assessment (CSWE 2013).

These four overarching themes within EPAS provide the framework for the detailed elements that are required for a social work education program to meet in order to gain full accreditation. An integrated curriculum design possesses each of these four areas. Program mission and goals means that the core aspects of social work's mission and values will be evident within the curriculum for each program that pursues accreditation. Integrity, competence and scientific inquiry are among the shared goals for social work, and are included here. Explicit curriculum identifies the specific components of pedagogy, including the curriculum content that makes up foundational coursework for generalist learning related to the BSW and curriculum for advanced practice to be learned at the MSW level. The EPAS competencies detail the foundational learning and practice behaviours that each program must provide in order to reach and to maintain accreditation. Implicit curriculum, the third of the four standards within the EPAS, involves the culture for learning social work, for each of the programs that seeks accreditation. Within this standard are topics that include transparency of policymaking, commitment to diversity, availability of resources, the environment for discovery and learning, and matters that relate to the climate for social work education in the program seeking accreditation. Assessment involves the assurance that competencies are met within the education structure for each school that seeks accreditation. Review, awareness and intentional change to the curriculum, both explicit and implicit, are elements of programs that reflect effective assessment and a self-examination to attain standards. Thus, these four standards detail how programs will attain academic excellence via models of curriculum design that are both traditional and reflect emerging types of learning. In this way, the EPAS 'support[s] academic excellence by establishing thresholds for professional competence' (CSWE 2008, 1).

Considering the rigorous standards and contributions of these agencies, CSWE's Office of Social Work Accreditation (OSWA) carries out a process of accreditation that involves numerous steps and includes a benchmarking process, site visits to the educational programs, program self-review and compliance guides, and reviews by the members of the Commission on Accreditation.

Social work core competencies

Colleges and universities that offer social work education and degrees utilise competency-based learning for development of the explicit and implicit curriculum that prepares students for either BSW and MSW practice. With competency-based learning, the focus is on the knowledge, values and skills required for either generalist or advanced social work practice.

To master the skills needed for social work practice, the BSW programs equip students for generalist practice, and the MSW programs produce advanced practitioners. Related directly to the prior discussion of accreditation of social work programs at US colleges, the BSW includes courses, projects and studies that relate directly to social work and issues specific to its generalist practice, social work values and ethics, and knowledge. These include the methods, approaches, communication skills, intellectual insight, and generalist knowledge required by professional social workers. At the MSW level, more sophisticated and complex skills and practice behaviours are required that include the application of research knowledge. These skills translate as core competencies that social workers at different levels must master for professional practice. Each of the ten competency areas details practice behaviours which illustrate, order and create operationalised measures for practice outcomes.

Table 14.1 EPAS ten core competencies for US social work education (CSWE 2008).

Specific competency	EPAS explanation of competency	Examples of competencies
1. Identify as a social worker and act accordingly.	Social workers serve as representatives of the profession, its mission, and its core values. They know the profession's history. Social workers commit themselves to the profession's enhancement and to their own professional conduct and growth.	• advocate for client access to the services of social work • practice personal reflection and self-correction to assure continual professional development • attend to professional roles and boundaries • demonstrate professional demeanor in behaviour, appearance, and communication • engage in career-long learning • use supervision and consultation.
2. Apply social work ethical principles in practice.	Social workers have an obligation to conduct themselves ethically and to engage in ethical decision-making. Social workers are knowledgeable about the value base of the profession, its ethical standards, and relevant law.	• recognise and manage personal values in a way that allows professional values to guide practice • make ethical decisions by applying standards of the National Association of Social Workers Code of Ethics and, as applicable, of the International Federation of Social Workers / International Association of Schools of Social Work Ethics in Social Work, Statement of Principles • tolerate ambiguity in resolving ethical conflicts • apply strategies of ethical reasoning to arrive at principled decisions.
3. Apply critical thinking in making judgements.	Social workers are knowledgeable about the principles of logic, scientific inquiry, and reasoned discernment. They use critical thinking augmented by creativity and curiosity. Critical thinking also requires the synthesis and communication of relevant information.	• distinguish, appraise, and integrate multiple sources of knowledge, including research-based knowledge, and practise wisdom • analyse models of assessment, prevention, intervention, and evaluation • demonstrate effective oral and written communication in working with individuals, families, groups, organisations, communities, and colleagues.
4. Engage diversity and difference in practice.	Social workers understand how diversity characterises and shapes the human experience and is critical to the formation of identity. The dimensions of diversity are understood as the intersectionality of multiple factors including age, class, colour, culture, disability, ethnicity, gender, gender identity and expression, immigration status, political ideology, race,	• recognise the extent to which a culture's structures and values may oppress, marginalise, alienate, or create or enhance privilege and power • gain sufficient self-awareness to eliminate the influence of personal biases and values in working with diverse groups

	religion, sex, and sexual orientation. Social workers appreciate that, as a consequence of difference, a person's life experiences may include oppression, poverty, marginalisation, and alienation as well as privilege, power, and acclaim.	• recognise and communicate their understanding of the importance of difference in shaping life experiences • view themselves as learners and engage those with whom they work as informants.
5. Advance human rights and social/ economic justice.	Each person, regardless of position in society, has basic human rights, such as freedom, safety, privacy, an adequate standard of living, health care, and education. Social workers recognise the global interconnections of oppression and are knowledgeable about theories of justice and strategies to promote human and civil rights. Social work incorporates social justice practices in organisations, institutions, and society to ensure that these basic human rights are distributed equitably and without prejudice.	• understand the forms and mechanisms of oppression and discrimination • advocate for human rights and social and economic justice • engage in practices that advance social and economic justice.
6. Engage in research-informed practice and practice-informed research.	Social workers use practice experience to inform research, employ evidence-based interventions, evaluate their own practice, and use research findings to improve practice, policy, and social service delivery. Social workers comprehend quantitative and qualitative research and understand scientific and ethical approaches to building knowledge.	• use practice experience to inform scientific inquiry • use research evidence to inform practice.
7. Apply knowledge of human behaviour in the social environment.	Social workers are knowledgeable about human behaviour across the life course; the range of social systems in which people live; and the ways social systems promote or deter people in maintaining or achieving health and wellbeing. Social workers apply theories and knowledge from the liberal arts to understand biological, social, cultural, psychological, and spiritual development.	• utilise conceptual frameworks to guide the processes of assessment, intervention, and evaluation • critique and apply knowledge to understand person and environment.
8. Engage in policy practice to advance social and economic wellbeing.	Social work practitioners understand that policy affects service delivery, and they actively engage in policy practice. Social workers know the history and current structures of social policies and services; the role of policy in ser-	• analyse, formulate, and advocate for policies that advance social wellbeing • collaborate with colleagues and clients for effective policy action.

vice delivery; and the role of practice in policy development.

9. Respond to the contexts that shape practice.	Social workers are informed, resourceful, and proactive in responding to evolving organisational, community, and societal contexts at all levels of practice. Social workers recognise that the context of practice is dynamic, and use knowledge and skill to respond proactively.	• continuously discover, appraise, and attend to changing locales, populations, scientific and technological developments, and emerging societal trends to provide relevant services • provide leadership in promoting sustainable changes in service delivery and practice to improve the quality of social services.
10. Assess, evaluate, and intervene with individuals, families, groups, and communities.	Professional practice involves the dynamic and interactive processes of engagement, assessment, intervention, and evaluation at multiple levels. Social workers have the knowledge and skills to practice with individuals, families, groups, organisations, and communities. Practice knowledge includes identifying, analyzing, and implementing evidence-based interventions designed to achieve client goals; using research and technological advances; evaluating program outcomes and practice effectiveness; developing, analysing, advocating, and providing leadership for policies and services; and promoting social and economic justice.	Engagement • substantively and affectively prepare for action with individuals, families, groups, organisations, and communities • use empathy and other interpersonal skills • develop a mutually agreed-on focus of work and desired outcomes. Assessment • collect, organise, and interpret client data • assess client strengths and limitations • develop mutually agreed-on intervention goals and objectives • select appropriate intervention strategies. Intervention • initiate actions to achieve organisational goals • implement prevention interventions that enhance client capacities • help clients resolve problems • negotiate, mediate, and advocate for clients • facilitate transitions and endings. Evaluation • critically analyse, monitor, and evaluate interventions.

Faculty credentials and scholarship

Social work educators in the US share several key credentials, beginning with the MSW degree, with the completion and award of the doctoral degree becoming the academic expectation for university instruction of social work. Other key traits of social work educators include active publications and peer-reviewed scholarship, research on issues of theory, practice and social justice, and participating in community service. Social work educators in the US serve as innovators in thinking, social work action and leadership for their educational institution, for the local community where they reside, and in global initiatives. Faculty development and collaboration among social workers across the US happen with research studies, data collection, scholarship, and programs that cross boundaries of university affiliation, state lines or geographical settings to allow social work practice and education to remain vital, immediate and relevant.

Education for social work practice

Field education

Field education is the critical element of learning and the signature learning format for study of social work at US universities and colleges. Field education is the direct placement of student social workers for supervised field instruction of the practice and performance of the core competencies in a professional setting that delivers social work services. The purpose is to provide real life learning experiences for the student learner in the profession to integrate theories, concepts, and skills. On site in the placement setting, social work professionals assist, guide and provide immediate oversight of the field education by communicating directly with the student, as well as with the academic liaison. According to the EPAS, a minimum of 950 hours of field education are required in graduate study, existing as 14 to 21 hours' field placement weekly. For the BSW, a minimum of 450 hours of field placement are required.

Key elements of field education are the development of social work values and ethics, critical thinking, and practice skills by the student. Field education is the means by which a student learns by firsthand practice in the work location of the demands, dilemmas, interactions and services that social work provides. Field instructors oversee the developing social worker as they perform tasks, witness ethical issues in social work and grow in judgment and professional practice skills. Field education placements are designed for hands-on experience, as the student gains in knowledge and insight and their tasks gradually grow in complexity. While the student's role, functions and duties grow at the field placement, competencies and confidence also grow in degree of complexity, responsibility, judgment and independence.

Coursework and community involvement

Social work classes include lectures, case studies, the use of role plays, and small group projects for collaborative learning and presentations. Collaborative learning and the discussion and response to real-world problems in the classroom are used as preparation for professional challenges to come. Courses also offer extensive reading assignments, research and writing, exams, and online learning experiences. In learning practice skills or clinical roles, theory and role play are used as a format for instruction, as well as case studies. The curriculum includes evidence-based practices as a focus for study of theory, research and practice behaviours.

Economic and social justice through cultural competency

In US social work education, a commitment to social justice and to improving the quality of life for all populations and humans is key. A recent review of the 2013 *Journal of Social Work Education* shows a range of topics including immigration issues, non-traditional and world spirituality practices for social work, an exchange program between a US university and Ghana, lesbian/gay/bisexual/transgender outreach and sensitivity for policy and practice, and communication as a priority in US multinational agency settings. Social workers share a goal to end the oppression, injustice and lack of opportunities for all groups and people. They do so via outreach, education, provision of services, the democratic political processes, advocacy and by consideration and execution of programs to connect with those who have less opportunity. Increasing global issues also affect US social workers. Due to the world's recovery from international wars, a severe rise in mental health issues in the US, the Arab Spring, and the economic issues impacting quality of life, US social workers are alert to social justice principles. These give social work education the goal of providing skills to respond to need wherever in the world it exists: essential services and support to those with restricted opportunity is a critical focus for social work education. More than ever, a multidimensional society exists in the US, reflecting a portrait of race, culture, class, sexual identity, religious or spiritual interests, and ethnic backgrounds.

Social work education seeks to prepare practitioners to meet the current and the anticipated concerns of marginalised groups, communities, personal histories and peoples. Methods of engagement, activism, and techniques for effective outreach, sensitive and culturally alert communication skills, inclusion, and culturally informed service delivery are among the social justice topics that US social workers practice and pursue. The concentrations that social work education offers for study of special topics reflect topics of special concern for US social welfare. These include gerontology and ageing, trauma, prevention and treatment of substance abuse issues, child and family welfare, military and veterans' issues, and advanced/clinical social work practices. Social work education seeks to heighten awareness, engage solutions, research vital alternatives, examine explanatory patterns, and intervene in progressive and helpful ways.

Resources of NASW and the Code of Ethics

With membership of around 150,000 and founded in 1955, another central organization coordinating social work issues in the US on a national level is the National Association of Social Workers (NASW). Among noted features and services of the NASW is their Code of Ethics, which offers a detailed design for ethical practice and values for professional social work practice. These are infused in the EPAS and are embedded in the BSW and MSW programs in the US.

The National Association of Social Work also supports and emphasises the importance of social justice, social work education, professional development, cultural engagement and sharing within and beyond social work, and service. The NASW publishes reference works, guides to professional standards and thematic concerns plus the aforementioned Code of Ethics and these may be accessed at the organisation's website at www.socialworkers.org.

Contemporary issues in US social work education

Dynamic response to current and upcoming topics in the field is an important component of social work education in the US. Thus awareness of the contemporary issues that affect social work students and their learning is crucial. These topics represent evolving trends related to US social work education. Financing a US social work education, social work licensure for US practice, global initiatives, the doctoral degree for social work, and distance learning are issues that represent concern, potential change, and close consideration by the US social work profession.

Tuition

The cost of social work study in the US varies and is determined largely by the university where the student enrols. A glimpse at tuition for MSW study in the US ranges from approximately $5000 to around $43,000 per year; often tuition and fees do not include living expenses for the student, such as room and board or transportation costs. Many universities offer scholarship programs, need-based tuition remission, or work study programs. For the BSW degree, annual costs for the period ending 2011 range from around $8000 per year at the most affordable institution to $32,671 for private four-year US institutions, with these figures including room and board.

Costs for social work higher education in the US are growing at a rapid pace and this is a serious concern for social work educational leaders and the social work profession. From 2000 to the current academic year, costs for undergraduate education in the US rose 42%, vastly higher than cost of living or income grew. CSWE reports that the median amount of loans, called student debt, for 2012–13 for US social work learners is $25,840 total borrowed to finance a baccalaureate degree. The median amount borrowed for MSW degree costs equals $36,337 (CSWE 2012/13 Annual Report).

Licensure and the Association of Social Work Boards

Independent of social work education, yet a logical and critical indirect link, is the licensure process for practitioners of social work in the US Individuals often pursue social work education in order to gain licensure as a social worker, which in the US is a separate process, distinct from higher education and the pursuit of social work education. For the US, social work licensure is coordinated through the Association of Social Work Boards (www.aswb.org/SWLE/SWLE.asp). The ASWB manages the US standards and content for examination of all US social work licensure within a central repository based upon individual states' exam content and cultural competencies.

Following completion and official verification of fulfilment of all educational standards and after the awarding of the relevant degree, BSW or MSW, a student may wish or need to seek licensure to practice. In many US states, an individual may not refer to themselves as a 'social worker' unless they hold the certification of that state's health professional licensure. Individual states have different eligibility for licensure, so a social worker interested in licensure would contact the state where that person resides. Commonly, licensure is offered at varying levels such as Graduate, Generalist, or Clinical social worker licensure, depending upon the university degree fulfilled, the level of field or professional experience, and the verified US professional social work supervision. Almost every state maintains a website outlining licensure types for all professions, including social work, via the Social

Work Board of Examiners for that state. These individual websites detail the requirements, fees, and timeline for earning licensure.

The implications of licensure requirements for social work students involve the added obligations, fees and requirements for state license. These regulations are embraced by social workers in the sense that they validate and make official the social work field, but licensure can involve time, registration and waiting periods for exams, and qualifying tasks that sometimes take years to complete. Social work education leaders in the US are vigilant regarding the need for the separate arenas of education and professional social work licensure to remain in sync, echoing the careful review of ethics, clinical procedures, diagnostic guidelines and other complex areas of social work practice.

Global awareness evident in the EPAS

Social work education remains aware and seeks to address through practice competencies for learning that ours is a global practice realm, and not merely a local one. The EPAS illustrate this, with emphasis for social work learning on diversity, engaging difference, human rights and socioeconomic justice. Essential human rights for all people, and outreach for those whose rights are restricted or limited, is a central theme in the EPAS, which emphasises a global perspective.

Related to CSWE's embrace of global concerns with commitment to solutions, is the Katherine A. Kendall Institute for International Social Work Education. Founded in 2004 with a commitment to outreach for international issues in social work education, the institute sponsors international conferences, research initiatives with a global scope, and promotes collaborative programs that link research and worldwide dialogues for social work learning. A world-renowned advocate for social justice and key to the development of social work education standards, Kendall was born in 1910 in Scotland and after emigration to the US at age ten later embraced the social work practice with an MSW from Louisiana State University in 1939 and a PhD from the University of Chicago in 1950 in social service administration. She served in leadership for national US social work bodies, and played a critical role in creation of the CSWE. Having served as associate director, executive director and other positions with CSWE, her passion for international unity of social work learning and for its causes governed her career. Around 1945 she was a staff member in the international office at the US Children's Bureau, and work at the United Nations (UN) followed in 1947. There, her research and writing on international social work issues led to publication of *Training for social work: an international survey*, prompting the UN passage of a resolution calling for professionalisation of social workers. The book greatly affected positive growth and development of social work education and the profession, worldwide.

From 1954 to 1963 in a voluntary role, Kendall served as Secretary of the International Association of Schools of Social Work (IASSW), helping to transform this organisation-from mostly European in scope to a global agency. She retired in 1978. Later, in 2004 – indicative of her passion for international learning in social work – she endowed the Katherine A. Kendall Institute of International Social Work Education, based at CSWE, for the promotion and enhancement of international understanding for social work. Numerous projects, conferences, and topics are evident within the Institute, including human rights, global migration and disaster management. Africa, Asia, Latin America, the US and the Caribbean are sites of some of the programs of the Institute.

Citing the broadening scope and myriad issues of a multinational community, the CSWE Katherine A. Kendall Institute aims to unite resources with the heightened and related skills social workers need to practice in an internationally informed context. The primary purpose of the institute is to support social work education for global awareness of the highest standards of social work learning with an international scope. Promoting programs to nurture solutions for worldwide topics, and building of needed skills, the institute urges collaboration and exchange of global ideas for international social work gains. The institute funds collaborative efforts to globalise and connect data collection, research initiatives and programs that improve international understanding. This is merely one example of growing awareness of the need to internationalise social work education and build contacts, effective solutions and social work standards worldwide.

Themes and special topics for social work education

A concern for global topics serves as a strong and ongoing issue for social work education in the US. Among the myriad issues of current research and dialogue for social work educators are found: internationalising social work education, issues of HIV-AIDS, evidence-based practices, treatment interventions and techniques for direct practice, innovations in social work learning, personal identity, communication techniques, strategies for self-care, the professional–personal balance, social policy, agency and university collaboration for community growth.

Doctoral education in social work

On the horizon appears debate and discussion in the profession regarding doctoral study in the field of social work. The Doctorate of Philosophy (PhD) in social work emphasises research, theory and intellectual contributions to the field, while the Doctorate in Social Work (DSW or Prof D) specialises in further study of clinical practices for social work. Different US universities offer these degrees each with unique characteristics, but a larger dialogue regarding the application of either degree to social work education remains. Some CSWE programs are discussing the implications of a change if the criteria for some federal clinical grant awards are to be awarded exclusively to DSW or clinical doctorates in social work. This beginning discussion begs clarification in the interest of committed students of social work who seek to maximise their learning and high level studies with demands of the profession and of the job market. The most recent document issued on Advanced Practice Doctorates is a report of an invitational think tank in September 2013 that addresses the question: 'Does the marketplace want or need doctoral level social work clinicians?' (Social Work Policy Institute 2013, 15). Some conclusions generated by the report indicate the need for further examination and wider discussion regarding the advance practice doctorate across the profession, inclusion of US federal agencies in the examination of options, and study of levels or patterns of interest in the DSW degree.

Online education and distance learning

Distance education where social work students complete classes online towards completion of degrees is growing in popularity. The trend is for continued increase in online degrees offered for both the BSW and MSW curriculum (CSWE 2014). With students juggling work obligations and their family life, the independence and virtual access are very popular for US students of social work. For the most recent period that CSWE has numbers available, five US universities offer online study for BSW degrees. There are 25 distance learning MSW programs available, as of 17 October 2013 (CSWE Annual Report 2012–2013). Individual schools' websites detail whether courses are available to take remotely, and outline how field education is coordinated during the degree studies. Students are urged to confirm CSWE's COA accreditation status of any college where they enrol for study of social work, and to examine all requirements and fees that relate to completion of the degree.

Conclusions

Social work education is continually evolving in the US, involving ongoing response by educators to environmental changes, social and cultural dynamics, and global issues. As shown, maintaining excellence via the highest standards for teaching and learning requires continued enhancement of programs and curricula. Priority consideration of values and ethics of the profession continues as a standard for US social work education. With vigilance for cultural competency, economic and social justice are upheld as hallmarks for US social work. Contemporary issues represent several topics of current concern and opportunity for leadership in these trends, and growth in the US social work profession.

References

Bureau of Labor Statistics (2014). Occupational outlook handbook: social workers, United States Department of Labor. Retrieved on 22 April 2014 from www.bls.gov/ooh/community-and-social-service/social-workers.htm.

Council on Social Work Education (CSWE) (2012/2013). Annual report. Retrieved on 22 April 2014 from www.cswe.org/File.aspx?id=69934.

CSWE (2012). 2012 statistics on social work education in the United States. Retrieved on 22 April 2014 from www.cswe.org/File.aspx?id=68989.

CSWE (2008). Educational policy and accreditation standards. Retrieved on 22 April 2014 from www.cswe.org/File.aspx?id=13780.

Social Work Policy Institute (2013). Advance practice doctorates: what do they mean for social work practice, research, and education. Washington, DC: National Association for Social Workers Foundation.

15

Social work education in the United Kingdom

Brian Littlechild and Karen Lyons

This chapter examines key areas in social work education theory, practice, and research in the UK, including the main methods used and the client groups with whom social workers engage.

The chapter sketches the origins and development of social work education and identifies key features currently framing social work education (SWE). The latter include factors associated with higher education systems and policies as well as those specific to social work in its organisational frameworks and as a profession. The staffing of social work programs and the role of research in relation to theory and practice development are discussed. A major section presents the predominant practice models, methods, theories and perspectives and their associated histories and epistemological challenges. Mention is made of contributing disciplines (e.g. sociology and law) and the key teaching and learning strategies utilised, including in relation to issues of cultural relativism and understanding, and international influences. Conclusions are drawn regarding the health of the discipline in the UK.

Social work as a recognised activity dates back to the late 19th century in the UK and social work education (SWE) has had a long and somewhat chequered history. One purpose of this chapter is to describe the context within which SWE has developed, with an emphasis on current contextual influences. More importantly, the chapter aims to analyse the contemporary features of social work, both as a discipline within higher education, and as a form of professional education with a primary task of preparing students for a variety of roles in 'real world' social work. The main organisational features of SWE are described, as are the regulatory frameworks and professional goals and ethics influencing the design and delivery of programs at a range of academic and professional 'levels'. It should be mentioned here that different factors have impacted on social work in Scotland and Northern Ireland in the relatively recent past and some of these have had implications for SWE. This chapter therefore relates specifically to England, although generic programs are the norm throughout the UK and a first degree (BA or BSc) in social work is currently the nationally accepted qualification.

A wide range of 'external factors' impact on social work and therefore on SWE. These include political direction and economic factors affecting the funding of social work agencies and education programs. In addition, the needs of service users; expectations of other professional groups and the wider public; and media pressures also influence professional and educational developments. Internally, debates reflect ambivalence about the purpose of SWE and the form it should take, raising questions about 'who teaches social work' as well as content and pedagogical approaches. Similarly, there are varied understandings of the role of research and therefore its form and focus. A major section presents the predominant practice models, methods, theories and perspectives and their associated histories and epistemological challenges. Mention is also made of contributing disciplines (e.g. sociology and law) and the key teaching and learning strategies utilised, including in relation to issues of cultural relativism and understanding; anti-oppressive strategies; and international influences.

Significant features of SWE in the UK have been expectations about the roles that social work employers (initially) and then service users would play in the structure and delivery of SWE, creating distinctive requirements on social work for close working relationships between university staff and social service agencies and those with whom they work. The major factors impacting on social work practice learning are identified and consideration is given as to how well students are prepared for practice. In addition, the special needs of newly qualified social workers and staff moving into specialist areas of work have been recognised leading to the establishment of various forms of post-qualifying and postgraduate education and training.

Following a section summarising the major trends in the development of SWE and its organisational context, this chapter focuses on the content of programs and their relationship to regulatory frameworks and 'readiness to practice' drivers. A further section discusses staffing and research issues as well as mentioning some new initiatives which may impact on social work in higher education. The chapter concludes with a consideration of the current state of SWE in England.

British social work education: history and organisational context

The first training opportunities for 'social workers' were afforded by a voluntary agency, the Charity Organisation Society (COS), in the late 19th century, and, by the early years of the 20th century, social work training had gained a place in various universities, notably in London, Birmingham, Liverpool and Glasgow. These were all cities with high rates of poverty with associated problems of squalid living conditions and ill health; and SWE included community work, allied to the earlier establishment of 'settlements' (forerunners of community centres) in the poorest parts of many cities. Some of the notable figures in the development of social work had their earliest experiences in the Settlement houses and subsequently made significant contributions to social work organisation and policy developments as well as education. One such person was Eileen Younghusband who, later in the 20th century, also contributed to international developments in SWE (Lyons 2008).

One outcome of World War 1 (1914–18) was an increase in interest in psychiatric conditions and treatments, and by the 1930s there had been significant growth in psychiatric (including psychoanalytical) services (as well as the beginnings of psychology as a discipline). These changes were reflected in SWE in the 'psychiatric deluge' (Payne 2005). On many courses this meant less concern about policies and interventions appropriate to the social conditions of poor people, relative to a greater emphasis on intra- and inter-personal relationships. This emphasis shifted again in the post-World War 2 period (1939–45) when a raft of welfare legislation laid the basis for the development of services and provisions broadly termed 'the welfare state'. One result of this was that sociologists and social policy analysts began to examine the outcomes of policies and programs aimed at general improvements in living standards and individual life chances, only to find, by the late 1960s, that old social divisions had resurfaced and new forms of social inequality had taken hold. Research had resulted in 'the rediscovery of poverty', a condition thought by many to have been eradicated, though it was now framed as a relative rather than absolute condition (Townsend 1979). As in previous eras, SWE was expected to mirror the shifts in political concerns and policy direction, although at this stage social work itself was being carried out in a range of agencies relating to different 'client groups' and courses tended to reflect the fragmentation of the field and provide 'training' in specialised fields.

In organisational terms, the earliest social work courses were established at postgraduate level in universities. These were usually allied to 'social studies' awards, constituting a continuous thread (with modifications) through to current forms of social work education and awards at master's level. The possibility of being awarded a professional qualification at two different academic levels has led to anomalies and complications in most recent organisational changes in the structure of SWE (see later). SWE has often recruited mature students but, apart from occasional efforts to adapt course length and attendance requirements to recognise this and the gendered nature of social work, gaining a professional qualification normally required attending a full-time course (at whatever academic level) until late in the 20th century.

From the 1970s, following the expansion in higher education through the establishment of a large number of polytechnics (similar to German Fachhochschulen), the majority of students qualified at Diploma in Social Work (DipSW) level, awarded by the academic institution after two years of study at undergraduate level, with the Certificate of Qualification in Social Work (CQSW) being awarded concurrently by the professional regulatory body, the Central Council for Education and Training in Social Work (CCETSW 1979–2001). Some universities continued to offer postgraduate courses to people who had gained undergraduate degrees in 'relevant subjects', affording some a postgraduate award in conjunction with a basic (rather than advanced) professional qualification. Organisational changes which took place in 1970, notably the establishment of unified Social Service Departments offering services across a wide range of client/user groups (with the exception of School Welfare and Probation Services), also resulted in shifts in the focus and content of social work courses which were now primarily 'generic'. A national division of responsibilities for youth and community services and for social services, between the Departments of Education and of Health respectively (and reflected at local authority and institutional levels), supported moves to establish separate courses and awards for youth and community workers. By the early 1980s the few remaining joint awards were ended with the establishment of separate bodies to regulate such courses and approve awards; and units or modules on CQSW courses equipping students for community work (and also often for group work) were largely discontinued. However, changes also reflected a moral panic about child abuse – most specifically, public concern about the deaths of children at the hands of their parents or primary care givers, particularly if these families were already under the supervision of social workers (Parton et al., 1997). Thus, there was an increased emphasis in many courses on work with individuals and families, including teaching and assignments aimed at developing skills in child observation and communicating with children.

Apart from a trend towards skills training rather than theoretical developments in social work education in the latter decades of the 20th century, there were also other shifts in course content. The first was related to developing racism awareness, equal opportunities and, eventually, anti-oppressive strategies, while the second laid an increased emphasis on teaching about the law. Anti-racism teaching and learning was required by CCETSW from the 1980s and inputs to courses were often first provided as short courses on anti-racism, add-ons to the main structure and content of programs. Subsequently, they were usually incorporated into mainstream teaching and extended into units or modules to address other forms of inequality and discrimination, e.g. based on gender, sexuality or disability.

In relation to the legal content of social work programs, a series of studies in the 1990s demonstrated that about 80% of students leaving social work education programs gained employment in local authority Social Service Departments, a statutory agency where legal requirements predominated in terms of the provision of services and the style of practice. Preventive work increasingly became a thing of the past or the responsibility of other agencies (including in the voluntary sector) and occupational groups. Many social workers complained that, in an increasingly managerialist environment, there was decreasing scope for relationship-based work and interventions beyond the assessment stage. It seemed as if what social work educators aimed to equip social workers to do was out of step with what they might be expected to do in practice.

The passing of the National Health Service and Community Care Act (1990) had signalled national moves to a mixed economy of care and increased emphasis on care management roles. This led in turn to the establishment of a parallel, employment-based route to a different qualification, Certificate in Social Services (CSS), which was offered in conjunction with some further and higher education institutions for about a decade. In addition, the government decided that changes should be made in the work of the Probation Service requiring the introduction of different training for Probation Officers and its complete separation from SWE. Thus, by the end of the 20th century, a more diverse range of awards existed in what might be called the 'social professions' and an increase in the modes of delivery was becoming apparent.

By the 21st century the government concluded that neither SWE nor its regulatory body were 'fit for purpose': approval was finally given for the replacement of the two year diploma/CQSW award by a three year degree, with provision for postgraduate conversion courses to continue as two-year masters' programs. These programs were to be regulated by a new agency, the General Social Care Council (GSCC, one each for England, Northern Ireland, Scotland and Wales 2001–12): this agency would not make a separate award but would require successful students to register in order to take up any post labelled as social work. Thus, social work finally achieved what many (including educators) had long argued for – provision of three-year educational programs and qualification at degree level (in line with many other countries in Europe and around the world) and restriction of use of the title social worker to those holding a professional qualification. However, the story does not end there since, by 2013, there have been further organisational changes in higher education and externally; several social work courses or departments have closed since the 1990s; SWE as a whole is in 2013 once again under review; the agency responsible for regulation has changed; and a new form of fast track training is being initiated, as we discuss later.

Course content, regulatory frameworks and readiness for practice

As indicated above, and in contrast to SWE in many other European countries, the content of British SWE courses has for some time been prescribed by regulations set out by government and its agencies. In 2010 the Social Work Reform Board was established as a government response to a child's death that raised severe doubts about the competence of social workers in protecting children already known to be at risk of abuse. Its purpose was to set out an agenda for social work and social work qualifying education and recommendations were made in 2012. Meanwhile, in 2011, a new body was established by government, the College of Social Work (with the aim of raising standards in social work and SWE. (It is intended that this should become a self-funding body, independent of government). The college has no regulatory powers, but its Professional Capabilities Framework (PCF, see later) and its standards are taken into account by the current regulatory body, the Health and Care Professions Council (HCPC) when validating programs (see later).

One stream of the Reform Board's work (of which one of the authors was part) focused on the 'Calibre of Entrants'. Traditionally social work courses have accepted some mature students with 'life experience' who may, however, lack good academic qualifications. Concerns were raised about how to assess at entry stage empathy for and understanding of service user issues and the potential to learn about and carry out the complex tasks of social workers, while also raising the academic standards on courses. The result was that academic entry requirements have been made more stringent, but concerns persist about both the suitability of students and the direction in which SWE is being pushed, i.e. to a more elite form of training (see also later) and away from a previous commitment to open access, providing opportunities to a wide range of applicants. The responsibility for driving this and other aspects of the agenda passed to the College of Social Work in England from 2012.

At the same time as the drive to raise academic standards, a key debate continues to be whether social work theory is sufficiently related to practice and, indeed, how much theory is needed to prepare students to become qualified social workers. The government's influence on the content and processes of SWE is now exercised through the Health and Care Professions Council (HCPC) which took over most of the responsibilities of the GSCC in 2012. As mentioned above, courses have increasingly phased out approaches such as casework (based on psychodynamic ideas) and community work, since they do not fit with government priorities, nor with the requirements of most employers. As with the GSCC before it, the HCPC stipulates that employers should have a substantial say in the development and ongoing review of courses.

The HCPC Standards of Proficiency for social workers in England

Approaches and focus: social workers must be able to

- understand the need to promote the best interests of service users and carers at all times

- understand the need to protect, safeguard and promote the wellbeing of children, young people and vulnerable adults
- understand the need to address practices which present a risk to or from service users and carers, or others
- be able to use practice to challenge and address the impact of discrimination, disadvantage and oppression
- be able to support service users' and carers' rights to control their lives and make informed choices about the services they receive.

Teaching and learning methods used to enable students to meet these requirements include lectures; seminars; small group and individual tutorials; problem-based learning; case studies and group exercises; visits to students on practice placements ('three-way meetings' between the student, practice educator and tutor); and, increasingly, online learning with the use of exercises, quizzes, online group discussions, etc.

One of the recommendations of the Social Work Reform Board was that there should be more emphasis on skills development, so, as from 2013, courses must include 30 days of skills training (assessed) before students can start practice placements. Considerable emphasis is placed on assessed practice learning in placements provided by social work agencies which are supported financially by the government's Department of Health (agencies get a daily fee for taking a student). Students usually undertake two or three assessed placements in different settings and these must total 200 days. A professional award cannot be made to anyone who fails a placement.

Practice learning therefore has a high priority in the assessment of students and great emphasis is placed by universities and the HCPC on the development and support of both placements and practice educators so that these are 'fit for purpose'. Panels have been established comprising university and agency staff and often also service users and/or carers to assess reports from the practice educators, who may be challenged to provide further evidence as the basis for decisions about passing or failing a placement. Prior to placements, practice educators are required to have undertaken training (provided by the universities) for their role. Guidance is issued for students and practice educators on the processes and regulations governing placements and these are monitored and supported through three-way meetings (usually two or three per placement) as well as workshops for the practice educators.

The main areas to be addressed in course content include:

- sociological ideas
- social policy
- psychology (e.g. human growth and development, mental health and learning disabilities)
- anti-oppressive practice
- law
- ethics teaching – this is variable, and often subsumed into the discussion of professional behaviour and regulation.

Key areas of policy and practice currently influencing SWE are individualisation; personalisation and individualised packages of care (with a new emphasis on 're-enablement'); adult and child safeguarding; inspection and regulation; legal aspects; interagency and inter-professional working (Wilson et al. 2011; Littlechild & Smith 2013), and risk assessment and management (Littlechild 2008; Littlechild & Hawley 2010).

The HCPC also takes into account the provisions of the College of Social Work; the central government's Department of Health; and the education sector's Quality Assurance Agency (QAA). The last body sets the academic descriptors of program levels for the BA/BSc in Social Work as well as for the master's degree which enables students with a relevant first degree to gain a professional qualification after two years. The HCPC validates social work qualifying courses which satisfy its Standards for Education and Training; its Standards of Proficiency (as described above); and also the Professional Capabilities Framework (PCF) issued by the College of Social Work. On qualifying, people wishing to work in social work designated posts must register with the HCPC, which also has powers to strike off social workers who are judged to have failed to meet its Standards of Proficiency and its ethical statement.

With regard to the Professional Capabilities Framework (PCF), this was developed by the Social Work Reform Board, but is now 'owned' by the College of Social Work. It was framed with the intention of moving SWE away from previous requirements regarding competences to a more rounded focus on capability. This reflects a move from a mechanistic tick box approach to a more holistic approach (The College of Social Work 2012b). The PCF sets out nine domains of social work, and how those entering the profession and then progressing through it attain those domains. Whilst not technically regulatory, this framework is being used extensively by the HCPC, social work agencies and qualifying social work courses (Figure 15.1).

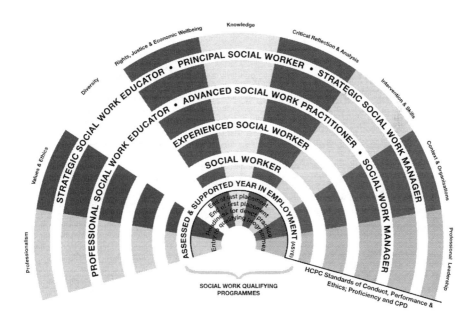

Figure 15.1 Professional capabilities framework for social workers (The College of Social Work 2012a).

Social work courses have to demonstrate to the HCPC that they are meeting the HCPC requirements for a qualifying course by having to map their learning outcomes to the elements of the PCF, and the HCPC's own Standards of Proficiency. For example, students should be enabled to:

Demonstrate a critical understanding of the application to social work of research, theory and knowledge from sociology, social policy, psychology and health. (Knowledge 5.1)

Demonstrate a critical knowledge of the range of theories and models for social work intervention with individuals, families, groups and communities, and the methods derived from them. (Knowledge 5.8)

Understand the inter-agency, multi-disciplinary and inter-professional dimensions to practice and demonstrate effective partnership working. (Contexts and Organisations 8.7)

In order for universities to be approved to run social work qualifying programs, they have to ensure that their students are able to 'meet all the standards of proficiency to register with us and meet the standards relevant to your scope of practice to stay registered with us'.

The following selection of a few key points from HCPC Standards for validating social work courses gives a flavour of the emphasis placed on different areas by them:

4.7 The delivery of the program must encourage evidence-based practice.

5.1 Practice placements must be integral to the program.

6.1 The assessment strategy and design must ensure that the student who successfully completes the program has met the standards of proficiency for their part of the Register.

The main aim of social work qualifying education from the HCPC's perspective is to prepare students at the point of qualification to be able to meet its Standards of Proficiency (see HCPC Standards for Education and Training 2012).

As a result of the policies and laws set out above, the new roles and skills for social workers have become the planning of care packages and services; resource allocation; assessment; and care management functions. Setting and reviewing performance indicators and outcomes based on the achievement of measurable objectives within predetermined procedures and resource allocation decisions based on government guidance and regulation have assumed greater importance than direct work with service users, with inevitable implications for the content of courses.

Earlier theories which emphasised social beings as members of social systems and the relationship between social problems and social and political systems have been discarded in the face of a general climate which places responsibility on individuals for their own behaviour and wellbeing (including income or lack of it). The individualisation of social problems has led to the teaching of theories and methods that are now focused on work with individuals and families, and formal organisations, at the expense of therapeutic, community and emancipatory approaches. The key elements of methods and models are individualised approaches, such as 'process' casework, often now focused on assessments for services, and referring on to other agencies, i.e. care management. Methods taught tend to be short term and time limited approaches; for example, task-centred work; crisis intervention; cognitive behavioural approaches; and targeted programs. Family therapy was popular in social work practice some 15 or so years ago, but the focus has moved to training-based work, such as in parenting programs. Solution-focused models based on strengths rather than deficits are examined in some courses. In summary, there has been a general move away from group and community work (seen by some as more likely to raise questions about and pose challenges to government policies) and from therapeutic work with individuals and families, in favour of more conservative and functional approaches. However, some have identified a renewed interest in direct work with children and also in relationship-based work (e.g. Wilson et al. 2011).

Staffing, research and new developments

Alongside the external pressures on SWE to move in particular directions, there have also been issues of visibility and identity within higher education, with implications for the staffing and research roles of social work educators themselves. Is it an academic discipline or a form of professional education (or even training)? Such debates are partly related to the alliances and organisational bases of social work courses – which have rarely been located in departments labelled Social Work. In the 1990s more than 50% of respondents to a survey described their alliances as primarily with staff in academic subject areas while the remainder were more allied with professional educators (Lyons 1999). Developments over the past decade or so, including the need for universities to cut their costs, suggest that possibly more programs are now located in professional departments and students may increasingly be taught some of their modules alongside other students in related fields for example, health or youth and community work.

With regard to staffing, for many years practice experience tended to be prized over academic qualifications in the appointment of staff, which, together with the responsibilities associated with the social work educator role (e.g. including placement visits), perpetuated a state in which theory and practice were divided; and the creation of new knowledge through research was not seen as the responsibility of social work educators themselves. Around 2000, a shift in this situation occurred, partly as a result of a series of seminars (initiated by social work academics with funding from the Economic and Social Research Council, ESRC) aimed at improving the theoretical base of social work and the research activities of staff. Further impetus was given by a national Research Assessment Exercise (RAE) in which social work educators from a minority of universities were amongst those whose work was included, resulting in specific funding for further research (to some institutions) and also the award of other funding for capacity building for research in social work. One outcome of this raised profile was what some hoped, and others feared, an increased academisation of social work education, with increased recognition given to the academic qualifications of newly appointed staff and increased expectations regarding their research activities.

In a demographic review of the UK social sciences, Mills et al. (2006) identified social work education as having high retirement and appointment rates and that 47% of the staff were aged 50 and over. In a subsequent research project into the implications of generational change in the social work academic workforce, Lyons and Maglajlic (2010) received 41 responses to a survey of 76 out of 100 programs in the UK (54% response rate, covering 479 staff). Data indicated that 10% of staff had retired in the past three years, that one in six were planning to retire in the next five years and that 60% of posts created by retirement were filled by first-time academics. Of the newly appointed staff, half came direct from social work practice, with 20% coming from research posts and the remainder mainly from other posts in social services (e.g. managers, training officers); 20% of the new entrants already held a PhD while 40% were undertaking – or intending to undertake – doctoral research. The findings also showed an increase in the proportion of women staff (already high) and a decrease in the numbers of staff from black and ethnic minorities (already low). A related analysis of 44 advertisements for social work posts identified that only three-quarters stated that a social work qualification was essential and this, with other anecdotal evidence, suggests that social work posts in some universities are open to colleagues from neighbouring disciplines. This is turn raises concerns about the implications for the development of professional identity in students at a time when social work in the field has been undergoing significant changes and a narrowing of its remit.

The situation regarding research has also changed over the past decade with the expectations of, and opportunities for, staff partly mirroring a continuing split between the old universities (established prior to 1992) and the new ones (based on the granting of university status to polytechnics in that year). Despite some notable exceptions, there has continued to be an emphasis on research in the old university sector while many new universities see themselves as primarily teaching institutions. In parallel, the competition for research funding from the main funding body (ESRC) and various charities has increased in anticipation of further rounds of national assessment exercises (e.g. the REF due in 2014), with the promise of further funding for the winners. This has led to a clearer concentration of a minority of social work staff in research centres and/or engaged in multi-disciplinary research teams (mainly in the old university sector), with staff in the new universities, whatever their inclinations, finding it increasingly hard to gain access to research funding and/or to undertake individual (unfunded) research programs (including for doctoral purposes). Sabbaticals, previously already rare in the new university sector, are now virtually unheard of and current anecdotal evidence of difficulties recruiting to social work posts (at various levels, up to and including professors) further reduces the time available for staff to undertake research.

The current staffing difficulties perhaps partly relate to the lack of a strong research culture in the profession as a whole and the lack of value placed on research in the wider political and policy context. However, a recent emphasis on evidence-based practice has pushed social work educators and those researching social work to reconsider the design of research projects (not least if they wish to win funding). The preferred mode of much social work research in the past has been in the qualitative paradigm, including the development of evaluative studies and approaches involving service users (e.g. Shaw 2012), but more emphasis has been given recently to adopting positivistic designs and quantitative methods (e.g. randomised control trials). This may put social work educators at a further disadvantage since few have had the necessary training in research skills and most do not include such teaching in their own qualifying and post-qualifying programs. However, some see this challenge as an indication of the maturing of social work into a proper discipline, gradually building the capacity to create its own knowledge base, for use in social work education and the wider professional field.

However, the regulatory developments described above suggest less valuing of research and staff development opportunities. For instance, there is now no regulatory framework for post qualifying continuing professional development (as previously existed in the provisions of the GSCC). Every three years, social workers need to demonstrate to the HCPC how they have kept up to date with their continuing professional development (CPD) but there are no specific links required in relation to research or academic awards. In addition, CPD is no longer one of the items included in government targets for local authority employers to meet and, given cuts in spending, there has been a decrease in support for CPD programs (including those provided by universities). Against this, in line with the government objective of raising the status and standards of the social work profession, two new training initiatives have recently been established, Step-up to Social Work (www.education.gov.uk/b00200996/step-up) and Frontline (www.education.gov.uk/a00225213/frontline). These are both intensive employer-led programs at master's level, that set out to attract academically high-achieving students, who may, if they continue in the profession, be more inclined towards research.

Finally, another recent external change which may impact adversely on university-based social work education is the reduction in the amount of money to be paid in bursaries to students gaining places on social work undergraduate and postgraduate degrees. These awards were introduced in the early 2000s following a fall in the number of recruits to SWE and calls for parity with other shortage occupations (including nursing and teaching). Bursaries have been effective in raising recruitment levels but it seems as if funding of the new initiatives mentioned above has now taken priority over maintaining traditional recruitment patterns.

Conclusions

SWE in England illustrates a number of points which may or may not resonate with readers outside the UK. A significant one is the extent to which it reflects national characteristics, culture and concerns in a particular time and place. Over a history spanning more than a century, social work has become a unified and apparently stronger profession, but, as with some other professions, it has also become increasingly subject to government expectations and requirements. These in turn are also reflected in other aspects of welfare changes which require individuals to take increasing responsibility for themselves, their relatives and neighbours (so-called 'care in the community'), only drawing on (or being referred for) public funding and/or social work services when a crisis is reached and/or the behaviour of individuals or families falls outside the tolerated norms. A culture of surveillance and regulation extends to the professionals who work with people in distress and social workers have found themselves increasingly subject to bureaucratic procedures and restrictions.

Similar drivers have been evident in government interventions and regulation of SWE which now shows some contradictory trends. On the one hand, there is an increased recognition of the need for developments in theory and research as these relate to practice, while on the other hand, students are required to spend more time on skills training and in practice placements and the money available to fund practice-related research is scarce. There is an increased recognition of the need for interprofessional cooperation, which theoretically could be achieved through increases in joint education, but the economies of scale required of universities usually mean delivery of generic courses to large groups without the opportunity to explore what the term might mean for different occupational groups in practice. There is also a recognition in some quarters that we live in an interconnected world where economics and migration are defining features of many societies – yet these topics are rarely addressed in the English SWE system due to crowded timetables and prescriptive guidance as to content relevant to a narrow form of social work – and perhaps the assumption that there is little to be gained from comparative or international study. Finally, the values of social work are compromised in a situation where policies aimed at extending opportunities to people who might otherwise not qualify for higher education – but who might make very good social workers – are overtaken by policies which emphasise academic qualities.

In all of this, the costs of SWE in England, the pressures on staff which prevent full engagement in research activities, and the various points of conflict which arise between institutions and professional bodies (e.g. around assessment) undoubtedly place SWE in a vulnerable position within the university sector – as demonstrated by the periodic loss of courses when universities seek to cut their costs and/or raise their research ratings. In parallel, the pressures and initiatives to increase the power of employers in relation to social work training and qualification suggest a future in which occupational standards prevail over critical thinking and professional practice and values. While we do not think that social work as a profession has been eroded to a point of no return in England nor that SWE is about to cease in universities, the situation with regards to future developments is, to say the least, uncertain.

References

Littlechild, B. (2008). Child protection social work: risks of fears and fears of risks – impossible tasks from impossible goals? *Social Policy & Administration*, 47(6): 662–75.

Littlechild, B. & Hawley, C. (2010). Risk assessments for mental health service users: ethical, valid and reliable? *Journal of Social Work*, 10(2): 211–29.

Littlechild, B. & Smith, R. (eds) (2013). *A handbook for interprofessional practice in the human services: learning to work together*. Harlow: Pearson Education.

Lyons, K. & Magajlic, R. (2010). Professional identity: generational change in social work academic workforce. Paper presented at Global Conference, Hong Kong, 13 June.

Lyons, K. (2008). Eileen Younghusband, 1961–1968. In F. Seibel (ed.), *Global leaders for social work education: the IASSW presidents 1928–2008*. Boskovice, Czech Republic: Albert.

Lyons, K. (1999). *Social work in higher education: demise or development*. Aldershot, UK: Ashgate.

Mills, D., Jepson, A., Coxon, T., Easterby-Smith, M., Hawkins, P. & Spencer, J. (2006). *Demographic review of the UK social sciences*. Swindon: Economic and Social Research Council.

Parton, N., Thorpe, D. & Wattam, C. (1997). *Child Protection, risk and the moral order*. Basingstoke: Macmillan.

Payne, M. (2005). *The origins of social work: continuity and change*. Basingstoke: Palgrave Macmillan.

Shaw, I. (2012). *Practice and research*. Aldershot, UK: Ashgate.

The College of Social Work (2012a). Reform resources. Retrieved on 11 June 2014 from www.tcsw.org.uk/uploadedFiles/TheCollege/_CollegeLibrary/Reform_resources/PCFfancolour.pdf.

The College of Social Work (2012b). Reforming social work qualifying education: the social work degree. London: The College of Social Work.

Townsend, P. (1979). *Poverty in the United Kingdom*. London: Allen Lane and Penguin Books.

Wilson, K., Ruch, G., Lymbery, M. & Cooper, A. (eds) (2011). *Social work: an introduction to contemporary practice* (2nd edn). London: Pearson Education.

Part 5
Social work and the welfare state

16

International social work education: the Canadian context

Mehmoona Moosa-Mitha

> In this chapter I analyse themes that emerge from scholarship on international social work education in the Canadian context. I focus on international student exchanges in my analysis through a centring of the multicultural/settler identity of Canadian society. I reflect on the definition of global oppression, student outcomes and the Canadian liberal welfare state, through the lens of the multicultural/settler identity of Canadian society, which serves to collapse the binary that exists between national and international as the basic assumption within which international social work education normatively operates. It also highlights different motivations present when minority students undertake international social work exchanges. It emphasises the geo-political nature of space and boundary crossing and makes explicit the colonial nature of power relationships that divide the world into a global north and south.

International social work education has rapidly become a desired educational objective in many schools of social work throughout Canada, largely through student/educator exchange programs (Tiessen 2012; Heron 2006; Lyons et al. 2012). This is the case for many reasons such as: the growing awareness of the global nature of social issues (Caragata & Sanchez 2002); neoliberal globalisation of the economy and university participation in it; and a long history of international social work practice by professionals in the global north working in the global south (Healy 2008).

According to Midgley (2001), international social work education is concerned with four broad categories:

1. impact of globalisation
2. impact of globalisation on social work practice
3. comparative enquiry and
4. professional collaboration and international exchanges.

In this chapter I will be focusing my analysis on the phenomena of Canadian student international social work practica as a part of a reciprocal exchange with countries in the global south or as a one-way placement of Canadian students in the south. International student exchanges are the predominant form within which internationalisation of social work education takes place, particularly in light of government support for such programs (Tiessen 2012). Moreover, a discussion on Canadian student international practica also serves as an entry point for analysis of the other aspects of international social work education identi-fied by Midgley.

In this chapter, I centre the settler/multicultural nature of Canadian society in the ex-isting scholarship and discussions of Canadian international social work education. My intention in doing so is twofold: firstly, to highlight racialised and Indigenous students' experiences and knowledge as subjects of international social work exchange programs. As Razack and Badwall (2006) have pointed out, much of the literature on social justice perspectives of social work focuses on the white subject as the learner; secondly, to con-textualise Canadian international social work education through a discussion of critical social work theory and practice. Centring the multicultural/settler character of Canadian society in theorisations of international social work education adds considerably to present scholarship. For example, it results in recognising the heterogeneity of Canadian society generally and the Canadian student population that participates in international social work education more specifically. It challenges the national/international binary within which analysis of international social work is conducted by presuming the national to be 'here' and international within a geographical space of 'there'. Canadian immigrant presence is built on a transnational identity with multinational ties that cannot easily be dichotomised as national and international (George & Delarosa 2009). It brings a geo-political analysis of colonial oppression that is manifest within a neoliberal international economic order and at the local level of nation-state boundaries, and it recognises the voices, experiences and subject positions of racialised and Indigenous Canadian students and scholars.

I begin my analysis by summarising the neoliberal, social justice and critical/postcolo-nial frameworks within which international education gets contested. I then focus on an analysis of the implications of a critical/postcolonial understanding of international social work education through a centring of the discussion on its multicultural/settler reality. I undertake this analysis by discussing three aspects of Canadian international social work education: 1) definition of global oppression; 2) student outcomes envisaged through par-ticipation in international social work education; and 3) globalisation and the neoliberal Canadian welfare nation-state.

Neoliberal, social justice and critical/postcolonial perspectives on international education

The impetus for internationalisation of education comes from many sources including students themselves who wish to enrich their learning through travel and work abroad programs of education (Tiessen & Epprecht 2012; Tiessen 2012; Heron 2011). There are also government funded initiatives for Canadian youth such as the Association for Uni-versities and Colleges in Canada (AUCC) who have been promoting internationalisation of education in order to encourage students to become 'responsible and engaged global citizens' (Tiessen 2012, Tiessen and Epprecht 2012; Heron 2011). Another source for in-ternationalisation of education in Canada is the Students for Development Program (SFD) that provides opportunities for students to participate in international education. This fed-erally funded program has provided more than 1000 students opportunities for practicum placements since 2005. In 2010, it significantly expanded its scope (AUCC 2010). Other Canadian governmental and non-governmental organisations are also active in promoting international education, in tandem with the AUCC, in the name of encouraging Canadian citizens take up the role of being 'global citizens' (Tiessen 2012).

Internationalisation of education, particularly as it is linked to the idea of the global citizen, can be understood in three ways, all of which are present, directly or otherwise, in the literature within the Canadian context. The first and predominant view can be characterised as a neoliberal perspective of international education. Within this perspective, international education is understood in instrumental terms as a means to promote globalised and corporatised education that can allow students from the global north a competitive advantage to benefit from global capitalism (Jorgenson & Shultz 2012). Post-secondary institutions see their particular role as being that of ensuring that students are linked to the knowledge economy, which forms an important basis to the running of globalised economies (Tiessen 2012; Heron 2011). Its neoliberal character is apparent in its instrumental view of education as a means to pursuing individual self-interest rather than as a means of pursuing collective notions of social justice (Rhoads & Szelényi 2011). Knowledge is viewed as a commodity and students as human capital studying within educational institutions that are aligned with the government's mandate of readying generations of Canadians to participate in a global marketplace (Jorgenson & Shultz 2012; Tiessen 2012).

The second is a social justice perspective that has its roots in international development theories often reflective of the philosophical orientations of non-governmental organisations from the global north engaged in social justice projects in the global south (Choudry 2010). The social justice perspective is concerned with an examination of the unequal power relations that characterise global relationships. In particular it criticises the role of transnational corporations and powerful governments like the US as engines of neoliberalism and proposes a greater strengthening of social democratic governance locally (Choudry 2010). Within this critical perspective, structural programs and the capitalist economic system are identified as resulting in global injustices (Heron 2006). An example of the structures in place that maintain global injustices are the structural adjustment debt programs and the various free trade agreements that privilege countries of the global north and maintain a north–south divide. Social democratic governance within countries of the global north is found to be lacking due to the neoliberalisation of the welfare state that is seen to have moved away from the heyday of social welfarism that was the liberal welfare state (Choudry 2010).

A third perspective, a critical postcolonial analysis of international education, builds on the social justice perspective by looking at both structural as well as a socio-historical-cultural analysis of the push to internationalise education (Jorgenson & Shultz 2012). In so doing, insights from the writings of postcolonial intellectuals are used to point out that internationalisation of education through exchange programs of students from the global north going to countries in the global south have to take into consideration that all these countries are former colonies (Heron 2006). Globalisation, as the context for the internationalisation of education itself is both a capitalist and a colonial project (Choudry 2010; Ife & Tesoriero 2006). As Heron (2006) points out, globalisation is defined as 'the integration processes of global economy that began with European exploration five centuries ago and that operate today to maintain the North/South divide'. Postcolonial theorists Androtto and De Souza suggest that international education needs to be 'other wise', by which they mean that critical examination of the genealogies of production and the effects of unequal relations of power and privilege have to be recognised (cited in Jorgenson & Shultz 2012). The damage of colonialism needs to be taken into account into the present as well as the new face of colonialism through the spread of the capitalist market economy and the global social injustices that result in its wake (Heron 2005). Having historical awareness, for example, results in critiquing social justice perspectives on international education for being nostalgic about a liberal social welfare state when in fact it was always exclusionary, and continues to be oppressive in relation to Indigenous people's welfare as well as those of racialised citizens in Canada (Choudry 2010).

Several scholars have spelled out the implications of a critical postcolonial analysis of international education as being the following: engaging in international education in ways that are widely inclusive of institutions in the global south; including a historical and sociocultural analysis of oppression (Rhoads & Szelényi 2011); and understanding the global nature of social issues as they relate to local ones (Jorgenson & Shultz 2012). Heron (2011) adds that a postcolonial analysis must not only be aware of the history of colonialism but also that of debt and mechanisms like the structural adjustment program and 'free trade' that keep the global south in a subjugated position relative to the global north. She points out that there is a direct relationship between the impoverishment of the south and the economic base of the middle class in the global north. According to Tiessen and Epprecht (2012), having this awareness means, amongst other things, that a mutuality of benefits must accrue as a result of international education exchanges and not a one-way benefit for students living in the global north, as is the case at present within neoliberal practices of international education.

I will examine the implications of critical postcolonial perspectives of international education in terms of social work education in the next section. I will do so through an examination of its definition of oppression, student outcomes and the neoliberal welfare state.

Global oppression and international social work education

A beginning entry point into understanding global oppression and the role of social work in it would be to clarify the relationship of social work to that of the Canadian nation-state. Social work as a profession is both nationalist in its practices and part of the liberal nation-building project in all Western welfare states including Canada (Moosa-Mitha, forthcoming). As an arm of the state, Canadian social workers are mandated to practice in line with state policies that have historically excluded racialised bodies on the basis of their precarious citizenship status and continue to do so. The nationalist basis of social work practices can be made clear to social work students, using postcolonial theoretical insights, by challenging the notion of space as being neutral (Razack & Badwall 2009). The geo-politisation of space can be undertaken by undertaking a historical examination of the colonising practices of the Canadian nation-state in relation to the Indigenous peoples of Canada and social work's role in it (Razack 2012, 2009). It is important that Canada's settler identity is made clear to social work students as an example of global capitalist practices that have a long history and are intimately connected with the nation-building project. Similarly a history of the Canadian nation-state's exclusionary practices in relation to immigrants arriving from countries from the global south must also be included as an example of the international dimension of the geo-politics of space. Understanding global oppression as the politisation of space in historical terms can also explain present day injustices as a legacy of colonialism, both locally and in relation to countries of the global south. Politisation of space can also explain injustices that occur presently such as the fortification of welfare states that increasingly seek to exclude immigrants and refugees fleeing from war and famine; itself a sign of the effects of globalisation. It can also make students aware of the rise of securitisation states that treat Muslims and Arab-looking people as suspect and are treated by social workers as such (Razack & Badwall 2006).

Aside from understanding the politics of geographical space and social workers' role in it as part of the nationalist project, postcolonial understandings of oppression will challenge social workers' perceptions of social problems in the global south as though they simply exist without any historical antecedents (Heron 2011). Rather than becoming objects of study by social workers from the global north studying in the south, it will help turn social work students' gaze to take on a more reflexive stance because it will help make clearer the complicity of social workers as a profession that enacts nation-states' exclusionary policies of social care and as people from the privileged north (Heron 2011; Tiessen 2012). Understanding the processes of colonisation of space will also make it easier for students to see the global dimensions of local issues.

Centring the multicultural/settler reality of Canada can also unsettle homogeneous and fixed understanding of global oppression. The narratives of indigenous peoples in relation to colonisation are multiple and changing as they resist and have continued to resist its many effects. Similarly countries of the global south have their own individual histories of oppression and colonisation that take on shifting contemporary manifestations. Razack (2012) reminds us that racialised students from Indigenous as well as other immigrant communities will have very different experiences of interlocking oppression that cannot be 'known' in advance with any degree of certainty. Critiques of international social work education have long noted the universalising tendencies of consultant social work educators from the global north advising on the development of social work education to universities located in the global south (Midgley 1981; Bogo & Herington 1988). Haug (2005) provides a pointed critique of social work educator exchanges when he accuses educators of conducting 'professional imperialism under which the dominant model of social work has been disseminated around the world where . . . primarily Western 'experts' teach or consult in non-Western countries, while ignoring power differences between them' (127).

What postcolonial analysis does provide for is a framework that is rooted in critical examination of relations of power, both locally and globally, that results in social injustices. It undertakes this analysis by recognising the historically derived nature of such injustices and the 'materially linked interlocking systems of oppression' (Tiessen & Heron 2012). It also means that the diversity of ways by which colonisation has occurred and continues to occur is not being acknowledged.

Centring the multicultural/settler nature of Canadian society also results in breaking down the binary of national/international in other ways. Immigration, which is largely defined in unilateral terms as the movement of people from one country to another, in fact represents a far more complicated reality. Immigrants who arrive from the global south into countries in the global north, for example, often move back to their countries of origin for periods of time, or may move to a third place, before re-settling into their host countries (Stasilius 2008). Their participation in their countries of origin may be more than superficial. For example, countries like India and Turkey have special status for non-resident Indian and Turkish people by allowing them voting and investment rights that recognise them as being transnational (Stasilius 2008). Moreover, many people around the world identify in ways that are not contained by nation-state boundaries. This is true of many Catholics, Jews, Muslims and Indigenous peoples. The world is in fact far more transnational than assumed in the literature on international social work.

Student outcomes when undertaking international social work education

Understanding the motivation behind undertaking international social work education projects is crucial to the pedagogical experiences that students will experience. George and Delarosa (2009) point out that international social work education could be undertaken for the sake of getting on the bandwagon of government sponsored programs in order to benefit from resources attached to such programs. Tiessen (2012) and Epprecht (2004) similarly question the motivations of students and educators who want to participate in international volunteer opportunities and student placements. A study examining the benefits that agencies in the global south accrue from the presence of students from the global north suggests that while the agencies were positive about student presence and felt that they brought in new ideas and had a greater knowledge of information technology, their contributions were rather superficial, particularly if their stay was under three month, as is generally the case (Tiessen 2012). This and other studies (Heron 2011) concluded that the benefits to the individual student from the global north were more likely greater in terms of greater appreciation of global realities and enhancement of resumes than it was to the agencies in the global south.

Using a postcolonial point of view Tiessen and Epprecht (2012) suggest that it is imperative for international student exchanges to be of mutual benefit and there be a mutuality of exchange of both benefits and burdens that come with globalisation. This translates into students becoming more aware of their own responsibilities as students coming from a privileged background as well as additional resources for social work agencies placing students in the global south. While there are some cases of students from the global south going to do their practica in the global north, by far the predominant model is of a one-way direction with students from the global north exceeding the number of students participating in an international student exchange (Razack 2009).

Examining motivations of students from the global north for undertaking international social work education is revealing. For most students the motivation is that it is an interesting way to travel, to get cross-cultural skills and to help countries that are perceived as being poorer and experiencing a lot of social problems (Heron 2011). Upon their return, Canadian students largely report feeling that the educational experience was a good one and cite increased global awareness of social issues, friendships with people from another part of the world and having a sense of adventure as some of the indicators of a successful international exchange program (Heron 2011; Razack 2009; Tiessen 2012). The motivations of students from the global north going to undertake international social work experiences or arriving from there are largely 'me'-centred (Heron 2011). In spite of the fact that some students talk about the desire to go for their practicum in the global south in order to 'help', it's a form of altruism that also tends to centre themselves rather than the other. This is largely the case because students tend to take an uncomplicated position vis-a-vis helping the other to produce a subject position of the social work helper who is innocent of the unequal power relations that result in social injustices in the first place (Heron 2011; Razack 2009).

One of the motivations cited most often by students interested in undertaking international social work practica is learning cross-cultural skills by immersing themselves in cultures that are foreign to them (Tiessen 2012). If we were to centre the multicultural/ settler reality of Canada, then the possibility of working across cultures can exist locally. Moreover, such a desire needs to be interrogated to understand it further. Neoliberal discourses on internationalisation of education also tend to use cross-cultural competency as a desired outcome of international education. In their case, having a cross-cultural aptitude puts students in the best position to compete within a global market by enabling them to move around a borderless world with relative ease (Jorgenson & Shultz 2012. The geo-political nature of nation-state boundaries is not simply about cultural differences but rather of racialised processes of colonisation.

Heron (2006) and Tiessen (2012) critique students' desire for cross-cultural skills on the basis of its consumerist orientation to learning. According to them, students perceive international social work education through the exchange program as consisting of the gaining of an 'authentic' experience of learning in exchange for the time and money students pay to receive it. Upon returning from an international exchange, they find that students still explain their learning in similar terms as when they left such as 'development of cross cultural skills' and 'increase in cultural understanding'. Aside from the fact that this learning is still couched in self-oriented terms, they find naïve the view, implicit in such articulations, that encountering difference is the same as knowing difference. They remark on the neoliberalism implicit in the view of social work students to acquire something that is couched largely in self-referential terms and is understood as being undertaken for instrumental reasons such as student enhancement of their resumes.

There has been a concerted attempt by social work educators intent on tapping the potential of international social work education to raise students' critical consciousness about global injustices in ways that are more than superficial (Fairchild et al. 2006). Larson and Allen (2006) did in fact set out to work with students to undertake international social work education with the explicit purpose of increasing their level of conscientisation – loosely defined as raising critical awareness of the structures of oppression that permeate globally. Having undertaken a preparatory program prior to undertaking their placement where students were exposed to the structural and historical reasons that keep Mexico (the destination for Canadian student placements) at a certain level of poverty, students were then placed with community development projects in Mexico. Larson and Allen (2006) found that there was indeed a rise in awareness of the global structural nature of oppression and a clear sense of implication of their own role in it. However, the real marker for having achieved conscientisation was theorised in terms of behavioural changes, and in their study Larson and Allen found that while there was some indication of behavioural change, it faded over time. Other studies (Tiessen 2012; Heron 2011; Razack 2011, 2009) have found that over time there is limited active engagement with issues of global social justice once students come back from their practica. George and Delarosa's study (2009) is an anomaly as it found that students remained actively engaged with issues of global injustice having come back from their practica in India. It is possible that these were students of colour with previous ties to India, although George and Delarosa do not make that explicit in their article. Suffice it to say that if the intention of educators is to ensure that students achieve a level of critical consciousness of the structural nature of oppression and privilege and can see their role in it through taking an activist stance in resisting global injustices locally, the evidence is dubious that this outcome is achieved, particularly over time.

Basing discussions on desired student outcomes as a result of undertaking international social work education adds to the critical perspective already present in the scholarship in a significant way. There is a propensity in relevant literature to assume that the students engaging in international social work education are white (Razack & Badwall 2006). As George and Delarosa point out, students of colour, particularly those who undertake international exchanges by visiting their countries of origin (or that of their parents), do not necessarily regard visiting these countries as 'international' but rather as 'national'. For example, South Asian-Canadian students, the case in point for George and Delarosa's analysis, consider engaging with agencies in India as an extension of their national identity; insofar as they identify both as Indians as well as Canadians. This of course does not mean that South Asian students should not need to understand their own privileged position in relation to residents of countries in the global south, but it does mean that their motivations for going may be very different and have not really been captured adequately.

To a degree it is possible to generalise from the evidence that we have regarding immigrant contributions and sense of responsibility towards their countries of origin. We know that countries like India greatly benefit from the patriotic sense of responsibility that results in Indian non-residents going back for a period of time to contribute to the knowledge base of such countries, particularly in relation to information technology (Stasilius 2008). Thus, much of the discussion on the neoliberalism embedded in 'I'-oriented student motivations may actually not bear relevance to students from immigrant backgrounds precisely because of their sense of responsibility to give back to the society from which they first arrived into Canada; and this desire cannot easily be critiqued as arising from a sense of entitlement to 'help elsewhere' (See Heron 2006). Perhaps these students are engaging in international social work as an instantiation of 'engaged and responsible global citizens' that Canadian Government agencies have identified as being the goal behind their support of internationalisation of education.

There are other ways that geo-politics can affect students from immigrant backgrounds. At the moment one such issue is the long-running war on terror that Canada as an ally of the US has been involved in. International exchanges for students of Middle-Eastern backgrounds or who are Muslims have a wholly different set of concerns that they engage in if they decide to undertake international exchanges in their countries of origin. Firstly, it is harder to organise such international exchanges, as governments do need to be working collaboratively at some level for such exchanges to be resourced. Secondly, the multinational identity that Canadian Muslims hold makes it hard to be representatives of two nation-states when the states themselves are in conflict with each other.

If the popular imagery of Canada is white, it is also non-native. The motivations and desired outcomes of Indigenous students are even less analysed or examined. Indigenous students crossing nation-state boundaries through international education programs have a different geo-political relationship to this border crossing than white settler students. It is not a movement from a colonial country to a former colon; rather, it is that of a colonised people going to a formerly colonised one, or if the exchange is latitudinal then to another colonial power. Pflanz (2011), an Indigenous Metis student who undertook an international student exchange practica from Canada to Denmark, reflected on the privileges that such a move carried precisely because of the fact that her own Indigenous status was often overlooked from both the sending and the receiving country and the resulting treatment of her as any other 'white' student.

In the end, recognising the realities of students of colour and Indigenous students engaged in international education exchanges may well be to recognise the difficulties that nation-states have with truly global identities that transcend nation-border states. Owning multiple national identities or indeed identities that have statehood boundaries imposed on them as a result of colonisation may prove to challenge the very notion of the international and hence of international social work education as it is currently defined.

The neoliberal welfare state

In considering the issue of internationalisation of social work education, it is important to ground it within both the profession of social work and the nature of the welfare state within which social workers in countries of the global north practice. The social justice perspective of international social work education, particularly due to the international development context within which it formulates its vision, tends to idealise liberal welfare states of the 1970s and 80s (see Choudry 2010). In doing so it ignores the nature of exclusions that resulted from the practices of the Canadian welfare state, particularly in relation to Indigenous and racial minority communities. This not only means that transposing the ideals of liberal welfare states in other parts of the world is another form of colonization; it also means that the narratives of an idealised past itself need interrogating.

International social work education must also take into consideration that the neoliberalisation of welfare states such as Canada is itself linked to globalisation. The Canadian state acts within a global arena to purchase social services, such as certain health care services, at a cheaper rate within a marketisation discourse of welfare states (Stasilius 2008). Another example of globalisation and its link to the neoliberalisation of the welfare state is the fast tracking of Filipino nannies who come to Canada to do care work for young children and the elderly to address the gap created by a retreating welfare state in Canada, resulting in care provision for those families who can afford to purchase it (Stasilius 2008). In the case of social work, globalisation is as much about disengagement of the responsibilities the state has towards its citizens as it is about citizens becoming more responsible for their own care by purchasing care within a global market.

Recognising not only the postcolonial reality of globalisation but also its increasingly neoliberal character, particularly in countries of the global north, facilitates student learning as a result of exchanges where alternative notions of care, such as community development models of care, help teach students from the global north other ways of doing social work (Larson & Allen 2006). Self-reflexivity about the drawbacks and absence of welfare states in the global north should facilitate the treatment of countries of the global south as viable resources for teaching alternative ways of undertaking social care. This is precisely what some educators from Canada have aimed to do when organising international exchanges for their students (see Larson & Allen 2006).

Moreover, social work, as I have already discussed, is an arm of the liberal welfare state in countries of the global north, and as such it is constituted by and within the nation-building project of colonial Canada. This is not the case only in historical terms, but continues to be so within 'postcolonial' Canada. Internationalisation of social work education must take into considerations the restrictions and barriers that social workers encounter when working with refugees, immigrants or generally anyone with a precarious citizenship status. Social workers themselves carry some of the biases against the presence of immigrants and refugees that emanate from the social policy context of liberal welfare states in the global north (Park & Bhuyan 2012). This hierarchical nature of citizenship as experienced by minority Canadians in their own society also has a bearing on how students of colour and Indigenous students understand their own sense of national belonging. It is important therefore that scholarship on international social work education does not treat Canadian students as constituting a homogenous group even within critical perspectives on international social work education by assuming that the basic aim of undertaking such education is to interrogate their own sense of 'innocence' and privilege in relation to countries of the global south. While this is true in some ways, differential citizenship claims and social exclusions experienced on the basis of race and indigeneity must also be recognised when undertaking preparation for international social work education exchanges.

Conclusions

In this chapter I have undertaken an analysis of some of the main themes that emerge within the scholarship on international social work education in the Canadian context. I have done so by focusing on one aspect of international social work education, namely international student exchanges from the global north to the global south. My thesis has been to insert and centralise the multicultural/settler identity of Canadian society in the scholarship on Canadian international social work student exchange programs in order to highlight some of the significant ways in which it adds to critical analysis on this topic.

Focusing on definition of global oppression, student outcomes and the Canadian liberal welfare state, I have suggested that centralising the multicultural/settler identity of Canadian society serves to collapse the binary that exists between national and international as the basic assumption within which international social work education normatively operates. I have also brought attention to the very different motivations and dynamics present when minority students undertake international social work exchanges. By examining the differential nature of experiences of Canadian citizenship based on students' social identity location, I have suggested that the scholarship on international social work education must treat Canadian students as a heterogeneous group.

Lastly I have argued that centralising the multicultural/settler identity of Canada brings to the forefront the geo-political nature of space and boundary crossing. Taking this seriously makes the historical and contemporaneous reality of the colonial nature of power relationships that divide the world into a global north and south more apparent.

References

Association of the Universities and Colleges of Canada (AUCC) & Canadian International Development Agency (CIDA) (2010). A world of possibility: highlights of the 2010 students for development program. Retrieved on 22 April 2014 from www.aucc.ca/wp-content/uploads/2011/11/sfd-a-world-of-possibilities-brochure-2010-e.pdf.

Bogo, M. & Herington, W. (1988). Consultation in social work education in the international context. *International Social Work*, 31(4): 305–16. DOI: 10.1177/002087288803100407.

Caragata, L. & Sanchez, M. (2002). Globalisation and global need: new imperatives for expanding international social work education in North America. *International Social Work*, 45(2): 217–38. DOI: 10.1177/00208728020450020601.

Choudry, A. (2010). What's Left? Canada's 'global justice' movement and colonial amnesia. *Race & Class*, 52(1): 97–102. DOI: 10.1177/0306396810371769.

Epprecht, M. (2004). Work-study abroad courses in international development studies: some ethical and pedagogical issues. *Canadian Journal of Development Studies*, 25(2): 687–706. DOI: 10.1080/02255189.2004.9669009.

Fairchild, S.R., Pillai, V.K. & Noble, C. (2006). The impact of a social work study abroad program in Australia on multicultural learning. *International Social Work*, 49(3): 390–401. DOI: 10.1177/0020872806063413.

George, P. & Delarosa, E. (2009). Nuance and subjectivity in international exchange: a response to 'The exchange experience in India'. *Canadian Social Work Review*, 26(1): 115–19.

Haug, E. (2005). Critical reflections on the emerging discourse of international social work. *International Social Work*, 48(2): 126–35. DOI: 10.1177/0020872805050204.

Healy, L.M. (2008). *International social work: professional action in an interdependent world*. NY: Oxford University Press.

Heron, B. (2005). Changes and challenges: preparing social work students for?Practicums in today's Sub-Saharan Africa context. *International Social Work*, 48(6): 782–93. DOI: 10.1177/0020872805057088.

Heron, B. (2011). Challenging indifference to extreme poverty: connecting southern perspectives on global citizenship and change. *Ethics and Economic*, 8(1). Retrieved on 22 April 2014 from ethique-economique.net/.

Heron, B. (2006). Critically considering international social work practica. *Critical Social Work*, 7(2). Retrieved on 22 April 2013 from www1.uwindsor.ca/criticalsocialwork/critically-considering-international-social-work-practica.

Ife, J. & Tesoriero, F. (2006). *Community development: community based alternatives in an age of globalisation*. Sydney: Pearson Education Australia.

Jorgenson, S. & Shultz, L. (2012). Global citizenship education (GCE) in? post-secondary institutions: what is protected and what is hidden under the umbrella of GCE? *Journal of Global Citizenship of Equity Education*, 2(1). Retrieved on 22 April 2014 from journals.sfu.ca/jgcee/index.php/jgcee/article/viewArticle/52/26.

Larson, G. & Allen, H. (2006). Conscientization – the experience of Canadian social work students in Mexico. *International Social Work*, 49(4): 507–518. DOI: 10.1177/0020872806065327.

Lyons, K. (2012). Introduction. In K. Lyons, T. Hokenstad, M. Pawar, N. Huegler and N. Hall (eds), *The SAGE handbook of international social work*. London: SAGE Publications.

Midgley, J. (2001). Issues in international social work: resolving critical debates in the profession. *Journal of Social Work* 1(1): 21–35. DOI: 10.1177/146801730100100103.

Midgley, J. (1981). Professional imperialism: social work in the Third World studies. *Social Policy and Welfare*. 16: 191–212.

Moosa-Mitha, M. (forthcoming). Using citizenship theory to challenge nationalist assumptions in the construction of international social work education. *International Social Work*.

Park, Y. & Bhuyan, R. (2012).Whom should we serve? A discourse analysis of social workers' commentary on undocumented migrants. *Journal of Progressive Human Services*, 23(1): 18–40. DOI: 10.1080/10428232.2011.605745.

Pflanz, S. (2011). Internationalising me: a look inside at the international social work practicum. Master's in Social Work research report. University of Victoria, Canada.

Razack N. (2012). International social work. In M. Gray, J. Midgley & S. Webb (eds), *The SAGE handbook of social work* (pp. 707–22). London: SAGE Publications.

Razack, N. & Badwall, H. (2006). Challenges from the North American context: globalisation and anti-oppression. *International Social Work*, 49(5): 661–66. DOI: 10.1177/0020872806066959.

Razack, N. (2011). Racism and anti-racist strategies. In L.M. Healy & R. Link (eds), *Handbook of international social work: human rights, development and the global profession* (pp. 237–42). NY: Oxford University Press.

Razack, N. (2009). Decolonising the pedagogy and practice of international social work. *International Social Work,* 52(1): 19–21. DOI: 10.1177/0020872808097748.

Rhoads, R. & Szelényi, K. (2011). *Global citizenship and the university: advancing social life and relations in an interdependent world.* Stanford, CAL: Stanford University Press.

Stasilius, D. (2008). The migration–citizenship nexus. In E. Isin (ed.), *Recasting the social in citizenship* (pp. 134–61). Toronto: University of Toronto Press.

Tiessen, R. (2012). Creating global citizens? The impact of learning/volunteer abroad programs, Report to IDRC. Retrieved on 22 April 2014 from cdnglobalcitizenship.files.wordpress.com/2012/10/oct-2012-final-report-for-gc-research.pdf.

Tiessen, R. & Epprecht, M. (2012). Introduction: global citizenship education for learning/volunteering abroad. *Journal of Global Citizenship & Equity Education,* 2(1). Retrieved on 22 April 2014 from journals.sfu.ca/jgcee/index.php/jgcee/article/viewArticle/54/27.

Tiessen, R. & Heron, B. (2012). Volunteering in the developing world: the perceived impacts of Canadian youth. *Development in Practice,* 22(1): 44–56. DOI: 10.1080/09614524.2012.630982.

17

Economic crises, neoliberalism, and the US welfare state: trends, outcomes and political struggle[1]

Mimi Abramovitz

The rise of neoliberalism in the US represents a response to the second economic crisis of the 20th century. Seeking to restore profits and economic growth, neoliberal proponents called for redistributing income upwards and downsizing the state. The resulting tax and budget cuts, privatisation, devolution and weakening of social movements led to greater economic insecurity/poverty, increased social problems, greater privatisation of services and increased regulation of the poor. Neoliberalism created enormous wealth for the top earners but it failed to produce the promised economic growth. Three intertwined political tactics helped to convince the American public to support polices that undermined their well-being and political power: the fabrication of a crisis, the generation of four panics and the exploitation of the resulting fears to impose policies that people would not otherwise stand for. Social workers are encouraged to engage in political struggle to reverse the unjust outcomes of the neoliberal assault on welfare states around the world.

Neoliberalism is a theory of political and economic practices and a set of economic policies that have become widespread in the last 30 to 40 years in the United States and internationally. It is most often associated with the structural adjustment programs administered by the World Bank, the International Monetary Organisation and the World Trade Organization. However, neoliberalism has also governed domestic policy in the United States, Canada, Great Britain and Western Europe during the last three decades. While the term is less familiar in the United States, Reaganomics, supply side economics, and conservatism – which refer to similar policies and practices – gained control of US public policy in the mid-1970s and early 1980s and remain in place today.

Based on a belief in the inherent wisdom of the market, neoliberal advocates regard market dynamics (e.g. private property rights, limited government, free markets, and free trade) as the central mechanism for governing economic, social and political life (George

---

1   This chapter is a shorter and revised version of M. Abramovitz (2012). Theorising the neoliberal welfare state for social work. In M. Gray, J. Midgley & S. Webb (eds), *The SAGE handbook of social work* (pp. 33–52). London: SAGE Publications.

1999; Harvey 2005). However, their call for limited government applies largely to domestic social programs. It does not rule out – and often supports – active state intervention on behalf of defence, national security, corporate welfare, and a range of policies that promote profitable economic activities (Harvey 2005). On the grounds that 'irresponsible' behaviour violates mainstream norms, neoliberalism also joins with social conservatism to endorse practices that monitor, regulate, and control the lives of the poor. These include greater use of welfare-to-work programs, stricter sentencing laws, zero tolerance policing, active deportation policies, increased policing of public schools and in general more surveillance of program clients among many other intrusive or punitive actions (Schram, Fording & Soss 2008).

Supporters defend neoliberal economic policies with two main arguments: (1) there is no alternative to the market economy, and (2) that a rising tide lifts all boats. The first view, popularised by conservative British Prime Minister Margaret Thatcher (1975–1990), holds that to avoid disaster, societies have no choice but to uphold free markets, free trade and globalisation. The second argument implies that the benefits of business-friendly neoliberalism will automatically trickle down to the average person. These ideas have become embedded in the taken-for-granted consciousness to the point where (1) they are regarded as 'common sense' by millions of people around the world (Ferguson 2004; Harvey 2005) and (2) have made anything other than cooperation with its principles appear both utopian and foolish. Critics, in contrast, say neoliberalism's 'survival of the fittest' approach to social welfare and civic life has transformed social welfare policy in ways that undermine the delivery of social services, increase poverty and inequality, create serious hardship for many individuals and families, conflict with social work values and ethics (Dominelli 1999; Garrett 2010) and have not produced the promised economic growth.

Despite the similar terminology, neoliberalism contrasts sharply with liberal political theory that guided the development of welfare states since the 1930s in the US, Britain, Western Europe and Scandinavia. Esping-Andersen (1990) identifies three types of liberal welfare states: the liberal welfare state (as found in the US and UK), the conservative-corporatist welfare state (e.g. Germany), and the social-democratic welfare state (e.g. Sweden and Denmark). Each reflects a different interpretation of the relationship between the individual, the market and the state. Liberal political theory remains pro-market but calls upon the government to mediate the market's excesses by ensuring a minimum level of wellbeing below which no one should have to live (Mullaly 2007; Wilensky & Lebeaux 1958). In the expanded social democratic version, this socially constructed standard of income, nutrition, health, housing, and education enables individuals to thrive, rather than just survive, and is provided as a right, not as charity (Marshall 1992; Mullaly 2007).

The US welfare state and 20th century economic crises

Neither the rise of the welfare state nor the neoliberal effort to dismantle it was merely accidental. Rather, both events in the US are best understood as a response by business and government to the two major economic crises of the 20th century. The first crisis – the collapse of the economy in the 1930s – brought the New Deal. The second crisis that arose in the mid-1970s gave rise to Neoliberalism (Bowles, Gordon & Weisskopf 1986; Kotz 2003a, 2003b; Lippit 2010; McDonough et al. 2010). The social structures of accumulation (SSA) theory (Bowles et al. 1986; Kotz 2003a, 2003b) explains that in the US and around the world each crisis surfaced when the institutional arrangements that had created the conditions for profit-making in the prior 50 years began to deteriorate. The policies no longer worked for the powers-that-be and had to be restructured or 'reformed'.

The first economic crisis in the US and the New Deal

The first crisis in the US marked by the 1929 stock market crash revealed that the social structures of accumulation (SSA) created in the 1890s to resolve a prior economic crisis had collapsed. The 1930s elite blamed their economic problems on the laissez-faire paradigm of minimal government action that had guided public policy during the preceding 50 years. They concluded that the nation needed a more active state to save capitalism from itself (Woolner 2011). However unwillingly, they called upon the federal government for help. Faced with extreme hardship, the poor, working class, and middle class also took to the streets to demand a new and stronger government response. With considerable political struggle Washington responded with a new SSA (i.e. the New Deal) designed to stimulate economic growth and mute the Depression-era social unrest.

The New Deal ushered in a major restructuring of the political economy based on *redistributing income downward and expanding the role of the state*. The new SSA included two major social welfare components: (1) the progressive income tax code – i.e. 25 brackets, a tax rate of 94% on the top bracket, and high corporate taxation (Tax Policy Center 2012a, 2012b); and (2) the transfer of social welfare responsibility from the states to the federal government. The latter created an entitlement to income support some 50 years after most other industrial nations had invested in social welfare. The sea change was legitimised in the late 1930s by two events. The US Supreme Court declared the constitutionality of federal responsibility for the general welfare, and leaders of business and government accepted the economic theory of the British economist John Maynard Keynes. Keynesianism called for greater government spending to increase aggregate demand and otherwise stimulate economic growth and argued that a modest degree of deficit spending usefully stimulated the economy. The wide range of New Deal programs helped business, banks, farmers, workers and some families (mostly white) get back on their feet (for years many programs excluded black domestic and farm workers). Despite this new spending, it took the stimulus of war production to produce a full economic recovery.

The post-World War 2 welfare state

From 1945 to 1975, often called 'the golden era of capitalism', the welfare state grew in response to population growth, the emergence of new needs, increased revenues, greater administrative capacity and the victories of the increasingly militant social movements demanding a larger share of the economic pie (Marglin 2000). The new welfare state won widespread support. It helped to 'save capitalism from itself' by carrying out a complex set of social, economic and political functions that mediated poverty, enhanced profits, and muted social unrest.

The *social functions* of the welfare state included both relief and regulation. Following the New Deal and into the 1970s, rising revenues enabled the government to provide a minimum level of income below which no one was expected to live, especially not the white middle class. Overall federal revenues rose from 16.5% of GDP (1947) to a peak of 19.7% (1969) (OMB 2012, Table 1.2) and payments to individuals rose from 3.9% of GDP (1947) to a high of 10.4% (1976) (OMB 2012, Table 11.1). The resulting downward redistribution of resources reduced poverty from a high of 22.4% of the US population (1959) to low of 11.1% (1973) (US Census Bureau 2013). The redistributive policies also narrowed the inequality gap causing the share of the national income held by the top 20% of earners to fall from 42.7% (1949/1950) to 40.6% (1974) while the much smaller share held by the bottom 20% rose from 4.5% (1949) to a high of 5.7% (1974) (US Census Bureau 2013). In exchange for greater economic security, program recipients often had to comply with white middle-class work and family norms or risk penalties for departing from these prescribed roles. That is, the rules and regulations of the expanding welfare state regulated the lives of individuals by enforcing the class, race and gendered status quo (Abramovitz 1996).

The *economic functions* of the welfare state helped to create the conditions for profitable economic activity and secured at least some corporate support for its programs. Less widely recognised than its social functions, on the economic front the welfare state also helped business by: (1) increasing purchasing power which ensured the daily consumption of goods and services; (2) supporting families who in turn supplied business with a healthy, educated and socialised workforce; (3) providing care to those too old, young or ill to support themselves, activities typically carried out by women's unpaid labour in the home (Abramovitz 1992a); (4) pressing down labour costs by supplementing wages; and (5) quieting social unrest resulting from market inequality. The expanded welfare state – combined with technological advances, pent up postwar demand, the Cold War arms race, and US control of world markets – fuelled economic growth. From 1947 to 1973 the real GDP increased an average of 4.03% a year (Officer & Williamson 2011). The expanding welfare state helped to raise the standard of living for many, if not all, US households, especially the white middle class, marked by the growth of both private sector wages and the median family income (Mishel 2012). Since wages rose in tandem with increased productivity, workers reaped a fair share of the enlarged economic pie that their efforts helped to create (Bernstein & Allegretto 2007).

The *political functions* of the welfare state promoted political stability. For one, welfare state rules and regulations typically enforced work and family norms and otherwise controlled daily behaviour. More systemically the welfare state mediated the contradiction between market inequalities and the democratic promise of equal opportunity for all. New Deal legislation, especially the Social Security Act (1935), the Wagner Act (1935) and the Taft Hartley Act (1947), reduced political conflict by establishing an informal set of mutual expectations known as the 'labour accord' in which trade unions exchanged higher wages, better working conditions and access to public benefits for longer contracts and fewer and less militant strikes, thereby contributing to the social peace (Lippit 2010; McDonough et al. 2010; Neumann & Rissman 1984). In the 1960s, business and government entered into similar race and gender 'accords' in which the civil rights and women's liberation movements exchanged an improved standard of living for less political conflict (Abramovitz 1992b). Overall employee compensation rose from 60.1% of the national income (1947) to a high of 66.7% (1980). While corporate profits rose, they fell from a high of 13.6% (1950) as a share of national income to low of 7.3% (1982) (Aron-Dine & Shapiro 2007). The capacity of the expanded welfare state to reduce poverty and lessen inequality eased the political discontent among the disadvantaged, legitimised 'the system' as fair to all, and otherwise contributed to economic stability and electoral calm on which business profits depended.

Second economic crisis

From 1935 to 1975, the expanding welfare state sustained its social, economic and political functions with reasonable success until the structural shifts in the domestic and global economies undermined the effectiveness of the postwar Social Security Act. Third World revolutions (e.g. Vietnam and others) reduced world power, US loss of access to cheap raw materials abroad, and mounting international competition signalled the end of post-war prosperity. The social movement victories also shifted the balance of power from the haves to the have-nots. Like a strike fund, the economic backup provided by unionisation and access to more substantial welfare state benefits emboldened workers to demand higher pay, women to challenge male domination, and persons of colour to challenge white supremacy. However, these gains also raised the economic costs of corporate investment and the political costs of maintaining the social peace. Taken together, all these changes weakened the SSA set up in the 1930s to promote profits, political stability and family wellbeing (Weisskopf 1981).

Faced with falling profits, the national elite decided that the New Deal, the post-war welfare state, and the war on poverty were part of the problem rather than part of the solution and argued for their demise (Harvey 2005). The welfare state, already an easy target owing to ongoing racism and hostility to the poor (Abramovitz 2011), became a poster child for the neoliberal attack on 'big government' for several reasons. Globalisation left US firms less reliant on US workers (Greenhouse 1983) and therefore less willing to support social programs that previously helped them to maintain the current and future workforce and to appease militant social movements. The elite also blamed welfare state spending for the enlarged deficit, rising interest rates, and other investment barriers (Amott 1993).

Neoliberal response: U-turn in public policy

Neoliberalism, the dominant response to the second economic crisis of the 20th century, surfaced in the mid-1970s and took hold in the 1980s. The new social structure of accumulation, best known as Reaganomics or supply-side economics, was launched in full by the Reagan Administration and pursued in varying degrees by every US administration since then. Seeking to restore the primacy of the market, redistribute income upwards and downsize the state, neoliberalism called for undoing the New Deal and Great Society. Hoping to dismantle the post-war welfare state, neoliberalism rejected government action as a way to mediate the contradictions between the requirements of economic production (e.g. low wages and high unemployment) and the foundation of family functioning (e.g. high wages and low unemployment).

The now familiar institutional arrangements put into place to achieve neoliberal goals and restore the primacy of the market included: (1) cutting taxes for wealthy individuals and corporations to reduce revenues and limit the progressivity of the tax code; (2) shifting social welfare responsibility from the federal government back to the private sector (privatisation); (3) shifting social welfare responsibility from the federal government back to the states (devolution); (4) reducing federal oversight of business, banks, labour markets as well as consumer and environmental protections (deregulation); and (5) weakening the influence of social movements best positioned to resist this austerity program. At the same time, the New Right gained ground and called for (6) restoring patriarchal 'family values' and (g) a colour-blind social order to undo the gains of the women's liberation and civil rights movements.

The impact of neoliberalism: more poverty, inequality, privatisation, and discipline of the poor

Neoliberalism represents a U-turn in public policy. From 1945 to 1975 US fiscal policy was governed by Keynesian economic theory that recommended modest deficit spending to stimulate the economy. A combination of numerous tax brackets and high marginal tax rates ensured that revenues nearly covered the costs of government in 21 of these 30 years with deficits running less than 1% of the GDP (OMB 2012, Table 1.3). During this now demonised era of big government, the nation prospered: the economy grew, poverty and inequality fell, wages and productivity increased in tandem and the standard of living rose for most people.

By the mid-1970s the neoliberal drive to downsize the welfare state began to take its toll. In 1981 Reagan declared, 'The taxing power of government must be used to provide revenues for legitimate government purposes . . . It must not be used to regulate the economy or bring about social change' (Weisman 1981, 1). Changes in the US tax code (fewer brackets and lower marginal tax rates for individuals and corporations) followed by the 2008 economic meltdown forced revenues down from 19.0% of GDP (1980) to 15.1% (2009/2010) and 15.8% (2011) – lower than in 1951 (OMB Table 1.2). At the same time, federal spending dropped from 21% or 22% of the GDP (1975 to 1996) to 18% or 19% (1997–2007). It might have continued to fall but for the economic collapse that required new and additional spending. The meltdown and the slow and jobless recovery, itself a product of prior policies, led to various government responses including a stimulus package, the bank bail-outs, emergency unemployment insurance benefits, foreclosure assistance, plus the cost of wars, all of which forced spending up to 24.1% of GDP (2011) – *the highest* level in any year since World War 2 after which it fell to 22.8% in 2012 (OMB 2012, Table 1.2). The gap between revenues collected and spending created an unusually large federal budget deficit.

The proponents of shrinking the state pointed to the growing deficit to press for more neoliberal tax and spending cuts. The resulting retrenchment undermined the social, economic and political functions of the welfare state that had previously fostered individual and family wellbeing, the conditions for profitable economic activity and social peace. Instead of generating economic growth as promised, the data show that neoliberal strategies increased economic insecurity, poverty and inequality, as well as the privatisation of social services, and efforts to discipline the poor. Given social work's location at the juncture of the individual and society, the profession once again faced picking up the slack.

Economic insecurity

Economic security in the US increased during the neoliberal period. In 2011, 46% of US residents did not earn enough to cover basic expenses, plan for important life events like college, or save for emergencies like unexpected health bills. They lived somewhere above the poverty line but constantly faced the danger of a financial catastrophe (WOW 2011). Wages that once increased in tandem with productivity now lagged far behind due to outsourcing production, technological change and weaker unions (Lach 2012; Mishel et al. 2009; Mishel et al. 2012). The Department of Commerce reported that during the 2000s big brand-name multinational corporations that employ a fifth of all American workers cut their US workforces by 2.9 million while increasing employment overseas by 2.4 million. At the same time, union membership fell from a peak of 35% of the civilian labour force (1955) to a low of 11.3 (2012) (US Department of Labor 2013a), but only 6.6 % in the private sector, the lowest level in a century (US Department of Labor 2013b). Reflecting these trends, the share of national income going to wages *fell* from a high of 66.3% (1970) to a low of 49.6% (2011), lower than in 1929 (Aron-Dine & Shapiro 2007; Norris 2011). Meanwhile the share going to profits rose from a low of 8% (1973) to an all-time high of 14.2% (2011) (Norris 2011). Alan Greenspan (1997), former chair of the US Federal Reserve Board and neoliberal champion, once explained how business benefited from workers' rising economic insecurity: a 'heightened sense of job insecurity . . . helps to subdue wage gains'

More poverty and inequality

In contrast to falling rates during the post-war period, poverty jumped from a low of 11.1% (1973) to a high of 15.2% (1983) and fell only slightly to 15.0% in 2012 (US Census Bureau 2012b). The inequality gap became an inequality chasm. In 2011, Latinos were most likely to receive poverty-level wages (43.3 %), followed by African Americans (36.0 %) and whites (23.4%) (Mishel et al. 2012)

The share of the national income held by the top fifth of earners (which had fallen during the postwar years) rose from 43.6% (1967) to 51% (2012), the second highest share on record; the share of the bottom fifth fell from a high of 5.7% (1974) to a low of 3.2% (2012) (US Census Bureau 2012a). Inequality increased in almost every state of the union (McNichol, et al. 2012) and the always wide racial disparities grew wider. More than 27% of blacks, 25% of Latinos, and 12.3 % of Asians lived in poverty in 2012 compared 9.7% of whites (non-Hispanics) (US Census Bureau 2012b). In 2012 white (non-Hispanic) earners comprised 78.5% of those in the top fifth of earners compared to 6.7% for blacks, 7.8% for Hispanics (of any race), and 7% for Asians (US Census Bureau 2012b).

More social problems

The growing poverty and inequality bred by neoliberalism generated economic hardship as more and more poor and working-class families earned too little or lacked the cash benefits they needed to buy food, housing, health services and childcare (Boushey et al. 2001). The long-term negative impact of cuts to health, training programs and all levels of education will be felt for generations to come, particularly in communities that are dispro-portionately younger, have less access to academic programs, fewer financial aid resources and diminished job-training opportunities (Cardenas 2012). In a study of more than 20 rich nations Wilkinson and Pickett (2009) found a linear relationship between inequality and presence of health and social problems. The nations with largest inequality gap suf-fered the most health and social problems and the inequality gap predicted the level of a country's health and social problems more accurately than its poverty rate. Sadly the US had the largest inequality gap in the world. 50 US, states with the greatest inequality gap also had higher rates of health and social problems. According to Nobel Laureate in eco-nomics, Joseph Stiglitz (2013), widening inequality (at its deepest level since before the Great Depression) is holding back the nation's economic recovery as it leaves the middle class less able to find work, consume, invest in education and pay taxes. He adds, 'market forces do not exist in a vacuum – we shape them. Other countries like fast-growing Brazil have lowered inequality while creating more opportunity and higher growth (Stiglitz 2013, 8).

Privatisation of services

Despite mounting social problems, neoliberal privatisation strategies that favoured the pri-macy of the market shifted social welfare responsibility from the public to the private sector. As early as 1997, a Council of State Governments survey found that of all gov-ernment departments, social service agencies were most likely to report increasing their use of privatisation over time (Johnson 2001). Privatisation has penetrated deeply into social work agencies. For example, *marketisation*, the earliest form of privatisation, trans-ferred services such as prisons, welfare-to work programs, and public school management into the hands of private, non-profit agencies and/or for-profit corporations. Since then, *managerialism* has begun to bring market principles into social services through the adop-tion of business management models. According to the Government Management Reform Act of 1994, 'To be successful in the future, government must, like the private sector, adopt modern management methods, utilise meaningful program performance measures, increase workforce incentives and flexibility without sacrificing accountability, provide for humane downsizing opportunities, and harness computers and other technology to strengthen service delivery' (Nightingale & Pindus 1997). More recently *financialisation* has deepened market penetration of social services by introducing the private investment model in social services (e.g. social impact bonds to fund social programs), defined as leveraging private sector capital to finance social services. For example, Goldman Sachs re-cently invested about $10 million in programs aimed at reducing the recidivism rates for Riker's Island correctional facility youth.

Privatisation advocates also support the renewed emphasis on efficiency, productivity, and performance outcomes while critics suggest that these emphases risk undermining the quality of care and increasing the commodification of interpersonal relationships embod-ied in caring work (Dominelli 1999; Ferguson 2004; Garrett 2010). In a study of the impact of the neoliberal welfare reform on non-profit human service agencies in New York City, Abramovitz (2005) found that social service workers were doing more with less. They re-ported running uphill just to fix the problems retrenchment created for their clients. They felt less effective, had less control over their work, and experienced troublesome ethical dilemmas leading to significant stress and burnout. Agency directors who adopted compensatory strategies to make up for lost funds reported 'mission drift'.

Disciplining the poor

Neoliberalism also promoted the welfare state's capacity to control or regulate the behaviour of the poor that had lessened during the more liberal postwar era. The greater directive, supervisory and punitive policies now disciplined subordinated populations for failure to integrate themselves into low-wage labour markets and/or to follow heterosexual marriage norms, most of which fall heavily on persons of colour (Schram et al. 2008). In *Regulating the Lives of Women*, Abramovitz (1996) found that neoliberalism's new rules and regulations penalised women viewed as departing from prescribed work and family roles and otherwise engaged in so-called 'irresponsible behaviour'. The latter included abortion, single motherhood, and same-sex marriage, among other personal choices.

How did this happen?

Social workers, among many others, have asked how it is that 'the people' were convinced to accept a U-turn in public policy that undermined their wellbeing, self-interest, and political power. Two explanations come to mind: moral panics and the shock doctrine

Moral panics

Since the mid-1970s, the war on the welfare state has played to four prevailing 'panics' that blinded people to their own self-interest: (1) the *economic panic* among the anxious middle class suffering falling wages and disappearing jobs; (2) the *racial panic* among white people which surfaced as persons of colour and immigrants began to institutionalise their hard-won gains and when the US elected a black president; (3) the *moral panic* induced by changes in women's role and family structures advancing women's and gay rights, and (4) *the political panic* among business and government leaders who feared the disaffected might rise up and blame them for the nation's mounting social and economic problems. By playing the race, welfare, gay marriage and/or immigration cards, neoliberal advocates convinced many people to vote for measures that undermined their economic security and the common good. The politics of fear and hate have kept people divided, blinded to their shared interests and, until recently, demobilised.

Shock doctrine

Neoliberals also resorted to what Naomi Klein (2007) calls the 'shock doctrine' to win support for their austerity agenda. The 'shock doctrine' refers to the creation or exploitation of a crisis or a disaster and the manipulation of the resulting panic to impose policies that people would not otherwise stand for. Neoliberals historically and to this day have stoked fears of the budget deficit to shock or frighten the American people into supporting deep tax and spending cuts. The federal budget deficit amounted to *less* than 1% of the GDP in most years from 1945 to 1980 (except for the mid-1970s recession). Nonetheless Reagan used the 'shock doctrine' to win the Presidency and launch the neoliberal agenda by telling the country that the federal debt was 'out of control' when in fact it was the lowest share of the GDP in 50 years. During the last 40 years neoliberals have enacted tax and spending policies that intentionally created federal deficits that *far exceeded* 1% of the GDP in all but four years (1998–2001). Deficits ranged from a low of 1.6% of the GDP (1979) to a high of 5%, climbed to 10% (2009), fell to 8.7% (2011) and then to 7% (2012) (OMB 2012, Table 1.2) still the fourth highest share of GDP since 1946 (Cove, Edwards, Rafferty, Regan, and Shakin (2012).

Echoing Klein's shock doctrine analysis, Nobel Peace Prize winner and economist Paul Krugman (2012) explained that: 'all the hyped up talk about the deficit . . . is yet another disingenuous attempt to scare and bully the body politic into abandoning many programs including the major entitlement programs that shield both the poor and the middle class from harm'(Krugman 2012, A29). He and other neoliberal critics explained that seeking to build public support for their anti-government agenda, neoliberals defined the deficits as a spending rather than a revenue problem and did so by ignoring the following important trends: (1) Economic growth during the tax hike period (1993–2001) exceeded growth in two tax cut periods (1981–1993 and 2001–2007) (Ettilinger & Irons 2008). (2) From 2001–2007, entitlement spending accounted for 10% of the deficit and discretionary spending for 7%, compared to 48% for tax cuts (Center on Budget and Policy Priorities 2008). (3) Current projections indicate that between 2012 and 2019 virtually the entire deficit will stem from the tax cuts (if extended in full), current wars and lingering effects of the recent downturn. (4) Finally, total spending (outside of health care) for low income programs oft-blamed and frequently targeted for major cuts is expected to fall below its prior 40-year average by 2020 (Kogan 2012). Based on these kinds of data, Krugman (2012) and others have concluded that the revenue gap is a side effect of the depressed economy rather than social spending and therefore cutting domestic programs or otherwise attempting to shrink the deficit rapidly will only make things worse. This is especially so for low-income programs whose costs (outside of health care) are not rising as a percent of GDP and thus do not contribute to the nation's long-term fiscal problems (Kogan 2012). On the other hand, social programs keep people out of poverty. Without the safety net, 28.6% of the population would have lived in poverty in 2010, *nearly twice the actual 15.5%* (Sherman 2011). Porter (2012) posits that cuts in discretionary spending 'would turn the government into little more than a heavily armed pension plan with a health insurer on the side' (Porter 2012, 5).

Future of neoliberalism

Proponents of neoliberalism promised their pro-market, anti-state strategy would generate economic growth that would trickle down to the average person. However, the data show that while wealthy individuals and large corporations benefited from the upward redistribution of income and wealth produced by neoliberal policies, the promised economic growth failed to materialise. From 1950 to 1976 real GDP growth averaged 3.98% per year (Officer & Williamson 2011). As the post-war social structures of accumulation that motored this growth lost steam, advocates of neoliberalism insisted that their tax and spending cuts would pay for themselves. However, this supply-side strategy failed. Instead, from 1976 to 2007 the economic growth rate fell from nearly 3.98% to 3.09% a year. During the subsequent economic meltdown (2007 to 2009) the average annual growth fell to *minus* 1.55%. As the economy began its slow recovery from 2009 to 2012, the growth rate increased slightly to an average of 2.38% per year. However, during the neoliberal period (1976 to 2012), overall growth averaged only 2.83% (Officer & Williamson 2011). Harvard economist Lawrence Katz told *The New York Times*, 'This is the first time in memory that an entire decade has produced essentially no economic growth for the typical American household' (cited in Herbert 2010, A7).

Even prior to the sharp drop in economic growth that accompanied the economic meltdown, some neoliberal moderates began to question the neoliberal strategy aimed at downsizing the state. As far back as 2004, Orszag (2004) – then Brookings Institute economist, observed that the deficit-financed tax cuts were unlikely to have significant positive effects on economic growth in the long term, and might well reduce it. In 2006, Robert Rubin, then director of the Hamilton Project at the Brookings Institute, former Treasury Secretary under Clinton, and Obama's economic advisor, issued a report that concluded that 'getting government out of the way' is fundamentally misguided since sound government policy is essential to maximising long-term economic growth. To ensure the productivity of workers and advance the US's 'promise of opportunity, prosperity and growth' the report called for government-supported access to financial assistance, educational training opportunities, and basic healthcare. Market forces, it added, must be supported and supplemented by an effective public role, one in which government ensured that the rules of the game were fair, transparent, and binding for all parties' (Altman et al. 2006, 14).

During the 2008 presidential primaries, even conservative *New York Times* columnist David Brooks (2008, n.p.) wrote: 'Supply Side Economics had a good run . . . today's Republicans [must] envision a different role for government than the 1980's Republicans because workers want a government that is on their side'. Brooks recommended child tax credits, universal healthcare, a tuition tax credit, and wage subsidies for laid-off workers forced to take low-paying jobs. Brooks (2008) and Rubin (2006) both concluded that the neoliberal tax cuts and hostility to government spending had become counterproductive. Both implicitly acknowledged the need for government to restore its traditional social (wellbeing), economic (profitable economic growth) and political (political stability) functions. The defeat of the Republican/Tea Party agenda in the 2012 US presidential election suggests that public opinion may be moving in the same direction. In his second inaugural address President Obama (2013) also pointed to the importance of an active government when he declared: 'Progress does not compel us to settle the centuries-long debate about the role of government for all time – but it does require us to act in our time'.

Others worried that the neoliberal strategy aimed at redistributing income upwards created too much inequality with problematic economic and political consequences. The data show that each time the share of income controlled by the top 1% (and top 10%) peaked, a major economic crisis followed. In 1928, after 50 years of *laissez faire* economic policy, the top 1% of US households claimed a record 23.9% of the pre-tax national income, the largest share since 1913. The following year the stock market crashed leading to the Great Depression. In 2007, after almost 40 years of neoliberal *laissez-faire* policies, the top 1% of US households again claimed a high 23.5% of the pre-tax national income, the highest share since 1928. In 2008, the US stock market crashed again, leading to the recession (Story 2010). Joseph Stiglitz (2013) suggests that this widening inequality is both holding back the nation's economic recovery and sending the 'American Dream' – a good life in exchange for hard work – to a slow death.

Others say that too much inequality undermines democracy. In 2006, Janet L. Yellen, President and CEO of the Federal Reserve Bank of San Francisco, declared: 'there are signs that rising inequality is ... impairing social cohesion, and could, ultimately, undermine American democracy' (n.p.). Supreme Court Justice Louis Brandeis (1856–1941) summed the problem up many years ago when he said 'We can have democracy in this county or we can have great wealth concentrated in the hands of a few but we cannot have both' (cited in Collins & Yeskel 2005, 13).

While the relationship between inequality, economic crises, and political democracy continues to be debated, one researcher suggested that inequality might have 'pushed people at the bottom of the ladder toward choices that put the financial system at risk' and that 'putting too much power in the hands of Wall Street titans enables them to promote policies that benefit them but that could put the system in jeopardy' (Story 2010, n.p.). As early as 1998, the author of a Morgan Stanley economic report stated:

> With worker rewards (compensation) lagging worker contributions (productivity) since the early 1980s, I have argued that it was only a matter of time before a politically inspired backlash would occur that would shift the pendulum of economic power from capital (shareholders) back to workers. While it hasn't happened yet, there is no reason to believe that such a reflex action won't occur at some point in the not-so-distant future. (Foster 2004)

In April 2000, William R. Cline, a trade expert at the Institute of International Finance, told *Business Week*: 'What worries many people about globalisation [linked to neoliberalism] is that the US does little to help those who lose out. You want to make sure that the benefits of trade are fairly shared' (in Bernstein 2000, n.p.). Former Federal Reserve Chairman Alan Greenspan stated, 'an increased concentration of income ... is not the type of thing which a democratic society, a capitalist democratic society can really accept without addressing ... because excluding significant parts of the population from the fruits of economic growth risks a backlash that can threaten prosperity' (in Altman et al. 2006, 18). Writing in *The New York Times*, Peter Goodman (2007) noted 'unease with market forces can be heard ... [t]he invisible hand is being asked to account for what it has wrought'.

It is unlikely these observers could have anticipated the 2008 economic meltdown or the Occupy Wall Street Movement that erupted in the US on September 17 2011 when 'the 99%' converged on Wall Street to let the 1% know 'just how frustrated they are with living in a world made for someone else' (Ryan 2012). Occupy Wall Street exposed the growing economic divide, put inequality on the public agenda for the first time in decades, and drew thousands of people into the streets in the US and around the world. President Obama (2013) also recognised the role of collective action in creating the conditions of the modern society when in his inaugural speech he celebrated Seneca Falls, Selma and Stonewall – historic makers respectively of US women's rights, civil rights and gay rights movements. By rebuking, however mildly, both the attack on big government and the assault on social movements, was President Obama rejecting the neoliberal paradigm launched by President Reagan 40 year ago? Reflecting on the US economic meltdown Kotz (2009) asked if rather than just another financial downturn, the US could be facing a systemic crisis of capitalism that would only be resolved through major restructuring of the political economy. As with prior economic crises, the answers depend on the outcome of the current political struggle represented by current legislative battles, electoral shifts and street protests.

Conclusions

This article reviews the trajectory of neoliberalism in the US and its impact on the US welfare state. Although the details differ from one country to another, neoliberalism has produced rather similar outcomes internationally. Social workers in the US and around the world downplay or ignore the need for political struggle at their own risk. If we become silent, tolerate, or promote neoliberal strategies, we implicitly align ourselves with principles and policies that foster hardship, decimate human services, and violate the social justice underpinnings of social work. Although some people think taking a stand politicises a previously neutral, objective, and apolitical profession, the historical record shows that social work has always been political in that it deals either with human consciousness or the allocation of resources. Since social workers cannot avoid the political, it is far better to address the issues explicitly than to pretend they do not exist. The history of the profession suggests activism on behalf of social work values offers a more ethical and effective option than calls for social work to avoid the political. Without such political struggles over the years, neither social work nor society would have changed for the better.

References

Abramovitz, M. (2011). The US welfare state: a battleground for human rights. In S. Hertel & K. Libal (eds), *Human rights in the United States: beyond exceptionalism* (pp. 46–67). Cambridge: Cambridge University Press.

Abramovitz, M. (2005). The largely untold story of welfare reform and the human services, *Social Work*, 50(2): 175–86.

Abramovitz, M. (1996). *Regulating the lives of women: social welfare policy from colonial times to the present*. Boston, MA: South End Press.

Abramovitz, M. (1992a). Poor women in a bind: social reproduction without social supports. *Affilia: A Journal of Women and Social Work*, 7(2): 3–44.

Abramovitz, M. (1992b). The Reagan legacy: undoing class, race, and gender accords. *Journal of Sociology and Social Welfare*, 19(1): 91–110.

Altman, R.C., Brodoff, J.E., Orszag, P.R. & Rubin R.R. (2006). *The Hamilton Project: an economic strategy for advancing opportunity, prosperity and growth*. The Brookings Institution. Retrieved on 22 April 2014 from www.brookings.edu/research/papers/2006/04/useconomics-altman.

Amott, T. (1993). *Caught in the crisis*. NY: Monthly Review Press.

Aron-Dine, A. & Shapiro, I. (2007). *Share of national income going to wages and salaries at record low in 2006*. Center on Budget and Policy Priorities. Retrieved on 22 April 2014 from www.cbpp.org/cms/?fa=view&id=634.

Bernstein, A. (2000). Backlash: behind the anxiety over globalisation. *Business Week Online*. Retrieved on 22 April 2014 from www.businessweek.com/2000/00_17/b3678001.htm.

Bernstein, M.J. &. Allegretto. S. (2007). *The state of working America, 2006–2007*. Economic Policy Institute. Ithaca, NY: Cornell University Press.

Boushey, H.G., Gunderson, C., Brocht J. & Bernstein J. (2001). *Hardships in America. The real story of working families*. Washington, DC: Economic Policy Institute.

Bowles, S.M., Gordon. D. & Weisskopf, T. (1986). Power and profits: the social structures of accumulation and the profitability of the post war economy. *Review of radical political economics*, 18(1&2): 132–67.

Brooks, D. (2008). Middle class capitalists. *The New York Times*, 11 January). Retrieved on 22 April 2014 from www.nytimes.com/2008/01/11/opinion/11brooks.html?scp=7&sq=brooks+david&st=nyt.

Cardenas, V. (2012). What is at stake for communities of color in the fiscal showdown debate? Centre for American Progress. Retrieved on 22 April 2014 from www.americanprogress.org/issues/race/news/2012/12/03/46635/what-is-at-stake-for-communities-of-color-in-the-fiscal-showdown-debate/.

Center on Budget and Policy Priorities (2008).Tax cuts: myths and realities. Retrieved on 22 April 2014 from www.cbpp.org/cms/?fa=view&id=692.

Collins, C. & Yeskel, F. (2005). *Economic apartheid in America*. NY: The New Press.

Cove, E.D., Edwards, B., Rafferty D., Regan D.S. & Shakin J. (2012). Monthly budget review. Congressional Budget Office. Retrieved on 22 April 2014 from www.cbo.gov/sites/default/files/cbofiles/attachments/43698-Nov-MBR.pdf.

Dominelli, L. (1999). Neo-liberalism, social exclusion and welfare clients in a global economy. *International Journal of Social Welfare*, 8(1): 14–22.

Esping-Andersen, G. (1990). *The three worlds of welfare capitalism*. Princeton, NJ: Princeton University Press.

Ettlinger, M. & Irons J. (2008). Take a walk on the supply side: tax cuts on profits, savings, and the wealth fail to spur economic growth. Center of American Progress & Economic Policy Institute. Retrieved on 22 April 2014 from www.americanprogress.org/issues/2008/09/pdf/supply_side.pdf.

Ferguson, I. (2004). Neoliberalism, the third way, social work: the UK experience. *Social Work and Society*, 2(1): 1–9.

Foster, J.B. (2004). The stagnation of employment. *The Monthly*, 55 (11 April). Retrieved on 6 June 2014 from monthlyreview.org/2004/04/01/the-stagnation-of-employment.

Garrett, P.M. (2010). Examining the 'conservative revolution': neoliberalism and social work education. *Social Work Education*, 29(4): 340–55.

George, S. (1999). A short history of neoliberalism: twenty years of elite economics and emerging opportunities for structural change. Paper presented at the Conference on Economic Sovereignty in a Globalising World, 24–26 March, Bangkok. Retrieved on 22 April 2014 from www.globalexchange.org/campaigns/econ101/neoliberalism.html.

Goodman, P.S. (2007). The free market: a false idol after all. *The New York Times*, 30 December. Retrieved on 22 April 2014 from www.nytimes.com/2007/12/30/weekinreview/30goodman.html?_r=1&scp=1&sq= T e+free+market%3A+A+False+Idol&st=nyt.

Greenhouse, S. (1983). The corporate assault on wages. *The New York Times*, 9 October. Retrieved on 22 April 2014 from www.nytimes.com/1983/10/09/business/the-corporate-assault-wages.html?scp=18&sq=employer+wage+reductions&st=nyt.

Greenspan, A. (1997). Testimony of chairman Alan Greenspan: the Federal Reserve's semiannual monetary policy report. Before the Committee on Banking, Housing, and Urban Affairs, US Senate, 22 July. Retrieved on 22 April 2014 from www.federalreserve.gov/boarddocs/hh/1997/july/testimony.htm.

Harvey, D. (2005). *A brief history of neoliberalism*. NY: Oxford University Press.

Herbert, B. (2010). Two different worlds. *The New York Times*, 17 September. Retrieved on 22 April 2014 from www.nytimes.com/2010/09/18/opinion/18herbert.html?_r=0.

Johnson, R.A. (2001). Policy documents: states expand privatization of social service. The Heartland Institute. Retrieved on 30 April 2014 from heartland.org/policy-documents/states-expand-privatization-social-services.

Klein, N. (2007). *The shock doctrine: the rise of disaster capitalism*. NY: Metropolitan Books.

Kogan, Richard (2012, Oct 23). The myth of the exploding safety net. Center on Budget and Policy Priorities. Retrieved on 22 April 2014 from www.offthechartsblog.org/the-myth-of-the-exploding-safety-net.

Kotz, D. (2009). The financial and economic crisis of 2008: a systemic crisis of neoliberal capitalism. Paper prepared for a panel on The Global Financial Crisis: Heterodox Perspective at the Annual Convention of the Allied Social Science Association, San Francisco, CA.

Kotz, D. (2003a). Neoliberalism and the SSA theory of long-run capital accumulation. Paper presented at the Allied Social Science Associations Convention, January, Washington, DC.

Kotz, D. (2003b). Neoliberalism and the US expansion of the 1990s. *Monthly review*, 54(11): 15–33.

Krugman, P. (2012). That terrible trillion. *The New York Times*, 17 December, p. A29 Retrieved on 22 April 2014 from www.nytimes.com/2012/12/17/opinion/krugman-that-terrible-trillion.html.

Lach, A. (2012). Five facts about overseas outsourcing. Centre for American Progress. Retrieved 22 April 2014 from www.americanprogress.org/issues/labor/news/2012/07/09/11898/5-facts-about-overseas-outsourcing/.

Lippit, V.C. (2010). Social structures of accumulation theory. In D. Kotz, T. McDonough & M. Reich (eds), *Contemporary capitalism and its crises* (pp. 45–71). NY: Cambridge University Press.

Magdoff, H., Bellamy, J. & McChesney, R. (2004).The stagnation of employment. *Monthly Review*, 55(11): 3–17.

Marglin, S.A. (2000). Lessons from the golden age: an overview. In S. Marglin & J. Schor (eds), *The golden age of capitalism: reinterpreting the post war experience* (pp. 1–38). NY: Oxford University Press.

Marshall, T.H. (1992). Citizenship and social class. In T.H. Marshall & T. Bottomore (eds), *Citizen and social class and other essays* (pp. 8–17). London: Pluto Press.

McDonough, T., Reich, M. & Kotz, D. (2010). Introduction: social structure of accumulation theory. In T. McDonough, M. Reich & D. Kotz (eds), *Contemporary capitalism and its crises* (pp. 1–22). NY: Cambridge University Press.

McNichol, E., Hall, D., Cooper, D. & Palacios, P. (2012). Pulling apart: a state-by-state analysis of income trends. Center on Budget and Policy Priorities. Retrieved on 22 April 2014 from www.cbpp.org/cms/index.cfm?fa=view&id=3860.

Mishel, L. (2012). The wedges between productivity and median compensation growth. Economic Policy Institute. Retrieved on 22 April 2014 from www.epi.org/publication/ib330-productivity-vs-compensation/.

Mishel, L., Bernstein, J. & Shierholz, H. (2009). *The state of working America 2008/2009*. Economic Policy Institute T.3.4: trends in average wages and average hours, 1967–2006 (2007 dollars). NY: ILR Press.

Mishel, L., Bivens, J., Gould, E. & Shierholz, H. (2012). *The state of working America* (12th edn). NY: ILR Press.

Mullaly, B. (2007). *The new structural social work* (3rd edn). NY: Oxford University Press.

Neumann, G.R. & Rissman, E.R. (1984). Where have all the union members gone? *Journal of Labor Economics,* 2(2): 175–92.

Nightingale, D.S. & Pindus, N.M (1997). *Privatisation of public social services: a background paper.* Retrieved on 22 April 2014 from www.urban.org/publications/407023.html.

Norris, F. (2011). As corporate profits rise, workers' income decline. *The New York Times*, 5 August. Retrieved on 22 April 2014 from www.nytimes.com/2011/08/06/business/workers-wages-chasing-corporate-profits-off-the-charts.html.

Obama, B.H. (2013) President Obama's second inaugural address (transcript). *The Washington Post*, 21 January. Retrieved on 22 April 2014 from articles.washingtonpost.com/2013–01–21/politics/36473487_1_president-obama-vice-president-biden-free-market.

Office of Management and Budget (OMB) (2012). Historical tables. Tables 1.2, 1.3, 11.1, 15.1. Retrieved on 22 April 2014 from www.whitehouse.gov/omb/budget/Historicals.

Officer, L.H. & Williamson, S.H. (2011). Annualized Growth Rate of Various Historical Economic Series. Measuring Worth. Retrieved on 22 April 2014 from www.measuringworth.com/growth/growth_resultf.php?begin%5B%5D=1947&end%5B%5D=1973&beginP%5B%5D=&endP%5B%5D=&US%5B%5D=REALGDP.

Orszag, P. (2004). The budget deficit: does it matter? Speech before the City Club of Cleveland. Retrieved on 22 April 2014 from www.brookings.edu/research/speeches/2004/07/16federalbudget-orszag

Porter, E. (2012). Goodbye government, under either fiscal plan, *The New York Times*, 19 December, p. 5.

Ryan, C. (2012). Allow us to introduce ourselves. We are the 99 percent. Retrieved on 22 April 2014 from wearethe99percent.tumblr.com/Introduction.

Schram, S.F., Fording, R. & Soss, J. (2008). Neo-liberal poverty governance: race, place and the punitive turn in US welfare policy. *Cambridge Journal of Regions, Economy and Society*, 1(1): 17–36.

Sherman, A. (2011). Without the safety net, more than a quarter of Americans would have been poor last year. Web log post. Retrieved on 22 April 2014 from www.offthechartsblog.org/without-the-safety-net-more-than-a-quarter-of-americans-would-have-been-poor-last-year/.

Stiglitz, J.E. (2013). Inequality is holding back the recovery. Web log post. Retrieved on 22 April 2014 from opinionator.blogs.nytimes.com/2013/01/19/inequality-is-holding-back-the-recovery.

Story, L. (2010). Income inequality and financial crises, *The New York Times*, 21 August. Retrieved on 22 April 2014 from www.nytimes.com/2010/08/22/weekinreview/22story.html?scp=1&sq=Story%2C+Louise+Slicing+Pie&st=nyt.

Tax Policy Center (2012a). Tax facts: individual income tax parameters (including brackets), 1945–2013. Retrieved on 22 April 2014 from www.taxpolicycenter.org/taxfacts/displayafact.cfm?Docid=474.

Tax Policy Center (2012b). Tax facts: historical corporate top tax rates and bracket 1940–2010. Retrieved on 22 April 2014 from www.taxpolicycenter.org/taxfacts/displayafact.cfm?Docid=65&Topic2id=70.

US Census Bureau (2013). Percent distribution of households, by selected characteristics within income quintile and top 5 percent in 2012. Retrieved on 22 April 2014 from www.census.gov/hhes/www/cpstables/032013/hhinc/hinc05.xls.

US Census Bureau (2012a). Historical income tables: income inequality. Share of aggregate income received by each fifth and top 5 percent of families: 1947–2012. Retrieved on 22 April 2014 from www.census.gov/hhes/www/income/data/historical/families/2012/F02AR_2012.xls.

US Census Bureau (2012b). Poverty Status of People, by Age, Race, and Hispanic Origin: 1959–201. Retrieved on 22 April 2014 from www.census.gov/hhes/www/poverty/data/historical/hstpov3.xls.

US Department of Labor, Bureau of Labor Statistics (2013a). Table 40: union affiliation of employed wages and salary workers by selected characteristics. Retrieved on 22 April 2014 from www.bls.gov/cps/cpsaat40.htm.

US Department of Labor, Bureau of Labor Statistics (2013b). Table 3: union affiliation of employed wages and salary workers by occupation and industry. Retrieved on 22 April 2014 from www.bls.gov/cps/cpsaat42.htm.

Weisskopf, T. (1981). The current economic crisis in historical perspective. *Socialist Review*, 57(11): 9–54.

Weisman, S.R. (1981). Intentionally or not, tax policy is a social policy, *The New York Times*, 2 August. Retrieved on 22 April 2014 from www.nytimes.com/1981/08/02/weekinreview/intentionally-or-not-tax-policy-is-a-social-policy.html.

Wider Opportunities for Women (WOW) (2011). *Living below the line: economic insecurity and America's families*. Retrieved on 22 April 2014 from www.wowonline.org/documents/WOWUSBESTLivingBelowtheLine2011.pdf.

Wilensky, H.L. & Lebeaux, C.N. (1958). *Industrial society and social welfare: the impact of industrialization on the supply and organisation of social welfare services in the United States*. NY: Russell SAGE Foundation.

Wilkinson, R. & Pickett, K. (2009). *The spirit level: why greater equality makes societies stronger*. NY: Bloomsbury Press.

Woolner, D. (2011). How Roosevelt saved capitalism: the 74th versus the 112th Congress. Web log post. Retrieved on 22 April 2014 from www.nextnewdeal.net/how-roosevelt-saved-capitalism-74th-versus-112th-congress.

Yellen, J. (2006). Speech to the Center for the Study of Democracy 2006–2007. Economics of Governance Lecture, University of California, Irvine. Retrieved on 22 April 2014 from www.frbsf.org/news/speeches/2006/1106.html.

18

The Nordic welfare model, civil society and social work

Gurid Aga Askeland and Helle Strauss

> Over several years the United Nations (UN) has been ranking the Nordic populations amongst the happiest in the world. One of the factors that seem to contribute to the happiness is an underlying trust between people. Another factor is the income equality with a small gap between rich and poor. Equality is one of the characteristic aspects of the Nordic welfare state. Equal communities produce less social problems, such as lower crime rates, less substance abuse and less mental health problems.
>
> The chapter introduces the Nordic welfare state model, and some of the characteristics of the civil society. It briefly discusses how the welfare state and civil society influence social work education and practice.

The Nordic welfare state is a well-known concept. It refers to the five Nordic countries of Sweden, Finland, Iceland, Denmark and Norway. While there are variations between these countries, there are major similarities that distinguish the Nordic welfare model from systems in other countries in the world. This chapter will primarily consider Denmark and Norway.

The welfare state developed in a period when Denmark and Norway were rebuilding after World War 2. It built on reforms and regulations from the late 18th century onwards when structures in communities were changing due to industrialisation and urbanisation. We are aware that our countries today are rich and prosperous, which influences the way our societies deal with welfare. Both countries have a population of about five million. While Denmark is a member of the European Union and Norway is not, both countries are to a much lesser degree affected by the financial crisis that has hit southern European countries.

A few decades ago several politicians and researchers predicted a cut-back of welfare state services. It was claimed that globalisation would put pressure on the Nordic welfare state and make it impossible to maintain this welfare model. But despite undeniable problems posed by globalisation, the Nordic welfare model has proven to be highly resilient and popular (Greve 2007).

Different welfare models

There exists no generally accepted definition of welfare, and the term is used with different meanings. In this chapter we refer to the welfare state as the way a country arranges for, creates, regulates and finances social institutions. The welfare society or regime are concepts which came into use in the 1990s when it was admitted that the responsibility for pursuing the welfare state lay in the cooperation and interaction between the state, civil society and the market.

Welfare models have been explained as three types by Esping-Andersen (1990):

- Liberal/Anglo-Saxon model (UK, US, Canada, Australia and New Zealand): social benefits reserved for the neediest. The state is responsible for core services, mostly in cooperation with non-governmental organisations (NGOs). Individual freedom and self-responsibility is valued.
- Corporatist–Conservative, also called the Continental Model: social security is funded mainly by mandatory regulated insurance linked to work.
- Social Democratic – Nordic countries: universal model characterised by progressive tax rates, and the state carries out most of the social welfare (Esping-Andersen 1990).

In many countries in the world, including the Mediterranean countries, social problems are expected to be taken care of by the extended family, the church or voluntary organisations. Today the three models mentioned above, are carried out in blended forms in various countries. Some general characteristics, however, are still recognisable as particular for the Nordic welfare model.

The Nordic welfare state is multi-dimensional and aiming at a high level of human wellbeing. Johansson defines this by nine components: 'health, employment, economic resources, knowledge and education, social integration, housing and neighbourhood, security of life and property, recreation and culture, and political resources' (Johansson cited in Kvist et al. 2012, 2).

Values behind the Nordic welfare states were consolidated by the social democratic parties in Norway, Sweden and Denmark. According to this understanding, citizens were born into a social community. A slogan created by the Social Democrats put people in the centre of the policy, 'Denmark for the People' (Christiansen 2007).

The seeds for the welfare state in the Nordic countries were planted long before the social democratic parties came into government. Nevertheless, the model is called a social democratic one as the growth of the welfare state happened when these parties were in power, and therefore have been credited for it. Nonetheless, it is important to emphasise that all political parties in Nordic countries have over the years and to a very large degree agreed with the basis of the welfare state.

Ideology of the Nordic welfare regime

Universalism is a central aspect of the Nordic welfare systems by which basic, standard support for every citizen is secured through social laws. This means that any individual or family, rich or poor, is entitled to social security. Universal rights are linked to illness, disability, unemployment, old age pension and child raising (child benefit). This system provides a basic feeling of security in everyday life, and as legally based rights, avoids conveying a sense of charity. Universalism was not primarily a social democratic principle, but a compromise of risk-sharing between different classes. Later on it has become a political and social value adhered to by all parties and a basic characteristic of the welfare state (Kuhnle 2012).

Solidarity is an important principle by which 'the broadest shoulders bear the greatest burdens'. The fortunate support the less fortunate, and stronger people take care of the weaker, because the individual sees itself as part of a unity, where the cohesion of the community is not just a political cliché, but a set of community rules – a way of acting – which is rooted in the common culture. There is an expectation that nobody exploits the system. Everyone does his/her duty and receives his/her rights.

Equality in relation to social security, free health care, education and job opportunities is an ideal of the Nordic welfare state. The state aspires to achieve formal equality in several ways, like by sex discrimination acts, and in Norway quotas for admission to various education programs, and board positions for women in the public and private sectors. Real equality, however, is difficult to obtain, as the state cannot make up for differences in private networks, informal resources and support systems. Equality in result is not obtained by universal rights alone as less advantaged people will need more support in order to achieve the same opportunities as more advantaged ones (Hansen 2007). Accordingly, social work and social care systems as well as means-tested benefits are necessary supplements to the universal rights.

Principles of the Nordic welfare state

The structure of the Nordic welfare model is based on politically agreed principles to enact or be responsible for:

- political conflict resolutions and decision making, based on consensus
- financing the welfare policy
- organising the services
- content and extent
- welfare policy resulting in less poverty and less income difference (Kuhnle 2012).

The welfare system builds on a long tradition. In Denmark the first poor laws mentioned were in 1708, in Norway 1755. Whether the governments are liberal, conservative or social democratic, the differences in their interpretation of the welfare system are rather small, as the majority of the populations agree with the ideological basis of the welfare state. It is based on a balance between the authority of the state and the freedom for the individual. Our parliaments consist of many different political parties and also our governments are often formed as a coalition of two or three parties. This model has been possible as the Nordic countries have developed a specific parliamentary democracy of consensus between the parties (Kuhnle 2012), made possible by there being less opposition between classes in the Nordic countries than in the rest of Europe. The welfare state deals with essentially democratic decisions on issues such as state investments, employment, housing, health, social security and education, and whether the state manages these in such a way that at least some minimum standards are achieved.

Globalisation has made the economy more complex. However, in this global market the Nordic welfare states have been, in spite of high wages, high taxes and with high levels of public intervention, very competitive. Some companies that have moved offshore have started to move their businesses back home. Competitive success has been due to high efficiency, know-how, innovation and a trusted public sector with minimal corruption. This has resulted in these countries maintaining prosperous economies as well as commitment to a state-supported welfare sector. One strategy has been an emphasis on human-capital formation and high labour-force participation.

The Nordic Governments have been following a mixed economy, which is a combination of a planned and market economy. The state constitutes a large part of the economy as it provides a good-sized amount of jobs in the public sector. This facilitates a strategy of active interventions with high public expenditure in order to maintain high employment and social welfare. Through the progressive tax system the necessary redistribution of wealth is provided. This progressive tax system is an important basis for financing the welfare state.

To pursue an extensive welfare state, a stable, sufficient tax income is necessary. This has been achieved by keeping up a high employment rate which also requires women to take part in the workforce and become taxpayers. As a consequence of most women working outside the home, the state has had to take over several of the obligations that used to be family responsibilities. Thus, a need emerged for care institutions for children provided by the public, as well as institutions and home care services for disabled and elderly people. This again created new workplaces, particularly for women. In order to secure a high quality service, institutions should be staffed with professional people, which relies on educational institutions to train them.

A basic idea is to make it possible for the society to alleviate its social problems and to enrich and equalise the living conditions of individuals and families (Greve 2007). In this way the most socially damaging effects of the market are reduced. The welfare system represents a compromise between the need for profit maximisation of the market and the consequent social insecurity for individuals, and, on the other side, individuals' need for a minimum of social security.

Administration of the welfare state

The distribution of public welfare state services in the Nordic countries is divided between the state and municipalities. While the social security scheme is rules-based, founded on universal rights and financed by the state, the social services are means-tested and covered by the municipalities. The majority of the social workers are employed by the municipalities and provide supplementary social services based on assessments. Social workers' tasks in the municipalities are primarily within child protection, integration into the labour market, social benefits, housing and supporting vulnerable people and families. Additionally, social workers are employed in hospitals, mental health, probation, refugee centres and in voluntary and private organisations.

User participation, which can be traced back to the social work original principle of client self-determination, has now been adopted and included as a principle in the social legislation. In reality, user participation is interpreted and practised to various degrees, from filling in various forms, to expecting users to express their opinions or to make their own decisions. An example of the latter is that disabled people are entitled to hire personal assistants paid by social security.

The public organisation and administration of social work in the Nordic countries has been influenced by neoliberal principles politically and economically (Høilund and Juul 2003). The new public management (NPM) approach has recently permeated the welfare regime, with its market orientation philosophy, privatisation, competition, standardisation, contracting, outsourcing, accountability and control. Citizens become consumers in the NPM system with purchase-provider arrangements. Language, titles and concepts are changing to fit with business and management ideology: people have become products; social workers are titled 'social entrepreneurs' and 'result managers'. Social work and social workers are less frequently used concepts in public documents and laws.

There is also a change from political and professional social work leadership to management leadership, followed by reorganising and merging of services into bigger units. The idea has been that transferring the NPM system, developed with business methods, into the public sector should increase the quality and efficiency of the latter, and reduce the encroachment of the state (Payne & Askeland 2008; Greve 2007). However work principles in a business sector might not work as well in a non-profit public sector. Thus the influence of NPM has resulted in increasing bureaucratization, creating dilemmas for social workers in relation to their values and professional approaches.

What is described above is supported by a Finnish study based on interviews of 24 social service workers. It shows that the social sector increasingly operates according to market principles and economic-rationalistic framing of time, contrary to the relational understanding of time in social work. 'To maintain their sense of self as skilled professionals, workers actively re-access and adjust their identities to exigencies of working life, but not without difficulties' (Hirvonen & Husso 2012, 351).

Social workers' potential to support individuals in their decisions for positive change is often based on a trusting relationship developed over time. In social work, following bureaucratisation the request for professional assessment has declined and professional autonomy reduced. Social workers experience less time and space for relationship building and individual needs-assessment based on a holistic approach (Røysum 2009, 2010).

For some time politicians and administrators have become more aware of how time-consuming administrative procedures are, detracting from resources that could be used in services that assist people. The new conservative Norwegian Government, in office from 2014, has as one of its goals a reduction of bureaucracy in public services. The municipality of Copenhagen in October 2013 decided upon an ambitious 'trust reform' making the social services more efficient and promoting professional core performances by dismissing demands for unnecessary time consuming documentation and procedures (Rasmussen 2013).

NGOs and private organisations

As a supplement to the services provided by the welfare state, NGO, private and volunteer organisations have always existed, partly supported by public funding. As mentioned above, the role the voluntary organisations play has been particularly acknowledged since the 1990s. Sometimes voluntary organisations function as an eye opener for the public as they may recognise and deal with people's immediate needs in a less bureaucratic way. Examples are crisis centres for women with violent partners, and drop-in centres for prostitutes, homeless people or drug addicts. NGOs have thus been forerunners before the state took over responsibilities. Private organisations may be non-commercial or commercial enterprises, which offer services for the public sector, for instance in foster care, child and youth institutions and services for people with substance abuse.

Civil society

A high percentage of the population use their voting rights compared to most countries. The voting rate for the national parliaments in Norway was 78% in 2013. In Denmark about 8% voted in 2011, which is the highest percentage achieved in that country. This may show that the population trusts the voting system and the political system and wants to make their contribution. Although voting not compulsory, many people consider voting a moral duty. Freedom of speech, free press, transparency in the public sector and access to social media makes it possible for people to express their opinions, and politicians are easily accessible. This has an ideological basis, and voter influence is greater due to the relative small population in our countries compared with many other countries.

In the Nordic countries about 40% of the population is engaged in voluntary organisations compared with 20% in the rest of Europe. On average people uphold 6.5 memberships in various organisations, which is twice as many as in Western Europe (Arnesen et al. 2013). Voluntary organisations contribute to the democratisation of a country. People are occupied with voluntary work in areas of sport, culture, health, in church and in other religious organisations. In addition, people might unite temporarily to pursue a common interest like refurbishing public institutions. Voluntary activities also provide people with social relations, social networks and may result in better health (Loga 2010).

Work is a deeply rooted value for Nordic people influenced by a protestant thinking (Kærgård 2007); although today the Nordic countries are secular societies. Employment serves two purposes: financial self-support and work as an activity which at the same time gives better self-esteem and accomplishment as well as access to social relationships and informal network in the workplaces.

Membership in trade unions is high although declining. The labour movement has had significant influence on the development of the welfare state (Wahl 2009). In negotiations with the employers' organisations salaries, standard working conditions, including average working hours (now approximately 37 hours weekly) and vacation (around five weeks a year) are settled. In case important national services are put at risk by strike or lockout, the state may become involved as a third party during negotiations. The parliaments in our respective countries will then launch impose compulsory mediation, whereby the conflict will be settled by arbitration.

Participation and influence on working conditions is legally stated, and decision-making about the future in public and private workplaces takes place in boards through democratic processes where employees are represented. The distance between management and employees is small and the relationship is based on mutual trust. Employees have high degree of autonomy and influence how their work is carried out, and in some professions possibly from a workplace at home. Similarly, parents are represented on boards in their children's institutions and schools (Gudmestad 2013).

The Nordic countries are considered to be family– and women friendly with a balance between work hours, family responsibilities and leisure time. Equality between women and men has been facilitated by women's participation in the labour market, which also made them independent of a male provider, and by many women taking up important civil and political positions, supported also by women's rights organisations.

Even if quite a few women have double workloads, it is fairly common that household responsibilities and tasks linked to children are approximately equally split between partners. Parental leave can be divided between parents according to different legal regulations. In Denmark the mother has 18 weeks of maternity leave. The parents can divide an additional 32 paid weeks according to their preference and 14 weeks without funding. Mandatory leave for fathers has been discussed but was not passed through legislation. In Norway parents may choose between 100% payment for 47 weeks or 80% for 57 weeks. Twelve weeks each are reserved for of the mother and father, the rest has to be divided between them according to their preference. Parental leave is an active policy instrument to change the male role, by emphasising the fathers' duties and rights, which have resulted in fathers strengthen their relationship with their children (Kabeer 2008).

Schooling is compulsory for 10 years in Denmark and 12 in Norway. Free education for everybody including university level has been an aim in the Nordic welfare state, which has resulted in a high degree of social mobility. Access to education is a feature of social justice and applies to any citizen regardless of life conditions and social class. Public grants and study loans have been supporting young people in their aspirations for higher education. Anybody who has skills and desire should have access to compete on equal terms for the highest posts in society regardless of social origin.

Children are trained in democratic processes and asked to express their opinions in kindergartens, schools, higher education, in pupils' councils and at home. They are used to having their voices heard and expect to be able to negotiate their rights. Children's opinions must be heard before formal decisions that affect them are made, even from a very early age. For instance, this includes decisions concerning parents' custody by divorce and interventions by child protection services.

Social work education – past and present

The welfare state developed particularly from the 1960s onwards with an expansion of the social security system and social services as well as in the health and educational sectors. The 1970s has been called the golden age of social services with a focus on prevention, education and rehabilitation.

Accordingly, there was a growing demand for a profession to staff the bureaucracy that was established to carry out tasks related to the social policy laws and regulations. Social work was found to be an appropriate profession to perform the functions, and separate schools of social work were established during this period, building on the short and few courses developed in the 1920s and 1930s. During the few last decades social work education has been expanded and merged into universities or university colleges.

Social work education has been reorganised to adhere to the Bologna system of higher educational programs. The countries' educational institutions offer bachelor's and master's degrees and some also PhDs. While the bachelor programs are based on a generalist model, masters' programs have different profiles and offer various specialisations. Some master's and PhD programs are primarily social-work oriented and others are interdisciplinary.

Who decides the content of the educational programs?

The state regulates the structure, length and content of the social work education through governmental frameworks and publicly funded evaluations organised by relevant government department, to ensure equal quality on a national level. Various stakeholders, such as government officials, the social worker union, labour union, educational staff, students and user organisations are invited to voice their opinions in hearings. Social work education has also been influenced by new public management.

Apart from the governmental framework, there is a certain freedom for the educational institutions and staff to prioritise specific courses and curriculum, and thus decide which ideologies and theories to emphasise. Sometimes professional unions will be invited to have their say. Students have their influence through membership on the institutional board.

Most social work programs on a bachelor level emphasise basic knowledge, skills and attitudes that prepare students to reflect on and adjust to various future jobs and organisational and political changes. In accordance with that social work in our context is closely related to the welfare state, social policy and social legislation are important courses in all bachelor programs.

The authorities expect social work students to graduate with ready-made knowledge and skills to practice in a bureaucratic social service field, and be familiar with various passing fashions in models and methods, although there are different opinions between social work employers and the government representing the above view. Educational programs, on the contrary, emphasise what constitutes social work as a profession. Social work is more than assisting people through a bureaucratic system, and thus social work students need to understand social problems in a holistic context, including obligations of the society as well as people's opportunities. It is important to prepare students for the challenge of finding the balance between support and control in their future work with clients. They need to learn how to analyse and influence administrative and political processes when social justice is pursued or resources are not sufficient in the organisations in which they are to perform their work. Students furthermore need to be able to integrate theory and practice, to critically reflect on values, various approaches, practices and social systems; to meet, understand and build relationships with people in various positions (Strauss 2012). Students' ability to reflect is usually more highly valued than mere reproduction of exact knowledge in assignments and exam papers. External examiners are used to various degrees, and students have a right to appeal the exam boards' markings.

In our secular societies spirituality and religion have to a large degree been overlooked in a holistic perspective in social work education. In this way the coping resources that people might find in spirituality and religion may get lost. Our students also need to learn to be aware how religion can be used as a tool for oppression.

A policy principle in all higher education is that students are responsible for their own learning. Students are expected to acquire the curriculum partly on their own, by reading and in study groups, as lectures will not give a thorough review of the literature, but rather widen the perspective of it. Educational programs offer various learning and teaching approaches and resources. The students teach each other, are actively involved in discussions and reflection, take part in skill training groups and in performing various oral and written assignments with or without staff supervision. Teachers invite students to engage and share their opinions in class, in order to train their competences in verbal expressions. This is also seen as an important tool in supporting their professional and personal development.

Student and staff exchanges

According to the Bologna Process, an extensive international student exchange is required. This takes place both in field placement and in theoretical studies within the frame of the different Nordic and European exchange programs, which also covers staff exchanges. In addition, quite a few students prefer to go to countries in Africa, Latin- and North-America, Asia or Australia. Regrettably, this seems to be a one way stream, as few foreign students are able to study in our countries, due to language barriers and the cost of living.

A few bachelor programs offer one semester in English inviting foreign students to study together with local students, and some master programs are offered totally in English. However, few students from developing countries succeed in getting funding for their studies in our countries, unless they are accepted as quota students.

Academisation and research

Over the years academisation of social work education has taken place, resulting in an increasing emphasis on research, theory building and publishing. Following from this, social work education has become highly independent of Anglo-American professional literature as Nordic social work literature is sufficient for study and research. However, to keep up-to-date in the various fields of social work and for inspiration, professional literature, particularly in English, is widely used. Except for Finnish, the Nordic people are able to read each other's languages, and thus social work literature can be used across the Nordic borders.

Contextualisation of the curriculum is important, not the least because of the strong legal aspects of social work in the Nordic countries. The teaching staffs do not only comprise social workers with different experiences and specialisation, but also other professionals teaching law, social policy, economy, sociology and psychology, and thus from different perspectives contribute to a holistic understanding of social problems, people and society.

Over the years there has been increasing expectations and financial support from the government to involve educational staff in research. Today there is a tendency for social work research to include users and practitioners. Practice research is attempts to build a closer relationship between research, theory and practice to make research more relevant and useful for practice and for education.

What are the challenges?

The welfare state secures basic conditions of existence and satisfaction, which is strongly supported by the majority of the Nordic people and the political parties. To maintain a welfare state requires a public bureaucracy. However to reduce bureaucracy is an aim of the political parties in our countries. The ultra-right wing parties would also like to reduce the level and amount of welfare services. Still, it must be kept in mind that even traditional liberal and conservative parties in the Nordic countries are in most aspects far more left than for instance the Democrats in the US.

The Nordic welfare state has been continuously exposed to criticism. The criticism falls in particular in three areas. Firstly, it has not reached it goals. We continue to have social problems like crime, substance abuse, relative poverty and not satisfying integration of refugees and immigrants. Secondly, the welfare state bureaucracy and security system is too expensive to maintain and in the long run may be unaffordable, especially since financial coverage may decrease with a declining tax paying workforce as the number of children is less than the growing elderly population. Expenses have gone up, due to an increased population and more extensive administration, which does not mean that the services have been better (Wahl 2009). Thirdly, it has been claimed that the welfare society produces dependency and irresponsibility (Hansen 2007). One criticism is that benefits are so high that some people prefer to live on those rather than support themselves by work. But it has also been found that some children, whose parents living on social security or benefits, cannot afford to participate in leisure and social activities together with their classmates (Andersen, Ejrnæs & Larsen 2010).

Even if the welfare state seems to survive, we also see signs of undermining and weakening of the welfare state through increasing individual responsibility, increasing poverty, social exclusion, bigger differences between rich and poor and commodification. So what we think should be the essence of a welfare state, will influence how we judge its status (Wahl 2009).

Despite the Nordic successes in stemming the tide of income inequalities better than most countries, inequalities have also somewhat increased in our region. However, even if there are slightly more poor people today in the Nordic countries, the proportion is still lower than southern Europe.

Furthermore, it has been maintained that high wages make it impossible to compete in the globalised world. The importance of formal education has been emphasised by the academisation process supported by politicians. However, some young people without particular academic skills have increasing difficulties as our communities have developed into knowledge societies. When practical skills are not appreciated in the schools, the schools produce drop outs, and these young people may later have difficulties in getting jobs, since almost any job requires some academic skills. Instead, guest workers are taking over.

Nordic countries had a very homogeneous population until the mid-1970s when immigration primarily from Turkey and Asian countries started. Later on there has been an increasing flow of refugees and asylum seekers from Latin America and Africa which continues to be a challenge to inclusion in society. Although it is an issue of concern, studies have shown that Nordic countries do not perform well enough when it comes to integrating immigrant in the labour market or preventing poverty among them (Gerdes & Wadensjö 2012). From former Eastern European countries our countries have had an increasing amount of guest workers, primarily doing manual work. In addition some people from these countries, including Roma people, arrive with no rights, nowhere to stay and try to make a living by begging in the streets. People from southern European countries now come in search of work because of the financial crisis.

The unemployment rate is low in Norway and Denmark, about 3% in the former and about 6% in the latter in 2013. Both countries are members of Schengen, the EU passport cooperation, which allows citizen to move freely within the borders of the member countries. With a youth unemployment rate of about 25% in Sweden, both Denmark and Norway have seen a flow of youngsters seeking work in our countries. In Norway 85 000 Swedes are registered in the labour marked. By living and working in the Nordic countries, guest workers earn social security rights, some of which are also valid after returning to their home countries. This is causing discussions about universal rights.

To combine support and control is often presented as a dichotomy between management and client orientation, and becomes especially a challenge when social workers are in positions where they provide means tested support. However, how to negotiate the balance between the two orientations is an old discussion (Christiansen 1990). According to Terum (2003), few models and methods exist that are developed for how to practice social work in a bureaucracy of the welfare system. They will not solve the dilemma, but it might have helped social workers more to be less prone to become influenced by and adjusting too easily to the ideology of the sociopolitical system and the bureaucratic management, and less likely to set aside the theoretical basis and social work values. A study of a critical reflection group in a social service agency showed that the social workers were not used to and felt uneasy about being asked about the value basis for their decisions (Askeland et al. 2011).

There are parallels between the Nordic social welfare state characteristics, like universalism, solidarity with the vulnerable, user participation, and social work principles such as users' self-determination and human rights. Following from this, the welfare state should be a work place where social workers should be able to work according to the principles of the profession. New public management which includes a high degree of control and less democratic processes (Wahl 2009) does not seem to fit well, either with traditions and culture in the Nordic countries, nor with social work values. Rather, the degree of control and accountability seems to demotivate employees, where quantity counts more than quality.

In some countries the efficiency and economic benefits of competition, reduction and fragmentations have been questioned, and they are looking for coordination and holistic thinking, which has been denoted as post-NPM-reforms (Stamsø 2009, 74). New public management has been influencing public administration in the Nordic countries, including social welfare over the last decades, but in several places critique is growing towards the weaknesses of the model and how resources are spent on procedures rather than on core performances towards service users. There seems to be a political awareness of this and a will to do something about it. However, the only reforms that have been introduced are intended to counteract the negative effects of the NPM, and not to counteract the ideology behind it.

Conclusions

The welfare state and equality of the civil society contribute to the wellbeing of people. According to the World Happiness Report people's experience of happiness has to do with how they experience confidence, security, prosperity, freedom, community, health and a balanced life in regard to work and family. The importance of these qualities is recognisable in the Nordic welfare principles and the society. For social work these values are key, and the values of the profession fit well with the values of the Nordic welfare system.

However, the lack of sufficient services in different areas of our community is pointed out all the time, and calls attention to service providers as well as politicians. The free press plays an important role in maintaining the values and the good condition of civil society and welfare state.

References

Andersen J., Ejrnæs, M. & og Larsen, J. (2010). Fattigdom, familie og børneliv. *Tidsskrift for pædagoger*, (50): 6–11.

Arnesen, S., Folkestad, B. & Gjerde, S. (2013). *Frivillig deltakelse i Norden – et komparativt perspektiv.* Bergen: Senter for forskning på sivilsamfunn og frivillig sektor.

Askeland, G.A., Oskarsen, E.M. & Unhjem, G. (2011). Holdninger og handlinger – bevisstgjøring gjennom kritisk refleksjon. In G.A. Askeland (ed.), *Kritisk refleksjon i sosialt arbeid* (pp. 168–81). Oslo: Universitetsforlaget.

Christiansen, K.U. (1990). Hva styrer sosialarbeidernes praksis? In K.U. Christiansen (ed.), *Perspektiver på sosialt arbeid: rapporter fra praksis*. Oslo: Tano.

Christiansen, N.F. (2007). Velfærdsstaten og det nationale. In J.H. Petersen, K. Petersen & L. H. Petersen. *13 Værdier bag den danske velfærdsstat*. Odense: Syddansk Universitetsforlag.

Esping-Andersen, G. (1990). *The three worlds of welfare capitalism*. Oxford: Polity Press.

Gerdes, C. & Wadensjö, E. (2012). Is immigration challenging the economic sustainability of the Nordic welfare model? In J. Kvist, J. Fritzell, B. Hvinden & O. Kangas (eds), *Changing social equality – the Nordic welfare model in the 21st century* (pp. 187–99). Bristol: Policy Press.

Greve, B. (2007). What characterises the Nordic welfare state model? *Journal of Social Sciences*, 3(2): 43.

Gudmestad, M. (2013). Samarbeidet hjem – skole som formidler av demokratiske verdier. In S. Sunnanå (ed.), *Skolehistorisk årbok for Rogaland: 1814 og demokratisk danning* (pp. 88–95). Stavanger: Skolemuseumslaget i Rogaland.

Hansen, E.J. (2007). Lighed og velferdsstaten. In J. H. Petersen et al. (eds), *13 verdier bag den danske velfærdsstat*. Odense: Syddansk Universitetsforlag.

Helliwell, J.F., Layard, R. & Sachs, J.D. (2013). World happiness report. Retrieved on 22 April 2014 from unsdsn.org/files/2013/09/WorldHappinessReport2013_online.pdf.

Hirvonen, H. & Husso, M. (2012). Living on a knife's edge: temporal conflicts in welfare service work. *Time & Society*, 21(3): 351–70.

Høilund, P. & Juul, S. (2003). Hvad er godt social arbejde? *Social kritik: Tidsskrift for social analyse og debat*, (89): 4–21.

Kabeer, N. (2008). Passion, pragmatism, and the politics of advocacy: the Nordic experience through a gender and development lens. In N. Keeber & A. Stark, with E. Magnus (eds), *Global perspectives on gender equality: reversing the gaze*. NY: Routledge.

Kærgård, N. (2007). Lyst og pligt til arbejde: kald og incitamenter i velfærdsstaten. In J.H. Petersen, K. Petersen & L.H. Petersen. *13 Værdier bag den danske velfærdsstat*. Odense: Syddansk Universitetsforlag.

Kuhnle, S. (2012). Den nordiske modellen: liberal, konservativ, sosialdemokratisk. Retrieved on 30 September 2013 from www.civita.no/2012/10/11/den-nordiske-modellen-liberal-konservativ-sosialdemokratisk.

Kvist, J., Fritzell, J., Hvinden, B. & Kangas, O. (eds) (2012). *Changing social equality: the Nordic welfare model in the 21st century*. Bristol: Policy Press.

Loga, J. (2010). *Livskvalitet. Betydningen av kultur og frivillighet for helse, trivsel og lykke: En kunnskapsoversikt*. Bergen: Senter for forskning på sivilsamfunn og frivillig sektor.

Payne, M. & Askeland, G.A. (2008). *Globalisation and international social work: postmodern change and challenge*. Aldershot, UK: Ashgate.

Rasmussen, T.J. (2013). Tilliden skal brede sig som ringe i vand. *Socialrådgiveren*, 12 (17 October). Retrieved on 22 April 2014 from socialrdg.dk/Default.aspx?ID=7033.

Røysum, A. (2009) Ulike forståelser av helhetlig oppfølging i NAV? *Tidsskrift for velferdsforsknining*, 12(3): 192–206.

Røysum, A. (2010). Nav-reformen: Sosialarbeidernes profesjon utfordres. *Fontene Forskning*, 1(3): 41–51.

Stamsø, M.A. (2009). New public management – reformer i offentlig sektor. In M.A. Stamsø (ed.), *Velferdsstaten i endring: norsk sosialpolitikk ved starten av et nytt århundre* (2nd edn, pp. 67–85). Oslo: Gyldendal norsk forlag.

Strauss, H. (2012). Socialrådgivere og beskæftigelsespolitik – profession og identitet. In I. Goli & J. Hansen (eds), *Beskæftigelsespolitik og socialt arbejde*. København: Hans Reitzels Forlag.

Terum, L.I. (2003). *Portvakt i velferdsstaten: om skjønn og beslutninger i sosialtjenesten*. Oslo: Kommuneforlaget.

Wahl, A. (2009). *Velferdsstatens vekst – og fall?* Oslo: Gyldendal.

Wilkinson, R. & Pickett, K. (2009). *The spirit level: why greater equality makes societies stronger*. NY: Bloomsbury Press.

Part 6
Social work and social change

19

Social work education in the post-socialist and post-modern era: the case of Ukraine

Tetyana Semigina and Oksano Boyko

During the last decade there have been significant changes in social work observed in many post-socialist and post-Soviet countries (Ukraine, Russia, Lithuania, Georgia etc.). The aim of this chapter is to introduce the international social work community to the context of social work developments in transition countries. The specific focus will be on Ukraine as a post-socialist country where social work as a professional project as well as social work education have been established quite recently.

Specific consideration is given to the existing post-socialist society's body of social work knowledge as the key feature of the social work professional project (Weiss-Gal & Welbourne 2008) and social work education. The interplay between political context, public values, social work teacher professionalism and professional practice development is considered.

The first social work training programs in Ukraine (as well as in some other post-socialist countries) were introduced at the beginning of the 1990s. At that time in the state which had just seceded from the USSR and announced its independence, there was a simultaneous process of social services development, social work emerging as an academic discipline, and formation of civic society institutes – in other words, all those things which did not exist during the socialist time. The background for all these social-political changes was chaotic organisation of market relations and rapid social stratification.

The history of social work education in Ukraine is both interesting and challenging at the same time (Bridge 2002; Ramon 2000; Semigina et al. 2005). In Ukraine social work as an academic discipline was officially established in spring 1991. The first professional school of social work in Ukraine was founded in 1993 with the support of the European Tempus British-Portugal project where outstanding British educators Shulamit Ramon, Steven Shardlow, David Brandon and others were engaged and the school became the part of the national university Kyiv-Mohyla Academy. The first master's degree program based on a generalist approach to social work and European values was launched in 1995.

The first bachelor programs in social work in Dnipropetrovsk, Chernigiv, Uzhgorod, L'viv and other Ukrainian cities were developed within the frames of European and Canadian projects. Experts and academics from various countries were eager to share with Ukraine the first-hand developments in social work, while every local university had been developing its own program of training of social workers which had been mirroring both a position of international project experts as well as the specific context and content of the University and the faculty within which the courses were to be housed. In some universities the accent in training was made on legal direction, the others made it on a sociological one, and some others on psychological or management ones. Thus, diversity was a key feature of introducing social work as an academic discipline in Ukraine.

Currently in Ukraine the social work specialty is delivered in nearly 50 educational establishments of different types and forms of ownership (Semigina et al. 2005). The social work degree programs have found their place at different faculties such as psychology, sociology, social management and others.

This chapter presents the results of the study on social work education development in the process of structural changes in Ukraine with regard to establishment of social work as a 'professional project' (Larson 1977). This chapter briefly establishes the context in which these changes are taking place and outlines the new arrangements. It indicates some of the complex factors that are shaping Ukrainian social work and discusses the significance of these changes with regard to post-socialist transformations in the country.

Theoretical background and methodology

The chapter is based on the idea of professional project which is developed in the sociology of professions and is based on Weber's concept of society as a scene where social groups compete for economic, social and political rewards, and the group creates the project. Supported and explained by Freidson (1970) and Larson (1977), the idea of professional project has been developed as a strategy.

Researchers claim that the social work profession is a modern profession (Weiss-Gal & Welbourne 2008; McDonald 2006). Social work education as well as social work academics are significant components of this project. It is mainly by their efforts that elements of the professional project are created as professional associations, ethical codes, academic journals, and the system of continuing professional education. With regard to the nature and status of teaching as a profession, there is, according to Larson (1977), agreement that professions are characterised by a combination of the following general dimensions: a body of knowledge and techniques professionals apply in their work; training to master such knowledge and skills; a service orientation; distinctive ethics, which justify the privilege of self-regulation that society grants them; and an implicit comparison with other occupations, which highlights their autonomy and prestige.

For the general overview of social work in Ukraine made in this chapter, there have been the indicators used identified by Weiss-Gal and Welbourne (2008) in the study of social work professionalisation. Based on the above, the indicators suggested for social work professionalisation study include: (1) public recognition of professional status; (2) professional monopoly over specific types of work; (3) professional autonomy of action; (4) possession of a distinctive knowledge base; (5) professional education regulated by members of the profession; (6) an effective professional organisation; (7) codified ethical standards; and (8) prestige and remuneration reflecting professional standing. These approaches to the core of social work professionalisation are completed with the important concept of social work professional ideology (Evetts 2003). This includes the professional values and beliefs motivate people to act, but it goes beyond that – being incorporated into relations and discourses about social problems and the ways to tackle them (Souflée 1993).

Besides this, important considerations are given in the chapter to the impact of international actors on development of national approaches to organisation of social workers' training and to the content of academic programs. At the same time, complex interactions are addressed between global and local levels of standardisation of social workers' training systems based on non-linear processes of glocalisation (an incorporation of the local and global) observed in post-socialist countries (Buzarovski 2001), and contextual effects which determine professionals' behaviour and mediate global imperatives (Burbank 1994). Thus, special attention was paid to different types of context that influence social work as a professional project in Ukraine.

The chapter is based on the analysis made in consultations with the local social work academics and educators during the meetings, professional round table discussions, and reflections from our own experience of creating the first social work program in Ukraine. It is well grounded on empirical literature on social work education in the country and review of relevant legal documents.

Societal conditions and political context

From 1991 Ukraine was undergoing a transition from centrally planned economy to a market-oriented one. It was the time when the country was experiencing the system crisis: numerous political, economic, social and cultural problems were intensified and suddenly became urgent. Break-up of the Soviet Union and the following collapse of the state economy resulted in shortages of goods and food, and triggered such social problems as unemployment, emigration, homelessness and poverty. Major political and social changes were accompanied in Ukraine, as well as in Russia and some other post-socialist countries, by dramatic growth of juvenile delinquency, drug and alcohol misuse, mental health issues and HIV/AIDS epidemics.

Interdependent difficulties and problems accumulated and aggravated with time, leading to increased numbers of people in need of social protection and support. Economic decline and increasing poverty led to greater inflows of those seeking residential care. The problems with social services and social exclusion were further exacerbated by scarcity of public resources and the fragmentised character of administrative, managerial and financial means.

The political, economic and social development of Ukraine as well as other post-Soviet countries shows that a certain continuum of political regimes emerged after the collapse of the USSR. Some countries (Latvia, Estonia, Lithuania) were oriented on integration with the European Union and implementation of democratic values, while others (like Russia, Uzbekistan and others) preserved the authoritarian political system. Ukraine is somewhere in the middle of this spectrum.

In 20 years of independence of Ukraine, the local political, economic and social context that has significant impact on social work and social work education can be characterised by:

- elitism in political and social life (the Constitution adopted in 1997 proclaims Ukraine a welfare state; however, standards of living are very low, the socialist-style system of privileges for elite groups was preserved)

- lack of cohesion of political actions (reforms of welfare services and higher education were announced and adopted by laws, but they were not implemented)
- social stratification (the current situation features high levels of economic inequality, poor remuneration of those employed by public services, including social workers, necessity to pay out of pocket for the services that are officially free of charge – medicine and education)
- ambivalent combination of state paternalism (with intention of state to regulate all areas of society) and neoliberalisation, including expanding of transnational corporation activities
- ambivalent and limited influence of international norms and actors (major international conventions were adopted in Ukraine, e.g. Convention on the Rights of the Child, UN Convention on the Rights of Persons with Disabilities, but they have not been implemented; international organisations provide huge financial support to the Ukrainian Government; however, they have minimal impact on political traditions in a country with deeply rooted corruption and non-transparency)
- socialist political rhetoric (power in country belongs to rich elite groups using populist proclamations of helping the poor; provision of social guarantees and social equality, while political actions are intended to support the position of rich groups and not the development of welfare programs).

Since 2010, the democratic values and civic society development in Ukraine are shutting down. The regression tendency of the last few years evidences further conservation of the bureaucracy system and authoritarian management in many areas, including medicine, education, and social work. The Ukrainian political situation has turned to become similar to Latin-American capitalism – oligarchic and dependent on patronage from the upper class (Montaño 2012).

While huge social problems demand the development of social work and social work education, the societal and political context has been a challenge for such a development.

Social services (institutional) context

McDonald (2006) stresses the institutional context which presents challenges for social work practice and education, which is also relevant for the Ukrainian context. The specific situation of Ukraine is that the social work development was not started from a 'zero' point. Ukraine, as well as other countries (Russia, Georgia, Latvia, Lithuania and others) inherited from the USSR the network of social institutions where there were no social workers and which were established based on the ideological perspective of social pathology. The prevailing general approach to addressing social issues was inherited too, with the understanding that they should be addressed similarly to medical issues or to those issues which the social control approach should be applied to.

During the Soviet times the system of social support was farmed out to bureaucrats. Existing social issues either were not addressed at all, or were ignored on ideological grounds. The public system of social welfare, created in the situation of lack of any charitable organisations, was characterised by extremely restricted social support with minimum social guarantees (Semigina et al. 2005).

Outreach services were launched in Ukraine in the 1990s. A network of territorial centres to provide day and home care to the elderly and disabled with no families were set up in every territorial district of Ukraine, although even now they still offer only a limited range of services provided to few categories of the eligible population.

In 1991 the first public social services for youth were organised to ensure positive socialisation of young people. These social services target disabled children, young families having problems, and preventing diseases in youth communities. The number of staff is insufficient, and in most cases they have small public financing which creates difficulties in running full-fledged programs aimed at social adaptation and rehabilitation of socially vulnerable groups of children and families.

Development of NGOs' activities offering social services and self-help groups (organisations of clubs and day centres for handicapped children and their parents, people with mental health problems, drug users and their families, and the HIV-positive) provides evidence for possible future changes while some new social work concepts have been introduced into the context (like foster care, family conferences etc.) and are legally bounded.

Despite existing innovative social services, the public social services system definitely requires further organisational, legal and personnel development. Major challenges that the public system of social services experiences are: its fragmentary structure, predominantly in-patient arrangement and little continuity in providing services to specific groups of clients. Still relevant is the actual reforming of social care that will address the issue of de-institutionalisation and introduction of community-based models of social care (Semigina et al. 2005). New methods of social work are often adopted through international cooperation and are supported by international donors. Usually, these changes are rooted in systemic models of social work, and in many cases they are not consolidated to make sustainable modification of practice. Institutional conditions, especially in public services, limit the initiative of employees of social services, as they have to perform mainly functional duties following a paternalist scheme of thought and action.

So, starting from the 1990s, the structural development of social services in Ukraine took place. However, these services are still far from the non-discriminatory ideology of modern professional social work and predominantly have personnel without social work education; moreover, they do not see the need for such personnel.

Professional context confronting the development of social work education

As a specialty, social work was approved by the Presidential Decree and by the relevant law of the Ministry of Education and Science of Ukraine in 1997. In 2004 social work was included into the current Ukrainian Occupations Classification, and since then it is an officially accredited profession in the country.

The important features of social work as a profession in Ukraine that influence the scope and the quality of social work education are:

- absence of licensing/registration for social workers or social services (in Lithuania and Estonia such procedures were introduced, while in Georgia they were only adopted, but not really implemented into practice)
- deficit of professional boundaries identification
- title of social worker may be granted to anyone working at social services; people without training may call themselves social workers
- the public's lack of knowledge of the functions of social workers.

- Despite the legal demand for managers of social services to have a social work education, the reality is far from this expectation (meetings in September 2013 with more than 50 managers of all public services from one of the Ukrainian regions revealed that none of them had education in social work and discussions uncovered lack of basic social work knowledge).

At the same time, most social workers – graduates of higher educational institutions – do not work in the profession due to low salaries, low status of social workers, poor working conditions and very few promotional opportunities. The status of social workers is considered to be lower than health care professionals such as nurses, physicians, psychologists and psychiatrists.

Iarskaia-Smirnova and Romanov (2013), while describing the Russian social services sector, stressed the persistence of the monopoly position of organisations providing public services and the limited possibilities of NGOs for creating a competitive environment, a lack of standardisation and standard regulation in this field, and a weak knowledge base concerning methods of working with clients. Similar context can be observed in Ukraine. The contemporary situation in Ukrainian social work demonstrates a lack of professional standards and training, lack of professional monopoly over specific types of work and lack of possession of a distinctive knowledge base, whereas these indicators are amongst the key ones (Weiss-Gal &Welbourne 2008) for social work professionalisation. These services do not build up a proper demand for educated social workers and do not cooperate with universities in training or retraining social workers.

An important challenge for the social work practice and education is the impact of international projects implemented in the country, which has a double effect. From one point, the impact can be considered to be extremely progressive and important in terms of professional developments and exchanges of ideas and practices. From the other perspective, a lot of paraprofessionals appeared because of short-term trainings the specialists had within the training programs (Semigina 2008). Those services that were the international projects' outcomes do not usually require any people with social work education. Both the state and the international structures supporting developments in the field of social work do not have any request for educated social workers. This creates challenges for the social work professional project formation in Ukraine, where, according to Freidson (1970) and Larson (1977), professionally trained social workers are starting to fight for control over the profession.

Another indicator of professionalisation – an effective professional organisation – is underestimated in Ukraine where such a professional association could play a leading role in developing social work nationwide. Currently there is a number of professional associations in the country with limited membership and leaders without social work education; none of them have real power to change the situation and to lobby social work professional development or influence what is taught in universities.

The professional values of social work are not promoted among workers of Ukrainian social services. In 2005, the Code of Ethics for social workers was adopted in Ukraine by the Order of Ministry of Youth, Family and Sport Affairs. This code is not based on the latest 'Ethics of Social Work – Principles and Standards' (approved by IASSW and IFSW in 2004) and is not embedded in day-to-day practice of social workers. Moreover, there are no state sanctions for violations of the Ukrainian Code of Ethics for social workers.

The professional ideology of social work in Ukraine, as in many transitioning countries, is heterogeneous. On the one hand, Soviet-style welfare programs (preserved to some extent) keep the tradition of state paternalism, pro-medical approaches to practice and fo-cus on 'helping relations'. Social workers develop public services, and clients expect that it is the social worker's responsibility to solve problems; the client is often in the passive role of a recipient and at times sees themselves as a victim of social circumstances.

At the same time, neoliberal context and its individualist perception of social prob-lems, enhanced by post-modernist views strengthening reflexivity and reciprocity in social relations, lays a new foundation of 'social work as a service'. This is a consumerist approach that may in the future be the norm in Ukraine. According to Otto and Schaarschuch (1999), this concept refers to a client as a highly individualised person who exercises choice according to her/his individual preferences. In Ukraine, as in many transitioning coun-tries, the tendency pointed out by Noble (2004, 291) for Western countries is evident: 'Social work is increasingly allowing the market to dominate its agenda by accepting that consumerism is the key paradigm in welfare reform'. The only difference is that welfare re-forms were not introduced in a systemic way, which created more fragmentation in the domain of social services.

Thus, the professional context of social work in Ukraine is rather challenging. Staff of the social services are predominantly not educated social workers, there is a limited pub-lic recognition of the profession and lack of professional monopoly. Professional practice is highly discrepant and contradictory; it sets ambivalent demands for social work educa-tion.

Broad academic context of social worker training

In the early 2000s, in Ukraine reform was announced of the highly centralised and over-regulated education system inherited from the Soviet time. It was expected that the coun-try should introduce the three cycles of the education system (bachelor, master and PhD) according to the requirements of the Bologna Declaration (1999). A broader understand-ing of the Bologna process principles and their adoption by Ukraine raises the issue of the commonality of the social work curriculum across national borders; promotion of mobility for students, teachers and researchers; and promotion of cooperation in quality assurance (the items stressed by Labonte-Roset 2004). The latter are included into the ob-jectives set by the European Ministers' Group to be reached in order to achieve greater compatibility and comparability of the educational systems. However, though officially modernising the education system according to the Bologna Declaration, the Ukraine ed-ucation system has not been transformed yet.

At present in Ukraine, according to Semigina et al. (2005), the system of training for social professions (social workers, social pedagogical staff and other professionals in the country) has four accreditation levels: (1) pre-professional training (vocational schools, lyceums); (2) professional training (colleges, technical schools); (3) graduate studies (uni-versities, institutes); (4) postgraduate studies (universities, institutes of postgraduate stud-ies, courses of advanced training).

There are two other levels in the Ukrainian education structure: (1) postgraduate or pre-doctorate studies (training that results in a scientific degree of a candidate of sciences, that is, an intermediate position between the master's and doctorate degree at US univer-sities; this degree is generally required to teach at the university level and to engage in scientific research); (2) doctorate studies (training that results in an academic degree of a

Doctor of Sciences which is equivalent to the Doctor of Philosophy degree at US universities).

In brief, degrees currently granted within the Ukrainian system of higher education are the following:

- Specialist Diploma level – refers to the normal university degree, five years of study
- Master Diploma level – refers to the normal university degree, one or two years of study (depending on previous qualification obtained)
- Candidate of Sciences (Candidate Nauk) level – refers to the postgraduate/aspirantura or pre-doctorate studies, 2–3 years of study. In EU terms it may be qualified equal to PhD
- Doctor of Sciences (Doctor Nauk) – refers to the highest doctorate conferred in Ukraine (Doctoral Studies).

The Ministry of Education and Science of Ukraine preserves its highly bureaucratic role in regulating all aspects of education. For example, postgraduate or pre-doctorate and doctorate studies offered at universities, institutes and research organisations should have the special authorisation of the Ministry of Education and Science of Ukraine. The degrees are granted following the presentation of a thesis to the specialised scientific committee, which is then reviewed in terms of content and procedural steps by the Ministry of Education and Science of Ukraine. At the same time, the ministry does not care about the international educational standards; for instance, the Global Standards for Social Work Education and Training (Sewpaul & Jones 2004). Universities have no autonomy and proper rights (for the selection of students into the program, to shape the program curricula including fieldwork and so on). The same situation can be observed in Russia (Iarskaia-Smirnova & Romanov 2013), while in other countries, e.g. Estonia (Raudava 2013), Lithuania (Vaananen et al. 2009), and Georgia (Shatberashivili 2012), the role of the governmental bodies in the higher education of social workers became more modest, and professional communities play quite an active role in the educational process.

To sum up, it is worth noting that Ukraine has an outdated system of degrees (not incorporated into new European reality) and the professional community has no influence on setting academic requirement for social worker training, as all standards and regulations are set up by the governmental bodies.

Specific social work education academic context

At the very beginning of social work introduction as an academic discipline in Ukraine, in the context of different Western projects, modern standards were brought and shared from the UK, Canada, Belgium, US, and Germany. However, the localisation process has affected the adoption of knowledge and values within the Ukrainian context. Reviews of Ukrainian textbooks and academic programs, results of research and discussions with academics demonstrate that social work education in Ukraine follows the tradition of those countries where the social work knowledge base consists of a combination of 'imported' knowledge (much of it developed in the US, Canada and the UK), and 'indigenous' knowledge that has been developed in the country itself (Weiss-Gal & Welbourne 2008). This 'indigenous' knowledge mainly refers to Soviet types of thinking, with the concepts of pathology, social control and positivism as the core vision of professional activities. Thus, most totalitarian ideas found their space within the approaches to the educational content. Populism and paternalism are the core ideas underpinning social work practice, facilitated much by positivism – the highly promoted basis for the vision and for the research evidence. It is supported by the view that social work is a highly utilitarian and pragmatic practice. This approach reduced 'theoretical knowledge' to an instrumental understanding of a situation or instrumental knowledge for action (Montaño 2012). Universal social change theories on which social work was founded (Noble 2004) are in many cases ignored or only briefly reviewed in the academic course 'Social Work Theories', but are not used in the courses in social work with different types of clients. The School of Social Work of the national university Kyiv-Mohyla Academy is one of the few Ukrainian faculties which incorporated the social change theories into its curriculum courses. Its lecturers used the frames of international projects and professional exchanges to get trained on the core social change theories as well as on the best practices mirroring them.

At the same time, students and professors may gain modern knowledge of social work theory and practice from local and translated textbooks, professional journals and communication. The key documents of the International Association of Schools of Social Work and the International Federation of Social Workers were translated and published in Ukrainian: *International definition of social work* (Semigina & Bryzhovata 2002), *Ethics of social work* (Ischuk 2008), the 'Global standards for social work education and training' (Yakovlyev 2010); and 'The global agenda for social work and social development commitment to action' (Semigina & Boyko 2012). Attempts are made to internationalise the existing curriculum via introducing different guests and optional courses with the updates on social work internationally (Boyko 2011; Kabachenko & Boyko 2011; and others).

The academic programs are overloaded with general courses of sociology, philosophy, history and languages introduced by the Ministry of Science and Education as mandatory, while the share of field placements is modest, being at some universities 5% of all academic time.

The existing system of higher education standards in Ukraine consists of a range of standards including the state and the branch ones as well as the special ones for higher education institutions. Before 2011 each Ukrainian university engaging in social work training was quite free to introduce different approaches to training, to identify a range of knowledge necessary for a social worker to have their own interpretations of social worker's competencies, and relevant formation of curriculums. In 2011, the branch standards for social work started to be developed; however, they have not been officially adopted yet. No service users or social work practitioners are invited or included into the Ministry Working Group on developing the branch standards for social work education in Ukraine. The indicative and disturbing fact is that, out of nearly 40 members of this group, only two persons have a master's degree in social work.

Underlying this inconsistent development is the profile of social work educators. We support the thesis of Kornbeck (2007) that the education profiles constitute a very valuable type of evidence which 'points to important aspects determining the identity and status of the discipline within academia, and of the profession – evidence of the ways in which social work knowledge is perceived in the national contexts' (98). Social work educators constitute a powerful factor that localises the international standards.

Before 1995 the only training for social work educators was provided via special courses, usually within the frames of international projects, and significant numbers of people came to social work education having education and professional backgrounds in other specialties, sometimes not related to social work. This had an impact on the content and quality of the knowledge delivered by them to the students.

Current requirements for social work education in the higher educational settings require the social work academic to have a relevant higher academic degree on the subject they deliver to students. Because of the lack of the third cycle of education (PhD programs) in social work in Ukraine, it does not seem realistic to meet such a requirement. To meet the general state standards in the country, social work faculties have to include lecturers of allied specialties with academic degrees but without any practice experience in social work. In most cases they deliver training to the students based on theoretical knowledge they have. Lack of relevant practice experience amongst social work academics seems to be critical as social work is essentially an applied discipline. This lack of trained social work academics and professionals teaching in the programs leads to fragmentation of the social work body of knowledge in the country and creates obstacles for its professionalisation (Boyko & Kabachenko 2011).

However, there is a strong belief amongst Ukrainian academics that introduction of the third level of education in social work in Ukraine will assist changing the current situation, where social work as a relatively new profession and academic discipline in Ukraine has a marginalised status – neither acknowledged as a separate field of education nor having completed the three cycle education. Because of this, those academics making attempts to advance their academic degree and to pass the third cycle of social work education (by studying for the PhD) have to find the space for their dissertation thesis within other fields of education such as Pedagogy, Sociology, Psychology. These disciplines integrate social work and create at its base 'new specialties'.

The first attempt made in Ukraine on introducing the third cycle of education in social work has been the first pilot project on introducing the first PhD in Social Work and Social Policy Program implemented at the School of Social Work at the national university Kyiv-Mohyla Academy in 2009–11, within the EU Tempus Project (Kabachenko, Savchuk & Boyko 2011). However, this program is still not recognised by the governmental bodies.

It is professed that, since the 1990s, there has been a process of 'academisation' in Europe (Otto & Schaarschuch 1999; Staub-Bernasconi 2009) which mainly refers to social work strengthening as an independent academic discipline. This process is being stimulated, in the first instance, by acknowledging social work as an independent professional area of activity which, in turn, needs its own research and academic centres, theoretical and practical approaches to conducting research, as well as the development of evidence-based social work practice. However, in Ukraine these issues so far have not been discussed amongst academics, lecturers and practitioners who are working in the social work education sector (Boyko & Kabachenko 2011).

One of the core challenges to social work education in Ukraine is its unclear mission and purpose. Should it prepare staff for current social services that actually do not need educated social workers with modern knowledge, or work to develop the professional project ahead of practice and then change this system?

The above vignette of social work education developments in Ukraine might be connected with many of the debates which have been identified globally. The issues raised are similar to those analysed internationally (Weiss-Gal & Welbourne 2008; Staub-Bernasconi 2009; Hugman 2010), i.e. the professionalisation of social work; contextualisation of social work knowledge, skills and values; differential access to resources and influence; and who plays what role in developing social work education.

Conclusions

Professionalisation of social work has not been completed yet in Ukraine, as there is a gap between the education and training and practice application. Social work as a profession and as a discipline has been introduced in the country, but it does not yet possess the whole range of specific features of the professional project. It is being trapped by ambivalent tendencies of preserving old paternalistic welfare traditions, strengthening of neoliberal societal conditions, and post-modern multifaceted paradigms of a 'new' social work practice.

The lack of the third cycle of education in social work in the country results in the lack of academics and researchers capable to conduct studies in social work, to create and to develop social work research centres and communities, and to educate and promote evidence-based practice. This, in turn, hampers the social work professionalisation and has a negative impact on social work education as the content and the requirements of social workers' competences have been permanently diluted by the significant impact of pedagogy, psychology and sociology.

The professional community is not commissioned to establish standards. Instead, this role is played by professional bureaucrats from relevant ministries. Policy decision-makers do not have the relevant education and experience, and do not share (in most cases they are even not aware of) social work values and professional requirements. Thus, such indicators of professionalisation like professional autonomy of action and professional education regulated by members of the profession are under threat. Thus, the system of social workers' education and training in the country does not seem to be corresponding to the Global Standards.

The international cooperation in social work education development in Ukraine was a useful catalyst in the initial stage; however, the paternalist scheme of thoughts and actions have gradually been substituted by a democratic egalitarian perspective 'imported' to the country in the 1990s.

Lessons from Ukraine (and their comparison to other post-socialist countries) might be interesting for those considering the contextualised behaviour of professionals and impact of political factors on social work education development.

References

Boyko, O. (2011). *International social work: methodological recommendations*. Kyiv: Makros.

Boyko, O. & Kabachenko, N. (2011). Social work as an academic discipline in Ukraine. *Social Work and Social Policy in Transition Journal*, 2(1): 79–104.

Bridge, G. (2002). Sustaining social work education in Ukraine: the second phase. *European Journal of Social Work*, 5(2): 139–147. DOI: 10.1080/714053064.

Burbank, M. I. (1994). How do contextual effects work? Developing a theoretical model. In M. Eagles (ed.), *Spatial and contextual models in political research*. NY: Tyler & Francis.

Buzarovski, S. (2001). Local environmental action plans and the 'globalisation' of post-socialist governance: the Macedonian experience. *Geo-Journal*, 55(2–4): 557–68.

Evetts, J. (2003). The sociological analysis of professionalism. Occupational change in the modern world. *International Sociology*, 18(2): 395–415. DOI: 10.1177/0268580903018002005.

Freidson, E. (1970). *The profession of medicine*. NY: Dodd, Mead and Co. ('Afterword' added 1988).

Hugman, R. (2010). *Understanding international social work: a critical analysis*. Basingstoke: Palgrave.

Iarskaia-Smirnova, E. & Romanov, P. (2013). Social workers affecting social policy in Russia. In J.I. Gal & L. Weiss-Gal (eds), *Social workers affecting social policy: an international perspective* (pp. 101–19). Bristol: Policy Press.

Ischuk, S. (2008). *Social work ethics*. Ternopil: TDPU.

Kabachenko, N. & Boyko, O. (2011). *Development of professional concepts in social work. Methodological guidelines*. Kyiv: Makros.

Kabachenko, N., Savchuk, O. & Boyko, O. (2011). *Doctoral Program (PhD) in Social Work and Social Policy*. Kyiv: Makros.

Kornbeck, J. (2007). Social work academics as humboldtian researcher-educators: discussion of a survey of staff profiles from schools in Denmark, England and Germany. *Social Work Education*, 26(1): 86–100.

Labonte-Roset, C. (2004). Social work education and training in Europe and the Bologna Process. *Social Work & Society*, 2(1): 98–104. Retrieved on 22 April 2014 from www.socwork.net/sws/article/view/234/294.

Larson, M. S. (1977). *The rise of professionalism*. London: University of California Press.

McDonald, C. (2006). *Challenging social work: the institutional context of practice*. NY: Palgrave Macmillan.

Montaño, C. (2012). Social work theory – practice relationship: challenges to overcoming positivist and postmodern fragmentation. *International Social Work*, 55(3): 306–19. DOI: 10.1177/0020872812437226.

Noble, C. (2004). Postmodern thinking. Where is it taking social work? *Journal of Social Work*, 4(3): 289–304. DOI: 10.1177/1468017304047747.

Otto, H.U. & Schaarschuch, A. (1999). A new social service professionalism? The development of social work theory in Germany. *International Journal of Social Welfare*, 8(1): 38–46. DOI: 10.1111/1468-2397.00060.

Ramon, S. (ed.) (2000). *Creating social work and social policy education in Kiev, Ukraine: an experiment in social innovation*. Cambridge: Anglia Polytechnic University.

Raudava, V. (2013). The impacts for developing the profession of social work in the post-communist context. *European Scientific Journal*, 9(20): 12–30.

Semigina, T. (2008). *Policy to combat HIV/AIDS epidemic in Ukraine: the role of the international support*. Kyiv: Agenstvo Ukraina.

Semigina, T. (2005). Professional social work: 10 years of sustaining in NaUKMA and outside. In O. Homilko (ed.), *Poklykannia universytetu* (pp. 203–13). Kyiv: Yanko, Veselka.

Semigina, T. & Boyko, O. (2012). The global agenda for social work and social development commitment to action. Retrieved on 22 April 2014 from www.eesrassw.net/documents/ga_ukraine.pdf.

Semigina, T. & Bryzhovata, O. (2002). International definition of social work. *Social Work and Social Policy* (3–4): 144–57.

Semigina, T., Gryga, I. & Volgina, O. (2005). Social work education in Ukraine. In F. Hamburger, S. Hirschler, G. Sander & M. Wobcke (eds), *Training for social professions in Europe*, vol. 3, *Finland, Russia, Belgium (Flanders), France, Luxembourg, Czech Republic, Ukraine, Hungary, Romania, Moldova, Liechtenstein* (pp. 152–170). Frankfurt am Main: Institut fur Sozialarbeit und Sozialpadagogik.

Sewpaul, V. & Jones, D. (2004). Global standards for the education and training of the social work profession. Adopted at the General Assemblies of IASSW and IFSW, Australia. Retrieved on 22 April 2014 from cdn.ifsw.org/assets/ifsw_65044–3.pdf.

Shatberashivili, N. (2012). Social work development in Georgia: challenges and perspectives. *Social Work and Social Policy in Transition Journal*, 3(1): 11–24. DOI: 10.1921/198787112X656225.

Souflée, F. Jr (1993). A metatheoretical framework for social work practice. *Social Work*, 38(3): 317–31. DOI: 10.1093/sw/38.3.317.

Staub-Bernasconi, S. (2009). Social work as a discipline and profession. In V. Leskosek (ed.), *Theories and methods of social work: exploring different perspectives* (pp. 9–30). Ljubljana: Faculty of Social Work.

Vaananen, A., Perttula, J., Godvadas, P., Malinaukas, G. & Gudliauskaite-Godvade, J. (2009). Representational identity of social work in academic context: comparison of Lithuania and Finland. *Socialiniaityrimai/Social Research*, 1(15): 52–63.

Weiss-Gal, I. & Welbourne, P. (2008). The professionalisation of social work: a cross-national exploration. *International Journal of Social Welfare*, 17(4): 281–90. DOI: 10.1111/j.1468–2397.2008.00574.x.

Yakovlyev, M. (2010). Global standards for the education and training of the social work profession. In *Innovations and Bologna process: the international conference papers* (pp. 23–36). Kyiv: University Publishing House 'Pulsary'.

20

Social work education in Eastern Europe: can post-communism be followed by diversity?

Darja Zaviršek

Social work education in Eastern Europe is marked by a historical period of state socialism and its socially constructed understanding of the person and the collective. Since the individual was subsumed by the collective, and social policy served the goals of the communist state, social work education in Eastern Europe has traditionally focused on the theories of collective social justice and equality. Theories of economic and social justice and universal social protection are still more represented than the theories of self-determination and the understanding of human rights from the universalist-particularist perspective. The key epistemological challenges are the understanding of diversity, empowerment and the ethical dilemmas in social work. There is a gap between social work education and social work practice, which opens some concerns about the methodological approaches of teaching, the selection of the students and the large numbers of newly qualified social workers every year. Educators previously came from sociology, psychology and law sciences, while today social work teachers most often come from the social work discipline and social work is taught at universities. Most social work departments have undergraduate and master programs and some have also developed doctoral programs.

The Eastern European region is geographically, historically and socially a wide and diverse territory and social work education depends and is influenced by two time periods and political as well as social regimes: state socialism (in some countries from 1921 but mostly after 1946 until 1991) and the post-socialist transition (1991 until present times). The region encompasses the former Soviet Union republics (Armenia, Azerbaijan, Belarus, Estonia, Georgia, Kazakhstan, Kyrgyzstan, Latvia, Lithuania, Moldova, Russian Federation, Tajikistan, Turkmenistan, Ukraine, Uzbekistan), Albania, Bosnia and Herzegovina, Kosovo, Macedonia, Montenegro, Serbia and countries that have become part of the European Union in 2004 (Czech Republic, Hungary, Poland, Slovenia, Slovakia, including the three Baltic countries already mentioned), in 2007 (Bulgaria, Romania) and in 2013 (Croatia). There is no single definition of what is Eastern Europe, but in order to understand the development of social work education the common denominator is state socialism.

In addition to state socialism, the pre-communist period of the three different empires (Habsburg, Ottoman and Russian Tsars), geographical and economic differences, large disparities between urban and rural areas, religious influences (Roman Catholic, Orthodox, Muslim), multiethnic territories, and relations between ethnic groups contributed to the state of today's social work education, social welfare institutions and professional practices. As the philosophy of social work sees the person within his or her context (biographical, social, political, structural), like social work practice itself which is always contextual and local, so also the development of social work needs to be understood within its impediments in different places, times and power contexts.

Social work schools and programs in the region

Despite the belief that social work did not exist in Eastern Europe prior to 1991, today there is considerable research which shows that professional social work education was established in some countries in the region after World War 1 (Poland, Hungary, Romania, Bulgaria), but was disrupted and closed down at the end of World War 2, or soon after (Hering & Waaldijk 2003; Schilde & Schulte 2005; Hering & Waaldijk 2006). For the communist leadership, social work was associated with capitalist ideology, seen as backward and a counter-ideology compared with the socialist idea that universal employment would ensure all other economic, social and emotional needs of people and establish the system of universal social and health protection.

Yugoslavia was the only communist country which had established schools for social work after the communist takeover (in 1952 in Croatia, in 1955 in Slovenia, in 1957 in Macedonia and Serbia, and in 1958 in Bosnia and Herzegovina), which is today perceived as a unique development of social work education under communism (Zaviršek 2005, 2008, 2012). The understanding of 'socialist social work' from the communist period was that 'social work carries out the goals of social policy' and social workers were primarily expected to work in the areas of social assistance delivery, family protection (which included foster care for children who had lost parents during the war or who were abandoned, and divorced and single mothers) and to prevent 'deviancies' (especially alcoholism and intentional unemployment). Social work education was imposed from above to influence the everyday life of people (Zaviršek 2008, 2012). The social work teachers were with rare exception members of the Communist Party and only ideas and practices acceptable to the regime were taught and practised. During the 1970s a social work teacher from Slovenia translated a classic social work book *Concepts and methods of social work* written by Walter Friedlander in 1958 and, after that, a respected party member teacher was asked to rescue him, otherwise he would be expelled from the school.

After 1991, all countries of Eastern Europe with the exception of Turkmenistan established social work education, mainly as a four or five year university program. Most of the programs were established with the support of international organisations, and in most cases Western academics (mainly from the US and Europe) were involved in the development of the departments, schools or programs. Some programs depend entirely upon Western funds. During the establishment of the first social work department in Ukraine at the Kiev Mohyla University in the early 1990, the classrooms were named after the names of the donors, like 'the Swiss room', while only social work students who were enrolled in a Western-funded educational project were entitled to drink English tea during the breaks to warm up their cold hands (D. Zaviršek, participant observation, Kiev, winter 1997). There were many Western 'social work missionaries' who didn't take account of culturally appropriate social work approaches and contexts and clearly dominated the local academics who struggled with poor language skills and lack of international experience. Simultaneously there were also a number of those who wanted to learn and to teach on an equal ground, carried books in their own suitcases in order to plant the seeds for the local social work libraries, helped students to get scholarships and accommodated them in their homes across the globe.

Due to such developments, social work education in Eastern Europe has become inevitably international. Eastern European social work students often knew more about social work in English-speaking countries, but had few ideas and almost no structural support to adopt and implement the transformed knowledge into the local context.

Until recently, educators in the region came from other social sciences (mostly sociology, psychology and law), while today social work teachers most often come from the social work discipline taught at the universities. Most social work departments have undergraduate and master's programs, but some developed doctoral programs too. The hierarchy between other social science disciplines (psychology, pedagogy, special education, law) remains untouched, with social work being at the bottom of them. One of the rare exceptions is Georgia today, where social workers are among the most wanted and best paid professionals within the caring professions in the country. They are seen as having a modern and good-quality education compared with the old-fashioned Soviet-type education of some other professionals (D. Zaviršek, personal communication, 23 November 2013, Tbilisi).

The country with the largest number of social work undergraduate programs is the Russian Federation (175 social work departments and programs), followed by Ukraine (with about 50 social work programs), Kazakhstan (22 social work programs), Czech Republic (15 programs), Azerbaijan and Kyrgyzstan (with seven universities where social work has been taught), Bulgaria (with five) and Romania (with four universities) (Iarskaia-Smirnova 2013). The universities with social work programs which have been developed lately are in Montenegro in 2003, Georgia in 2004, Uzbekistan in 2004, and Kosovo in 2012. After the year 2000, intensive development in international collaboration in teaching and student exchange took place and many postgraduate master's studies appeared across the region; for instance in Armenia in 2000, in Belarus in 2001, in Azerbaijan in 2005, in Kyrgyzstan in 2006, in Moldova in 2007, in Georgia in 2008, etc. (Rutgers University Center for International Social Work 2008). The processes of the academisation of social work are seen in research and the establishment of doctoral studies in social work in Armenia, the Czech Republic, Estonia, Georgia, Romania and Slovenia. A cross-national collaboration is shown also in the first International Doctoral Program in Social Work and Social Policy – Indosow, from 2009, which is run by a consortium of the schools of social work from the East and the West and was initiated, quite unusually, by an Eastern European school of social work (Zaviršek 2009a).

Today, most of the countries have national associations of social workers and some of them, like the Czech Republic, also have an association of social work educators (since 2009). Social work academics have been active in establishing a number of academic journals mostly in local languages; for example: *The Journal of Social Policy Studies* based at Saratov University, *Social Work* based at the University of Ljubljana and established already in 1962, *Social Policy and Social Work* based at the University of Belgrade and established in 1971, and many more. Some of the journals contain a mixture of local and foreign languages (e.g. *Social Work Review* based at the University of Bucharest, *Social Work Yearbook* based at the University of Zagreb), while some of them are published in English only, like for example *Social Work in Transition* from the Kyiv-Mohyla Academy and Sheffield Hallam University. In 2008, the schools of social work from the region have established the East European Sub-regional Association of the Schools of Social Work which brings together a large network of social work schools and scholars from the region. Most of the schools in the region follow the work of the International Association of the Schools of Social Work including its global documents and the global social work definition, although only a handful of the schools are its members.

One of the disturbing characteristics of social work education in some countries from the region is a high number of social work students who are enrolled in the universities due to the lack of employment. The quantity of the students threatens the quality of social work education, especially when the topics of professional values and ethics are in question. Some social work programs have become hybrid academic-welfare institutions which 'care' for young people in the way that they keep them within the educational system until the age of 25 or more in order to prevent their early unemployment. The schools of social work in Slovenia or in Bosnia and Herzegovina are examples of such trends, but not the only ones. The Department of Social Work at the University of Sarajevo enrols 500 undergraduates on a yearly basis. All of them are taught and supervised by not more than 11 academic staff, mostly hard-working and under-paid female academics employed at the department. One of the social work teachers bitterly complained: 'The government is buying itself social peace while offering 500 social work students' placements at the university!' (D. Zaviršek, personal communication, 16 March 2013, Sarajevo). Social work education itself has become a form of state social welfare intervention in neoliberal conditions. In Bosnia and Herzegovina the official rate of unemployment is more than 44% which is higher than in Greece with the deepest economic crisis among European countries (Sladojević 2012). The students, who experience this form of welfare-educational system, also know that they have little chance for employment as social workers, which influences their motivation and the learning atmosphere.

This is one of the reasons why most social work programs across the region have been lacking reflective and practice oriented learning, close supervision during the practice placements, and training in social work ethics. Many social work topics are contested and demand time and space in order to transform students' value systems and taken-for-granted assumptions about people's needs, dignity, ability and social work interventions. The medical model in the area of people with disabilities and mental health problems travels from one generation to another as taken-for-granted knowledge which needs – in order to be transformed into a social and holistic model of human beings – time, student and teacher engagement and a safe atmosphere. While state socialism has focused primarily on one type of inequality – economic injustice and consequently poverty – which social workers across Eastern Europe still today recognise as the main danger for human dignity, other human situations which could also cause discrimination and inhumane conditions, like multidimensional gender inequality, ethnic discrimination and hatred, and homophobia, are not seen as equally important as the right for economic redistribution.

Eastern European societies have difficulties with diversity (similar to postcolonial and remaining communist countries globally) and therefore social work education has an even bigger responsibility to teach diversity as a conscious learning process. Therefore, it goes beyond the feasible to accommodate large numbers of students with supported practice placements and to teach an engaged community-based and advocacy-oriented practice or even individual and collective empowerment. In many parts of Easter Europe the theories of diversity are not taught at all and at some schools they remain solely theories without practice.

The well-known quandary experienced in many local contexts with the word 'empowerment' is a symptom of how the theories travel and become local specific. In Slovenia, empowerment is officially translated as 'krepitev moči' (strengthen the power) (Videmšek 2014), which does not recognise historically founded oppression and the existence of unjust social structures including the welfare ones. Similarly, where the word 'diversity' is used, it most often means 'the difference' and 'difference' is mostly understood as otherness. When social work students or professionals express their respect towards diverse human conditions, they say they respect 'those who are different'. This is a highly normative understanding of diversity, because the idea of 'being different' encompasses all conditions and appearances which are seen as not 'normal'.

Social work education, therefore, mostly fails to lead the students to make some major paradigm shifts in thinking and to take a critical stance about the normative construction of normality which is mostly constructed and transmitted by a common sense old-fashioned medical, psychological, pedagogical and social work knowledge about the lives of the service users and their decisions.

Contextualising social work education in Eastern Europe

After the change of the political regimes in 1991, the region of Eastern Europe faced fragmentation due to ethnic wars, massive economic crises, migration and the appearance of state building among the former Soviet Union and Yugoslav republics alongside international political players (World Bank, the International Monetary Fund, and institutions of the European Union) which influenced economic life and social policy/legislation of the countries in the region.

The 'emergency welfare state' (Inglot 2009) processes after 1991 included new social policy legislation and the development of the mixed system of social services (governmental, non-governmental organisations (NGOs) and private). The times of economic liberalisation were harsh for most Eastern European countries and for the majority of people (Jäppinen et al. 2011; Bessudnov et al, 2011). The existing industries and state enterprises collapsed and a period of enormous unemployment, among men, women and ethnic minorities (especially Russian in the Baltic countries, and Roma people in the Czech Republic, Slovakia, Slovenia, Croatia, Romania, Hungary and Bulgaria) started to dominate everyday life. Poverty expanded and has remained the central fact of life. It has affected most heavily the rural areas of the region, from where people migrated to the capital cities, or from more eastern parts of the region towards the Western parts, and from more southern parts towards the north (from central Asia to Russia; from Ukraine to Poland; from Kosovo and Albania to Croatia and Slovenia). In Albania, rates of poverty in rural areas are almost 70% higher than in the capital city (Ymeraj 2007).

People faced many breaks in their everyday routine: privatisation of publicly created goods and services during state socialism (kindergartens, local health centres, factories); flexibility of labour and consequently unemployment after a long period of full employment; early retirements of a huge number of workers in some countries; ethnic conflicts and wars; economic migration and consequently the transformation of extended family care systems and family life; the development of huge economic inequalities ('the new rich'); and the return of religious powers as the key political and social players in secularised societies. Eastern European countries moved from the period of state socialism to the era of neoliberalism. Vanhuysse (2009) has observed that the large-scale early retirement of Eastern European workers in Poland and the Czech Republic during the 1990s was a deliberate governmental strategy against potential workers' resistance and protest towards the neoliberal reforms from a decade ago. Many researchers show that the international financial institutions heavily influenced national governments' decision-making in the economic and social policy areas and worked towards the neoliberalisation of the whole region (Deacon et al. 2007).

Violent ethnic conflicts (Croatia, Macedonia, Georgia), ethnic wars (Armenia, Azerbaijan, Chechnya), ethnic cleansing and mass killings (Bosnia and Herzegovina, Kosovo) which appeared almost immediately after the fall of Yugoslavia and Soviet Union caused deaths, disability, forced migration, a big number of refuges, internally displaced persons, as well as voluntary and compulsory re-migration, increased poverty, trans-generational losses and trauma. In Bosnia and Herzegovina 100,000–300,000 persons were killed and out of 4.4 million population one million fled the country between 1992 and 1995 (Holiček & Rašidagić 2007). Similarly, 850,000 persons fled from Kosovo in 1999 and 360,000 Kosovans sought refuge in neighbouring Macedonia which was about 17% of the whole population of Macedonia (Mitev 2007; Cocozzelli 2007). After Kosovo proclaimed the independent state in 2008, social work students disputed whether they were ethnically 'Albanians', 'Moslems' or 'Kosovans', and remained divided into three different ethnic identities (personal notes, University of Pristine 2008). Georgia with less than 5 million population has formally 250,000 internally displaced persons, and half of them still today live in Collective Living Centres (since the Russian occupation of Abkhazia and South Ossetia regions in 2008).

During state socialism, the 19th and 20th centuries' primordial understandings of the blood-kin relationship based on singular ethnic belonging were replaced by the pragmatic communist ideology which suppressed the ethnic identity in order to construct again a singular but new identity of a socialist proletariat. After 1991, ethnicity became for the vast majority of people almost a 'new' political and social identity, not formally recognised and mostly not individually lived for almost half of the 20th century. The imagined identities were mobilised by political elites for a new political project of shifting the national and state borders. The revival of the ideology of blood was criticised by many world humanists including Nelson Mandela, who expressed it very clearly: 'They [the leaders] thought through their blood and not through their brains' (Crwys-Williams 2010, 25).

In 1992 the new Slovenian Government deprived more than 25,000 persons (official holders of Yugoslav passports who came to Slovenia as economic immigrants) of their citizenship rights and erased them from the register of permanent residents of the Republic of Slovenia. They lost all social and political rights and were treated as illegal migrants vulnerable to detention and deportation (Zorn 2009). In the Baltic countries, too, the exclusion of the internal 'others' (the Russian ethnic minority) helped to construct seemingly ethnically homogeneous states.

Roma people, who are today the largest ethnic minority in Europe, have suffered severely during the last 20 years. There are nine to 12 million Roma people in the region, most of them in Romania (2.5 million). The figures are estimates and include people who have defined their ethnicity as Roma during national censuses and those who have not (mostly because of racism). Roma men have lost their jobs due to the closing down of heavy industry and their poor education. Additionally, they have lost the alternative sources of earning (e.g. collecting iron, plastic bottles, simple craft, music) and remained largely without income, dependent on social assistance money. Many Roma fled ethnic wars. In Kosovo, for instance, Roma villages were burnt after the war, as the local population deemed the Roma as Serb collaborators. Many of them became asylum seekers, illegal migrants and long-term homeless. Unemployment levels among Roma people in all countries of Eastern Europe are extremely high, currently ranging from 60–90%. Roma women are transgenerationally marginalised, living mostly in segregated settlements that they hardly leave. They are unemployed, sometimes illiterate, but receive welfare assistance if they have children. Regardless of whether they have small or large Roma populations, all Eastern European countries articulate from moderate to extreme nationalist rhetoric against Roma peoples, some ethnically motivated hate speech and violent attacks against Roma settlements (Vermeersch & Ram 2009). The ethnic hatred has been a product of a long history of exclusion in the pre-communist period, during communism (since Roma lacked long-term industrial employment, they were categorised into the lowest class among socialist citizens, and called the lumpen-proletariat) and continues today.

Economic crises and the neoliberal transformation of the national governments, made thousands of people migrate to Western countries to seek jobs and support those who stayed in their country of origins. In Albania (3.1 million population) a quarter of its population (mostly young men) left the country between 1990 and 2005 mostly to Greece and Italy (Ymeraj 2007). Thousands of women from Ukraine and Lithuania have become care workers and are today part of the phenomena known as 'global motherhood' (Ehrenreich & Hochschild 2003). They care for the family of the employer abroad while providing economic care for their families at home, especially their children. In Germany there are about 200,000 female care workers from Eastern Europe with more than 30,000 from Lithuania. In the Ukraine, some estimates show that in every third family at least one female member is a migrant worker abroad (Tolstokorova 2010).

Remittances from Eastern European emigrants have become either a crucial income source or the only family income which helps numerous families to survive. Only recently has the large-scale female migration become a governmental concern. In Lithuania, the mass media speaks about the immigration of large numbers of women while in the Ukraine social workers and other social service professionals speak about the 'Italian syndrome' (abandoned and lonely children but with monthly income from their mothers working mostly in Italy). Some creative responses by social workers were developed to support children who are left alone. For instance, Lithuania introduced temporary guardianship for grandparents who care for children of migrant workers (Malinauskas 2011). Not only relatives, but also friends, neighbours and school teachers provide some social parenthood for these children. Social parenthood has become a reality for a growing number of adults and children (Zaviršek 2009b).

Nevertheless, many researchers express concern that, in poorer Eastern European countries, the system of home care is entirely based on the unpaid care work of the family members, mostly women, who are today leaving home to seek paid care work abroad (Prochazkova & Schmid 2009). Older people who are left alone can neither afford to pay state-run nursing homes nor even more expensive private ones. In some countries social workers are involved in poorly paid community-based home assistance services for the elderly.

Social work and the needs of people living in Eastern Europe

Since the individual was subsumed by the collective, and social policy served the goals of the communist states, social work education has traditionally focused on the theories of collective social justice and equality. The consequence is that social work theories of economic and social justice and the universal social protection are still more represented than the theories of diversity, self-determination and the understanding of human rights from the universalist-particularist perspective. The key epistemological challenges are understanding of diversity, empowerment and the shift from formal participation towards the actual one.

The delivery of social assistance money to people who are unemployed, poor families, ethnic minorities, elders and persons with disabilities is the main part of social workers' activities. In wealthier countries in the region with a wide range of long-established governmental institutions and community-based welfare services (day centres for people with multiple diagnoses, sheltered workshops, crises centres for children in need, family-helpers system, women refuges and the group homes for people with mental health problems and other disabilities) social workers provide placements to these institutions and organise payment contracts usually covered by local municipalities, the state and the person and his or her relatives. Most of the welfare facilities are located in the cities and people from rural areas hardly reach them or must send relatives far away from home to long-stay institutions. Since the economic crises after 2008 and radical cuts in social protection in national states by the international financial organisations, even more social work activities are focused on social transfer delivery, and fewer activities happen in the area of community development.

Many types of welfare organisations, styles of work and approaches have remained the same until the present, e.g. long-stay institutions for disabled people despite pilot projects on deinstitutionalisation; the denial of most legal and actual rights of children with intellectual disabilities; the non-existence of independent advocacy work especially for children; the denial of self-determination of service users; and absence of social action approaches in deprived communities. At the same time, many social work educators, students and social workers have been involved in the process of deinstitutionalisation (funded and often initiated by the Western donors), which most often got stuck half-way due to the lack of local governmental support and lack of adequate professional support for carers (Anghel 2011; Russell & Iarskaia-Smirnova 2013).

The local and international NGOs cover many different social work areas. Especially in the countries of the former Soviet Union and the south-east of Europe, social work innovations were only possible with the use of the international money (violence against women and support for victims of rape, the development of personal assistance projects and independent living of persons with severe disabilities, deinstitutionalisation initiatives especially for children, cooperatives for people with long-term mental health problems, support services for mothers with a child with impairments, counselling for stigmatised LGBT people, medical aid and counselling for people affected with HIV and AIDS, and projects against human trafficking). In Belarus, disability activists try to make the government sign the UN Convention of the Rights of People with Disabilities and a well-known organisation for the prevention of women's slavery, La Strada, works across the borders of Russia, Belarus and Ukraine against women's and children's trafficking.

Local and international NGOs usually work in Roma settlements, mostly organising different projects with children and sometimes doing women's empowerment work. Children's maltreatment and the early marriages of Roma girls as well as violence against Roma women are the areas which are avoided and silenced by social workers as much as by the general public. A small number of gojim (non-Roma) social workers have developed a strong relationship of trust with the Roma and there are innovative projects in Bulgaria and Romania, where international NGOs together with social work students and local people set up Roma cooperatives in their settlements.

The economic crises and the neoliberal governments across the region have today caused more poverty among the retired workers, single-headed households, the elderly, people with disabilities and elderly single women. The consequence is that the religious organisations and the staff without academic education started to offer 'social work' services. These organisations have become the only anchor for people in extreme poverty. It seems like two parallel processes exist in the region: on the one hand, the academisation of social work and on the other the growing number of organisations practising charitable activities that are replacing the state social work services and professional support. The revival of the religious social services can be observed across the entire region. Church power has been re-established ideologically and economically after states returned some (or even all, like in Slovenia) of its confiscated property from the times before communism. Despite the regained power of the religious institutions which suffered persecutions during the communist era, the religious authorities see themselves as the victims of the former political regime and in need of compensation for previous atrocities. With the increased neoliberalisation the state abandonment of people in need of social assistance money, housing and other forms of support, the church got involved in social welfare work by 'serving the poor' (religious kitchens, help for families with many children, the elderly, the disabled, individual counselling).

At the same time, the religious authorities became front-runners in morally driven debates and are together with the leading political parties responsible for the increased level of intolerance and violence across Eastern Europe. In November 2013 the Patriarch of the Georgian Orthodox Church prohibited the local NGO to open a shelter for homeless families in the capital city Tbilisi. The organisation called Identoba ('Identitiy') has become known for its liberal views on same-sex partnerships and the promotion of the equal rights of LGBT community members. Religious spokesmen publicly condemned members of the NGO, claiming that their progressive attitude towards sexuality was dangerous and would negatively influence the homeless children under their care. Identoba got hundreds of anonymous threats from people across the country, which eventually stopped them opening the first shelter for homeless people and families in the country (Robakidze 2013; D. Zaviršek, personal communication, 23 November 2013, Tbilisi). Between 2009 and 2012 the Catholic Church in Slovenia started a campaign against the government proposal of the new Family Act which was meant to disallow physical punishment of children by parents and carers, give more rights to children with intellectual disabilities, and equalise families of same-sex parents with heterosexual ones. The ideological church campaign followed by right wing supporters constructed gay people as dangerous paedophiles, who posed a threat not only to an individual child but to the health of the nation as a whole (Zaviršek & Sobočan 2012). The proposed Act was banned. Similarly in Croatia the Catholic Church and the right wing parties succeeded in preventing a national referendum on a similar matter in December 2013. Those who attended it were in fact the minority of the national voting pool, but most of them supported the religious claim, saying that the constitutional changes should clearly define the marriage as only possible between a man and a woman (Ugrešić 2014). All of these examples show that Eastern Europe remains the zone of sameness, where diversity and difference are seen to be a threat to the homogeneous.

Social work theories and social work schools don't necessarily challenge such values. Social work is seen, rather, as a neutral profession which helps, assesses, transfers, evaluates, measures, but does not criticise the existing social order and, with rare exceptions, does not teach social work students to become critical of social inequalities and injustices.

Conclusions

Social work education as well as social work practice in the region is very diverse and varies from a descriptive normative transmitting of knowledge about welfare systems, legislation and formal social work tasks prescribed by the national ministries and the political parties in power to critical teaching of distributive and recognitional justice.

When social work teachers and professionals from the region want to contextualise their professional activities, they most often use an expression that they work and live in a society which is in a transition. The 'transition' has become a cover-word which can be translated in variety of ways: as the justification of the given situation of economic hardship, an excuse for poor practice and services, and as an expression of a fatalistic world-view where little can be changed. Eastern Europe and its social work teaching and practice seem to be in 'transition' for decades or at least for more than 20 years. Nevertheless, the recent social protests of students, social workers and the general public which started in 2012 and are spreading across many countries (Ukraine, Bosnia and Herzegovina, Kosovo, Slovenia and Croatia) speak very loudly against the local elites as well as the neoliberal power-players and government cuts of social transfers and salaries, and are advocating for diversity and democratic changes in societies including at the universities. These social movements are today re-shaping the post-communist Eastern Europe countries as well as their social work educational institutions and welfare practices.

References

Anghel, R. (2011). Transition within transition: how young people learn to leave behind institutional care whilst their carers are stuck in neutral. *Children and Youth Services Review,* 33(12): 2526–31.

Bessudnov, A., McKee, M. & Stuckler, D. (2011). Inequalities in male mortality by occupational class, perceived status and education in Russia 1994–2006. *European Journal of Public Health,* 22(3): 332–37.

Cocozzelli, F. (2007). Kosovo. In B. Deacon & P. Stubbs (eds), *Social policy and international interventions in South East Europe* (pp. 203–20). Cheltenham, MA: Edward Elgar.

Crwys-Williams, J. (ed.) (2005). *In the words of Nelson Mandela.* Johannesburg: Penguin.

Deacon, B., Lendvai, N. & Stubbs, P. (2007). Conclusion. In B. Deacon & P. Stubbs (eds), *Social policy and international interventions in South East Europe* (pp. 221–42). Cheltenham, MA: Edward Elgar.

Ehrenreich, B. & Hochschild, A.R. (eds) (2003). *Global woman: nannies, maids and sex workers in the new economy*. London: Granta Books.

Hering, S. & Waaldijk, B. (2006). *Helfer der armen – hueter der oeffentlichkeit. Die Wohlfahrtsgeschichte Osteuropas 1900–1960*. Opladen, Germany: Barbara Budrich.

Hering, S. & Waaldijk, B. (eds) (2003). *History of social work in Europe (1900–1960)*. Opladen, Germany: Leske + Budrich.

Holiček, R. & Rašidagić, E. K. (2007). Bosnia and Herzegovina. In B. Deacon & P. Stubbs (eds), *Social policy and international interventions in South East Europe* (pp. 149–66). Cheltenham, MA: Edward Elgar.

Iarskaia-Smirnova, E. (2013). Social work in post-socialist countries: divergence and common ground. In H. Homfeldt, C. Bähr, C. Schröder, W. Schröer & C. Schweppe (eds), *Weltatlas soziale arbeit. Weinheim*. Munich: BELTZ Juventa.

Inglot, T. (2009). Czech Republic, Hungary, Poland and Slovakia: adaptation and reform of the post-communist 'emergency welfare states'. In A. Cerami & P. Vanhuysse (eds), *Post-communist welfare pathways. Theorizing social policy transformations in central and Eastern Europe*. Hampshire, NY: Palgrave.

Jäppinen, M., Kulmala, M. & Saarinen, A. (eds) (2011). *Gazing at welfare, gender and agency in post-socialist countries*. Newcastle upon Tyne: Cambridge Scholars Publishing.

Malinauskas, G. (2011). *This child is also mine: a narrative approach to the phenomenon of atypical custodial grandparenthood*. Rovaniemi: Lapland University Press.

Mitev, G.M. (2007). Macedonia. In B. Deacon & P. Stubbs (eds), *Social policy and international interventions in South East Europe* (pp. 130–48). Cheltenham, MA: Edward Elgar.

Prochazkova, L. & Schmid, T. (2009). Homecare aid: a challenge for social policy research. In S. Ramon & D. Zaviršek (eds), *Critical edge issues in social work and social policy* (pp. 139–64). Ljubljana, Slovenia: FSD.

Rasell, M. & Iarskaia-Smirnova, E. (eds) (2013). *Disability in Eastern Europe and the former Soviet Union*. Abingdon: Routledge.

Robakidze, A. (2013). Controversy over NGO homeless shelter, *The Messenger*, 14 November, pp. 1, 4.

Rutgers University Center for International Social Work (2008). Social work education and the practice environment in Europe and Eurasia. United Stated Agency for International Development (USAID). Retrieved on 1 February 2014 from crin.org/docs/ Best%20Practices%20in%20Social%20Work%20_final_121008.pdf.

Schilde, K. & Schulte, D. (eds) (2005). *Need and care: glimpses into the beginnings of Eastern Europe's professional welfare*. Opladen: Barbara Budrich.

Sladojević, D. (2012), Nezaposlenost u BiH duplo veća nego u Grčkoj. Nezavisne novine. Retrieved on February 2014 from www.nezavisne.com/novosti/drustvo/ Nezaposlenost-u-BiH-duplo-veca-nego-u-Grckoj-145761.html.

Tolstokorova, A. (2010). Where have all the mothers gone? *Anthropology of the East Europe Review*, 28: 184–214.

Ugrešić, D. (2014). Fašizacija Hrvatske već je izvedena [The fashization of Croatia has happened already]. Radio Free Europe, 17 February. Retrieved on 1 February 2014 from www.slobodnaevropa.org/content/ugresic-za-rse-fasizacija-hrvatske-vec-je-izvedena/ 25187616.html.

Vanhuysse, P. (2009). Power, order and the politics of social policy in Central and Eastern Europe. In A. Cerami & P. Vanhuysse (ed.), *Post-communist welfare pathways. Theorizing social policy transformations in Central and Eastern Europe* (pp. 53–72). Hampshire, NY: Palgrave.

Vermeersch, P. & Ram, M. H. (2009). The Roma. In B. Rechel (ed.), *Minority rights in Central and Eastern Europe* (pp. 61–75). London: Routledge.

Videmšek, P. (2014). From definition to action: empowerment as a tool for change in social work practice. In A.L. Matthies & L. Uggerhoj (eds), *Participation, marginalisation and welfare services. Concepts, politics and practices across European countries* (pp. 86–105). Farnham: Ashgate.

Ymeraj, A. (2007). Albania. In B. Deacon & P. Stubbs (eds), *Social policy and international interventions in South East Europe* (pp. 187–202). Cheltenham, MA: Edward Elgar.

Zaviršek, D. (2012). Women and social work in Central and Eastern Europe. In J. Regulska & B.G. Smith (eds), *Women and gender in postwar Europe: from Cold War to European Union* (pp. 52–70). London: Routledge.

Zaviršek, D. (2009a). Can development of the doctoral studies in social work resist the neo-liberalism within academia? Some comparisons. In S. Ramon & D. Zaviršek (eds), *Critical edge issues in social work and social policy. Comparative research perspective* (pp. 219–37). Ljubljana: FSD.

Zaviršek, D. (2009b). Between blood and care: social parenthood as the enlargement of the concept of parenthood in the current societies. *Socialno delo*, 48: 3–16.

Zaviršek, D. (2008). Engendering social work education under state socialism in Yugoslavia. *British Journal of Social Work*, 38(4): 734–50.

Zaviršek, D. (2005). 'You will teach them some, socialism will do the rest!' The history of social work education 1945–1960. In K. Schilde & D. Schulte (eds), *Need and care: glimpses into the beginnings of Eastern Europe's professional welfare* (pp. 237–74). Opladen: Barbara Budrich.

Zaviršek, D. & Sobočan, A.M. (2012). *Rainbow families go to school. Perspectives of children, parents and teachers*. Ljubljana, Slovenia: FSD.

Zorn, J. (2009). A case for Slovene nationalism: initial citizenship rules and the erasure. *Nations and Nationalism*, 15(2): 280–98.

21

Social work education as a catalyst for social change and social development: case study of a Master of Social Work Program in China

Angelina W.K. Yuen-Tsang, Ben H.B. Ku and Sibin Wang

In response to the urgent need for professionally trained social workers to help in alleviating emerging social problems in China after the introduction of the market economy, the Hong Kong Polytechnic University and the Peking University launched a Master of Social Work (China) Program for social work educators in 2000, with the aim of developing a critical mass of social work educators to take up the future leadership in developing social work and social work education in China. To date, seven cohorts of over 230 students consisting of social work educators, NGO and government officials have been admitted to the program, and graduates of the program are playing a pivotal role in spearheading the development of social work education and fostering social development through the process. In this paper, the authors will present the vision and mission of the Master of Social Work (MSW) Program, the teaching and learning strategies adopted, and the ways in which the program has facilitated social change and social development through its educational process.

China is undergoing rapid social and economic transformation as a result of the introduction of the Open Door Economic Policy since the late 1970s. As a measure for alleviating emerging social problems, the Chinese Government has re-introduced social work education programs to the universities since the late 1980s after a lapse of over 30 years. In view of the acute need to train social work educators, the Hong Kong Polytechnic University and Peking University launched a MSW (China) Program in 2000, with the aim of developing a critical mass of social work educators to take up the future leadership in developing social work and social work education in China. Moreover, it is also expected that the program will help in bringing about social change and social development through its educational process.

In addition to the academic contents of the program, fieldwork practicums have been developed in different locations in China, partly to provide sites for fieldwork training and partly to facilitate the generation of indigenous practice models and theories relevant to the Chinese context. The numerous practicum projects developed by the MSW Program have played a catalyst role in impacting on positive social change in the local communities concerned and in facilitating social service development in the country. Moreover, graduates of the program have worked zealously in their different capacities to spearhead major breakthroughs in social policy initiatives and to institute social work as a profession in China. In this paper, the authors will first provide a snapshot of the development of social work education in China and will highlight the vision and mission of the MSW (China) Program and illustrate with examples the catalyst functions of social work education in facilitating social change and development in the Chinese context.

The re-emergence of social work education in China

Social work training programs were first introduced to the most prestigious universities in China in the 1920s, but they were all eliminated in the 1950s because of the belief that socialist China had no social problems and therefore had no need for social work education (Lei & Shiu 1991). The introduction of China's 'Open Door' economic reform in 1978 by reformists within the Communist Party of China led by Deng Xiaoping steered China away from a welfare state model towards the neoliberal welfare model, based mainly on economic efficiency and aimed at providing only basic welfare benefits to maintain social stability. It was anticipated that there would be a significant re-emergence of social inequality and class division (Leung & Nann 1995; Preston & Haacke 2003). In view of the escalation of social problems, the Chinese Government searched for ways to resolve these problems and to maintain social stability. After the re-introduction of sociology as a discipline to the universities in 1979, some leading academic and political leaders who were previously trained in social work and applied sociology, such as Lei Jieqiong and Fei Xiaotong (Lei & Shui 1991), fervently advocated the reintroduction of social work as a discipline into the university curriculum. In 1989, Peking University started to launch its social work program at both the undergraduate and postgraduate levels and was gradually followed by other universities and cadre training colleges in China.

During the 1990s, the development of social work education in China was confronted with a host of problems, including the lack of public recognition of the social work profession; unclear role distinction between the social work professionals and government cadres; lack of career prospects for social work graduates; direct borrowing of Western concepts; lack of practice experience to facilitate theory building; shortage of professionally trained social work teachers to help in the development of social work programs; and the lack of support from the government (Yuen-Tsang 1996). The number of social work programs remained limited during this period and the expansion was slow.

But, since 1999, the number of social work programs expanded dramatically because of the massive expansion in higher education in China and the rising demand for professional social workers to help in developing the rapidly expanding social service provisions in China. The number of universities offering social work programs suddenly surged to over 200 in the early 2000s, though the majority of the teachers of these programs had not received any professional training. It was in such a context and in response to the acute need to develop the capacity for social work educators to take up the future leadership to develop social work in China that the Hong Kong Polytechnic University and the Peking University decided to join hands to launch the first MSW Program in China in 2000.

The social work profession was given a major boost in 2006 when the Chinese Government formally announced its intention to 'build up a strong team of social workers to help in the development of the harmonious society'. Numerous measures were also introduced to support this national policy, including the establishment of pilot social work schemes in different parts of China; the establishment of social work positions in different pilot cities; and the introduction of the professional examination system for social workers. Realising the need to develop high level professional training programs for social workers, the Ministry of Education of China has, in early 2009, endorsed the proposal to introduce China's own Master of Social Work (MSW) Program in Chinese universities. This is one of very few professional master's programs endorsed by the Ministry of Education. In 2012, 61 major universities in China were selected to launch the MSW programs. In view of the introduction of China's local MSW Program and the gradual maturing of the social work profession in China, the Hong Kong Polytechnic University and the Peking University decided not to continue our joint MSW Program beyond the seventh cohort, but rather, to focus our effort on building the capacity of universities in China to develop their own MSW Programs. In this connection, the 'Peking University-Hong Kong Polytechnic University China Social Work Research Centre' was established in 2008 with the mission to provide a national platform for dialogue, exchange, research and learning pertaining to the continuing advancement of social work in China.

Vision and mission of the MSW (China) Program of the Hong Kong Polytechnic University and Peking University

In 2000, the Department of Applied Social Sciences of the Hong Kong Polytechnic University, in collaboration with the Sociology Department of the Peking University, decided to launch a MSW (China) Program in China with the aim 'to develop a critical mass of committed, competent, reflective and culturally sensitive social work educators to take up the future leadership in developing social work and social work education in China'. Moreover, the program endeavours 'to develop indigenous social work theories and practice appropriate to the Chinese context' and 'to make positive impact on social work, social services, social policy and social development in China'.

The program is basically a 'training of trainers' program which is designed primarily for experienced social work educators and is being offered on a three-year part-time basis so as to allow the students to stay in their jobs while pursuing their studies. The curriculum is characterised on the one hand by its insistence to adhere to international standards, and on the other hand by its emphasis on the need to contextualise and indigenise social work theory and practice in the Chinese context. Students are required to take 18 subjects, including ten required subjects, two elective subjects, three social work practicums, and a three-staged social work dissertation (see Figures 21.1 and 21.2 for details of the curriculum and the conceptual framework of the program). Though most of our students are experienced social work educators with impressive credentials and most of them will not be involved in direct practice after graduation, we insist that all of them have to undergo three rigorous supervised fieldwork practicums so as to develop their capacity for theory–practice integration and to cultivate their commitment to serving the needy and the vulnerable groups at the grassroots. Most of the subjects and practicums are carried out in the Chinese mainland using an intensive block-mode. Students will spend their last semester at the Hong Kong Polytechnic University so as to engage in a period of intensive full-time study and to gain direct practice experience in social work organisations in Hong Kong. The majority of the professional subjects, including the practicums, are taught by professors and instructors from the Hong Kong Polytechnic University, while Peking University professors are primarily responsible for teaching subjects relating to social science and policy issues and provide co-supervision in dissertations.

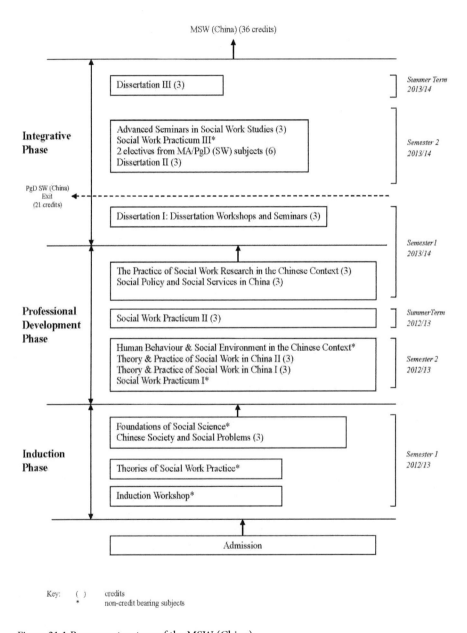

Figure 21.1 Program structure of the MSW (China).

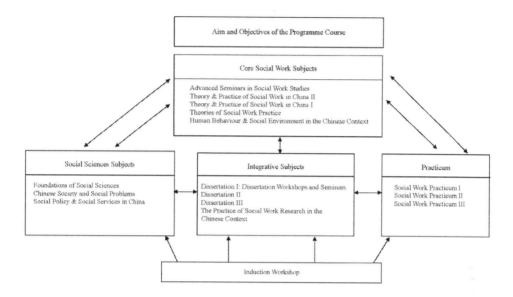

Figure 21.2 Curriculum of the MSW (China) program: a conceptual model.

In line with our social development mission, deliberate efforts have been made to enhance university–community collaboration and to link the curriculum to the social realities of contemporary China. Both the academic staff and students are encouraged to develop 'scholarship of engagement' (Boyer 1990) through combining teaching, research and professional service to the community to address social issues and to foster social betterment.

The planning team of the program has adopted a social developmental perspective which endeavours to improve the welfare of the population as a whole through integrated social and economic development initiatives emphasising capacity building of individuals, families and communities (Hall & Midgley 2004; Midgley and Livermore 1997; Xiong 1999). We believe that the integrated and comprehensive nature of the social developmental perspective in social work education provides a viable way to tackle the massive poverty, deprivation and inequality experienced by the Chinese population. Moreover, this perspective provides opportunities for capacity building, and promotes social and economic change that produces improvements in standards of living, social wellbeing and citizen participation (Hall & Midgley 2004).

Transferring these beliefs to social work education in the Chinese context, our team strongly believes that all students should be the key actors in their own learning processes, and that strengthening the capacity of students to make policy and practice decisions in their local contexts guided by social work values and to be able to carry out their interventions in a professionally competent and critically reflective manner is the core concern of our teaching endeavour. Moreover, we encourage our students to actively engage their service-users and to strengthen the capacity of their service users in their service-delivery process, so that the service-users will become partners and key actors and in social change and development processes in their own communities.

Fostering social change and social development through the education process

In order to achieve the intended objectives of the program and to foster social change and social development through the education process, the curriculum design, fieldwork practicum, as well as teaching and learning strategies have been diligently designed to reflect our concerns and commitments. The following are some of the key strategies adopted by our program.

Educating reflective practitioners as change agents

We believe that it is impossible to foster social change and social development without first changing the mindset of the change agents themselves. As social problems are becoming more and more complicated in contemporary society, conventional skills of social work practitioners are found to be increasingly inadequate for dealing with complex social issues and problems. Social work practitioners need to be competent, flexible, versatile and reflective and be able to respond proactively to the changing socioeconomic environment.

We do not expect our graduates to directly apply technical-rational solutions acquired from textbooks to resolve practical problems since there are few standard formulae for solving real life problems. Instead, we endeavour to develop among our students critical awareness towards issues and problems which they confront, and their capacity to relate these issues to a holistic understanding of social work practice.

In the program, we emphasise critical thinking and self-reflection and we help students to examine values and attitudes which are embedded within their social and cultural structures. We encourage students to deepen their understanding about how their beliefs and knowledge may affect their practice, and we encourage them to engage in critical dialogue with their teachers and service users throughout their learning process. Students are encouraged to develop a contextual understanding of social work practice in contemporary China and to engage in critical reflections on the competing values and ethical dimensions underlying these practices, so that they will become active learners who are able to develop their own personal perspective of and approach to social work practice in the Chinese context (Ku et al. 2005). We hope that our students will be aided through these processes to develop their capacity as independent and active learners who are able to construct, deconstruct and reconstruct their professional practice in the Chinese context through critical reflection. It is only when they become reflective practitioners that they could become effective change agents.

Participatory action research as pedagogy for change

In order to facilitate our students to become reflective practitioners and effective change agents, we have adopted the participatory action research model as our education pedagogy. In particular, the 'reciprocal-reflection theory' developed by Schön (1983, 1987), which offers an alternative way to understand and explain the processes through which a novice develops professional scholarship through reflective practice. It was used as the guiding framework for our practicum.

In the past few decades, an increasing number of social science theorists and human service practitioners have become dissatisfied with traditional models of integrating theory and practice. The 'applied model', as a dominant approach, is primarily based on technical rationality and derived from positivist philosophy (Schön 1983, 1987) and it stresses the professionals as instrumental problem-solvers whose competences rest on the skilful application of 'objective, consensual, cumulative and convergent' theories into practice (McCartt Hess & Mullen 1995; Schön 1983, 1987). Because of the dissatisfaction with the dominant models, social science theorists and human service practitioners have actively sought alternative models. In recent years, participatory action research is increasingly being recognised as a viable approach to deal with the problem of the theory–practice gap because it enables practitioners to integrate research with practice and to generate practice theories from the ground (Greenwood 1991; Lanzara 1991; Pace & Argona 1991; Oja & Smulyan 1989; Sarri & Sarri 1992; Sung-Chan 2000; Yuen-Tsang & Sung-Chan 2002; Whyte 1991). Participatory action research involves change experiments on real problems in actual practice contexts and involves interactive cycles of identifying, planning, acting and evaluating a problem through rigorous reciprocal-reflection-in-action processes between educators and students (Sung-Chan 2000; Yuen-Tsang & Sung-Chan 2002).

With the above understanding, we have developed practicum sites in different parts of China using the participatory action research model. We strive to cultivate among our students a strong sense of commitment to theory–practice integration and a keen interest to generate indigenous practice theories from the ground. We believe that it is only when our students have developed the passion to serve the vulnerable and deprived in real-life contexts that they could become effective change agents to bring about constructive social change and social development.

Partnering with local communities to effect change

Universities worldwide have a long tradition of community participation and social involvement. The Settlement House Movement at the beginning of the 20th century is an early example of community participation. According to this model, social engagement, actively addressing the pressing social, political, economic and moral ills of society, is an integral part of higher education (Marullo & Edwards 2000; Mayfield et al. 1999). However, the strong link between higher education and community has gradually weakened as academics increasingly assumed a pose of scientific objectivity and focused on the creation of new knowledge within the academy, thus detaching themselves from direct involvement in reform and activism. The dominance of the paradigm of scientific objectivity in universities has been reinforced by the emergence of reward and incentive systems, selective recruitment, disciplinary evolution, and institutional structures that emphasise the discovery and pursuit of academic knowledge. Academics are thus increasingly divorced from social reality and have lost their early aspiration to become pillars of social justice and vehicles for social change (Harkavy & Puckett 1994).

During the last decade, there has been renewed discussion of the need for universities to exercise their social responsibility through revitalising links with communities (Boyer 1990; Gronski & Pigg 2000; Weinberg 1999; Wang 2003; Yuen-Tsang & Tsien 2004). Boyer (1990) advocates a broader interpretation of scholarship and advises an application of knowledge that moves towards social engagement. He argues that universities need to adopt a model of 'scholarship of engagement' and that both faculty and students, in collaboration with community residents, should apply their knowledge to the solution of social issues and problems. Boyer maintains that it is only through the pursuit of 'scholarship of engagement' that the learning experiences of students and faculty are enhanced and revitalised.

It is based on the above values and beliefs that the both the academic and the practicum curriculum have been planned and developed. Deliberate efforts have been made to develop collaborate relationship with community stakeholders, including local government departments, universities, NGOs, community leaders and residents throughout the planning and implementation processes of the action projects related to each of the practicum sites developed by the program. Through university–community partnership, we hope to foster a strong sense of ownership of the projects among community stakeholders. The partnership relationship has not only facilitated our easy entry into the community and the smooth implementation of our projects, but it has also helped in fostering community participation and cultivating a support among local stakeholders towards the sustained development of these projects.

Networking among students, graduates and stakeholders to sustain change

A total of 238 students have been admitted to the MSW (China) Program in the seven cohorts. There are 15 graduates in the first cohort, 22 graduates in the second cohort, and around 40 students in the third to seventh cohorts. These students come from 150 universities, 81 NGOs and 28 provinces from all over China. These graduates are dispersed in different parts of the country, and it is extremely difficult for them to maintain close contacts among each other. Moreover, since many of them are located at rather isolated locations where the social work profession is relatively undeveloped, it is essential that measures are introduced to provide support for our graduates so that they could sustain their commitment to the furtherance of social work practice and social development.

We understand that social networks are powerful instruments to connect people and to sustain relationships. Social networks can also play important supportive functions and can facilitate the exchange and transmission of resources among network members. In order to provide continuing support for our students and graduates and to sustain the change efforts made, the curriculum team has therefore developed a networking strategy which aims to link the students, graduates and stakeholders in the social work education and social welfare sector in a supportive network and to facilitate them to become a reflective learning community to promote social change and social development through collaborative efforts.

In view of the urgent need to establish a strong supportive network among the students and graduates and to sustain their commitment to social change and social development, an alumni association was formed in 2005 consisting of all graduates of the program. They hold regular functions and maintain close contacts through participation in national and regional social work education functions. Moreover, a China Social Work Research Centre has been established jointly by the Hong Kong Polytechnic University and the Peking University, housed in a beautiful courtyard within the Peking University campus since 2008 to facilitate joint research projects among network members, to organise seminars and provide continuing education opportunities for graduates, and to provide a forum for dialogue among social work educators, students, practitioners and government officials on issues relating to social policy and social work practice. Members of the network can participate in research projects and training activities initiated either by the Centre or by network members. The centre has become a hub not only for our graduates but also for other interested social work educators and practitioners both from China and overseas to interact, to provide support and consultation for each other, and to activate social change and social development initiatives for social betterment.

Fieldwork practicum as contexts for social change and social development

Fieldwork practicum provides excellent contexts for the students to develop their practice competence, to engage in critical reflection, to integrate theory with practice, and to nurture their commitment to social change and social development. The second practicum takes place in the summer of their second year of study, during which the students have to engage in an eight-week block placement where they will live and work together in a practicum site of their choice in China. Since 2000, we have developed many practicum sites in different parts of China, using participatory action research as our pedagogy.

Each practicum site is carefully selected, developed and sustained through the joint effort of our teaching team, students and local stakeholders. In each practicum site, we usually focus on one area of emerging social need and we use the participatory action research model in demonstration projects through the joint effort of students, teachers, service-users, and sometimes involving local government officials. In order to ensure that the demonstration projects could be continued and sustained, we usually involve a local university (where at least one of our MSW students to be placed in the practicum comes from) as our partner, so that the practicum site will be used by the respective university as a future practicum site for their own social work students. Usually a cluster of at least five students will be placed at one site and they will be supervised by the same supervisor so that they can form a learning community and can provide mutual support for each other throughout the practicum process. Moreover, it is expected that the different cohorts of students taking part in the same practicum site, together with the strategic partners involved in the process, can form a critical mass to further develop the model of practice that they have evolved and can help in spearheading the development of the practice model in China.

During the past 13 years, the MSW (China) Program has developed numerous practicum sites in different parts of China and many of these have now become common models of practice in the country through the powerful demonstration of the effect of the projects, and the zealous effort of our graduates to campaign for these models of practice through teaching, research and policy advocacy. These include:

- strength-based mentorship project to support the social integration of migrant children in Beijing
- home–school–community integrated service project on delinquency prevention in Shanghai
- community-based social inclusion projects to foster social integration of deprived families in Wuhan and Xiamen
- holistic elder care projects in institutions for senior citizens to enhance active ageing in Hangzhou and Beijing

- community-based rehabilitation project to promote community care for physically disabled persons in rural villages in Hunan
- community-based mental health project to build social support networks for persons with mental health challenges in Kunming
- rural capacity-building projects to build community solidarity and reduce rural poverty in Yunnan and Sichuan
- rural–urban alliance projects to promote eco-farming and fair trade through social enterprises in Guangdong and Sichuan
- occupational social work project to foster labour welfare and industrial harmony in Harbin
- asset-building projects to foster post-disaster social reconstruction in Sichuan.

Case illustration: the Yunnan Rural Capacity-building Project

The curriculum team has made diligent efforts to plan and develop the fieldwork practicums as contexts for social change and social development. The following case study on our rural social work development project in Yunnan illustrates the typical process in which our practicums are being implemented and how our social development goals are being realised.

Stage I: Mapping of existing indigenous practice approaches through the use of oral history

One of the foremost social problems haunting China is rural poverty. Poverty in rural villages has been accelerated by market globalisation and China's entry to the World Trade Organization. In 2012, there are a reported 167 million migrant workers who have been pushed from their villages because of rural poverty to take up low-paying jobs in urban cities. As a consequence of rural–urban migration, many rural villages are left with only children, the elderly and the disabled, and this has created acute social disintegration and social problems. Moreover, increasing incidences of popular resistance and loss of authority of rural cadres have further weakened the social fabric and long-standing social control mechanisms and has threatened the stability and harmony of the vast rural population in China.

While the Chinese Government has already launched macro-level anti-poverty programs to combat rural poverty and has made impressive progress in rural poverty reduction, most of the efforts are directed towards economic development and income generation, and relatively little attention has been devoted to social and community development using social work approaches. As such, the curriculum team of the MSW (China) Program decided to experiment on a rural social work project in the Yunnan Province through the development of a practicum site, using the capacity-building model as a guiding theme. The chosen field site for this practicum is located in the Wu Township in the northern part of Yunnan and the area is an officially designated poor township by the government. The aim of the project is to enhance the capacity of local villagers and stakeholders through integrated community development.

The Yunnan project started in the summer of 2000 and has been used as a site for participatory action research and for providing practicum opportunities for our MSW

(China) students and social work students from Yunnan University. During each practicum, a cluster of at least five MSW students together with one experienced social work supervisor and one assistant supervisor from the Hong Kong Polytechnic University resided in the village for a period of eight weeks. Social workers cum researchers graduating from the Yunnan University had been employed to take charge of the development of the project on a full-time basis. The participatory action research method was used to guide the development of the practicum project.

The focus of the first stage of development was to listen to the voices of local villagers, to understand their concerns and problems, and to identify their capacity for development. The teachers and students did not come with preconceived ideas and a fixed agenda for intervention prior to their entry to the village. Instead, they partnered together to discover the needs of the people, to map the existing approaches that were being used by local villagers to deal with their problems, and to reflect on the strengths and weaknesses of existing local practices, using the reciprocal-reflection-in-action approach in the process.

As the students did not understand the local dialect, they partnered with young villagers who spoke Putonghua (the national language) to collect oral histories and these young villagers became the interviewers, translators and partners in the process. Guided by the basic principles of the reciprocal-reflection-in-action approach, the teachers, students and the villagers collaborated in a mutual process in analysing and reflecting on the oral history testimonies collected. The teachers, students and some active villagers developed into a learning community of independent and active learners who were able to construct, deconstruct and reconstruct their social work practice in the local context through critical reflection.

In this stage, the students were able to build trust and rapport with the local villagers, discover the needs and problems of the local community, and map the existing practice approaches used by local villagers. They were also encouraged to discover their own strengths and weaknesses as learners and practitioners through the reciprocal-reflection-in-action process. While the learning process was often painful for most of the students because they were more used to the authoritative teaching and learning approach, most of them were elated at the end because of the sense of joy which they experienced in the process of discovery and growth.

Stage II: Constructing a rural capacity- building practice framework through community participation and partnership

The teachers, students and researchers developed a critical understanding of local needs and existing practices in the local community through the reciprocal-reflection-in-action process. The next step was to organise some sharing sessions and analyse the oral histories with local villagers who participated in the oral history collection process. This was a deliberate process to involve the active local villagers in community analysis so as to build their capacity for critical reflection and for future leadership.

The students were then divided into different teams and each team consisted of one student and a few selected active villagers. Each team was responsible for one village and they visited local villagers, local cadres and stakeholders and discussed with them issues of concern identified through analysis of the oral history testimonies. Attempts were made to facilitate the villagers to discuss their vision of their desired community and their suggestions on preliminary steps to achieve their goals through realistic community involvement projects. The villagers participated enthusiastically in the discussions and developed a strong sense of ownership of the problems identified and the concrete suggestions made. Different small groups gradually emerged through the process, including youth groups, women's groups, senior citizens' groups and local leaders' groups. The small groups started to propose and plan concrete community-based social development projects such as the generation of methane gas, adult education programs, income-generating handicraft projects, and the building of a community centre.

In the process, the students employed a capacity-building approach, and took the role of facilitators rather than experts in community development. They modelled after their supervisors who had assumed non-expert roles in the teaching and learning process and had partnered with them throughout the process of discovery. They learned to internalise social work values and ethical principles and had also developed a sense of passion towards the plight of the local villagers and became committed to the cause of poverty alleviation and social development in China.

Stage III: Implementing the rural capacity-building practice framework

After having developed the rural capacity-building practice framework, the framework was implemented through the use of the participatory action research approach. The students facilitated the villagers to work on the ideas that they had proposed in the previous stage and helped them to actualise their plans through group work and community organisation strategies. Concrete projects were carefully deliberated on and subsequently implemented, taking into consideration the realities and constraints of the local context. Projects that were finally chosen for implementation include: the generation of methane gas for fuel; the formation of support groups for women and the elderly; the provision of adult education programs for the illiterate; leadership training for young villagers; training programs for children and young people on ethnic songs and dances by elderly villagers in order to preserve the cultural heritage; constructing a local museum on ethnic history and culture; and the development of income-generating handicraft projects. All these projects were being discussed, planned and implemented collectively by involving the practicum students, teachers, researchers, villagers and local stakeholders concerned. The local people also proposed to build an integrated community service centre to serve as a hub for local villagers to meet and to engage in communal activities. With funding for the building materials raised in Hong Kong, the community centre was planned, designed and built by villagers.

Many of the villagers had been transformed by their experience in the project. Many of them were very passive and pessimistic in the past and they felt hopeless in view of the grave poverty in their village. In the past, their only way out was to go outside of their villages and to seek jobs in urban factories. With the development of the rural capacity-building project, many of them realised that they could find ways to enhance their social and economic wellbeing through collective efforts. Moreover, instead of despising their traditional ethnic culture, many of them began to discover the richness of their cultural heritage and were keen to preserve and transmit it to their future generations.

The major challenge of our students in this stage was to make a shift from their familiar expert-oriented approach to the collaborative and facilitative approach. This problem became more apparent in this stage of development when they had to work closely with the villagers to develop concrete plans for action. The students were used to providing consultation and giving expert ideas in their normal roles as university professors and re-searchers. They had great difficulty in holding back their suggestions in a directive manner in order to listen to the voices of the people in a humble and empathetic manner. But they were alerted to their lack of awareness of this through continuous reciprocal-reflection-in-action processes.

The students discovered that the villagers were actually full of ideas and had great capacity for development despite their lack of education, resources and exposure. Given the opportunities and encouragement, the villagers could become highly motivated and could join together to do amazing things to improve the quality of life not only for them-selves and their families, but also for the collective good of their community. Moreover, the students also experienced the thrill of actually being involved in the real-life process of conceptualising, planning and implementing social change and social development. The experience greatly inspired them and transformed their conception of social change and how social change could be actualised in the Chinese context.

Stage IV: Reflecting on the experimentation and ensuring sustainability of change efforts

Besides the engagement in continuous reciprocal-reflection-in-action throughout the en-tire action research process, a major evaluation was carried out in the summer of 2005 to reflect on the whole project since its inception in 2000. The purpose of the evaluation was to reflect on past experiences, to identify the gaps and limitations of the approach, to refine and improve the rural capacity-building practice framework and to ensure the long-term sustainability of the project. Students, teachers and researchers involved in the project during the period were invited to attend the meeting and to share their views about the project.

The most critical problem confronting us in the process was the difficulty to change the mindset of people. Even though the project emphasised social development and had adopted a capacity-building approach to the process, most of the teachers and students in-volved in the project found it extremely difficult to practise their values and beliefs in the real-life context. While they advocated for equity, justice and fairness, they found that they were often the ones who violated such principles and asserted their power and domina-tion in the decision-making processes. While they were educating the villagers to exercise gender equality, some of the male students and teachers exhibited chauvinistic behaviours towards their female colleagues which had caused much embarrassment and unhappiness. While they themselves were zealously promoting social change and social development, they could be using methods and strategies which, though seemingly efficient and effec-tive, were contradictory to the core beliefs of social development. Fortunately, the use of the reciprocal-reflection-in-action paradigm had helped in minimising these problems, sharpening critical reflection, and creating an environment for open dialogue and mutual support among key players involved in the project.

Another issue of concern was the sustainability of the change efforts. The project had started many worthwhile initiatives at the community level, but it was not at all easy to sustain these initiatives on a long-term basis. While it was relatively easy to sustain the in-terest of the villagers in the various interest groups and support groups, it was extremely difficult to sustain the momentum of the income-generating projects. For instance, the handicraft project was developed with a view to help local women to generate income through production of local handicrafts and cloths. But the project was not too success-ful and could only provide minimal supplementary income for a few families because of reasons such as the difficulty to market the products, the low quality and unattractive de-sign of the products, the lack of resources to buy raw materials, and the difficulty to evenly distribute the income generated from the project. The team reflected on the underlying causes of the problems and discussed ways to enhance the sustainability of the income-generating projects. The core issue was again related to the mindset of the people. It was felt that the women involved in the project were only concerned about generating income from the project to improve their own household income and were not concerned about improvement of the collective good and social development. The team reflected that they had not done enough preparation to enhance local villagers' knowledge and understand-ing about social development before the commencement of the project. It was therefore suggested that more efforts have to be made not only to enhance the capacity of the par-ticipants in income generation, but, more importantly, the capacity to promote collective good through mutual support. Moreover, it was suggested that efforts have to be made to involve the local and provincial officials as partners of the projects so that government resources and support could be drawn upon to help the local villagers. The team also suggested that we had been over-emphasising the 'social' aspect of development, and not paying adequate attention to the 'economic' and other related aspects of development. As such, it was suggested that we should strengthen our team by drawing upon the help of economists, designers, health professionals and others so that we could provide a holis-tic and inter-disciplinary approach to social development. All these insights generated through the reflection process have been used to guide the further improvement of the rural capacity-building project in its subsequent stage of development.

Finally, the team also deliberated on issues related to knowledge building and knowl-edge dissemination. During the previous years the project staff accumulated a host of experience and data collected through the action research process. We have been illumi-nated by our experience and especially by the insights gained through the participatory action research process. We have generated ideas on rural social work practice through our project and have gradually evolved an indigenous rural capacity-building model for the Chinese context. In order to share our experience and ideas with fellow social workers in China, we have developed a series of workshops and training programs so as to pop-ularise the rural capacity-building model in other parts of China. A Rural Social Work Research Centre has subsequently been established at Yunnan University in 2007 to fur-ther our work on rural social work development. The centre has now become a national hub for social workers and other related practitioners and researchers to meet, to have dia-logue, to promote the rural capacity-building model, and to advocate for social change and social development in rural China.

Conclusions

The MSW (China) Program is committed to the development of social work and social work education in China and to the furtherance of social change and social development. We position ourselves as catalysts for social development through our numerous cur-riculum initiatives and especially through our active engagement in participatory action research projects in connection with our fieldwork practicums. Through these action research projects, our students have been facilitated to actively engage in initiatives to foster social change and social development. Efforts have been made to address critical social issues in contemporary China such as poverty, unemployment, marital breakdown, population ageing, street children, mental illness, and social exclusion. Through personal involvement in these action research projects, our students have gradually gained the awareness and confidence that social work education can become a powerful catalyst for social change and development. It is indeed our hope and aspiration that more social work educators in China could take up the social responsibility and the mission to promote social change and social development in China to enhance the quality of life of the Chinese people.

References

Boyer, E.L. (1990). *Scholarship reconsidered: priorities of the professoriate.* Princeton, NJ: Carnegie Foundation for the Advancement of Teaching.

Greenwood, D.J. (1991). Collective reflective practice through participatory action research: a case study from the fagor cooperatives of mondragon. In D.A. Schön (ed.), *The reflective turn: case studies in and on educational practice* (pp. 84–108). NY: Teachers College Press.

Gronski, R. & Pigg, K. (2000). University and community collaboration. *The American Behavioral Scientist,* 43(5): 781–92.

Hall, A. & Midgley, J. (2004). *Social policy for development.* London: SAGE Publications.

Harkavy, I. & Puckett, J.L. (1994). Lessons from Hull House for the contemporary urban university. *Social Science Review,* 68(3): 299–321.

Ku, H.B., Yeung, S.C. & Sung, P. (2005). Searching for a capacity-building model in social work education. *Social Work Education,* 24(2): 213–33.

Lanzara, G.F. (1991). Shifting stories: learning from a reflective experiment in a design process. In D.A. Schön (ed.), *The reflective turn: case studies in and on educational practice* (pp. 285–320). NY: Teachers College Press.

Lei, J.Z. & Shui, Z.Z. (1991). The thirty years of the social work programme of Yenjing University. In N. Chow et.al. (eds), *Status quo, challenge and prospect: collected works of the seminar of the Asian-Pacific region social work education* (pp. 10–16). Beijing: Peking University Press.

Leung, J.C.B. & Nann, R. (1995). *Authority and benevolence: social welfare in China.* Hong Kong: Chinese University of Hong Kong Press.

Marullo, S. & Edwards, B. (2000). From charity to justice. *The American Behavioral Scientist,* 43(5): 895–912.

Mayfield, L., Hellwig, M. & Banks, B. (1999). The Chicago response to urban problems: building university–community collaborations. *The American Behavioral Scientist,* 42(5): 863–75.

McCartt Hess, P. & Mullen, E.J. (eds) (1995). *Practitioner–researcher partnerships: building knowledge from, in, and for practice.* Washington, DC: NASW Press.

Midgley, J. & Livermore, M. (1997). The developmental perspective in social work: educational implications for a new century. *Journal of Social Work Education,* 33(3): 573–85.

Oja, S.N. & Smulyan, L. (1989). *Collaborative action research: a developmental approach.* NY: Falmer Press.

Pace, L.A. & Argona, D.R. (1991). Participatory action research: a view from Xerox. In W.F. Whyte (ed.), *Participatory action research* (pp. 56–69). London: SAGE Publications.

Preston, P.W. & Haacke, J. (2003). Change in contemporary China. In P.W. Preston & J. Haacke (eds), *Contemporary China: the dynamics of change at the start of the new millennium.* London: Routledge Curzon.

Sarri, R.C. & Sarri, C.M. (1992). Organizational and community change through participatory action research. In D. Bargal & H. Schmid (eds), *Organisation change and development in human service organisations, administration in social work* (pp. 99–122). NY: Haworth Press.

Schön, D.A. (1987). *Educating the reflective practitioner: toward a new design for teaching and learning in the professions*. San Francisco: Jossey-Bass.

Schön, D.A. (1983). *The reflective practitioner: how professionals think in action*. NY: Basic Books.

Sung-Chan, P. L. (2000). Learning from an action experiment: putting Schön's reciprocal-reflection theory into practice. *Cybernetics and Human Knowing*, 7(2–3): 17–30.

Wang, S.B. (2003). The social responsibility of social work in a changing society. In S. Wang et al. (eds), *China's social work in transition: essays from 2001 annual symposium of China Association for Social Work Education* (pp. 3–12). Shanghai: East China University of Science and Technology Press.

Weinberg, A.S. (1999). The university and the hamlets: revitalising low-income communities through university outreach and community visioning exercises. *The American Behavioral Scientist*, 42(5): 800–13.

Whyte, W.F. (ed.) (1991). *Participatory action research*. London: SAGE Publications.

Xiong, Y.G. (1999). Problems and challenges confronting the development of social work education in the 21st century. In *Journal of China Youth College for Political Sciences*, special issue, *Reflections, Choices and Development: Special Issue on Social Work Education* (pp. 32–37).

Yuen-Tsang, W.K.A. (1996). Social work education in China: constraints, opportunities, and challenges. In J. Cheng & T.W. Lo (eds), *Social welfare development in China: constraints and challenges* (pp. 85–100). Chicago: Imprint Publications.

Yuen-Tsang, W.K.A. & Tsien, T. (2004). Universities and civic responsibility: actualising the university–community partnership model through the anti-SARS project in Hong Kong. *The Asian and Pacific Journal of Social Work and Development*, 14(1): 19–32.

Yuen-Tsang, W.K.A & Sung-Chan, P.P.L. (2002). Capacity building through networking: integrating professional knowledge with indigenous practice. In N.T. Tan & I. Dodds (eds), *Social Work around the world*, vol 2, *Agenda for global social work in the 21st century* (pp. 111–22). Berne: IFSW Press.

Part 7
Social work and political activism

22

Reflections of an activist social worker: challenging human rights violations

Linda Briskman

Activism in social work can arise from practitioner wisdom that prompts action to respond to human rights violations. This paper offers reflections on the Eileen Younghusband keynote address in South Africa in 2008. I lament the lack of human rights advancement in subsequent years where infringements on the rights of many of the world's most vulnerable people receive negative responses from governments and scant attention from professions. The paper calls for ascendancy of the active moral practitioner, born from outrage and a desire to combat racism, the marginalisation and demonisation of those 'othered' in dominant discourse. Social work values and principles provide leads.

In 2008 the International Association of Schools of Social Work (IASSW) held its international conference in Durban, South Africa. The conference theme of transcending global and local divides was timely as, despite the catchcry of globalisation, many nation states were increasingly bunkering and drawing themselves into what anthropologist Ghassan Hage (2003, p. xii) refers to as a 'pervasive paranoid nationalistic culture of neo-liberal capitalism'. Alongside this a human rights discourse was rapidly sinking into a security discourse. Reflecting on this conference and updating the keynote address I gave on this occasion brings little joy, for the human rights trajectory has increasingly spiralled downwards. This chapter offers some reflections on social work responses to human rights violations and reflects on my own activist journey as a way of advancing critical engagement of social workers in issues of global concern. It builds on Eileen Younghusband's keynote address delivered in 2008 at the IAASW conference.

I have personally traversed a long and bumpy personal and political journey to where I position myself today as an academic activist in the Australian context. The further I travel on this journey, I become increasingly convinced, maybe even doctrinaire, about the moral and ethical duty of social workers to move beyond the realm of everyday practice to explore critical issues that impact on the wellbeing of our nations and the world at large, however small the contribution. Although social work has a courageous reputation in dealing with questions of injustice, this is by no means universal; settings where social work's political activism is ingrained in its mission are not the majority. Political action can be a contentious and risky business. I believe, however, that in order to create a just and peaceful world the concerted actions of people, ordinary and extraordinary, are needed to work towards the principle of 'never again'. In this, social work has much to contribute in both international and local contexts.

My two main areas of social work political endeavour are in the areas of Indigenous rights and asylum seeker rights. In this I am spurred on by the words of Australian Aboriginal activist Lowitja O'Donoghue, who poses the question: 'How is it that this nation's First Peoples, and its last peoples, should suffer similar indignity?' (O'Donoghue 2003). These are questions that permeate in too many countries.

The question is partly answered by understanding the pervasiveness of Western dominance and how 'the other' is represented in societies where power and privilege accorded to 'the West' creates a climate of ongoing colonialism where the non-conforming are represented as ignorant, deviant, dark and dangerous. In this, as a global community, we are still so far from recognising Indigenous wisdom or accepting the gifts that those 'othered' in mainstream discourses can bring to our societies in order that we can all flourish in inclusiveness.

The focus of my chapter is on the social work response to the here and now, within the supposedly 'democratic' west, where the rhetoric of the rule of law is often misleading as it masks pernicious practices that take place under its aegis. In many countries monocultural doctrines are increasingly taking hold and this results in tragic consequences for many groups, damage to the reputation of nations and denigration of the professions which implement the policies arising from such canons. In this way the professions, including social work, are both victim and perpetrator within prevailing paradigms and frameworks. The example of social work resistance and political activism that I will later be drawing upon illustrates a human rights challenge by social work educators – the People's Inquiry into (immigration) Detention in Australia.

But first I widen the context to refer to some of the human rights issues that ought to be of concern to social workers. In doing so I propose four interconnected junctures for social work in carving out its role in the political realm: recognising human rights abuses; responding through political activism; identifying guiding principles; and responsibility of educators.

Recognising human rights abuses

In many countries we are observing the imposition of malevolent acts, and see governments of the West level accusations of human rights abuses on 'the tyrannical'. Without discarding the need to be informed commentators on the international stage, regrettably this emphasis may render us blind to brutalities in our own countries, such is the strength of government propaganda machinery and media collusion. The examples below relate to 'the war on terror', the Indigenous sphere and racism.

An over-arching concern is the erosion of civil liberties in the wake of the attacks in New York on 11 September 2001 when a number of Western governments introduced draconian anti-terrorist laws (Burnside 2007, 145) that were enabled by producing a politics of fear that bordered on mass hysteria. By what logic, we should ask, has the so-called war on terror upturned the protections that were once considered sacrosanct? The results of this upheaval have been dire and engendered by fear imposed on an unsuspecting and uncritical citizenry.

In a number of countries we have observed acceptance of rendition and the outsourcing of torture. In Australia we saw one of our nationals, David Hicks, spend five years in captivity in Guantanamo Bay. Another Australian, Mamdouh Habib, was tortured by Egyptian and American authorities with Australia's knowledge. Later an Indian national and medical practitioner, Mohammed Haneef, was held without trial and removed from Australia on now discredited and flimsy grounds that were constructed around the linking of his mobile phone SIM card to botched terror attacks in Britain in 2007. This man's life and career were destroyed by an over-zealous government and Australia's reputation was further scarred. Australian social worker Aloysia Brooks (2013) is one of the few social workers who has ventured into exploring the social work response to torture.

On a global scale there is ongoing suffering and maligning of Indigenous peoples. It took far too many years for the declaration on the rights of Indigenous peoples to find its way through the United Nations. Australia, Canada, the United States and New Zealand were condemned by the international human rights community for initially voting against it. Social workers are acutely aware of the harms done to Indigenous family life through the removal of children from their families and communities in a number of countries. But in 2007 in Australia many stood helplessly by when the conservative government invoked an Emergency Intervention. Ostensibly to deal with problems of child sexual abuse in remote Northern Territory Aboriginal communities, the federal government cast aside provisions of the *Racial Discrimination Act* and deployed, into localities where memories of abuse at the hands of authorities were very much alive, the army, police and medical practitioners. Taken away were the minimal but hard fought for rights of those communities and the government introduced legislation which did not even mention children. The election of a Labor government led to an apology for past wrongs by Prime Minister Rudd that went some way toward healing past wounds, but has not resolved the socioeconomic status of Indigenous peoples who still lag in having their human rights realised in such fields as health, housing, education, employment and income (Briskman 2014). Social work increasingly strives for engagement with Indigenous communities including through centring Indigenous Australians in its most recent Code of Ethics (AASW 2010).

Social workers are familiar with tenets of anti-racist and anti-oppressive practice but this is more likely to be directed inward to social work practice at a micro level. Racism is not always named yet the lack of care of society toward those 'not like us' is directed at the marginalised, the excluded, the despised – those struggling for belonging and identity. This very year of 2014 has seen the 'race debate' ignite in Australia following an announcement by the federal government that it would replace a section of the Racial Discrimination Act that makes it unlawful to offend, insult, humiliate or intimidate on the grounds of race, colour or ethnicity. Commentator David Marr (2014, 7) dispels the notion that the move is about free speech, stating that Prime Minister Tony Abbott is instead persuading a slice of the electorate that 'he is running a government after their own hearts – one that understands, even respects what they feel about Aborigines, immigrants, Muslims and boat people', the latter term referring to asylum seekers who make their journeys to Australia by boat.

Eurocentric paradigms of knowledge increasingly dominate and are imposed as universal truths (Seidman 1994, 257). In Australia this represents an insidious revival of the White Australia Policy which we believed had been cast aside, the rise of unfettered nationalism based on imperial principles of British heritage that we thought had vanished and the demise of multiculturalism which we thought was here to stay. Globally we are observing what Kundnani (2007), in the British context, refers to as the end of tolerance and what Barthes (1997, 88) describes as inoculation; practices that immunise society against difference. There is an insidious rise in Islamophobia, with organisations world-wide preaching hate and propagating myths directed at Muslims implying that Muslim immigration is something to fear. In a climate of fear, now an entrenched universal phenomenon, the protection of human rights becomes extraordinarily difficult (Burnside 2007, 159). The limits of international law present an imperative for both local action and international pressure. Proactively, the Australian Association of Social Workers (2010) calls upon social workers to recognise and challenge racism and other forms of oppression.

Responding to human rights abuses through political activism

Rather than being on centre stage, social work is a profession that is often misunderstood, ignored, practised within contradictory paradigms and sometimes lacking in self-confidence within the hierarchy of professions. The question is how to position social workers as actors in the political realm.

To explore this point, I discuss the social work response to asylum seeker policy in Australia for it is in the realm of asylum seeking where nation states have bunkered themselves most successfully against people fleeing their homelands in search of safe haven. Invasion anxiety and border security become privileged over human security. By way of countering this stance, social work academics in Australia initiated a major undertaking spurred by shame and disgust at the brutal treatment of asylum seekers in our country, where we reached a new moral threshold that meant it was possible to push away unarmed people seeking refuge in our waters (Perera 2002). It should be noted that this activity has recently accelerated in the form of a policy named Operation Sovereign Borders, with its centrepiece of intercepting asylum seekers at sea and retuning them to their staging post of Indonesia in specially designed orange life rafts. The extent of this operation is covert as it is intentionally hidden from the public, with the Immigration authorities refusing to speak about what it calls 'on-water' matters. The quest for transparency in government is a failed project.

Australia's policy of mandatory detention was secured for the long-term in 1992, which means that all 'unauthorised arrivals' arriving without travel documents are removed from the human circle and placed in immigration detention centres for indeterminate periods, until granted a protection visa (now only temporary visas) or removed from Australia. These detention prisons have been primarily located in remote desert or island sites or offshore in Nauru or Papua New Guinea (Manus Island), the latter of which has been the scene of extreme violence that resulted in the vicious killing of an Iranian asylum seeker in 2014.

Around this shame of the nation an advocacy movement formed, which was faced with the monumental task of countering highly effective government propaganda that had duped the public into becoming accomplices to the prevailing view that we were in danger of being invaded by fleeing asylum seekers whom, we were told, could even be a terrorist threat. Although increasingly harsh measures exist on a global scale, Australia has stood out in its application of mandatory detention to all unauthorised arrivals and became a testing laboratory (Pickering 2005) for other countries wanting to eradicate what they see as the asylum seeker scourge.

The People's Inquiry into Detention, auspiced by the Australian Council of Heads of Schools of Social Work, sought to change asylum seeker policies in Australia and to have the stories of this reprehensible era of social policy on the public record for the future of the nation. It was particularly the policy of indefinite mandatory detention that spurred us on and harsh prisons where people were enveloped by a punishing power (Browning 2006) and reduced to what Agamben (1998) refers to as 'bare life'.

The Australian heads of social work, representing more than 20 social work schools in Australia, undertook the inquiry as government would not. The policies and practices of the government were seen by us as a catastrophic response to a global humanitarian issue that had only minimally reached Australian shores. We were incensed by the resistance of government to investigate its own policies and practices even though it had called an inquiry into the wrongful detention of a mentally ill Australian resident, Cornelia Rau, who had been locked away in a detention centre by convincing the authorities that she was a German called Anna. She had been meted out the very same treatment as the asylum seekers whose plight did not create the media and public eruption that followed Cornelia's detention. We were further impelled by the increasing despair of those who had been detained for many years and for whom the courts effectively deemed could remain there for the rest of their lives. The People's Inquiry was born from outrage. As a group of academic social workers, we considered it beholden on our knowledge, expertise and passion to conduct a national investigation.

After announcing the inquiry we were overwhelmed by the response to what soon became a collective, organic and transparent process. Immediate support emerged from all around Australia and from people from all walks of life (Briskman and Goddard 2007). Before long, a team of advisors, organisers, counsellors, panel members, researchers and others rallied to join in the quest to expose the evils of the detention regime. Students joined for social work placements or internships from other disciplines. We commenced with no money but gradually attracted some funds from philanthropic trusts and organisations which believed in our quest. The inquiry process demonstrates how social work, despite its diversity of practice models and organisational constraints, can garner the support of others to challenge human rights abuses (Alston, in Briskman et al. 2008).

Ten public hearings were held across Australia and heard the gruelling testimonies of almost 200 people, one-third of whom had been in detention and the rest who were advocates, professionals or people who had worked within the detention system. We received a similar number of written submissions. Our research assistant trawled through masses of public documentation, media reports and information that came to us informally from 'the back of a truck'. The strength of the work is the documentation of the stories, told by those affected, while they were still current. At the end of our deliberations we could only conclude that asylum seekers had been portrayed as less than human, that the media colluded with the portrayals and that the public (most of whom supported mandatory detention) were deceived.

By world standards there are very few unauthorised arrivals in Australia due to tyranny of distance. And we, from a vast and wealthy nation with an ethos of a 'fair go', have seen an increasing range of policies introduced that make us among the world's worst. The policies are so evil that Julian Burnside (2007, 129) has accused a former prime minister John Howard (1996–2007) of being guilty of crimes against humanity when judged by his own laws.

Although the detention of all people has been shocking, the detention of children, often for many years, has shaken to the core social workers and others in the Australian community. Even when notifications under state government child protection provisions were made by social workers and other advocates, they were ignored as the children were bounced between the question of federal and state jurisdictions (immigration being a federal responsibility and child protection in the domain of the states). Child and family welfare is something that should be the centre of social work concern and, like the Stolen Generations of Indigenous children removed from their families before it, the detention of child asylum seekers is sure to stir future generations into harsh condemnation of this era of Australian history.

Children were detained in immigration detention facilities until 2005 when the policy changed following agitation from within the ranks of the government. It later re-emerged and now there are more than a thousand children in closed detention facilities in Australia or on Nauru. The caging of children is perhaps the greatest human rights violation in Australia since World War 2 (Ozdowski 2008, 1). It has been described by two of the authors of the book that arose from the People's Inquiry (Goddard & Briskman (2004, 17) as organised and ritualised abuse of children. More recently we have described the transfer of unaccompanied children to Nauru as human trafficking (Briskman & Goddard 2014). The Australian Human Rights Commission is conducting an inquiry into the detention of children, the second on this topic in a decade.

The People's Inquiry began as a somewhat subversive endeavour with no formal authority to conduct the inquiry except for the authority of 'the people'. In 2008 it entered the mainstream with the three social work authors (Briskman et al. 2008) winning the Australian Human Rights Commission Award for Literature.

Guiding principles

Arguably, social work has an obligation to engage in the type of political activism that underpinned the inquiry. Tiamelo Mmatli (2008, 306) tells us it is dereliction of our professional duty not to comply with what Mullaly (1997) calls the promotion of political will to develop a humanised society. There is also urgency to overturn secretive activities of governments, and to invoke our expertise and value base for transparency and public interest. In this there are a number of core social work underpinnings.

First, there are the directives and principles enshrined in social work ethics, national and international, that call on social workers to affirm human rights and to challenge unjust principles. The international Statement of Principles on ethics in social work proclaims that the principles of human rights and social justice are fundamental to social work (IFSW & IASSW 2004). The Australian Code declares that the social work profession opposes and works to eliminate all violations of human rights (AASW 2010).

Then there is the knowledge base of social workers, much of it derived from practice wisdom as critical ethnographers – participant observers in our work where we are witness to the impact of subjugation, oppression, racism and structural disadvantage. The International Federation of Social Workers (IFSW 2012) states, 'As part of civil societies' ground force, social workers have inside access to the people most affected by poverty and human rights injustices'.

And there are the critical theoretical leads – including postcolonialism, and anti-op-pressive and anti-racist paradigms – that assist us in working towards emancipation and liberation (Mullaly 1997, 143). Through our connections and observations there is the prospect to challenge taken-for-granted ways of doing things that for practitioners may equate with complacent and unquestioning compliance.

This leads on to the question of complicity. If social workers fail to act on what they know, are they collaborators? I have conducted research that examines the 'dual loyalty' question – loyalty to the client or loyalty to the employing body. Much of the exploration on this question arose in South Africa through Physicians for Human Rights, bringing to the forefront complicity of health professionals during the apartheid era. In Australia, to-gether with Deborah, Zion, Bebe Loff, I explored the involvement of professional workers – mainly psychologists, psychiatrists, general practitioners and nurses – with the immi-gration detention regime in Australia. All are professions with codes of ethics. There were contrasting responses: collusion, advocacy and silence. Some health professionals are disturbingly associated with actions that fall under the Convention against Torture's defin-ition of cruel, inhuman and degrading treatment (Briskman et al. 2010).

For social workers facing dual loyalty conflicts, there is a need to reconsider roles and principles. Social work is largely organisational practice and there is a wealth of literature that discusses how organisations can be sites of tension for social workers as their practice ideals are subsumed by the organisational mission (e.g. Lymbery & Butler 2004; Hough & Briskman 2003). Social workers have been among those employed on Nauru by a non-gov-ernment organisation and were among those who spoke out publicly about the brutality they witnessed. A human services practitioner with the organisation said, 'We were ex-pected to show allegiance to the Australian government and the organisations that worked on Nauru, ergo helping the men was a form of treason' (Isaacs 2014, 59).

Responsibility of educators

How do social work educators inspire future social workers to take a lead and become what I heard a participant at the 2008 Durban social work conference refer to as morally active practitioners? One important strategy is to demonstrate to students the passion for human rights work as role models. The People's Inquiry involved students in every aspect of the process and invariably the students stayed with us when their placements ended as they believed that what they were doing was important. We did not fear accusations of parti-sanship when human rights were on our side. We set aside concerns about whether or not we were adequately preparing students for the realities of practice for they will face those soon enough, but student-time may be the only opportunity for supported engagement in political reflection and political practice. Furthermore, academics are less constrained than others and universities may be the last bastion of freedom for the exercise of our core values and principles. The role of universities is essential, for, as Hamilton and Maddison tell us (2007, 13), they:

> are essential for producing educated, informed and questioning citizens with some ca-pacity to scrutinise government decisions. The academics who staff these institutions require a high level of academic freedom to pursue research that may, at times, challenge a government's values and agenda.

Speaking out can occur in non-conventional ways. One of my heroes is former British social work academic Roy Bailey, who together with Mike Brake wrote an early radical social work text. Roy Bailey is now a folk singer of renown, spreading the word on a range of oppressions.

Moral courage

Jim Ife, in the Eileen Younghusband address in Montreal in 2000, made a comment that resonates. He spoke then of how many social workers have an interest in international issues by supporting Amnesty International, for example, but in their role as a private citizen. What are the ways to move social work to more direct action? I return to the example of refugees to pave the way forward.

For human services workers casting their gaze on refugees, there can be passive or active ways of acting and we must be alert to the fact that decisions that impact on the social work agenda are not usually made by social workers or even by people who share our value base. Refugees can be seen as a practice issue in dealing with torture and trauma, mental health and settlement. Another mode of working is through minimising harmful policies in order to provide better service outcomes. A third mode of intervention sees asylum seeking as a political issue requiring direct political action. There is an inherent difficulty of working across all practice boundaries requiring an exploration that draw upon on a mix of ethics, theory, values, methods, ideology and dual loyalty concerns. Ultimately social workers need to decide whether to work in settings where the values are in contradiction to personal values and professional ethics and whether speaking out and protest is the best choice in particular settings. This has been the stance of some social workers employed in Nauru detention who resigned from their positions.

Conclusions

The recommendations from the People's Inquiry called upon the Labor government of that time to remove racism, restore human rights and reinstate accountability. These three tenets transcend the local, but these universal themes are often understated in the lexicon of social work. These three basic principles represent a gateway for the emancipation of ourselves from the tyranny of organisational practice and for the liberation of those suffering at the hands of cruel regimes.

Academic Brian Martin (2006) calls upon scholars to speak out. He warns against fear of imagined risk saying:

> You think that if you offend someone powerful, this may jeopardise your tenure or promotion application. Your grants might be blocked. You might be sued for defamation . . . You could even be hauled in by ASIO and interrogated.

To counter such fears, we can take inspiration from the words of lawyer and head of Reprieve, Clive Stafford Smith. In his book titled *Bad men: Guantanamo Bay and the secret prisons*, he states, 'I am under no illusion that I have the skill to do justice to the stories of these prisoners, but the greatest sin would be not to try' (Stafford Smith 2007, x).

Confidence can be gained by noting that our dissidence received massive support, our academic careers have not suffered and security officials have not entered our doorways. As Martin (2006) states, the biggest risk to free speech is not reprisals but self-censorship. The best antidote is for more people to speak out.

And finally, I refer to a small but significant book by Stephane Hessel titled *Time for outrage*. He wrote this call to action in 2010 when he was 93 years old, 'on the last leg of my journey' as he put it. He used the time before he died to reflect on events that laid the foundation for his lifelong commitment to politics, which was the resistance movement challenging inequality, discrimination and oppressive acts against those without social, political or economic power. Hessel spoke of the unbearable things around us and implores us to open our eyes so we will see. The worst attitude, he says, is indifference. He invoked the duty of all to ensure that our society remains one of which we are proud, not a society that is among other things wary of immigrants and intent on their expulsion. Social workers have an ethical responsibility to use our precious freedom wisely and before we too lose this right.

References

Agamben, G. (1998). *Homer sacer: sovereign power and bare life*. Stanford: Stanford University Press.

Alston, M. (2008). Preface. In L. Briskman, S. Latham & C. Goddard. *Human rights overboard: seeking asylum in Australia*. Melbourne: Scribe.

Australian Association of Social Workers (2010). *Code of ethics*. Canberra: Australian Association of Social Workers.

Bailey, R. & Brake, M. (eds) (1975). *Radical social work*. London: Edward Arnold.

Briskman, L. (2014). *Social work with Indigenous communities: a human rights approach*. Melbourne: The Federation Press.

Briskman, L. & Goddard, C. (2014). Australia trafficks the asylum seeker children. *The Age*, 25 February, p. 20.

Briskman, L. & Goddard, C. (2007). Not in my name: the people's inquiry into immigration detention. In D. Lusher & N. Haslam (eds), *Yearning to breathe free* (pp .90–91). Sydney: The Federation Press.

Briskman, L., Latham, S. & Goddard, C. (2008). *Human rights overboard: seeking asylum in Australia*. Melbourne: Scribe.

Briskman, L., Zion, D. & Loff, B. (2010). Challenge and collusion: health professionals and immigration detention. *The International Journal of Human Rights*, 14(7): 1092–106.

Brooks, A. (2013). Torture and terror post-9/11: the role of social work in responding to torture. *International Social Work*. DOI: 2013 0020872813487932.

Browning, J. (2006). States of exclusion: narratives from Australia's immigration detention centres, 1999–2003. PhD thesis, University of Technology, Sydney.

Burnside, J. (2007). *Watching brief: reflections on human rights, law and justice*. Melbourne: Scribe.

Fook, J. (1999). Critical reflectivity in education and practice. In B. Pease & J. Fook (eds), *Transforming social work practice: towards critical perspectives*. Sydney: Allen & Unwin.

Gilbert, S. (2001). Social work with Indigenous Australians. In M. Alston & J. McKinnon (eds), *Social work: fields of practice* (pp. 62–72). Melbourne: Oxford University Press.

Goddard, C. & Briskman, L. (2004). By any measure it's official child abuse. *Herald Sun*, 18 February, p. 17.

Goddard, C. (2004). Baby Ghazal's got a new name: No. 390, *The Age*, 13 April. Retrieved on 1 November 2006 from www.theage.com.au/articles/2004/04/12/1081621892083.html.

Hamilton, C. & Maddison, S. (2007). Dissent in Australia. In C. Hamilton & S. Maddison (eds), *Silencing dissent: how the Australian Government is controlling public opinion and stifling debate* (pp. 1–23). Sydney: Allen & Unwin.

Hessel, S. (2010). *Time for outrage*. NY: Hachette.

Horton, D. (2008). Are we civilised? *On Line Opinion*, 11 June. Retrieved on 15 May 2014 from www.onlineopinion.com.au/print.asp?article=7477.

Hough, G. & Briskman, L. (2003). Responding to the changing socio-political context of practice. In J. Allan, B. Pease & L. Briskman (eds), *Critical social work: an introduction to theories and practices*, pp. 202–13. Sydney: Allen & Unwin.

Ife, J. (2000). Local and global practice: relocating social work as a human rights profession in the new global order, Eileen Younghusband Memorial Lecture, 31 July, IFSW/IASSW Biennial Conference, Montreal.

IFSW (2012). Poverty eradication and the role for social workers. Retrieved on 7 April 2014 from ifsw.org/policies/poverty-eradication-and-the-role-for-social-workers/.

IFSW & IASSW (2004). Ethics in social work: statement of principles. Retrieved on 27 January 2008 from www.ifsw.org/en/p38000324.html.

Isaacs, M. (2014). *The undesirables: inside Nauru*. Melbourne: Hardie Grant Books.

Kundnani, A. (2007). *The end of tolerance: racism in 21st century Britain*. London: Pluto Press.

Lymbery, M. & Butler, S. (2004). *Social work ideals and practice realities*. Hampshire: Palgrave Macmillan.

Marr, D. (2014). Race, votes and free speech. *The Saturday Paper*, 5–11 April, p. 7.

Martin, B. (2006). The answer is blowing in the whistles. *The Australian*, 15 November, p. 34.

Mmatli, T. (2008). Political activism as a social work strategy in Africa. *International Social Work*, 51(3): 297–310.

Mullaly, B. (1997). *Structural social work: ideology, theory and practice* (2nd edn). Toronto: Oxford University Press.

New South Wales Council for Civil Liberties (2007). Shadow report prepared for the United Nations Committee Against Torture on the occasion of its review of Australia's third periodic report under the Convention Against Torture and other Cruel, Inhuman or Degrading Treatment or Punishment, 27 July.

New Zealand Association of Social Workers (1996). *Code of ethics*. NZASW, Christchurch.

O'Donoghue, L. (2003). Return to Afghanistan: resettlement or refoulment, Public forum on Afghanistan: resettlement or refoulment, Adelaide, 27 February. Retrieved on 5 June 2014 from www.safecom.org.au/lowitja.htm.

Perera, S. (2002). A line in the sea. *Race and Class*, 44(2): 23–39.

Pickering, S. (2005). *Refugees and state crime*. Sydney: Federation Press.

Rogalla, B. (2003). Modern-day torture: government-sponsored neglect of asylum seeker children under the Australian mandatory immigration detention regime. *Journal of South Pacific Law*, 7(1): 1–18. Retrieved on 17 September 2007 from www.paclii.org/journals/fJSPL/vol07no1/11.shtml.

Sandoval, C. (1997). Theorising white consciousness for a post-empire world: Barthes, Fanon and the rhetoric of love. In R. Frankenburg (ed.), *Displacing whiteness: essays in social and cultural criticism* (pp. 86–106). London: Duke University Press.

Seidman, S. (1994). *Contested knowledge: social theory in a postmodern era*. Malden, MA: Blackwell.

Stafford Smith, C. (2007). *Bad men: Guantanamo Bay and the secret prisons*. London: Weidenfeld and Nicolson.

23

Contesting the neoliberal global agenda: lessons from activists

Maureen Wilson, Avery Calhoun and Elizabeth Whitmore

With the ongoing failure of governments to protect their citizens from impacts of the neoliberal global agenda, civil society groups worldwide have moved into the breach. Social workers, as allies of these groups, are uniquely positioned to help maximise their effectiveness in confronting the threats of corporate globalisation to democracy, economic justice, the environment and protection of the commons.

How do activist groups know when they're making a difference? This chapter builds on a four-year collaboration with nine diverse activist groups to see what we could learn together about effective practice in social/environmental justice work. We report on what activists told us about what 'success' means in their work, and what facilitates those successes. Reflecting on the implications of these findings in relation to social work skills and capacities, we suggest how social work educators might enhance our capabilities to contribute to the critical work of challenging and replacing the global neoliberal project.

> Principles of human rights and social justice are fundamental to social work . . . Every social worker has the opportunity to matter and, hopefully, the capacity to do so.
>
> Gayle Gilchrist James, Past President, International
> Federation of Social Workers

The continuing global hegemony of neoliberalism presents a special challenge to social work. By virtue of our ethical obligation to address issues of social justice, social work is inevitably at odds with the neoliberal agenda and its exacerbation of social inequalities and environmental degradation.

National governments, generally speaking, have been spectacularly ineffective in either challenging the neoliberal global agenda or in protecting their citizens from its impacts. This failure – whether for reasons of ideological complicity with the forces of neoliberalism, or of constraints imposed by international financial institutions or trade agreements – has led civil society groups worldwide to move into the breach. Social workers are active with many of these organisations and movements, and they and those with whom they work are increasingly looking for means of maximising their impact in transforming policies and practices detrimental to human welfare.

Yet in spite of the growing importance of the role of civil society organisations in protecting human and environmental welfare, there is a dearth of tools to assist citizens and the social practitioners who accompany them in assessing the effectiveness of different strategies in achieving successful outcomes. In this chapter, we hope to help inform the efforts of social work educators in developing the capacities of social workers to both carry out and evaluate social change practice.

The study

The impetus for the study discussed here was in two ethical obligations of social workers – to address issues of social justice, and to evaluate the effectiveness of our practice as we do this – and in our underdeveloped understanding of 'what works' in this area of practice.[1]

In this four-year project we collaborated with nine activist groups across Canada to see what we could learn together about effective practice in social/environmental justice work. Our objectives were to develop a better understanding of the meanings of 'success' for activist groups, to learn about factors and conditions that contribute to those successes, and to support our collaborating groups in reflecting on these questions in relation to their own work. Following a brief discussion of challenges to neoliberal hegemony among which we locate this project, we will share what we have learned that might support the efforts of social workers in their pursuit of social and environmental justice.

Neoliberalism and its discontents: consequences, critiques, challenges

Neoliberalism, a marriage of 18th century liberal ideas on individual liberties and freedoms and modern-day market fundamentalism, found impetus in the 1970s in the context of the inflation and falling rates of profit affecting economic elites. Its ideas on free markets, free trade and a non-interventionist state have found expression in structural adjustment programs involving cuts in government spending, privatisation of public enterprises, removal of controls on trade and exchange, deregulation of wages and prices, weakening of environmental protections, and in general the removal of any laws or regulations interfering with commercial interests. The neoliberal view, advanced by transnational corporations and their allies, and sectors hegemonised by these, is that labour markets need to be more 'flexible', and social programs cut, to deal with international competition. Thus, neoliberals advocate cuts in unemployment insurance, repeal of labour protective laws ('labour market deregulation'), weakening of union power, and cuts to social programs. As economist Raj Patel puts it, 'from the 1970s onward, our economy was hijacked by free-market fundamentalists whose mantra was "greed is good, regulation is bad" ' (2009b).

Perhaps the most contentious tenet of neoliberal ideology is the principle that the rules of the market should govern societies, rather than the other way around. This belief in the

1   We are grateful to the Social Sciences and Humanities Research Council of Canada for funding for this research. Parts of this chapter were published in Wilson, M. G., Calhoun, A. & Whitmore, E. (2012). Contesting the neoliberal agenda: lessons from Canadian activists. *Canadian Social Work Review*, 28(1): 25–48.

inherent wisdom of the market[2] is combined with the assumption that competition will get things done in the most efficient ways possible, allowing the talents of the most able to find expression and eventually benefitting everyone: the rising tide of capitalism will lift all boats.

Some boats, however, prove more seaworthy than others. It follows naturally with the application of this doctrine – promoting competition between individuals, businesses and nations – that there will be winners and losers. Globalisation, operating under neoliberal rules, is producing a small number of fortunate winners and an overwhelming world majority who are excluded from its benefits (WB 2013; Yalnizyan 2013). Notwithstanding claims of free trade advocates that the majority will inevitably benefit from global economic integration, fulfilment of the promised broad improvements to human welfare resulting from deregulation and global competition has been little in evidence. Rather, the disparities that have grown over past decades between rich and poor – within and between countries – persist (Anand, Segal & Stiglitz 2009; Rosling 2013; Slater 2013).

Noting the extent to which this over-reliance on market forces and economic liberalisation has worked to the detriment of the world's poor, the United Nations Department of Economic and Social Affairs, in its 2010 *Report on the world social situation*, pleaded for a shift away from the market fundamentalist thinking, policies and practices of recent decades. It urged national governments to implement sustainable development and equity-oriented policies appropriate to their own national conditions. This plea, however, has fallen largely on unresponsive ears, as have other similar reports and exhortations. For poor nations, the tying of their loans to structural adjustment requirements has meant that this shift in policies was not an option. The leadership of most rich nations, on the other hand, has largely bought into the 'common sense' of growth/trickle-down economics and the neoliberal axiom of 'bad state/good market' (McMichael 2010, 3).

Further, to many, 'free' trade agreements represent threats to democracy and to national sovereignty, as they constrain governments to act in accordance with commercial considerations at the expense of the interests of their own citizens or the environment. Trade agreements giving corporations the power to sue governments, should laws or regulations interfere with commerce, it is argued, result in the concentration of economic and political power in the hands of corporate élites. This expansion of 'rights' and 'freedoms' for corporations, with the dismantling of trade and investment barriers, has disempowered people and governments and transferred power into the hands of global corporations (Korten 1996, 2009; Trew 2013).[3] Thus, free trade agreements that allow the interests of corporations to trump those of governments, and the structural adjustment policies associated with globalism, have the effect of reducing the capacity – and right – of governments to protect their citizens from these impacts (Klein 2008; Cazes & Verick 2013).

Equally seriously, the growing economic and political power of businesses and investors in recent decades (Stanford 2008) has produced a mounting concern that inequali-

---

2   Resonating with Polanyi's (1944) historical research demonstrating national markets are not 'natural' but created and maintained by an infrastructure of laws and institutions, Kozul-Wright & Rayment (2004) note, 'It is a dangerous delusion to think of the global economy as some sort of "natural" system with a logic of its own: It is . . . the outcome of a complex interplay of economic and political relations' (3–4).

3   Yet, as Korten commented, 'even CEOs are extremely limited by imperatives of global competition from acting socially responsibly. When they do, they are quickly replaced. When they do not, they are rewarded greatly' (IFG 1996, 12).

ties in wealth and power are fuelling the global climate crisis (Klein 2013; Nikiforuk 2008; Worth 2009b). Climate change, in turn, disproportionately affects the poorest of the poor through flooding, malaria, malnutrition, diarrhoea, rising world food prices, and the increasing numbers of 'natural' disasters (*New Internationalist* 2009; IPCC 2013). Thus, there is an additional sense in which 'the rich world owes the poor world an ecological debt' (Worth 2009a, 8).

The globalised opposition to the hegemony of neoliberalism is perhaps best summed up in the 'one no, many yeses' theme of the World Social Forum (WSF). Meeting in various places around the world as a counterpoint to the annual World Economic Forum in Davos, Switzerland, the WSF represents a broad-based civil society rejection of the neoliberal global agenda (the 'no') and an affirmation of the multiplicity of alternatives that are generated through the creative genius of ordinary people (the 'yeses'). In the context of the shrinking role of governments, popular and civil society groups globally have stepped in to respond to the consequences of neoliberal rule – working at social and political levels, and also at the level of economic survival (Wilson & Whitmore 2000). Challenges to neoliberal globalism have come also from within corporate and political elites, as 'cracks in the Washington consensus'.[4]

How can citizen organisations make the most of their scarce resources as they work to strengthen civil society and broad democratic participation in impacting policies and practices detrimental to human and environmental welfare? And how can social workers contribute to these efforts? This is work of critical importance, yet while a wide range of civil society organisations has engaged in addressing these themes, remarkably little has been done by way of monitoring the effectiveness of these civil society interventions. There are daunting methodological and practical challenges in doing this, not the least of which is what has been described as a 'positivist resurgence' in the academy, particularly pronounced in the practice professions (Brown & Strega 2005). To the extent that this positivist perspective – with its illusion of neutrality – predominates, issues of how knowledge is socially constructed, and whose interests it serves, are obscured.

Evaluating activism

The challenges notwithstanding, the need of activists to understand whether and how their efforts are making a difference has increasingly engendered efforts to assist in this work.[5] While no consensus has emerged on any 'best' approach to assessing the effectiveness of activist work, two limitations are widely recognised in academic and professional literatures and in the 'grey literature' of activist organisations and funding agencies. First, the voices of activists themselves tend to be missing; the use of narrative has been suggested as a way of bringing these in while '[letting] the story be told' (Egbert & Hoechstetter 2007; Innovation Network 2008). Also missing has been the identification of outcomes beyond

---

4   By the turn of the 21st century, as economic, social, environmental and political crises proliferated throughout the world, increasing numbers of people at the 'centre' questioned the neoliberal 'miracle' (Soros 1998). The Tobin Tax, Nobel Prize–winning economist James Tobin's (1978) proposal for a punitive tax on short-run speculative financial transactions, was one initiative proposed to rein in out-of-control capital. The 2008 market collapse created overnight neo-Keynesians in corporate circles, with recognition of the need for re-regulation in the interest of capital accumulation (Martinez 2009).
5   See, for example, Chapman 2002; Coffman 2009a; Klugman 2010; Masers 2009; Pyrch 1998; Reisman, Gienapp & Stachowiak 2007; Stephens 2009; Young and Everitt 2004.

specific policy change (Coffman 2007; Guthrie et al. 2005; Miller 1994; Miller 2004). This project attempts to respond to these gaps.

Methodology

In our view, social inquiry and practice are both at their best when grounded in praxis, 'developed out of a dialogue between activism and reflection – practice and theory' (Carroll 2006, 234). This combines the unmasking of the intersecting workings of capitalism, sexism, racism, ableism, heterosexism and other sources of marginalisation and exploitation[6] with action to bring about social transformation. In the study described here, we sought to serve as allies of activist groups in the construction of knowledge for practice.

While working alongside counter-hegemonic civil society groups and with a critical perspective, we used tools of appreciative inquiry (AI), the origins of which are in the very different discourse of management/organisational development. Unlike Grant and Humphries (2006), we find no contradiction in this. Rather than assuming methods are automatically linked with particular ideologies or interpretive paradigms, we consider any method to be potentially useful to the extent to which it can contribute to emancipatory ends.

As an action research method, AI builds knowledge through continuous/iterative processes of inquiry and change. It makes use of narrative to draw out success stories, to identify key elements for success, and to build on these. The narrative, or story, is evoked initially by using appreciatively phrased questions (see below) that guide the conversation. Although there are several variations, the process of AI generally includes four phases: discovery (from stories about high points, discovering strengths and potentials in the organisation), dreaming (creating a vision of a desired future), design (choosing what to work on now) and destiny (implementing the design).[7] The appreciative process, by engaging people in storytelling, captures nuances, emotions and energy that could be missed by other data collection strategies.(Bushe 2011; Cooperrider, Whitney and Stavros 2008). Further, as Patton notes, '[there is] evidence that some problems and weaknesses can be easier to surface when evaluation takes an appreciative stance' (2003, 91).[8]

Recruitment of collaborating groups

We recruited groups to work with us in this project not for representativeness, but for diversity and potential theoretical payoff. We issued invitations through several networks asking for activist groups interested in exploring with us the question 'how do you know when you're making a difference?' From the responses and by reaching out through our own networks, we deliberately selected groups that varied in terms of focus of work, organ-

---

6 This requires the courage and intellectual honesty to carry out 'a ruthless criticism of everything existing, ruthless in two senses: the criticism must not be afraid of its own conclusions, nor of conflict with the powers that be' (Marx 1978, 13).

7 The 'dream' phase of this process addresses the criticism that AI 'ignores the negative'. In the dream phase, people are asked to envision a positive future, implicitly providing information about what they see as deficits in a current reality.

8 See also Bushe 2011; Dick 2006; Elliot 1999; Cooperrider 2008; Fals Borda 1986; Patton 2010; Reason & Bradbury 2007, 2008; Whitney & Stavros 2008; Zandee & Cooperrider 2008.

isational size and complexity, demographics, support base, funding, and geography. These included:

- a grassroots group of older women with no staff, budget or organisational structure
- a national environmental research/advocacy organisation with a large professional staff
- a gay/lesbian/bisexual/transgender youth group
- the national chapter of an international development advocacy organisation
- a Quebec-based social justice advocacy group focusing on international issues
- a high profile self-advocacy group of disabled activists
- a rural/Aboriginal-based group affirming remote and rural life
- the Canadian chapter of an international body advocating for the rights of children
- a provincial organisation of professional social workers addressing social justice issues.

The process

Our approach with each of the nine groups varied depending on the needs and capacities of both the group and the research team. Generally, the process began with an introductory workshop for the group followed by in-depth individual interviews of group members, with appreciative framing of the questions.

The individual interviews were semi-structured, allowing for interviewer–participant probing and dialogue. The interview guide included questions such as the following:

- Can you tell us about a successful project/campaign/social action you have experienced in your work? [Probe: What were the things that helped to make that successful?]
- What are you most proud of about your group/organisation?
- When is this group at its best? [Probe: Can you tell us about a time like that?]
- Can you talk about a time when your group/organisation successfully overcame an obstacle or challenge? [Probe: What made that possible?]
- Imagine that you fall asleep for five years. When you wake up, what would you hope to see in your group/organisation? [Probe: What does it look like? How is it working?]

Eighty-six in-depth interviews were carried out with individual activists, with a range of 5–15 interviews per organisation. Following the transcription of the interviews for a particular group, a preliminary thematic analysis of the interviews formed the basis for a second workshop, co-facilitated by the researchers, to assist the group in clarifying its 'dreams' and moving to the creation of shared vision, action and reflection. Additional workshops were available to follow up on this work, to allow groups to make further use of what we had learned. Assuming that most groups would have time and financial constraints, we built in funding for each to hire a research assistant to manage logistics and serve as liaison with us.

We held a two-day symposium to discuss the preliminary results, offer space for representatives from each collaborating group/organisation to talk about their experiences and learning, and to refine our understandings of the meanings and facilitating factors for success. The symposium also provided an opportunity for participants to network with each other. The discussions were animated, with exchanges of insights, good energy and lots of laughter as we grappled with ideas about success and how to put it all together. An appreciative spirit infused these conversations, as participants focused attention on what works and why.

Making sense of what activists told us

Analysis of the individual interviews involved a continuous process of coding and categorising the data using the constant comparison method. At least two researchers coded each interview. As interviews were completed and the project progressed, we developed successively more finely tuned categories. At the broadest level, our codes reflected the two main research questions: what does success mean to social/environmental justice activists, and what do activists think contributes to their success? Within each of these two main codes, multiple categories, subcategories, and sometimes sub-subcategories, emerged as we tried to honour both the differences and the similarities in the stories our participants were telling us.

Activists' perspectives on success

What did activists convey to us about the range of meanings, for them, of success or effectiveness in their work, and about factors that facilitate success? Not surprisingly, there was considerable overlap between the two – an achievement that was a step along the way to an ultimately desired outcome was often, in the moment, experienced as a success in itself. In the following, we highlight themes emerging in this study that are of particular relevance to social work's pursuit of social justice in the context of the dominance of the neoliberal agenda.

What does success mean?

For the activists participating in this study, success or effectiveness in their work has a number of interrelated meanings. While sharing a desire for transformational change – for broad social, political, economic and environmental justice – they described to us a rich range of other specific indicators to them that their work has been successful. These included themes of concrete changes in policies, practices or laws; citizen engagement; aspects of the functioning of the activist groups themselves; the raising of awareness or changing of attitudes of politicians, decision-makers and the general public; and personal change for activist group members themselves.

Broad transformational change

Activists from all groups in this project described success as achieving social/environmental justice: 'Well, you know, success comes when people who are poor and oppressed are no longer poor and oppressed'. People told us of envisioning a time when 'the world is at peace and we have a handle on all of the environmental problems'. Some described 'the total elimination of racism, the total elimination of sexism and homophobia', and others 'no poverty in the world for children. All children are going to school. No child is dying of HIV/AIDS'.

Changes in specific policies, practices or laws

While keeping goals of broad social/environmental transformation always in mind, activists told us they assess success in terms of specific 'concrete' outcomes – changes in policies, practices or laws in their own spheres of activity. For example, 'Canada did cancel the debts . . . Yeah, it was a major success', or 'Finally we got [the accelerated capital cost allowance] removed from the federal budget in 2007. And by doing so, we put back in the pockets of Canadians . . . hundreds of millions of dollars in revenue'. Success was celebrated when laws were enacted: 'to have inclusion of sexual orientation [in the Individual Rights Protection Act]' and policies changed: 'McMaster and Guelph adopted a fair trade policy'. Having roles in framing decision-making processes and constructing debates were often described as victories: 'The fact that there was a public review process for us was a victory in that we had been calling for that to happen. And there were certainly certain elements of how the panel undertook its work that reflected our recommendations'.

Citizen engagement

Democratic participation or citizen engagement was widely identified by activists as an end in itself. The numbers of people engaged was identified as an important outcome especially in relation to public gatherings such as rallies or demonstrations and for letter-writing campaigns or signatures on petitions. The engagement of people from a broad range of social sectors was also seen as a positive indicator: 'Marching down that street, that feeling in Calgary, with such a wide range of middle class people and people with children . . . soccer mums'. The diversity of people engaged in social justice activities is widely valued: 'There will be First Nation kids, white kids, older people, all together. To me, I think that's just the most amazing part'. Many groups see it as important that people engaging in social action are not just 'the usual suspects', the ubiquitous hard core activists.

The nature or quality of people's engagement is sometimes even more celebrated than the numbers or identities of the people engaged. Valued are nonviolence, civility, risk-taking, collaboration, self-advocacy and, to some most importantly, just the fact that people are standing up and making themselves heard.

Engaging people of opposing views in civil public dialogue is considered a particularly important aspect of success by many activists:

> So four of them came together and then they had a conference . . . And to me, something like that is especially good, because it brings people together, and people from different perspectives. Even though they don't agree with each other, but this is a place where they can exchange ideas, you know. And trying to understand better . . . Just the fact that we could bring people together to talk about the issue, to me, it's a success.

The act of speaking out, or making one's voice heard, is often defined as an important achievement in itself. For example, for a disability action group, advocating for one's own and others' rights, publicly voicing one's opinion is highly valued:

> I feel proud when we do our Louder and Prouder Rallies every year. Because we're able to come out and show, 'Yes, we have a disability and we're not shy to show that we have one, that we can be loud, like loud and proud about it.

The presence of energy and enthusiasm was widely identified as indicative of engagement and an important sign that things are going well: 'People investing their energy is always a measure or a sign of success. And people just being enthusiastic' and 'when we were at the activity . . . the atmosphere, the enthusiasm, the pride, just the participation was over-whelming.'

Changing attitudes or atmosphere around an issue

Shifting attitudes or atmosphere surrounding an issue is often considered mainly a means to an end. However, for specific pieces of work, attitude change in itself is seen as a sign of the success. For example, for members of the disability action group, reframing the meaning of disability was described as having hugely empowering implications both for their self-esteem and for their approach to activism.

> I really appreciate those opportunities where you make someone question. They ask . . . 'Why are you . . . celebrating disability?', 'Why are you calling [your campaign] Freak Out?' Like, 'That's so wrong, you shouldn't be proud'. And then someone with disability goes, 'But I am and what's wrong with that?' [A certain group member] has been confronted a few times by people who are TABs (temporarily able bodied, he calls them). And he just . . . challenges people.

Shifting attitudes and/or raising awareness among specific target groups was identified as important to all groups in this study. Politicians (or their constituents) and decision-makers, for example, are frequently singled out for attention: 'we visited targeted [Members of Parliament] across the country and we made sure to get to MPs of all different stripes. And our ask was that they would take this campaign to the respective caucuses'. Attracting media coverage and bringing awareness to the general public were also often mentioned as evidence of success: 'We could see every night on the news . . . if we were successful, if we got media attention and our particular voice was heard. And it quite often was'. The importance of enhanced public awareness is evident in this statement: 'Fifteen years ago, if you were to ask someone, 'What is a sweatshop?' [the answer would have been] 'I don't know'. Whereas now, if you ask people 'What is a sweat shop?' there is a fairly good idea about what a sweatshop is'.[9]

Personal experience, meaning, learning

The struggle for social justice can be difficult and discouraging work. Change can be slow – at times, barely perceptible. Sometimes activists have a feeling of 'tilting at windmills, because we're trying to take on big issues'. People in this study told us they are heartened in their desire to 'do the right thing' when a 'concrete' objective has been met. 'There is a good feeling when you help make something happen, like a Starbucks recognising Ethiopia's rights to their own brand names for coffee'.

Many activists are motivated by a feeling of 'being part of something that's bigger than yourself'. '[When] you can see sort of a global movement – people taking action and that you're a part of that.' Others speak of a sense of belonging. One participant summed up what many felt about his organisation: 'one of the things this place offers . . . is a sense of community'. For groups in which membership is based on personal identification with the

---

9   A workplace typically involving long hours, poor pay, unsafe conditions, flouting of labour/child protective laws.

cause they are working on, success is to some extent defined by feelings of acceptance and validation of identity.

> I think it was successful for me because through the course of being together, sharing stories, talking about issues, talking about systemic barriers . . . we came to realise a lot of what we share, and also the gathering was not just about the discussion of problems . . . We all left feeling a tremendous surge of pride in who we are and in what we do.

Sometimes that personal validation and acceptance morphs into a politicised involvement in the struggle for social justice, in a shift of focus from the personal to the political: 'The Youth Project slowly built me up as a stronger individual, of being a LGBT youth and all of a sudden, the following year, I became . . . this big youth advocate for gay and lesbian students in my school'.

Also widely mentioned by participants in this study was the importance of having fun. In an echo of Emma Goldman's (1931) 'If I can't dance, I don't want to be part of your revolution', one youth observed that 'There's a lot of laughter, there's a lot of fun involved . . . So the process itself is kind of as rewarding, I find, as the result . . . And that's definitely one of the motivators of being here . . . it's important work, but it's also fun'.[10]

Facilitating factors

We were impressed by how clearly they highlighted the importance of the ability to identify, analyse and act strategically in relation to the environments in which they are operating. Conversations about relationships between broader social structures, local contexts, and individual experience were among the most passionate, perhaps because the commitment to positive change derives in large part from activists' profound understanding of the structural causes of social inequities. Many participants expressed the view that the world could really change if only all of us were to understand that 'everything is connected'.

Because structural analysis – understanding the broad social forces and opposing social/economic interests determining social structures – is considered foundational to achieving social justice goals, many groups develop strategies designed to help themselves and their constituencies (policymakers, politicians, their own members, the general public) to understand these connections. Some identify this process as 'consciousness raising' or 'connecting the personal and political'. A stakeholder described how effectively one advocacy organisation made these connections:

> They [workers in the advocacy organisation] deal with social implications, they deal with economic implications, they deal with ecological implications, and they're very good at getting people to understand that all of these things are integrated.

---

10   Attributed to Emma Goldman based on a passage in her Living My Life: 'I did not believe that a Cause which stood for a beautiful ideal, for anarchism, for release and freedom from convention and prejudice, should demand the denial of life and joy' (1931, 56).

In addition to the need for this structural analysis as a foundation for their work, activists also emphasised the critical importance of conjunctural analysis. That is to say, they pointed out the importance of examining the moment (conjuncture) in which they are operating – and of understanding how current forces, actors, and events represent constraints or opportunities for action in a given moment. Sometimes, it is a matter of taking advantage of an unexpected opportunity: 'there was a new Minister . . . who was looking for something to hang her hat on and we got her at the right time'. Sometimes considerable study and preparation is required:

> I mean, first off, you have to actually analyse [the situation]. You have to step back and analyse who holds power. And which players directly influence decision-makers who hold power. And the second thing you have to do is understand what buttons they have to push . . . what are the interests the power holders have . . . so that you're in a position to change their thinking by pressing the buttons.

Other facilitating factors for success participants mentioned included their organisations' credibility or reputation, various aspects of the internal functioning of their groups, their ability to attract, engage and retain participants, and a range of additional specific strategies they have found to be effective. These included clear focus, careful planning and preparation, mobilisation of support around an issue, judicious use of strengths/resources/ talents within the group, creativity in strategies/activities/approaches, and persistence/ tenacity.

Evaluation: attribution vs contribution

In relation to 'concrete' changes particularly, attribution was frequently identified as an issue, especially by groups accountable to funders. Where many forces, conditions and players are involved, it is difficult to credit a success to any particular group:

> When we define success . . . it is changing government policy. Changing bad policy into good policy. Now the problem with that is there's always an attribution question, so we can play a role in that, but there are so many other roles . . . You could have a really progressive Prime Minister, you could have huge public concern, and again, environmental groups can play a role in that, but they're only [a] part . . . You could have a spate of news media stories . . . a huge number of factors that go into a political decision.

Many participants identified pitfalls related to characterising only these observable or measurable types of outcomes as successes. In one way or another, achieving a change means 'a long, slow process' of which they may never see the full results. Others worry that too much reliance on 'measureable' outcomes might 'force people to choose, as advocacy targets, quantifiable things that aren't necessarily systemic change'.

Conclusions

Challenging neoliberalism

What does all of this tell us about how social workers can best respond to the global and local challenges of neoliberalism? Clearly social work values have much in common with the goals and aspirations of the activist groups with whom we've collaborated. And it can be argued that some of the most promising countervailing forces to neoliberal hegemony, both in practice and in the development of accompanying theory, tend to come from those rooted in popular struggles. Thus, it is not surprising that social workers all over the world are already allied with the popular movements they hope will help to build a more equitable and sustainable world. However, how we work in relation to these processes is more complex than simply deciding whose 'side' we're on.

The findings of the study discussed here illuminate some of the ways in which activists, in large and small ways, are working to respond to injustices in the context of a neoliberal world. Without doubt, their aims are about 'changing the world'. But they have told us that the large or small social and personal changes that happen along the way are not separate from, but an integral part of, those goals. We have heard them talk about the importance of both structural and conjunctural analysis, of the linking of the personal and the political, and of the compelling sense of being a part of something larger than oneself as they engage in this work.

We were struck by the yearning evident in the words of many of the activists for an alternative to the unrelentingly individualistic, competitive ethos associated with the ascendancy of neoliberalism. And as they spoke about their coming together to work for change, we could not help but be inspired by the energy, excitement and profound commitment that were communicated along with their words. The untapped power of this yearning can represent an important asset as individuals, groups, networks and alliances come together as formidable adversaries of the existing order – collectively, 'the other superpower'. Max Neef (1997) likened this to the power of a 'cloud of mosquitoes' which 'hangs together but has no chief'. No one caught in that cloud doubts its effectiveness.

Implications for social work and social work education

We opened this chapter with a quotation from the late Professor Gayle Gilchrist James (2003), asserting the importance for social workers of the opportunity and the capacity to work for human rights and social justice. It is with building this capacity that social work education must concern itself.

Social workers can bring a range of roles and skills to this work. As noted by participants in the study discussed here, what are needed are skills for both conceptualising this reality, and for effective means of acting to change it – though not necessarily in that order. Most of these needed skills are already present in social work, which owes a debt to both Gramsci (1976) and Freire (1973) for their explication (Whitmore, Wilson & Calhoun 2011). As Susan George (1997) has pointed out to us, the Gramscian recognition of the importance of the struggle for ideological hegemony – the 'war of ideas' – in recent decades seems to have been taken more to heart by the champions of neoliberal economic doctrine than it has by more progressive forces. This work needs to be reclaimed by those united in the search for social and environmental justice.

It is perhaps also time to revisit another Gramscian notion: the leadership potential in 'organic intellectuals' who contribute not by virtue of holding the social role of an intellectual, but by virtue of their intimate connection to, and reflections on, the struggles of daily life (Gramsci 1976). This lesson, developed by Freire (1973) to dramatic effect in popular education (education for critical consciousness) with Latin-American and African underclasses, has come to significantly impact how social work is conceived (Alayón 2005; Wilson & Prado Hernández 2012).

Along with their value orientation (Wilson 2012), social workers can bring important conceptual and practical skills to work both on the terrain of the 'war of ideas' and on the terrains of political and economic action. These include the ability to analyse the historical contexts in which we work, as well as the ability to distinguish, carry out and share the skills of both structural and conjunctural analysis. This must include knowledge of the nature of neoliberalism (the rules of engagement), of its current manifestations, of its human and environmental consequences, and of current government and civil society responses to these impacts. It implies the ability to work with others to analyse historical moments and their possibilities, and to use and share these insights in relation to the intersection of personal troubles and public issues, as well as in practice directly addressing structural issues.

With these, as Professor James reminded us, social workers are uniquely equipped to make ourselves effective allies as we work for and with activist groups, organisations and movements addressing issues of human rights and social justice. More conscious and systematic attention to the development of the conceptual and practical skills needed in this area of practice, and to the range of participatory and collaborative research approaches available to support it, will enhance the capacity of social workers to contribute in this way. Since there will never be a road map for this kind of work, the thoughtful application of these skills becomes critical as we 'make the road by walking'. (Horton & Freire 1990).

References

Alayón, N. (ed.) (2005). *Trabajo social latinoamericano: a 40 años de la reconceptualización.* Buenos Aires: Espacio Editorial.

Anand, S., Segal, P. & Stiglitz, J. (eds) (2009). *Debates in the measurement of global poverty.* Oxford: Oxford University Press.

Brown, L. & Strega, S. (2005). Introduction: transgressive possibilities. In L. Brown & S. Strega (eds), *Research as resistance: critical, indigenous and anti-oppressive approaches* (pp. 1–17). Toronto, ON: Canadian Scholars' Press.

Brown, L.D., Bammer, G., Batliwala, S. & Kunreuther, F. (2003). Framing practice-research engagement for democratising knowledge. *Action Research*, 1(1): 81–102.

Bushe, G.R. (2011) Appreciative inquiry: theory and critique. In D. Boje, B. Burnes & J. Hassard (eds), *The Routledge companion to organisational change* (pp. 87103). Oxford: Routledge.

Carroll, W.K. (2006). Marx's method and the contributions of institutional ethnography. In C. Frampton, G. Kinsman, A.K. Thompson & K. Tilliczek (eds), *Sociology for changing the world: social movements/social research* (pp. 232–45). Halifax, NS: Fernwood Publishing.

Cazes, S. and Verick, S. (2013). *The labour markets of emerging economies: has growth translated into more and better jobs?* Basingstoke: Palgrave Macmillan.

Chapman, J. & Wameyo. A. (2001, January). *Monitoring and evaluating advocacy: a scoping study.* Retrieved on 22 April 2014 from www.eldis.org/vfile/upload/1/document/0708/DOC21800.pdf.

Chapman, J. (2002). Monitoring and evaluating advocacy. *PLA Notes*, 43: 48–52.

Coffman, J. (2007). What's different about evaluating advocacy and policy change? *The Evaluation Exchange*, XIII(1): 2–4.

Coffman, J. (2009a). *A user's guide to advocacy evaluation planning*. Cambridge, MA: Harvard Family Research Project. Retrieved on 22 April 2014 from www.innonet.org/resources/node/460.

Coffman, J. (2009b). Framing paper: current advocacy evaluation practice. Los Angeles, CA: The California Endowment. Retrieved on 22 April 2014 from www.calendow.org.

Coghlan, A. T., Tzavarus Catsambas, T. & Preskill, H. (2003). An overview of appreciative inquiry in evaluation. In H. Preskill and A.T. Coghlan (eds), *Using appreciative inquiry in evaluation* (pp. 5–22). San Francisco, CA: Jossey-Bass.

Cooperrider, D.L., Whitney, D. & Stavros, J.M. (2008). *Appreciative inquiry handbook* (2nd edn). Brunswick, OH: Crown Custom Publishing.

Egbert, M. & Hoechstetter, S. (2007). Evaluating non-profit advocacy simply: an oxymoron? *The Evaluation Exchange*, XIII(1&2): 20. Retrieved on 22 April 2014 from www.hfrp.org/evaluation/the-evaluation-exchange/issue-archive/advocacy-and-policy-change/evaluating-nonprofit-advocacy-simply-an-oxymoron.

Elliot, C. (1999). *Locating the energy for change: an introduction to appreciative inquiry*. Winnipeg, MB: International Institute for Sustainable Development.

Fals Borda, O. (1986). *El problema de cómo investigar la realidad para transformarla* (3a. edn). Bogotá: Tercer Mundo.

Freire, P. (1973). *Pedagogy of the oppressed*. NY: Seabury Press.

George, S. (1997). How to win the war of ideas: lessons from the Gramscian right. *Dissent*, 44(3): 47–53.

Goldman, E. (1931). *Living my life*. NY: Knopf.

Gramsci, A. (1976). *Selections from the prison notebooks*. Edited and translated by Q. Hoare & G.N. Smith. NY: International Publishers.

Grant, S. & Humphries, M. (2006). Critical evaluation of appreciative inquiry: bridging an apparent paradox. *Action Research* 4(4): 401–18.

Guthrie, K., Louie, J., David, T. & Crystal Foster, C. (2005). The challenge of assessing policy and advocacy activities: strategies for a prospective evaluation approach. Los Angeles, CA: California Endowment. Retrieved on 22 April 2014 from www.calendow.org/uploadedFiles/challenge_assessing_policy_advocacy2.pdf.

Horton, M. & Freire, P. (1990). *We make the road by walking: conversations on education and social change*. Philadelphia, PA: Temple University Press.

Intergovernmental Panel on Climate Change (IPCC) (2013). Climate change 2013. The physical science basis. Retrieved on 22 April 2014 from ww.ipcc.ch/report/ar5/wg1/#.UtHOqf1M7nc.

International Forum on Globalisation (IFG) (1996). *IFG News*, 1(Fall).

Innovation Network, Inc. (2008, September). Speaking for themselves: advocates' perspectives on evaluation. A.E. Casey Foundation and the Atlantic Philanthropies. Retrieved on 22 April 2014 from www.innonet.org/client_docs/File/advocacy/speaking_for_themselves_web_basic.pdf.

James, G.G. (2003). Address to students, Social Action Day, Faculty of Social Work, University of Calgary, Alberta, Canada.

Klein, N. (2008). *The shock doctrine: the rise of disaster capitalism*. NY: Metropolitan Books.

Klein, N. (2013). How science is telling us all to revolt. *New Statesman*, 29 October. Retrieved on 22 April 2014 from www.newstatesman.com/2013/10/science-says-revolt.

Klugman, B. (2010). Evaluating social justice advocacy: a values based approach. Retrieved on 22 April 2014 from www.evaluationinnovation.org/sites/default/files/Klugman%20Brief.pdf.

Korten, D. (2009). Beyond bailouts, let's put life ahead of money. *Yes!* 48(Winter): 12–15.

Korten, D. (1996). *When corporations rule the world*. West Hartford, CT: Kumarian Press.

Kozul-Wright, R & Rayment, P. (2004). *Globalisation reloaded: an UNCTAD perspective. Discussion Paper 167*. NY: United Nations.

Martinez, M.A. (2009). *The myth of the free market: the role of the state in a capitalist economy*. Sterling, VA: Kumarian Press.

Marx, K. (1978). For a ruthless criticism of everything existing. In R.C. Tucker (ed.), *The Marx-Engels reader* (pp. 7–10). NY: Norton.

Masers, B. (2009, October). Evaluating policy change and advocacy: the funder's perspective. Retrieved on 22 April 2014 from www.innonet.org/client_docs/File/center_pubs/advocacy_funders_perspective.pdf.

Max Neef, M. (1997). On human economics. Presentation at Convergence: The World Congresses of Action Research, Action Learning and Process Management and Participatory Action Research. Cartagena, Colombia.

McMichael, P. (2010). Changing the subject of development. In P. McMichael (ed.), *Contesting development: critical struggles for social change*. NY: Routledge.

Miller, C. (2004). Measuring policy change: assessing the impact of advocacy and influencing work. Unpublished report prepared for One World Action.

Miller, V. (1994). *NGO and grassroots policy influence: what is success?* Washington, DC: Institute for Development Research and Just Associates.

New Internationalist (2009). Special issue, *Climate Change Denial*: January/February.

Nikiforuk, A. (2008). *Tar sands: dirty oil and the future of a continent*. Vancouver, BC: David Suzuki Foundation-Greystone Books.

Patel, R. (2009a). *The value of nothing: why everything costs so much more than we think*. Toronto, ON: HarperCollins.

Patel, R. (2009b). The value of nothing. Video posted on 11 November. Retrieved on 22 April 2014 from www.rajpatel.org.

Patton, M. Q. (2010). *Developmental evaluation: applying complexity concepts to enhance innovation and use*. NY: The Guilford Press.

Polanyi, K. (1944). *The great transformation*. NY: Rinehart.

Preskill, H. & Catsambas, T.T. (2006). *Reframing evaluation through appreciative inquiry*. Thousand Oaks, CA: SAGE Publications.

Pyrch, T. (1998). Introduction to the action research family. *Studies in Cultures, Organizations & Societies*, 4(2): v–x.

Ranghelli, L. (2009). Measuring the impacts of advocacy and community organising: application of a methodology and initial findings. *Foundation Review*, 1(3): 131–48.

Reason, P. & Bradbury, H. (eds) (2008). *SAGE handbook of action research: participative inquiry and practice* (2nd edn). London: SAGE Publications.

Reason, P. & Bradbury, H. (2007). Editorial. *Action Research* 5(4): 339–40.

Reilly, M. (2007). An agenda for change in the USA: insights from a conversation about assessing social change in Washington DC. Retrieved on 22 April 2014 from www.ids.ac.uk/idspublication/an-agenda-for-change-in-the-usa-insights-from-a-conversation-about-assessing-social-change-in-washington-dc.

Reisman, J., Gienapp, A. & Stachowiak, S. (2007). A guide to measuring advocacy and policy. Prepared for the Annie E. Casey Foundation by Organisational Research Services. Retrieved on 22 April 2014 from www.aecf.org/upload/PublicationFiles/DA3622H5000.pdf.

Ringsing, B. & Leeuwis. C. (2008). Learning about advocacy: a case study of challenges, everyday practices and tensions. *Evaluation*, 14(4): 413–36.

Rosling, H. (2013). Global trends: wealth & health of nations. Gapminder. Retrieved on 22 April 2014 from www.gapminder.org/world/ 29 October 2013.

Slater, Jon (2013). Annual income of richest 100 people enough to end global poverty four times over. Oxfam. Retrieved on 22 April 2014 from www.oxfam.org/en/pressroom/pressrelease/2013-01-19/annual-income-richest-100-people-enough-end-global-poverty-four-times.

Soros, G. (1998). *The crisis of global capitalism: open society endangered*. NY: Public Affairs.

Stanford, J. (2008). *Economics for everyone: a short guide to the economics of capitalism*. Halifax, NS: Fernwood Publishing.

Stephens, M. (2009). *Toward good practice in public engagement: a participatory evaluation guide for CSOs*. Ottawa, ON: Canadian Council for International Co-operation.

Tobin, James (1978, July/October). A proposal for international monetary reform. *Eastern Economic Journal*, 4(3–4): 153–59. Retrieved on 17 April 2014 from ideas.repec.org/a/eej/eeconj/v4y1978i3-4p153-159.html.

Trew, Stuart (2013). CETA: what's in the deal? *Canadian Perspectives*, Autumn: 17.

United Nations (2010). Rethinking poverty. UN report on the world social situation. Division for Social Policy and Development of the Department of Economic and Social Affairs. Retrieved on 22 April 2014 from www.un.org/esa/socdev/rwss/2010.html.

Whitmore, E. & Wilson, M.G. (2005). Popular resistance to global corporate rule: the role of social work. In I. Ferguson, M. Lavalette & E. Whitmore (eds), *Globalisation, global justice and social work* (pp. 189–206). London & NY: Routledge.

Whitmore, E., Wilson, M.G. & Calhoun A. (eds) (2011). *Activism that works*. Winnipeg, MB & Halifax, NS: Fernwood Publishing.

Wilson, M.G. & Prado Hernández, I. (2012). Solidarity, common cause, relationship. In Julie Drolet & Tuula Heinonen (eds), *International social development: Canadian social work experiences and perspectives* (pp. 170–90). Winnipeg, MB & Halifax, NS: Fernwood Publishing.

Wilson, M.G. (2012). Globalisation. In L. Healy & R. Link (eds), *Handbook on international social work* (pp. 16–23). NY: Oxford University Press.

Wilson, M.G., Calhoun, A. & Whitmore, E. (2012). Contesting the neoliberal agenda: lessons from Canadian activists. *Canadian Social Work Review*. 28(1): 25–48.

Wilson, M.G. & Whitmore, E. (2000). *Seeds of fire: social development in an era of globalism*. Halifax, NS: Fernwood Publishing, the Canadian Consortium for International Social Development (CCISD) and The Apex Press.

Wilson, M.G., Whitmore, E. & Calhoun, A. (2011). Building success in social activism. In E. Whitmore, M.G. Wilson & A. Calhoun (eds), *Activism that works* (pp. 11–28). Winnipeg, MB & Halifax, NS: Fernwood Publishing.

World Bank (WB) (2013). Gini index. Retrieved on 22 April 2014 from search.worldbank.org/data?qterm=International%20income%20inequality&language=EN# 29.

Worth, J. (2009a). Four principles for climate justice. *New Internationalist*, January/February: 419.

Worth, J. (2009b, April). Can climate catastrophe be averted? The first tipping point to climate disaster is already here. *CCPA Monitor*, April: 10–13.

Yalnizyan, A. (2013). Study of income inequality in Canada – what can be done. Ottawa: Canadian Centre for Policy Alternatives. Retrieved on 22 April 2014 from www.policyalternatives.ca/publications/reports/study-income-inequality-canada—what-can-be-done.

Young, L. & Everitt, J.M. (2004). *Advocacy groups*. Vancouver: UBC Press.

Zandee, D.P. & Cooperrider, D.L. (2008). Appreciable worlds, inspired inquiry. In P. Reason & H. Bradbury (eds), *The SAGE handbook of action research: participative inquiry and practice* (2nd edn, pp. 190–98). Thousand Oaks, CA: SAGE Publications.

24

No issue, no politics: towards a New Left in social work education

Mel Gray and Stephen A. Webb

This chapter articulates a new politics for social work education in light of its public statements on confronting injustice and inequality (Global Agenda, International Federation of Social Workers, International Association of Schools of Social Work and International Council on Social Welfare (IASSW, ICSW, IFSW 2012). With social justice as a guiding value, we exhort social workers to take an ethical and political stance and define how commitments can be mobilised. Students come to social work motivated by change: they want to make a difference but the crucial question is 'How do we make this happen?' To answer this we need to understand the centrality that issues play in mobilising a politics of controversy for social work and gain salience with publics in political activation. We argue that the displacement of politics to a global forum, in which a cross-national alliance of social workers can hold an international institution to account, requires a concrete set of controversies over which mobilisation can be configured. Our intention is to conceive of public involvement in politics – in this instance by social work students and their educators – as being occasioned by, and providing a way to settle, controversies that existing institutions are unable to resolve. This chapter is in part a call for social work educators to renew their engagement with radical thought through issues that impact on students and practitioners alike.

Undoubtedly, one of the great virtues of social work is that it continues to think politically in these unpropitious times of austerity and the dismantling of public services. Its foundational values of equality and justice have always been compounded with freedom as core political ideals. The search for structures that might realise these moral ambitions and taking a political stance in their defence has been a consistent feature of social work. Therefore, the complete absence of a political charter in the Global Agenda for Social Work and Social Development (IASSW, ICSW, IFSW 2012) gives cause for concern. This chapter presents current research on political mobilisation to explain why this is a problem for social work. Recent sociological research suggests that people tend to get organised around an issue of common concern or an object of controversy (Marres 2005, 2007, 2012). Therefore, for social workers to organise around the objectives of the Global Agenda, the issue being contested or around which we want social workers to get organised needs to be named and fully articulated. There is widespread agreement in social work that, at root, the issue it constantly has to address in daily practice is the manifestations of neoliberal capitalism and its partner public management regimes of power. The pernicious effects of neoliberal market-oriented policies are seen daily in austerity measures, welfare rationing, punitive managerial regimes, zero-hour employment contracts, growing inequalities and discriminatory labelling of welfare recipients which are impacting negatively on social workers and service users alike. It is therefore important to ask what the relationship is between the Global Agenda set out by the various international professional social work associations and the issues impacting directly on daily social work practice. The fact that the Global Agenda does not name the underlying issue it seeks to address is thus deeply problematic. Gray and Webb (2013) have taken this a step further by arguing for a renewed progressive political Social Work Left to articulate its role in combatting the exploitative capitalist, neoliberal economic order and its new public management regime. If the goals of the Global Agenda and a new Social Work Left were aligned, and the issue named as neoliberal capitalism, only then would the forces defacing the realisation of the moral standards to which social work commits itself be eradicated. However, having said this, political action requires more than adherence to principles and values. As current research shows, it needs a materiality of practices or object of participation to effectively mobilise social workers around an issue of contestation. We need to identify clear cases of the displacement of politics from sites of local, regional and national politics to a global forum. In short, contemporary social research tells us issues call publics – and protests – into being.

This chapter articulates this 'new politics' for social work in light of its public statements on confronting injustice and inequality (IASSW, ICSW, IFSW 2012). Social work explicitly adopts justice as a normative value. This means it exhorts social workers to take an ethical and political stance. However, it does not necessarily define how its commitments might be mobilised. Hence, this chapter is in part a call for social work educators to renew their political commitments and engagement with radical thought and issues and impart this to their students.

Reisch and Andrews's (2002) examination of radical social work in the US shows social work's lack of militancy in confronting the system of capitalist power that delimits and rejects the core values of social work. Politically, social workers are unorganised and do not usually have the energy, time, resources or assertiveness to take up active political roles (Gray et al. 2002). This exposes the weakness of social work as a professional pressure group and helps explain the strength of the neoliberal capitalist state and its managerial agents in determining our ability to respond with political verve, courage and commitment (Marston & McDonald 2012). These ultimately are the central objectives of a renewed social work politics, which begins with grappling with enduring ideas about what a 'just society' might look like and how injustice manifests itself in everyday relationships and institutional structures of domination and exclusion that lead to injustice. It continues with locating the issues leading to this unjust state of affairs, taking a stance and confronting, unsettling, agitating, and seeking to transform the oppressive relations and unjust structures that maintain them. In this respect, building solidarity across borders in social work education means providing examples of social protest successfully staged in the transnational arena and focusing on the 'materiality of struggle' (Marres 2005, 2007, 2012).

A renewed politics of social work

A first step in conceiving a renewed politics of social work education hinges on two important contemporary incursions within the social sciences, one from social theory and the other from political philosophy. The fact that they criss-cross in instantiating new forms of political action is particularly helpful in advancing a new politics for social work education. The former focuses exclusively on debates in theoretical sociology, galvanised chiefly by Nancy Fraser and Axel Honneth (2003) and often referred to as the 'integrated model of social justice' framework. The latter is derived from French political philosopher Alain Badiou, particularly his reworking of the communist hypothesis as part of his larger project of reconstructing a model of political action derived from Marx's historical materialism (Badiou 2010). Taken together, they have the potential to galvanise a new politics for the education of social workers by innovatively reworking agendas on social justice, and of political possibility. Each rests on transformative ideas relating to universal emancipation and freedom from exploitation and oppression (for a fuller discussion of the social and political theory underpinning the arguments in this chapter, see Gray & Webb 2013).

These fresh insights from sociology and political philosophy observe a significant shift in social and political thought that can act decisively on social work education. Broadly, this shift is based on renewal and crisis:

- Renewal is situated largely at the level of political ideas and values, especially as they relate to the development of a progressive left agenda that emphasises social justice, freedom and equality.
- Crisis refers to the vulnerabilities of neoliberalism and state capitalism on a global scale to the extent that many political commentators believe we are now entering a new phase: a protracted, long downturn in the fortunes of capitalism.

These shifts are particularly relevant in considering how we devise a critical role for the education of social workers in confronting the contradictions of the logic of capital accumulation and greed based on the notion of endless growth (Coates 2003; Gray et al. 2013). Social work owes it, as much to itself as to its clients, to confront the dominant capitalist and neoliberal apparatus with every tactic at its disposal. Social workers have to get organised and find one another. This quest for solidarity underlies the Global Agenda but without any direct reference to the problems we are confronting or their causes.

Those in social work seeking a new politics are situating the debate within this much invigorated New Left grouping of thinkers that coalesce around critical considerations of community and progressive political agendas who believe universal justice is not possible without the abolition of capitalism. Having abandoned 'class struggle essentialism' for the plurality of antiracist, feminist and postmodern resistances, 'capitalism' is now clearly re-emerging as the name of the problem social work must confront (Ferguson 2008; Ferguson & Lavalette 2004; Ferguson & Woodward 2009; Ferguson, Lavalette & Whitmore 2004; Lavalette 2011; Garrett 2013).

As a consequence, today we are witnessing within social work the return of a new theory and practice of resistance that focuses on public controversy and issues of democracy (Garrett 2013, Gray & Webb 2013). This fertile ground of thought can frame the way a radical social work can be instantiated under the banner of a 'New Social Work Left' and take a political stance that is inherently antagonistic to its adversaries: neoliberal capitalism and new public management. This has long been the object of the emancipatory activism of new social movements, not least the green or environmental politics gaining ground in social work that seek to tackle the longstanding problems of economic inequality and social injustice head-on.

It heralds a new phase for social work education faced with the difficult challenge of persuading educators and students that there is something worthwhile to be gained in engaging with the radical project of a new issues-based politics. Through curriculum design and content, mainstream social work education can limit and even dislodge student experience of what is important and urgent (Lingis 2007). Importantly, for social work students, inculcating a critical approach to politics means becoming involved in public controversies around issues of local and regional significance that can take on global proportions, such as discriminatory forms of employment, climate change, population overshoot, capitalist austerity measures, and freedom from censorship.

A New Social Work Left can inspire core supporters and win over potential allies by demonstrating the chain of equivalences that exist among the various issues impacting on social workers – from the ecological crisis to the exploitation of the poor – against different forms of subordination (Gray et al. 2013). It can do this by reactivating older radical traditions in social work and, if there is a real shift in the point of contestation with this new politics of social work, it is precisely because of the signs of innovation and controversies that are happening on the wider social, economic and cultural plane under which social work is operating.

Within this context, the International Association of Schools of Social Work and the International Federation of Social Workers together with the International Council on Social Welfare have produced a Global Agenda for Social Work and Social Development (IASSW, ICSW, IFSW 2012). In our endorsing a critical social work agenda for education, a challenge for these international organisations would be to openly declare their opposition to neoliberalism and the destructive nature of state capitalism. These organisations should be launching militant agendas, around issues of poverty, unemployment and workplace relations. We wonder what it would take for these international organisations to lead such a progressive agenda and to stand up in defiance?

An important locus for a new politics is social work education, given students come in motivated by a desire for change, searching for fresh perspectives around social justice. Thus, as it did in 1968, this reactivation of the radical project might well begin with students. However, it is not merely a matter internal to mainstream social work. Many issues and events central to contemporary understandings of society belong to fields of operation that are external to social work and cannot be reconceptualised in terms of social work categories alone. We therefore need students to have a strong grounding in the social sciences, with a sound knowledge of political philosophy and theoretical sociology. This is because we are working within a discursive rupture that has recently occurred within progressive left thought that gains salience only through continuous critical discourse about the oppressive and violent regimes we wish to oppose and replace. For certain, social work has been shaped by wider political attitudes towards class, gender and race. Moreover, social work operates in a position of objective structural disadvantage, which has been vividly exposed in European countries currently undertaking public sector austerity measures and the aggressive de-funding of social services, such as Greece and Spain. External structures impact decisively on social work, and social work students need to understand this broad macro context that shapes their work. This is one very good reason why contemporary social and political theory offers a sound basis for constructing a new politics. The strands drawn upon, indebted to progressive thought, demonstrate how a New Social Work Left must be concerned with new political forms of resistance, interruption and struggle (see Smith 2012).

To this end, social work education needs to forge new ways of 'thinking the political' and devising strategies and tactics for active political engagement (Gray & Webb 2013). It needs to engage in real debate over fundamental principles as well as concrete public issues and controversies. The desire here is for a testing and proving of critical thought around specific public issues which should be capable of bringing together social work's role in demands for justice and anti-oppression. The New Social Work Left seeks to renew and re-activate the radical tradition of the 1970s and develop a more solid base for political and ethical work to which the Global Agenda might align itself.

Initiating a 'new' politics for social work education

Any new ways of thinking about politics must be constructed in a way that enables students to imagine a different world than one enslaved to capitalism and neoliberal man-agerialism. Politics then becomes about imagining a better future – one in which justice and equality prevail, in which people have an equal share of earth's finite resources. For some, the environmental crisis is forcing us to envision and implement a new ecological paradigm because voracious capitalism is no longer tenable or sustainable (Coates & Gray 2012; Gray & Coates 2012; Gray et al. 2013). Capitalism has significantly contributed to the crisis over climate change. It is this view of politics that motivates a new politics of social work, one that will enable us to envision a new future for social work. Though social work-ers fight daily in their organisations against punitive welfare cuts and oppressive policies, through their acts of resistance and interruption, they also need to envisage alternative ways of imagining political life, relations between professionals and service users, and jus-tifications for militant opposition: a new politics is needed to articulate this new political agenda for social work to oppose the injustices of capitalism and its neoliberal economic rationality, austerity measures and managerial control.

It is in this spirit that the 'new politics' of social work must be approached by adopting a backward and forward gaze as we face challenges reminiscent of radical social work in the 1970s and 1980s and seek to revivify radical action, given its ongoing relevance in contemporary social work (Ferguson 2008; Ferguson & Lavalette 2004; Ferguson & Woodward 2009; Ferguson, Lavalette & Whitmore 2004; Lavalette 2011). There is ongoing relevance in collectivist-based activism and resistance to specific instances of public unrest and oppression. Ideologically situated on the left, most critical social workers continue to see merit in ethical socialist ideas, though are faced with the need for a reconstructed rad-ical agenda since the demise of European communism.

Social work educators need to be aware that the 'overtly academic' nature of radical social work has, over the years, enjoyed little support from frontline practitioners (see Carey & Foster 2011). However, in their teaching, they need to emphasise the importance of the critique that a critical social work brings to emancipatory practice. By enlarging students' critical thinking, more effective methods to counter restrictive procedural and managerialist practices can be envisioned. Out of this comes tangible, practical ways of meeting the pressing, crisis-oriented, micro needs of service users that practitioners en-counter on a daily basis. The strength of critical social work has always been its broad, general, 'macro' dynamic or ontological themes, 'such as the role of social work within a diminishing welfare state apparatus, the underlying causes of greater regulation within social work organisations, [and] the wider impact of globalisation' (Carey & Foster 2011, 577). However, we use the word 'global' too uncritically in social work (Gray et al. 2008, 2013; Gray & Webb 2008). What exactly does it mean? If we are to grapple with the meaning of solidarity in the 'global' agenda, we need to be mindful of research that repeatedly shows that, rather than participate in mass action or public dissent, social workers tend to engage in small acts of interruptive resistance. The nature of such resistance must remain surprising and unanticipated, so as to defy managerialism, regulation and control. In exercising discretion, managers, too, resist and undermine hegemonic 'managerial' discourses (Aronson & Smith 2010; Carey 2009).

Carey and Foster (2011) highlight why radical social work must, to some extent, remain at a level removed from the daily practice of social work. Its role is to engender a political understanding of how managerial 'prescriptions connect . . . with the day-to-day practice of social workers and the organisational conditions of social welfare' (Pearson 1975, 140). Its function lies in the generation of ideas and a language through which practitioners filter their daily experiences. This critical lens creates a space for separate 'realms of theory' (Althusser 2003) essential to progressive social change. It is in this spirit that we need to approach the 'new politics' of social work, which inevitably will contain something of the old while providing a new language with which to analyse what is wrong with the world and the policies engendering injustice. The 'global' agenda would benefit considerably from more overt statements about the causes of poverty, inequality and injustice it seeks to attack and by aligning itself with the New Social Work Left (Gray & Webb 2013).

Though critical social work thinkers are up against a profession of social workers prepared to surrender or compromise their 'technical' and 'ideological' autonomy within a 'highly rationalised care management labour process' (Harris 2003), we would do well to remember that employee resistance and rule breaking remains common, and recalcitrant social workers have 'not disappeared but merely adapted their behaviour or attitudes to accommodate changing circumstances' (Carey & Foster 2011, 583) as they have always done. As Kemshall (2010) points out, even highly regulated systems can be negotiated, circumvented and resisted in myriad ways by skilful social workers. Rather than the 'new politics' of social work being in grand, overambitious ideals, there is a trend which highlights the importance of a 'micro politics' – small deviant acts of resistance at the coalface. For radical social workers, social work has always been about how the personal connects to the political, and educators need to teach students how this 'micro politics' connects with 'public' issues and structural change.

The making of politics around public controversy and issues

Central to recent empirical research on what constitutes a politics for the public is the question of the extent to which the material spaces we inhabit and the objects with which we interact shape our politics and, in turn, become the issues and targets of political struggles. Here the public is seen to comprise a set of material elements that intermediate collective relations. As Dewey (1991) noted, 'indirect, extensive, enduring and serious consequences of conjoint and interacting behaviour call a public into existence having a common interest in controlling these consequences' (15–16). His politics of the public is best described as an entanglement of relations among entities that do not belong to the same social world but are connected through an issue that affects them jointly.

This has direct resonance for social work and its Global Agenda, which can draw immediately from contemporary social research showing that democratic politics in contemporary society involves particular practices of issue formation (Marres 2005). This insight comes from an 'object-oriented' perspective on politics in Science and Technology Studies (STS) which gives pride of place to the 'objects' of politics, i.e. to defining and solving issues. Emulating Dewey's ideals of participatory democracy and his 'socio-ontological' understanding of issues, it suggests that people's involvement in politics is mediated by problems that affect them (Marres 2007). It holds that public involvement in politics is dedicated to the articulation of public issues. Issues drive people to involve themselves in democratic processes, not democratic values or democratic ideals of inclusive opinion-making and accountable decision-making (De Vries 2007). Several points bear emphasis here for social work education:

- Relevant communities involved in decision-making are demarcated on the basis of issues rather than democratic values like 'citizen representation', 'inclusive debate' and 'rational deliberation' (Amin 2012). Contemporary research on social capital supports the need for more, not less, public involvement in politics (Putnam 2004).
- 'Theories of agenda setting regard issue definition as the decisive factor in democratic institutional politics, as it determines which actors can get involved in political process, and on what terms' (Marres 2007, 761). The goal is to counteract tendencies in modern society to leave the big decisions to the experts in the belief that only they understand the complexity of the political structures and processes they themselves have created.
- Public affairs are defined by the networked entanglement of social associations.

In learning from this fresh perspective, social work may ask who are the actors in the Global Agenda? How are they summoned into being around concrete issues and controversies? Are they merely the IASSW, ICSW, IFSW or their representatives working at a national or international level? How will they involve national social work associations and how do they plan to move social workers beyond mere advocacy of a Global Agenda towards a more considered involvement and their implication for wider publics, such as service users? How are they going to persuade social workers of actions they need to take to fulfil the goals of the Global Agenda? How binding is the agenda and exactly what do issues do in making them a reality? We argue here the answers to these questions lie in a clear articulation of the issues around which to mobilise social workers to combat social and economic injustice. To this end, there is a need for new theoretical resources to bring the missing politically active social work 'public' back into the profession, and social work education can provide this.

Certainly the Global Agenda is a first step in making issues publicly visible, thereby forcing them onto the political agenda (Habermas 2001). But social work draws too heavily on perspectives on democracy that adopt procedural models of public participation developed in political science, with discussions on participation, particularly service-user participation, being preoccupied with the method and processes of democracy: participatory procedure and representative participation. Social work education would do well to embrace the insights that the new sociology of material practices offers, such as its commitment to follow practices-in-the-making, and the more general conviction that prescriptions are likely to impose impossible demands (Hinchliffe 2001).

Most importantly for the Global Agenda, the politicisation of an issue is an essential precondition for a democratic processing of these matters of concern. Social work needs to find and teach examples where social workers have attained political success in entanglements around a particular issue and achieving change for service users. By studying 'best practice' models of political entanglement they might discern the processes that placed the issue on the political agenda and led to direct action to address the problems caused by the issue.

So what is to be done?

So what can the Global Agenda do about our main adversaries – neoliberalism, capitalism and managerialism? First it needs a perspective on the issue, a particular way of framing the problem that comes from the way in which we think about it. This is what theory provides. Contemporary social theory tells us that, despite the global financial crisis, neoliberalism, with its global ambitions for profit and accumulation, is far from done (Harvey 2011). It has proved impervious to the uncertainties facing capitalism, the fragility of national governments and risks associated with marked increases in inequality and remains in ascendancy across the globe (Harvey 2005, 2011). In Marxist terms, this is confirmation of 'the long-term systemic risks that capital poses to life on planet earth' (Harvey 2011, 262).

In 'Down with existing society', French political philosopher Alain Badiou (1987) railed against this state of affairs:

> If the lamentable state in which we find ourselves is nonetheless the best of all real states this simply proves that up to now the political history of human beings has only given birth to restricted innovations and we are but characters in a pre-historic situation. If, in terms of political thought and practice, of forms of collective life, humanity has yet to find and will not find anything better than currently existing parliamentary states, and the neoliberal forms of consciousness associated with them, this proves that as a species, said humanity will not rank much higher than ants and elephants. (3)

From a social work perspective, what is required is a more detailed examination of power relations at work: how they are configured as part and parcel of capitalism and how social relations and control structures are managed. A key focus for social work is managerialism and oppressive micro-management regimes, since the main stalwarts of the neoliberal apparatus are its managers (Boltanski & Chiapello 2005). Management is crucial in authoritatively accepting, legitimating and delivering the justifications for profit and greed in this phase of capitalism, since management discourse does its most decisive work in the economy. In effect, if state law and the military are always ready in reserve, it is managers who are the glue that hold capitalism together, delivering its command and regulatory structure at the level of the everyday. As such, it is the rationality of management, its agenda and micro practices that must be a central target for a sustained social work critique and radical confrontation, for social services management supports, maintains and deepens the neoliberal apparatus.

A Global Agenda aligned with a New Social Work Left could develop counter-acts and oppositional tactics against the totality of neoliberal and managerial domination. In identifying with the ones excluded from community, it could mobilise groups, such as poor slum dwellers, migrant workers or what is being called the 'precariat' as a political community of issues involving the entanglement of social work and those excluded (Standing 2011). The violence of neoliberalism, aided and abetted by its policing state and law, has led to Italian historian and political philosopher Giorgio Agamben's (2005) claim that we live in dangerous and unprecedented times, under what he calls a state of exception whereby, at any time, law can be suspended to preserve a juridical state order predicated on the blurring of legal and illegal, public and private, citizen and criminal, terrorist and freedom fighter. Stephen Graham (2010) critically examines the subtler and more familiarly overt modes of social control and surveillance that are being put to use in troubling ways in modern cities, not least an increasing dependence on methods of local policing eerily similar to Western military behaviour on the battlefield. At times of emergency or crisis, the State abandons all pretence to popular democracy and takes on a militarised, legal mode often against its own citizens:

Indeed, the state of exception has today reached its maximum worldwide development. The normative aspect of law can thus be obliterated and contradicted with impunity by a governmental violence that – while ignoring international law externally and producing a permanent state of exception internally – nevertheless still claims to be applying the law (Agamben 2005, 87).

Where does social work situate itself in relation to the evil of neoliberal capitalism? And what stance does it take in constructing new political forms? In the words of the World Social Forum, 'Is another world possible' or is capitalism the only game in town? Where is the vanguard of a progressive politics in all of this? Who will magically work the transformation of subordination and exploitation into political agency? And where are the sustained acts of resistance with which writers from Althusser to Foucault tried to console us?

What most diagnoses fail to offer, including postmodern social work, is any working out, in a meaningful fashion, of concrete forms of resistance. We may speculate, however, whether it is possible to identify a rising opposition to confront the situation that has been imposed upon us. Moreover, does a radical alternative inhere in Marxism and, by implication, a Marxist social work when 'Marxist literature, although plentiful . . . has a depressing air of sterility and helplessness' (Kolakowski 1978, 29). Does this suggest a deep structural fault line in the thinking of the Left that should be avoided at all costs in developing any new politics? British Leftist historian, political scientist and one-time editor of the *New Left Review*, Perry Anderson (2000), thinks so. In confronting present forms of neoliberal violence, he urges us to avoid the 'consolation' of the Left, which is based on the need to have some message of hope and has a 'propensity to over-estimate the significance of contrary processes, to invest inappropriate agencies with disinterested potentials and to nourish illusions in imaginary forces' (10). Hence, we are often left with a pluralistic politics resting on the activation of new social movements that embody a hesitant and weak critique of advanced capitalism, but does this best capture the uneven journey and immediate prospects for a new politics of social work?

There is little doubt that social work reflects aspects of the wider impasse in contemporary political activism: 'There are innumerable blueprints for utopian futures that are, in varying degrees, egalitarian, cosmopolitan, ecologically sustainable, and locally responsive, but no solution to the most intractable problem of all: who is going to make it happen [and how]?' (Bull 2005, 19) This absence of agency is a structural effect conditioned by the disappearance of a politically influential working class.

The vexed issue of identifying a primary agent of radical change links explicitly to social work's agenda because of its foundational consideration of equality, justice and emancipation; but are social workers, too, subject to 'the seductions of the market, the norms of disciplinary power, and the insecurities generated by an increasingly unbounded and disorderly human geography' (Brown 2011, 55)? Like the majority of Westerners, have they, too, 'come to prefer moralising, consuming, conforming, luxuriating, fighting, simply being told what to be, think, and do over the task of authoring their own lives' (Brown 2011, 55). Are they, too, 'largely oriented 'towards short-run gratifications rather than an enduring planet, towards counterfeit security rather than peace, and disinclined to sacrifice either their pleasures or their hatreds for collective thriving' (Brown 2011, 56)?

The winds of political change

How can social work education actively pursue an agenda of emancipatory politics fashioned towards freedom, justice and equality? The practice of social work inevitably operates within a 'grand tension' of refusing the dominant order, while at the same time being contaminated by and maintaining this order. For radicals, the tensions to which this situation gives rise are best dealt with by political discipline, developing local clusters of solidarity and being critically reflective. This will enable social workers to live with these tensions and sustain their refusal of neoliberal management practices.

Radical interventions in social work are tactically best suited to specific issues via small groups. In our recent empirical work on community engagement, we were most surprised to discover just how multinational corporations and local state bureaucrats are terrified of social protest and radical mobilisation. This is especially true when a public issue gains salience with the media. Many protest groups are not aware of the panic they excite in the minds of the bosses. Big business and their state bureaucrat allies are utterly risk aversive about inciting public protest and controversy. They neither understand nor can account for what they see as the 'emotive and irrational public'. Thus talking about and organising around social inequality and injustice is a threat to political power. Badiou (2012) constantly reminds us that successful protests and uprisings in different domains have often taken place because of the actions of minorities.

Through education, social work can become a politics of refusal or what Agamben (1999) refers to as an 'I would prefer not to' strategy. It can discover a new sense of promise and negate and react against the violence of neoliberalism and the social inequalities it engenders. In these dark times of neoliberal violence, social workers have to, once more, stand together in solidarity. Social work educators can invite students to consider what new forms of collective life are possible and how social work may take part in a fresh demand for equality, justice and universal emancipation.

References

Agamben, G. (2005). *State of exception*. Chicago, IL: University of Chicago Press.
Agamben, G. (1999). *Potentialities: collected essays in philosophy*. Stanford, CA: Stanford University Press.

Althusser, L. (2003). *The humanist controversy and other writings*. London: Verso.

Amin, A. (2012). *Land of Strangers*. London: Polity Press.

Anderson, P. (2000). Renewals. *New Left Review*, 2(1): 5–24.

Aronson, J. & Smith, K. (2010). Managing restructured social services: expanding the social? *British Journal of Social Work*, 40(2): 530–47.

Badiou, A. (2012). *The rebirth of history: times of riots and uprisings*. London: Verso.

Badiou, A. (2010). *The communist hypothesis*. London: Verso.

Badiou, A. (1987). À bas la société existante! [Down with existing society]. *Le Perroquet*, 69: 1–3.

Boltanski, L. & Chiapello, E. (2005). *The new spirit of capitalism*. London: Verso.

Brown, W. (2011). We are all democrats now ... In G. Agamben, A. Badiou, W. Brown & J.L Nancy (eds), *Democracy in what state?* (pp. 44–58). NY: Columbia University Press.

Bull, M. (2005). The limits of the multitude. *New Left Review*, 35: 19–29.

Carey, M. (2009). The order of chaos: exploring agency care managers' construction of social order within fragmented worlds of state social work. *British Journal of Social Work*, 39(3): 556–73.

Carey, M. & Foster, V.L. (2011). Introducing 'deviant social work': contextualising the limits of radical social work whilst understanding (fragmented resistance within the social work labour process). *British Journal of Social Work*, 43(1): 576–93.

Coates, J. (2003). *Ecology and social work: toward a new paradigm*. Halifax, NS: Fernwood Publishing.

Coates, J. & Gray, M. (2012). The environment and social work: an overview and introduction. *International Journal of Social Welfare*, 21(3): 230–38.

De Vries, G. (2007). What is political in sub-politics?: How Aristotle might help STS. *Social Studies of Science*, 37(5): 781–809.

Dewey, J. (1991 [1927]). *The public and its problems*. Athens, OH: Swallow Press/Ohio University Press.

Ferguson, I. & Lavalette, M. (2004). Beyond power discourse: alienation and social work. *British Journal of Social Work*, 34(3): 297–312.

Ferguson, I. & Woodward, R. (2009). *Radical social work in practice: making a difference*. Bristol: Policy Press.

Ferguson, I. (2008). *Reclaiming social work: challenging neo-liberalism and promoting social justice*. London: SAGE Publications.

Ferguson, I., Lavalette, M. & Whitmore, E. (eds) (2004). *Globalisation, global justice and social work*. London: Routledge.

Fraser, N. & Honneth, A. (2003). *Redistribution or recognition? A political-philosophical exchange*. London: Verso.

Garrett, P.M. (2013). Active equality: Jacques Rancière's contribution to social work's 'New Left'. *British Journal of Social Work*, 1–17. DOI: 10.1093/bjsw/bct188.

Graham, S. (2010). *Cities under siege: the new urban militarism*. London: Verso.

Gray, M. & Coates, J. (2012). Environmental ethics for social work: social work's responsibility to the non-human world. *International Journal of Social Welfare*, 21(3): 239–47.

Gray, M. & Webb, S.A. (eds) (2013). *Social work theories and methods* (2nd edn). London: SAGE Publications.

Gray, M. & Webb, S.A. (2008). The myth of global social work: double standards and the local-global divide. *Journal of Progressive Human Services*, 19(1): 61–66.

Gray, M., Coates, J. & Hetherington, T. (eds) (2013a). *Environmental social work*. Abingdon, Oxon: Routledge.

Gray, M., Coates, J., Yellow Bird, M. & Hetherington, T. (eds) (2013). *Decolonising Social Work*. Farnham, Surrey: Ashgate.

Gray, M., Coates, J. & Yellow Bird, M. (eds) (2008). *Indigenous social work around the world: towards culturally relevant education and practice*. Aldershot, UK: Ashgate.

Gray, M., Collett Van Rooyen, C.A. J., Rennie, G. & Gaha, J. (2002). The political participation of social workers: a comparative study. *International Journal of Social Welfare*, 11(2): 99–110.

Habermas, J. (2001). *The postnational constellation: political essays*. Trans by M. Pensky. Cambridge: Polity Press.

Harris, J. (2003). *The social work business*. London: Routledge.

Harvey, D. (2011). *The enigma of capital and the crises of capitalism* (2nd edn). Oxford: Oxford University Press.

Harvey, D. (2005). *A brief history of neoliberalism*. Oxford: Oxford University Press.

Hinchliffe, S. (2001). Indeterminacy in-decisions: science, policy, and politics in the BSE (Bovine Spongiform Encephalopathy) crisis. *Transactions of the Institute of British Geographers*, 26(2): 182–204.

IASSW, ICSW, IFSW (2012). The global agenda for social work and social development. Retrieved on 22 April 2014 from cdn.ifsw.org/assets/globalagenda2012.pdf.

Kemshall, H. (2010). Risk rationalities in contemporary social work policy and practice. *British Journal of Social Work*, 40(4): 1247–62.

Kolakowski, L. (1978). *Main currents of Marxism*. Oxford: Oxford University Press.

Lavalette, M. (2011). *Radical social work today: social work at the crossroads*. Bristol: Policy Press.

Lingis, A. (2007). *The first person singular*. Chicago, IL: Northwestern University Press.

Marres, N. (2012). *Issue mapping: demonstrating the relevance for participatory social research*. London: ESRC Digital Social Research Demonstrator Project.

Marres, N. (2007). The issues deserve more credit: pragmatist contributions to the study of public involvement in controversy. *Social Studies of Science*, 37(5): 759–80.

Marres, N. (2005). *No issue, no public: democratic deficits after the displacement of politics*. Amsterdam: Ipskamp Printpartners.

Marston, G. & McDonald, C. (2012). Getting beyond 'heroic agency' in conceptualising social workers as policy actors in the twenty-first century. *British Journal of Social Work*, 42(6): 1022–38.

Pearson, G. (1975). *The deviant imagination: psychiatry, social work and social change*. London: Macmillan.

Putnam, R. (2004). *Better together: restoring the American community*. NY: Simon & Schuster.

Reisch, M. & Andrews, J. (2002). *The road not taken: a history of radical social work in the United States*. NY: Brunner-Routledge.

Smith, R. (2012). Castells, power and social work. *British Journal of Social Work*, 42(2): 283–99.

Standing, G. (2011). *The precariat: the new dangerous class*. NY: Bloomsbury Academic.

Part 8

The past and the future of social work

25

Learning from our past: climate change and disaster interventions in practice

Lena Dominelli

> Social work has a lengthy history of intervening in disaster situations – natural and human-made, especially in philanthropic work with faith-based organisations and individuals. This changed with institutional forms of solidarity enshrined in the welfare state following World War 2. These impulses were coupled with the formation of the United Nations and its affiliated bodies, formed to rebuild a war-devastated Europe. These now have a remit to respond to any humanitarian disaster anywhere. In this chapter, I describe these developments, and include how the International Association of Schools of Social Work (IASSW) also became involved in such initiatives, highlighting the creation of co-produced solutions in locality-specific culturally relevant ways through community partnerships that include the social sciences like social work working alongside the physical sciences. I also argue that disaster interventions should form part of mainstream social work curricula and that humanitarian aid workers should have a social work qualification.

Social work has a lengthy history of involvement in delivering humanitarian aid following disasters. Desai (2007) describes how social work academics at the Tata Institute of Social Sciences have been responding to disasters in India since 1947, and have developed sophisticated infrastructures for doing so. The simple act of helping someone in crisis is a form of social work. History is replete with such examples, but these are normally not claimed as social work interventions. This is because such helping is provided as charitable good neighbourliness or kindness displayed to strangers rather than that provided by specially trained professionals who are embedded in institutionalised helping relationships. Institutional forms of helping have sought to harness acts of goodwill, under both the aegis of religious institutions rooted in beliefs about philanthropic giving and/or through state-endorsed forms of giving formulated on notions of collective solidarity and rights-based entitlement to services such as the welfare state. Humanitarian aid workers have tended to consider themselves as continuing philanthropic traditions and not linked up with the profession, although many qualified practitioners work in and manage humanitarian bodies, and humanitarian workers do social work by another name. Currently, humanitarian aid workers are seeking to professionalise and create regulatory mechanisms independently of social work, thereby replicating the creation of an ethical code, sanctions and other regulatory mechanisms. It is essential that a dialogue ensues between these two groups of professionals to ensure that they do not go their separate ways if social work is not to be fragmented further.

Philanthropic giving is associated with institutions such as: Christian churches through charitable giving; Muslim mosques disbursing zakat; Sikh gudwaras observing vand chhako; Judaism has tzedakah; Hinduism promoting dana; Buddhists urging selfless giving; and so on. Professional social work which began in Europe over 100 years ago (Kendall 2000) has deep roots in philanthropic thought and charitable giving. Since then, professional social work has moved into institutionalised giving through publicly financed provisions including the welfare state which Dominelli (2004) termed 'institutional solidarity', voluntary agencies, and increasingly through philanthro-capitalists who give money to favoured projects in the Global South, e.g. mosquito nets to reduce malaria (Bishop and Green 2008).

Other charitable responses occur when disasters, whether natural or human-made, strike and usually entail governmental, professional and individual giving. Contemporary humanitarian aid provided in such situations is structured around institutions linked to the United Nations, government departments such as Emergency Planning, international civil society organisations such as the International Federation of the Red Cross and Red Crescent (IFRC), not-for-profit organisations and local non-governmental bodies (NGOs) that provide charitable giving and assistance. Additionally, social workers are involved in government bodies specially created to provide safety and services during both natural and human-made disasters. These include: aid distribution departments such as the British DfID (Department for International Development) that provides aid for countries in Africa and Asia; Canada's CIDA (Canadian International Development Agency) that operates in many countries including those in Latin America; and Sweden's SIDA (Swedish International Development Agency) that funds projects globally including in former Yugoslavian nations after the Balkan Wars of the 1990s; or disaster management agencies such as FEMA (the Federal Emergency Management Agency) in the United States. Yet, while social workers can be involved at all levels and in all bodies that distribute caring services, their voice is seldom heard in the media covering disaster interventions. And, more worryingly for the profession, there is scant attention given to these activities in most mainstream social work curricula (Dominelli 2013a).

In this chapter, I highlight the roles that social workers have played in disaster interventions, including their capacity to work in multidisciplinary teams to enhance the humanitarian services provided. And I consider the relevance of lessons from past disasters that are useful in addressing 21st century conditions including those linked to climate change, which, along with poverty, are proving extremely difficult to eradicate. These two problems expose virtually intractable contemporary challenges for social workers to address. Moreover, they are inextricably linked. Poor people have fewer resources available to reduce or mitigate the impact of either climate change or other types of disasters, and so when these occur, these groups suffer most. Populations in the global South, indigenous peoples, women, children, and black people in the global North are the most adversely affected groups while they have contributed least to creating such problems in the first instance. I draw on empirical research from several projects, one based on the 2004 Indian Ocean tsunami, another on climate change and older people in the UK, and others based on disaster interventions linked to earthquakes and floods[1] and activities conducted under the aegis of the Disaster Intervention and Climate Change Committee of the International Association of Schools of Social Work (IASSW) which I have headed since its inception in 2010. All of these examples indicate that climate change creates new vulnerabilities, has a deleterious impact on people's existing vulnerabilities and reduces their capacity to demonstrate resilience during a disaster and afterwards in the post-disaster reconstruction and prevention processes. Moreover, this work reveals how social workers' transferable skills and values enable them to mobilise people in locality-specific and culturally relevant approaches to mitigate the risks that they will face to livelihoods and wellbeing and demand more accountable and socially and environmentally just solutions that will benefit everyone.

Social work's disaster interventions: historical beginnings

Professional social work began in Europe, with important developments occurring in the UK and the Netherlands towards the end of the 19th century. In the UK, the Settlement Movement and the Charity Organisation Societies (COS) worked on issues of poverty, unemployment and housing among white British working-class people and immigrant groups in East London. The COS focused on casework interventions that focused on individual responsibility and change, while the Settlement Movement sought to address the same problems through community-based collective action and brought in university students including those from Oxford University to foster self-help initiatives. Jane Addams, when she visited community workers in the British Settlement Movement, was so impressed by Toynbee Hall and its initiatives in East London that she imported its model of working into the US and set up Hull House in Chicago. Meanwhile, in the Netherlands, the University of Amsterdam beat the UK in establishing the first university-based course for training social workers by a couple of years. Social work education at tertiary level entered the American academy a few years later (Kendall 2000; Dominelli 1997).

Professional social work's involvement in disaster situations came later. It formally commenced after World War 2 to help rebuild a war-devastated Europe and involved American funding through the Marshall Plan. This included Fulbright Scholarships which allowed selected academics to go to the US to train in social work at doctoral level. Such exchanges promoted the Americanisation of European social work, and impacted heavily upon locality-specific and culturally relevant forms of social work practices[2] in Europe. Many of these were lost as many returning academics and those accessing American literature utilised this external knowledge in the educational programs in their countries of

---

1   The projects are the: Internationalising Institutional and Professional Practices: Community Participation models in the 2004 tsunami in Sri Lanka, funded by the British Economic and Social Sciences Research Council; Built Infrastructures, Older People and Health and Social Care under Conditions of Climate Change (BIOPICCC) funded by the British Engineering and Physical Sciences Research Council (EPSRC); Earthquakes without Frontiers (EwF) project funded by the British Natural Environmental Research Council (NERC) and the ESRC; activities facilitated by the International Association of Schools of Social Work (IASSW) Disaster Interventions and Climate Change Committees, including attendance at the United Nations Framework Convention on Climate Change (UNFCCC), Conference of the Parties (COP) meetings.
2   I invented the term 'locality-specific culturally relevant' forms of social work to avoid using the term 'indigenous' because this term carries so much colonial baggage that I wished to avoid (Dominelli 2000).

origins. There was a certain cachet of sophistication and modernity associated with American social work over local brands. For some countries, the imperialistic mandate was more obvious. Ioakimidis (2010), for example, describes how Greek social work was destroyed through the deliberate policy of Americanising the local curriculum. Similar concerns have been raised by others, including Yip (2005) and the rise of the movement promoting indigenous social work (Hart 2010).

The United Nations (UN) and its associated agencies were crucial in both spreading professional social work across the globe and developing its disaster intervention dimensions. Under its aegis, disaster intervention, or humanitarian aid as it has become known, has grown into a big business involving millions of professional relief workers and volunteers (Pilger 2005). At the same time, governments who have promised substantial sums of aid either do not deliver the full amount, or donate it as tied aid which does not always provide the goods and services that local people either need or want.

The UN opened the Office of the High Commissioner for Refugees (UNHCR) in Geneva in 1950 to take over relief functions previously performed by its Relief and Rehabilitation Administration (UNRRA) in a Europe devastated by war. Expert-led models provided the dominant paradigms for practice, even though the Office of the High Commission on Human Rights (UNHCHR) had underpinned its operations with a commitment to human rights. The UNHCHR was replaced by the Human Rights Council (UNHRC) in 2006 to accommodate objections raised by several countries including the US. A number of other changes occurred in the UN's disaster work infrastructures in the intervening years. They are too detailed for coverage here, but today the main body for delivering humanitarian aid is the Office for the Co-ordination of Humanitarian Affairs (OCHA) which is led by a UN Under-Secretary for Humanitarian Affairs. OCHA replaced the UN's Department of Humanitarian Affairs in 1998 and Valerie Amos has been in charge of OCHA since 2010. OCHA's work is undertaken through the Executive Committee for Humanitarian Affairs, an Emergency Relief Coordinator (Amos), and the Inter-Agency Standing Committee (IASC). Social workers have helped IASC develop the guidelines for psycho-social interventions amongst others, and IASSW (International Association of Schools of Social Work) members helped to translate these into a number of different languages. Other UN agencies with an interest in humanitarian aid are the UNDP, UNFPA, UNHABITAT, UNHCR, UNICEF; the WHO and World Bank; and international non-governmental bodies including the International Committee of the Red Cross and Red Crescent, Oxfam, Save the Children, Christian Aid, World Vision, USAID, and local civil society organisations.

The OCHA-driven infrastructure was created to improve coordination of aid, and integrate inter-agency, multi-sectoral interventions and multi-professional involvement to deliver services more effectively to recipients. While progress has been achieved, the Haiti earthquake of 2010 and the ongoing Syrian civil war have highlighted extensive difficulties in achieving these objectives in complex situations, especially those further complicated by armed conflict and the loss of governance structures. Although lessons have been learnt from these experiences, they indicate the intractable nature of humanitarian aid that gets trapped in the interstices of political power plays in which national sovereignty trumps state duties to care for their citizens and ensure that they can access food, clothing, shelter, medicine, education, health and social services as endorsed by Articles 22 to 27 of the Universal Declaration of Human Rights (UDHR) which all UN member states have ratified.

Observing the implementation of the provisions of the UDHR is a task that social workers can promote (George 2003).

Selected disasters involving substantial social work contributions

The UN defines a disaster as 'widespread extensive damage that is beyond the coping capacity of any community and thereby requires external intervention' (Perez and Thompson 1994). This potentially covers both natural and human-made disasters like earthquakes, tsunamis, flooding, drought and chemical spills respectively. Dominelli (2009) has extended this definition to include poverty as the largest 'human-made' disaster and argues that there is an interaction between these which blurs the boundaries between these two broad types. Additionally, the impact of disasters is exacerbated by poverty, leaving women, children and older people as the most vulnerable groups (Bizzari 2012). Additionally, Dominelli (2012a) builds on Bullard (2000) to suggest that urbanisation and industrialisation based on capitalist social relations jeopardise sustainable solutions to the fundamental causes of many avoidable disasters and highlight the role of sexist, classist and racist power relations in structurally undermining the resilience of exploited and vulnerable populations following a disaster. Social workers, with their concerns about social justice and human rights, are well-placed to advocate for environmentally sound, equitable and socially responsible disaster interventions and cover these in mainstream social work curricula (Dominelli 2013c).

The number of instances in which social workers have worked as humanitarian aid workers is legion and beyond the scope of this short article, so I focus on examples of recent disasters that IASSW has utilised to raise awareness of various issues encountered in providing humanitarian aid. These have drawn upon research and IASSW members' commitment to developing disaster interventions as important arenas for the development of theory and practice. I choose instances that produced developmental milestones in IASSW's recent contributions to the field.

I begin with an initiative emanating from Durham University (Dominelli in the UK) and Metropole University College (Strauss in Denmark) endeavouring to secure support from the IFSW (International Federation of Social Workers) and ICSW (International Council for Social Welfare) to provide a conference on social workers' role in climate change interventions as a side event in the COP (Conference of the Parties) 16 Summit in Copenhagen in December 2009. For this event, given my research on the 2004 Indian Ocean Tsunami, I spearheaded the development of a policy document on social work's role in disasters and another on climate change which were discussed and unanimously ratified at this conference and subsequently approved by the IASSW Board of Directors at its Copenhagen meeting in January 2010. The Copenhagen event raised the profile of climate change and disaster interventions in all three sister organisations (IASSW, ICSW and IFSW). This was followed up by an article challenging practitioners and educators to take this work forward as an integral part of the social work profession (Dominelli 2011). Additionally, the then President of IASSW (Yuen) had the vision to request that I seek IASSW's accreditation to the UNFCCC. Consequently, IASSW has been accredited at UNFCCC and, as head of the Disaster Intervention and Climate Change Committee, I have ensured social work representation at the Cancun (2010), Durban (2011), Doha (2012) and Warsaw (2013) meetings of the UNFCCC. Exhibitions, side-events and media interviews have enabled policy-makers and NGOs to appreciate the role of social work in climate change debates.

However, IASSW's recent involvement in disaster interventions had commenced earlier – in response to the 2004 Indian Ocean Tsunami through the RIPL Network (Reconstructing Peoples' Lives after Disasters) which was agreed by the board at the first meeting chaired by President Abye Tasse to provide both direct aid and capacity-building initiatives in affected communities. This endeavour is described in detail in Dominelli (2013b). Although this began with various universities in the UK, Canada and Slovenia intervening in Sri Lanka and working with local universities (Colombo, Sabaragamuwa, Rahuna) and the National Institute for Social Development (NISD) (the educational body responsible for delivering social work education in that country) only Ljubljana and Durham universities remain involved, primarily through staff and student exchanges that continue to the present. These revolve primarily around assisting long-term reconstruction initiatives and capacity building aimed at improving social work education in Sri Lanka. This work has been conducted primarily through voluntary initiatives funded largely through university staff and student goodwill. However, CIDA funded non-social-work staff at Queen's University to assist NISD in replacing its diploma program in social work with an undergraduate degree in 2006. It helped initiate MA-level studies at NISD as well. The issue of bringing social work education into the university remains a live one, and although there is support for NISD joining Colombo University at staff level, the money needed to do this has not been forthcoming from the Sri Lankan Government which is responsible for NISD through the Ministry of Social Welfare as well as holding the purse-strings for the University Grants Committee (UGC) which then distributes funds amongst all Sri Lankan universities.

IASSW's role in disaster interventions was given a huge boost through President Yuen's support for social work development in the People's Republic of China, particularly following the 2008 Wenchuan earthquake which destroyed large numbers of lives and livelihoods across huge swathes of Sichuan Province. These interventions are strongly embedded amongst staff based at Hong Kong Polytechnic University and described at length in Sim et al. (2013). Along with other IASSW colleagues, I have made modest contributions to training events focusing on disaster interventions aimed at capacity building and curriculum development in China. Other crucial developments here have involved community development initiatives (Ku et al. 2009), psychosocial work (Sim 2011), and interdisciplinary work that crosses the physical and social sciences to build resilience before, during and after disasters (Dominelli 2012a, 2012b). Additionally, Yuen's energy resulted in the creation of other joint initiatives including the formation of the Institute of Disaster Management and Reconstruction (IDMR) with Sichuan University in Chengdu which was launched in early 2013. These diverse threads are being woven together and are highly influential in the future development of green or disaster-based interventions in social work in China. Additionally, the Sichuan experience, along with the Sri Lankan one which were presented at an ESRC Festival of Social Science Event in Durham in late 2012, inspired local residents who listened to these presentations in a disadvantaged part of that city and saw the picture exhibition based on Sim's work in Yingxiu to consider using photography to enhance their own resilience and tell their stories in surviving poverty locally. This provides an excellent illustration of how Asian experiences can influence developments in the West. Social workers can undertake more work that encourages flows of information and lessons from abroad to the West, in what I term reciprocated knowledges (Dominelli 2004).

The 2010 earthquakes in Haiti and Chile also provided opportunities for IASSW to contribute to disaster interventions both in providing practical help, increasing awareness of the issues involved in developing community preparedness and promoting capacity-building initiatives. IASSW members from universities in the Caribbean, Canada and the UK sought to provide practical help and support for victim-survivors in Haiti. Colleagues from the Caribbean highlighted inappropriate interventions in Haiti, including the limited distribution of aid amongst those affected; the treatment of children by some agencies; fragmented service provision; and the implications of inadequate health care for the future health of victim-survivors. Funding from Durham University facilitated the engagement of Haitian-origined staff in the University of Montreal to strengthen their links and interventions with affected social work educators in Port-au-Prince and contribute to seminars aimed at building capacity in social work in the Haitian capital city which was virtually totally destroyed – its infrastructure, public institutions, governance structures – and resulting in huge casualties. It also provided the first instance in which physical scientists and social scientists at Durham University were able to highlight landslide hazards for social scientists and for the IASSW member to pass this information on to practitioners on the ground

In Chile, IASSW members from the UK, Hong Kong and different parts of Latin America provided seminar training aimed at building capacity for disaster intervention. During the course of their visit to the country, Chileans' own contributions to capacity building and curriculum development, housing construction and preparedness initiatives were shared amongst those present, and highlighted the importance of local initiatives led by the indomitable Malvina Ponce de Leon in strengthening the knowledge held by social work practitioners and educators in the country. The many lessons the overseas visitors took away with them covered the importance of sound housing construction in reducing the number of fatalities during earthquakes; networks of support at local and international levels; and the constant updating of curriculum materials to ensure the inclusion of the latest research data and the mainstreaming of disaster interventions in what is taught to social work students

The lessons learnt through these disaster interventions culminated in the creation of the Christchurch Virtual Helpline and the development of a virtual means of support for hard-pressed practitioners responding to endless aftershocks (11,000 in one year) and stressed victim-survivors of the 'double-whammy' inflicted by the 2010 and 2011 earthquakes in Christchurch, New Zealand. Using the insights of IASSW initiatives, those collected through data arising from the research projects identified below (in note 1) and the Disaster Intervention and Climate Change Committee, I sought to gather the energies of many IASSW members who wanted to respond to a request that IASSW assist practitioners and victim-survivors in Christchurch (Dominelli 2012a). Without any additional resources to help reach this objective, I used technologies offered by the internet and mobile phone to lead the development of ethical guidelines and bring together a group of social work educators and practitioners who were willing to support people in Christchurch who could contact them by telephone, email and Skype in dealing with the traumas that arose from these two earthquake events. The ethical procedures and Christchurch Virtual Helpline model were offered to IASSW members responding to the Fukoshima multiple-hazard disaster in Japan (Akimoto) later in 2011.

The 2013 Lushan earthquake in China led to the further integration of knowledge held by physical and national scientists, utilising the expertise held in the Earthquake without Frontiers (EwF) Project funded by the Natural Environmental Research Council (NERC) in the UK which involved a multi-stakeholder consortium in studying the Alpine-Himalayan Continental Plate (i.e. Earthquake Belt), with particular emphasis on Kazakhstan, Nepal, Bihar (India) and the Ordos Plateau (near Xi'an) in China. This consortium, based on British universities – Cambridge, Durham, Hull, Leeds, Northumbria and Oxford – expanded to include Hong Kong Polytechnic University and the Institute of Disaster Management at the Tata Institute of Social Sciences in India. Responding to the needs of the victim-survivors in Lushan involved a different form of virtual, voluntary support and was led by Durham University's social sciences head for the in-country EwF project in China. This disaster struck a few weeks before the head of the IASSW Disaster Intervention and Climate Change Committee and the current IASSW President (Nadkarni) were to go to Chengdu to celebrate the launch of the IDMR.

As the social sciences lead for EwF's work in China, I had met physical science colleagues at the Chinese Earthquake Administration (CEA) and practitioners linked to Red Cross China earlier. Consequently, I was able to find out what was happening on the ground through the internet-based information technologies, particularly email and Skype. As I had already distributed the Humanitarian Aid and Disaster Intervention Toolkit, Manual and Handbook, based on the ESRC 2004 Indian Ocean Tsunami Project at an OCHA meeting in Copenhagen in March 2013, it was available for me to offer for utilisation in this incident. Colleagues in the CEA and Hong Kong Polytechnic University volunteered to translate parts of it for use by practitioners responding to the needs of the Lushan earthquake victim-survivors, a number of whom had been adversely affected by both the 2008 Wenchuan and 2013 Lushan earthquakes. Additionally, I was able to call upon the landslide hazard expertise at Durham University and passed their maps identifying these hazards to practitioners on the ground in Lushan. These maps identified the areas where camps should not be sited because the risk of landslides would be too high. Thus, physical and social scientists showed that, by working together, knowledge could be shared and used to inform decision-making and practice in complex, dangerous situations.

This model of interdisciplinarity utilisation of physical sciences and social sciences knowledge through collaborative endeavours was used subsequently to inform practitioners and academics involved in supporting those affected by the Uttarkhand floods during the summer of 2013. IASSW members including Nikku, Dominelli and President Nadkarni worked together to support local people and apply for funds to conduct research to improve preventative responses to future floods. The Tata Institute and Nepal School of Social Work sent staff and students to assist the local universities. Durham did not because lack of local knowledge and funds meant doing so was inappropriate and could jeopardise local initiatives and also place additional pressure on scarce resources including those linked to helping people reach safety. The stress they place on hard-pressed resources is something volunteers should think about before they go into a disaster situation (Dominelli 2012a). Once again, the landslide expertise at Durham University was harnessed to provide much needed information about this particular hazard and then given to academic staff, students and practitioners on the ground in Uttarkhand. Funds to further develop this work in this area are being sought. Academics at the Hemwati Nandan Bahuguna Garhwal University and their students are key players in these initiatives to ensure that all interventions are locality-specific and culturally relevant.

Although these interdisciplinary, multi-stakeholder approaches to disasters are discussed to some extent in Dominelli (2012a, b), these instances highlight the importance of further development in this newly emerging area of professional practice – green social work. Green social work has sought to develop theory and practice to a different level than either ecological social work or disaster social work which has either largely ignored the physical environment as in ecological social work (see Gill & Jack 2007) or environmental social work which ignores a holistic approach rooted in a structural critique of current models of socioeconomic development including hyper-urbanisation, structural poverty and political marginalisation according to diverse social divisions and neoliberal social relations (van Wormer et al. 2011; Sim et al. 2013). Although IASSW activities have drawn upon and disseminated the green social work model in response to requests for help, as a flexible, locality-specific culturally relevant one, it is essential that the lessons learnt from the examples considered above are made known more widely and developed further to ensure that social work's roles and responsibilities in disaster interventions and climate change are better debated, understood, theorised and practiced. Crucial to this is partnership working within an egalitarian, social justice and human rights–based framework that is led by local people. I now turn my attention to considering some of the opportunities and challenges entailed in conducting such work.

Learning from past disaster interventions for future responses

The combination of direct action and research illustrated through the above discussion reveals that with leadership, commitment and energy, social work can innovate and foster practice in new directions and promote the production of shared knowledge and learning. IASSW can play a crucial role in growing this emerging aspect of the profession – green social work – by:

- developing interdisciplinary approaches to both natural and human-made disasters
- co-producing solutions with local players
- enhancing local initiatives and resilience
- developing disaster intervention curricula that are locality-specific and culturally relevant
- promoting locality-specific and culturally relevant practices under the leadership of local players, even when they draw upon knowledge and expertise emanating from countries based overseas and contribute to the interrogation and further development of such knowledge and expertise
- promoting the translation of scientific knowledge for local use while passing on local knowledge that can inform scientific discussions
- strengthening the role of the social work profession in disaster interventions and climate change discussions locally, nationally and internationally.

Challenges that need addressing include:

- lack of resources to innovate in theory and practice
- difficulties in implementing socially just and environmentally sustainable approaches to disaster interventions, especially in complicated situations where local resources and expertise have been destroyed by the disaster and/or armed conflict

- tensions in co-producing solutions among local players themselves and between overseas and local players
- compassion fatigue among donors and helpers
- overcrowded social work curricula for mainstreaming to occur easily
- including humanitarian aid workers in the social work profession
- low levels of social work influence amongst practitioners and policy-makers.

The identified opportunities are useful in developing social work's potential to contribute to debates about and interventions in disaster interventions. The Global Agenda developed by IASSW, IFSW and ICSW has one of its four pillars based on sustainable development. This can facilitate the compilation of good practice and relevant theories that are being used to promote social workers' practical engagement with the issues raised above across the world, but also to strengthen the profession's voice within the UN and other international bodies (Truell and Jones 2012).

The above challenges will require extensive action at the local and national levels to ensure that political commitment to supporting disaster victim-survivors is given priority and resources, and people are given dignity in having their needs met as they determine them. It is also about enabling local populations who might provide funds and resources to do so. This might involve social workers providing information about how earlier funds were used and which groups were covered by their distribution. And it is about convincing national governments and politicians to uphold their promises of aid, but also to remove any conditions that restrict their use to advantage the donor-country, not the receiving one.

Social workers have transferrable skills in interviewing people, mobilising resources, raising consciousness about social problems that affect the wellbeing and livelihoods of people, flora, fauna and the physical environment and facilitating the development of solutions and actions that bring communities together in institutional expression of solidarity, individual initiatives promoting goodwill, and enhancing understandings of the interdependent connectivities that mean that finding solutions to the problems initiated by climate change will benefit every living being on planet earth.

References

Bishop, M. & Green, M. (2008). *Philanthro-capitalism: how the rich can save the world*. London: Bloomsbury Press.

Bizzari, M (2012). Protection of vulnerable groups in natural and man-made disasters. In A. de Guttry, M. Gestri & G. Venturini (eds), *International response law* (pp. 381–414). The Hague: TMC Asser Press.

Bullard, R. (2000). *Dumping in Dixie: race, class and environmental quality* (3rd edn). Boulder, CO: Westview Press.

Desai, A. (2007). Disaster and social work responses. In Dominelli, L. (ed.), *Revitalising communities in a globalising world* (pp. 297–314). Aldershot, UK: Ashgate.

Dominelli, L. (2013a). Social work education for disaster relief work. In M. Gay, J. Coates & T. Hetherington (eds), *Environmental social work* (pp. 280–97). London: Routledge.

Dominelli, L. (2013b). Empowering disaster-affected communities for long-term reconstruction: intervening in Sri Lanka after the tsunami. *Journal of Social Work in Disability and Rehabilitation*, 12(1–2): 48–66. DOI: 10.1080/1536710X.2013.784175.

Dominelli, L. (2013c). Gendering climate change: implications for debates, policies and practices. In M. Alston & K. Whittenbury (eds), *Research, action and policy: addressing the gendered impacts of climate change* (pp. 77–94). Sydney: Springer.

Dominelli, L. (2012a). *Green social work.* Cambridge: Polity Press.

Dominelli, L. (2012b). Social work in times of disasters: practising across borders. In M. Kearnes, F. Klauser & S. Lane (eds), *Critical risk research: practices, politics and ethics* (pp. 197–218). Oxford: Wiley-Blackwell.

Dominelli, L. (2011). Climate change: social workers' roles and contributions to policy debates and interventions. *International Journal of Social Welfare,* 20(4): 581–89.

Dominelli, L. (2010). *Social work in a globalising world.* Cambridge: Polity Press.

Dominelli, L. (2009). *Introducing social work.* Cambridge: Polity Press.

Dominelli, L. (2004). *Social work: theory and practice for a changing profession.* Cambridge: Polity Press.

Dominelli, L. (2000). International comparisons in social work. In R. Pearce & J. Weinstein (eds), *Innovative education and training for care professionals: a providers' guide* (pp. 25–42). London: Jessica Kingsley.

Dominelli, L. (1997). *Sociology for social workers.* London: Macmillan.

George, S. (2003). Globalising rights? In M. J. Gibney (ed.), *Globalising rights* (pp. 15–33). Oxford: Oxford University Press.

Gill, O. & Jack, G. (2007). *The child and family in context: developing ecological practice in disadvantaged communities.* Lyme Regis, UK: Russell House Publications.

Hart, M. (2010). Critical reflections on an aboriginal approach to helping. In M. Gray, J. Coates & M. Yellow Bird (eds), *Indigenous social work around the world: towards culturally relevant education and practice* (pp. 129–40). Aldershot, UK: Ashgate.

Ioakimidis, V. (2010). Expanding imperialism, exporting expertise: international social work and the Greek project. *International Social Work,* 54(4): 505–19.

Kendall, K. (2000). *Social work education: its origins in Europe.* Alexandria, VA: CSWE Press.

Ku, H. B., Yuen-Tsang, A. & Liu, H. C. (2009). Triple capacity building as critical pedagogy: a rural social work practicum in China. *Journal of Transformative Education,* 7(2): 146–63.

Perez, E. & Thompson, P. (1994). Natural hazards: causes and effects. *Pre-Hospital Disaster Medicine,* 9(1): 80–88.

Pilger, J. (2005). The other tsunami: cover story, *The New Statesman,* 10 January. Retrieved on 20 January 2006 from www.johnpilger.com.

Sim, T. (2011). Developing an expanded school mental health network in a post-earthquake Chinese context. *Journal of Social Work,* 11(3): 326–30.

Sim, T., Yuen, A., Chen, H.Q. & Dong, Q. H. (2013). Rising to the occasion: disaster social work in China. *International Social Work,* 56(4): 544–62.

Truell, R. & Jones, D. (2012). The global agenda. *International Social Work,* 55(4): 454–72. DOI: 10.1177/0020872812440587.

van Wormer, K., Besthorn, F.H. & Keefe, T. (2011). *Human behavior and the social environment, macro level: groups, communities and organisations.* NY: Oxford University Press.

Yip, K. S. (2005). A dynamic Asian response to globalisation in cross-cultural social work. *International Social Work,* 48(5): 593–607.

26

Social work education: current trends and future directions

Vishanthie Sewpaul

This chapter deals with changing patterns of social work education in a rapidly globalising world. Neoliberalism and advances in information technology are creating spaces for cross-border, virtual education as never before. The chapter interrogates the impact of neocolonial, capitalist expansion of higher education as a tradable commodity, and reviews some of the debates around the universal and the particular with regard to cross border virtual education. The universal-particular debate is further probed by reviewing global initiatives of the International Association of Schools of Social Work (IASSW) and International Federation of Social Workers (IFSW), such as the Global Definition, program consultations linked to the Global Standards, and the proposal to form regional centres of excellence. While well-intentioned, neither the processes nor the outcomes of these initiatives are neutral, often reflecting geo-political power, the project of legitimation, hegemonic discourses and neoliberal and new managerialist thrusts towards standard setting, performance appraisals and external reviews within modernist notions of progress and development.

Neoliberalism, fuelled by the profit motive and the exponential rise in the use of information technology in offering cross-border education, has serious implications for social work education where process, relationship building, reflexivity and ethical reasoning and practices are core. Social work education must be underscored by an emancipatory pedagogy, designed to engage students as active social citizens, skilled in the art of truly being there for the other (Bauman 1993). Yet, the offering of whole degrees online is reducing the complexities of teaching and learning to transferable skills to be applied in the labour market (Martin & Peim 2011; Tomusk 2004), and it compromises the ethical imperatives of social work education (Reamer 2012a) and practice (Reamer 2012b). The International Association of Schools of Social Work (IASSW) and the International Federation of Social Workers (IFSW), as global bodies representing social work educators and practitioners, respectively, have been engaging in a number of global initiatives. These include the Global Definition, program reviews linked to the Global Standards for Social Work Education and Training (Sewpaul & Jones 2004 – hereafter referred at as the 'Global Standards'), and proposals to initiate regional centres of excellence. While well-intentioned, neither the processes nor the outcomes of these initiatives are neutral, often reflecting the complexities of geo-politics, hegemonic discourses and the neoliberal and new managerialist thrusts towards standard setting, performance appraisals and external reviews within modernist notions of progress and development. One of the defining features of neoliberal capitalist expansion is for-profit cross-border online education.

Neoliberalism and cross border education in the digital age

Neoliberalism refers to a combination of socioeconomic and political discourses and policy choices based on the values of an unregulated market, the reification of individual freedom and choice, and faith that market fundamentalism would promote economic growth, efficiency, progress and distributional justice, primarily through trickle-down effects. Neoliberalism, which privileges the market above human wellbeing and welfare (Coburn 2006; Clegg 2011; Harvey 2005; Giroux 2002; Roberts 2009; Shumar 1997; Sewpaul & Hölscher 2004), is underscored by maximising exports, reduced social spending and reorganising 'national economies in order to become parts of a broader regime of transnational economic activity' (Rizvi & Lingard 2000, 423). Higher education has not escaped the impacts of neoliberalism, with educators confronting 'the harsh realities of commodity production: speed-up, routinisation of work, greater work discipline and . . . the insistent managerial pressures to reduce labour costs in order to turn a profit' (Noble 1999, 46), and neglect of the development of critical thinking with managerialist discourses on what works, narrowly defined evidence, throughputs, effectiveness and efficiency (David 2011; Giroux 2002; Sewpaul & Hölscher 2004; Sewpaul 2013a). Neoliberalism has intensified racialised and gender inequality (Clegg 2011; Sewpaul 2013a); reconstructed students into consumers or customers (Noble 1999; Clegg 2011; Shumar 1997) and professors into entrepreneurs with their roles increasingly being mediated by digital technology; and increased surveillance (Lewis 2010; Noble 1999). It has replaced collegiality and trust with contracts, competitiveness, individuality and performance indicators (Roberts 2009). While there is some resistance in response to the corporatisation and commodification of higher education, the danger is that universities are taking on the dominant discourse, treating neoliberalism as inevitable and actively participating in its reproduction by self-consciously embarking on bureaucratic rationalisation (Coburn 2006). Roberts (2009) contends that neoliberalism, through its state apparatus (Althusser 1971), fosters an ideologically compliant, adaptable and technically skilled workforce – unthinking workhorses that serve the needs of the market. Rationalisation of resources; down-sizing of staff; privileging of research, particularly funded research at the expense of teaching; generating third stream funding; and extending university offerings to maximise profits, are becoming naturalised features of universities. These are accompanied by incentives for staff who do comply, and disincentives and/or threats for those who do not. Meyer (2000) argues that 'world society does not simply arise, rather, it is built by agentic state and non-state actors, who (often eagerly) participate in (its) formation' (241, brackets in original).

One of the major agents of the neoliberal agenda is the World Bank (WB). Salmi (2000), a WB educationalist, in valorising the rapid changes in higher education powered by information technology, said:

Imagine a university without classrooms or even a library. Imagine a university 10,000 miles away from its students. Imagine a university without required courses or majors or grades . . . Imagine ranking institutions by their degree of Internet connectivity. Imagine a country whose main export earnings came from the sale of higher education services. Imagine a socialist country that charged full-cost tuition fees in public higher education. (2)

Linked with the WB is the World Trade Organization (WTO) in the higher education business. Nation states are increasingly engaging in free trade agreements in compliance with WTO obligations of trade in the service sector, including the buying and selling of higher education (Coburn 2006; Knight 2008; Naidoo 2007; Walsch 2009). Educational neo-colonial, capitalist expansion has become consolidated through online distance education and virtual learning environments, with commercial vendors playing a major role (Knight 2008). Education has become a new form of 'academic colonialism' (Tomusk 2004, 156). The US leads the world in educational export, with education being one of its top five service exports, followed by the UK, Australia and New Zealand (Martin and Peim 2011). These countries have become the biggest sellers of education on the international market, especially with the increasing demands from countries such as India, China and Malaysia (Department of Foreign Affairs and Trade 2005). Higher education has become a multimillion-dollar business (Kaur & Manan 2010), with many richer countries becoming dependent on income from fee-paying students from poorer countries (Stanley 2012). It is estimated that the e-learning market will be worth about $69 billion by 2015 (Martin & Peim 2011). In 2003/2004 education services were worth AUD$5.9 billion to the Australian economy (a 13% increase from 2002/2003); 95% of this was earned from international students living in Australia, where education is the fastest growing service export (Department of Foreign Affairs and Trade 2005). According to Vincent-Lancrin (2011), in 2010 education became Australia's number one service export item, earning $17.7 billion. Salmi (2000), the WB educationalist, in the face of all things not being equal, proclaimed a blatant untruth: 'The best universities of any country can reach out across borders by means of the Internet or satellites, effectively competing with any national university on its own territory' (2). Furthermore, as Marginson (2006) avers, 'emerging nations are colonised by the "brain drain" of key personnel and ideas, by foreign research conversations and agendas, and by the in-your-face visibility and robustness of the leading foreign institutions' (20).

Developing countries in Asia and Africa, for various reasons, including increasing domestic demand, poor infrastructure and resources, the ubiquitous devaluing of knowledge that emerges from these contexts, and the valorising of so-called Western knowledge that enables its universalisation, are unable to export education, thus reinforcing unequal power relations and patterns of domination and subordination (David 2011; Naidoo 2007; Shumar 1997; Tomusk 2004). Courses designed in the developed world are exported into developing countries, with the quality of such programs being brought into question (Knight 2008; Naidoo 2007; Noble 1999; Walsch 2009). Tomusk (2004) writes of the immorality of 'making developing countries pay for a random selection of Western trivialities delivered through global distance learning consortia' (147). Cross border education provides a lucrative market for Western course packages and textbooks that are transferred wholesale, e.g. from the US or Australia into China, with nothing changed except translation from English into Chinese. Such academic imperialism ignores local contexts and cultures (Coburn 2006; Naidoo 2007; Tomusk 2004; Walsch 2009). Cross border offshore and online providers are also more likely to have English as the medium of instruction, while local universities retain the vernacular (Knight 2008; Kaur & Manan 2010). Kaur and Manan (2010), for example, write about this in the context of Malaysia, warning that with transnational private Western providers using English as the medium of instruction while local public providers use the Malay language, ethnic polarisation is likely to ensue. They also warn about potential class conflicts, as highly marketable courses get priced out of the reach of those in low-income brackets. These are inconsistent with the broad objective of education, promoting the public good, and with social work education's particular emphases on social inclusion, human rights, social justice and peaceful co-existence.

While online distance education might have increased access to some, it has, at the same time, contributed to greater inequalities (Altbach 2010; Naidoo 2007; Tomusk 2004). David (2011) asserts that 'the hyper-marketisation of education as a commodity [and] . . . the embeddedness of neoliberal forms of markets, competition and league tables' (160) has seen more entrenched structural inequalities, both within countries and across the global North and the global South. Chau (2010) argues that the range of technologies required in online learning widens the digital divide between the rich and the poor. The growing hype about technology-mediated education masks the reality that not everyone has the resources for it. According to Walsch (2009), in 2006, 98.5% of Africans were without internet. In Brazil access to the Internet reflects the stark difference between the rich and the poor – with 58.7% of the rich and only 5.7% of the poor having Internet access in 2006.

Of particular salience to social work education is neoliberal capitalist engendering of greater inequality, decreased social justice, and the offering of skills training via vocationally oriented curricula rather than knowledge and critical reflexivity (David 2011; Kaur & Manan 2010; Roberts 2009; Sancar & Sancar 2012). The mechanistic use of online learning recasts students as passive consumers of pre-packaged instructional commodities, and deprives teaching and learning of the 'delight of the warm and caring human voice and touch' (Sancar & Sancar 2012, 247). This has implications for emancipatory social work education, where the aim is to have graduates who are critically and actively engaged social citizens who are willing to use their voices in the interests of deepening democracy and social justice. There is a difference between the use of technology to enhance teaching, the use of blended on and off-campus teaching, and the offering of whole qualifications online.

Social work's and social work education's major strength is that it is context specific (Sewpaul & Jones 2004), yet with global shifts, and with online offering of social work degrees, education is becoming de-contextualised. Reamer (2012a), while not eschewing the use of technology in education, raises a number of ethical concerns about the offering of whole social work qualifications online. He asks the following questions: 'Does an online program sufficiently honor social work's longstanding commitment to human relationships?'; 'Can we be assured that online programs provide sufficient quality control?'; 'Are online programs meeting their ethical duty to be forthright in their representations to the public?' On deliberation, these questions are answered in the negative. Reamer points to the deleterious effects of online social work education (2012a) and online social work therapeutic intervention (2012b). The human experience cannot be understood outside of its social context. This applies as much to educators and students and the people whom we educate students to work with. Universalising discourses vis-a-vis contextualisation, and their link with dominant neoliberal and neocolonial practices, are some of the challenges facing IASSW as it embarks on global processes.

IASSW global processes

It is in the light of the above processes of globalisation, the commodification of higher education and new managerialist practices that the global processes of the IASSW must be understood. The IASSW does not exist in a vacuum. It is embedded within broader societal processes and discourses that have become inscribed into it. The IASSW deals with these global hegemonic discourses with a somewhat uneasy tension: on the one hand developing polices and guidelines that might serve to challenge and contest them, while at the same time adapting to and embracing the perceived inevitability of the global patterns. Like universities and other societal institutions, IASSW, as part of the ideological state apparatus (Althusser 1971) reinforces dominant discourses and patterns, and engages in projects of legitimation. Reflecting the broader schizophrenic world that we live in, IASSW tries to integrate into a coherent whole disparate threads and dichotomies. While the visioning and ideological underpinnings speak to research, knowledge, social development, civic engagement, social inclusion, human rights and social justice, these are juxtaposed against an instantiated geo-political inequality, the cloak of cultural diversity that might work against universal human rights discourses and practice, and new managerialist endeavours favouring global-standards setting, quality assurance and program reviews, and setting up regional centres of excellence and knowledge hubs that are part of the wider neoliberal, competitive agenda.

Setting up of regional hubs of excellence

In facilitating a process and structure wherein institutions compete to become regional hubs in higher education, IASSW inscribes into itself the function of validation and legitimation, as do national governments. Naidoo (2007), for example, writing in relation to the impacts of neoliberalism in higher education, highlights the Malaysian Government's aim to become an Asian hub for higher education, whilst developing partnerships with foreign institutions in Qatar, UAE and Kuwait. These countries are similarly competing to transform themselves into regional centres of excellence for the Middle East. Many countries aspire to host world-class institutions of higher learning. Singapore's education minister, Teo Chee Hean (cited in Altbach 2000), spoke of making Singapore 'the Boston of the East' (7), with world-class universities that are productive, lucrative and globally competitive. Despite Singapore's success, Altbach (2000) warned that this was not easy. What makes it difficult are the 'formidable' structural challenges in relation to geography, history, and the more inflexible governance that influences the epistemological foundations of education, that Singapore experiences relative to Boston's advantages (Altbach 2000, 8). Brezis (2012) attributes the high ranking of US universities primarily to flexibility of governance with minimal state interference – 'the sine qua non of quality and success' (173). He argues for greater public funds for research, while discouraging all other state intervention. These advantages ensure that the US holds prime position in global university rankings. Brezis

(2012) reports that in terms of the Shanghai rankings, among the 50 top ranked universities, 75% are from the US.

By 'endorsing regional centres of excellence (IASSW Social Work Educational Resource Centres)' (www.iassw-aiets.org/uploads/file/20121025_iassw-12-uk.pdf), the IASSW will allow institutions to gain legitimacy, increase their positional goods (Marginson 2006), attract more elite and fee-paying students, reproduce global competition in qualification offerings and 'uni-directional student flows and asymmetrical cultural transformation' (Marginson 2006, 18), as discussed above. Given the criteria set by the IASSW for institutions to become regional hubs, existing patterns of inclusion and exclusion will be reinforced. One can hardly envisage, for example, an institution in Somalia having the infrastructure and the capacity to compete with an institution in South Africa to become a regional hub. Amongst the criteria set by the IASSW are the following:

- Evidence of being an accredited institution, recognised by the local government / professional association, signifying their mandate to offer social work education programs at the postgraduate level and above.
- Strong track record in offering high quality social work education and training programs.
- Commitment to regional development and culturally appropriate practices based on a demonstrable track record of such activities.
- Access to venues and facilities suitable for accommodating capacity-building programs for IASSW member institutions and participants from the region. (IASSW Regional Resource Centres, Operational guidelines for establishing and monitoring Regional Resource Centres, 1 September 2013)

Global standards and program consultations

Similar arguments apply to IASSW program reviews – what has been recast as program consultations. IASSW offers 'a globally diverse team of consultants', 'the use of globally agreed standards' and 'extensive experience, through its membership, in delivering and promoting high quality social work education' (IASSW program consultation, operational guidelines for peer consultations, dated 9 July 2013) to undertake program reviews. This document, which speaks of engaging with host institutions as 'critical friends' in a collaborative manner, represents a radical shift from its earlier version (Operation and guidelines for curriculum review, dated 24 January 2013), where IASSW represented itself as an external agent, doing reviews of institutional programs, with no participation from members of host institutions, except as providers of information. In terms of process, the earlier document read: 'The IASSW team will request meetings with all stakeholders including the management, teaching faculty members, administrators, students in the program, field instructors, other agency representatives and any other/s identified by the university/social work program. These key interest groups will also be invited to give feedback on the review process and findings' (Operation and guidelines for curriculum review, dated 24 January 2013). So normalised was this top-down paradigm that it took much to challenge the gulf between the rhetoric, that spoke to 'peer reviews', 'partnerships' and 'cultural appropriateness', and the operationalising process that reflected a tokenistic view of participation.

In an email dated 5 February 2013, I communicated the following to the board:

I have a problem with the very idea of IA doing audits/reviews. IA does not have any legitimate authority to do so; it is top-down and reflects an assertion of power. Should an institution ask for a review we should encourage them to use national/regional bodies responsible for quality assurance (where they exist). Even in the absence of national/regional structures, we should ... encourage the institution's staff to engage in a self-assessment exercise ... Should the institution – via this self-assessment – recognise the need for capacity building with regard to e.g. strengthening of the curricula or research development, they can make a request to IA. This is within our scope and what we can do. In this way we play a facilitative role without the top-down approach. If we do the reviews directly we run risks as we have no control about how our conclusions/judgments/recommendations would be read and interpreted by institutional authorities. Our overarching principle: First do no harm!

Bourdieu (1996) cogently argued that the power and impact of legitimation is proportional to the distance between the legitimating agency and the legitimised. The greater the distance between the legitimating agency and the legitimised, the greater is the power and perceived impact. Thus, scholars and institutions in their home countries are likely to be less validated and validating than those that are external. IASSW, aware of its legitimating power relative to national/regional bodies, persists in its aim to engage directly in program consultations/reviews. Sakaguchi and Sewpaul (2009) indicated how developing countries often enthusiastically and unreservedly accede to the demands of Western professional legitimising. They argued that 'the Global Standards, the international definition and the international code of ethics ... represent a universalising discourse around what excellent social work ought to be' and they ask: 'If IASSW and IFSW are perceived to be the authorised truths, then might it not become a self-imposition that national endeavours emulate global aspirations?' (Sakaguchi & Sewpaul 2009, 8). Fraser (2008) writes of transnational bodies that are 'apparently emancipatory ... which may contain elite biases and do not always manage to live up to their democratic aspirations' (140).

In the 9 July 2013 version of the program consultation document, IASSW asserts that it will play no role in 'Higher Education validation processes or to any professional accreditation activities'. While the latter might entail a formalised statutory process and one that IASSW can easily disengage from, the very engagement in the consultation/review process is an act of validation. If institutions are not seeking validation and legitimacy they are unlikely to engage IASSW in program reviews/consultations. With its offering of a globally diverse team of consultants, with extensive experience in promoting high quality social work education, and with benchmarking against globally accepted standards, programs endorsed by IASSW will be, or perceived to be, validated at the highest level. In a recent national program review of the Bachelor of Social Work at the University of KwaZulu Natal (where the author is employed), mileage was gained by reflecting how the BSW was benchmarked against the Global Standards. In a world of audits, accreditation, reviews and evidence-based credibility, programs do and will seek validation that global institutions, documents and processes proffer. It is part of the legitimation game-playing in higher education, as is the game of publishing, rating and rankings for self and institutional preservation and survival in an increasingly commercialising academic environment. The dominant contemporary message is that individuals and institutions have to 'get with it' or 'get left behind'. There is simultaneously external coercion and repression and internal self-regulation, where individuals are coopted as agents of social control (Fraser 2008).

While promoting the 'development and expansion of social work education' is an overtly stated objective of program reviews, possible covert legitimation and neoliberal objectives remain unacknowledged. IASSW serves as a consultant for a fee. The operational guidelines reflect that the process will generate huge costs for host institutions that are 'expected to cover all direct expenses such as air travel, accommodation, meals and local transport for the IASSW Consultation Team members' with the following fee structure attached to the consultation: for country income of less than US$2000 per annum – $200; earning capacity of between $2001 – $10 000 per annum a proposed fee range of $350–$1000, and for those earning above $10,000 a fee range of $500–$2000. Regional associations are expected to cover a proportion of the consultation fee. The principle underlying the latter proposal is not addressed. Given the structure of IASSW, it is not uncommon for institutions to be fee-paying members of IASSW and not a regional association. Thus, a host institution, which a regional association might be expected to support, might be a member of IASSW but not the regional body.

Apart from validating and legitimating institutions through its global processes, international bodies also engage in their own self-legitimation. Evetts (1995) argued that professions maintain their influence on internationalising processes by placing increased emphasis on the legitimacy and authority of their international bodies. Williams and Sewpaul (2004) acknowledged that the specification of criteria in the Global Standards document, albeit in the form of ideals to be aspired toward, fall within a reductionist, modernist mode of thinking. They asked, 'Are we in modernist fashion continuing the 'discourse of legitimation' (Lyotard 2003, 259) in respect of the status of social work?' Writing six years after the adoption of the Global Standards, Sewpaul (2010), who was co-chair of the Global Standards Committee and the chief architect of the document, answers this question in the affirmative and addresses her uneasy tension about some of the compromises made in the process and the Western inscriptions into the document. Writing earlier, Sewpaul (2005) acknowledged possible pitfalls in developing the Global Standards. As products of our sociopolitical world, we (I write 'we' as I am equally constitutive of the process) are susceptible to ideological hegemony designed to manufacture consent in the interests of capital and the ruling elite. So successfully insidious and embedded is this hegemonic discourse that Sewpaul (2013b) used the metaphor of it being 'inscribed in our blood'.

Although ideology is false consciousness, it is, according to Althusser (1971), about the only consciousness we have. As products of our world, 'those who are in ideology believe themselves by definition outside ideology' (Althusser 1971, 175). Given its non-conscious nature, the 'accusation of being in ideology only applies to others never to oneself' (Althusser 1971, 175) – thus we rarely recognise our own collusion in reproducing prejudices, stereotypes and patterns of inclusion/exclusion and inequalities that we so vehemently oppose. It is difficult to think outside the box, but what Althusser offers us is a critical self-consciousness, that might serve as a precursor to change. Supporting the complexity of the relationship between structure and agency, Althusser (1971) points out the paradox implied by the term 'subject': it means both a 'free subjectivity, a centre of initiatives, author of and responsible for its actions' (182). It also means a 'subjected being ... stripped of all freedom except that of freely accepting his submission' (Althusser 1971, 182); what Sewpaul (2013b) calls 'the voluntary intellectual imprisonment of the free subject' (120). Hall (1985) asks the following:

A critical question in developed liberal democracies is precisely how ideology is reproduced in the so-called private institutions of civil society – the theatre of consent . . . How
a society allows the relative freedom of civil institutions to operate in the ideological field
– day after day, without direction or compulsion by the State. (100)

The normalisation and naturalisation of neoliberalism and new managerialism in social
work education and practice is manifest in an increasing production and dissemination of
quality standards, codes of ethics, procedural manuals, program reviews and assessment
schedules. Thus, global bodies like the IASSW come to serve as 'the theatre of consent' in
reproducing the ideology of neoliberalism and new managerialism.

Review of the global definition

The unacknowledged and perhaps unrecognised reproduction and pursuit of legitimation
and neocolonialism might underlie the global definition processes and outcomes. Since
the adoption of the international definition by the IFSW in 2000 and the IASSW in 2001
there have been criticisms. Despite its popularity, and being one of the most cited definitions, it is a short-lived one. A global definition formulated by the IFSW before this was
in 1957, developed by representatives from Belgium, Denmark, France, Germany, Italy,
Netherlands, Scotland, Sweden and Switzerland. The 2000/2001 definition is radically different from the conservative thrust and gender-biased language of the 1957 definition. The
short-lived nature of the current definition must be viewed positively, reflective of greater
inclusivity of different regions of the world, more robust debate and democratic participation made possible by global communication.

On account of the critiques of the current definition, IASSW and IFSW have, for the
past few years, jointly engaged in processes of consultation to review it. Given the contextual realities of social work, questions have been raised about the wisdom of having a
single definition on a global level. Yet, there is a sense that there must be some unifying
characteristics of social work that grant legitimacy to the existence of international bodies
such as the IASSW and the IFSW. There is also a sense that there are some shared visions
on a global level about what social work is. Even with acceptance, in principle, of the need
for a global definition, the consultation processes have generated huge debates about what
is included or excluded in a global definition, with every word in the proposed new definition scrutinised, and its relevance for all contexts critiqued.

In an email dated 21 July 2013, a colleague Professor Bruce Hall from Colorado State
University made the following observation: 'when all is said, it is essentially a political
process . . . Definitions may be useful at the core, but all fail at the margins'. He referred to
the pseudo-scientific

attempt to define in order to assert . . . power and claim to authority . . . 'The Global Definition' is a good academic exercise. It may help elaborate the core . . . The exercise,
however, has little immediate value for the practice of social work, globally. That practice
is besieged by more dangerous challenges . . . Public and political approbation is unlikely
to sustain social work unless the profession supports and demonstrates commitment to
the claims it already makes.

Notwithstanding the salience of these observations, there are others who believe that definition is of substantive and immediate import. Ioakimidis (2013, 184) asserts that the current definition has 'informed the practice and aspirations of a great number of frontline social workers . . . who have joined the profession out of a commitment to social justice'. The main criticisms, particularly from the Asia-Pacific region, centred on the 2000/2001 definition representing a Western bias with its emphasis on individual rights and social change, to the exclusion of collective rights and the societal imperatives for continuity, stability and social cohesion. Henrickson (2011), for example, argued that: 'Social change, empowerment and liberation, social justice and human rights are not concepts that have shared understandings throughout the world. Concepts such as social harmony, interdependence, and collectively are concepts that are more highly valued in many Asian and indigenous Pacifika communities' (4). Sewpaul (2007) has strongly challenged East–West value dichotomies; the world is not either/or. There is a tendency to idealise Asian culture based on collectivism, respect for family, embodying unifying and holistic principles and intuitive functioning as opposed to Western culture which is represented as fragmented, individualised and reductionistic, which must be challenged.

In contrast with the views of some colleagues from the Asia-Pacific is the Latin-American view that the current definition does not sufficiently speak to radical structural changes. What also emerged very strongly from the Asia-Pacific region was the proposal to include 'indigenous knowledges' in the definition. This is by no means an un-contentious issue. If, for example, a person who self-defines as indigenous writes and publishes in an internationally recognised 'Western' journal, is that knowledge then indigenous or Western? Indigenous peoples have, over the centuries, been making invaluable contributions to knowledge development, which they might not be given credit for. Thus, the dichotomy between indigenous and Western knowledge might be at the peril of indigenous peoples. It might cogently be argued that all knowledge is indigenous to whatever context it originates in. Even where colleagues vehemently argue for culturally appropriate/indigenous social work practices, they often cite Western authors to support their claims – perhaps a reflection of the acceptance of what emerges in the West as authorised truths or the lack of opportunities for non-Western scholars to have their work published. Sen (2005) comments on the 'dual role of the West: the colonial metropolis supplying ideas and ammunition to postcolonial intellectuals to attack the influence of the colonial metropolis!' (133). However, as reflected in the commentary to the proposed new definition, Western hegemony does remain a problem. Knowledge that originates in the West becomes valorised and universalised; the voices of indigenous peoples remain marginalised and silenced; and the West often appropriates indigenous knowledge. There are, nevertheless, some who believe that the inclusion of 'indigenous knowledges' reflects the growing hegemony of the Asia-Pacific region in the IASSW, and the resurgence of conservatism (Ioakimidis 2013) or perhaps a nostalgic throwback to an ordered and gendered society, underscored by Confucian values and practices (Sewpaul 2007).

The 2000/2001 definition was the first to explicitly endorse the principles of human rights, social justice and the liberation of people, inscribing social work with its political and emancipatory mandate. Ioakimidis (2013) expresses concern about 'a power struggle that could potentially endanger the achievements of the previous definition' (184). He refers particularly to the power of China and Japan, 'whose large membership base in international social work organisations allows them to promote the idea of "harmony and stability" over "social change and justice"' (Ioakimidis 2013, 195). There is, according to

Ioakimidis, 'a risk of a backward looking socially conservative definition' (184). This also emerged as a major source of tension in the development of the Global Standards. To accommodate the needs of colleagues from the Asia-Pacific region, while not reneging on the human rights and social justice aims of social work, the Global Standards document dealt with the issues by constantly adding qualifiers e.g. 'Enhance stable, harmonious and mutually respectful societies that do not violate people's human rights' and 'Promote respect for traditions, cultures, ideologies, beliefs and religions amongst different ethnic groups and societies, insofar as these do not conflict with the fundamental human rights of people'. It is the awareness of risk of regressing to conservatism that prompted the committee to add qualifiers in the commentary to the proposed new definition, for example, 'insofar as such stability is not used to marginalise, exclude or oppress any particular group of persons'.

Recognising the diversities of contexts, the Joint Global Definition Committee of the IASSW and the IFSW have taken a principled decision to create space for layered definitions at the global, regional and national levels. Colleagues representing the Asia-Pacific spearheaded this decision. In order to accommodate the particularities of different regions and/or nation states, the committee decided to have a brief, concise and aesthetically appealing definition that will be easily translatable into different languages, while encouraging the amplification of the definition at regional and/or national levels. This is a pragmatic solution to addressing the universal-particular conundrum – acknowledging contextual realities while conceptualising social work as a global profession. Despite making this very clear during the consultation processes, what became evident was that many colleagues wanted their views reflected in a global definition. Given Bourdieu's (1996) thesis of legitimacy resting on the distance between the legitimising agency and the legitimised, it is likely that colleagues will place greater premium on a global definition rather than on a national or regional one.

The final round of consultations ended in September 2013, and it is envisaged that IASSW and IFSW would have approved a definition to be put to their membership for adoption at the General Assemblies of IASSW and IFSW in Melbourne in 2014. A major recommendation that emerged during the latest round of consultations, that generated much debate within the Board of the IASSW, was that social work as a discipline is included in the definition. To this end, the committee proposes that the first line begins with: 'Social work is a practice-based profession and an academic discipline that facilitates social change' rather than: 'The social work profession facilitates social change'. Yet, Sewpaul (2010) pointed out that reference to social work as a profession is a double-edged sword, with the shift from the earlier version of the Global Standards adopted in Adelaide in 2004 (Sewpaul & Jones 2004) to its final version (Sewpaul & Jones 2005) being one of the sources of disquiet for her.

Whether or not the definition will have substantive impact will depend on the extent to which social workers own it, and whether or not, as Hall above states, 'the profession supports and demonstrates commitment to the claims it already makes'. To this end, global bodies like the IFSW and the IASSW, that serve as substantive and symbolic embodiment of social work, must be all the more cognisant of living up to the goals and ideals reflected in the global definition, rather than capitulate to the imperatives of neoliberalism and new managerialism.

Conclusions

For profit online, virtual education challenges all of the major principles and values underscoring social work and social work education. Successful pedagogy rests on the power of the educator to: stimulate students' thinking and imagination; engender a spirit of love of knowledge; link theoretical knowledge to daily lived experiences; engage students in controversial debate and discussion; provide a sense of hope for the future, and encourage students to challenge injustices at local, national and/or international levels (Palmer 2006; Giroux 2002; Freire 1970; 1973; Sewpaul 2013b). Palmer's (2006) first principle is: 'We teach who we are . . . good teaching cannot be reduced to technique . . . good teaching comes from the identity and integrity of the teacher' (6). Online education, driven by neoliberalism, privileges information and vocational instruction, that eschews such constructionist, emancipatory and radical approaches. Clegg (2011) challenges the 'no choice' mantra about adopting new technologies in teaching and asks that we 'puncture the emerging narratives of inevitability and efficiency' (176). Therein might lie an invaluable role for the IASSW.

The commodification of higher education is linked to neocolonial and imperialist capitalist expansion manifested in the language of knowledge/information society, where 'the main beneficiary . . . is the Western supplier of knowledge' (Tomusk 2004, 161). It is also manifested in the way higher education has turned its attention to standards setting; audits and reviews; performance measurement; inputs and outputs; outcomes and targets; and efficiency and effectiveness, conjuring the imagery of excellence and inevitability. Neoliberalism penetrates daily consciousness to the extent that it becomes normalised and naturalised and considered necessary for social order despite the gross race, class, gender and geographic inequalities engendered (Sewpaul 2013a). Haiven (2011) contends that 'we all participate in hierarchies of race, class gender and privilege. No one is a pure victim in this economic system' (1). It is in the light of these processes that universities, and global bodies like the IFSW and the IASSW, must critically reflect on the processes that they adopt and their potential outcomes in reproducing geo-political power and neoliberal and imperialist practices.

As with individuals, global bodies with the benefit of reflexivity have the power to disrupt or to reinforce dominant thinking and taken for granted assumptions. The discourse on legitimation, introduced above, may not in itself be the problem. Reflexivity demands that we question and unmask the veneer of altruism, and the geo-political power that might underlie such legitimation processes. We need to acknowledge both the positive and the possible shadow motivations for our actions, and reflect on our possible complicity in reproducing neoliberalism, neocolonialism and their concomitants. In doing so we might allow the free subject to trump over the subjected being.

References

Altbach, P. (2010). Trouble with numbers. *Times Higher Education*, 23 September, pp. 48–50.

Altbach, P. (2000). Asia's academic aspirations: some problems. *International Higher Education*, 19(1): 7–8. Retrieved on 22 April 2014 from www.bc.edu/content/dam/files/research_sites/cihe/pdf/IHEpdfs/ihe19.pdf.

Althusser, L. (1971). Ideology and ideological state apparatuses. In *Lenin and philosophy, and other essays*. Trans. by Ben Brewster. London: New Left Books.

Bauman, Z. (1993). *Postmodern ethics*. Oxford: Blackwell Publishing.

Bourdieu, P. (1996). *The state nobility*. Stanford: Stanford University Press.

Brezis, E.S. (2012). Why are US universities at the top of the international rankings? In W. Bienkowski, J.C. Brada & G. Stanley (eds), *The university in the age of globalisation* (pp. 155–76). NY: Palgrave Macmillan.

Chau, P.J. (2010). Online higher education commodity. *Journal of Computing in Higher Education*, 22: 177–191. DOI: 10.1007/s12528-010-9039-y.

Clegg, S. (2011). Academic identities re-formed? Contesting technological determinism in accounts of the digital age. *Contemporary Social Science: Journal of the Academy of Social Sciences*, 6(2): 175–89.

Coburn, E. (2006). Commodification or rationalisation? Yes, please!: technology transfer talk in the Canadian context. In G. Krüken & M. Torka (eds), *Diffusion and transformation of higher education models: universities between national traditions and global trends* (pp 235–59). Bielefeld, Germany: University of Bielefeld.

David, M.E. (2011). Overview of researching global higher education: challenges, change or crisis. *Contemporary Social Science*, 6(2): 147–63.

Department of Foreign Affairs and Trade (2005). Education without borders: international trade in education. Australian Government, Economic Analytical Unit. Retrieved on 22 April 2014 from www.dfat.gov.au/publications/eau_education/education_without_borders.pdf.

Evetts, J. (1995). International professional associations the new context for professional projects. *Work, Employment and Society*, 9(4): 226–51.

Fraser, N. (2008). *Scales of justice: reimagining political space in a globalising world*. Cambridge: Polity Press.

Freire, P. (1973). *Education for critical consciousness*. NY: The Seabury Press.

Freire, P. (1970). *The pedagogy of the oppressed*. Harmondsworth: Penguin Books.

Giroux, H.A. (2002). Neoliberalism, corporate culture, and the promise of higher education: The university as a democratic public sphere. *Harvard Educational Review*, 72(4): 425–63.

Haiven, M. (2011). From NYC: 'Occupy Wall Street has no agenda' is an alibi for apathy. *The Media Co-op* (Halifax). Retrieved on 22 April 2014 from www.mediacoop.ca/blog/max-haiven/8378.

Hall, S. (1985). Signification, representation, ideology: Althusser and the post-structuralists debates. *Critical Studies in Mass Communication*, 2(2): 91–114.

Harvey, D. (2005). *A brief history of neoliberalism*. Oxford: Oxford University Press.

Henrickson, M. (2011). An Asia-Pacific response to the discussions on social work definition. Keynote address at the International Symposium on the International Definition of Social Work Review: A voice from Asia and the Pacific, 16 July, Waseda University, Tokyo, Japan.

Ioakimidis, V. (2013). Arguing the case for a social justice based global social work definition. *Critical and Radical Social Work*, 1(2): 183–200.

Kaur, S. & Manan, S.A. (2010). Market forces and globalisation: implications for higher education in Malaysia. Retrieved on 22 April 2014 from www.mohe.gov.my/portal/images/utama/doc/artikel/2012/05–04/Market%20forces%20and%20globalisation.pdf.

Knight, J. (2008). Higher education in turmoil: the changing world of internationalisation. Rotterdam, Netherlands: Sense Publishers.

Lewis, M. (2010). Knowledge commodified and the new economics of higher education. *Journal of Curriculum Theorising*, 26(3): 1–4.

Lyotard, J.F. (2003). From the postmodern condition: a report on knowledge. In L. Cahoone (ed.), *From modernism to postmodernism: an anthology*. Oxford: Blackwell Publishing Ltd.

Marginson, S. (2006). Dynamics of national and global competition in higher education. *Higher Education*, 52(1): 1–39. DOI 10.1007/s10734-004-7649-x.

Martin, G. & Peim, N. (2011). Cross-border higher education, who profits? *Journal for Critical Education Policy Studies*, 9(1): 127–48.

Meyer, J. (2000). Globalisation: sources and effects on national states and societies. *International Sociology*, 15(2): 233–48.

Naidoo, R. (2007). Higher education as a commodity: the perils and promises for developing countries. London: The Observatory on Borderless Higher Education. Retrieved on 22 April 2014 from www.une.edu.au/chemp/projects/monitor/resources/he_global_commodity_observatory.pdf.

Noble, D. (1999). *Digital diploma mills*. London: Monthly Review Press.

Palmer, P.J. (2006). The heart of a teacher: identity and integrity in teaching. Retrieved on 22 April 2014 from www.nvcc.edu/loudoun/cte/HTMLobj806/Parker_Palmer_on_Teaching_and_Learning.pdf.

Reamer, F.G. (2012a). The elephant in the (virtual) classroom: the ethical implications of online social work education. Retrieved on 22 April 2014 from www.socialworktoday.com/news/eoe_080312.shtml.

Reamer, F.G. (2012b). *Boundary issues and dual relationships in the human services*. NY: Columbia University Press.

Rizvi, F. & Lingard, B. (2000). Globalisation and education: complexities and contingencies. *Educational Theory*, 50(4): 419–26.

Roberts, P. (2009). A new patriotism: neoliberalism, citizenship and tertiary education in New Zealand. *Educational Philosophy and Theory*, 41(4): 410–23.

Sakaguchi, H. & Sewpaul, V. (2009). A comparison of social work across Japan and South Africa in relation to the global standards for social work education and training. *International Journal of Social Welfare*, 20(2): 192–202.

Salmi, J. (2000). Facing the challenges of the twenty-first century. *International Higher Education*, 19: 2–3. Retrieved on 22 April 2014 from www.bc.edu/content/dam/files/research_sites/cihe/pdf/IHEpdfs/ihe19.pdf.

Sancar, C. & Sancar, M. (2012). Neoliberal mechanisation of education. *The Turkish Online Journal of Educational Technology*, 11(3): 246–54. Retrieved on 22 April 2014 from www.tojet.net/articles/v11i3/11323.pdf.

Sen, A. (2005). *The argumentative Indian: writings on Indian culture, history and identity*. London: Penguin Books.

Sewpaul, V. (2013a). Neoliberalism and social work in South Africa. *Critical and Radical Social Work*, 1(1): 15–30.

Sewpaul, V. (2013b). Inscribed in our blood: challenging the ideology of sexism and racism. *Affilia: Journal of Women and Social Work*, 28(2): 116–25.

Sewpaul, V. (2010). Professionalism, postmodern ethics and global standards for social work education and training. *Social Work/Maatskaplike Werk*, 46(3): 253–62.

Sewpaul, V. (2007). Challenging East–West value dichotomies and essentialising discourse on culture and social work. *International Journal of Social Welfare*, 16(4): 398–407.

Sewpaul, V. (2005). Global standards: possibilities and pitfalls for re-inscribing social work into civil society. *International Journal of Social Welfare*, 14(2): 210–17.

Sewpaul, V. & Hölscher, D. (2004). *Social work in times of neoliberalism: a postmodern discourse*. Pretoria: Van Schaik Publishers.

Sewpaul, V. & Jones, D. (2005). Global standards for the education and training of the social work profession. *International Journal of Social Welfare*, 14(3): 218–30.

Sewpaul, V. & Jones, D. (2004). Global standards for social work education and training. *Social Work Education*, 23(5): 493–513.

Shumar, W. (1997). *College for sale: a critique of the commodification of higher education*. London: The Falmer Press.

Stanley, G. (2012). Challenges in the quest to create global qualifications and standards are driving change in educational systems. In W. Bienkowski, J.C. Brada & G. Stanley (eds), *The university in the age of globalisation* (pp. 3–25). NY: Palgrave Macmillan.

Tomusk, V. (2004). *The open world and closed societies: essays on higher education policies 'in transition'*. NY: Palgrave Macmillan.

Vincent-Lancrin, S. (2011). Cross border higher education: trends and prospects. *Revista Innovacion Educativa*, 11(56): 86–100.

Walsch, P. (2009). Global trends in higher education: adult and distance learning. Retrieved on 22 April 2014 from www.icde.org/filestore/Resources/Reports/FINALICDEENVIRNOMENTALSCAN05.02.pdf.

Williams, L.O. & Sewpaul, V. (2004). Modernism, postmodernism and global standards setting. *Social Work Education*, 23(5): 555–65.

27

Global education for social work: old debates and future directions for international social work

Lynne M. Healy

Social work is enmeshed in the context of globalisation, offering new opportunities as well as threats to the profession and its educational sector. As a result, interest in international social work has expanded, yet the area remains without a clear definition. This chapter explores three different directions for international social work: as a movement for increased universality in standards for practice and education; as a form of specialised practice; and as the profession's actions and impact on global policy, especially following the adoption of the Global Agenda for Social Work and Social Development. The continuing debates over imperialism and indigenisation are acknowledged and the salience of these for each of the directions is discussed. Implications and recommendations for social work education are addressed.

'By 2020, the question of whether and how to internationalise social work curriculum will have vanished from professional discourse'. Instead there will be 'a long overdue recognition that all is global and that it is counterproductive to divide what is local from what is international' (Healy 2002, 179). It has been more than a decade since these words were published and they were identified as possible fantasy at the time. The idea behind the statement was that social work would come to fully recognise the importance and impact of the global environment, and therefore social work education would seamlessly incorporate relevant global content. With 2020 rapidly approaching, this chapter will assess current and quite diverse directions for international social work and relevant educational strategies. Major debates will be addressed as well as the fact that debates plaguing the field of social work remain the same after decades of scholarly work.

Many scholars recognise that social work practice is enmeshed in the context of globalisation, offering new opportunities as well as threats to the profession and its educational sector (Dominelli 2010; Payne & Askeland 2008; Healy 2008; Lyons 2006). Globalisation has continued to revitalise old debates about international social work, and raised new issues in the 21st century. Contemporary authors continue to discuss the optimal ways for social work and social work education to address the impacts of globalisation. Two issues that continue to shadow international social work are definitional confusion and concern about professional imperialism and accompanying arguments urging indigenisation. Debates continue on these issues and have different salience depending on how international social work is understood. In this paper, three diverse definitions and directions for international social work are discussed, with reference to the recent literature. These are: international social work as a movement for universality in the profession and its standards; international or global social work as a form of practice; and international social work as the roles and impacts of the profession on the global stage and global issues. All address the book's theme of 'crossing borders and blurring boundaries'. However, they have very different implications for social work education and intersect the imperialism/indigenisation debates differently.

There are many definitions of globalisation and it is assumed that readers of this book will be familiar with at least some of these. Deepak, quoting from Gunewardena and Kingsolver, gives a comprehensive and non-judgmental definition of globalisation as 'a set of social and economic processes that entail intensified global interconnectedness via the mobility and flows of culture, capital, information, resistance, technologies, production, people, commodities, images and ideologies' (2012, 781). Embedded here are many elements germane to social work, beginning with the flow of people, and including culture, information, ideologies, resistance and information.

Intensification of the forces of globalisation has increased attention to international aspects of social work. Scholars and practitioners recognise that local manifestations of problems often have global roots. Alphonse, George and Moffatt (2008) write that current problems in India, such as farmer suicide, result from the impact of globalisation on local communities as global markets and control of intellectual property for essential seeds by multinational corporations disrupt the potential for livelihood. Despair also grows among former factory workers in industrialised countries, as outsourcing to distant factories leaves them among the long-term unemployed. Other negative manifestations of globalisation include pollution, new diseases, structural adjustment policies, migration caused by conflicts, climate change, or economic dislocation, and many more. More positively, there are opportunities for global exchange and networking, participation in global civil society movements, and rapid diffusion of helpful technologies including social work knowledge and interventions. In many ways, the 'distance' between the local and the global has been shrinking, resulting in recognition that we face problems that cannot be solved within the boundaries of a nation-state. Furthermore, communication technologies bring an onslaught of information on global conditions easily to our computers or other devices. Recognition of the impacts and opportunities of globalisation are partly responsible for a renewed interest in international aspects of social work.

History of development of the concept of international social work

Although the use of the term international social work can be traced back to the 1928 First International Conference of Social Welfare (Jebb 1929), it is within the past 15 years that scholarship in the field has burgeoned. Beginning with a text by Lyons in 1999, there is now a modest library of books titled 'International social work' or variations on the theme. These are supplemented by journal articles and numerous conference presentations. The expansion of interest and attention to the topic is illustrated by the publication of two major reference works on international social work by well-respected publishers in 2012 (Healy & Link; Lyons, Hokenstad, Pawar, Huegler & Hall). These developments signal a partial maturation of the area, but much remains to be elaborated and negotiated.

The definition and purpose of international social work is still somewhat vague. As recently as 2012, Huegler, Lyons and Pawar stated that international social work 'has a long genesis but unclear definition' (1). Numerous definitions have been proposed, including some that are value or goal based, some that emphasise professional functions or roles, and others that merge the two dimensions (Ahmadi 2003; Cox & Pawar 2006; Healy 2008; Hugman 2010). Hugman and colleagues defined the field as follows: 'international social work refers to education, practice, research, policy and exchanges concerned with the realities of global processes in human wellbeing' (Hugman et al. 2010, 634). They also introduce the idea of crossing borders into the definition, and note that this can be understood in various ways as 'transcending, transmitting, transforming or transgressing borders' (634). The idea of 'globalisation' is discussed as describing the impact of global forces on local realities and the impact of local developments on the global (633), a concept also explored by Lyons (2006). Of note is that definitions have been proposed, critiqued and debated in the professional literature for many decades.

Haug (2005) criticised the dominance of Western scholars in defining international social work. Others have identified the growing interest in international social work as a resurgence of imperialism or a form of neo-colonialism, in which professionals from the global North are drawn to practice or consult in the global South. A further critique is that this practice is sometimes or often irrelevant and perhaps harmful in effect as it imposes theories and modes of intervention that do not fit local circumstances. Briefly, I would point out that Haug's critique captures only a partial view of the field. The scholars she refers to built on the work of earlier experts from South Asia, transplanted to the US, but writing from the perspectives of their roots. We could also more broadly conceptualise the many African, Caribbean and Asian writings on indigenisation, especially those cast in juxtaposition to globalisation, as a part of the literature on international social work. The imperialism debate will be revisited later in the chapter.

To more adequately engage with relevant debates, I turn to examine three quite diverse ways of approaching the purpose and intent of international social work.

International social work as a move to universalise the profession

Cox and Pawar (2006) expanded upon Healy's (2001) functional definition of social work to add a fifth purpose: the promotion of social work and social work education globally. As they state it: 'International social work is the promotion of social work education and practice globally and locally, with the purpose of building a truly integrated international profession' to address significant global issues (20). Trygged (2010) notes the 'universalist tendency in international social work'; as such, 'international social work is a modernity project, since it is looking for a common understanding of social problems and is consequently more focused on sameness than on diversity' (647). He concludes that 'it is a modernity project in recognition of its striving towards universal principles and to overcome some of the contradictions between the universal and the local, as well as in its attempts to find a role for social work in the globalisation process' (653).

Along these lines, we can view the major documents agreed to by the International Association of Schools of Social Work and the International Federation of Social Workers since the beginning of this century as outputs of this modernity and universalism project. Beginning with a new global definition of social work in 2000, the organisations adopted a statement of ethical principles and the first ever set of global standards for social work education in 2004. These documents and the homogenising and universalising implications of international social work have been the target of critiques viewing such efforts as imperialist at worst, or needing to be balanced by significant attention to indigenisation. The Global Standards for the Education and Training of the Social Work Profession in particular has drawn criticism as too Western in orientation (Yip 2004) and for privileging a universalist orientation (Williams and Sewpaul 2004); however, the document was welcomed by many newer programs in Asia and Africa for helping them negotiate with university administrators to strengthen social work. Alphonse et al. (2008), writing from India on the impact of globalisation on local conditions, offered: 'Professional training can no longer happen in isolation, insulated from international processes. Globalisation has necessitated a search for global standards in education and practice' (153).

Rankopo and Osie-Hwedie (2011) contradict this view, emphasising the importance of indigenisation as the development of culturally relevant interventions, recognising and privileging local contexts. They emphasise that social work cannot simply be transplanted, and that the distinguishing feature of social work – that it intervenes at the point where people intersect with their environment – necessitates an indigenous approach. They conclude that 'cultural explanations of social reality are more relevant than those that seek to transcend all cultures' (145). As catalogued by Gray, Coates and Yellow Bird (2008), Rankopo and Osie-Hwedie's article is one of many calling for indigenisation of social work, a theme that dates back to the beginning of the 1970s and has been addressed by authors from Africa, Asia, the Middle East, Europe and North America.

But there are other forces encouraging a more universal approach. Lyons (2006) addressed the growing mobility of social workers as another push factor for global standards. As social workers migrate internationally for employment opportunities, their readiness for the workforce in the new country becomes an issue. If social work training becomes more uniform, there will be less concern about adequacy of educational preparation for those who move from country to country to practice social work. The move to free labour mobility within Europe is noteworthy, but there is also significant recruitment of social workers by the UK, often from countries outside the EU, and migration of professionals from the Caribbean and other areas to the US and Canada. Global standards, now only voluntary, would support increased labour mobility. Therefore, it might be argued that global standards improve social workers' capacity to work abroad, but diminish their effectiveness at home according to those pushing more indigenisation.

The educational implications of the push for recognition of social work as universal would be to do further work to develop globally relevant curriculum. Issues of professional mobility would be taken into account in designing curricula. Further efforts to improve the Global Standards are needed, and we could also expect consideration of systems of accreditation of social work programs globally or at least more agreements for mutual recognition of degrees.

International social work as a practice

One dimension of crossing borders is global or international practice. A number of authors support the concept of an international social work practice (Cox & Pawar 2006; Healy 2008; Hugman 2010) and there are schools of social work in diverse countries, including

Canada, Denmark, Israel and the United States, offering specialisations in global or international practice. The term international social work or global social work has sometimes been used to refer to this, usually inferring that a practitioner from the global North is serving as a development specialist or consultant in the global South, whether working for an international organisation or directly contracted by a global South institution. Interestingly, 'global practice' does not seem to be used as a label for practitioners who may be recruited from the global south to staff social agencies in the UK or the US. If international practice is understood mainly as physically crossing borders, then all practitioners who migrate, whether from North to South or South to North, can be considered practicing international social work. More narrow definitions, however, reserve this label for those working with international organisations and/or on global problems.

Several questions emerge: the first is whether there is such a thing as 'international or global practice' and secondly, if so, whether this is a good idea or something that should be discouraged as inherently imperialistic. And, if there is an international or global practice, how would social work educational programs prepare students for these roles? Are current educational models adequate preparation?

Social work education prepares students to address people's issues in their interactions with their social environment or context. Educational models have long recognised the need for social workers to intervene with systems of varying sizes – indeed some programs claim to prepare students to intervene in systems of 'all sizes'. Rarely, however, is 'all sizes' conceptualised to fully accommodate the global environment and the impact of globalisation. In a 1962 article that apparently attracted little discussion, Goldman suggested international social work as a fourth practice level to address international social problems, complementing the traditional levels of individual, group, and community. Although not entirely a practical notion as stated, his idea could be further interrogated to discern what forms of social work intervention could address international problems effectively.

Webb (2003) contested the idea of international social work, arguing that social work practice requires deep knowledge of local environments, including institutions, culture, laws, and ways of relating. He continues that the very definition of social work—that it is the profession that intervenes at points where people intersect with their environments—means that 'global practice is a practical impossibility' (193). Others raise the concern over imperialism or neo-colonialism when Western professionals design development and relief programs and when staff trained in the global north work on the ground in developing countries. These efforts and interventions may be ineffective due to lack of fit with local realities, or damaging due to the attitudes of superiority and insensitivity of the foreign professionals. The efforts that 'rescue' child labourers without realising or recognising the conditions of their families living in poverty is an example of a well-intentioned, but often inadequate or harmful, approach to a complex problem (Deepak 2012).

Another example comes from the response of Western therapists, including some social workers, to 'rescue' victims of mass disasters, such as the Banda Aceh tsunami. As Bragin said, 'there have been all too many reported instances in which outsiders have been permitted to practice in situations of extreme gravity and do harm through importing external methods of coping while marginalising rather than strengthening indigenous systems' (2012, 514). But – is the answer to withdraw from the arena of international practice or to increase education on appropriate responses? In fact, much was learned from these unfortunate responses to disaster. A committee of representatives from both non-governmental humanitarian agencies and United Nations agencies developed and published the

Inter-Agency Standing Committee Guidelines on Mental Health and Psychosocial Support in Emergency Settings (IASC 2007). Social workers were among those representing NGOs that developed the new guidelines; social work educators can take up the responsibility of including these guidelines in its preparation of professionals, thereby improving practice and strengthening the role of the profession.

Education for international social work practice

Concern over imperialism may have led social work to largely cede the arena of international development practice to other professions less concerned about Western imposition. Yet, social workers may offer some real advantages in this work. Among them are that social work education includes content on appreciation of diversity and some level of cross-cultural skills, appreciation of the interplay between person and environment, a strong value base, and endorsement of the importance of participatory approaches to planning and development. Thus, social workers could be expected to be more respectful of local knowledge than professionals without this foundation. Through cross-national connections to local practitioners, social workers can tap into sources of knowledge at the grassroots, so crucially needed in development projects. Indeed, in advocating indigenisation, Rankopo and Osie-Hwedie (2011) remind us that 'Indigenisation does not negate collaboration with external partners and experts, and seeking resources for capacity-building' (141).

To respond, social work educators should acknowledge that global practice will remain a relatively specialised sub-area of the overall arena of international social work. But I argue that the profession should shed its ambivalence and encourage committed social workers from all parts of the world to pursue roles in international development and relief. It is up to educators to ensure that practitioners from social work programs are well prepared to be partners with local experts and communities and to challenge negative models. Leaving the arena to other professions will neither improve practice nor enhance the profession's contributions globally. Social work programs aiming to prepare students for international work must address a number of critical content areas. Practitioners need skills including planning, proposal development, training of trainers, and community engagement, plus a subject area of expertise such as HIV/AIDS, child welfare, or disaster mitigation and response. These should be blended with a solid foundation in human behaviour, cultural diversity, and social work ethics. International practice and educational preparation for it should demonstrate social work's capacity to respond appropriately and effectively, in education and practice terms, to the various global challenges 'that are having a significant impact on the wellbeing of large sections of the world's population' (Cox & Pawar 2006, 20).

International social work as a profession in global policymaking

Work at the policy level is another form of international or global social work. In a joint article, the leaders of IASSW, IFSW and ICSW declared that 'social work is well placed to play a key role in responding to the individual, community and global social problems facing the world' (Jones et al. 2008, 849). They announced a new era of increased collaboration among the three organisations to achieve 'enhanced global influence of the social work profession' (Jones et al. 2008, 847). An important outcome of this collaboration was the launch in 2012 of the Global Agenda for Social Work and Social Development.

The Global Agenda

The Global Agenda calls for the profession to engage more fully with the critical global social issues of the decade. It identifies an expansive range of action areas for social work engagement in four broad priority areas: social and economic inequalities within and between countries; dignity and worth of the person (including human rights); environmental sustainability; and the importance of human relationships (IASSW, ICSW, IFSW 2012). For each of these, there are commitments for social work organisations to work at the level of the United Nations and other global bodies, for social work practitioners at the community level, for the organisations themselves, and for social work education. They include some specific commitments, such as work to achieve the Millennium Development Goals (MDGs), social work involvement in defining the post-2015 agenda, efforts to achieve universal ratification of key human rights treaties, addressing global inequalities through such initiatives as the Global Social Protection Floor, and increased engagement with climate and environmental issues.

These commitments identify an important third direction for international social work—that of influencing policy on global social problems and collaborating with other groups for global action. In explaining the Global Agenda, Jones and Truell (2012) discuss the profession's duty to 'inform policy development and priority-setting by engagement with global and regional political institutions' (465). They note that 'global visibility and engagement' are important for the stature of the profession, but can also make a difference in outcomes for people on the ground. They refer to and echo Mmatli (2008) who encouraged social workers in Africa to lobby for improved policies within the region; as Mmatli explained the multiple benefits of engagement, 'social work's contribution to social development will become more apparent; its presence and prominence among professions will be perceived; and social work clients will stand to benefit' (303).

There are opportunities to bring social work values and strengths into play in the profession's representation work at the United Nations and other global bodies. Currently, small teams of members represent IFSW and IASSW at several offices of the United Nations. In IASSW's work with the UN NGO Committee for Social Development, for example, representatives have been able to advocate for rights-based approaches and have participated in several projects to bring voices from the grassroots into UN deliberations. IASSW submitted an intervention on the importance of participatory approaches to poverty eradication to the 50th session of the UN Social Development Commission, and hosted a panel on participation at the meeting of the commission (IASSW 2012). ICSW has made numerous interventions and connections as part of the campaign for the Global Social Protection Floor. These initiatives and others showcased social work values and strategies to UN representatives and other globally active NGOs. Challenges are to expand these efforts and develop better ways to engage colleagues from diverse countries in these inputs.

Need for advocacy in global higher education

Another important arena for professional involvement is higher education policy at the global level. Growing trends risk further disadvantaging locally relevant knowledge and knowledge generation from new sources. More and more universities in both global North and South are relying on rankings and journal impact factors. This is an insidious way of re-introducing elements of professional imperialism. The highly ranked journals are those based in Western nations, with long-established universities and social work education. Global ranking of journals and programs will undermine the regional social work journals that are adding important knowledge building to professional understanding of problems and theory. Rankings based on citations also disadvantage newer and less popular topics, as fewer scholars work in these areas.

Accreditation and the potential incursion of foreign bodies of accreditation may exacerbate the domination of Western/Northern standards for higher education, and in worst cases, impose culturally irrelevant standards on programs in Africa and Asia. Midgley (2008) mentions a proposal that surfaced in 2002 that the US Council on Social Work Education (CSWE) consider accrediting programs in other countries; he labelled this a 'new imperialism' that results from the elevation of Western standards and educational systems. Schools of social work in the Global South may seek external accreditation as a way to bolster their academic standing and reputation. Midgley does comment that the 2002 proposal 'was fiercely resisted by members of the organisation's [CSWE's] Global Commission who explained that this would require educational programs in developing countries to conform to the curricular requirements prescribed for American schools', resulting in inappropriate education (41). The re-emergence of discussions of accreditation and increased emphasis on journal rankings makes engagement with the politics and policymaking of higher education on the regional and global scales essential to combat this new form of imperialism.

Educational implications: building global literacy as a goal for social work education

If taken seriously, the Global Agenda and the call for more social work impact on global issues puts huge responsibilities on the educational sector to prepare professionals with sufficient knowledge to engage. Social work education needs to prepare students with a minimum level of global literacy. This is essential to improve the practice of social workers in their local contexts that are increasingly affected by global forces, especially the influx of large migrant populations, and would enable professionals to fulfil their roles as informed participants in political systems at home. Global knowledge will also serve as a foundation for a smaller number of professionals who will focus their entire practice locally on work with international migrant populations, or go on to careers with a focus on international work where they can apply their professional values and skills in inter-disciplinary teams in development and disaster response. More importantly, global knowledge may inspire and prepare more social workers to engage actively in tackling global social problems on the policy level, whether on the national or inter-governmental level.

Although data are scarce, there are indications that social work education is currently failing miserably in globally relevant teaching. The results of newly conducted studies in East Africa on social workers' capacity to contribute to achievement of the Millennium Development Goals (MDGs) are discouraging. Among Kenyan social work students surveyed in 2012, a dozen years after adoption of the MDGs and only three years from the achievement target, only 14.4% said they knew the MDGs in detail (Wairire et al. forthcoming); 31% either were not aware or only slightly aware, meaning that they had heard of the term, but did not know what the goals constituted and therefore, of course, could not link their practice to these goals in any way. There were similar, in fact slightly worse, findings among practicing social workers, only 10.9% of whom knew the MDGs in detail (Wairire et al. forthcoming); findings in Uganda paralleled the Kenyan study (Twikirize et al. 2013). An in-class survey of MSW students in one US school in 2013 revealed that only 25% knew what MDGs stood for; more discouraging was that this was an elective course on international social work; attracting students with a strong interest in the content (Healy 2012). Scores on other items of basic global knowledge were similarly dismal.

Specific content and curriculum models can vary across countries, but practitioners in all countries need preparation for practice in environments increasingly affected by global influences. The preparation provided to students should also assist the profession to secure and enhance a role for social work in the global policy and action network addressing the issues in our profession's arena of concern and expertise.

Shifting the priority of international social work to global policy may alleviate some concerns about imperialism. As Kreitzer and Wilson describe it, in solidarity the profession can recognise that 'we are all in this together and that there are global problems that need to be addressed by all of us, for the benefit of all of us' (2010, 716). It fits with Ahmadi's call to refocus international social work on working for human rights, social justice, conflict prevention and peace and to emphasise partnership as the model of work (2003).

Revisiting the debates: imperialism and indigenisation

At the outset, I noted that debates over imperialism and indigenisation have been regular themes in the literature. Perhaps we should question our profession's tendency to revisit the same issues for decades, with little substantive change in the arguments put forth. More than four decades ago, the journal *International Social Work* published an editorial message that it would no longer accept articles that focused on the lack of fit of Western social work in developing countries because the editors concluded that the topic was 'threadbare' due to the many submissions on the topic (Irvine 1972). Yet, the theme persists in our literature. Gray, Coates and Yellow Bird (2008) catalogued dozens of articles on the need for indigenisation dating back to 1972 as well. If these are simply repetitive articles, then perhaps little harm is done. But, the messages of the dangers of imperialism may impede the profession's capacity to act and discourage North–South partnerships on issues of mutual concern. Perhaps it is time to relabel use of inappropriate models as just bad practice, and to recognise that there may be complex reasons why curricula haven't been fully indigenised after so much intellectual capital has been spent in calling for this to occur.

Deepak (2012), in calling for transforming the approach to international social work, human rights, and development by giving attention to global inequalities, power relationships and structural inequalities, recognised that there are many sources of oppression, including those imbedded in traditional power structures and indigenous practices. The strategy she identified as 'global scattered resistance' (788) fits well with the Global Agenda and with the recommendation made here to expand global impact. Deepak accepts that resistance can occur at multiple levels. Social workers can contribute to human rights and social justice within organisations such as the UN and World Bank where they can work to publicise and educate on the impacts of globalisation on marginalised groups, while others can work from the outside in opposition to these organisations and their actions. Part of the responsibility of education for international social work is to address the global structures and policies that create gross inequalities, and help students see the linkages between global forces and the problems they can identify on the ground and to show them points of access to make change (Deepak 2012). For scholars and practitioners seeking to extend social work's influence on global issues, the need is to recognise that progress can be made in engagement with mainstream global bodies, in global and local movements of resistance and advocacy, and in local practice. Disparaging or privileging some of these over others has not been productive for the profession.

Conclusions

International social work is still a work in progress and an arena with diverse definitions, interpretations, and directions. Rather than continuing to debate definitions, this chapter has explored three current directions for international social work and their educational implications. It is possible that all three directions are appropriate for social work in the 21st century. Forces to universalise aspects of the profession—its definition, ethical principles, and education—are intensifying even as they remain controversial. Some educational programs in diverse countries are identifying global or international practice as an area of specialisation, while others question its very feasibility. The international professional organisations have committed social work to an ambitious agenda for addressing global challenges. It should be easiest to secure agreement that increasing the global knowledge of social workers will only strengthen the profession. Low global literacy is not desirable and puts our professionals at a disadvantage. Secondly, global knowledge is necessary if social work is to have an impact on global issues and fulfil the Global Agenda. Most, unless they hold their profession in very low esteem, would also agree that social work does have something to offer for efforts to address global social problems and strengthen respect for human rights.

Considerable work remains to be done. The specific content that would make up minimal global literacy needs to be identified, and this should be done as a partnership project with efforts to develop both universal concepts and content and locally specific elements. Language will present some obstacles to building global knowledge and will demand more effort to ensure translation of social work scholarship into diverse languages. Some relevant sources, especially those from the United Nations, are published in multiple languages, increasing their accessibility. The dominance of English language in publishing and professional conferences creates barriers for non-English speakers. In some ways, it also leads many scholars whose first language is English to narrow their search for alternative sources of knowledge. Thus, translations should also be encouraged both from and to English and other languages. Theory building is another, perhaps more challenging, project. Although Trygged notes that, since there is no single theoretical base for social work, 'it is hardly possible to achieve a common set of theories for international social work' (651), Healy (2012) writes that theory is beginning to emerge through the blending of social work methods and perspectives with globally relevant concepts of human rights, development, and social inclusion. This work remains in its infancy.

Finally, although it will likely be later than 2020, social work may come to recognise a more holistic perspective. The global and the local can no longer be easily divided. Globally aware, knowledgeable and active professionals are needed in every context and will eventually be identified simply as competent social workers in the 21st century.

References

Ahmadi, N. (2003). Globalisation of consciousness and new challenges for international social work. *International Journal of Social Welfare,* 12(1): 14–23.

Alphonse, M., George, P. & Moffatt, K. (2008). Redefining social work standards in the context of globalisation: lessons from India. *International Social Work,* 51(2): 145–58.

Bragin, M. (2012). The IASC guidelines on mental health and psychosocial support: a quick guide for social workers. In L.M. Healy & R.J. Link (eds), *Handbook of international social work: human rights, development and the global profession* (pp. 514–16). NY: Oxford University Press.

Cox, D. & Pawar, M. (2006). *International social work: issues, strategies and programs.* London: SAGE Publications.

Deepak, A.C. (2012). Globalisation, power, and resistance: postcolonial and transnational feminist perspectives for social work practice. *International Social Work,* 55(6): 779–93.

Dominelli, L. (2010). *Social work in a globalising world.* Cambridge: Polity Press.

Goldman, B.W. (1962). International social work as a professional function. *International Social Work,* 5(3): 1–8.

Gray, M., Coates, J. & Yellow Bird, M. (eds) (2008). *Indigenous social work around the world: towards culturally relevant education and practice.* Aldershot, UK: Ashgate.

Haug, E. (2005). Critical reflections on the emerging discourse of international social work. *International Social Work,* 48(2): 126–35.

Healy, L.M. (2012). Defining international social work. In L.M Healy & R.J Link. *Handbook of international social work: human rights, development, and the global profession* (pp. 9–15). NY: Oxford University Press.

Healy, L.M. (2008). *International social work: professional action in an interdependent World.* NY: Oxford University Press.

Healy, L.M. (2002). Internationalising social work curriculum in the 21st century. In N.T. Tan & I. Dodds (eds), *Social work around the world,* vol. 2, *Agenda for global social work in the 21st century.* Berne, Switzerland: IFSW Press.

Healy, L.M. (2001). *International social work: professional action in an interdependent World.* NY: Oxford University Press.

Healy, L.M. & Link, R.J. (2012). *Handbook of international social work: human rights, development, and the global profession.* NY: Oxford University Press.

Huegler, N., Lyons, K. & Pawar, M. (2012). Setting the scene. In K. Lyons, T. Hokenstad, M. Pawar, N. Huegler & N. Hall (eds), *The SAGE handbook of international social work* (pp. 1–33). London: SAGE Publications.

Hugman, R. (2010). *Understanding international social work: a critical analysis.* Basingstoke, Hampshire: Palgrave Macmillan.

Hugman, R., Moosa-Mitha, M. & Moyo, O. (2010). Towards a borderless social work: reconsidering notions of international social work. *International Social Work,* 53(5): 629–43.

Inter-Agency Standing Committee (IASC) (2007). Inter-agency standing committee on mental health and psychosocial support in emergency settings. Retrieved on 22 April 2014 from www.humanitarianinfo.org/iasc/pageloader.aspx?page=content-subsidi-tf_mhps-default.

IASSW (2012). Statement for the 50th Session of the United Nations Commission for Social Development. Retrieved on 22 April 2014 from undesadspd.org/ CommissionforSocialDevelopment/Sessions/2012/NGOsStatements.aspx.

IASSW, ICSW, IFSW (2012). The global agenda for social work and social development. Retrieved on 22 April 2014 from cdn.ifsw.org/assets/globalagenda2012.pdf.

Irvine E.E. (1972). Editorial. *International Social Work*, 15(4): 1–3.

Jebb, E. (1929). International social service. In *First International Conference of Social Work: proceedings of the conference, July 8–13*. Paris: International Conference of Social Work.

Jones, D. & Truell, R. (2012). The global agenda for social work and social development: a place to link together and be effective in a globalised world. *International Social Work*, 55(4): 454–72.

Jones, D., Yuen, A. & Rollet, C. (2008). News and views: rising to the global challenge: IASSW, ICSW, and IFSW join hands to build an agenda for the next decade. *International Social Work*, 51(6): 847–49.

Kreitzer, L. & Wilson, M. (2010). Shifting perspectives on international alliances in social work: lessons from Ghana and Nicaragua. *International Social Work*, 53(5): 701–19.

Lyons, K. (2006). Globalisation and social work: international and local implications. *British Journal of Social Work*, 36(3): 365–80.

Lyons, K. (1999). *International social work: themes and perspectives*. Aldershot, UK: Ashgate.

Lyons, K., Hokenstad, T., Pawar, M., Huegler, N. & Hall, N. (2012). *The SAGE handbook of international social work*. London: SAGE Publications.

Midgley, J. (2008). Promoting reciprocal international social work exchanges: professional imperialism revisited. In M. Gray, J. Coates & M. Yellow Bird (eds), *Indigenous social work around the world: toward culturally relevant education & practice* (pp. 31–45). Aldershot, UK: Ashgate.

Mmatli, T. (2008). Political activism as a social work strategy in Africa. *International Social Work*, 51(3): 297–310.

Payne, M. & Askeland, G.A. (2008). *Globalisation and international social work: postmodern change and challenge*. Aldershot, UK: Ashgate.

Rankopo, M.J. & Osie-Hwedie, K. (2011). Globalisation and culturally relevant social work: African perspectives on indigenisation. *International Social Work*, 54(1): 137–47.

Trygged, S. (2010). Balancing the global and the local: Some normative reflections on International social work. *International Social Work*, 53(5): 644–55.

Twikirize, J.M, Asingwire, N., Omona, J., Lubanga, R. & Kafuko, A. (2013). *The role of social work in poverty reduction and the realisation of millennium development goals in Uganda*. Kampala: Fountain Publishers.

Wairire, G.G., Zani, A., Mutie, P.M. & Machera, M. (forthcoming 2013). *The role of social work in poverty reduction and realisation of millennium development goals in East Africa: Kenyan perspective*. Kampala, Uganda: Fountain Publishers.

Webb, S. (2003). Local orders and global chaos in social work. *European Journal of Social Work*, 6(2): 191–204.

Williams, L. & Sewpaul, V. (2004). Modernism, postmodernism and global standards setting. *Social Work Education*, 23(5): 555–65.

Yip, K.S. (2004). A Chinese cultural critique of the global qualifying standards for social work education. *Social Work Education*, 23(5): 597–612.

Contributors

Mimi Abramovitz, DSW, Bertha Capen Reynolds Professor of Social Policy, Silberman School of Social Work, Hunter College, CUNY and The CUNY Graduate Center, New York, NY . Email: Iabramov@hunter.cuny.edu

María-José Aguilar-Idáñez, Senior Professor in Social Work and Social Services and Director of GIEMIC (Research Interdisciplinary Group about Migrations, Intercultural studies and Citizenship) & Director of Master in Migration and Interculturality (UCLM)University of Castilla-La Mancha (Spain). Email: mariejose.aguilar@uclm.es

Gurid Aga Askeland, PhD, Diakonhjemmet University College, Institute of social work and family therapy, Norway. Email: g.askeland@diakonhjemmet.no

Frank R. Baskind, PhD, School of Social Work, Virginia Commonwealth University, Richmond, VA, USA. Email: fbaskind@vcu.edu

Oksano Boyko, PhD, National University of Kyiv-Mohyla Academy Ukraine. Email: boykoo@ukr.net

Linda Briskman, Professor of Human Rights at the Swinburne Institute for Social Research. School of Arts, Social Sciences and Humanities, Faculty of Health, Arts and Design. Email: lbriskman@swin.edu.au

Cerita Buchanan, MSW, Lecturer in Social Work at The University of the West Indies, Open Campus Mona Jamaica. Email: cerita.buchanan@open.uwi.edu

Daniel Buraschi, GIEMIC (Research Interdisciplinary Group about Migrations, Intercultural studies and Citizenship)University of Castilla-La Mancha (Spain). Email: buraschidaniel@hotmail.com

Avery Calhoun, PhD, Associate Professor in the Faculty of Social Work, University of Calgary (Edmonton). Email: calhoun@ucalgary.ca

Lena Dominelli, PhD, Professor, School of Applied Social Sciences, Durham University, UK. Email: lena.dominelli@durham.ac.uk

Sandra Elizabet Mancinas Espinoza, PhD, is Professor at Universidad Autónoma de Nuevo León, Mexico. Email: sandramancinas@hotmail.com

Christine Fejo-King, PhD is an Aboriginal woman from the Northern Territory of Australia. She is a practising social worker and author. Email: christine@fejoking.com.au

Mel Gray, PhD, Professor, School of Social Work, Newcastle University, Australia. Email: mel.gray@newcastle.edu.au

In-young Han, PhD, Professor in Graduate School of Social Welfare, Ewha Womans University, Seoul, Korea. Email: yhan@ewha.ac.kr

Lynne M. Healy, PhD, Board of Trustees Distinguished Professor/ University of Connecticut School of Social Work, USA. Email: lynne.healy@uconn.edu

Mark Henrickson, PhD, Associate Professor of Social Work at Massey University, Auckland, New Zealand. Email: m.henrickson@massey.ac.nz

Sandra Joseph, PhD, Associate Professor and Head, Dept of Social Work, Stella Maris College (Autonomous), Chennai, India. Secretary of the Indian Association of Social Work Education. Email: sanjose.smc@gmail.com

Ben H.B. Ku, PhD, Associate Professor, Department of Applied Social Sciences, Hong Kong Polytechnic University. Email: hok.bun.ku@polyu.edu.hk

Jung-won Lim, PhD, Associate Professor, College of Social Welfare, Kangnam University, Yongin, Korea. Email: jungwonlim@kangnam.ac.kr

Brian Littlechild, PhD, Professor of Social Work at the University of Hertfordshire, UK. He is joint chair of the IASSW Publications Committee. Email: b.littlechild@herts.ac.uk

Karen Lyons, PhD, CQSW, Emeritus Professor (International Social Work) at London Metropolitan University, (UK). Email: Karen@the-lyons.co.uk

Mehmoona Moosa-Mitha, PhD, Associate Professor in School of Social Work, at the University of Victoria, British Columbia, Canada. Email: mehmoona@uvic.ca

Carolina Muñoz-Guzmán, Assistant Professor Pontificia Universidad Catolica de Chile, School of Social Work. Email: cmunozgu@uc.cl

Rodreck Mupedziswa, PhD, Professor and Head of Department of Social Work at the department of Social Work. University of Botswana, Botswana. Email: mupedziswa@mopipi.ub.bw

Vimla V. Nadkarni, Ph.D. President, International Association of Schools of Social Work (IASSW)Former Dean & Professor, School of Social Work, Tata Institute of Social Sciences, Mumbai India. Email: vimla@iassw.net or vimla1912@gmail.com

Carolyn Noble, PhD is Emertia Professor at Victoria University, Melbourne and Inaugural Professor of Social Work at ACAP in Sydney, Australia. Email: Carolyn.noble@vu.edu.au or carolyn.noble@acap.edu.au

Bala Raju Nikku, PhD, School of Social Sciences, Universiti Sains Malaysia (USM) and Nepal School of Social Work. Email: Nikku21@yahoo.com

Nelly B. Nucci, PhD, Senior Professor, School of Social Work at Universidad Nacional de Cordoba Argentina. Email: nellybn@gmail.com

Fentiny Nugroho, Ph.D is Head of the Department of Social Welfare, University of Indonesia. She also serves as the President of Asian Pacific Association for Social Work Education and Vice President of International Association of Schools of Social Work. Email: fentiny@yahoo.co

Letnie Rock, PhD, Senior Lecturer in Social Work at The University of the West Indies, Cave Hill Campus Barbados. Email: letnie.rock@cavehill.uwi.edu

Kanya Eka Santi, MSW, Lecturer and Head of Bandung College of Social Welfare (STKS). Currently she serves as a Vice-Chair of Indonesian Association of Social Work/Social Welfare Education. Email: kanyaekasanti@yahoo.co.id

Tetyana Semigina, PhD, Professor National University of Kyiv-Mohyla Academy Ukraine. Email: tetyanasemigina@gmail.com

Vishanthie Sewpaul, PhD, Professor in School of Applied Human Sciences, University of KwaZulu Natal, Durban, South Africa. Email: sewpaul@ukzn.ac.za

Clara Shockley, Virginia Commonwealth University Graduate Research Assistant School of Social Work, Virginia Commonwealth University. Email: shockleycs@mymail.vcu.edu

Refilwe P. Sinkamba, MSW,Lecturer at the Department of Social Work, University of Botswana, Botswana. Email: Refilwe.sinkamba@mopipi.ub.bw

Barbara Staniforth, PhD, Associate Professor in School of Counselling, Human Services and Social Work Faculty of Education, University of Auckland. Email: b.staniforth@auckland.ac.nz

Silvia Staub-Bernasconi, PhD, Professor, School of Social Work, University of Applied Sciences and Arts Northwestern (FHNW), Switzerland. Email: staubernasco@bluewin.ch

Helle Strauss, Senior Lecturer, Metropolitan University College, Institute of Social Work, Kronprinsesse Sofiesvej, Denmark. Email: hest@phmetropol.dk

Isidor Wallimann, Ph.D. is a Visiting Professor at Syracuse University, NY, and Professor Emeritus from the School of Social Work Basel, Switzerland. Email: isidor.wallimann@sunrise.ch

Sibin Wang, PhD, Professor, Department of Sociology, Peking University, China Email: wsbpku@sina.com

Stephen Webb, PhD, Professor, Department of Psychology, Social Work and Allied Health Sciences, Glasgow Caledonian University, UK. Email: Stephen.webb@gcu.ac.uk

Elizabeth (Bessa) Whitmore, PhD, Professor Emerita from Carleton University, Ottawa, Canada. Email: Elizabeth.whitmore@carleton.ca

Maureen Wilson, PhD, Professor Faculty of Social Work and the Consortium for Peace Studies at University of Calgary, Canada. Email: mwilson@ucalgary.ca

Angelina W.K. Yuen-Tsang, PhD, Vice President (Institutional Advancement and Partnership) and Professor, Department of Applied Social Sciences, Hong Kong Polytechnic University, Hong Kong. Email: angie.yuen@polyu.edu.hk

Darja Zavirsek, PhD, Professor Faculty of Social Work, University of Ljubljana Slovenia. Email: darja.zavirsek@fsd.uni-lj.si

Made in the USA
San Bernardino, CA
16 October 2016